For Anna Eraut

Contents

List of illustrations	viii
List of boxes	ix
Acknowledgements	x
Publisher's acknowledgements	xi
Maps	xii
Preface	xvii
Glossary	xviii

1 From tsarism to revolution, 1894–1917 — 1

Social and political conditions in tsarist Russia	1
The war with Japan	3
The 1905 Revolution	5
The time of the Dumas	8
Stolypin's reforms	10
The alliance system	13
The First World War	15
The February Revolution	18
The return of Lenin	22
The July Days	24
The Kornilov revolt	26

2 The October Revolution, 1917–1921 — 31

The Constituent Assembly	37
Making peace with the Central Powers	39
The Cheka and the beginning of the Red Terror	41
The start of War Communism	44
The start of the civil war	45
Red victory	49
The war with the Poles	51
The end of the civil war	52
The Kronstadt rebellion	53

3 NEP and the rise of Stalin, 1921–1928 — 58

The formation of the USSR	58
The start of the New Economic Policy	62
The development of a Soviet bureaucracy	65

The rise of Stalin 68
The death of Lenin 71
The formation of the United Opposition 74
Propaganda, literacy, and education 76
Foreign policy in the 1920s 82
Summary: the 1920s 89

4 Collectivization, industrialization and the Great Purge, 1929–1940 91

Introduction 91
The decision to collectivize agriculture 92
Mass collectivization begins 94
The Great Famine in Ukraine 98
Completion of collectivization 102
The start of industrialization 103
The purges 108
Socialist Realism begins 116
Foreign policy in the 1930s 120
Popular Fronts 122
Toward the Nazi–Soviet Pact 124

5 The Great Patriotic War and aftermath, 1941–1953 135

Early stages 135
The assault on Leningrad and Kyiv 141
Operation Typhoon: the attack on Moscow 142
The Partisan movement 145
Stalingrad 146
Wartime culture: the peak of Socialist Realism 150
The Battle of Kursk Salient 154
Stalin and his allies 156
Victory in the West and in the East 161
The results of the Great Patriotic War 162
Economic recovery 165
Armed resistance 167
The period of High Stalinism 169

6 Khrushchev's reforms, 1953–1964; and postwar foreign policy 176

The succession question 176
The Virgin Lands Program 181
The 20th Party Congress 183
The attack on the Russian Orthodox Church 190
Cultural thaw 191
Foreign policy during the early Cold War, 1945–1963 194
Another plot 217

7   The Brezhnev regime and its successors, 1964–1984   **222**

Introduction   222
Leonid Ilich Brezhnev   224
The economy   225
The Constitution of 1977   230
Language and political questions in the national republics   231
Foreign policy under Brezhnev   234
Culture under Brezhnev   249
The dissident movement   253
The last years of the Brezhnev regime   254
The interlude: Andropov and Chernenko   255

8   Gorbachev, Glasnost and Perestroika, 1985–1991   **260**

Introduction   260
The Chernobyl disaster   263
The development of Glasnost   269
Politics under Gorbachev   275
The perils of Perestroika   282
Foreign policy   285
The national question   290
1991 – the year of collapse   295
The Soviet legacy in retrospect   299

**9   From Yeltsin to Putin: Russia's decline and recovery,
1992–2008**   **304**

Vladimir V. Putin   312
Political events, 2000–2008   314
The attack on the oligarchs   315
Presidential elections of 2004   317
Russia and its neighbors   319
Chechnya: terrorism and the resumption of war   322
Partnerships   324
The 2007 parliamentary elections   325
Gazprom and economic revival   328
Historical memory and the modern state   329

Bibliography of older works   338
Index   351

List of illustrations

2.1	Russian peasants preaching communism	46
3.1	Lenin in a wheelchair	68
4.1	Portrait of Stalin hanging on a building	107
4.2	Nikolay Bukharin	116
5.1	Families identify the dead in Kerch, Crimea	145
5.2	War on the Eastern Front, 1942	150
6.1	Soviet soldiers watching the Czechoslovakian Independence Day parade	200
6.2	Nikita Khrushchev taking a walk	219
7.1	Kuznetsk coal basin	226
7.2	Dachas and gardens	230
7.3	Leonid Brezhnev and Helmut Schmidt	239
8.1	Mikhail Gorbachev	264
8.2	Police officers in Red Square	281
8.3	Daily life in Russia, 1989	284
9.1	Dmitry Medvedev and Vladimir Putin	327

List of boxes

1.1	Lev (Leo) Nikolaevich Tolstoy (1828–1910)	12
1.2	Mikhail Vladimirovich Rodzyanko (1859–1924)	13
2.1	Feliks Edmundovich Dzerzhinsky (1877–1926)	41
3.1	Russian Association of Proletarian Writers (RAPP)	78
3.2	Mikhail Bulgakov (1891–1940)	79
3.3	Anna Akhmatova (1889–1966)	80
3.4	Osip Mandelstam (1891–1938)	80
4.1	Reaction of Soviet citizens to the Terror	111
4.2	Vladimir Mayakovsky (1893–1930)	117
4.3	Vera Mukhina (1889–1953)	118
4.4	Aleksandr Moravov (1878–1951)	119
5.1	Ilya Ehrenburg (1891–1967)	151
5.2	Aleksandr Gerasimov (1881–1963)	153
5.3	Sergey Prokofiev (1891–1953)	154
5.4	Fyodor Reshetnikov (1906–1988)	170
5.5	Dmitry D. Shostakovich (1906–1975)	171
5.6	Aram Khachaturian (1903–1978)	172
6.1	Boris Pasternak (1890–1960)	192
7.1	Andrey Sinyavsky (1925–1997)	250
7.2	Aleksandr Galich (1918–1977)	251
7.3	Bulat Okudzhava (1924–1997)	251
7.4	Vladimir Vysotsky (1938–1980)	252
9.1	Anna Politkovskaya (1958–2006)	324
9.2	Dmitry Medvedev (1965–)	326
9.3	Tatyana Tolstaya (1951–)	332

Acknowledgements

I am grateful to Christina Wipf-Perry of Pearson Education for commissioning this book; to Jessica Harrison for her editorial assistance; and to the five anonymous reviewers, as well as to a number of people who have helped me at various stages. They include Peter Rutland of Wesleyan University, who provided several useful sources; University of Alberta student Gem Shoute, who helped to update the bibliography and, together with Kim Shoute, worked on biographies; and my former graduate student Meaghan Bernard, who helped with information on the Putin period. I am especially grateful to Anna Eraut for editing the text and for assistance with sources; and to Serhy Yekelchyk, University of Victoria, for his careful reading of the text and very helpful suggestions. The inspiration for the current version came from students at the University of Alberta, particularly those in my classes and seminars on 20th-century Russia. Although a book designed for university students in an English-speaking environment does not list Russian sources, I have consulted many of them in producing this volume. I would like to express my appreciation in particular to Sh. M. Munayev, V. M. Ustinov, V. I. Menkovsky, O. A. Yanovsky, and G. M. Sevostyanov, as well as to Salavat Iskhakov, a Moscow colleague with whom I have worked on recent projects.

David R. Marples
Edmonton, Alberta, Canada
December 2, 2009

Publisher's acknowledgements

We are grateful to the following for permission to reproduce copyright material:

Maps

Map 1, Map 2 and Map 3 from *The Soviet Union 1917–1991*, 2nd edition, Longman (McCauley, M. 1993); Map 4 from http://www.lib.utexas.edu/maps/commonwealth/russia_auton_92.jpg, Courtesy of the University Libraries, The University of Texas at Austin.

The publisher would like to thank the following for their kind permission to reproduce their photographs:

Corbis: Bettman / CORBIS (Plate 2.1, Plate 3.1, Plate 4.1, Plate 4.2, Plate 5.2, Plate 6.1); Dmitri Baltermants / The Dmitri Baltermants Collection / Corbis (Plate 5.1); Wolfgang Kaehler / CORBIS (Plate 7.2); The Dmitri Baltermants Collection / Corbis (Plate 6.2); Bernard Bisson / Sygma / Corbis (Plate 7.1); pa / dpa / Corbis (Plate 7.3); Reuters / Corbis (Plate 8.1); David Katzenstein / CORBIS (Plate 8.2); Ed Kashi / CORBIS (Plate 8.3); Alexander Zemlianichenko / epa / Corbis (Plate 9.1).

Every effort has been made to trace the copyright holders and we apologise in advance for any unintentional omissions. We would be pleased to insert the appropriate acknowledgement in any subsequent edition of this publication.

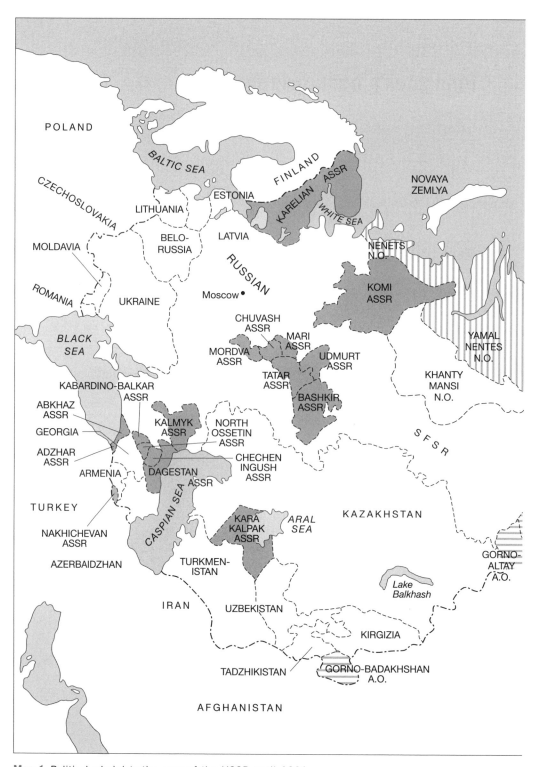

Map 1 Political-administrative map of the USSR until 1991.

Martin McCauley, *The Soviet Union 1917–1991 @ Longman Group UK Limited 1982, 1993*

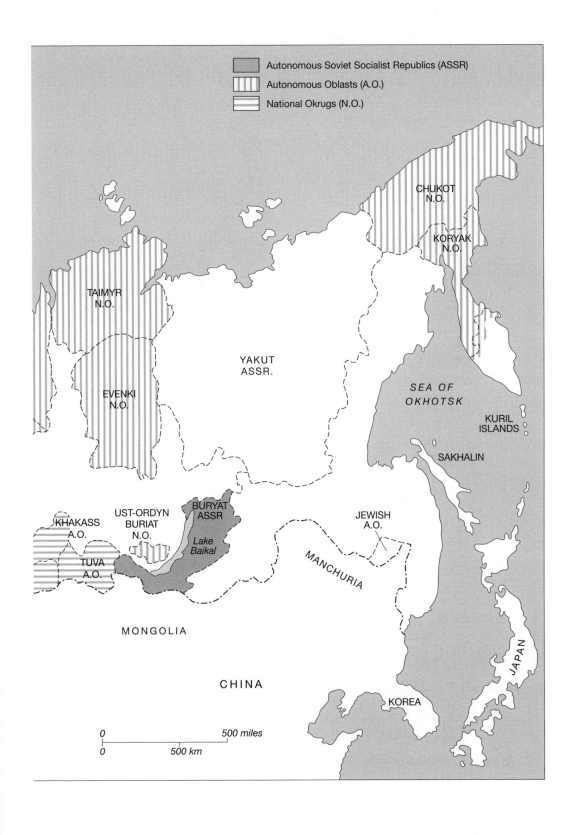

Autonomous Soviet Socialist Republics (ASSR)
Autonomous Oblasts (A.O.)
National Okrugs (N.O.)

CHUKOT
N.O.

KORYAK
N.O.

TAIMYR
N.O.

YAKUT
ASSR.

SEA OF
OKHOTSK

EVENKI
N.O.

KURIL
ISLANDS

SAKHALIN

BURYAT
ASSR

UST-ORDYN
BURIAT
N.O.

JEWISH
A.O.

KHAKASS
A.O.

Lake
Baikal

TUVA
A.O.

MANCHURIA

MONGOLIA

JAPAN

CHINA

KOREA

0   500 miles
0   500 km

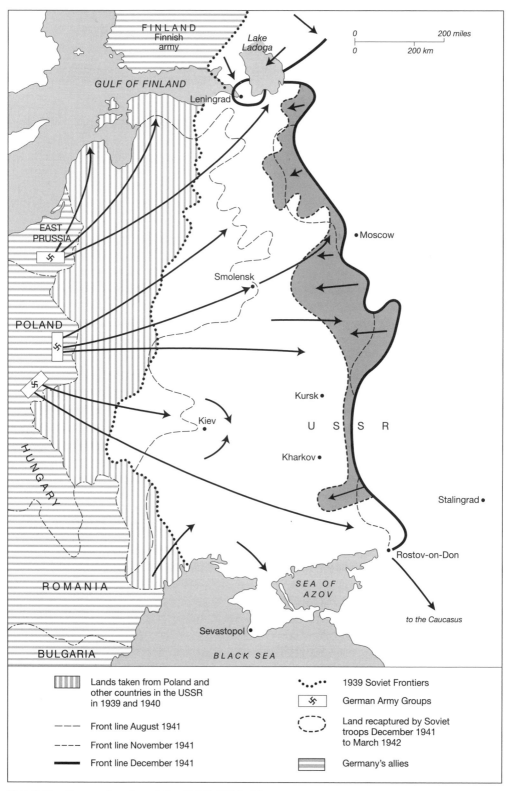

FINLAND
Finnish army

Lake Ladoga

GULF OF FINLAND

Leningrad

0   200 miles
0   200 km

EAST PRUSSIA

• Moscow

Smolensk

POLAND

Kursk •

HUNGARY

U   S   S   R

Kiev

Kharkov •

Stalingrad •

Rostov-on-Don

ROMANIA

SEA OF AZOV

to the Caucasus

Sevastopol •

BULGARIA   BLACK SEA

| | | | | Lands taken from Poland and other countries in the USSR in 1939 and 1940

•••••• 1939 Soviet Frontiers

⌐卐⌐ German Army Groups

– – – Front line August 1941

– – – – Front line November 1941

—— Front line December 1941

Land recaptured by Soviet troops December 1941 to March 1942

Germany's allies

Map 2 The German invasion of the USSR 1941–42.

Martin McCauley, *The Soviet Union 1917–1991 @ Longman Group UK Limited 1982, 1993*

Map 3 Soviet territorial gains in Europe 1939–49.

Martin McCauley, *The Soviet Union 1917–1991 @ Longman Group UK Limited 1982, 1993*

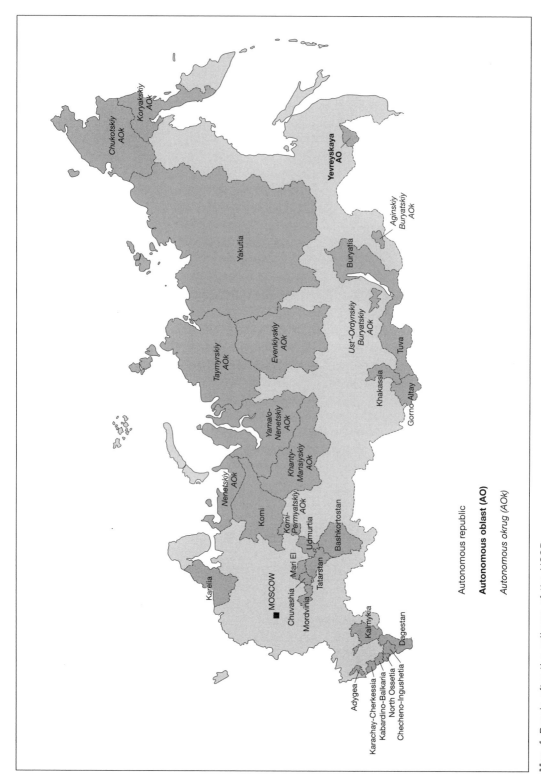

Map 4 Russia after the collapse of the USSR.
Courtesy of the University libraries, the University of Texas Austin

Autonomous republic

Autonomous oblast (AO)

Autonomous okrug (AOk)

Chukotskiy AOk

Koryakskiy AOk

Yevreyskaya AO

Aginskiy Buryatskiy AOk

Yakutia

Buryatia

Taymyrskiy AOk

Evenkiyskiy AOk

Ust'-Ordynskiy Buryatskiy AOk

Tuva

Khakassia

Gorno-Altay

Yamalo-Nenetskiy AOk

Khanty-Mansiyskiy AOk

Nenetskiy AOk

Komi

Komi-Permyatskiy AOk

Udmurtia

Bashkortostan

Karelia

MOSCOW

Chuvashia

Mari El

Mordvinia

Tatarstan

Kalmykia

Dagestan

Adygea

Karachay-Cherkessia

Kabardino-Balkaria

North Ossetia

Checheno-Ingushetia

Preface

An earlier version of this work appeared under the title *Motherland: Russia in the Twentieth Century* in 2002. The current text has been heavily revised, and a number of sections and chapters have been added. This edition represents an attempt to explain the "long twentieth century" from 1894 to 2008, i.e., in terms of rulers, from the time of Nikolay (Nicholas) II to the end of the presidency of Vladimir Putin. It is intended for students at universities and sixth-form colleges, though it is hoped that general audiences will also find it easily comprehensible. The book is divided chronologically, and for the most part based on the time in office of state leaders – largely for convenience, but also because, for much of the period, direction came from the top in an increasingly centralized society. Also the leaders of the time always initiated some changes and imposed a particular stamp on a period. I have tried to give due attention to social and cultural trends and developments as well as to foreign and domestic policy. Key cultural figures are highlighted in mini-biographies because they are less well known than political and military leaders. The bibliography is divided into two sections: well-known works for each chapter, which are provided at the end of the book; and newer publications (2002–2009), which are listed immediately at the end of each chapter, along with questions for discussion.

Glossary

The following Russian terms or acronyms appear in the book.

AKhRR Association of Artists of Revolutionary Russia (*Assotsiatsiya khudozhnikov revolyutsionnoy Rossii*)

artel cooperative association; a term used to categorize a type of collective farm that allowed its members a few personal items and a private plot of land

BAM Baikal–Amur Railway (*Baykalo-Amurskaya Magistral'*)

bednyak poor peasant

Cheka Extraordinary Commission to Combat Counter-Revolution and Sabotage; the abbreviation is taken from the first two words – in Russian, *Chrezvychaynaya komissiya*. See also OGPU, NKVD, and KGB.

chernozem black soil

Cominform Communist Information Bureau (*Informatsionnoye byuro Kommunisticheskikh partiy*)

Comintern Communist International (*Komintern*)

CPSU Communist Party of the Soviet Union (*KPSS: Kommunisticheskaya partiya Sovetskogo Soyuza*)

Duma Russian parliament

FSB Federal Security Service of the Russian Federation (*Federal'naya sluzhba bezopasnosti Rossiyskoy Federatsii*)

GKO State Defense Committee (*Gosudarstvennyy komitet oborony*)

GOELRO State Commission for the Electrification of Russia (*Gosudarstvennaya komissiya po elektrifikatsii Rossii*)

Gosplan State Planning Commission

guberniya an administrative-territorial unit in Imperial Russia

GULAG Chief Administration of Corrective Labor Camps and Colonies (*Glavnoye upravleniye ispravitel'no-trudovykh lagerey i koloniy*)

KGB Committee for State Security (*Komitet gosudarstvennoy bezopasnosti*), the name of the Soviet security agency from 1954 to 1991

Kombedy Committees of the Village Poor (*Komitety derevenskoy bednoty*)

Komsomol Young Communist League (*Kommunisticheskiy soyuz molodezhi*)

kulak rich peasant

magnitizdat taped copies of underground music or literature

MGN Ministry of State Security (*Ministerstvo gosudarstvennoy bezopasnosti*)

mir village community; the word also means "world" and "peace". See also *obshchina*.

MTS Machine-Tractor Station (*mashinno-traktornaya stantsiya*)

narodnost' nationality, or people; when applied to literature it signified particular qualities, themes or values that supposedly appealed to the common worker

NEP New Economic Policy (*Novaya ekonomicheskaya politika*)

NKVD People's Commissariat of Internal Affairs (*Narodnyy komissariat vnutrennikh del*)

NTS National Alliance of Russian Solidarists (*Narodno-trudovoy soyuz Rossiyskikh solidaristov*)

oblast province

obshchina village community

OGPU All-Union (United) State Political Administration (*Ob'yedinennoye gosudarstvennoye politicheskoye upravleniye pri SNK*); known earlier as the GPU, or State Political Administration

Okhrana literally "protection"; the name of the Russian secret police in the tsarist era

otlichniki excellent workers; a term used in the 1930s for those who exceeded planning targets in industry

partiynost' party membership or spirit; in literature it signified that writing must adhere to the party line

Peredvizhniki the Wanderers, a Russian school of realist painters formed in the 1870s, which later influenced Socialist Realism in art

pood unit of measurement (one pood is equal to 16.38 kgs)

Proletkult Proletarian Culture

RAPP Russian Association of Proletarian Writers (*Rossiyskaya assotsiatsiya proletarskikh pisateley*)

rayon district or county

RBMK graphite-moderated nuclear reactor (*Reaktor bol'shoy moshchnosti kanal'nyy*)

samogon home-distilled alcohol

serednyak middle peasant

sovkhoz state farm

Sovnarkhoz Economic Council (*Sovet narodnogo khozyaystva*)

Stakhanovites record-breakers in Soviet industry, named after the coal miner Aleksey Stakhanov

Stavka military headquarters

TASS Soviet news agency (literally, the Telegraph Agency of the Soviet Union)

TOZ association for the joint cultivation of land (*Tovarishchestvo po sovmestnoy obrabotke zemli*)

ukaz decree or edict

UPA Ukrainian Insurgent Army (*Ukrains'ka Povstans'ka Armiya* in Ukrainian)

volost the smallest administrative division of Imperial Russia

VVER water-pressurized nuclear reactor (*Vodo-vodnyanoy energeticheskiy reaktor*)

Yezhovshchina the time of Yezhov, the term used for the period of the Stalin purges when Nikolay Yezhov was head of the NKVD

zagradotryady blocking units established by the NKVD in the German–Soviet war to prevent retreats

zemstvo district or local assembly that originated with the reforms of Tsar Aleksandr II (1855–1881)

Zhdanovshchina the time of Zhdanov, the term used for the period of cultural uniformity under the leadership of Andrey Zhdanov

1

....

From tsarism to revolution, 1894–1917

Social and political conditions in tsarist Russia

Russia at the turn of the century was a peasant nation with a population of about 129 million, a feudal empire of vast territory that was reliant almost exclusively on agriculture for its national income. It was the world's main agricultural producer in 1897, though the situation in the villages, home to 97 million people, was strained. The emancipation of the serfs in 1861 had alleviated the worst vestiges of the economic system of serfdom, which had tied the peasants to the land, but it had hardly ameliorated their plight, burdening them with redemption payments that ultimately exceeded the value of the land now in their possession. Often the plots of land these peasants worked were smaller than the amount required for subsistence, forcing them to lease land, often from their former landlords. Methods were primitive, and manual labor was the norm. The late 19th century also saw a rapid expansion of the population, causing the further division of the land plots and the departure of many peasants from the villages to the growing towns, or else to Siberia or even abroad. Droughts and famines occurred frequently, partly as a result of the adverse climatic conditions, and partly as a consequence of the way in which Russian agriculture was organized. The basic issues of village life were dealt with by the village community – the *mir* – an organization that many political agitators had envisaged as the instrument of a social revolution.

The period was also one during which the vast Russian Empire slowly began to experience the beginnings of major industrialization. Russian industry at the turn of the century was characterized by the workshop and by seasonal workers, who would return to the villages to assist with the harvest in the fall. In the larger cities, such as St Petersburg, however, the factories springing up were often huge affairs, employing thousands of people. Under Prime Minister Sergey Witte, Russia embarked on a campaign to build railways, and in the last decade of the 19th century some 16,800 miles of railways were constructed. By the turn of the century, the empire had several established industrial centers – regions of Poland, such as Warsaw and Lodz, the major cities of St Petersburg and Moscow, and the Donbass region of Ukraine. For the most part, the major investors in the development were foreign – French, German, Belgian, and British. By 1913, the urban population had risen to 18 percent of the total, and was mostly occupied in industry, construction, trade, and technical industries. Nevertheless over 70 percent of the population remained in the agricultural sphere.

The tsarist autocracy represented a forbidding but weakening leadership. Russian expansion since the 16th century had been chaotic, often unplanned, frequently conducted by individualistic freebooters, and partly as a result of conquests arising from warfare. In the 19th century, a small group of the intelligentsia devised different revolutionary ideas and methods to bring about change. None came to fruition, other than the assassination of Tsar Aleksandr II in 1881. Terrorism as a means to bring about change was discredited by this time. Populism, the attainment of a socialist revolution through the village community, also appeared to have failed. Increasingly those who wished to bring about political change in Russia considered that it was no longer possible for Russia to avoid the capitalist stage of its development. More traditional political parties began to emerge. The Socialist Revolutionary Party, using a peasant base, was formed in 1900 and was generally the largest of all Russian political parties, though lacking in organization and leadership. The Russian liberal party, the Constitutional Democrats, or Kadets, was founded in 1905 after a Congress of Rural and Urban Activists. Russian Marxism was not new, but for some years it had been confined to emigration. In 1898, however, the Russian Social Democratic Workers' Party held its first "congress" in a wooden hut in the city of Minsk. It was attended by nine delegates from Social Democratic organizations, with others from the Jewish Bund, and *Rabochaya gazeta* (*Workers' Newspaper*). Most of the participants were well known to the secret police, the Okhrana, and were arrested immediately afterward. Little that occurred in the 1898 meeting seemed to herald anything of import.

The 2nd Congress held in 1903 had to be convened abroad, though it was still facing pressure from the police, this time of Germany, eventually moving from Stuttgart to London. The immediate goals of the party were radical enough – to overthrow at once the tsarist autocracy and establish a democratic republic, while introducing rights for workers such as an eight-hour day, eliminating the remains of the feudal system in the village, and allowing full rights to non-Russians, including self-determination. The maximal goal was even more utopian – the establishment of the dictatorship of the proletariat through a socialist revolution. The goals were more deep-rooted than those of the European trends of the day, particularly in Germany where Economism had taken root: the belief that the workers' demands could be satisfied gradually through the trade union movement without having to resort to outright revolution. Such views were anathema to the Social Democratic leaders. The Russians were also divided on tactics, however. One group, initially the largest, and led by Yuly Martov (the pseudonym of Yuly Tserderbaum), considered that the party could incorporate not only committed and hardened revolutionaries but also sympathizers. The other, led by Vladimir Ilich Ulyanov (Lenin), following guidelines laid out in his 1902 pamphlet *What Is to Be Done?*, preferred a small, disciplined party that could guide rather than be guided by the mass of the workers. As the Congress progressed, and disputes led to the departure of several delegates, this faction was found to be in the majority, and designated by Lenin with the title of Bolsheviks. Martov and his now-minority group were termed the Mensheviks. Though the divide seemed frivolous and temporary, it proved to be permanent, mainly thanks to the intransigence of Lenin.

Though the revolutionary Marxist party was very small, there appeared to be some hope that it could have an impact on Russian political life. By the turn of the century, Russia was suffering from unemployment in the towns. On the initiative of Count Witte, the working day had been reduced to a maximum of 11.5 hours by 1897, but many workers considered this excessive. There was also widespread peasant unrest after the difficult years of famine. In the period 1900–1904, 1,205 peasant "disturbances" were recorded. Many of the intelligentsia also demanded reforms. Partly at the behest of the authorities, and specifically of V. K. Plehve, appointed Minister of Internal Affairs in 1902, the Jews became a scapegoat for the difficulties, and 1903 was notorious for its anti-Jewish pogroms in cities in Moldavia, Belarus, and Ukraine. At the turn of the century, the Jews, confined to the Pale of Settlement, formed a majority or plurality in the major towns of the western borderlands. In the summer of 1903, oil workers in Baku initiated a general strike, and were quickly joined by workers in other parts of the Caucasus, comprising more than 100,000 people, again reiterating the demand for better working conditions, including an eight-hour day. The industrial centers of Ukraine and south Russia then joined in. The Social Democrats did not organize these strikes but they did join in and were able to spread effectively their propaganda. The first legal trade union – the Assembly of Russian Factory Workers – was formed in this same year. Its leader was a priest, Georgy Gapon, who was a double agent working for the tsarist Okhrana. As often happens in such cases, however, it was difficult to know where Gapon's real sympathies lay. The police would try to control such movements through infiltration, but often the movement seemed to be beyond their reach. By April 1905, when the 3rd Congress of the RSDWP was held in London, and Lenin had been elected as the Chairman of the Congress, the possibility of a "bourgeois-democratic" revolution in Russia appeared to be much greater than hitherto. The party issued a new newspaper, the *Proletarii*, and divided activities between a Russian section and one abroad, with Lenin appointed as the chairman of the latter.

The war with Japan

The main possibility for further expansion lay in the Far East, and at the expense of China. Nikolay II, who had ascended to the throne upon the death of his father Aleksandr III in 1894, had no clear ambitions. Rather his approach was traditional – to continue the legacy inherited from his robust father and to maintain and strengthen the existing realm. Thus he was far from averse to colonialism, but had run into a new problem – the emergence of Imperial Japan as a new colonial power in the Far East. To date, the Japanese had not posed a serious threat to the Russians, but they were equally anxious to benefit from the weakness of China, and in Japan's case the goal was to use Korea as a springboard for further encroachment. In

1894–1895, Japan had defeated China, using the victory to gain control over part of the Liaotung Peninsula – including, at its tip, Port Arthur. Almost at once the Great Powers had intervened to prevent this "outrage" by an Asian power; and Japan, resentfully, had been forced to relinquish its conquests. The immediate beneficiary was Russia, which in 1897 obtained a lease over both the Liaotung Peninsula and Port Arthur, which was linked to the new Trans-Siberian Railway through the Chinese territory of Manchuria. Japan was concerned that the next target for the Russians would be Korea, and decided that the most preferable alternative was a war with Russia.

There were several disadvantages for Russia at the outset of the war. The main one was logistics. To fight a war so far from the center of the empire required the transportation of the Russian army and supplies and equipment over a lone route, that of the Trans-Siberian Railway, which was single-tracked. The Japanese by contrast could easily replenish their resources from the Japanese islands. Both the Russian Pacific Fleet and the Russian Far Eastern Army were based on the Liaotung Peninsula, but both were put under immediate pressure by Japan. On January 27, 1904 the war began when Japanese units attacked the Russian fleet at Port Arthur. Though the attack was repelled, the fleet was effectively hemmed in, and it became the focus of further Japanese assaults. In May the attack was renewed, when Japanese forces based in Manchuria began a long siege of Port Arthur. Though Japanese losses were extraordinarily high, the port finally fell on December 20, 1904, after the Japanese had begun to use 11-inch howitzers that weighed almost 500 pounds. Russian losses in the battle were considerably less than those of their Japanese counterparts; but the Russian commander at Port Arthur, General Anatoly Stessel, had to scuttle the Pacific Fleet's ships. Thereafter, the fate of the Russians at sea would depend on the Baltic Fleet, which was dispatched on a remarkable journey of 20,500 miles in October 1904, with the aim of reaching Vladivostok.

In the meantime, the Russians suffered a series of defeats in land battles. Military operations had begun in April 1904, with the Japanese deploying four armies. Two great battles were fought, neither of which was conclusive, but the outcome of each was that the Japanese army held the battlefield at the conclusion. At the Battle of Liaoyang between August 11 and 21, 1904, a slightly larger Japanese force defeated a Russian force led by General Aleksey Kuropatkin, and both sides suffered more than 17,000 casualties. A Russian counter-offensive at Sha Ho was a disaster, resulting in around 40,000 casualties. Generally, however, the trench warfare was equally catastrophic for both sides and a prelude to what was to occur during the First World War. In February 1905 the two sides met at Mukden with enormous armies. One estimate maintains that over 600,000 troops from both sides took part in this battle, and casualties were huge (more than 150,000). The Japanese victory, though a narrow one, was achieved largely because of the army's numerical superiority in machine-guns. Mukden proved to be the most decisive land engagement of the war, and the Russian defeat was a major embarrassment for the government of Nikolay II. An expected easy victory over an Asian opponent had failed to materialize.

At sea, matters were to take an even worse turn for the Russians. The Baltic Fleet, under the command of admirals Z. P. Rozhestvensky and N. I. Nebogatov, managed the considerable feat of circumnavigating most of the globe, only to run into an ambush by the large Japanese fleet under the leadership of Admiral Togo Heihachiro. The Russian losses were unprecedented at sea, and included nineteen major warships out of the thirty dispatched. Only four ships out of the Baltic Fleet ever reached the port of Vladivostok, and almost half the Russian sailors lost their lives. However, mainly through the diplomatic skills and wiles of Witte, the Russian side did not fare particularly badly as the Treaty of Portsmouth, mediated by the Americans in September 1905, moderated considerably Japanese demands for the transfer of the entire Liaotung Peninsula to Japanese control, the seizure of the entire Sakhalin Island, control over Korea, and the removal of the Russian army from Manchuria. Japan did receive the southern part of Sakhalin, and was permitted to control Korea, and Russia agreed to transfer its lease over the peninsula. Though the results of the treaty were less harsh than might have been anticipated, the military and naval defeats reduced the prestige of the tsarist government at a time when outright revolution had broken out in the capital, St Petersburg. The first real dent in the 300-year-old Romanov dynasty had been rendered. In later years, Soviet leaders, and particularly Stalin, were to avenge the disastrous defeat by Japan – a sign of how deeply such an event rankled, even among avowed socialist activists.

By 1905, Russian standing as a world power had fallen sharply. Less than a century earlier, the Russian tsar, Aleksandr I, had been in Paris helping to supervise the abdication of Napoleon Bonaparte. By contrast, Nikolay II, a pleasant and courteous family man, had suffered the most ignominious defeat in living memory. Britain, one of Russia's main rivals in the Near East, no longer regarded Russia as a serious threat to its empire, and to India in particular – the two countries would sign an alliance agreement in 1907. Henceforth, Russia would seek to re-establish itself on the international stage, often as a means of diverting attention from growing domestic (and especially economic) problems. The tsarist autocracy was in theory the most powerful ruling family on the continent and landmass of Eurasia. In practice, the tsars had become vulnerable. A weak tsar, like Nikolay, was dependent on his ministers and on Russia's international standing. His ministers gave him contradictory advice: Witte seeking cordial links with China and Korea, and Plehve preferring a more aggressive and warlike attitude toward these states, which were under Japanese influence. Partly as a result of circumstances beyond his control, but partly through his own inadequacies, such a goal proved beyond his power.

The 1905 Revolution

The revolution of 1905 began with a strike movement – something quite common in the Russian Empire during this period. Working conditions were extremely difficult. Employers generally ignored a flurry of laws issued in the later part of the 19th century to reduce working hours and improve labor conditions. However, the demands of the strikers at the outset suggest that there was already a political dimension to the protests. The strike began on January 3 at the giant Putilov munitions factory in St Petersburg, and spread to several other factories throughout the week. The strikers demanded an eight-hour working day, a rise in wages, and the cessation of indirect taxes, but also the transfer of lands to the peasants and the convocation of an assembly based on equal and general voting rights. Less than a week later, a large group of demonstrators took their protests directly to the Tsar, with a peaceful procession to the Winter Palace. The priest Gapon led the marchers. The Tsar was absent, but the Cossacks under the command of the Grand Duke Vladimir fired on the protestors, killing an estimated 1,000 of them, and injuring about five times as many. The event became known as Bloody Sunday and catalyzed the protests of 1905. By the end of the month over 400,000 Russian workers had joined the strike.

The strike movement continued over the next several months, despite an abortive government commission to ascertain the causes of the workers' discontent. Another famous event was the mutiny in the battleship *Potemkin*, immortalized by the Soviet film director Sergey Eisenstein, which took place in Odesa in mid-June. The sailors had refused to eat poor-quality meat, taken command of the ship, and hoisted the red flag. The battleship made a raid on Odesa before returning to the Black Sea. Lacking fuel, the mutineers eventually landed in Romania and gave themselves up to the local authorities. By October the strike had spread to the Russian railway workers, on the main lines between Moscow and several cities further east and south, such as Kursk and Kazan. Altogether some 120 cities and towns saw mass strikes, with thousands of protestors in the streets demanding the convocation of an Extraordinary Assembly. By October 13, various factories in St Petersburg had begun to elect representatives to a new council (soviet) of workers' deputies. In the meantime, the tsarist regime had agreed reluctantly to establish a state parliament (Duma) provided with legislative authority. The Duma was to comprise representatives from the landowners and factory managers, and the peasants were to receive one out of every eight seats. The workers, however, were not enfranchised because they did not own property. Thus the initial law antagonized the very forces that had initiated the strike. On October 17, as the worker discontent reached a climax, Nikolay II agreed to freedom of speech and of assembly, along with a parliament that wielded real authority – the concession was termed the October Manifesto. Two days later the monarchy also agreed to the creation of a Council of Ministers under the chairmanship of Witte.

The period of the 1905 Revolution also saw the formation of two new political parties. The Kadets were fortunate that Witte was seeking liberal support for the government in a move to drive a wedge between those groups prepared to compromise and the more hardened revolutionary elements. By late October a number of Kadet leaders, including the historian P. N. Milyukov, took part in discussions with the government. The Kadet goal was for the party's leaders to be invited into the government – a prospect that began to fade with time. In mid-October the Kadets held an Extraordinary Congress in Moscow which combined the goals of two organizations – the Union of Liberation and the Union of Land Constitutionalists. Though a relatively small party, the Kadets remained influential for many years, and included members of the landed aristocracy and the liberal intelligentsia, along with academicians. The party's guiding light was Milyukov. The Kadets sought a constitutional monarchy (close to the British model), freedom of assembly and of the press, universal suffrage, and the establishment of a Duma that would exert significant control over the government. Their goals were radical in 1905, and the prominence of their members in public life ensured that the party would not be ignored. However, the eventual polarization of political life in Russia ensured that the Kadets gradually began to move further away from the more radical tendencies that followed the military defeats during the First World War.

Another party was formed as a result of the tsarist Manifesto, namely the Union of October 17 or Octobrists. They represented a more affluent group of merchants and landowners, and were led by M. V. Rodzyanko and A. I. Guchkov. The latter, a well-known banker from a thriving Moscow family, emerged as the main leader. The party had around 75,000 members within its first two years of existence (making it larger than the Kadets), and preferred a more conservative monarchical system, though the existence of the party ostensibly was to ensure that the regime adhered to the concessions made in its Manifesto. The party included some of the more prominent landowners, such as D. N. Shipov. Both the Kadets and the Octobrists were moderate parties with limited goals. In 1905 they constituted the major parties at a time when the direction of events was never very clear. The 1905 Revolution, as opposed to a general strike and mass protests, was confined to a brief period at the very end of the year, when the more radical elements tried to unite the workers and the more disaffected elements of the peasantry. The tsarist Manifesto was used as the spark for numerous meetings and demonstrations against the autocracy in the larger cities of the empire. On October 18, the Central Committee of the Russian Social Democratic Workers' Party denounced the Manifesto as a betrayal of the working masses. In fact, it was a dangerous document to the revolutionary movement as it threatened to divide the protestors into the satiated and those who sought outright revolution.

The events of the 1905 Revolution occurred rapidly. On October 13, the St Petersburg Soviet had been formed, and eventually it came under the chairmanship of a Social Democrat, L. D. Trotsky, at that time somewhat distant from Lenin and the more hard-line Bolshevik members of the RSDWP. On October 26, sailors at the Kronstadt naval base began a revolt, and were arrested by the authorities. The ensuing trial in St Petersburg led to a general strike in the capital on November 2. Martial law had been declared by this time in Poland as a result of bloody clashes between demonstrators and the authorities in Warsaw and Lodz. On November 11, sailors of the Black Sea Fleet mutinied. Ten days later, a Moscow Soviet of Workers'

Deputies was formed that included members of the RSDWP (Bolsheviks and Mensheviks), Socialist Revolutionaries, and members of the Jewish Bund. The Bolshevik leadership in Moscow at once demanded of the Soviet that it declare a general strike in the city, with the hope that it would lead to an armed uprising. By December 8, the strike was widespread, involving more than 150,000 workers. From Moscow, the strike spread to other cities, notably St Petersburg and Minsk. Next day, barricades appeared in the streets of Moscow, and ultimately the uprising embraced more than thirty major cities of the empire, including some in Poland, Ukraine, Siberia, and southern parts of Russia. Yet the protests died as quickly as they arose, mainly because of the lack of unity among the demonstrators. The more moderate elements were contented with the offer of a legislative assembly; the revolutionaries wished to overthrow the regime, expropriate lands for the peasantry, and introduce a republic in Russia – all demands that in this period were perceived as unrealistic and frightening to the majority of the merchants and landowners. Despite the presence of Trotsky in the capital, the 1905 Revolution was essentially leaderless. No single leader had a vision of where the protests should lead or was prepared to provide direction.

On the other hand, the two events of 1904–1905 – the catastrophic war with Japan and the 1905 uprising – had, whatever the short-term outcome, seriously undermined the tsarist autocracy of the Romanovs. Thereafter, there would always be the Duma in place – an arena in which potential orators could sound off against the worst excesses of the tsarist system. Moreover, the tradition of a general strike would remain, always a threat beneath the surface when the economic situation became bleak. The revolutionaries also learned lessons from 1905, and the organization of the Soviet signaled that the workers were prepared to turn to their own devices if the new legislature could not satisfy their demands. The royal family, in turn, had lost credibility as a result of Bloody Sunday, which created an impression of remoteness and distance from the masses. Hitherto there had always appeared to be a link between the Tsar and the mass of impoverished workers and the peasantry, hence the naivety with which a petition was offered directly to Nikolay II. However, only the combination of factors rather than one key issue can explain the gradual demise of the Russian monarchy after the 1905 Revolution. For the moment, the Tsar seemed to have avoided a disaster even worse than the defeat by Japan. The question was how to consolidate the situation and ensure that such protests did not re-emerge. The first matter was the convocation of the new assembly, the First Duma.

The time of the Dumas

On December 11, 1905 the electoral law was modified, providing a complex system of voting that disenfranchised several groups of the population, including women, those under the age of 25, those in the military, and those people without a fixed abode. The voting of delegates was weighted in favor of the propertied classes and the wealthier merchants. Whereas the nobility could elect one delegate per 2,000 people, for workers this was one per 90,000. In addition, as the regime recovered from the anarchy of recent events, it placed a barrier between the new Duma and the monarchy, namely the manifesto of February 1906, which permitted the State Council the right to approve any laws issued by the Duma. The First Duma, elected in March–April 1906, provided a plurality of votes for the Kadet Party, which received 279 seats, followed by the Labor Group (*Trudoviki*) with ninety-seven. Non-party groups received 105 seats. Though the results from the perspective of the monarchy could have been worse, the Octobrists and other right-wing groups had fared poorly. On the left, the Bolsheviks had boycotted the election, but the Mensheviks also remained on the periphery with only eighteen seats. By April, the State Council and the State Duma gained legal authority through the issue of the Basic (Fundamental) Laws of the Russian Empire. Less than four months later, the regime dissolved the Duma, leading several deputies to flee to Vyborg where a rival parliament was hastily established. The government had been dissatisfied with demands to remove the restrictions imposed on the Duma by the Fundamental Laws. It had also requested control over the state budget and agrarian reforms that included the division of landowners' estates among the peasantry. The Tsar was so dissatisfied with the lack of compliance in the new legislature that he dismissed Count Witte on April 14, 1906, replacing him with I. L. Goremykin.

The Second Duma, which lasted only from February to June 1907, was even less satisfactory in the eyes of the monarchy. Though the Octobrists and supporters of the monarchy had performed much better, gaining fifty-four seats, they were outnumbered by the Social Democrats (including the Bolsheviks) with sixty-five. The Labor Group was now the largest faction, followed by the Kadets. Before the convocation of the Third Duma, therefore, the electoral law was altered, raising the number of electors from the nobles and merchants and reducing the number of seats allocated to the peasantry and lower-middle stratum of the towns. More than 200 members of the nobility were elected, while the monarchists and the Octobrists had gained almost 270 seats. The Third Duma sat from November 1907 to June 1912. Making sense of these three elections is not easy. The overlap between the various groups prevents any clear deductions. One can discern some trends, however. On the far right were extremist and pro-monarchy groups. The most fervent were the Black Hundreds, notoriously anti-Semitic, but prominent in several areas. Their closest allies were the Octobrists, since both groups were happy to preserve the monarchy intact and to accept a Duma without any significant powers. At the center of political life were the Labor Group, the Kadets, and occasionally the more moderate of the socialist groups, though it would seem an error to ascribe to the Mensheviks and the Socialist Revolutionaries the tactics of compromise that they embraced in 1917. The Bolshevik faction in parliament also was not notably more extreme than its socialist counterparts, but it was more isolated. The Duma continued into the war years (the Fourth Duma); and, though reduced in power from the original body, its significance should not be underrated.

Stolypin's reforms

On April 26, 1906, Petr Stolypin became the Minister of Internal Affairs, and on July 8 he was appointed Chairman of the Council of Ministers. Born in 1862 in Dresden, he had run the distant western *guberniya* of Grodno and subsequently was head of the Saratov region. There, as governor, he had succeeded in quelling all revolutionary activity during the time of the 1905 Revolution. Politically it is hard to place Stolypin. He was a man who saw the need for progressive reforms in agriculture, while seeking to preserve the powers of the tsarist autocracy and promote the cause of Russian nationalism. Yet he had been known to curb the excesses of the Black Hundreds in his own area of administration. Considered the scourge of the revolutionary movement, he was also disliked by the nobility for his sudden rise to prominence. Stolypin's attention turned primarily to agriculture and the *mir* or the *obshchina*, the society that effectively ran the village. He proposed that the peasants should have the right to consolidate their landholdings – a move that would prevent the desired division and redistribution of the estates of the landowners, but would also allow the peasants to become small landholders in their own right. Through a *Ukaz* of November 9, 1906, the peasants gained the right to leave the village society. The goal was the dissolution of an institution that had gained authority after the Emancipation of 1861 but which in Stolypin's view was the chief impediment to real change at village level. Aleksandr Krivoshein, the Minister of Agriculture, and Vladimir Kokovtsov, the Finance Minister, supported his reforms.

Another goal of the reform was to resolve the problem of rural overpopulation, particularly in the central regions of Russia. By dividing the lands this way, the government considered that a portion of the population, freed from the ties of the village community, would seek employment in the towns, whereas those more inclined to agriculture would become established smallholders. The reform worked in so far as it was implemented prior to the outbreak of war. By 1916, for example, some 3 million heads of households had left the village community, with the bulk of the departures taking place in 1908–1909, and more than 25 percent of community households had consolidated their lands by this date. The newly consolidated farms took the form of *otrubs*, uniting several smallholdings, or else enclosed farmsteads known as *khutors*. Altogether about 1.6 million new farms were established. A large number of people (more than 2.5 million) had migrated from their villages, mostly east of the Urals. By the first year of the war, these new farms accounted for about 50 percent of the grain production of the Russian Empire, and they were particularly successful in the key agricultural regions, such as the Volga region, the Ukrainian steppes, and Siberia. In 1912 the Russian harvest reached a new peak, and grain exports rose accordingly.

The reform, however, was not an unqualified success because the bulk of the peasants (around 75 percent of the total) remained in the village community, and even the mass migration was insufficient to resolve the problem of rural overpopulation. About 18 percent of the migrants eventually returned to their former homes. In general, the peasantry was not well disposed toward change, and initially the new farms were not very profitable. The transformation of the village envisaged by Stolypin was to be a protracted reform that might take twenty years to complete. Stolypin himself, however, did not live to see its implementation. On September 1, 1911, D. G. Bogrov, an anarchist reputed to be working for the Okhrana, assassinated him in Kyiv. His death limited the effects of the agrarian reform, and prevented a concomitant reform of industry that would have seen significant benefits accrue to the workers. Stolypin's plan was to ensure that workers' demands were met in a similar way to those of their counterparts in Germany, so that revolutionary tendencies could be assuaged. He also planned to introduce a system of general education in Russia. On the other hand, while these goals might be considered progressive, the Prime Minister sought only to enhance the power of an autocracy weakened by revolution. As a result, Stolypin was almost universally unpopular. Could the tsarist system have been reformed? In the prewar years, despite revolutionary outbreaks and peasant revolts, there are signs that the Russian economy was developing rapidly. But the reforms were not sustained, and there is little indication that the monarchy was seriously interested in changing the social structure of the country. Stolypin, like Witte, seems to have been a brilliant choice of minister (the latter, though, was appointed initially by Aleksandr III rather than by Nikolay II). But there were far fewer inspired – and even some highly dubious – choices; and under the tsarist system, with a tsar uninterested in the affairs of state, the poor quality of ministers was to be a critical factor.

In the period 1906–1912, the revolutionary movement ostensibly faded, and the possibility of the emergence of more democratic parties increased. The Bolshevik Party determined to go its own route. In 1912, at a conference in Prague, the party formally separated from the Mensheviks and launched its own newspaper, *Pravda*. This move coincided with the rekindling of the strike movement in the empire, which was sparked in turn by an incident in the gold mines of the Yakutia region, when the militia fired on striking workers, killing more than 250. In 1912–1913, the empire again seemed to be engulfed in strikes and protests. The Bolsheviks now had six deputies in the Fourth Duma, but there was little common ground between the Duma and the government. In 1912, I. V. Stalin first emerged as a Bolshevik theoretician with a pamphlet entitled *Marxism and the National Question*, in which the native Georgian stressed the right of non-Russians to self-determination within the empire. Such sentiments appealed to groups that were gradually losing their autonomy, such as the Finns and the Poles, and those regions in which national consciousness was developing rapidly, like Ukraine and Armenia. On the other hand, in 1913 the Romanovs could celebrate 300 years in power with an ostentatious ceremony, featuring

Nikolay II and his German wife Aleksandra, both descendants of the English queen Victoria, and seemingly oblivious to the coming storm of war and revolution. Through Victoria, the then incurable disease of hemophilia had struck the heir to the throne, Aleksey, leading the royal couple to turn to a series of mystics and faith healers in an effort to ensure their son's survival. In 1912, Rasputin was introduced to the court, where he would remain a critical influence for the next few years.

Rodzyanko chaired the Fourth Duma, replacing Guchkov, who was soon recruited to the State Council. The two bodies grew increasingly further apart. Although the Fourth Duma was a very conservative body, with the clergy now alongside the landowners as its leaders and a notable contingent of far-right deputies, it nevertheless sought to maintain its constitutional rights vis-à-vis the monarchy. Rodzyanko was the key figure in this regard. The government, through the State Council, grew increasingly reactionary, promoting a policy of Russian nationalism by trying to reduce the territories of Finland by detaching the southern part of Vyborg province – the move failed – and turning public wrath against the Jewish population of the Pale of Settlement, which was made a scapegoat for Russia's problems. One of the far right factions, the Union of the Russian People, had the backing of the Russian Orthodox Church, increasingly a mouthpiece of the government and criticized heavily by writer Lev Tolstoy, who was excommunicated in 1901 but remained one of the most influential figures in Russia until his death in 1910. Many leading church figures became compromised by their tolerance of or support for Rasputin. In the spring of 1912, Rodzyanko also took the unusual step of warning the Tsar that Rasputin's ready access to the royal family was damaging the prestige of the monarchy.

BOX 1.1

....

Lev (Leo) Nikolaevich Tolstoy (1828–1910)

One of Russia's greatest writers and most influential figures, Leo Tolstoy was born into an affluent noble family at the Yasnaya Polnaya estate in Tula province, 100 miles south of Moscow, on September 9, 1828. Orphaned at the age of 9, he nevertheless lived a privileged life, spending a fairly dissolute youth marked by gambling, drinking bouts, and associations with various women before joining the army to take part in campaigns in the Caucasus as well as in the Crimean War of 1854–1856. Many of his novels are based on his real-life experiences. They include an autobiographical trilogy, *Childhood*, *Boyhood*, and *Youth* (1852–1857), *The Cossacks* (1857), his most famous work, *War and Peace* (1869), *Anna Karenina* (1877), and *Resurrection* (1899). Tolstoy dropped out of Kazan University, where he had studied oriental languages and law, and developed philanthropic enterprises at Yasnaya Polnaya. In 1862 he married Sofya Andreevna Behrs, with whom he had ten surviving children. In the 1880s and 1890s the great author became increasingly devoted to religion, renouncing material wealth and authoritarian institutions. Though difficult to categorize precisely, his views were close to an anarchistic Christianity marked by non-resistance to tyranny, a fascination with death and asceticism, and a

Box 1.1 continued

rejection of the Orthodox Church. His views are outlined in his voluminous diaries. After 1884 he adopted the look of a white-bearded patriarch that was captured effectively in a painting by Ilya Repin in 1887. During his own lifetime he became a cult figure, and travelers and pilgrims flocked to Yasnaya Polnaya. In 1901, the Holy Synod of the Russian Orthodox Church excommunicated him. His choice of lifestyle caused much conflict within his family, and only his youngest daughter Aleksandra stood by him in his later years. In the fall of 1910 the two left the estate and set out secretly, evidently without a destination in mind, but Tolstoy contracted pneumonia and died at the house of the railway stationmaster of Astapovo, Ryazan province, on November 20, 1910.

BOX 1.2

Mikhail Vladimirovich Rodzyanko (1859–1924)

A prominent politician of the early 20th century and self-described as "the fattest man in Russia," Rodzyanko was born on February 9 (21), 1859 into a landowning family in the *guberniya* of Ekaterinoslav (Dnipropetrovsk). One of the founding members of the Octobrist Party, he was a member of the State Council in 1906–1907, and a deputy of the Third and Fourth State Dumas between 1907 and 1917. After 1911 he was the chairman of the Duma, succeeding Aleksandr Guchkov. During the First World War he formed an alliance with the Constitutional Democrats (Kadets) in an effort to secure some authority for the assembly during the ascendancy of Rasputin. Rodzyanko denounced Rasputin as a German spy and counseled the Tsar, unsuccessfully, to remain in Petrograd in 1915 rather than lead the Russian army in the war. During the February Revolution of 1917 he played a key role in the abdication of Tsar Nikolay II and was chairman of the Temporary Committee of the State Duma. Following the Bolshevik uprising of October 1917 and the outbreak of the Russian Civil War, Rodzyanko joined the army of General Anton Denikin. He emigrated to Yugoslavia in 1920, and died there on January 24, 1924.

The alliance system

International diplomacy in the late 19th and early 20th centuries revolved around an alliance system that was complex and restrictive. The defeat in the war with Japan paradoxically led to an improvement in relations with the main enemy, the British Empire, which had clashed several times with Russia in the Near East (Afghanistan and Iran) and in Tibet. The Anglo-Russian Entente of 1907 in effect formed a triple alliance, as both countries already had agreements in place with France. It was signed in St Petersburg by A. Nicholson, the British ambassador, and A. P. Izvolsky, the Russian Minister of Foreign Affairs, and the weakened Russia renounced its interests in Afghanistan while dividing Iran into a neutral zone in the center, a zone of Russian influence in the north and of British influence in the south. Both sides agreed to recognize China's prevailing influence in the nominally independent Tibet. Instantly the new entente appeared to be directed against the other alliance system in Europe, embracing Germany, the Austro-Hungarian Empire, and Italy. In this same year of 1907, Russia also signed an agreement with Japan. It did not yet mean, however, that two hostile alliance systems had permanently divided Europe. Such an outcome developed because of the various policies pursued by these powers in the interim. The alliance with France and Britain received support from the noted Kadet leader Petr Struve, who considered Russia's correct path to be toward Europe rather than adventurism in the Far East.

From Russia's perspective, the most important factor about the alliance system was the tension in the Balkans. Russia felt obliged to come to the aid of Serbia, which in turn appeared to threaten the stability of the Austro-Hungarian Empire. In 1907–1908, it seemed possible that an Austro-Russian compromise would be reached on several key questions – Austria agreed that Russia should have the right to send its naval vessels through the Dardanelles, and in return Russia supported Austria's wish to annex the territory of Bosnia-Herzegovina and incorporate it into its empire. In practice, nothing went right for Russia. The Austrian government acted very swiftly to occupy these territories, whereas the Western Powers resisted the Russian move through the Dardanelles, as it would have further weakened the crumbling Ottoman Empire. In 1909, S. D. Sazonov was appointed Russian Foreign Minister. Sazonov saw Germany as the main impediment to Russia's interests and tried to solidify the Triple Entente. Once war had started, Sazonov was at the forefront of demands for Russia's territorial expansion at the expense of Austria and Turkey. Germany, in turn, supported Austrian interests in the Balkans with impunity, in the belief that the area was beyond the sphere of British and French interests, and would not be the cause of a rise in international tension.

For the Russians, the alliance system brought few tangible gains and numerous problems. Two agreements were made with Japan in 1910 and 1912, the first of which allowed Japan a free hand in Korea, and the second divided the two countries' spheres of interest in northeast China and Mongolia. Thus Russia could avoid the threat of a two-front war. The Tsar visited Berlin in November 1910 for talks with his cousin, Kaiser Wilhelm II, and the two countries reached an agreement at Potsdam the following year, in which Russia accepted the German request to build a railway to Baghdad, while the Germans recognized Russian control over northern Iran. How seriously the Germans tried to wrench Russia from the Entente is a matter for debate, but the Western Powers took the threat seriously and raised objections. Two factors should be noted in the events that led to the outbreak of war in August 1914: first, Russia was as ambitious as any of the other powers in its wish to expand its territory and defend its interests in the Near East and Eastern Europe; but, second, of the major powers (with the possible exception of Britain), Russia had the least to gain from the outbreak of a new war. Russian prestige was at stake, however; the Austrian decision to punish Serbia after the assassination at Sarajevo of the Archduke Franz Ferdinand, heir to the Austrian throne, followed two setbacks for Russian diplomacy during the Balkan Wars of 1912–1913, when the Serbs were unable to fulfill their demands for an outlet to the sea. Austria, for its part, had to deal with a multi-ethnic empire that had long been divided between German-speakers and Slavs. A dual monarchy with Hungary since 1867, the old empire could not withstand a stronger Serbia, which would provide encouragement to fellow Slavs seeking more powers.

The First World War

After the death of the Archduke, Austrian artillery bombarded Belgrade on July 29, 1914, before Vienna had mobilized its army. Russia responded with a general mobilization on July 30, following a period in which it had tried to mobilize forces against Austria, but not against Germany. The Tsar still hoped to come to terms with the Kaiser, and a flurry of notes was exchanged. For the Entente, the readiness of the Russian army was paramount; though the full details of the Schlieffen Plan were not known to the Entente powers, it was anticipated none the less that the bulk of the German forces would be thrown against France, and thus Russia was asked to mount an offensive in order to divert German troops eastward. Mobilization, however, made war far more likely. The Central Powers (Germany and Austro-Hungary) had anticipated that any Russian mobilization would be slow, taking up to six weeks to complete. The amended version of the 1905 Schlieffen Plan (devised by Count Alfred von Schlieffen, chief of the German general staff from 1891 to 1906) therefore foresaw a rapid German thrust into France, sweeping to the Channel and to the west of Paris, in an effort to end the war in the West before Russian mobilization had been completed. Hence, once the Russians mobilized, it became essential that Germany do the same, unless the Russians could be persuaded to desist. When the Russians did not respond to a German ultimatum, Germany declared war on Russia on August 1, 1914.

In retrospect, the German plans, while ingenious, were seriously flawed. For one thing, the adherence to such a strict timetable was contingent upon Belgian neutrality and an undamaged railway system. For another, it ignored the fact that, while the Russian mobilization would take time, Russia none the less could have a substantial army (up to 800,000 troops) in place within two weeks. It has often been said that Russia was unprepared for war in 1914. The point is accurate, but needs to be qualified. Russia's main weakness lay in its artillery and in the readiness of its fleet. But it was not wholly unprepared. It had planned for both a defensive and an offensive operation, depending on German action. The defensive plan would have been put into play had there been a major German assault from East Prussia at the outset of the war. However, under pressure from the French and the British, it was the offensive operation, known as Plan A, that was used, which encompassed a Russian assault on both East Prussia and the Austrian territory of Galicia. The Russian army, under the Grand Duke Nikolay, an imposing figure of 6 feet 7 inches, did not assign clear priority to either campaign, though once the German army began to move through Belgium the French ambassador in Petrograd (as the capital had been renamed at the war's outset) requested an immediate Russian attack on East Prussia. The area was a difficult one to tackle, as it consisted of forests, swampy land, and numerous lakes, and Russian communication was amateurish, being made over open radio. The East Prussian operation lasted from August 17 to September 15, 1914, and from Russia's perspective it was an unmitigated disaster.

Russia used two armies in this assault. The 1st Army was under General P. K. Rennenkampf, a 60-year-old cavalry general who had commanded an army group in the war against Japan. Rennenkampf was ordered to attack from the north, in an attempt to cut off the German 8th Army from the main city of Koenigsberg. The Russian 2nd Army was under the command of A. V. Samsonov, a man five years Rennenkampf's junior, but with whom he had a history of bad relations. According to the Russian plan, Samsonov was to attack from the south and west, joining up with the 1st Army and encircling the German troops. At Gumbinnen on August 17, Rennenkampf achieved initial success, but did not follow up his gains – indeed, he seems to have been over-apprehensive of the threat of a German counter-attack. The inertia of the 1st Army raised the confidence of the Germans, who had hitherto considered the complete abandonment of the East Prussian territory. Instead they transferred two army corps and a cavalry division from the Western Front, thus providing much-needed relief for the French. Samsonov meanwhile was trying to ascertain his exact position, seemingly unaware that German armies had encircled him, and they inflicted a severe and crushing defeat on the Russians at Tannenberg. In this battle, the Russians suffered over 50,000 casualties, and some 150,000 were taken prisoner. Samsonov committed suicide. At the ensuing Battle of Masurian Lakes, Rennenkampf's 1st Army, still intact despite defeat on the battlefield, was driven out of East Prussia. Thereafter the Russian army never set foot on German soil for the remainder of the war. Russia may have saved the French, but it had suffered a grievous loss.

Further south, the Russians fared better. The Galician Operation took place from August 18 to September 21, 1914. The Russian army of the Southwestern Front under General N. Ivanov drove the Austrians back over the Danube, while four Russian armies attacked the L'viv region, virtually eliminating the Austrian 3rd Army. Both sides suffered heavy losses in this campaign, which saw the Austrian troops retreat to the Carpathian Mountains. That they were able to recover at all was a result of the Russian failure to capitalize on the successful attack. By November, with the Austrians on the verge of a total defeat, the Germans were obliged to divert troops to their aid, and a portion of the German army was transferred to Upper Silesia. On November 12, Turkey joined in the war on the side of the Central Powers, but suffered a major defeat at Sarykamysh, when its 3rd Army suffered over 90,000 casualties. By 1915, the

Germans, having failed with the Schlieffen Plan, redirected their major operations to the Eastern Front. In May 1915 the Germans and the Austrians achieved a decisive breakthrough in southern Poland, and by the following month the Russians had pulled out of Galicia. As the year continued, with German forces consolidated, Russia suffered a series of setbacks, vacating the whole of Poland, western Ukraine and Belarus, and the western districts of the Baltic States. To this point, the Russians had suffered over 3.5 million casualties. In addition, on the advice of his wife, the Tsar himself took over command from the Grand Duke on September 18, 1915, leaving the capital in the hands of Aleksandra and her chief advisor, the disreputable Rasputin. It was to prove a fateful decision because it left the country leaderless at a critical economic and political period, and it also directly associated the monarchy with the results of the military confrontations.

The year 1916 is best-remembered for two colossal battles on the Western Front: Verdun, in which the Germans tried to defeat France at its eastern-border fortress through a battle of attrition; and the Somme, which lasted from June until November, and constituted a disastrous British offensive to relieve the French. The Russians again were asked to play a contributory role, with a new offensive that would be preceded, for the first time in the war, by the provision of adequate artillery, machine-guns, and rifles to the Russian troops. In March 1916, General A. A. Brusilov was appointed commander-in-chief of the Russian army of the South-western Front. He had been in charge of the Russian 8th Army in Galicia. Reserves were moved covertly to the front, and plans were made to link an artillery barrage with a sudden surprise attack on Austrian troops. The tactics worked well, and on a wide front the Russians advanced in waves all the way to the foothills of the Carpathian Mountains. Austrian losses were enormous, and were estimated at about 1.5 million. Once again, the Russians appeared to be very close to a decisive victory over Austro-Hungary, but Brusilov's problems increased as the attack continued. He lacked reserves and had no answer to the German response, which was to transfer thirty-four divisions from the Western and Italian Fronts to prevent its ally from being defeated. Once again, the Russians had come to the rescue of their French ally (there was no French defeat at Verdun), but at too high a cost. Brusilov's offensive came to a halt by the end of September 1916.

Further south, Russia had gained some ground against the Turks at Ezerum, a Turkish citadel defended by the 3rd Turkish Army. In this battle, which took place from January to March 1916, Turkish casualties were as high as 50 percent, and Russia received the plum from its Entente allies of the potential annexation of Turkey's lands in the Black Sea area at the end of the war. However, Russia's position at the end of 1916 was far from secure. Its troops were suffering from supply problems, heavy casualty rates, and disillusionment with the war. At home, there were already long lines for food and acute shortages in the towns. Further, the population began to believe rumors of pro-German sentiment at the Russian court, with Aleksandra widely regarded as treacherous to the Russian cause. Such sentiments were fueled by the retirement of Sazonov in the summer of 1916 and his replacement by B. V. Shturmer, the Chairman of the Council of Ministers, who took temporary control of foreign policy between July 7 and November 10. Aleksandra, meanwhile, refused to heed the advice of the Duma. Russian plans were often orchestrated by Rasputin, who retained the confidence of the royal family because of his apparent ability to stop the Tsarevich's bleeding when he fell, a result of his hemophilia. Rasputin's debauched behavior served to discredit the monarchy and led to his assassination by members of the royal family in December 1916. By this time, Russia's situation in the war was desperate. Fierce attacks that could not be sustained had resulted in major losses of the empire's western lands. As the Germans continued to advance into the Baltic States, they posed a threat to Petrograd itself.

Tsarist Russia was on the verge of collapse. The causes were varied. First, one needs to look at the historical context. Several old empires were to be eliminated by the First World War – the Ottoman, the Austro-Hungarian, and the Russian (in addition to the Prussian Hohenzollern monarchy, a relatively new empire). In each case their demise followed several cataclysmic military defeats; but, in the case of the first two, the fall of the monarchies might have been predicted. In the Russian case, the situation appears less clear-cut. Was there any one factor that caused the sudden end to the Romanov dynasty? Can it be ascribed to the folly of entering another war, the earlier defeat by Japan, revolutionary ferment in the capital, peasant discontent, or the personal inadequacies of the ruling family? The key element seems to have been the general dissatisfaction in the major cities of Petrograd and Moscow, combined with a mutiny in the Russian army – in the end the generals and their men lost confidence in the Tsar and persuaded him to abdicate, but it is hard to discern what sort of system they wished to see in place of the monarchy. A constitutional monarchy seemed to be one possibility; but once the Tsar, along with his brother the Grand Duke Mikhail, declined to rule further there was surprisingly little desire among the population to resuscitate the autocracy. Of the famous cousins of Europe, only George V remained in place in Britain, and his powers were severely limited. However, even he felt insecure enough to deny his homeland as a haven to the deposed Romanovs. The First World War had brought great suffering everywhere, and no monarchy remained untarnished by it. It was almost as though the postwar era constituted not only an end to conflict but also a new world in which the defeated nations, especially Germany and Russia, would need to find their own direction.

The February Revolution

The revolution of February 23–27, 1917 (March 8–12 New Style by the Georgian calendar) was directly linked to the economic and social problems that had been exacerbated by the war. In Petrograd the crisis had begun at least two years earlier, and the course of events repeated those of 1905 and 1912, with added impetus.

No common ground could be found between the Duma and the Cabinet, and in the former a Progressive Bloc had been formed that sought a new Cabinet that could inspire the confidence of the public. At the beginning of the year, there were widespread protests in the capital at the lack of bread. At the giant Putilov factory, which had been a catalyst for many earlier protests, workers again downed tools, demanding a rise in wages and the re-employment of workers who had been laid off. Mass protests coincided with International Women's Day (March 8, NS) and continued unabated for four days, developing into a general strike in Petrograd. The fate of the government depended on the Petrograd Military Garrison, and its response to the demand of the Tsar on March 10 that it put an end to the disorders in the capital. Its commander, General Sergey Khabalov, had formed a special military district in Petrograd to deal with the mass protests some three weeks earlier. He complied with the order, and within a few hours more than 130 protestors had been killed. The following day, however, troops began to fraternize with the workers. The government had lost control over the capital. On this same day, the Duma was dissolved and barricades reappeared on the streets. By March 12, both the main arsenal and the Winter Palace had fallen into the hands of revolutionaries.

The main question at this juncture was whether a new source of authority would emerge. Because of its dissolution, the Duma could form only a temporary committee. Some of its prominent members, such as Rodzyanko, wished to preserve the monarchy, and began in effect to occupy the main ministerial functions, though without significant popular backing. Rodzyanko communicated several times with the Tsar, whose train had reached the headquarters of the Northern Front in Pskov, on March 14. With no support from any of his generals, the Tsar quietly agreed to an act of abdication on March 15, initially in favor of his son, but after a change of heart in favor of his brother. The latter had no desire to take over in such circumstances, and indeed it appears unlikely that he would have survived long had he done so. He declined the throne on the following day, placing hopes instead in the convocation of a new Constituent Assembly that would decide the future of Russia. By March 15, the Petrograd Soviet was re-created, occupying, like the temporary Duma committee, a room in the Tauride Palace. These two bodies would between them determine the immediate direction of Russia. The temporary committee retained the semblance of continuity with the Duma, but lacked popular backing; the Soviet represented the demonstrators on the streets, but was from the beginning a large and unwieldy body.

In these early days of the revolution, about 3,000 delegates sat in the Soviet, though most of them were not members of any political faction. The country's future direction, however, was under the influence of the more politically aware members, particularly those of the Menshevik and Socialist Revolutionary parties who began to play a dominant role. The Socialist Revolutionaries (led by Viktor Chernov) remained the largest political grouping in the country with around 800,000 members at their peal, while the Mensheviks perhaps numbered around 200,000, and had several notable leaders including I. G. Tsereteli, and F. I. Dan, with a leftist section led by Lenin's former comrade, Yuly Martov. The Mensheviks perceived the revolution in strictly Marxist terms – as a bourgeois revolution that now should be supported and consolidated, in order to prevent a return to a monarchy. The temporary committee of the Duma, together with the Petrograd Soviet, decided that a new Provisional Government should be formed, which would rule the country until the elections to the new legislature. A compromise candidate for prime minister was found – Prince G. E. Lvov, a prominent landowner known to hold progressive views. Lvov had been the head of the Zemstvo Union. Within the new government, the Kadets played the major role (supported by the Octobrists), occupying six out of the twelve established Cabinet posts. In particular, the historian P. N. Milyukov, as Minister of Foreign Affairs, began to play the leading role. Milyukov had been an outspoken critic of the tsarist regime in the former Duma. At first there were no socialists in the Cabinet, the Menshevik faction's leader N. S. Chkheidze having declined to join the "bourgeois" government. However, Aleksandr Kerensky, a prominent Socialist Revolutionary lawyer who had made a name for himself with speeches in the Duma, agreed to join the Cabinet as Minister of Justice, and became the only leading figure to have a foot in both the new organizations.

In theory, the Soviets, as the representatives of the popular masses, could have taken power in March 1917. Instead, they confined themselves to the more immediate goals, such as ensuring that soldiers based in the capital did not have to return to the front. The most notable example of this goal was Order No. 1, issued on March 14, which the Soviet forced on the government, and the details of which were published in the Soviet newspaper *Izvestiya* before it officially became law. The order ended the primacy of officers in the Russian army, banned ranks and saluting, and enforced the supremacy of committees in making major decisions. The Soviet also encouraged peasants to take over landowner estates in the countryside and advocated workers' control in the factories. Essentially, however, its main role was as a watchdog over the actions of the government and to ensure that it carried out the progressive reforms advocated by the Soviet. It formed an inside pressure group that could not be ignored, but at the same time did not wish to take over power. Though some Bolsheviks had joined the body, the party was in no position to dictate policy. It had suffered more than the other revolutionary parties from tsarist repressions. Most of its leaders were abroad or in exile, and those who had remained in Petrograd were unsure of how to react to the tumultuous events. The Bolsheviks thus supported the policy of compromise with the government.

The countryside had lost much of its workforce during the war years, but the key institution there remained the peasant commune (known as the *obshchina* or *mir*), which was in the position of dealing with growing peasant demands for the division of lands. The latter belonged to the nobility, landowners, church, and state. Once the requests were made, the village commune then decided how to distribute them, and this institution rather than the Soviet was the key element, as it began to authorize the expropriation of such lands without authorization from Petrograd.

Simultaneously, the peasant Socialist Revolutionary Party was playing a decisive role in the Soviets, which were trying to expand their organizational base outside the towns, taking over the functions of the Zemstvos, where landowners held sway.

The early measures of the Provisional Government brought about a dramatic transformation of Russia. An eight-hour working day was introduced, and a seven-point program embraced many of the demands advanced by the Soviet, such as an amnesty for political prisoners, freedom of the press and of assembly, and the rights and freedoms of all citizens regardless of nationality or background. In late March, tsarist holdings became state property, and a Central Bureau of Trade Unions was created in Petrograd and Moscow. The government also recognized in principle that a permanent government would only be decided once the Constituent Assembly had been elected. The scope of the new measures, however, was limited by two key factors. The first was Russia's continuing participation in the First World War and its commitment to its Entente allies, Britain and France. Though the two countries welcomed the democratic changes taking place in Russia, they were more concerned that Russia did not renege on its agreements, thus allowing the German army to divert divisions back to the Western Front. The seven-point program avoided mention of the war, though Order No. 1 implied that the Russian army would become severely restricted as a fighting force. The Lvov Cabinet was also reluctant to commit itself to the goals of the past. On April 9, Milyukov declared that what was needed was a just peace without annexations. The Entente powers, however, dispatched a special mission to Petrograd in the same month to ensure that Russia abided by its obligations. In the Soviet, the Mensheviks and the Socialist Revolutionaries also advocated the signing of an immediate peace without annexations.

The war question came to the fore on May 1 when Milyukov sent a note to the Entente allies, confirming that Russia would adhere to its wartime aims and commitments. The War Minister, A. I. Guchkov, also approved the statement. The note was intended primarily to appease the Western partners, but its contents became known from the telegraph office. By May 3, there were mass demonstrations in the streets of Petrograd demanding the resignation of Milyukov. Some historians have perceived this event as the first uprising against the Provisional Government, but the protests were limited to the capital, and the crowd was assuaged by the dismissal of Milyukov and Guchkov. Though there were some pleas for the Soviet to take power, the Menshevik and Social Revolutionary majority had no such desire. The protests – sometimes referred to as the April Days – indicated the extreme sensitivity of the war question. Nevertheless, the Provisional Government made no attempt to end Russian participation in the war. Guchkov's replacement as War Minister was Kerensky. In addition, the new Cabinet formed in mid-May 1917 (the First Coalition Government) included several Menshevik and Socialist Revolutionary leaders, such as Tsereteli (Posts and Telegraph), M. I. Skobelev (Labor) and V. M. Chernov (Minister of Agriculture). Henceforth, the flaws of the government would reflect on these parties and undermine their standing in the Soviet.

The return of Lenin

The Bolshevik leader Lenin had failed to predict revolution in Russia in 1917. A firm opponent of Russian participation in the First World War, the events of February–March found him in Switzerland, desperate to return home, and furious at the tactics being applied by Petrograd Bolsheviks. The main culprits were Stalin and L. B. Kamenev, who had taken over the editorial direction of *Pravda*, and produced some articles conciliatory toward fellow socialist parties and in favor of working with the Provisional Government. In his "Letter from Afar," Lenin advocated that the Soviet refrain from further support for the government and take power itself. He maintained that the revolution was in transition to a second phase when the workers, together with the "toiling" peasantry, would take over the reins of power. At this point, Lenin's comments were inconsequential. He was simply out of touch and, away from the capital, could do little to influence events. His return in the so-called "sealed train," along with some twenty of his comrades (including his wife Nadezhda Krupskaya and close associate Grigory Zinoviev) occurred at the behest of the Germans, who were willing to make a small investment to cause further chaos in the capital of Russia. In some ways it was a necessary sacrifice for Lenin, though it was a rash one as he never quite escaped the accusation that he had collaborated with an imperial power – and an enemy of Russia – in order to return home. After a long journey to the Baltic coast, by boat to Sweden, and then by train through Finland, Lenin arrived at the Finland Station in Petrograd on April 16. There, a brass band and representatives from the Soviet, including its chairman Chkheidze, greeted him, only too happy to welcome a seasoned socialist leader to the new utopian Russia. Lenin, ignoring Chkheidze, immediately gave a speech in which he welcomed the forthcoming social-ist revolution. The "bourgeois" revolution was hardly over, and already he was antici-pating the next phase in Marxist doctrine. Lenin had grown hungry for power.

The following day, Lenin elaborated his thoughts in the April Theses, a doctrinaire and angry collection of slogans, entitled "Concerning the tasks of the proletariat in the revolution." The Theses attacked the Provisional Government for its continuation of the war, and reiterated that the time was ripe for the change from a bourgeois government to one ruled by the workers and the poorest stratum of the peasantry. The Soviet had to take power, stated Lenin. The Bolshevik demand in the future must be "All power to the Soviets!" Land should be socialized, and all banks merged into a single socialist bank. The course of events had produced a remarkable and unprecedented situation, in Lenin's view:

> The second highly important feature of the Russian Revolution is the fact that the Petrograd Soviet of Soldiers' and Workers' Deputies, which, as everything goes to show, enjoys the confidence of most of the local Soviets, is *voluntarily* transferring state power to the bourgeoisie and *its* Provisional Government, is voluntarily *ceding* supremacy to the lat-ter, having entered into an agreement to support it, and is limiting its own role to that of an observer, a supervisor of the convocation of the Constituent Assembly. . . . This

remarkable feature, unparalleled in history in such a form, has led to the *interlocking of two* dictatorships: the dictatorship of the bourgeoisie . . . and the dictatorship of the proletariat and the peasantry.

In short, the usual path of a bourgeois revolution, which might be expected to result in a lengthy period of bourgeois rule, had been diverted, mainly because many "ordinary citizens" had begun to take an active role in politics. As a result, according to Lenin, the normal laws of Marxism no longer applied. It was possible to give the revolutionary process a push in order to attain a dictatorship of the proletariat.

As for dual power, the Mensheviks and the Socialist Revolutionaries were already in league with the government, and had become bourgeois themselves. Only the Bolsheviks, therefore, represented the workers. The Bolshevik Central Committee debated the theses briefly and rejected them by thirteen votes to two. Lenin had become isolated in his own party, the leading members of which believed that he had misjudged the situation. G. V. Plekhanov thought the comments "nonsense." Over the next several days, however, Lenin began to persuade individual Bolsheviks to change their mind, using the force of his personality as much as arguments. Gradually his views began to prevail – they did after all offer a clear path for the future – and, when the party held its 7th All-Russian Conference between May 7 and 12, Lenin's views were widely accepted. By then they could be reduced to three basic, yet appealing slogans, "Bread, peace, land." The Bolsheviks were to become the political opposition of 1917, and the only party seeking actively to overthrow the Provisional Government (something of a contradiction in terms).

Gradually the exiles began to return to the capital. They included Aleksandra Kollontay, a 45-year-old feminist veteran of the Russian Social Democratic Workers' Party, and another member of the post-February *Pravda* editorial board. By mid-April, Kollontay had become a member of the Executive Committee of the Petrograd Soviet. In May, Lev Davidovich Trotsky, leader of the Interdistrict Group, returned to the capital from the United States. Trotsky approved of Lenin's new course of action, which he believed was much closer to his own line. In fact, like Lenin, Trotsky foresaw an armed uprising as the immediate route to power. The alliance, with Lenin as the leading partner, may have been opportunistic, but was to prove a critical factor in the later Bolshevik triumph. Trotsky had abilities that Lenin could not match – his oratory, his rapport with the workers, and his activism. For all his leadership qualities, Lenin was hardly the man to be fighting at the barricades alongside workers (the American historian Richard Pipes [Pipes, 1990] goes so far as to imply an innate cowardice). Trotsky's arrival coincided with a dramatic rise in tempo of revolutionary sentiment among the masses. Between April and July 1917 there were three increasingly strong demonstrations in the capital. The Bolsheviks participated fully only in the third, but the Soviet in all three cases placed its support behind the government. However, the sentiment in the capital and in Moscow was often out of step with the feeling in the provinces, where much of the population had suffered several years of deprivation. The revolution had been welcomed, but the number of those who now sought further political changes was limited. For some time, therefore, the Bolsheviks remained on the periphery of political life.

At the 1st Congress of Soviets on June 16, out of 822 delegates there were 105 Bolsheviks. The Mensheviks and the Socialist Revolutionaries, with 248 and 285 delegates respectively, composed a clear majority. However, the mood of the Congress was falling out of step with that of the masses in the streets, who were demonstrating with slogans demanding that the Soviets take power. In the meantime, Kerensky, the Minister of War, and easily the dominant figure in the government after the dismissal of Guchkov and Milyukov, made the fatal error of embarking on a new military offensive in the summer of 1917. Progress was almost a carbon copy of the assault of the previous summer under Brusilov. Initially, progress was good, and Russian forces pushed back the Austrians in Galicia. However, the Central Powers regrouped, and Germany came to the aid of its ally. As the Russian army retreated, the retreat turned into a rout, and by mid-June the soldiers began to desert en masse. On July 1, a massive demonstration in the capital attracted around 500,000 people, many of them carrying red banners and bearing revolutionary slogans identical or similar to the Bolsheviks'. Lenin was always exceptionally sensitive to the mood of the masses. The Mensheviks and SRs in the Soviet had supported the attack. Its failure led to renewed demonstrations in Petrograd, the so-called July Days of July 16–17, which for the first time were also directed against the Soviet for backing the Kerensky offensive.

The July Days

The July Days upheaval was the most serious in the capital since the overthrow of the monarchy. The Bolsheviks were forced to respond, though there seems to be little evidence that Lenin welcomed the opportunity to lead the masses into an armed uprising. Sailors from the Kronstadt naval base joined the workers and soldiers on the streets of Petrograd. The Bolsheviks could not ignore the events without losing credibility, but their contribution seems to have been half-hearted. They did not have the numbers or the authority to take power, even though by this time they were the only party that was firmly opposed to the war, supported workers' control over industry, and backed peasant demands to take over landowner estates. Lenin's response was to dismiss the protestors who appealed to him to lead the uprising, reportedly leaving them confused. Left to their own devices, the crowd degenerated into a looting and drunken mob without any clear directions.

Ultimately the rising failed, and the government and the Soviet attempted to restore order in the capital. Several Bolshevik leaders were arrested, including Trotsky, who would have been insulted not to have been included among those locked up. The government also disseminated widely the rumor that Lenin was a German agent, along with Zinoviev and the other exiles who had traveled to Russia from Switzerland. The government ordered the arrest of the Bolshevik leader for espionage. Rather than suffer arrest, Lenin fled to Finland, where he remained for the next several months, his main activities limited to writing frantic letters to his comrades in the capital. Meanwhile troops burst into the Bolshevik headquarters and dismantled the printing equipment of the newspapers *Pravda* and *Trud*. The former newspaper, along with the soldiers' organ, *Soldatskaya pravda*, was closed down. New order was established in the Russian army. The death penalty was reinstated, and the more militant protestors among the troops based in Petrograd were sent to the front. The Lvov government was dissolved, and Kerensky formed a Second Coalition Government that combined Kadets, Socialist Revolutionaries, and Mensheviks.

The youthful Kerensky, like Lenin, was born in Simbirsk in 1881, eleven years after the Bolshevik leader, and was a lawyer by training. He had been elected a member of the Fourth Duma in 1912 as a member of the Labor group, and gained prominence with his passionate speeches. Kerensky's period of office, however, was brief, and he failed to gain the support of any major faction. Once in power, he seemed to be assailed from all sides and yet unable to resolve any of the burning issues. He received support from the Entente powers as long as he was prepared to continue the war effort, and he is widely regarded today as presiding over a brief period of democracy in Russian history. On the other hand, he vacillated, frequently changed direction, and ultimately became little more than a convincing orator, but one who could not sway the masses or convince them to be patient. Kerensky's Cabinet in July included seven Socialist Revolutionaries and Mensheviks, and four Kadets. In political terms, as the situation became polarized as a result of mass demonstrations in the streets, Kerensky began to move toward a more hard-line position, relying on the military to enforce his wishes. Consequently, several historians have perceived that, had the Kerensky era continued, it would likely have led to a harsher regime backed by the army. However, the issue is rarely discussed. Following the Kornilov uprising, and after some hesitation, Kerensky resolved to defend the gains of the February Revolution against the threat of a military dictatorship.

Following the failure of the July Days, the Bolsheviks changed tactics at the 6th Congress of the RSDWP, which was held between August 8 and 16. It was no longer feasible to retain the slogan "All power to the Soviets!" as long as the Mensheviks and the Socialist Revolutionaries – regarded as counter-revolutionary forces – held the majority. At the same time, the program for an armed uprising was affirmed, as was the main goal to conduct work to take over the Soviets through the support of the masses. Trotsky's group was now officially incorporated into the Bolshevik Party and its leader elected as a member of a Central Committee that included Lenin, Kamenev, Zinoviev, and Stalin. Both Stalin and Sverdlov were principal speakers, in the absence of Lenin and Trotsky, but they relied on messages from Lenin urging new party tactics in the light of the rapidly changing political situation. Not all delegates supported a direct path to revolution. Some, such as Evgeny Preobrazhensky, maintained that a revolution in Russia should not precede a socialist revolution in Europe, and could not succeed without one. By August 1917, the power of the Bolsheviks had grown considerably. Its membership had tripled since April, rising from 80,000 to 240,000; but, at the same time, delegates recognized that more time would be needed before the working class was solidly behind the party.

The Kornilov revolt

On July 31, on the orders of Kerensky, General Lavr Kornilov replaced General Brusilov as commander-in-chief of the Russian army. Brusilov had been a tolerant figure. Kornilov was adamantly opposed to Bolsheviks and committed to restoring order in Russia. A dour figure of limited intelligence, he had served in the Far East and gained a reputation for efficiency and ruthlessness. Once appointed by Kerensky, he immediately initiated a power struggle with the Prime Minister. The first opportunity he had to express his views was at a State Assembly in Moscow, set up by Kerensky to try to find a new basis for a stable government in Russia. The arrival of Kornilov and his armed guards caused a sensation in Moscow, and the general made a speech supporting the establishment of a military dictatorship. The State Assembly itself seemed to signal a new move by Kerensky to consolidate power and dispense with the Soviets, and as such generated a major protest in Russia's largest city, involving about 400,000 people. What is less clear, and has engendered a protracted debate, is Kerensky's attitude toward the statements and goals of his new commander-in-chief. Had Kornilov simply reneged on his agreement to serve the Kerensky government from the outset? Or had Kerensky appointed him simply to restore order by imposing a military-backed regime in which, presumably, Kerensky would retain his position as the head of the government?

Soviet sources hold to the latter view, arguing that Kerensky had prepared the revolt from Petrograd with the support of the Kadet Party, and with the backing of the Entente powers. In this way, a simplistic "move to the right" can be established, opposed by the democratic populace with the support of the Bolsheviks. However, it seems more likely that Kerensky wished to restore order without conceding the vestiges of the democratic Russian state. He maintained in retrospect that the Kornilov revolt was the decisive factor leading to the Bolsheviks seizing power. The pro-revolution forces in the capital had to be armed, and Bolshevik prisoners released, and a virtual civil war situation developed in Petrograd. On September 7, Kornilov ordered the 3rd Cavalry Corps under General Aleksandr Krymov to march on Petrograd, along with the so-called Savage Division from the Caucasus, and put an end to disorder fomented by the Bolsheviks. At the same time, Kornilov arrogated to himself supreme power over the military and the Russian government. Kerensky's response was to amass similar powers. He announced that Kornilov had been dismissed, and formed a Directory of four members, of which he was the head. No Kadets were included. However, he needed above all the support of the popular masses, and thus appealed to the Soviet and to the factory workers, soldiers, and sailors to support the gains of the revolution against a military dictatorship. The result was an outpouring of support for the only party that had stood resolutely against the Provisional Government and the war effort, namely the Bolsheviks. In defense of the capital, the Red Guards could muster 25,000 volunteers, provided with weapons. The Petrograd Garrison and the Baltic Fleet were also firmly against Kornilov. Revolutionary agitators established control over most of the railways leading from the major cities to the Western Front, and including the route taken by Krymov's army. The road to Petrograd was blocked.

The Kornilov revolt petered out very quickly. Krymov's troops fraternized with local workers and refused to march on Petrograd, and their commander committed suicide on September 13. Kornilov himself was arrested and eventually confined in Bykhov prison near Mogilev (Mahileu) in contemporary Belarus. However, he escaped from confinement on November 19, thanks to his sympathetic jailers, not long after the Bolsheviks came to power in Petrograd and, together with some followers, traveled southward where he eventually was placed in charge of the White forces on the Don. He was an early casualty of the Civil War in Ekaterinodar when a shell landed on the farmhouse in which his headquarters were based on April 13, 1918. When the Bolsheviks discovered where he was buried, they dug up his coffin, burned his corpse, and left it at a nearby garbage dump.

In the immediate term, Kerensky benefited from the collapse of the uprising. He appointed himself the commander-in-chief on September 12, and had Russia proclaimed a republic two days later. In late September he convened yet another body, the Democratic Assembly, which had the task of laying down the principles of a future government prior to the election of a Constituent Assembly. Its first step was to form a Pre-Parliament. On October 8, Kerensky formed the Third Coalition Government, which included ten Mensheviks and Socialist Revolutionaries. By this time, the country was in a state of deep chaos. The transport system had broken down, resulting in widespread shortages of bread in the towns. Many of the larger factories stopped work. Industrial output had fallen by 50 percent compared to the level of 1916. Prices rose sharply for key goods, such as coal and iron. In the countryside, peasant disturbances continued unabated. Kerensky seemed incapable of preventing the descent of the country into anarchy. On September 13, the Petrograd Soviet accepted a Bolshevik resolution that demanded an end to further cooperation with the bourgeoisie. A new election had brought about a Bolshevik majority. Soon, Trotsky was released from prison and within a week was to be elected once again the Chairman of the Soviet. By September 18, the Moscow Soviet also came under the control of the Bolsheviks.

Under such circumstances, the slogan of "All power to the Soviets!" could now be revived with a realistic chance of success. The Bolsheviks now possessed the largest political grouping in the capital and clearly had the support of the revolutionary elements. Lenin's role was minor. He was confined to writing letters, demanding an armed uprising that combined the soldiers, workers, and sailors at such a critical moment. He feared the opportunity might be missed. By October 20 (NS) he had returned to Petrograd in disguise, and a meeting of the Bolshevik Central Committee was convened three days later to discuss the possibility of an armed uprising. Only Zinoviev and Kamenev were opposed. They had argued, not without reason, that the party should await the forthcoming 2nd Congress of Soviets (scheduled for November 7) and the formation of the Constituent Assembly. The majority, including Lenin, Trotsky, Stalin, and Sverdlov, believed that only the Bolsheviks could carry out an armed uprising. A compromise with other socialist parties was not necessary, nor was it wise to await a decision of the 2nd Congress of Soviets. The Bolsheviks must seize power and then present fellow socialists with a *fait accompli*. The alternative was to become involved in endless discussions that would achieve nothing. In his letter "Marxism and the Uprising," Lenin discussed details of the takeover of power, which was to be undertaken through a combination of the Red Guards, the Kronstadt sailors, and the soldiers of the Petrograd Garrison (at that time not yet committed to the Bolshevik cause). These troops were to occupy the key points of the city (government buildings, train stations, telegraph offices) and to place under arrest the members of the Provisional Government and leading generals at the front who did not support the rising.

Questions for discussion

1. How were the Japanese able to defeat the Russians in the war of 1904–1905?
2. How was the tsarist regime able to survive the revolution of 1905?
3. Did Rasputin really have a significant impact on the downfall of the Russian monarchy of Nicholas II?
4. What were the achievements and failures of the Russian Provisional Government of 1917?
5. What were the main points of Lenin's April Theses? Were they feasible as a program in the spring of 1917?

Recent works

Ascher, Abraham. *The Revolution of 1905: A Short History*. Stanford, Calif.: Stanford University Press, 2004.

Bowlt, John E. *Moscow and St. Petersburg in Russia's Silver Age, 1900–1920*. London: Thames & Hudson, 2008.

Cohen, Aaron J. *Imagining the Unimaginable: World War, Modern Art, and the Politics of Public Culture in Russia, 1914–1917.* Lincoln, Nebr.: University of Nebraska Press, 2008.

Easley, Roxanne. *The Emancipation of the Serfs in Russia: Peace Arbitrators and the Development of Civil Society.* London: Routledge, 2009.

Ericson, Steven, and Allen Hockley. *The Treaty of Portsmouth and Its Legacies.* Hanover, NH: Dartmouth College Press, published by University Press of New England, 2008.

Fuller, William C. *The Foe Within: Fantasies of Treason and the End of Imperial Russia.* Ithaca, NY: Cornell University Press, 2006.

Gatrell, Peter. *A Whole Empire Walking: Refugees in Russia during World War I.* Bloomington, Ind.: Indiana University Press, 2005.

Haimson, Leopold H. *Russia's Revolutionary Experience, 1905–1917: Two Essays.* New York: Columbia University Press, 2005.

Harcave, Sidney. *Count Sergei Witte and the Twilight of Imperial Russia: A Biography.* Armonk, NY: M. E. Sharpe, 2004.

Heretz, Leonid. *Russia on the Eve of Modernity: Popular Religion and Traditional Culture under the Last Tsars.* Cambridge: Cambridge University Press, 2008.

Holoquist, Peter. *Making War, Forging Revolution: Russia's Continuum of Crisis, 1914–1921.* Cambridge, Mass.: Harvard University Press, 2002.

King, Greg. *The Court of the Last Tsar: Pomp, Power, and Pageantry in the Reign of Nicholas II.* Hoboken, NJ: Wiley, 2006.

King, Greg, and Penny Wilson. *The Fate of the Romanovs.* Hoboken, NJ: Wiley, 2003.

Lohr, Eric. *Nationalizing the Russian Empire: The Campaign against Enemy Aliens during World War I.* Cambridge, Mass.: Harvard University Press, 2003.

MacKean, Robert B. *Late Imperial Russia: Problems and Prospects.* Manchester: Manchester University Press, 2005.

McNeal, Shay. *The Secret Plot to Save the Tsar: New Truths behind the Romanov Mystery.* New York: William Morrow, 2001.

Nation, Craig R. *War on War: Lenin, the Zimmerwald Left, and the Origins of Communist Internationalism.* Chicago, Ill.: Haymarket Books, 2007.

Polunov, Alexander. *Russia in the Nineteenth Century: Autocracy, Reform, and Social Change, 1814–1914.* Armonk, NY: M. E. Sharpe, 2005.

Sanborn, Joshua A. *Drafting the Russian Nation: Military Conscription, Total War, and Mass Politics, 1905–1925.* DeKalb, Ill.: Northern Illinois University Press, 2003.

Stoff, Laurie. *They Fought for the Motherland: Russia's Women Soldiers in World War I and the Revolution.* Lawrence, Kan.: University Press of Kansas, 2006.

Weeks, Theodore R. *Nation and State in Late Imperial Russia: Nationalism and Russification on the Western Frontier, 1863–1914.* DeKalb, Ill.: Northern Illinois University Press, 2008.

Wood, Alan. *The Origins of the Russian Revolution, 1861–1917.* London: Routledge, 2003.

Wortman, Richard. *Scenarios of Power: Myth and Ceremony in Russian Monarchy from Peter the Great to the Abdication of Nicholas II.* Princeton, NJ: Princeton University Press, 2006.

2

···················

The October Revolution, 1917–1921

Such is the controversy surrounding one of the pivotal events of the 20th century that it is worthwhile to discuss the various perspectives briefly. For some historians, the word "revolution" may be inappropriate. It took place from November 6 to 8 (NS) 1917, and involved the seizure of power by a relatively small, urban-based party led by a fanatical leader backed by Trotsky's leadership over the Soviet. Richard Pipes (Pipes, 1990), one of the most prolific historians of the period, maintains that the uprising was in fact a coup d'état rather than a revolution. Other historians (Acton, 1990; Suny and Adams, eds, 1990) have pointed to the strong sentiment toward the Bolsheviks by the fall of 1917, their control over the Petrograd and Moscow Soviets, the growing dissatisfaction with the Kerensky government and its inability or unwillingness to resolve the major questions of the day: the ending of Russian participation in the war; the division of land among the peasantry; and the provision of enough food to the people. The concept of a change of regime was hardly unusual. In fact the Bolsheviks could easily have gained a foothold in the Cabinet, given their support, or a fully socialist government could have come to power. Such ideas were completely alien to Lenin. For the Bolshevik leader, the route was clear. The Bolsheviks could never link themselves to the unpopular government, and could never compromise with their fellow socialists (already denounced as counter-revolutionaries). The party that had been created essentially through the principles outlined in Lenin's 1902 pamphlet *What Is to Be Done?* had to seize control over the state. In adhering to such a rigid procedure, Lenin was acting like a Marxist, albeit one who did not adhere closely to doctrine.

In the years between the end of the Soviet Union in December 1991 and Putin's accession to the presidency in 2000, very little of the official Soviet version of the events of November 1917 retained any credibility either in Russia or in the West. The image of a Lenin as a quasi-deity changed to that of an almost comical figure – a small man dressed in a shabby suit and cap. (In Moscow's Red Square for some time in the independence period, two actors made a good living from tourists by impersonating Lenin and Marx, and posing for photographs.) Lenin's voluminous works vanished from bookstores. Only small groups of elderly Communists retained much affection for him, though the curious still formed long lineups to examine his mummified corpse in its mausoleum. In brief, the country was "de-Leninized." The process only occurred after the Soviet period. Conversely, the dethroning of Stalin, whose crimes were either much more pronounced or much better known, took place over several decades, from 1956 to the Gorbachev period (with a notable break during the leadership of L. I. Brezhnev). In general, Russian historians are not devoting much of their research in the 21st century to a re-examination of Lenin. Western historians have presented their views over a lengthy period in such an out-pouring of literature that one might assume that there is nothing new to say about the subject. What new can possibly emerge from the events of November 1917? Were these events really so important in the context of Russian history? Are not the signs of continuity between the tsarist and Soviet regimes more significant than the changes that occurred in a relatively swift and bloodless change of power? As long as the Soviet regime remained in power in the 20th century, in other words, the revolution could retain its majesty. But in the post-Soviet era, when the social and economic situation changed with such definitive rapidity, and a new generation appeared that did not merely scorn Lenin but ignored him, then *ipso facto* the historical image changed, too.

Did the image become more accurate? The denigration of Lenin's role by histor-ians may have been equally as harmful as their earlier uncritical stances. Lenin should be acknowledged as the key figure in the October events. Without him there would have been no uprising, whatever his personal participation or lack of it. One should note also that Western historians have continued to publish new studies of Lenin that have added considerably to our knowledge of the Bolshevik leader (Service, 1985–1995, 2000; White, 2001; Lih, 2006; Budgen, 2007). More than any other player, his motivation seems to have been power. Taking over the state in the conditions of November 1917 was not so difficult, but the correct moment had to be picked. In theory, the Soviet could have taken power at any time. In the spring of 1917 it would have received the support of the military garrison. Matters were simplified when the Soviet resolved to create a Military-Revolutionary Committee (MRC) on October 25, 1917, ostensibly for the defense of Petrograd, but covertly to be the organ that pre-pared forces for an armed uprising. It included not only Bolsheviks but also mem-bers of the splinter groups that had broken away from the other socialist parties: the Left Socialist Revolutionaries and the Internationalist wing of the Mensheviks, in addition to some anarchists. A. S. Bubnov, M. S. Uritsky, Stalin, Sverdlov, V. A. Antonov-Ovseenko, P. Ye. Dybenko, and N. V. Krylenko, all prominent Bolsheviks by this time, joined the MRC. Its activities were under the guidance of Trotsky, the Chairman of the Petrograd Soviet. Within a week, and largely thanks to the work of Trotsky, the Petrograd Garrison had ended its neutrality and committed itself to the Bolshevik uprising.

The change of regime was unspectacular, though well organized. Its main archi-tect played a relatively minor role, other than to harangue those who stood in his way. On October 29 there took place another meeting of the Bolshevik Central Committee that also included the Petrograd committee's military organization, factory committees, and trade unions. Though most of those who attended supported the idea of the uprising, Kamenev and Zinoviev again voiced their disapproval. Two days later, they published their views in the pages of an opposition newspaper,

Novaya zhizn (*New Life*), an extraordinary act of disloyalty, but one that also demonstrates their desperation, a belief that the uprising would destroy the party. In this way, they gave the authorities advance warning of Bolshevik intentions (though the Kerensky government could hardly have been so ill-informed as to be completely ignorant of Bolshevik goals). On November 2, the Central Committee reconvened to discuss the fate of the two dissidents. Several Bolsheviks were unwilling to act harshly, including ironically Stalin and Uritsky, later two of the more intolerant personalities. Lenin had been angry enough to want the dissidents' expulsion from the party. Instead the committee let Kamenev and Zinoviev off with a warning, ordering them never to speak out in future against an officially accepted decision of the party.

As the Pre-Parliament lapsed into rather meaningless debates – Kerensky having refused to deal with the questions of the war and of land – the Provisional Government made a weak attempt to forestall Bolshevik plans. It ordered the cruiser *Avrora* to leave its mooring opposite the Winter Palace and put out to sea, knowing that its fleet was heavily pro-Bolshevik. Army officers, meanwhile, targeted the Bolshevik press. They cut off the telephone links to the Bolshevik headquarters at the Smolny Institute, closed down bridges over the Neva river, and ordered troops to defend the Winter Palace. At best, those involved carried out the orders half-heartedly. Within a few hours, the cruiser had returned to its base, and the Bolshevik papers were being printed; the forces defending the Winter Palace were never substantial. The government sent the Death's Head Women's Battalion to the palace, evidently in order to shame regular troops into joining it. No more than 3,000 soldiers were present, and their commitment to the cause of the ailing government was questionable. The Bolshevik Central Committee, meanwhile, gathered at the Smolny Institute to divide up final duties for the uprising. Compared to the traumatic and very public revolution of March 1917, the "Great October" was a quiet affair. The MRC sent its proclamations via *Avrora*'s radio. The armory at the Peter and Paul Fortress was secured. Dzerzhinsky led forces that took over the post and telegraph facilities. Others led by Bubnov were sent to take over the railways. Little could be done of a military nature until the arrival of the most committed revolutionary element, the Kronstadt sailors, and they were late. By the evening of November 6, the capital was basically secured by the Bolsheviks, including the Neva bridges and the post and telegraph offices. Lenin arrived in disguise at the Smolny Institute, frantic with worry that something could still go wrong.

Early on the morning of November 7, the main railway stations and electric power station were taken over by the insurgents. Next they occupied the State Bank and the Central Telephone Exchange. There was little opposition. After his rather feeble attempt to curb the uprising, Kerensky fled from the capital in the US ambassador's car and made his way to the headquarters of the Northern Front. Members of his Cabinet remained debating issues in the Winter Palace. The Marinsky Palace, where the Pre-Parliament had been convened, was in Bolshevik hands by midday on November 7. About 5,000 sailors had by now arrived from the Kronstadt base on

Kotlin Island. The force was to be more than sufficient to ensure the success of the uprising. Compared to the July Days, the capital appeared relatively quiet. This same morning, the MRC had issued an appeal "To the citizens of Russia," declaring that the Provisional Government had been dissolved, and that state power had been transferred to the Petrograd Soviet. Only the Winter Palace had yet to be taken. The assault began at 6 p.m., though once again it appears to have been delayed for several hours. In Soviet historiography and films, the storming of the Winter Palace is the key event of the Revolution. In fact, the Red Guards and the Kronstadt sailors, under the leadership of Vladimir Antonov-Ovseenko, entered by the main gate, burst into the palace, and arrested the Cabinet members of the government. Six people were dead. The mob looted the palace.

That same evening, the 2nd Congress of Soviets convened at the Smolny Institute with 673 delegates. The Bolsheviks outnumbered their rivals, with 390 delegates, compared to 160 Socialist Revolutionaries and seventy-two Mensheviks. The Menshevik leaders (about fifty people) protested bitterly at the Bolshevik takeover of power and promptly walked out of the assembly – ridiculed as they did so by Trotsky, who confined them to "the garbage heap of history." Only at 4 a.m. could the impatient Congress publicize the news that the Winter Palace had fallen. It then accepted decrees on peace and on land, and the "Declaration of the Rights of the Peoples of Russia." A new Central Executive Committee of the Soviet was elected, with 101 members, of whom sixty-two were Bolsheviks and twenty-nine members of the Left Socialist Revolutionaries. In this way, Lenin could claim to be sharing power. In these early hours after the uprising, these declarations were more symbolic than actual since few people in Russia could have been aware of another change of government. The Declaration on Land, for example, which transferred ownership of all land to district Soviets of Peasant Deputies and Volost Land Committees, was merely a reflection of changes that had already occurred without Bolshevik guidance. Opposition seemed very likely. The Mensheviks and Socialist Revolutionaries met at the city Duma with the Kadets, and established a Committee for the Protection of the Motherland and the Revolution. Kerensky had escaped and was likely to return with military backing, though the extent of his support was by now questionable. The 2nd Congress confirmed the success of the uprising, and the takeover of power by the Bolsheviks. The uprising itself posed few problems, despite Lenin's nervousness. The Congress announced the formation of a new government on November 8, called the Council of People's Commissars, and headed by Lenin as its Chairman. The other Cabinet members were as obscure as had been those of the Provisional Government in March, with the exception of Trotsky.

Despite the ease of the takeover, several early difficulties presented themselves. The first was the threat from forces raised by Kerensky and led by General N. N. Krasnov from the Northern Front in Pskov, numbering at their peak about 5,000. These troops began to occupy settlements en route to the capital, including Gatchina and Tsarskoe Selo, but the gains were temporary. The Bolshevik government sent a delegation to Gatchina, and it had little difficulty persuading the troops to desist and even to arrest their leaders. Kerensky's threat was over, and he fled the country. Krasnov promptly switched sides. The second threat came from the large union of railway workers, which was not opposed to the general course of events, but which demanded a government that included all socialist elements, rather than just the Bolsheviks and Left Socialist Revolutionaries. The union was under the leadership of committed Mensheviks. Kamenev and Zinoviev, who seem to have been out of step with Lenin at every juncture in these events, were not averse to this idea. Another prominent figure that supported a coalition government was Aleksey Rykov, like Lenin educated at the law faculty of Kazan University. Rykov had been a member of the Central Committee since August, and of the Petrograd Soviet since September. After the uprising he had been appointed the People's Commissar of Internal Affairs. However, Lenin would not accept the notion of sharing power, and the three figures were removed from their positions in the Central Committee and the government. Sverdlov took over from Kamenev as Chairman of the Soviet Central Executive Committee; and Grigory Petrovsky, a native of Kharkiv, Ukraine, replaced Rykov in Internal Affairs, a position he was to hold until March 1919.

The change of Cabinet was important but not a decisive break with the dissidents. Lenin still valued the contribution of figures like Zinoviev, Kamenev, and Rykov, and their demise was temporary. All three were to be given key roles in the future Soviet government. The issue did signal, however, some serious differences in outlook within the party, particularly concerning the legality of the takeover. It still seemed inconceivable to many that a party with such a narrow base of support – the major urban centers – could rule alone in a largely peasant country. Power-sharing would have resolved the issue of Bolshevik legitimacy, but it would have prevented Lenin from wielding the sort of authority he desired. Above all he feared the prospect of endless debate and being unable to get his way on a number of issues. The Mensheviks in particular were perceived as more doctrinaire Marxists. As far as Lenin was concerned, he had broken with them five years earlier. Yet to some Bolshevik leaders it seemed unlikely that power could be retained if the Bolsheviks elected to rule alone. However, Lenin and Trotsky in particular were convinced that revolution in Europe would soon solidify the change of government in Russia. Though the majority of the party followed their line, their authority was never as pronounced as it may have appeared. Time and time again, the Central Committee would prove unable to secure unanimity of opinion on a key issue, despite the cajoling and persuasion of Lenin.

Though the uprising had succeeded in Petrograd, the situation in Moscow was never so clear-cut, and dividing lines between the parties were not fully demarcated. By the time the MRC was formed in Moscow, an open conflict had broken out. Moreover, the MRC comprised both Bolsheviks and Mensheviks, and was not the decisive force that it had been in the capital. A Committee for Public Safety (CPS) had also been created. Rather than seizing power, the MRC (led by such figures as P. G. Smidovich and V. P. Nogin) held extensive discussions with the forces of the CPS under the Socialist Revolutionary military officer K. I. Ryabtsev. The MRC agreed to leave the Kremlin and to relinquish control over post and telegraph. Ryabtsev and military officers declared martial law and prepared to defend Moscow with about 10,000 troops. After a brief but decisive clash, the troops took over the Kremlin. In panic, Lenin began to send loyal forces to assist the MRC in Moscow, including Red Guards from various centers, Baltic sailors, and others. Railway workers began to occupy the main Moscow stations. A sustained conflict seemed likely. In fact, the process took about a week before revolutionary units moved into Red Square and surrounded the Kremlin. On November 15, the CPS gave up the struggle, and Bolshevik forces took over the Kremlin the following day.

Only the troops at the front were still to be pacified. Few were loyal to the Kerensky regime. General N. N. Dukhonin, who had replaced Kerensky as the commander-in-chief of the armed forces, proved to be unreliable. He was in contact with Entente missions, which discouraged him from approaching the Germans for an armistice. The Soviet Russian government dismissed him, replacing him with Nikolay Krylenko, a reliable member of the Petrograd military organization of the party. Various missions were sent from major cities to military headquarters, including one to Mogilev (137 miles east of Minsk) headed by Krylenko himself on December 1. The MRC soon took over the town and the headquarters, while Dukhonin was lynched by an angry mob. The Northern and Western Fronts had joined forces with the Bolsheviks. They had also gradually begun to control several towns of European Russia. Thus, within less than a month, the main events of the uprising were over and the new authority consolidated. For the people of Russia the change of power at first meant very little. The Bolsheviks were not unwelcome, because they had made promises to alleviate the major problems. At least they could be given a chance. Lenin's government never enjoyed the sort of euphoria that had occurred after the fall of the monarchy. In March, tsarist authority had collapsed without any certainty as to what would replace it. In November, however, Lenin's group had seized power, isolating itself from the other socialist parties. It now followed up with a flurry of decrees, most of which aimed to centralize power in the hands of the party.

The main measures of the early period of Bolshevik rule were as follows. The Declaration of the Rights of the Toiling and Exploited Peoples announced the equal standing of all citizens of Russia regardless of religion or national background. On November 27, the Soviet Executive Committee proclaimed workers' control over production, establishing factory committees and a new organization – the Council of Workers' Control. The next day, the former army was officially demobilized, following the disbanding of the police service and the judiciary. The new commissariats took over the buildings of the former ministries. In general, they were staffed with new and usually inexperienced personnel. The Bolsheviks were obliged to rely on the expertise of many specialists and technicians, regardless of their political orientation. By December, further progress had been made in bringing economic life under state control. The principal organ was the Supreme Council of the Economy, which had branches throughout the country. The new leadership nationalized many former international holdings in what had been the Russian Empire by the end of 1917, though a formal decree on heavy industry coming under state control was issued only in June 1918. The government nationalized banks on December 27, 1917, and foreign trade in April 1918.

The Constituent Assembly

Lenin and the Bolsheviks, like the other socialist parties of 1917, had consistently supported the convocation of a Constituent Assembly. By November 1917, in Lenin's eyes at least, there was no longer any need for elections since the wishes of the working masses were embodied in the institution of the Soviet. Elections had been scheduled for November 25, however, and duly took place. They have been termed the last free elections in Russia (at least until the spring of 1989). The Bolsheviks performed relatively well, gaining more than 50 percent of the votes in Petrograd and Moscow, which evened out to 24 percent in the country as a whole. Sheila Fitzpatrick notes that the Bolsheviks attained a majority of votes from the armies of the Northern and Western Fronts, as well as from the Baltic Fleet, but did less well on the southern fronts and among sailors of the Black Sea Fleet (Fitzpatrick, 1984). Though these results may have owed something to intimidation, they reflected the notable transformation in urban opinion over the previous eight months. Elsewhere, however, the party remained on the fringe of Russian politics. The Constituent Assembly was to have 800 seats, though only 715 were elected. Of this number, the Socialist Revolutionaries (in their united form on the ballot) received 370, the Bolsheviks 175, the Kadets seventeen, and the Mensheviks fifteen. Clearly, the Socialist Revolutionaries would dominate the new assembly. Lenin and the Bolshevik leaders, therefore, decided to delay the convocation for as long as possible, partly to "educate" the masses, and partly to eliminate the Kadets as a force in political life. Before the Assembly met, Lenin issued his "Declaration of the Rights of Toiling and Exploited Peoples," the goal of which was to encompass all the new laws issued by the Bolshevik government to that point, which were to be presented to the Assembly for acceptance.

When the Assembly duly met on January 18, Sverdlov for the Bolsheviks tried to take over the podium and push through the recognition of the Bolshevik proposals. The majority did not support such a move, nor did it refrain from sharp criticism of the Bolshevik uprising. Chernov, head of the Socialist Revolutionaries, initiated a lengthy debate on the agrarian question. In the gallery, armed sailors playfully pointed rifles at the speaker. In fact, many delegates feared the atmosphere in Petrograd, as the city had become a committed Bolshevik camp. After the failure to persuade the majority to accept their proposals, the Bolsheviks and their Left SR allies walked out of the Assembly. Lenin decided that it should be dissolved. In the early hours of January 19, the weary guards demanded that the delegates should leave the building. When the delegates returned later the same day they found the doors closed. The Soviet Executive Committee duly issued a decree on Lenin's instructions dissolving the Assembly. The delegates returned home to their villages, leaving the Socialist Revolutionaries and their Menshevik allies to seek alternative means of support. Though there were few initial protests at the dissolution of the Constituent Assembly, it proved to be a uniting force for the anti-Bolshevik socialist and liberal forces during the Civil War.

It would surely have been surprising had the Bolsheviks given up power in January 1918 and agreed to follow the demands of the Assembly. Few Russian citizens were accustomed to a democratic parliament; and, moreover, the Constituent Assembly lacked a military force capable of maintaining it or willing to maintain it. By January the Bolsheviks had begun to consolidate power, and they had not begun badly. At that point, the regime was beginning to live up to its promises. Negotiations were under way with the German High Command, redistribution of land had been accepted and passed into law, and a start had been made to resolving economic chaos. The Assembly, on the other hand, threatened like the Pre-Parliament to get sidetracked by long-winded and inconclusive discussions. Lenin's view that the Soviet was a more democratic institution was mere propaganda, but there is no doubt that the Soviet was the decisive force in the capital. As if to prove the point, three days after the dissolution of the Constituent Assembly, the 3rd All-Russian Congress of Soviets convened, and immediately "legalized" the Declaration of the Rights of Toiling and Exploited Peoples. It declared the All-Russian Congress of Soviets to be the highest organ of power in Russia, and in between Congresses this distinction applied to the Soviet Executive Committee. Though neither the Congress nor the Executive Committee could take the place of the party or of Lenin, they served as a symbol of the new "democracy." The dissolution of the Constituent Assembly epitomized Lenin's break with the past, his willingness to resort to force to maintain power, and his final rift with fellow socialist parties.

Two months later, at the 8th Congress of the Bolshevik Party, the old appellation of RSDWP was dropped, and replaced by the more impressive Russian Communist Party (RCP). Gradually, the other parties of 1917 were outlawed, even though they had never formally rejected the new government or threatened to take action that might undermine it. By mid-1918, the Socialist Revolutionaries and the Mensheviks were formally excluded from the Soviets, however. Increasingly the Soviets in Soviet Russia became mouthpieces for party decrees, organs with no real authority. Lenin had used them to take power, but had little need for them once power had been secured. In July the first Soviet Constitution was issued, that of the RSFSR or Soviet Russia. The Constitution did not mention the leading role of the party, though it proclaimed the dictatorship of the proletariat in alliance with the poorest stratum of the peasantry. In essence Russia had become a workers' state. The period 1918–1920 can be considered one in which Lenin and his party tried to transform Russia on the basis of ideology. In the long term it was anticipated that other republics would join the

new federation, with solidarity from neighboring European countries once pro-
letariats had taken control in them. Whether the Bolsheviks could remain in power,
however, depended upon resolving the most important question – that of extracting
Russia from the quagmire of the First World War. In this instance, Lenin was to prove
the most pragmatic of the Bolshevik leaders.

Making peace with the Central Powers

On taking over the reins of state, the Bolsheviks had immediately issued a Decree
on Peace, a utopian document that presumed that the warring powers would
declare a peace without annexations. A second premise was that the European states
were on the verge of revolution, and that the working class of each country would
find common ground against an imperialist conflict. The Central Powers had the most
to gain from such a decree. Should Russia leave the war, the Germans would be able
to transfer forces to the Western Front for a final assault on the Allies, possibly before
the main contingent of American troops arrived on European soil. The war had been
a crucial stumbling block for Kerensky's government. He had staked much on a final
and successful assault through Galicia. Lenin had no such illusions. An armistice
was essential if the Bolshevik state was to survive. The Central Powers were coming
perilously close to Petrograd, as the German army moved through the Baltic
States. After negotiations in the town of Brest-Litovsk, an armistice was signed on
December 14, 1917, a temporary interlude that was to expire in January the following year. The Germans, however, demanded territorial gains and saw no reason why
they should compromise with the bedraggled group of revolutionaries that had
come to make terms.

The war issue illustrated the limits of Bolshevik internationalism. The party
could reach no consensus. Trotsky, the War Minister, adopted a supercilious attitude
from the outset, convinced that the Imperial and Austrian Germans were living
on borrowed time. On a personal level, Trotsky hardly endeared himself to the
Germans in particular (the Austrians being strictly a subsidiary partner). He was
particularly incensed that the new Ukrainian government had been permitted its own
delegation during the peace discussions. Bukharin led a group within the Bolshevik
leadership that considered it possible, following the example of the French in the late
18th century, to fight a revolutionary war. Lenin was prepared to sign a treaty under
almost any terms, save the relinquishment of state control, but he lacked support.
Ultimately, the 3rd Congress of Soviets approved a meaningless formula put forward
by Trotsky which declared that the Bolsheviks would not continue the war, but nor
would they sign a shameful peace treaty. In the meantime, the Bolsheviks hoped that
their delaying tactics would allow them greater leeway once the Imperial government
of the Hohenzollerns had fallen. They waited in vain. The impatient Germans issued
an ultimatum on February 9, and the following day Trotsky issued his declaration of

"No peace, no war." General Max Hoffmann, commander of the German army in the east, responded to this nonsense in appropriate Prussian tradition. One week later, the Germans resumed their advance, meeting almost no opposition. The Russians had not even bothered to destroy bridges in their path.

For the Bolsheviks, it was a moment of crisis. There seemed every possibility that the Soviet Russian government would be overthrown and, equally worrying, that Russia itself would fall under the occupation of the Central Powers. The German advance was relentless. Ukraine and Belarus were quickly occupied. The seizure of Latvia and Estonia cleared the way to Petrograd. Lenin's reaction was to demand the immediate signing of a peace treaty. He threatened to resign if this decision was not taken. Simultaneously, all forces once more gathered to protect the capital, but on this occasion the aggressor was not the hapless Kornilov but the most efficient army in Europe. Germany, ignoring the pleas of American president Woodrow Wilson to abide by his Fourteen Points, issued new peace terms that could not be amended. The Russians had three days in which to agree. Even so, the Bolshevik Central Committee agreed to terms by the narrowest-possible margin, seven votes to five. Trotsky refused to return to Brest to sign a humiliating treaty. Instead, second-rank Bolshevik leaders like G. V. Chicherin, L. M. Karakhan, Petrovsky and G. Ya. Sokolnikov signed the Treaty of Brest as Russia's representatives on March 3, 1918. Soviet Russia lost one-third of the population of the former Russian Empire – more than 56 million people, and a total of 485,000 square miles of territory. Many prized territories were lost – Poland, Ukraine, Lithuania, Finland, Latvia, and Estonia. Russia recognized the new government of Ukraine, disbanded its army and fleet, and was also asked to pay reparations. In the south, Turkey took over several disputed territories.

Was the sacrifice worthwhile? In retrospect, the harshest treaty in living memory would not last long, though Lenin and his colleagues could hardly have anticipated that the war would end only eight months later. The capital and the revolution had been secured, and many of the territories ceded had been won by Russian imperial expansion – in the case of Poland, by brutal partitions in the late 18th century. By leaving the war, the Bolsheviks retained the support of the peasantry, who made up the bulk of the disintegrating Russian army. They could look to the creation of a new army, and to the restoration of economic life (at least in theory). Such was the fury at the treaty in some circles, however, that the Left Socialist Revolutionaries could no longer serve as partners in the Soviet government. At the 4th Extraordinary Congress of Soviets, which took place from March 14 to 16 to ratify the Brest-Litovsk Treaty, the Left Socialist Revolutionaries walked out in protest, vacating their three Cabinet posts of Agriculture, Justice, and Posts and Telegraph. The alliance had never been an easy one, however, and it had served its purpose, namely to present an image of a worker–peasant alliance, which showed that the Bolsheviks were not averse to power-sharing. By November 13, the Treaty was declared null and void following the end of the war in Europe two days earlier. The Paris peace treaties confirmed some of Russia's losses – Poland and the three Baltic States became independent. Over the next three years, however, the Bolsheviks were to attempt to regain lost territories in Ukraine, Belarus, and the Caucasus, albeit under the guise of spreading the cause of the Revolution.

The Cheka and the beginning of the Red Terror

Between 1918 and 1921, Lenin and the Bolsheviks were preoccupied with security. Retaining power proved to be exceptionally difficult, not least because of the uncompromising nature of the new regime. In the period of underground existence and exile, the Bolsheviks had cultivated an image of martyrdom. The Okhrana infiltrated the party (rumors abounded for years that Stalin was an agent of the tsarist police) and other radical groups. Before November 1917, many Bolsheviks had deplored the existence of a secret police. However, Lenin in particular recognized its value. The use of terror to subdue members and potential members of the opposition was an important tactic. Lenin was always willing to dish out merciless retribution on his enemies, often as an example to the people (though his rhetoric was often more venomous than his deeds). Consequently, the founding of the All-Russian Extraordinary Commission for the Struggle with Counter-Revolution and Sabotage (Cheka) was regarded as a necessary means for preserving the Bolshevik government. Ostensibly, it was meant as a temporary measure, one that could be rescinded once the period of struggle was over. There was little chance of that, however, given the polarization of political life. In any case, the Cheka was less a watchdog over government security than an instrument of power and terror. Under its fanatical leader Feliks Dzerzhinsky, it had few restraints, wielding authority to try and execute suspects without having to go through the courts.

BOX 2.1

Feliks Edmundovich Dzerzhinsky (1877–1926)

Born into a family of Polish landholders in the Dziarzhynava estate in the Russian Empire (now part of Belarus) on August 30 (September 11), 1877, he was raised mainly by his devoutly Catholic mother, who trained him for the priesthood before he converted to Marxism as a young man. He attended the Russian gymnasium at Wilno (Vilnius), from which he was expelled for revolutionary activity. In 1895 he joined the Lithuanian Social Democratic Party and thereafter was arrested several times. Between 1897 and 1900 he was twice sent to Siberia by the tsarist authorities, but each time managed to escape captivity. In 1899, after one such escape, he went to Warsaw where he founded the Social Democracy of the Kingdom of Poland and Lithuania. Arrested again in 1912, he was moved eventually to Butyrki prison in Moscow, and released only with the advent of the February Revolution in 1917. In April he joined the Bolshevik Party as a member of the Moscow Soviet, and in July he was elected to the Bolshevik Central Committee at

▶

Box 2.1 continued

the 6th Party Congress. From this time he was a close associate of Lenin, who came to rely on the ascetic and incorruptible figure. Dzerzhinsky was a member of the Military Revolutionary Committee during the October Revolution, and subsequently was made Chairman of the Extraordinary Commission to Combat Counter-Revolution and Sabotage (Cheka), the Bolshevik secret police force founded in December 1917. His role was to conduct the Red Terror, which reached extreme proportions during the Civil War. After the war ended, the Cheka was transformed into the State Political Directorate (GPU), and Dzerzhinsky became Minister of the Interior (1921–1924), Minister of Transport (1921), and head of the Supreme Council of the National Economy (1924). He died in Moscow on July 20, 1926, after a Central Committee meeting at which he had made an impassioned speech in defense of Stalin and his policies. The famous statue of Dzerzhinsky in Moscow's Lubyanka Square, outside the headquarters of the secret police, was torn down in 1991 after the failure of the August 1991 putsch against President Mikhail Gorbachev. However, other memorials remain across the former Soviet Union, including a monument in Minsk, and a museum in his birthplace in contemporary Belarus in the town Dzyarzhinsk (formerly Koydanava). He is regarded as the founding father of the secret police (known by its various acronyms – GPU, OGPU, NKVD, KGB, and currently the Russian FSB).

The Cheka was founded on December 20, 1917, i.e. before the convocation of the Constituent Assembly. By this time, the government had formally outlawed the Kadet Party. The Kadets, however, were not the main threat to the Bolshevik regime – the military situation was the most immediate danger. On March 11, 1918 the capital was transferred from Petrograd – perilously close to the front – to Moscow. Almost immediately the Cheka swung into action to eliminate Anarchist organizations there, and they quickly became figures that aroused fear in the people. Ironically, the Left SRs, the Bolsheviks' partners, were also playing a leading role in the Cheka. Once the Mensheviks and the mainstream SRs had been expelled from the Soviet, the Left SRs emerged as the main domestic threat to the Bolsheviks from the spring of 1918. There were several reasons for this. First and foremost, the Left SRs were bitterly opposed to the Treaty of Brest-Litovsk and tried to sabotage it. Second, as representatives of the rural regions, they opposed the bitter class warfare taking place in the countryside under War Communism and in particular the Committees of the Poor, which represented Bolshevik authority. They also felt that the Bolshevik regime was reneging on some promises it made upon taking power, most notable of which was the abolition of the death penalty.

Matters came to a head at the 5th All-Russian Congress of Soviets in Moscow on July 4, 1918. Ukrainian delegates present demanded that the party support Ukrainian guerrillas in their struggle to remove German forces; but Sverdlov, Chairman of the Congress, with strong backing from Trotsky, refused to take any action that might provoke the Germans. In addition, the ruthless policies of grain requisition in the countryside also received approval, against the opposition of the Left SRs. Two days later, the Left SRs started an uprising in Moscow. In order to undermine the Treaty of Brest-Litovsk, two members of the party got into the German embassy and assassinated the ambassador, Count Wilhelm Mirbach. Dzerzhinsky, who was investigating the incident (according to some historians, he was implicated to some extent), was detained by the Left SRs, who took over the Office of Posts and Telegraph in Moscow and claimed power. However, the Bolshevik government in the Kremlin was not seriously threatened, and Bolshevik troops were able to round up thirteen of the leaders of the putsch. All were executed. Lenin and Trotsky offered their condolences and apologies to the German government, averting the threat of a renewed German invasion. The summer of 1918, however, was to mark the beginning of Red Terror, directed against what appeared for a while to be a serious threat to the Bolshevik regime.

Among the first victims of the early Cheka terror were the former tsar Nikolay Romanov and his family. Though their deaths were also linked to the progress of the White Army in the civil war, they were connected more closely to events in the capital. Since March 1917, the royal family had been under house arrest. They had been refused permission to leave the country after their most likely host, Great Britain, declined to accept them. Incarcerated near Ekaterinburg in the Urals, they posed little real threat to the Bolshevik regime. During the civil war, none of the White leaders supported a revival of the monarchy. On July 17, however, the family was executed in the cellar of the house in which it was staying on the orders of local Bolshevik leader Yakov Yurovsky. The story of the execution needs no elaboration, but the grisly nature of the deed continues to repel. The bodies were doused in gasoline and thrown down a mineshaft. Back in Moscow, Lenin and Sverdlov denied all responsibility. One Bolshevik who regretted the executions was Trotsky, who would have preferred to put the former tsar on trial, while taking on the role of prosecutor in a dramatic public spectacle. Lenin had no time for such notions. The royal family had been eliminated with the ruthlessness that became typical of the secret police. Arguably the former tsar himself might have been seen as an unacceptable symbol of the past. The same argument could hardly be applied to his family and less still to its bodyguards and servants. Nevertheless, every member of the Romanov family in Soviet Russia was hunted down and executed.

On September 3, two events provided some justification for the increased vigilance. In Petrograd, a student member of the SRs assassinated Moisey Uritsky, the Chairman of the Petrograd Cheka. In Moscow on this same day, Lenin was to address two meetings. After the second speech, a young Anarchist – also affiliated at one time to the SRs – named Fanya Kaplan shot him twice, leaving the Bolshevik leader badly wounded. Lenin refused hospitalization, fearing that he might be poisoned by hostile doctors, and was tended at home. The two events do not appear to have been linked. They did, none the less, lead to two changes in Russia. First, Lenin became well known to the Soviet public for the first time. The Bolsheviks put a lot of publicity into the internal threat to a leader who before this had been able to walk down many Moscow streets unrecognized by passers-by. Second, the events led to organized terror. Hundreds of people were rounded up and executed as a result of the shootings. In Petrograd, some 500 people were shot, including a number of officials prominent in the tsarist period; and the police chief, G. I. Petrovsky, proclaimed a new period of state terror on September 2. The Left SRs, the Anarchists, and the British and French embassies were implicated in counter-revolutionary plots to overthrow Lenin, Trotsky, and other leading Bolsheviks. (Hitherto, only the German embassy had been openly involved in political intrigue; but Bruce Lockhart, the British unofficial representative at the embassy, was widely believed by the authorities to be involved in espionage.) The Mensheviks, fearing for their lives, proclaimed their loyalty to the Soviet government.

The start of War Communism

In 1918 the Bolshevik regime launched an economic program known as War Communism, a system of extreme state control and nationalization of industry, accompanied by forced requisition of grain from the peasants. In some respects, the system represented ideological Bolshevism in operation, but Soviet sources claimed that the new authorities had little choice over the policy adopted. The land issue was a sensitive question, and one on which the Bolsheviks could find little common ground with their temporary partners, the Left SRs. However, as Russia was a peasant country, the Bolsheviks could not afford to ignore the land question. Lenin in 1917 was happy to agree to the peasant demand for land. There was little responsibility involved; and, for the most part, the peasants were quick to take control of the estates of the former landowners once an opportunity arose. Early in 1918 the Bolsheviks established norms for usage of land. The peasants now began to demand the distribution of the lands of the better-off farmers and the enclosed farmsteads that had been formed after the Stolypin reforms. The Bolsheviks for their part preferred to transfer these lands to newly established state farms (*sovkhozy*), the ideal form of state control in the countryside. Elsewhere some artels and communes were formed, but the process was a slow one, embracing only a small percentage of peasant households. Grain prices had been fixed in the time of the Provisional Government, and the Bolsheviks also adhered to the same pattern of commodity exchange, whereby industrial goods could be exchanged for agricultural. The difficulty with such a program was the lack of industrial goods in the early years of Bolshevik power; there was little incentive for the peasant to provide grain. Instead, many individual peasant farms simply sowed less, and this policy led to a critical situation as the political tensions in Russia mounted with the outbreak of civil war.

Those observers who sympathized with the Soviet Union tended to place emphasis on the necessity of grain collections during civil war conditions. E. H. Carr, the noted British historian, believed that the civil war rendered it a "matter of life and death" (Carr, 1979). The question, however, is which came first – the assault on the countryside or the beginnings of civil conflict? The Bolsheviks maintained that kulaks had taken over grain supply and were unwilling to release it to the state – and, moreover, that foreign imperialist powers were supporting such action. The German occupation of Ukraine exacerbated the crisis. By April 1918 the daily allowance of bread in Moscow was 100 grams; in Petrograd it was only 50 grams. The Bolsheviks believed that starvation would bring about the fall of the Soviet regime. The result was the establishment of a "food dictatorship" in May 1918, when extraordinary powers were given to the People's Commissariat of Food Supply. To this body the Bolsheviks transferred all authority for state purchase of grain at fixed prices. If the peasants were unwilling to relinquish the grain, the authorities would requisition it by force. On paper, they would requisition grain from the kulaks, though in practice there was often little distinction made between the kulaks and the middle peasants.

Evidence suggests that Lenin and his party fomented the class war in the countryside. The squads of workers formed an alliance with the Committees of the Poor (*Kombedy*), depicted as the natural allies of the Bolshevik regime. The grain collected from the peasants – the surplus – was to be used for the army and to feed the towns. In the atmosphere of conflict, the peasants often tried to conceal the grain. In these cases, the Bolshevik forces often took the entire surplus, leaving the peasant with barely enough on which to subsist. In Soviet parlance, it was a war against an internal enemy, and it was the first time that Bolshevik policy toward the peasantry took a clearly hostile line. Their supporters in the villages suffered heavily from peasant assaults, and much of Russia was in a state of uprising. However, the Left SR uprising, initiated partly in response to such policies, came only in July 1918 with the assassination of the German ambassador, Count Wilhelm Mirbach. Up to that time a semblance of unity existed within the government. Thus one should see War Communism as the application of pure Bolshevik ideology rather than as a response to the growth of kulak power, or the obstinacy of richer farms in refusing to give up surplus grain to the state. (Plate 2.1)

The start of the civil war

The Russian army had been in a state of mutiny since late 1916, but it had never formally been disbanded. It had twice been asked to embark on new offensives during the last two years of Russian participation in the First World War. Though it had begun to disintegrate in the spring of 1917, especially after Order Number 1, the army remained in place because of the justifiable fear of a foreign invasion. On January 28, 1918, a government decree announced the formation of a new force, the Red Army. Trotsky, the Commissar for War, recruited volunteers for the new "worker–peasant"

Plate 2.1 Russian peasants preaching communism. Russian peasants spread the word about communism to their fellows, ca. 1918–1924. A picture of Lenin hangs in the background.
Image: Bettmann/CORBIS

army. They had to be Soviet citizens over the age of 18, who could receive support from either a trade union or army committee, and sign up for three months. They would receive a regular salary and be provided with food, but in the vast majority of cases no uniform. Under the harsh conditions prevailing in early 1918 these incentives were enough for a mass movement to the new army. Before long, more than 100,000 volunteers had joined the makeshift force that operated according to committees, did not recognize officers, rarely had weapons, and consisted of inexperienced and raw recruits. Such an army could not fulfill any of the considerable tasks Trotsky anticipated. It was unlikely that it could stand up to even a partial assault by one of the European armies that had fought in the war. By April, Trotsky had realized that a viable army would need the services of former officers in the tsarist and Provisional Government armies. Discipline would have to be restored, which meant reviving many traditions, such as an officer caste, saluting, and the prompt fulfillment of orders. But how was the old officer class to be persuaded to join the new army?

The answer was to hold families of former officers hostage. Those who did not volunteer would be given menial and burdensome manual labor. Gradually the Red

Army began to take shape. On May 29, a new decree stipulated that all citizens were required for duty in the Red Army except those unworthy because of their "moral qualities." Ultimately the decision to use tsarist officers was a success, and perhaps one-third of the officer corps of the former tsarist army joined the new Communist version. The most notable figures were Ioakim Vatsetis (1873–1938), the son of an impoverished peasant family from Lithuania, who joined the Bolsheviks during the October Revolution; and Sergey Kamenev (1881–1936), a Kyiv-born First World War veteran, who rose rapidly through the ranks of the Red Army, thanks to the support of Trotsky, and gained a reputation for using his own initiative at the front, often ignoring orders from the political leaders if the situation on the ground did not seem to warrant them. The deployment of former tsarist officers was one reason why the Bolsheviks ultimately triumphed in the Russian Civil War.

As early as May 1918, it seemed that a new army would be required urgently. On March 6 to 8, British troops had landed at Murmansk and Arkhangelsk to safeguard their supplies of military goods, which they had placed at the disposal of the Russians in 1916–1917. There was no immediate indication that the landings were hostile to the Bolshevik government. Before long, however, French and American units joined these troops. By the beginning of August there were further landings at Arkhangelsk. Among signs of more sustained opposition to the Bolsheviks had been the formation of the Voluntary Army of the Don on November 2, 1917. Several generals had escaped from loose captivity, including Kornilov and Anton Denikin, but their initial intention was to form a new army to continue the patriotic conflict with the Germans. By the spring of 1918, generals Alekseev, Kornilov, and Denikin had joined forces in the regions of the Don and the Kuban. Officers fleeing from Trotsky's enforced recruitment made their way eastward to the Urals and Siberia, ready to lead any future campaign against the Bolsheviks. On January 19, 1918, the Russian Patriarch Tikhon had condemned the Bolshevik regime. Toward the end of the month the Germans had recognized an independent Ukraine. Further conflicts seemed inevitable. On April 5, the Japanese army occupied Vladivostok, clearly intent on further encroachment on Russian territory. American forces reluctantly began to disembark there several weeks later.

The Allies, recognizing that the Bolsheviks would have to be removed from power before Russia returned to the Entente, began a half-hearted effort to build up forces in support of the White armies. Eventually they decided to use the services of the Czechoslovak Corps, prisoners of war captured from the Austro-Hungarian army, who had been formed and trained as a potential army of the future government of Czechoslovakia. The Entente had wanted to use this force in the First World War, but first it had to be taken out of Russia. Trotsky insisted that it should be disarmed, and that it had to travel on the Trans-Siberian Railway to the east rather than take the shorter route to Europe through one of the northern ports. The Corps did manage to retain some weapons, but skirmishes broke out as it traveled east – one of them was with a trainload of Hungarian prisoners who had stopped as they traveled in the opposite direction. In the spring of 1918, the Czechoslovak Corps was the best-organized military force in Russia. By May, it had begun to control several towns along the rail route, evidently fearing that its men would be interned in a special camp were they to surrender to local Bolshevik forces. In Chelyabinsk it soon displaced the local Bolshevik government. The rebellion of the Czechs coincided with a largely Bolshevik-created class struggle in many towns and most of the countryside. The formation of the Committees of the Poor to requisition grain was perhaps the main factor in the intensification of the conflict. Thus what was rather a motley band of anti-Bolshevik military leaders soon acquired the force of a mass movement, which was swelled by expropriated peasants, merchants, Socialist Revolutionaries, Mensheviks, and disaffected Orthodox church members. Politically these forces often had little in common and they would find it difficult to obtain support from sections of the population.

The opposition group was called "Whites" because of the aim of preserving Holy Russia from the Antichrist, namely the Bolsheviks. Anti-Bolshevik uprisings spread across Siberia, where Bolshevik control had always been nominal. In the summer of 1918 there were anti-government uprisings in Yaroslavl and Ashkhabad. In August the British occupied Baku, and Entente troops also arrived in Central Asia. In the Caucasus, the invaders gradually moved northward, capturing Grozny after a battle in November 1918. The Whites by this time had occupied huge tracts of land, larger than that held by the Bolsheviks in the European part of the country. The first leader of the Volunteer Army was Kornilov. When he was killed in April 1918, Denikin replaced him. General P. N. Krasnov was named Ataman of the Great Army of the Don in April 1918, and with the help of Cossack troops launched an attack on Tsaritsyn in mid-August. The Whites occupied towns along major rivers – on the Volga, for example, they captured Samara, Simbirsk, and Kazan during the summer. Various anti-Soviet governments were created in occupied towns (Ufa, Samara and Omsk being three of the main centers). On the Volga and in large parts of Siberia, peasants generally supported the SRs – in Omsk, for example, the SRs had formed the Siberian Provisional Government. The situation for the Bolsheviks looked desperate. In September, the Revolutionary Military Council was formed to fight the new war. Trotsky was its chairman, and I. I. Vatsetis the commander-in-chief of the Red Army. Trotsky once again took on the main role in a critical situation.

The development of the civil war was determined largely by events in Europe. Lenin, having broken with the Entente, was not prepared to sever the agreement made with Germany at Brest-Litovsk. But once the war in Europe ended, on November 11, the situation in Soviet Russia also changed dramatically. The Allies became foreign occupiers. Revolution soon broke out in Germany and Austria-Hungary, as Lenin and Trotsky had predicted. The great monarchies of central Europe – the Habsburgs and the Hohenzollerns – collapsed. The Germans began to evacuate their forces from occupied regions of the former Russian Empire – the Baltic States, Ukraine, Belarus, and the Caucasus. Lenin denounced the Brest Treaty on November 13. Several days later, the White forces were reorganized. Admiral A. P. Kolchak, based at Omsk, was designated "Supreme Ruler of Russia," and Denikin was his subordinate in the southern part of Russia. In the north of Russia, by early 1919, the effective ruler was General E. K. Miller, even though on paper he was answerable to an SR government. Entente ships entered the Black Sea, and troops were put ashore at major ports – Novorossiisk, Odesa, and Sevastopol. In Estonia, where the Bolsheviks managed to take power during November–December 1918, General N. N. Yudenich began to build up his forces. By late 1918 and early 1919, a bitter struggle had developed on (for the Bolsheviks) the Eastern Front as Kolchak's forces advanced, sustained by recognition from the forces of the Entente, who now hoped for a rapid end to the conflict in Russia.

Red victory

The White forces were unable to coordinate fully their assault on the Bolsheviks, hindered by geographical and communication difficulties, although in the spring and early summer of 1919 they appeared close to success. Kolchak's great march westward was an impressive military feat along a front almost 1,450 miles long. In March 1919 his army approached the Volga river. Izhevsk and Ufa had fallen into his hands. Trotsky frantically began to extend recruitment. Large numbers of Communists and Komsomol workers were sent to the front. In May, Yudenich attacked Petrograd. The former capital mobilized all men aged between 18 and 40, and by June 19 the threat had been dealt with. Yudenich's forces were pursued through the Baltic States. Trotsky divided the army of the Eastern Front into two forces to counter Kolchak – the Northern Group under V. I. Shorin, and the Southern Group under M. V. Frunze and V. V. Kuibyshev. Overall command was given to S. S. Kamenev and S. I. Gusev. Trotsky was able to halt Kolchak's attack, but felt obliged to divert troops to meet a threat from the south. Kolchak's prospects, however, now appeared slim. Frunze was placed in command of the Eastern Front on July 13, 1919. He was aided by commanders such as M. N. Tukhachevsky, head of the Russian 5th Army, which advanced from Central Asia to occupy Chelyabinsk in late July.

The political tactics of the Whites contributed to the Bolsheviks' success. Aristocratic military commanders and the mass of peasants had little in common; the peasants were generally loyal to the SR cause, but for the most part were more anxious to sustain their livelihood. Under Kolchak, the authorities confiscated peasant land, and forced peasants to join the White Army. Before long, peasant revolts against his administration were common. There was much resentment against "White Terror" – the ready execution of deserters or those unwilling to take up arms for the White cause. Kolchak's aid from the Entente powers also began to decline. Intervention in the civil war was unpopular in Britain and France, with both governments needing to deal with the unprecedented costs of the First World War. By the spring of 1919, the Allies began to pull their armies out of occupied regions of the Caspian and Black Seas (Odesa, Sevastopol, and Baku). The northern ports of Murmansk and Arkhangelsk would be abandoned by September and October. Kolchak was in full retreat. Early in 1920 he would be captured by the Czechoslovak Corps, which, disillusioned with the protracted conflict, had little hesitation in handing him over to the Bolsheviks, who executed him in February 1920. However, in July 1919, the main threat to the Bolsheviks came from Denikin, who advanced from the south with the goal of capturing Moscow. He applied a scorched-earth policy as his army advanced, making him unpopular with the local peasants in Ukraine.

Denikin's advance was the most dramatic moment of the civil war. The fact that he was moving through European, rather than remote Asian, territories accentuated the threat. By the end of June, he controlled much of Ukraine, including the major cities of Kharkiv and Ekaterinoslav, in addition to Tsaritsyn on the Volga river. On July 3, the White general ordered an attack on Moscow on three fronts. Lenin issued an appeal "All for the struggle with Denikin!" The Bolsheviks mobilized all those over the age of 16. The Whites' progress was slow, impeded at every stage by frantic resistance, but it was also relentless. They occupied the major cities of Kursk and Belgorod in southern Russia, as well as Kharkiv in north-east Ukraine. Orel and Voronezh would soon fall to the White Army as well. By mid-October, Denikin's forces were approaching Tula, the last step before the attack on Moscow. In the north-west, Yudenich was now quite close to Petrograd with another White army. The period from mid-summer to the early fall of 1919 was the most dangerous time for the new Bolshevik state. However, Bolshevik organization and resistance were improving. Again, Denikin's policies did not advance his cause. He was marching, he declared, "for one and indivisible Russia," a proclamation that would hardly endear him to many non-Russians in the former empire (Ukraine, the Caucasus, and other regions). It was obvious that Denikin would support the return of the landowner. The peasantry had little to gain by supporting him. Also, despite his slogans, Denikin could not win the backing of Russian patriots. Instead it was the Bolshevik regime that could appeal to fellow Russians to preserve Russia against an army supported and financed by foreign powers. To many peasants, homegrown Bolsheviks were preferable to a return of the landowner and foreign occupation (distant though that prospect may have been in reality). The Bolsheviks' use of terror to enforce conscription and deal with deserters and cowards was not significant – the Whites also used terror as a means of coercion. The people of Russia were in fact caught in a ruthless conflict, with neither side showing any mercy. There could be no moral crusade against the Bolsheviks in 1919.

Through counter-attacks starting in October 1919, the Bolshevik forces were able to check the advance of Denikin's army. By January 10, 1920, Tsaritsyn and Rostov had fallen into Red hands (Stalin, the party leader on the Southern Front, would claim credit for the former victory). Budenny's First Cavalry Army and Tukhachevsky's new Caucasus Front were also instrumental in turning the tide of the civil war. By

January the Allies had evacuated the remnants of Denikin's forces from the Crimea. One month earlier, the Red forces had virtually destroyed Yudenich's army in the northwest region. The British lifted their blockade of Russia this same month. In February the Bolsheviks reached peace terms with Finland and the Baltic States (all former territories of the Russian Empire). Much of Siberia was now in Bolshevik, or pro-Bolshevik partisan hands. Japanese forces still occupied the area around Lake Baikal, where the remnants of the White Army had congregated. Bolshevik forces had even occupied Vladivostok in late January 1920. However, Lenin recognized the difficulty in maintaining control over the Far East, particularly after the Japanese returned to occupy Vladivostok in early April 1920. Instead he approved the formation of a buffer state – the Far Eastern Republic (April 6, 1920) – that would not be linked directly to Soviet Russia, but would serve as a means to end Japanese intervention on Russian soil. In the summer of 1920, Japan agreed to remove its forces from the Baikal region provided the Bolsheviks did not interfere with the authority of the Far Eastern Republic. This agreement ended the conflict in the Russian Far East.

The war with the Poles

Following the end of the First World War, a debate began among the Western Allies, the Poles, and affected neighboring territories regarding the precise demarcation lines of the new Polish state. The Polish attack on territories to the east coincided with the advance of Denikin in the spring of 1919. The first towns occupied were those in Belarus and on the Lithuanian border, including Grodno and Wilno (Vilnius), which were captured between February and April, along with areas of Western Ukraine. The occupation of Minsk followed in August, but the Poles were unable to advance further than the Berezina river. In April 1920, Jozef Pilsudski joined forces with the Ukrainians under Symon Petlyura, and by May 6 the joint armies had occupied Kyiv. The Bolsheviks belatedly recognized the new danger and began to transfer forces from other fronts to the west. Two new fronts were formed to combat the Poles – the Western Front under Tukhachevsky and the Southern Front under A. I. Yegorov. The Soviet forces, hardened by the civil war, made rapid progress against the stretched Polish forces. The Red Army reoccupied Kyiv on June 12 and began a rapid advance to the west, facing relatively weak opposition. By mid-August, the Bolshevik forces were nearing Warsaw. Further south, Budenny's cavalry reached the western Ukrainian city of Lviv.

For Lenin and Trotsky, an enticing prospect now opened up – the formation of a Soviet government in Poland that would be the prelude to revolutions in Europe. The nascent Bolshevik regime could thus export revolution, supported by the working class in the occupied countries. Poland would be the test case. On July 31, 1920, the Bolsheviks created a Provisional Revolutionary Committee as the basis of a future Polish government. Among its leaders was Dzerzhinsky, head of the Cheka, along with another Polish Communist, Yulian Markhlevsky. Circumstances, however, did not favor such ambitious plans. The Polish workers were content to see the restoration of an independent Poland after more than a century of subjugation by foreigners. They had no wish to see the arrival of a new conquering army from the east. Tukhachevsky's advance had carried his army well ahead of its supply lines and – perhaps even more important – it had lost contact with Budenny's cavalry, which was still engaged in operations in Western Ukraine. The gap between the two Soviet armies allowed the Poles to mount a counter-attack around Lublin. The Warsaw battle continued from July 30 to August 2, and resulted in a resounding defeat for Lenin's army. The Poles, assisted by French military advisors, threatened to encircle the Soviet forces. Following the recovery at Warsaw, Polish forces were able to recapture much of Western Ukraine and Western Belarus.

Before an armistice was signed on October 12, 1920, the Poles had advanced beyond the Curzon Line,[1] putting them in a good bargaining position for the peace treaty that would eventually be signed in Riga on March 18, 1921. For Soviet Russia, the campaign had been the least successful of the period of conflict between 1918 and 1921. Poland was able to hold on to significant territories occupied by Ukrainians, Belarusians, and Jews (Eastern Poland), in addition to the Wilno region. The three Baltic States were to gain independence. The Soviet territory once again contracted. More important, the goal of exporting revolution to the West had now to be shelved. In any case, the Soviet economy could not cope with the continuation of the war. Transport was in a deplorable state, affecting the supply lines, and the army was underfed and underequipped. Tukhachevsky's initial success was especially impressive given the state the Red Army was in. Peasant uprisings had broken out across Russia in the summer of 1920, the most notable being that in Tambov under the leadership of A. A. Antonov, which spread into the Saratov and Voronezh regions and encompassed about 30,000 insurgents. Smaller movements developed in late 1920 and early 1921, particularly in the vast spaces of Siberia, where a Siberian Peasant Union attempted to form an anti-Communist government. At its peak, the movement comprised about 60,000 people.

The end of the civil war

In June 1920, the last surviving White commander, Baron Petr Wrangel, had used the diversion of the Polish–Soviet war to advance from the Crimea. Though the White cause was already lost, he caused major problems and proved a more skilled and efficient commander than his predecessors with grander titles. In early October he mounted an attack on the Reds at Kakhovka. The Bolsheviks set up a new Southern Front in September 1920, under the command of Frunze and the Revolutionary Military Council, backed by the First Cavalry Army. By November 3, Wrangel had been forced back into the Crimea, where he barricaded himself in at the fortified outpost of Perekop. Five days later, the Red Army stormed into the Crimea and attacked Wrangel's stronghold. The remaining Whites were soon overcome. On November 12, the Bolsheviks took Simferopol; the great prize of Sevastopol was seized three days later. The British and the French were no longer prepared to be involved in the fading White cause, but they did consent to evacuate Wrangel and his troops via the Black Sea. The main fighting of the civil war was over. In some regions it dragged on, however, causing a drain on the Soviet state without really threatening its survival. The Ukrainian anarchist Nestor Makhno led his band on raids throughout Ukraine, often switching sides; but by November 1920, with the Soviet authorities victorious, he turned all his forces on the Bolsheviks. On October 25, 1922, Vladivostok came under the control of the Far Eastern Republic, as the Japanese withdrew their forces. The following month, however, the republic was merged with the Soviet authority in the Far East. The war had been devastating, but with the victory Bolshevik power had at last been secured. Lenin had made few compromises, and had managed to sustain his state despite the policy of War Communism, the application of terror and coercion with his army, and without any form of collaboration with his fellow social-ists. In the process, the conflict had left the country in a deplorable state. Famine spread through much of central Russia and Ukraine. The upper estimate is that more than 23 million people died during 1918–1921, a figure more than double the total casualties of all sides in the First World War, though the more conservative figure of 15 million deaths between 1917 and 1920 is perhaps more accurate.

The Kronstadt rebellion

The rebellion at the Kronstadt naval base does not fit easily into the developments of the civil war as it involved a sector of society hitherto pro-Bolshevik and indeed one of the pivotal forces of the October Revolution. In the spring of 1921, a mutiny broke out on the battleship *Petropavlovsk*, signaling the beginning of the Kronstadt rebellion. The uprising involved some 14,000 sailors of the Baltic Fleet, along with Kronstadt workers. The rebels demanded the release of political prisoners, the restoration of political freedom, and new elections to local Soviets. M. I. Kalinin, Chairman of the Soviet Executive Committee who had been visiting Kronstadt, was hustled off the base. On March 2, the insurgents issued a slogan calling for an end to the "regime of commissars." There are a variety of interpretations of this uprising. Soviet and some current Russian historians maintain that the revolt received its inspiration from the capitalist West and/or Russian émigrés. These sources maintain further that the Socialist Revolutionary Party, and its leader Viktor Chernov personally, received substantial sums from London and Paris in an attempt to remove the Bolsheviks from power despite the failure of intervention dur-ing the civil war. They note the high percentage of sailors with a peasant background and comment that some of them served earlier with the White Army. However, it seems more likely that the insurgents were made up of workers as well, and Lenin noted that many were hungry and dissatisfied with the consequences of Bolshevik rule to date (i.e. War Communism and lengthy years of warfare).

The Bolsheviks could have reacted in a variety of ways; but Trotsky, Commissar for War, regarded the uprising as an outright rebellion and demanded that the sailors lay down their weapons. Only those who surrendered voluntarily would be granted an amnesty. On March 7, Trotsky ordered Tukhachevsky to occupy the base. Twice, however, Soviet forces were repelled, and only on March 18 did Soviet troops succeed in overcoming the resistance. The leaders of the revolt were executed. The Bolsheviks gained little from this uprising. Officially the insurgency was blamed on Anarchist agitation among the sailors. It was obvious to Lenin, however, that large segments of the population had become disaffected with the Bolshevik government. There could be no clearer warning than the demands of the Kronstadt sailors, once the most reliable pro-Bolshevik force in the former capital of Petrograd. Enemies, internal and external, had been overcome. It was now time to restore the country, both politically and economically. Ideological Bolshevism had failed. The civil war had been won, at least in part, through uniting disparate forces to fight foreign occupation – Bolshevik propaganda consistently exaggerated the extent of international commitment to the Whites since it was in the interests of the government to do so. The Bolsheviks won because they had better leadership, were better organized, and they occupied key centers of industry and communications in the very heartland of Russia. To many they were merely the most preferable of several poor alternatives, mainly because they did not threaten a return of the landowners or subjugation to a foreign power.

Note

1 The Curzon Line was a proposed demarcation line between Poland and Soviet Russia put forward by the British Foreign Minister, Lord Curzon. The line corresponded roughly to the border between Prussia and the Russian Empire after the Third Partition of Poland in 1795.

Questions for discussion

1. Was the October Revolution a popular uprising?
2. How were the Bolsheviks able to stay in power?
3. What territories and resources did Soviet Russia lose as a result of the Treaty of Brest-Litovsk?
4. What were the main features of the policy of War Communism, and why was it so unpopular?
5. Why did the Red Army succeed in the Civil War?

Recent works

Bainton, Roy. *A Brief History of 1917: Russia's Year of Revolution.* London: Robinson, 2005.

Bisher, Jamie. *White Terror: Cossack Warlords of the Trans-Siberian.* London: Routledge, 2005.

Borrero, Mauricio. *Hungry Moscow: Scarcity and Urban Society in the Russian Civil War, 1917–1921.* New York: Peter Lang, 2003.

Brooks, Jeffrey. *Lenin and the Making of the Soviet State: A Brief History with Documents.* Boston, Mass.: Bedford/St. Martin's, 2007.

Budgen, Sebastian. *Lenin Reloaded: Toward a Politics of Truth.* Durham, NC: Duke University Press, 2007.

Carrère d'Encausse, Hélène. *Lenin.* New York: Holmes & Meier, 2001.

Chamberlain, Lesley. *Motherland: A Philosophical History of Russia.* New York: Rookery Press, 2007.

Corney, Frederick C. *Telling October: Memory and the Making of the Bolshevik Revolution.* Ithaca, NY: Cornell University Press, 2004.

Crownover, Roger. *The United States Intervention in North Russia, 1918–1919: The Polar Bear Odyssey.* Lewiston, NY: Edwin Mellen Press, 2001.

Dowswell, Paul. *The Russian Revolution: October 25, 1917.* Chicago, Ill.: Raintree, 2004.

Dunn, Bill. *100 Years of Permanent Revolution: Results and Prospects.* London: Pluto Press, 2006.

Edwards, Judith. *Lenin and the Russian Revolution in World History.* Berkeley Heights, NJ: Enslow, 2001.

Fevzi, Altug. *Thornbush: Memoirs of a Crimean Tatar Nationalist and Educator Relating to the Russian Civil War and the Famine of 1921–1922.* Istanbul: Isis Press, 2004.

Finkel, Stuart. *On the Ideological Front: The Russian Intelligentsia and the Making of the Soviet Public Sphere.* New Haven, Conn.: Yale University Press, 2007.

Gooding, John. *Socialism in Russia: Lenin and His Legacy, 1890–1991.* Basingstoke: Palgrave Macmillan, 2002.

Gregory, Paul R. *Terror by Quota: State Security from Lenin to Stalin. An Archival Study.* New Haven, Conn./Stanford, Calif.: Yale University Press/Hoover Institution, Stanford University, 2009.

Kiaer, Christina and Eric Naiman. *Everyday Life in Early Soviet Russia: Taking the Revolution Inside.* Bloomington, Ind.: Indiana University Press, 2006.

Kinvig, Clifford. *Churchill's Crusade: The British Invasion of Russia, 1918–1920.* London: Hambledon Continuum, 2006.

Le Blanc, Paul. *Marx, Lenin, and the Revolutionary Experience: Studies of Communism and Radicalism in the Age of Globalization.* New York: Routledge, 2006.

Lih, Lars T. *Lenin Rediscovered: What Is to Be Done? in Context.* Boston, Mass.: Brill, 2006.

Malle, Silvana. *The Economic Organization of War Communism 1918–1921.* Cambridge: Cambridge University Press, 2002.

Mawdsley, Evan. *The Russian Civil War.* New York: Pegasus Books, 2007.

Murphy, Brian, and Erik C. Landis. *Bandits and Partisans: The Antonov Movement in the Russian Civil War.* Pittsburgh, Pa: University of Pittsburgh Press, 2008.

Palat, Madhavan K. *Social Identities in Revolutionary Russia.* Basingstoke: Palgrave Macmillan, 2001.

Pannekoek, Anton. *Lenin as Philosopher: A Critical Examination of the Philosophical Basis of Leninism.* Milwaukee, Wis.: Marquette University Press, 2003.

Pearson, Michael. *Lenin's Mistress: The Life of Inessa Armand.* New York: Random House, 2001.

Read, Christopher. *Lenin: A Revolutionary Life.* London: Routledge, 2005.

Renton, David. *Trotsky.* London: Haus, 2004.

Rosmer, Alfred. *Trotsky and the Origins of Trotskyism.* London: F. Boutle, 2002.

Service, Robert. *Trotsky: a Biography.* London: Macmillan, 2009.

Smele, Jonathan D. *The Russian Revolution and Civil War, 1917–1921: An Annotated Bibliography.* London: Continuum, 2003.

Smith, S. A. *Revolution and the People in Russia and China: A Comparative History.* Cambridge: Cambridge University Press, 2008.

Swain, Geoffrey. *Trotsky.* Harlow: Longman/Pearson, 2006.

Thatcher, Ian D. *Reinterpreting Revolutionary Russia: Essays in Honour of James D. White.* Basingstoke: Palgrave Macmillan, 2006.

Transchel, Kate. *Under the Influence: Working-Class Drinking, Temperance and Cultural Revolution in Russia, 1895–1932.* Pittsburgh, Pa: University of Pittsburgh Press, 2006.

Trotsky, Leon. *History of the Russian Revolution.* Chicago, Ill.: Haymarket Books, 2008.

Turton, Katy. *Forgotten Lives: The Role of Lenin's Sisters in the Russian Revolution, 1864–1937.* Basingstoke: Palgrave Macmillan, 2007.

Vatlin, Alexander. *Piggy Foxy and the Sword of Revolution: Bolshevik Self-Portraits.* New Haven, Conn.: Yale University Press, 2006.

Wade, Rex A. *The Bolshevik Revolution and Russian Civil War*. Westport, Conn.: Greenwood Press, 2001.

Wade, Rex A. *Revolutionary Russia: New Approaches to the Russian Revolution of 1917*. London: Routledge, 2004.

White, James D. *Lenin: The Practice and Theory of Revolution*. Basingstoke: Palgrave Macmillan, 2001.

3

....

NEP and the rise of Stalin, 1921–1928

The formation of the USSR

The civil war period meant that any early formation of a state embracing non-Russian republics and regions would be complex. By the end of the war there were six Soviet socialist republics – the RSFSR, the Ukrainian SSR, the Belarusian SSR, Azerbaijan, Armenia, and Georgia. In Central Asia, Bukhara and Khorezmsk had founded people's soviet republics in 1920, in the latter case comprised mainly of Uzbeks. Lenin's compromise Far Eastern Republic also remained in place. The events of the civil war reached a peak in Ukraine, where governments changed hands several times, and the Bolsheviks lacked substantial support among the indigenous population. In March 1919 the Bolsheviks issued a Constitution of the Ukrainian SSR, for example, proclaiming the "sovereignty and independence" of Ukraine. In February 1919 the fledgling and highly insecure Belarus received a Constitution at the 1st Belarusian Congress of Soviets, held in February 1919. The three republics of the Caucasus region did not receive a Constitution until 1921–1922.

Within the Russian Federation, several autonomous republics and oblasts (provinces) were formed, including the Bashkir Autonomous Republic in March 1919, and the Kyrghyz–Kazak, Dagestan, Gorsk, and Tatar autonomous republics in 1920. In other areas, communes were formed rather than republics – this applied particularly to long-established groups such as the Volga Germans. One can say simply that the Russian Federation was under construction but that its final form had not been determined during the civil war period, a time when the entire state seemed ready to self-destruct into many fragments. For the most part, the Russian regions were not yet ready to give up acquired powers. As early as the summer of 1919, L. B. Kamenev, who was given responsibility for federation-building, proposed to unite several commissariats in the Soviet republics with the Russian variant, i.e. to try to centralize administrative control. Some agreements were duly made in the spheres of defense, economic activities, and foreign relations. For the most part, however, the regions still wanted to exert control over these areas, resulting in friction with Russia.

With the end of the civil war, the immediate question facing the Bolshevik leaders was how to form a state that went beyond the territory of Soviet Russia to include the five smaller republics, the largest and most desired of which was Ukraine. The Transcaucasian states of Armenia, Azerbaijan, and Georgia, which historically, ethnically, and in terms of religious persuasion were radically different, were lumped together in one Transcaucasian SSR. Matters were not made easier by the fact that the debate over the future entity coincided with Lenin's first serious illness. In this period Lenin alternated between periods of activity and anger at what he perceived as the development of Great Russian chauvinism in the Bolshevik ranks, and times of almost total incapacitation. The only viable thesis on the national question in the Bolshevik past had been a plea for self-determination of nations penned by Stalin in 1912, though Lenin clearly had an influence on the final product.

At the 10th Congress of the Russian Communist Party in March 1921, Stalin, as the People's Commissar for Nationality Questions, delivered a speech in which he glorified the Russian SFSR as the ideal form of a state union republic. In Stalin's view, the non-Russian SSRs, together with the autonomous republics and oblasts, and the communes, had to unite with a Great Russian state under Bolshevik control. He noted that the process was already well under way in the period 1918–1920, and thus it was only necessary for the Bolsheviks to bring the question to its natural fruition. The idea was the antithesis to the sort of vision that Stalin espoused in 1912, and it reflected in part an emerging Great Russian view that owed much to the trials of the civil war period. At the Congress, G. I. Safarov, a member of the Turkestan Commission, accused the party of neglecting the national question, and declared that the Bolsheviks had already made numerous blunders in Central Asia.

Many Bolsheviks also found Stalin's views unacceptable, and after objections at the Congress a special commission under Valerian Kuibyshev was formed to examine the matter. Implicit in the formation of the commission was the notion that Russia would gain overall control, but the various components of the new formation would be granted some autonomy. Lenin, meanwhile, condemned Stalin's ideas and supported the formation of a Union state, in which the Russian Federation would not be accorded any special rights over the other constituent republics. Stalin and his associates, while obliged to heed Lenin's views, which were approved by a Plenum of the Central Committee of the Russian Communist Party, were at liberty to interpret decisions their own way, backed by military force and a crude approach to dealing with the complex issues of nationality.

Such an approach was illustrated in Georgia, where on October 21, 1922 the entire Central Committee of the republican Communist Party resigned. The Georgians demanded that they should enter the new Union state as a separate nation rather than as part of Transcaucasia. Their chief obstacle was a fellow countryman, Stalin's associate Sergo Ordzhonikidze, secretary of the Transcaucasian regional committee, who physically attacked one of the Georgian leaders. Both Stalin and Ordzhonikidze acted more outrageously toward the regional leaders of their own national group than toward ethnic Russians. Georgia was under the control of a popular Menshevik government before the arrival of the Red Army in February 1921, and the territory had been "cleansed" of Mensheviks over the following month. The Red Army's invasion represented little more than an act of local power-grabbing by the Bolsheviks, engineered by Stalin and Ordzhonikidze. The republic was not yet fully pacified, however, and the question of Georgia continued to trouble Lenin, who was rapidly losing any control over events in the Soviet periphery.

On December 30, 1922, the 1st All-Union Congress of Soviets, comprising delegates of the four major republics, sanctioned the declaration and agreement of a new Union state, the Union of Soviet Socialist Republics. The USSR's ultimate goal was declared to be "the uniting of workers of all countries in a global union of Soviet republics," i.e. the eventual attainment of world revolution. The Union state was to be a federation of sovereign republics. The central government in Moscow gained control over defense, the state budget, state security, border control, external trade, international representation, and transport. The four republics retained control over internal matters, healthcare, justice, and education. The highest organ of the USSR was declared to be the All-Union Congress of Soviets; and, in the periods when the Congress was not meeting, the Central Executive Committee would run the country. This latter committee consisted of two organs: the Council of the Union, and the Council of Nationalities. Its initial chairmen were M. I. Kalinin (RSFSR), G. I. Petrovsky (Ukrainian SSR), A. G. Chervyakov (Belarusian SSR), and N. N. Narimanov (Transcaucasian SSR). Kalinin then chaired a commission to come up with the draft of a Constitution for the new state.

Once this was done, the new Union acquired legitimacy through the Basic Law (Constitution) of the USSR, which was approved on January 31, 1924 by the 2nd All-Union Congress of Soviets, and issued in two parts. Part 1, the declaration about the formation of the USSR, focused purely on politics and propaganda. It noted the contrast between capitalism, with its national hostility, colonial plundering, inequality, oppression, and pogroms, and "imperialist aggression and war", and socialism, which allegedly brought about the fraternal cooperation and harmony of peoples, in addition to national equality, peace, and freedom. Part 2 consisted of an accord about the formation of the USSR, which consisted of eleven sections. Section 2 was the most significant. It declared that the borders of the USSR were inviolable, and that all residents of the republics of the Union were eligible for citizenship. However, the republics had the right to secede from the Union. Section 4 noted that the number of delegates to the Congress of Soviets would depend on the population of the constituent republics, while the Soviet of Nationalities would be based on representatives from Union and autonomous republics. Sessions of the Central Executive Committee had to be held three times a year, and in the interim the highest executive authority lay with the Presidium of the CEC, which consisted of twenty-one people.

The formation of the USSR and the first Constitution helped to consolidate the process that had begun in November 1917, while allowing the Russian Federation to take on some of the responsibilities of the former empire. Initially, there was no clear indication that the new formation would result in national oppression. The form of republican government that took shape in the 1920s was embraced by the slogan "National in form, socialist in content," and the Union republics were encouraged to develop their national cultures, and to use their native languages in schools and in official business. However, from the outset, the problem with the formation of the USSR and the first USSR Constitution lay with the development of the party bureaucracy rather than with the fiction of a Soviet form of power. The Constitution (as well as the later Stalin Constitution of 1936) made good reading, but it hardly conveyed the reality of power in Moscow, and the innate tendency of the post-Lenin party leadership to amass power in its own hands, initially in the form of a triumvirate, but ultimately in the single dictatorship of Stalin. The party, not the Soviets, ruled the Soviet Union and dictated policy for much of the period of Communist rule.

The granting of powers to the republics was a masterstroke of Lenin. For the moment, it pacified areas that had little desire to return to rule from Russia. It could be argued equally that republics like Ukraine and Belarus were not yet ready for self-rule. Both areas had suffered greatly in the civil war, as indeed had the territories of the Caucasus. The formation of the Union followed seven years of more or less constant warfare for Russia, which had led to the devastation of the economy and mass starvation among its people. Gradually the USSR expanded, and changes were made to the benefit of the new national republics. Between 1924 and 1926, for example, the Belarusian SSR expanded through the inclusion of territories from Russia (from Vitebsk and Gomel regions), which more than doubled its population. In 1923–1924, Azerbaijan received two autonomous regions, Nakhichevan and Nagorno-Karabakh (the former had a large Armenian minority, while the latter was predominantly Armenian). In 1924 also, the authorities created an autonomous Moldavian SSR within the composition of Ukraine, ostensibly to protect Moldavians from further encroachments of Romania, which had occupied Bessarabia after the end of the First World War. Gradually the Soviet domain penetrated Central Asia also, as a result of which two new Union republics were created by 1925 – Turkmenistan and Uzbekistan, along with autonomous Tajikistan within Uzbek territory.

Elsewhere in this region, Soviet power had been established in the Kyrghyz–Kazak region by March 1918, which was declared an Autonomous Soviet Socialist Republic (ASSR) on August 26, 1920. By October 27, 1924, the area had been greatly expanded through the addition of lands from the Kyrghyz–Kazak part of Turkestan. The population of the ASSR thus rose to more than 5 million. The capital of the republic, originally Orenburg, was moved to Ak-Mechet at this time, and by the following February it had switched again, this time to Kzyl-Orda. In April the ASSR was officially renamed the Kazakh ASSR, and by 1929 its capital had been transferred to Alma-Ata, where it was to remain until the end of the Soviet period. Between 1936 and 1938, the ASSR was transformed into the Kazakhstan SSR, which became in area the second-largest of the Union republics. In similar fashion, Tajikistan, which had been part of Uzbekistan until 1929, acquired status as a Union republic in 1929; and Kirghizia became an autonomous part of the Russian Federation in 1929, and a Union republic by 1936. Meanwhile, the Transcaucasian SSR divided into its three constituent parts – the republics of Georgia, Azerbaijan, and Armenia. Before the Second World War, eleven Union republics had been formed (later Moldavia would be appended to Bessarabia as the Moldavian SSR, and the three Baltic States were annexed in 1940). The formation of the Soviet Union in its final form was thus a haphazard affair, often undertaken without regard for the sensitivity of borders with occasional isolation of ethnic groups from their titular territories.

The start of the New Economic Policy

The system of War Communism had necessitated state control over most of the industry of the country. Nationalization had been carried out on large and moderate-sized factories, and even on many of the smaller ones. By the end of 1920, all enterprises that employed more than five people had been nationalized, and over 60 percent of these factories had officially instituted "workers' control." The Bolsheviks had been woefully short of cadres with sufficient skill and experience to operate the factories and consequently had called on the services of former non-working-class specialists for such tasks. Under War Communism – and particularly under civil war conditions – industrial output in Russia dropped sharply. Periodically, many factories fell into the hands of the White forces, particularly in the oldest industrial region of Ukraine, where the Donbas Basin supplied vital fuel and raw materials. However, in the territory that had remained most firmly under Bolshevik control – the center of European Russia, with Moscow as the focal point – industry began to grow once again in wartime conditions. Working conditions in the period of War Communism were harsh. Everyone over the age of 14 had to work, and the working day was constantly increased to meet production needs.

In the rural areas, the Bolshevik encouragement of class warfare through the Committees of Poor Peasants resulted in the dismantling of the remaining large estates and the severe reduction of peasant farms in the more affluent (kulak) category. Thus the proportion of kulak farms had been reduced from about 15 percent of all households in 1917 to around 5 percent by the end of the civil war period. War Communism had also seen the first experiments in communal farming, though without any one form of socialist agriculture prevailing. Thus there were artels, communes, TOZ (Associations for the Joint Cultivation of Land), etc., but they constituted a meager proportion of all farms and added very little to the material base of the Soviet village. The Bolsheviks generally supported the concept of collective farms, but the earlier experiments hardly augured well for the future. Most villages saw a substantial fall in food products in the period 1918–1920, and particularly of bread. The peasants could hardly develop much experience of collective farming while the country was in a state of war, and also at a time when the farms lacked any kind of mechanical base. Lenin had noted at the 8th Party Congress that once the farms could be provided with 10,000 tractors Russian peasants might support socialized agriculture.

Of all the policies pursued by the Bolsheviks in the countryside, that of grain requisitioning was the most unpopular and bound to alienate the most peasants. Initially, from the time that the Bolsheviks had merged the Congress of Workers and Soldiers' Deputies with the Congress of Peasants' Deputies in January 1918, the regime had espoused an official union of the workers and the peasants. Under War Communism, this union took on a more militant and radical hue, as the Bolsheviks officially linked themselves with the poorer peasants in a contrived conflict against their richer brethren, the kulaks. The middle peasant was also expected to join in this struggle on the government side, though often kulak divisions of estates and the general impoverishment blurred the distinctions in the countryside (in so far as they were ever really evident). The policy was a disaster, and the majority of the peasants were alienated from a regime that they had at best tolerated, or regarded as the least of several evils – generally because the Bolsheviks, unlike the Whites, never threatened to bring back the landowners.

In early 1921, several delegations from the villages came to Moscow to request that Lenin's government change its policies. There is no clear consensus about when Lenin decided to embrace the New Economic Policy, though the idea had been discussed as early as 1918. During the late 1980s, the Gorbachev regime frequently maintained that the NEP was the natural policy of Lenin once the civil war was over. On the other hand, the NEP seems to have been as much a matter of necessity as of ideology. It was essential to give the peasants some incentive to provide food for the country. Grain requisitions had to be stopped and replaced with a more appropriate system. The 10th Party Congress took place as the revolt of the Kronstadt sailors reached a climax, and there could be no better example of how a group that had wholeheartedly embraced the causes of October had become totally disillusioned with the bureaucratic and harsh leadership that now emanated from Moscow. The Congress therefore resolved on a switch to the NEP, and the replacement of grain requisitions by a flat tax. This turned out to be much more lenient in the reservation of grain supplies to the state, lowering the peasant quota from 423 million to 240 million poods (one pood is equivalent to 36 lb), after which the peasant was free to do with surplus grain as he liked. Once administered, the tax could not be raised.

Though the 10th Congress introduced the NEP, one cannot say that its formulation and goals were complete. Lenin did not even use the words "New Economic Policy" at the time. Moreover, other aspects of this same Congress indicate that the party was tightening rather than relaxing its grip on the country. It accepted decrees on ending party factionalism; for example, it condemned the platform of the Workers' Opposition (particularly on the need for an independent movement of trade unions), and it condemned what it termed "anarcho-syndicalist" deviations. It was to this Congress that Stalin was to refer when citing the need for party unity. Thus what had been introduced by Lenin was described not as something new, but as a "tactical retreat," a period of recovery for the country, and an end to the conflict in the villages. For the time being, old and new systems had to work together – small-scale capitalism returned to the village. No doubt, in Lenin's view, a socialist state would eventually emerge triumphant from the brief experiment of two systems working parallel to each other. But the timing of this success remained uncertain.

What were the goals of the NEP? In the first place, the key areas of government were to remain under the firm control of the party. The government was also to maintain control over the "commanding heights" of the economy: heavy industry, banks, transport, and foreign trade. The peasant–worker union heralded in early 1918 was to return. At the same time, the Bolshevik leaders needed to take steps to endear their regime to the mass of peasantry. There were several possible ways to do this, but the first step was clearly to try to eliminate illiteracy, and in so doing ensure that the peasants were subjected to a daily round of Bolshevik propaganda. In short, Bolshevik newspapers, agitators, and party officials had an opportunity to engender a new source of support while carrying out a progressive reform, the elimination of illiteracy.

The introduction of the NEP was made more difficult by a major famine that occurred in many regions of Russia and Ukraine in 1921. It affected the population of twenty-two districts, and an estimated 23 million people may have died from hunger. The famine encompassed the Volga region, the southern part of the Urals, and areas of Ukraine that had seen several armies engaged in bitter conflict, depriving the land of its sown area and ensuring disastrous harvests. The regime's grain-requisitioning policies also played a role, and the famine was the natural end product of War Communism, a signal that this system had manifestly failed. In August 1921, Soviet Russia signed an agreement with the United States for famine relief, through an Administrative Aid program. The government also set up a relief commission under Kalinin, though its efforts were relatively negligible. However, by 1922, Russian harvests had begun to improve.

Under the NEP, it was anticipated that the peasant and the urban worker would embark on a natural exchange of goods in a non-monetary system. Each would satisfy the other's need for products in a complementary fashion. The problem for the peasants was the noted lack of attractive or necessary goods being produced by the factories at this time. The conditions of Russian towns in 1921 saw a mass exodus of the urban population to the countryside. The government was forced to close factories or to lease them to foreign companies. Those that could survive were merged into larger groups, or trusts, and workers received their wages in cash. The Soviet government wanted to control the economic recovery of the country, and had already formed a State Planning Commission (Gosplan) in February 1922. On the other hand, it was always likely that agriculture would recover slowly, whereas the tempo of industrial development – which had been rapid prior to the outbreak of the First World War – would be considerably faster. The question for the government was how to control a periodic "scissors crisis" in pricing, whereby agricultural goods would be sold to the towns at prices that the sellers, the peasants, considered to be unreasonably low.

The NEP, nevertheless, permitted the recovery of agriculture. In sown area and production of livestock the prewar totals had been surpassed by 1927. The chief supporter of the NEP, Nikolay Bukharin, gave a speech to peasants in the spring of 1925 in which he assured them that the policies of War Communism would not return. Instead, he declared, they should "enrich themselves." Bukharin believed in a gradual route to socialism, using profits from agriculture to fund a very slow industrial build-up. This policy did not meet with favor among the more ideological Bolsheviks, such as Evgeny Preobrazhensky or indeed Trotsky, now engaged in a power struggle with Stalin and the members of the triumvirate. The Bolsheviks, after all, relied for their mandate on the proletariat. The NEP catered to the peasant in many ways, but it did not resolve all problems in the villages. While the amount of bread reaching the towns was now considerably better than in the past, it hardly met the needs of the population.

The NEP period was a time of revival, but it also saw the emergence of acute social problems, especially in the urban centers. Unemployment was a key factor, embracing around 1.5 million workers. Wages were low, and did not even approach the prewar level. Housing was an acute problem, as thousands of workers were forced to live in barrack-like huts with few amenities. When the workers did go to the factories, they were faced with old and dilapidated equipment that frequently broke down. Accidents led to a high death rate. More familiar urban problems returned in the relatively tolerant atmosphere in Russian cities of the 1920s – a high crime rate and prostitution among them. The figure of the "Nepman" (a trader during the New Economic Policy) appeared in the towns, while small farmers re-emerged in the countryside. Bukharin's slow route to socialism seemed to the more idealistic Bolshevik leaders less of a compromise than a return to small-scale capitalism and bourgeois habits. Though the situation was much improved since 1921, the population remained on a sparse ration of bread and potatoes. By the mid-1920s therefore, the NEP had brought about the economic revival of the country without ensuring rapid growth. The differentiation in prices for industrial and agricultural goods caused considerable concern. The low purchase prices for basic peasant products, in the view of the regime, limited incentives in the village to produce more of a surplus.

The development of a Soviet bureaucracy

The years of revolution and civil war had been remarkable for the degree of popular activity and civic life. In those extraordinary times, the role of the "masses" on the streets of Petrograd and then of Moscow had appeared to take on a momentum of its own. Following the Red Terror and the bleak period of civil war, the regime developed a duality whereby the official organs of authority, the Soviets, were gradually deprived of power, and instruments within the party came to the fore. What Trotsky had feared when the Social Democratic Workers' Party split into two factions in 1903 became a reality – a growing bureaucratic structure that developed into a dictatorship not of the working class, but of the party leadership and ultimately of one man. The conditions of terror applied by the summer of 1918 were a factor in this development. During that period it became all too easy to circumvent the normal legal processes, and to deal with suspected criminals or counter-revolutionaries with tribunals and "kangaroo" courts. The first Soviet prime minister, the noted administrator Yakov Sverdlov, died in 1920 and was replaced by the more placid and passive M. I. Kalinin, a man who remained prominent in the Soviet system until his death in 1946 without leaving upon it a discernible stamp. The government faded into the background while the party organization came to the fore. The various organizations that had developed since the revolution – trade unions, cooperatives, and others – were subordinated to the control of the party.

As the party took control over most facets of life in Russia, it exhibited a general intolerance of old institutions and rival political parties. In the 1920s could be discerned the distinction between the relative liberties of the Union republics and the narrowness of the political spectrum in Moscow. During the period, publicly the party leadership tried to demonstrate the unity demanded by Lenin in March 1921. This cohesion was a façade masking an acute power struggle that was taking place at the center, and over which the Bolshevik leader Lenin could wield little control once weakened by illness. However, it was Lenin who prepared the groundwork. By the spring of 1922 he had already turned on the Russian Orthodox Church and informed members of the Politburo that it was time for a ruthless struggle against an institution that had been deprived of political power for more than 200 years. The goals were twofold – to obtain for the state the assets of the church, and second to ensure that the church did not become a focal point for opposition to the regime.

Lenin had long remained critical of rival socialist parties, and by 1922 he had redirected his attacks from his former unwillingness to share power with them to accusations that the Mensheviks and the Socialist Revolutionaries were counter-revolutionary in outlook. The successor organization to the Cheka, the GPU (State Political Directorate), was given the task of undermining and eventually eliminating all opposition parties, which led to the demise of the Mensheviks by 1926 and the Socialist Revolutionaries two years later. During the same period, the Communist Party structure was gradually turned into an all-encompassing bureaucracy, whereby the key posts were assigned from the central party apparatus in Moscow, often on a very personal basis. Thus reliable workers at the center of the party hierarchy had their own mirror image at the regional levels, in which local bosses could amass considerable power. Officials were nominated to the key posts rather than appointed through ability.

In the past, and especially within the Soviet Union, historians maintained that the development of the Soviet bureaucracy was a direct result of the machinations of Stalin. However, as historians such as Richard Pipes (Pipes, 1996) have demonstrated, it was Lenin who began the process. Whether matters would have proceeded differently had Lenin remained healthy is a moot point, but everything that had occurred under Lenin's leadership after the takeover of power would suggest that his main goal was centralization. One can say that the key distinction between the first two Soviet leaders was less in accumulation of power than in the concept of the state that had been created. Lenin's vision was of a federal union in which the working classes of each republic would participate for the good of the whole. Stalin's view was a more traditional Russia-dominated structure that would pursue ultimately Russian national interests. Though it was generally adorned with socialist slogans and propaganda, Stalin's Great Russian view was in place from the early 1920s.

After Lenin suffered his first stroke in 1922, he began to consider the question of a successor. The result was his "Letter to the Congress" in late 1922, a document that provided a biting character study of each of the main party leaders at that time – Zinoviev, Kamenev, Bukharin, Stalin, and Trotsky. In the case of the former three figures, it seems unlikely that Lenin seriously thought that they had the ability or the wherewithal to lead the party that he had controlled through his personal influence since 1902. Zinoviev and Kamenev had shown themselves to be hesitating and even cowardly at critical moments in 1917. Bukharin had acted rashly during the crisis of Brest-Litovsk and negotiations with the Germans. He was regarded in any case as a young theorist, not as someone regarded as a potential leader. Trotsky was a more difficult case, as a relative latecomer to the party and yet a man who had overshadowed Lenin in the events of both the revolution and the civil war. Nevertheless, Trotsky had never been a rival for party leadership. His arrogance and conceit did not endear him to other long-time party members, and he appeared to be naïve when it came to political in-fighting. Trotsky was perhaps the ideal subordinate for Lenin, believing as he did in the original vision of a socialist revolution that would spread to other parts of the world.

Stalin, on the other hand, was a discovery of Lenin, the "marvelous Georgian" with supreme administrative and organizational abilities. His early role in the Social Democratic Party was noted for a number of spectacular bank robberies (Sebag Montefiore, 2007), and a number of historians have focused on his possible role as a double agent. The suspicion itself indicates Stalin's closed and enigmatic personality, his distrust of both friend and foe, and his ability to conceal what views he had, or to nurture grudges (particularly against Trotsky) over long periods of time. Stalin recognized from an early stage the wisdom of supporting Lenin on various issues – other than the occasions when Lenin was outside Russia or very ill – often being in a minority when doing so. The last, sick years of Lenin and the rise of Stalin in the period 1918–1922 are critical for an understanding of the Soviet state that was to emerge after Lenin's death. (Plate 3.1)

Plate 3.1 Lenin in a wheelchair, ca. 1924.
Image: Bettmann/CORBIS

The rise of Stalin

It is not necessary to go into great detail about Stalin's early life. He has been the subject of more biographies than Hitler, including in recent times a two-volume psychological portrait by the American scholar Robert C. Tucker (Tucker, 1974, 1990), an intriguing and controversial depiction by the late Soviet military historian Dmitry Volkogonov (Volkogonov, 1991), and speculative and imaginative narration by the Russian playwright Edvard Radzinsky (Radzinsky, 1992). In the first fifty years after his death, Stalin was vilified within and without Russia, while generating a certain admiration in a number of circles, including some in his native Georgia. In several respects, the past is no clearer for the plethora of research; indeed, it is not even certain when Stalin was born (1878 or 1879), though his place of origin was Gori, or of what parentage (a drunken Georgian shoemaker who beat him frequently or a prominent Russian general). The important aspects of Stalin's upbringing appear to have been his dependence on his mother, education at a seminary in Tblisi, and his conversion to Marxism (or, perhaps more accurately, to the revolutionary movement) and eventual allegiance to the Russian Social Democratic Workers' Party. His early career as a party operative saw him as an organizer of strikes in Georgia and Azerbaijan in the early years of the century, as a bank robber, as a leader who was frequently sent for periods of exile in the Russian north (where he fathered a child with a native woman) and Siberia. He took Lenin's side in the great rift of 1902 with the Mensheviks, though he was not to meet his leader until 1912.

What was important during these years was the need for secrecy and suspicion. The Bolshevik organization was penetrated thoroughly by the Okhrana and contained a number of double agents. Stalin's most famous portrait is from the file kept on him by the tsarist secret police. Despite the success of the treatise on the nationality issue, Stalin was not a prominent Bolshevik before 1917, though he was better-known than some historians have given him credit for. One can say that he was among the leaders of the second-rank Bolsheviks, along with Sverdlov, Molotov, and Sokolnikov, a reliable party worker devoted to the cause, without the ideological background and cosmopolitanism of Trotsky, the personal magnetism of Lenin, or the seasoned European training of a Kamenev or a Zinoviev. He appears to have been utterly without scruples, incapable of strong attachments (he even neglected his mother for years, and his callous behavior was certainly one of the reasons why his second wife committed suicide in 1932), a manipulator of men and events with limitless patience. He was possessed of an innate cunning and intelligence that rendered him a superb political in-fighter. Though his speeches and writings make dull reading, he was able once he came to power to create an image of himself as an irreproachable, kind, even saintly figure who had taken on responsibility for all Russians.

Stalin's appearance was also unlikely to attract undue attention. He was 5 feet 4 inches, stocky, and had gray-yellow eyes, a trademark moustache, a face pockmarked from smallpox in his youth, and one arm longer than the other. Yet he seems to have had some ideals. He initially changed his surname Djugashvili to that of Koba, a revolutionary hero in 19th-century Georgian folklore, by which name some of his contemporaries from that period always addressed him. The name Stalin, or "man of steel," was a better indication of the image he wished to create, and in addition it complemented the name of Lenin. Like his contemporary and rival Hitler, he seems to have taken on the mantle of his adopted nation, though Georgia had been part of the Russian Empire, whereas Austria remained outside Germany until the 1930s. It seems an obvious statement that Stalin could not have come to power but for Lenin's premature death. On the other hand, even Lenin in his weakened state could not fail to see that Stalin was amassing extraordinary authority. Stalin benefited more than any single figure from the Bolshevik takeover, the weaknesses of his opponents, and the illness or death, at critical times, of his leader and rivals, Lenin, Sverdlov, and Trotsky.

Stalin is one of the few leaders of the 20th century who seem to rise above historical events, but for whom it is hard to discern one overriding goal other than that of personal power. Is it possible to say that Stalin initiated the concept of a Soviet Motherland, that he identified the cause of the Communist Party with that of a Russian homeland? The difficulty is trying to ascertain at what point he made the transition from the leader of a revolutionary state with ambitions of world revolution to one with a vision based on more traditional Russian motives. That Stalin was a revolutionary for good motives or bad is not in doubt. One of his abilities, however, was to maintain the status quo, to provide an image of a quiet and hardworking figure without any personal ambitions (prior to Lenin's death), or any strong views on the issues debated so fiercely at the time, such as the virtues of the NEP vis-à-vis a program of mass industrialization and the forced collectivization of peasant households. This apparent reticence may have been a result of Stalin's inability to take part in a discussion at so high a level, or it may have been that he did not hold strong personal views, other than a strong animosity toward Trotsky that eventually became pathological.

Stalin's one key mistake in the period after the Revolution was the personal insult he rendered to Lenin's wife, Nadezhda Krupskaya, which caused Lenin to break off relations with him and demand his removal as General Secretary of the Party in the postscript to his Testament. For some time this document hung over Stalin like a noose because it undermined the image he wished to portray of a faithful follower and interpreter of Lenin, one without personal ambitions for whom the good of the party superseded all (an epitaph that might have been reserved for Trotsky in the 1920s). But Lenin had been severely weakened. As his grasp on the country slipped, so the real power moved from the hands of the man who had led the party for so long and into the newly created bureaucracy. All sources agree that within this bureaucracy the authority of Stalin was immense, partly because he was one of the few leaders willing to take on such a heavy administrative load. He was a member of the Politburo, the Organizational Bureau, and the Secretariat, the key apparatus for deciding who entered the party, or who was promoted or demoted. Stalin also directed the Workers' and Peasants' Inspectorate (though he did not remain in this post), and was Commissar for Nationalities. In all of these posts, and especially during the civil war, Stalin's crude and vindictive personality frequently emerged. He may not have made many political errors during these years, but he had a foul temper and offended many people. He was safe, however, within a party that protected its own and which maintained a fragile unity during the period of crisis in 1918–1921. Stalin was not expendable, and as such he was able to use his various positions to take over power from rivals with better credentials as intellectuals and long-term Bolshevik leaders.

The death of Lenin

Lenin became very ill in 1922, though he recovered and returned to work in October of that year. His last major speeches were written between October and December 1922, and part of his Testament as late as January 1923, along with his final "Letter to the Congress" (cited above). Throughout 1923, Lenin stayed in the village of Gorki, near Moscow, deprived of the power of speech and increasingly remote from political events. The severity of his illness is evident from the photographs of that period, which reveal a gaunt figure with protruding eyes and vacant stare. Despite a slight improvement in his health at the end of the year, Lenin died on January 21, 1924 at the age of 53. He had become a legendary figure and appears to have been genuinely popular among Soviet citizens well before it became obligatory to praise him as a virtual deity. For four days, Muscovites came to pay respects to Lenin's corpse, which was placed in the House of Unions. Then, on January 26, the 2nd All-Union Congress of Soviets decreed that henceforth January 21 would be commemorated as a day of mourning. It also decided that Lenin would not be buried, but placed in a mausoleum and preserved, that a new edition of his works would be published, and that henceforth, the city of the revolution, Petrograd, would be renamed Leningrad.

Trotsky was absent for the funeral, recovering from one of his many real or imagined ailments. Stalin was to use the occasion for a quasi-religious speech in which he vowed that the party would follow Lenin's path in the future. Krupskaya also spoke, as did Voroshilov, Kalinin, and Klara Zetkin, on behalf of the international Communist movement. Lenin, who had always been modest in appearance and had little time for ceremonies, would not have approved of the way his corpse was to be used by those who succeeded him, and initially by a triumvirate of Zinoviev, Kamenev, and Stalin, united only by the desire to prevent their great rival, Trotsky, from taking over as leader. For a brief time, there seemed to be a real possibility that, given Lenin's new eminence, his Testament would put an end to Stalin's political ambitions. For the moment, however, Stalin's new allies needed him; and, although the contents of Lenin's letter were read out before the 13th Congress of the Russian Communist Party in May 1924, the delegates resolved that, happily, in this instance, Lenin's fears had been unfounded. There was thus no need to remove Stalin. The occasion was one of the few on which Stalin might have been ousted. By remaining silent, Trotsky showed his complete failure to grasp the political occasion, ostensibly his loyalty to the party remaining uppermost in his mind.

However, Trotsky was losing patience with the ruling triumvirate and the way the Soviet state was moving away from the goals closest to his heart – the theory of permanent revolution and a socialist uprising in Europe. His article "New Course," published in December 1923, advocated tighter party jurisdiction over the growing Bolshevik apparatus. Then, in October 1924, he published an explosive monograph, *The Lessons of October*, a fairly vindictive and angry work that ridiculed the role of Zinoviev and Kamenev in the October Revolution, and also maintained that as the leader of the Comintern it had been Zinoviev who was responsible for the failure of the Communist revolution in Germany. Zinoviev and Kamenev were now seriously threatened. The former had his power base in Leningrad where he was head of the party organization, in addition to his prominent, but largely symbolic, role as chairman of the Comintern. Kamenev's power base was Moscow where he also led the city party organization. In theory his was a powerful position, but his party organization had supported the cause of the Workers' Opposition in 1923 and had subsequently been purged. The new members for the most part owed their allegiance to Stalin.

Trotsky's pamphlet paved the way for a bitter power struggle within the Soviet leadership and became the focus of debate for the remainder of 1924 and in 1925. The Plenum of the party's Central Committee denounced the pamphlet and made reference to Trotsky's Menshevik past. He was now described as an infiltrator among the Bolsheviks who sought to revise "Leninism," a nebulous word that signified only the way Lenin was interpreted by the triumvirate. A new term of abuse emerged, namely "Trotskyism," one that was to be regurgitated over and over during the 1930s as the most dangerous possible threat to the Soviet regime. In truth, Trotsky remained highly critical of the government in the 1920s but was never disloyal to it. In January 1925 he was deprived of his position as Commissar of War without a struggle – clearly, as the popular leader of the army, this position was his one opportunity to make a bid for power, had he so desired. Either Trotsky did not wish to take such a drastic step, or else he placed party loyalties above all, or he underestimated the threat to his own position within the hierarchy.

By April 1925, the 14th Conference of the Russian Communist Party had accepted a treatise of Stalin on the concept of *Socialism in One Country* – one that Trotsky scorned, and even Zinoviev and Kamenev opposed. There was nothing very original about this document, but it did reflect the political reality: that revolution outside Russia for the moment had failed, and thus the Bolshevik-founded state needed to survive without outside allies. Stalin had advanced himself as a political thinker, as a potential leader of the country. It was followed by another pamphlet entitled *On the Problems of Leninism* (January 1926), which pointed out that Trotsky's earlier writing demonstrated a lack of faith in the Russian peasant and his revolutionary élan. In addition, Trotsky had now shown that he did not have much faith in the Russian proletariat, either. Russians lacked the revolutionary experience of their European counterparts, and they were backward both in history and in development. According to the Soviet leadership, Trotsky and his supporters were also too bound up with theory and dogma, without due regard to the reality of the situation in Russia.

The initial plan of the triumvirate appears to have been to overload Trotsky with meaningless positions that took up much of his time. Already Trotsky could not go anywhere without being followed by Stalin's agents, who monitored his every move. He was appointed as chairman of the Electro-Technical Board, as the head of a Concessions Committee, and the Scientific-Technical Board of Industry. None of these positions came with any real power, but they did keep Trotsky busy, and the idea was to ensure that he had little time for high-level politics. However, Trotsky seems to have taken an interest in at least some of these activities. He visited several power stations, for example, which was enough to concern the authorities that he was involved in some plot to redeem his authority. By the middle of 1925, Zinoviev and Kamenev were growing more distant from Stalin. Both were finding that, even in their personal fiefdoms, party members owed their loyalty to Stalin. In Leningrad workers were unhappy with the NEP and the concessions that were being made to the richer peasants.

Zinoviev and Kamenev had an ally in Lenin's widow. She disapproved of the treatment of her late husband's corpse, and the fact that the party had not seen fit to follow Lenin's directions in removing Stalin as General Secretary. Based in Leningrad, she grew closer to Zinoviev, the city party boss, and requested that the Central Committee debate the concept of Socialism in One Country. Stalin, however, was already too firmly entrenched, and no such discussion ever took place. At the 14th Party Congress, held between December 18 and 31, 1925, the opposition made its position clear, and many of its members anticipated that Trotsky would make a stand on their behalf. Once again, however, Trotsky appeared reluctant to become involved in something as distasteful as political in-fighting, and remained silent. Either Trotsky had no conception of the force that Stalin had accumulated, or else he felt that he could rely on his reputation and presence to turn delegates his way.

The Congress was stacked with Stalin's supporters, who heckled the efforts of Zinoviev and Kamenev as they tried to air their views. Zinoviev took a bold step by bringing up Lenin's Testament and citing Lenin's warnings that Stalin would abuse his power. Kamenev also pointed out the growing autocracy within the party. But, less than two years after Lenin's death, the figment of triumvirate rule had already ended. The majority of delegates accepted Stalin's views, though certainly not all of them. Krupskaya was also given a hearing, and she criticized the use of Lenin as a cult figure, and the practice of including quotes from his speeches and writings at every public occasion. Other speakers felt that it was time to end personal animosities among the leadership and praised the past contributions of Trotsky and Zinoviev. In retrospect, the 14th Party Congress was the last occasion when the possibility of unity still existed. Trotsky would never attend another Congress.

The Congress ended with the removal of Zinoviev from his Leningrad stronghold. There was little protest, and Stalin sent Sergey Kirov to Leningrad with the orders to take over all branches and offices of the city's party organization. This was made easier by the fact that Zinoviev had never been a popular figure, and had been noted for his cruelty and malice. Kirov, at that time a loyal Stalin supporter, took on the mantle of First Secretary of the city of Leningrad in January 1926. The alliance between Zinoviev and Kamenev had continued for years with barely a hint of any dissension between them. They had been united initially by their fear of Trotsky and his possible quest for supreme power, and had perceived Stalin as their ally. However, Stalin had in turn become the most powerful figure in the party through his various positions. Stalin, dismissed as a "gray blur" by Trotsky during the Revolution, had even elevated himself as a party theorist and the main arbiter of Lenin's will. The difficulty for the old Bolshevik leaders lay in their past. For Zinoviev and Kamenev, it consisted of years of loyalty to Lenin in the wilderness period, but there was also the forgettable period in 1917 when they had lacked the will to support an armed uprising. Trotsky, above all, had revived those memories with his bitter *Lessons of October*. But Trotsky had lost some serious battles almost by default. He was no longer the threat he once appeared to be. The possibility arose that the three new outsiders in the leadership might find common cause. The focal point had to be economic policy and the Stalin leadership's continued adherence to the NEP and to Socialism in One Country, long derided by Trotsky as contrary to the interests of developing socialism.

The formation of the United Opposition

The emergence of the United Opposition was to be the last serious attempt to unseat Stalin, though its once powerful members were already seriously weakened by the time of its formation. The Central Committee held a plenum in April 1926, at which Kamenev, Zinoviev, and Trotsky were all present. Though Kamenev spoke disparagingly about Trotsky at the meeting, Trotsky supported an amendment put forward by Kamenev to Rykov's proposals on Soviet economic policy. As a result, the former enemies agreed that it was time to halt the NEP and start an expansive industrialization program. Once the session was over, Zinoviev, Kamenev, and Trotsky had a private meeting and formed an alliance, hoping that Krupskaya would shortly join them. Before the trio could come up with some sort of program, however, Trotsky once again became ill and was obliged to go abroad for six weeks. Nevertheless, an opposition had been formed, and by May some important Bolsheviks had joined its ranks, such as Antonov-Ovseenko, K. B. Radek, and Pyatakov. The United Opposition demanded a halt to the growing bureaucracy within the party and a return to the sort of policies espoused during the period of War Communism.

By July, at a joint plenum of the Central Committee and the Central Control Commission, Trotsky announced the "Declaration of the Thirteen," which linked his platform of Permanent Revolution and a merciless struggle against the kulaks. The plenum rejected the declaration, and in the aftermath removed Zinoviev from the ruling Politburo. None of the opposition seems to have been willing to undertake a sustained campaign. By October, the United Opposition had issued an apology for its indulgence in a factional struggle and declared itself a supporter of party unity. The October Plenum of the Central Committee also banished Trotsky and Kamenev from the Politburo, and the Committee instructed the Comintern that Zinoviev should be replaced as its president. The Plenum was followed by the 15th Party Conference, which dutifully reaffirmed Stalin's policy of Socialism in One Country. This maneuver was tantamount to a renewal of faith in the NEP. The rebels were clearly torn between allegiance to the party of Lenin, and their wish to remove Stalin and return to what they saw as "ideological normality." They did not approve of the "Russian way" that Stalin was treading, or of the alliance between the working class and the peasantry. Ultimately, they did not see the power struggle in the same terms as Stalin. The General Secretary and his then colleagues, such as Bukharin, Rykov, and Tomsky, the chairman of the trade unions, admonished the dissenters, but always appeared to allow them a route back into the good graces of the party. This pattern is exemplified by the lengthy debate that occurred in August 1927 within a joint plenum of the Central Committee and Central Control Commission as to whether Trotsky and Zinoviev should be excluded from the former body. The Plenum criticized their actions but allowed them a reprieve. Within a month, the thirteen main opposition leaders had openly attacked the Central Committee's policies in a letter. And so the struggle continued.

Matters continued in this fashion until the decisive event in the demise of the United Opposition, namely the 15th Party Congress. Thus, at another joint plenum on October 21–23, 1927, Trotsky and Zinoviev were expelled from the Central Committee for constantly opposing party policy. They were also accused of counter-revolutionary activities and setting up an illegal printing press. Trotsky still believed in his power to move a crowd, and chose as his next occasion for protest November 7, 1927, the tenth anniversary of the revolution, when he and his supporters planned a counter-demonstration in Moscow. Through the OGPU (United State Political Administration, the successor to the GPU), Stalin quickly learned of these plans, and the protests were inconsequential. One week later, Trotsky and Zinoviev were expelled from the Communist Party, a decisive step, while the milder Kamenev was removed from the Central Committee. The Party Congress in December confirmed these actions and issued a decree "On the Opposition." This stated that the dissidents had become open enemies of Soviet authority and had adopted Menshevik and counter-revolutionary attitudes. Seventy-five more people were expelled from the party, including Kamenev, Radek, Kh. G. Rakovsky, and Pyatakov.

By early 1928, the "rebels" had been thoroughly defeated. Trotsky was not to be forgiven. In mid-January he was sent into exile in Kazakhstan, and several other prominent colleagues were removed from the capital, including Radek and Rakovsky. Zinoviev and Kamenev were permitted to stay at the price of confessing their sins in the pages of *Pravda*. For the present it appeared that they might find a way back into the good graces of Stalin. Trotsky's long and often half-hearted struggle against the wiles of Stalin ended when he left for Turkey in January 1929 from his native port of Odesa, along with his wife and older son. Just before his departure he had called on world Communists to struggle against Stalin. Trotsky's name would become an anathema in Soviet propaganda. His role in the Revolution was not merely forgotten; rather it was erased from the pages of history, along with his photograph. The difference between the two men lay more in personality than in program; indeed, Stalin was shortly to adopt policies long advocated by Trotsky. The two contemporaries embodied different versions of the Bolshevik revolutionary – the one an eloquent intellectual, a visionary who was persuaded by the will of Lenin to join the Bolshevik cause; the other a man rooted in the Russian Empire, who looked at the world in terms of a power struggle, but rarely in international terms. To Stalin, the fate of Communism and the fate of Russia were closely tied together.

Propaganda, literacy, and education

Before Lenin's death, in 1923, the Soviet authorities conducted a survey of people in the age group 11–40 and learned that more than 27 million citizens were functionally illiterate. As a result, a society to eliminate illiteracy was created under the chairmanship of Kalinin. First, it focused on the urban centers, and permitted workers time during the working day to learn to read and write. By the mid-1920s, the Soviet regime had succeeded in reducing levels of illiteracy in the towns, partly through the auspices of the trade unions. One of the most convenient ways to enhance the program was through propaganda, and particularly through newspapers. Bolshevik and later Soviet newspapers were relatively crude vehicles, full of slogans and admonitions to the population, with modern-day scandals substituted by outrageous statements about the threats of foreign intervention or the machinations of the British in particular. The date May 5 was declared to be a Day of the Press, as it was also the date that marked the tenth anniversary of the appearance of *Pravda*. A host of newspapers followed in the 1920s, of which the military newspaper *Krasnaya zvezda* (*Red Star*) and the youth newspaper *Komsomolskaya pravda* (*Young Communist Truth*) became the best-known.

The format of these newspapers was generally four pages, with the pronouncements of the party (with requisite quotations from Lenin, and later Stalin, along with his photograph) on the front page. They were easy to read and digest, and the messages were always simple. Before long, the authorities began to establish journals, the most important of which was the party's theoretical journal, called *Bolshevik*. By the mid-1920s, about 1,750 journals circulated in the Soviet Union (somewhat more than in the prewar period), but the 1,100 or so newspapers enjoyed a circulation of about 8 million, more than double the level of 1913. Alongside the message of Marxism, the Bolsheviks also promoted atheism through the media. By the early 1920s over 700 monasteries had been demolished, and by the middle of the decade a Union of the Militant Godless had been founded. Its organs were the newspaper *Bezbozhnik* (*Godless*) and the journal *Antireligioznik*; and the central and republican newspapers propounded similar themes, alongside Marxism-Leninism. Reportedly the membership of the Union of the Militant Godless was around 350,000 by 1925.

At first under the Bolsheviks the network of schools was reduced, though in Lenin's time the educational system became part of the regime's propaganda network. In 1921 the famous Institutes of Red Professors were founded in Moscow and Leningrad, and the universities focused their attention on the social sciences, and particularly on courses examining the October Revolution, the USSR Constitution, and the dictatorship of the proletariat. Around the same time, the Pioneer organization was formed, with the goal of training young minds from an early age. After Lenin's death they became the Lenin Pioneers. The Bolsheviks made great efforts to ensure that entry into the universities was weighted in favor of the working class, and the party was given special tasks to ensure ideological work in these institutions and to struggle against "bourgeois ideology." In 1918 a Socialist Academy was created, which concentrated on the natural sciences. By 1925, however, the highest rank was bestowed on the Russian Academy of Sciences, which was renamed the Academy of Sciences of the USSR. In this same period, the national republics, particularly Belarus and Ukraine, were allowed to make substantial gains in the sphere of education. Ukraine alone, led by Oleksandr Shumsky, Minister of Education, and encouraged by Stalin's henchman Lazar Kaganovich during his tenure as Ukraine's First Party Secretary, boasted twenty-five universities by the mid-1920s, and the much smaller Belarusian SSR had three. The process of national development continued in some form into the early 1930s when it was abruptly halted. In Ukraine in particular the movement began to take on a distinct anti-Russian hue as Ukrainians tried to establish their own identity and historical antecedents.

There was a widening gap, however, between the increasingly rigid cult of Leninism at the center and the growth of national culture in the peripheries of the new federation. Though he was not the founder of such a cult – that honor belongs to Zinoviev and Kamenev – Stalin was its perpetuator. The party guided the state based on the writings and speeches of Lenin, and since such works were more notable for their inconsistencies and contradictions than for a common or even an original doctrine Lenin could be used to justify virtually any policy (other than a return to a system of the past). Lenin gave the Soviet state a certain legitimacy, not as a ruthless revolutionary who had advocated rounding up and shooting several thousand bourgeoisie in order to bring the nation to order, but as a kind and saintly figure, wise beyond his years. In 1923, even before his death, but after he had left the political scene, an institute was founded with Lenin's name. A Lenin Library for the working classes was established, and the second and third editions of his *Collected Works* were published. It has been estimated that by the years 1924–1925 the state publishing house had issued over 20 million copies of Lenin's books and pamphlets. The propagation of Lenin became an industry in its own right. Vladimir Mayakovsky, the Futurist poet, wrote a poem entitled "Conversation with Comrade Lenin" in 1929.

Soviet literature gradually became organized and centrally directed, though it was a rather tortuous process. The movement called Proletarian Culture (Proletkult) predated the October Revolution, but it was a natural beneficiary of the Bolshevik victory. By 1920 the authorities had agreed to the creation of literary studios for writers of working-class background, about 80,000 in total. Virtually none of them left any impression. Lenin, an avid reader of 19th-century Russian classics, did not subscribe to the view that only proletarian literature was of value. In 1920 the People's Commissariat for Enlightenment took over control of Proletkult. In the following year, the government and several private firms began to publish literary works on a large scale. The period 1921–1924 is regarded as one of civil war literature, but it also provided the first works associated with the Soviet regime. Many of them were romantic in nature, praising the Revolution and its progressive nature. Literary giants such as Aleksandr Blok, Andrey Bely, and Valery Bryusov all supported the Bolshevik Revolution. Other adherents included Mayakovsky and the pro-peasant poet Sergey Yesenin. Few of these figures were to survive the 1930s; many grew disillusioned with the Soviet system even by the end of the 1920s, but they made a significant impact on Soviet culture.

Other groups also abounded alongside Proletkult. One, called Oktyabr, was formed in Moscow in 1922, and introduced the following year a new literary journal called *Na postu* (*On Guard*). In 1925 it was renamed *Na literanom postu* (*Guarding Literature*). The Oktyabr group faithfully supported government policy, eventually forming several groups of the Association of Proletarian Writers, with acronyms dependent on their place of abode – thus the Moscow group became MAPP, the Leningrad group LAPP, and so forth. In Russia by the late 1920s the dominant association was the Russian Association of Proletarian Writers, RAPP, which became quite powerful, exercising virtual control over literary output in Russia until its incorporation into the new Union of Writers in 1932. RAPP also began a crusade against writers considered anti-Communist, who at this time included figures like A. N. Tolstoy (who had emigrated in 1918) and A. M. Gorky, who, somewhat ironically, both became icons in the Stalin years. By the late 1920s, these writers were back in vogue, as well as the publications of A. A. Fadeyev and Mikhail Bulgakov, but there was still a plethora of literature on a more mundane and blatantly political level.

BOX 3.1

Russian Association of Proletarian Writers (RAPP)

Founded in 1924 by various proletarian writers, RAPP's main objective was to promote and dominate proletarian literature in the Soviet Union. Its literary style was known as "psychological realism." The group was known as the All-Union Association of Proletarian Writers (VAPP) until it was renamed RAPP in 1928 when its political power reached its peak and remained so until 1932. Early membership included recruits from the Komsomol and the Proletkult movement. In 1928 the organization received instructions from the CPSU to make the 1st Five-Year Plan the sole theme in Soviet literature.

Box 3.1 continued

Fulfilling this order rendered RAPP the most influential artistic group. As a result, literary works that were either non-proletarian, containing "bourgeois" elements ("formalist"), or ambivalent with regard to Communist ideology were usually heavily criticized or ridiculed as anti-Soviet. The organization made life for dissident authors difficult by forcing them into unemployment or by having them arrested. By politicizing the literary scene, the association's power continued to grow under the leadership of Leopold Averbakh. Though powerful, it failed to produce the cadres it had promised. By the spring of 1932, it was replaced by the Union of Soviet Writers.

BOX 3.2

Mikhail Bulgakov (1891–1940)

A contemporary Russian writer and playwright who opposed the Soviet regime throughout his life, Mikhail Bulgakov was born in Kyiv, Ukraine, on May 15, 1891. He graduated with a medical degree in 1916 from Kyiv University. During the First World War, he served in the Russian army as a medical aide. In the Civil War period, he served with the White Army against the Bolsheviks. After the war, he gave up medicine to pursue his love of literature. His first book, *Future Perspective*, was published in 1919. Bulgakov gained Stalin's favor in 1926 with a play about life during the Civil War called *Days of the Turbins*. However, his opposition to the Soviet regime did not go unpunished: in 1927 his works were considered openly anti-Soviet. His career was ruined when all his works were forbidden to be published and his plays were no longer staged after 1929. In 1928 he began writing his most famous fantasy satirical novel, *The Master and Margarita* (1966). The novel contained a harsh satire on Soviet society and its literary establishment. He was employed as an assistant producer in the Moscow Arts Theater in 1930, with the aid of Stalin, which protected him from arrests and executions. However, Bulgakov's works remained banned even past his death on March 10, 1940. Only in the 1980s, in the period of Gorbachev's Perestroika, were all his works published in the Soviet Union.

The 1920s were a relatively liberal period for the arts, and several groups operated outside the control of the state. One was the Fellow Travelers, authors of non-worker background, and not linked to state policies, but who did not openly oppose Communist doctrine. Many of the most important literary figures of the 1920s were members of the Fellow Travelers, including Boris Pilnyak, A. N. Tolstoy, Isaak Babel, and Ilya Ehrenburg. In Petrograd, the organization Serapionovy Bratya (The Serapion Brothers), which began its activities in February 1921, operated in the same vein. A new group called Pereval (Mountain Pass) started in Moscow in 1923, and included many party members who felt that the horizons of literature should remain faithful to the Soviet worker but could none the less be fairly broad. Its members included Eduard Bagritsky, a well-known poet, Andrey Platonov, and Nikolay Zarudin. Writers and poets who were too outspoken, on the other hand, remained isolated. Into this category fell Anna Akhmatova and Osip Mandelstam. By the late 1920s, restrictions on Soviet literature were becoming more apparent, though the Stalin leadership was inclined to focus first on literary developments in non-Russian republics, which were perceived as more threatening.

BOX 3.3

Anna Akhmatova (1889–1966)

Anna Akhmatova (born Anna Andreevna Horenko) was a distinguished Russian poet considered to be among the greats of the 20th century. The themes of her work were often centered on love, culture, and the decadence of Russian society. She was born in Boshoy Fontan, Odesa, on June 28, 1889, and began writing poetry at the age of 11. In 1910, she became a member of the Acmeist group (a neo-classical reaction to Symbolist poetry), and married its leader, Nikolay Gumilyov. Her first collection of verse, *Vecher* (*Evening*), was published in 1912. She gained prominence two years later with *Rosary* (1914). Both poems broached themes of love that are seen today as precocious for the time. Married three times, she also had a number of prominent affairs, mostly with other poets. By 1922, her work was accused of being anti-Soviet after Gumilyov was executed for illegal activities the year before. From 1925 to 1940, all publication of her works was banned. However, in 1939, at the behest of Aleksandr Fadeyev, head of the Union of Soviet Writers, she was provided with a room in Leningrad and a small pension. This permitted her to complete *Iz Shesti Knig* (*From Six Books*), which was nominated for, but did not win, the Stalin Prize in 1940. One of the most famous works by Akhmatova is *Requiem* (eventually published abroad in 1963), which depicted the terrors of the Stalinist regime. It was not released in Russia until 1987. During the war years, she was evacuated to Tashkent, where she wrote *Courage* (1942), after witnessing the siege of Leningrad, which appeared on the front page of *Pravda*. Despite this honor, in 1946, she was expelled from the Union of Soviet Writers. Subsequently, her son Lev Gumilyov was imprisoned, and her works were banned. To ensure the release of her son from the Gulag, Akhmatova wrote several poems exalting Stalin in the magazine *Ogonek*, including a eulogy for the dictator after his death. Her son was freed in 1956, and Akhmatova was also rehabilitated during the period of the Thaw under Khrushchev. She died on March 5, 1966 in Leningrad.

BOX 3.4

Osip Mandelstam (1891–1938)

A Russian poet and essayist born to a Jewish family in Warsaw on January 15, 1891, Osip Mandelstam was a pioneering member of the Acmeist school of poetry. After the first Russian Revolution in 1905, his poems focused on Russian symbolism, which

Box 3.4 continued

was popular at the time. In 1911, to counter the Symbolist movements, the Acmeist movement, based in St Petersburg, called for a return to the use of concrete imagery. Mandelstam gained fame for the collection *Kamyen* (*Stone*) in 1913, followed by *Tristia* (1922), which secured his role as a major poet. Though initially a supporter of the Bolsheviks, Mandelstam opposed the October Revolution and condemned the work of poets who were sympathetic toward the revolution, such as Mayakovsky. Between 1925 and 1930, he took to prose and produced works such as *On Poetry* (1928) and *The Egypt Stamp* (1928). Mandelstam was arrested in 1934 for his well-known "Epigram," which harshly criticized the leaders and Soviet policies, as well as for his poetry attacking the collective farm system. After his suicide attempt in Cherdyn, his sentence was softened and he was instead exiled to Voronezh. He continued to compose poetry; and, like most of his works, it failed to conform to the Socialist Realism doctrine. Consequently, in 1938, Mandelstam was arrested again for counter-revolutionary activities and sentenced to five years in the Gulag where he died of an unspecified illness on December 27, 1938. His career became known through the memoirs of his wife Nadezhda, which were published in the West in the 1970s.

This early period of Soviet literature saw the influence of several major writers of a newer generation. Two may be cited here. Boris Pilnyak (1894–1937) was the predominant prose writer of the early 1920s, particularly after the appearance of his novel *Goly god* (*The Naked Year*), which led to a movement known as "Pilnyakism." Soviet propaganda extolled Pilnyak as the first of a younger generation of writers to support the Revolution and become a mentor to others. Yevgeny Zamyatin (1884–1937) was already an established writer when the Bolshevik regime arrived. In Petrograd (Leningrad) in the 1920s he was a father figure to younger writers, known best for his 1920–1921 novel *My* (*We*). Gradually Zamyatin lost his faith in the Soviet system, and he felt that the dynamism of the Revolution had given way to conservatism and reaction. The Serapion group nurtured an entire generation of talented writers, including Vsevolod Ivanov, Lev Lunts, Isaak Babel, and Nikolay Tikhonov. Maksim Gorky, who was already 49 at the time of the Bolshevik Revolution, watched the new movement from afar. Gorky, who was to become the leading "official" writer during the period 1933–1936, was a maverick as far as the Bolsheviks were concerned. From April 1917 he had been the editor of the newspaper *Novaya zhizn*, and he had disapproved of the methods and reasons for the Bolshevik takeover. He opposed the dogmatism of Lenin and his censorship of the press. In July 1918, *Novaya zhizn* was shut down. That December, however, Gorky became a member of the Petrograd Soviet, and played a prominent role in the establishment of the first worker–peasant university, the Bolshoy Drama Theater (not to be confused with the more famous Bolshoy Theater founded in 1825) and the publishing house World Literature. To the Bolsheviks, whatever his real views, Gorky was the best-known Russian literary figure and thus an important symbol for their new regime. In October 1921, however, Gorky left the country, living in Germany, Czechoslovakia, and later Italy. Only in 1933 did he return permanently to live in Moscow, by which time his dissident past remained a dangerous impediment to his long-term survival. However, it was Gorky who was the main force behind the creation of the Union of Writers of the USSR in August 1932.

Foreign policy in the 1920s

The civil war had been a serious strain for the government of Soviet Russia. The regime of Lenin and Trotsky had been obliged to respond to attacks on several fronts, and while none of those assaults proved to be capable of removing the Bolsheviks from power they remained a threat for some time. During these years, the most severe Red Terror had been inflicted on a people weary of fighting. Episodes in the war took place mainly at distant outposts – Admiral Kolchak operating from central Siberia and General Denikin in south Russia, reaching his zenith with the capture of Tsaritsyn, the city that was soon to bear the name of Stalin himself. As for the Allies, one can assume that their initial goal was to secure the military bases that had been set up on Russian soil. The Americans had little desire to become involved in the Russian civil war, whereas the British and the French were angered by Lenin's apparent volte-face in the spring of 1918 and his decision to abide by the agreement made with the Germans. The Allies none the less imposed a fairly effective blockade on Russia during this period, and the suffering of the Russian population was made all the more acute because of it.

The period 1919–1921 also saw the end of Lenin and Trotsky's dream of socialist uprisings throughout Europe in unity with the cause of Soviet Russia. The Communist International, an unwieldy body that held three congresses between March 1919 and June 1921, embodied Lenin's hopes for the spreading of the Revolution, under the chairmanship of Lenin's long-time associate Zinoviev. Though the Comintern reflected the early enthusiasm for the revolution in Russia, it would soon be badly divided on a number of issues, not least the authoritarian nature of its chairman, and Russia's desire to maintain its influence as the world's first Communist state. After Lenin's death, it was probably doomed to failure. Zinoviev was soon to be involved in a power struggle that would eventually destroy him. His successor, Bukharin, was to suffer a similar fate. Stalin was also innately suspicious of foreign parties, and in this period narrowed his focus to hard-line Communist parties rather than mainstream socialist ones. In Germany, for example, Stalin ordered the Communists (KPD) to oppose the much larger and well-established Socialist Party (SPD) throughout the turbulent 1920s.

However, the Comintern at first appeared to Western democracies as dangerously subversive. The platform of the Comintern was one of world revolution, and in its

"Twenty-One Conditions" of 1920 it advocated that Communists take over from the more traditional "bourgeois" socialist parties in controlling trade unions, that they should infiltrate organizations in capitalist states, including the armed forces, and play a role in anti-colonial movements. Simply put, it was a call to arms to Communists everywhere to follow the lead of Soviet Russia in achieving a socialist state. The very existence of the Comintern rendered Soviet foreign policy ambiguous. It signified that there were always two foreign policies being followed – the official one, which in the early period can be termed "peaceful coexistence," and the long-term, more covert policy of Soviet involvement in Communist parties world-wide in the cause of revolution.

The Comintern, ultimately, was more a symbol of an international movement than one endowed with any real power, though this weakness did not become apparent until later. The Bolshevik version of a revolution was a narrow one, and one geared to the needs of Russia – an alliance between the workers and the poorer stratum of the peasantry, which made up the majority of the population without really exhibiting strong loyalty to the Soviet regime. Was it really possible to export a Russian revolution to countries that even the Soviet leaders (Stalin excepted) considered more advanced both economically and culturally? Lenin noted that the seeds of European revolution already existed. The end of the war had seen the collapse of the Austro-Hungarian Empire and the German monarchy. Both those countries had been defeated, the Austrians and the Hungarians disastrously so.

The Germans, on the other hand, had appeared to be close to victory even in the early months of 1918. Defeat came suddenly and, to many, inexplicably. One problem of Germany was the relative strength of the socialist movement that brought benefits to the workforce even in the 19th century. The giant SPD was proof that a gradualist approach to revolution might bring success. The SPD had supported the war, but it was not heavily compromised by this support. Any hope of a Soviet government succeeding in Germany, however, was undermined by the general sentiment that the politicians in Berlin had betrayed the German army in the field. In turn, this feeling crystallized with the harsh provisions of the Versailles Treaty. Germany had not experienced any conflicts on its soil, other than Russia's brief incursion into East Prussia in August 1914, but it had been made a scapegoat for the outbreak and the course of the war.

That Lenin felt some commitment to Germany as a potential partner appears plain, even though he was far-sighted enough to recognize that a Germany restored to its full powers would likely become the fiercest enemy of the Soviet regime. Though the Soviet leader never viewed the world in great-power terms, and long advocated the theory of self-determination for the peoples of the various empires, his relationship with Germany has never been satisfactorily explained. It was the Germans who allowed Lenin to return to Russia, who financed his revolution, and then had been chosen by Lenin as the potential partner at the outset of the civil war. Germany at the same time was the best hope for a socialist revolution, the homeland of Marx and Engels, a new state that had come into being only in 1871, but which already had a powerful and demanding workforce. On the other hand, one recalls Trotsky's fury at the Germans for their recognition and promotion of an independent Ukraine. In Russia, what Lenin called Great Power chauvinism had not been eradicated as a result of the October Revolution. It had merely taken new forms, which, while Lenin was alive, were concealed behind democratic rhetoric. But they were never far from the surface, epitomized perhaps by the behavior of Stalin and Ordzhonikidze in their native Georgia, which had sought independence from Soviet Russia.

Initial optimism at the course of events in Germany and Hungary was shortly followed by harsh reaction. Of the states that were established in Europe after the First World War, only one – Czechoslovakia – could be described as a genuine democracy. The death knell to the hopes of the Bolshevik leadership was the Polish–Soviet war. Marshal Pilsudski and his Polish army had captured Kyiv, but had then been repelled by the enthusiastic army of General Tukhachevsky, a former tsarist officer. The Poles had been forced back to their own capital of Warsaw, pursued by an overextended Red force that anticipated a workers' uprising on its behalf in the city on the Vistula. To the Poles, however, patriotic fervor replaced any such feelings of support for a workers' state. Poles have long memories, and Russia's role in the three partitions of Poland in the late 18th century was of far more import than the rabble army at the gates, with its pro-Soviet propaganda. The Poles, after all, had not enjoyed national statehood since 1795. Though neither side could really claim to be the victor in the Polish–Soviet war, the Poles regained much of their lost territory and were to retain it with the 1921 peace treaty at Riga.

The treaty itself established the eastern border of Poland well beyond the so-called Curzon Line. It did not satisfy Poland's original decision for going to war against Soviet Russia – the return to the political boundaries prior to the first partition of Poland in 1772. It did none the less extend Poland's eastern border by about 125 miles, signifying that Poland would rule territories with large minority populations – Jews in the cities, Ukrainians and Belarusians in the countryside. The Entente powers secured from the new Polish government a promise that these areas would be permitted some autonomy, but the promise was never close to being kept. The Soviet state, on the other hand, had already begun to take up some of the causes of the former Russian Empire. From the Riga Treaty onward, Poland was regarded as an enemy state, and throughout the interwar period its relationship with Soviet Russia and the USSR was uniformly hostile. The USSR, especially in the 1920s, would strongly encourage the subversive activities of the Communist Party of Poland and its two ethnic subdivisions, the Communist Parties of Western Ukraine and Western Belarus. It referred to the Polish state as the "landowner government of Poland," and coveted the territories therein (especially Volhynia) that had once belonged to the Russian Empire. Similarly, Soviet Russia never accepted the loss of the lands of Bessarabia, which were given to Romania after the Paris peace treaties that followed the First World War.

As the civil war came to a close, the Soviet government began to conclude a series of alliances with its neighboring states, beginning on the southern borders of the former Russian Empire. In February 1921, treaties of friendship were signed with Iran and Afghanistan, and also with Turkey in mid-March. Although the Western powers, and particularly the United States, had condemned the Brest-Litovsk Treaty, they had not formally invited Russia back into European structures. Subsequently, the United States began to follow a policy of isolation and did not participate formally in the meetings of the early 1920s. Lenin's regime was fortunate that the world's most powerful country had temporarily stepped off the world stage. Moreover, Britain and France had suffered great losses during the war, particularly in costly and futile battles on the Somme and at Verdun. Though the two states were recognized as the leading powers of Western Europe in the early 1920s, neither was in a position to dictate policy. France for its part was reliant on coalition governments throughout the interwar period, while Britain's wartime Liberal coalition was falling apart. Under the circumstances, the survival of the Soviet state, after its "baptism of fire" during the civil war, was virtually assured. However, it badly needed new partners, a restoration of trade, and contacts with the "outside world."

The first such gathering was an International Economic Conference in Genoa in April 1922, to which Soviet Russia was invited, along with thirty-three other countries, including Germany, at that time regarded as something of an international pariah and saddled with "war guilt" from the long conflict. Lenin himself was named as the head of the Russian delegation, but some Russian leaders were fearful that he might be the victim of a terrorist attack if he were to leave Russian soil. Never a particularly bold leader, Lenin's trepidation at such attacks had increased as a result of his near-assassination by Fanya Kaplan in 1918. Thus Georgy Chicherin, the People's Commissar of Foreign Affairs, went to Italy in Lenin's place. The Soviet team also included the diplomats V. V. Vovosky, L. B. Krasin, and M. M. Litvinov. Russia attended the conference apparently because, now that the civil war and foreign intervention on Russian soil had ended, the country was interested in developing trading links.

From the outset some of the underlying differences between the Entente powers and their former ally came to the fore. Manifestly the goals of the Allies, on the one hand, and of Soviet Russia, on the other, were always going to be far apart, and so it proved in practice. The ideological and utopian Bolsheviks gave speeches demanding a general reduction on arms and the banning of the more barbaric means of waging warfare. The Western democracies, on the other hand, maintained that the Soviet government should honor the debts of the former tsarist regime, which, they declared, amounted to R18 billion. They also asked that Russia should return to the rightful owners the foreign firms that had been subjected to nationalization, or pay compensation. The Bolsheviks never seriously considered such requests, even though they had hinted prior to the conference that they would be prepared to discuss them. Their attention was directed more toward an agreement with Europe's other outcast power, Weimar Germany.

The result of this focus was a separate agreement signed between Chicherin on behalf of Russia and Walther Rathenau for Germany at Rapallo, just outside Genoa, on April 16, 1922, when Russia and Germany restored diplomatic relations and established trade and economic connections. Germany also refrained from requesting the return of nationalized enterprises as long as Russia did not extend that privilege to any other power. In return, Germany acquired the status of a "most favored nation" and benefited from generous trade agreements. The Russians also allowed the German army to test new weapons on Soviet soil, contrary to the stipulations of the Versailles Treaty. Rapallo provided a more positive outcome for the Soviet delegation than the Genoa conference itself, which eventually switched venues to The Hague and ended inconclusively, particularly in view of Russia's refusal to recognize any obligations of the current government to the governments of the past and the fact that two of the delegates had chosen to make a private agreement that appeared duplicitous to the Western allies. Relations with Germany were to remain warm; and, indeed, it was with the future enemy that Soviet Russia and later the USSR established the closest links in Europe. The sequel to Rapallo was an expansion of the original agreement on November 5, 1922, in Berlin, and then the Treaty of Berlin on April 24, 1926, which was a neutrality agreement between the two sides for a five-year period. This was extended on June 24, 1931 and again shortly after Hitler came to power. By the mid-1920s, Russia and Germany had embarked on active economic and military cooperation. German officers were teaching in Soviet military academies, while Germany was able to use Soviet territory as a training ground for its army. Before Hitler, Germany was to remain the USSR's closest partner in Western Europe, and one could argue that in this period the relationship was mutually advantageous. The direction of Soviet foreign policy at this time certainly owed something to the diplomacy of the erudite and cultured diplomat Chicherin, whose time as Commissar of Foreign Affairs was characterized by the restoration of diplomatic links with much of the world. Chicherin (no doubt under the sway of Lenin and then subsequently of Stalin) also appears to have nurtured a view of the world that was first and foremost anti-British. The British were regarded as the major victorious power to emerge from the First World War and, given the reticence of the United States, to be enjoying a period of renewed domination of European affairs.

Generally Britain and France were overtly hostile to the new Russian government until 1924. The hostility was illustrated at an international conference, which took place from November 1922 to July 1923 in Lausanne, and at which the Soviet role was limited to comments on the Black Sea region. The Allies insisted that the Dardanelles remain open for the free passage of commercial and military vessels; whereas the Bolsheviks, having witnessed the results of this during the civil war, angrily demanded that all powers other than Turkey should be banned from sending military ships through the Straits either in times of peace or in times of war. Before this conference had ended, Lord Curzon the British Foreign Minister had ordered the Soviet government to cease what he called its anti-British activities in the Near

East, particularly in Afghanistan and Iran. The Soviet response of May 11 was that the country should not be treated like a colony, and that it would retain its current ambassadors in the aforementioned countries.

Gradually, however, the Soviet Union emerged from international isolation and followed the policy that Lenin termed "peaceful co-existence." Plainly Russia could not remain in a state of virtual war with the capitalist West. It needed to open its borders to trade, and the threat of revolution in central Europe had receded. After Lenin's death, in February 1924, the USSR established diplomatic relations with Britain, and this significant breakthrough for the Soviet side was followed by diplomatic recognition from several major states, including China, France, Mexico, Denmark, Austria, Sweden, Norway, and Italy. Relations with China were further clarified in late May 1924 with an agreement of mutual recognition through which the USSR retained control over the Chinese Eastern Railway and Outer Mongolia. In turn, the Soviets accepted the current territorial borders of China and the sovereignty of the republic, and promised not to interfere in its internal affairs. In both France and Britain, the change in the nature of the relationship came about largely through the election in those two countries of governments more sympathetic to the USSR – Eduard Herriot's "Leftist Bloc" in France, and Ramsay MacDonald's Labor government in Britain.

The culmination of this period of peaceful co-existence was the restoration of relations with Japan, a country with which Russia had been at loggerheads since the beginning of the century. Normal diplomatic links were resumed in January 1925, and Japan made a major concession to pull its troops out of the northern half of Sakhalin Island. This occupation had violated the provisions of the 1905 Treaty of Portsmouth that had ended the Russo-Japanese War. Henceforth, Japan restricted itself to the southern portion of the island. The respite from external pressure provided the Soviet government with a breathing space, albeit a very brief one. By early 1925, the benefits of Lenin's NEP were also becoming apparent. It seemed possible that the Soviet Union might emerge as a valuable trading partner with the Western democracies. However, there was always a significant gap between Soviet conciliation toward the capitalist states and the revolutionary rhetoric of Moscow. The respite in hostilities was always likely to be temporary as long as the Western democracies and the relatively weak China believed that the Bolsheviks continued to try to interfere in their domestic affairs and undermine the structure of their states.

In Britain this view became apparent during the general strike of British trade unions that began on May 4, 1926. Some eighteen months earlier, a forged letter, supposedly signed by Comintern chief Grigory Zinoviev and the leaders of the British and Finnish Communist Parties, inciting English workers to penetrate the trade unions and the army and to prepare for a socialist revolution, was published in a popular British newspaper. The letter may have been one factor behind the subsequent fall of the Labor government and the failure of attempts to ratify a trade agreement with the USSR. Later in 1924, the Labor government lost its mandate, and the Conservatives came to power and quickly renounced the trade agreements with the

Soviet Union. For a brief period, however, some links remained between the USSR (mainly through the Comintern) and the British trade union movement, and in April 1925 an Anglo-Russian Joint Advisory Committee was set up. It came to little because British trade unions, in the Soviet view, were insufficiently committed to revolutionary policies.

In 1926, therefore, when the British General Strike occurred, the Soviet leaders were taken by surprise. Zinoviev doubted that such a strike could succeed. Soviet trade unions, little more than mouthpieces of the government, were obligated to provide material aid to striking English coal miners, once again leading to accusations that the USSR was interfering in Britain's internal affairs. The British Trades Union Congress refused the aid, and Soviet intrusion was clearly exposed. Once the British government, and Churchill in particular, succeeded in ending the strike by harsh methods, Anglo-Soviet relations faced a seemingly inevitable decline. On May 27, 1927, British police raided the London office of Arkos, the Soviet trade delegation, and found various items of Soviet propaganda. Charges of espionage followed. Britain at once broke off diplomatic and trading relations with the USSR, a situation that was to last until 1929 when Labor once again was in office. The British government was genuinely afraid of the spread of "Bolshevism" in the country, particularly in view of the seriousness of the General Strike and its impact on a country that had been hard-pressed by the sacrifices of the First World War.

The impression of the increasing isolation of the USSR was reinforced by the sudden and rapid deterioration of relations with China, which began with a massacre of Chinese Communists in Shanghai by the forces of the Nationalist leader, Chiang Kai-Shek, on April 12, 1927. This slaughter followed a raid by Chinese police on the offices of the Soviet mission to Beijing. Within two years, a new conflict broke out in China when the Manchurian Army seized the telegraph facilities of the Chinese Eastern Railway and raided the Soviet Consulate in China. In the process Soviet control over the railway was ended, and Soviet organizations based there were forcibly dissolved. Soviet citizens were subject to arrest, and the Manchurian Army crossed the Soviet border on more than one occasion. Stalin in response appointed General V. K. Blyukher, formerly the chief military advisor to the government of Sun Yat-Sen, to command a new military unit called the Special Red Banner Far Eastern Army. Diplomatic relations with China were broken off, and the Far Eastern Army won a few skirmishes with the Manchurians, most of which took place on Chinese territory.

This new Soviet aggression worried the Western democracies. In February 1929, some five months before the conflict broke out in China, the Soviet Union had been a witness to the Briand–Kellog Pact, along with Poland, Romania, Turkey, Iran, Estonia, and Lithuania – an ambitious and wordy document that advocated general disarmament. The Soviet government was once again pursuing dual aims – on the one hand, arguing that the world should cut back on weaponry and refrain from war; and, on the other hand, using its military to retain its authority in an area of former tsarist influence in the Far East. In the former campaign, the Soviet delegation had played a formative role in the preparatory commission of the League of Nations on Disarmament in November 1927, with a plea for general and full disarmament. The commission, however, degenerated into a talking shop. Concerning its more aggressive stance, Stalin argued that Soviet troops had crossed into China for the cause of self-protection. Before long, the conflict was over. On December 3, the USSR and China signed a preliminary peace agreement, followed by a full protocol at Khabarovsk on December 22, 1929. The status quo was restored in Manchuria with neither side having made any appreciable gains, but the Soviet state was living precariously.

Summary: the 1920s

The new personality cult established in the USSR signified that the regime had taken on a certain pattern, that it was no longer a country in a transitional period, en route to a pure form of socialism or ideology. The guidelines had been clearly demarcated. At the center a power struggle had occurred concomitantly with an intense debate over the correct economic path. The victor of the first had been Stalin, allied with the so-called Right forces in the Politburo – Bukharin, Rykov, and Tomsky. Trotsky had been defeated, and Kamenev and Zinoviev rendered ineffective. The second debate had continued throughout the 1920s, with Stalin remaining in the background, content to support the NEP as long as it seemed to be yielding results. The relatively tolerant economic policy and the freedom allowed for national-cultural development of the non-Russian areas, however, only aroused his suspicion and fear of forces that might emerge to threaten his personal power. It was time therefore for a radical change on both those fronts.

Questions for discussion

1. Why did the Bolsheviks change course to the New Economic Policy in the 1920s?
2. How did the death of Lenin result in Lenin's cult?
3. How can one explain Stalin's rise to power by 1928?
4. Was the decade a relatively liberal one for Russian culture? What caveats might be applied to that statement?
5. How was the Soviet Union able to emerge from isolation in the 1920s?

Recent works

Agnieszka, Knyt. *The Year 1920: The War between Poland and Bolshevik Russia.* Warsaw: KARTA Centre, City of Warsaw History Museum, 2005.

Baron, Nick. *Homelands: War, Population and Statehood in Eastern Europe and Russia, 1918–1924*. London: Anthem Press, 2004.

Calhoun, Daniel F. *The United Front: The TUC and the Russians 1923–1928*. Cambridge/New York: Cambridge University Press, 2008.

Carleton, Gregory. *Sexual Revolution in Bolshevik Russia*. Pittsburgh, Pa: University of Pittsburgh Press, 2005.

Chatterjee, Choi. *Celebrating Women: Gender, Festival Culture, and Bolshevik Ideology, 1910–1939*. Pittsburgh, Pa: University of Pittsburgh Press, 2002.

Gabel, Paul. *And God Created Lenin: Marxism vs. Religion in Russia, 1917–1929*. Amherst, NY: Prometheus Books, 2005.

Gregory, Paul R. *The Lost Politburo Transcripts: From Collective Rule to Stalin's Dictatorship*. New Haven, Conn.: Yale University Press, 2008.

Heinzen, James W. *Inventing a Soviet Countryside: State Power and the Transformation of Rural Russia, 1917–1929*. Pittsburg, Pa: University of Pittsburgh Press, 2004.

Lyandres, Semion, and Dietmar Wulff. *A Chronicle of the Civil War in Siberia and Exile in China: The Diary of Petr Vasil'evich Vologodskii, 1918–1925*. Stanford, Calif.: Hoover Institution Press, 2002.

Montefiore, Simon Sebag. *Young Stalin*. New York: Alfred A. Knopf, 2007.

Nelson, Amy. *Music for the Revolution: Musicians and Power in Early Soviet Russia*. University Park, Pa: Pennsylvania State University Press, 2004.

Robinson, Paul. *The White Russian Army in Exile, 1920–1941*. Oxford: Clarendon Press, 2002.

Roslof, Edward E. *Red Priests: Renovationism, Russian Orthodoxy, and Revolution, 1905–1946*. Bloomington, Ind.: Indiana University Press, 2002.

Viola, Lynne. *The War against the Peasantry, 1927–1930: The Tragedy of the Soviet Countryside*. New Haven, Conn.: Yale University Press, 2005.

Ward, Chris. *Russia's Cotton Workers and the New Economic Policy: Shop-Floor Culture and State Policy, 1921–1929*. Cambridge: Cambridge University Press, 2002.

Wynot, Jennifer J. *Keeping the Faith: Russian Orthodox Monasticism in the Soviet Union, 1917–1939*. College Station, Tex.: Texas A&M University Press, 2004.

4

Collectivization, industrialization and the Great Purge, 1929–1940

Introduction

After his victory over the Left Opposition, which had made its goals known publicly, Stalin turned on the supporters of the NEP within the Politburo before making a radical change in policy direction. The principal members of what became known as the Right Opposition were: Bukharin; Aleksey Rykov, who had occupied Lenin's former position as the Chairman of the Council of Ministers from February 1924 to May 1929; and Mikhail Tomsky, chairman of the Soviet trade unions, who had headed the Soviet trade union delegation to London in 1924. These three figures did not pose a serious threat to Stalin and never mounted a public campaign against him. Between June and July 13, 1930, at the 16th Party Congress, Stalin and his supporters announced that the Right Opposition had been defeated. Tomsky lost his position in the Politburo, which now appeared to be packed with Stalin's closest associates, such as Voroshilov, Kaganovich, Kirov, Molotov, and others. For the moment, Rykov retained his seat.

In the late 1920s, worker dissatisfaction with the Soviet leadership began to manifest itself in several areas, and particularly in the Donbas region. In 1928 there occurred the so-called Shakhty affair, during which workers and engineers in the Donetsk Basin were accused of gross violations of working safety, flooding and wrecking coal mines, and other acts of vandalism. A trial followed in Moscow in 1929, presided over by a man who was to become notorious as the State Prosecutor during the great show trials of the 1930s: Andrey Vyshinsky. Conditions in the mines were without doubt dangerous, and there may have been isolated attempts to damage the mines. Corruption and theft of property were rife. On the other hand, the miners did not pose an overt threat to the regime. They were the first of many scapegoats for the problems in industry during the Stalin period. Five of the accused were executed (though eleven had originally been sentenced to death), and the majority received prison sentences of four to ten years.

The late 1920s also saw the atmosphere in the country change from one of relative toleration to one of fear. By 1927, we recall, there appeared to be an authentic possibility that the Soviet Union would be involved in another war, most likely with Britain or China. Stalin thrived on periods of tension when the problems within the country could be attributed to external enemies seeking to subvert the system. Repeatedly Soviet propaganda declared that the capitalist states would use any opportunity to overthrow the world's only Communist state. Already, by early 1930,

Stalin had begun to expand the camp administration that became known as the GULAG (Chief Administration of Camps), which was made subordinate to his secret police, the OGPU (United State Political Administration). Initially most of these camps were located in the remote areas of the White Sea, but soon they would be set up across the country, and particularly in Siberia and the Far East. Arrests became commonplace, and more specifically the authorities exposed a number of groups, real and imagined, within the country. In January 1930, for example, several officers of the tsarist army were placed under arrest. In July, a Toiling Peasants' Party was uncovered and declared to consist of counter-revolutionary elements, including several well-known Soviet economists. In Ukraine, another fictitious organization, the League for the Liberation of Ukraine, was supposedly revealed. In the fall of 1930, the OGPU announced the discovery of a dangerous espionage organization made up of former landowners; and two former property-owners from the tsarist period, Professor A. V. Ryazantsev and General E. S. Karatygin, were shot along with forty-four others.

The decade closed with a much-publicized trial of industrialists who were accused of paving the way for foreign intervention in agreement with Russian émigrés based in Paris. In December also, Rykov lost his seat in the Politburo, and Molotov took over his position as Premier – Chairman of the Council of People's Commissars. The arrests and trials were minor compared with what was to follow in the USSR, but they marked a departure from the tolerance of the earlier 1920s and reflected the consolidation of power by Stalin. In December, Stalin celebrated his 50th[t] birthday, and the event was marked by extravagant pageants and by odes to Stalin in the Soviet media. Though the cult of Lenin started even before Lenin's death in January 1924, the cult of Stalin dates from this occasion. Henceforth, official propaganda overflowed with adulation of Stalin's personal attributes. One well-known poet even suggested that the country should dispense with the official calendar and replace it with a new one based on the birth of Stalin. Stalin's wise nature, his sentiments for the Soviet people, and his position as heir to Lenin were now features of Soviet propaganda. The entire issue of *Pravda* was devoted to Stalin on his birthday, an attitude that was rather typical of Russia's autocratic past, eastern rather than western in origin, though it has all too frequently been compared with the propaganda for Hitler.

The decision to collectivize agriculture

By the time of the 15th Party Conference in 1927, the party leadership was already developing plans to adopt a Five-Year Plan for the development of industry. In turn, this new development required a guaranteed supply of grain from the countryside to the towns, to compensate for the massive exodus of workers from rural to urban centers. Theoretically, as people like Bukharin argued, the NEP might have financed this new development, had the party believed that the peasants would supply an adequate amount of grain. But agricultural output had begun to taper off and did not meet the state's requirements. Before the Revolution, great estates or private smallholdings had produced about half the grain. By the late 1920s, however, the structure of the countryside had begun to change. The peasantry still made up the vast majority of the population – about 108 million people lived in rural areas, and the urban workforce constituted less than 8 percent of the population. But, within the villages, the NEP period had seen the rapid expansion of the so-called middle peasant – the *serednyak* – who now made up about 80 percent of the rural population. At the same time, there were some 21 million poor peasants (*bednyaks*) and 5.9 million kulaks (4 percent of the total rural population). Stolypin's program of the early part of the century seemed to be coming to fruition. The Revolution, followed by the NEP, had produced a petty-bourgeois village.

Perhaps the key problem in agriculture was the reluctance of the peasants to sell grain to the state at low prices. When the harvest was poor, as in 1928, the state authorities had to force some peasant households to sell grain. The scissors crisis that had developed in 1923 returned in force. In the winter of 1927–1928, the government introduced bread rations in the towns and raised the agricultural taxes of the better-off peasants. Grain exports, which had been lucrative for the government of Nikolay II, were by now twenty times less than they had been in 1913. Official propaganda announced a "grain crisis," and Stalin made an unusual visit to Siberia, where he informed local peasants that the problems were being caused by farmers hoarding grain, and in particular the culprits were kulaks, the class enemies of the Soviet state. How accurate this statement was can be discerned from our earlier observation that kulak farms made up only 4 percent of the total. Was there a campaign by kulaks to hoard grain? The answer is that many peasants needed the grain to survive. The period had seen a significant population-growth, and thus peasants were consuming more of the grain produced than was the case before the war.

The year 1928 marked a turning point in Soviet agriculture. The USSR was now suffering from a shortage of grain needed to feed the towns and to supply the Red Army, particularly troops in the Far East on the volatile border with China. The problem lay not only in the villages but also in the towns, which had failed to provide the peasants with useful industrial goods. There had also, it was alleged, been a certain lack of vigilance by state organizations and cooperatives, which were fighting with each other rather than uniting against attempts by kulak farmers to raise the price of grain. Already, by December 1927, the 15th Party Congress had issued a decree "Concerning work in the village," which advocated the development of collective farming, to create a socialist basis in agriculture and ensure the movement of grain to the towns. The peasants were not to be forced into new farms, but were to be persuaded and enticed, with high taxes on those who chose to remain as individual farmers. In this same period, Bukharin, the firmest supporter of the NEP, advocated that the state could buy grain abroad rather than revert to drastic methods of procurement and isolation of the kulaks. His idea was rejected, however.

The regime was ready to return to the sort of class warfare perpetuated in the period of War Communism. By February 1928, for example, the Central Committee of the party instructed local party organizations to find various methods of waging a class struggle in the village.

Particular attention was paid to alleged speculators, whose lands were confiscated: 75 percent were retained by the state, and the rest distributed among the poorer peasantry. By the fall of 1929, collectivization of farms was again under way, but progress was slow. Most of the new farms were Associations for the Joint Cultivation of Land (TOZ), which permitted the peasants to retain their draught livestock and agricultural implements. A much greater transformation, however, was on the horizon: the enforced mass collectivization of agriculture that has been described by some scholars as the second Soviet revolution. It was not literally a revolution since the goal was to consolidate rather than change the existing government; but it did represent a huge change, and an end to the working alliance with the peasantry that had permitted economic recovery during the 1920s. In Stalin's view, the new class war had to subordinate the peasant to the worker – the key goal was to ensure that the party controlled the countryside. In order to achieve this aim, the regime had to entice the middle peasants to join collective farms. Hitherto the farms had been weak affairs since they were comprised of the poorest strata of the population, precisely those who had nothing to lose by joining. Many of them had no land or livestock, and since the government was not in a position to provide machinery to the collective farms it made little economic sense to establish them. Again it is worth emphasizing Stalin's priorities – collectivization was undertaken in order to support and maintain the great industrialization drive, which in turn was to transform the country from a backward agricultural nation to an advanced industrial one. Stalin believed that the USSR was ten years behind the advanced nations of the West in industrial development. Not only did it have to bridge this gap, but it also had to achieve economic self-sufficiency. The atmosphere created in the country was one of a state of war – enemies were everywhere and being uncovered anew by the secret police. The new directions in economic policy would eradicate these enemies and strengthen the country.

Mass collectivization begins

Mass collectivization began in the summer of 1929 and at a rapid rate. About 4.3 million peasants had joined kolkhozes by the end of the year, which comprised about one-fifth of the poor and middle peasant households. On November 7, 1929, the 12th anniversary of the Bolshevik Revolution, Stalin published an article in *Pravda* entitled "The Year of the Great Transformation." However, at first the great mass of middle peasants did not give up their property, and the regime's focus was on the key grain-growing regions, such as the Volga region, the Ukrainian steppes, and the north Caucasus. By the summer of 1929, in these regions, the authorities declared some villages to be fully collectivized, and by the end of the year several districts had also completed the process. At the same time the TOZ, which might be described as a more autonomous form of organization, was replaced by the artel, whereby land, draught animals, and equipment became the property of the collective farm, while the peasant farmer retained only a small household plot and a few chickens or rabbits. Not until 1935 did the government formalize this development with an official decree that denoted the structure and operation of the agricultural artel as the principal form of collective farming.

On January 5, 1930, a Central Committee decree addressed the issue – "Concerning the tempo of collectivization and means to aid the state with kolkhoz construction." The Soviet party and government envisaged that collectivization would be completed in a very short period in the priority regions, and as early as the spring of 1931 in the regions on the Volga and the northern Caucasus. Ukraine, the Central Chernozem region, then Urals and Siberia would follow by the spring of 1932. It would not be necessary to attain the same sort of tempo in the other parts of the country, such as within the vicinity of the major cities of Moscow and Leningrad, or western and northern Russia, until later in the 1930s. It made sense to focus resources on a few areas, ensure that they were fully collectivized, and then turn to areas closer to the main industrial centers.

Such was the determination of the early part of this drive to collective farms that it was possible for the kulak farms to join the new structures. It was always difficult for the authorities to differentiate the kulaks from the middle peasants; and, since the priority was to achieve full collectivization in grain-growing regions, some areas did not deny kulak farms that had given up their property to the new collective. Stalin himself put a stop to this development by issuing a declaration of war on the kulak at an all-union conference of agrarian Marxists in late December 1929. According to Stalin, the country had moved to the second stage of the Revolution. The first had been the expropriation of the landowner estates, and the second was the transition to collective farming. The Soviet Union would become, it was announced, the world's richest source of grain; but, in doing so, it was essential not merely to remove the kulak from the collective farms but also to "liquidate [him] as a class." Why was this action necessary? The response was that the kulaks were allegedly in league with the international bourgeoisie and supported by internal and external enemies. They had entered the collective farms only in order to destroy them from within. The first task, then, was to expose the kulaks within the farms and in the regions of full collectivization to remove them.

In mid-January, the Politburo created a special commission under the chairmanship of Molotov, which made recommendations to the Politburo regarding the expulsion of kulak households from regions that had been fully collectivized. This was followed by a Politburo decree of January 30, which ended leasing of land, hiring of labor, and enforced the confiscation of kulak property, livestock, residential buildings, and others. In short, the kulak farms were to be eliminated, though the decree – cynically – suggested that no more than 3–5 percent of kulak farms should be destroyed, i.e. precisely the number of estimated kulak farms according to earlier calculations. Another decree followed on February 1, 1930: "Concerning measures to strengthen the socialist reconstruction of agriculture in the regions of full collectivization and in the struggle against the kulak." This decree obligated the local authorities to transfer all the lands taken from "kulak households" to the indivisible funds of the kolkhoz, and thus they could not be leased out. The kulaks were isolated and deprived of their livelihood. In the meantime, the reliable party activists and sympathizers descended on the villages like locusts, led by the 25,000 volunteers selected from about 70,000 urban residents who wished to take part in the social upheaval.

Despite the figure of 3–5 percent for the number of farms to be destroyed, this total was soon exceeded. There was no clear definition of a kulak farm. The peasants themselves might recognize one farm as being wealthier than another, and petty jealousies may have existed, but they did not think in class terms. The class nature of "dekulakization" was something external, almost foreign, introduced by townspeople with no links to the villages. If a farmer had more than one horse or cow, then the more enthusiastic participants in Stalin's program would consider him a kulak. In several regions about one in every six households was deprived of its possessions and evicted. Once the family had been removed, then frequently the house would be looted of its remaining contents. The speed of the process ensured that families did not have time to take with them all their belongings. Those supervising the evictions consisted of various sectors of local party and government authorities and the outsiders from the towns – members of the regional executive committee of the Soviet, representatives of village Soviets, the local party organization (if there was one), and the Committees of the Poor Peasants, which had been resurrected. According to plans worked out within the OGPU, the kulak residences were to be used by the new farms and the village Soviets.

As for the kulaks themselves, the authorities divided them into three groups, the smallest of which was the first – counter-revolutionaries or terrorists who were opposed to the Soviet state and persecuted as criminal; in some cases they were shot. Others were either transferred to distant parts of the country, or else moved to administrative regions. The second and third categories were in theory allowed to retain some possessions, but in practice local powers did not adhere very closely to these conditions. Many lost all their possessions and were sent to remote regions of the Urals and Siberia, or else to the far north, where they were employed in chopping down trees for the mining industry. The overwhelming impression of these events is of a virtual civil war conducted on a demographic basis. An urban-based party organization uprooted so-called class enemies while itself taking over the administration of the villages. The towns sent not only the 25,000ers, but also other workers to assist with sowing and harvest, members of the party, Komsomol, and urban Soviets. The main source of this urban army was the two main Russian cities, Moscow and Leningrad. Under a decree of January 30, 1930, the Red Army also had to play a significant role and commit 100,000 soldiers for work in the villages. The local party organizations were obliged to join in, despite the fact that in some areas the problems and pain of the changes were self-evident.

For the peasants, there was often no resort other than active or passive protest. Collectivization may have taken some years in its preparation, but it was introduced with such brutality and haste that there could be nothing voluntary about it. Unless they were very poor, peasants could see little advantage in joining the new kolkhozes. The new farms had almost no equipment and, as it turned out, few animals, either, as many peasants chose to slaughter their own livestock rather than see animals they had raised transferred to the alien structure of a collective farm. There was also the matter of subterfuge. By slaughtering their livestock, a kulak household could render itself instantly to a middle-sized or even a poor one. Some households sold off their property and then joined the kolkhoz. As for the new farms, they were unlikely to be very successful. The chairman of the kolkhoz was invariably an outsider – perhaps a member of the Red Army, a 25,000er, the chairman of the village Soviet, or someone the party felt it could trust. Rarely did the person chosen have much experience of farming, let alone of a complex structure like a kolkhoz. The lack of machinery and animals also deprived the kolkhoz of any advantage derived from its size. Often the villages established "paper kolkhozes," which existed on paper for the benefit of the authorities but soon dissolved after the local activists moved on to the next region.

Over a period of six months, Stalin and the then Premier, Kalinin, received 90,000 letters of protest about the behavior of the local authorities, and peasant insurgencies broke out across the Soviet Union, in virtually all of the chief grain-growing regions. Viola argues (Viola, 1998) that peasants were far more active in their resistance than has often been surmised, and notes the significant role played by women in the protests. The chaos caused by the enforced removal of kulaks and creation of collective farms is almost unimaginable. The local authorities may have been overzealous. They frequently dispensed with the limited type of collectivized farm and formed pure communes, meaning that the peasants did not even retain a cottage or hut of their own. There is also no doubt that local officials were preoccupied with creating large structures, which were held *ipso facto* to be superior to small farms. These giant farms were simply unworkable in the early 1930s because they lacked machinery. The Stalin regime had not only succeeded in creating a civil conflict once again; it had also alienated perhaps the majority of the Soviet population. Ultimately even Stalin had to pay attention to the new dilemma. On March 2, 1930, he published in *Pravda* an article entitled "Dizzy with Success," which held that local zealots had placed unwarranted pressure on the peasants, damaging the voluntary nature of the collective farm movement. The "little father" thus separated himself from the movement he had created – a fiction that appeared quite credible to many peasants who did not associate Stalin with the violence inflicted on the villages. Measures were to be introduced to put an end to the "distortions." Two weeks later, Stalin's comments resulted in a new party decree – "About deviations from the party line in the kolkhoz movement." Collectivization, it declared, must not be enforced but had to be a voluntary process. Most important, it was necessary to pacify the middle peasant, the *serednyak*, the largest stratum in the country, and turn him into an ally of the regime.

As a result of Stalin's article and the decree of March 14, the peasants deserted the collective farms in droves. The percentage of households collectivized fell from 50 percent in March to just over 21 percent by August 1930. The respite was only temporary. The authorities resorted to pressure rather than physical force, increasing taxation on individual farms or refusing them credit, and raising obligatory deliveries to the state to levels beyond the capacity of most farmers. By September 1931, 60 percent of peasant households were in collective farms. The results for Soviet agriculture were little short of disastrous. Because of mass slaughter, the country suffered the sort of livestock losses hitherto seen only in wartime. By the summer of 1930, livestock numbers had fallen by 25 percent. One area particularly hard hit was Kazakhstan, where most farmers were nomadic, but the Communist officials pushed through collectivization without any regard for local conditions. There was little incentive for the peasants to stay on the new collective farms. Wages, which were very low, were paid in kind, rendering the peasant dependent on the kolkhoz. After a harvest had been collected, the immediate requirement of the kolkhoz was to fulfill state grain deliveries, but the prices being offered for grain and other products were about ten times lower than the market level. Many peasants chose to uproot themselves and head for the cities in a reversal of the situation at the beginning of the 1920s. The Soviet authorities put a stop to this by introducing a passport system for urban residents in December 1932. Peasants did not receive such passports and thus were officially as tied to the village as they had been under serfdom.

The Great Famine in Ukraine

The state purchases of grain and the losses of livestock led to acute problems in several key agricultural areas of the country, particularly in Ukraine, the Don region, Kazakhstan, and the north Caucasus. The situation was aggravated by a drought that spread through the Lower Volga, the western regions of Siberia, and the north Caucasus; and full-scale famine had occurred in many regions by 1932. The famine reached a crisis in Ukraine, where, according to studies undertaken by the Ukrainian demographer Maksudov, a minimum of 4 million peasants died (Hryn, 2009). On August 7, 1932, the authorities passed a Law for the Protection of Socialist Property, which made it a criminal offense to steal even an ear of grain from the harvest, with a penalty of execution and confiscation of property, or ten years in exile. This draconian law was applied most harshly in Ukraine, where the new passport system prevented the starving masses from entering the towns, or crossing the internal border into Russia or Belarus to find food. The famine caused massive loss of life, but the Soviet regime denied its existence until late 1987, thereby exacerbating the suffering. These events led to a major scholarly debate about the cause and consequences of the Ukrainian famine that has never reached a consensus.

The debate began more than twenty-five years ago when the Ukrainian Research Institute at Harvard University commissioned a book on the Ukrainian famine, which, after some delay, was entrusted to the British-born writer Robert Conquest, who worked with an assistant, James E. Mace, who had recently completed a doctoral thesis on Ukraine in the 1930s. Conquest was best-known for his book on the 1930s Soviet purges, which had been published in the mid-1960s. His new book on the Ukraine famine, published in 1986, was entitled *Harvest of Sorrow*, and came out to general acclaim but some significant criticisms. Among these was the fact that the photographs used to depict famine victims were not always authentic: several showed victims of the 1921 famine that occurred in various parts of the former Russian Empire after the civil war. Conquest had also relied for some of his source material on a book with the dubious title *The Black Deeds of the Kremlin*. Given the year that *Harvest of Sorrow* was written, it could hardly be expected that he would have had access to Soviet archival material. Indeed, given his past research, he above all people might have expected to encounter difficulties getting such access. There were also disputes over figures, the number of victims, and whether too much emphasis was being placed on Ukraine as opposed to other regions. Kazakhstan, after all, had lost about one-third of its rural population during the collectivization campaign of 1929–1931.

Concerning the famine itself, there were several issues that proved hard to resolve. Some sources – particularly those emanating from the Ukrainian Diaspora – put the death toll at anywhere between 7 million and 10 million. The last Soviet census prior to the famine had been in 1926. Stalin had banned the next census, conducted in 1937, and purged its gatherers. Only in 1939 did a new Soviet census appear, and it indicated that the population of the Ukrainian SSR had fallen by more than 3 million since 1926 whereas the population of Russia (RSFSR) had risen by 16 million over the same period. The key question, however, was what the population-loss might have been in the banned 1937 census (another reason for its suppression may have been the extent to which it revealed continuing adherence to religious beliefs on the part of the population). In addition, the interim period between the two censuses had seen upheavals other than the famine, such as collectivization itself, and the purges that began on a major scale from 1937, but which had been in place since 1932 in the local party organizations. To some observers, it was inconceivable that Stalin's policies could have led to such severe consequences, largely unknown to the rest of the world (other than through private diplomatic dispatches). The supporters of the Soviet system were also consistent in their denial.

In December 1987, Ukraine's hard-line party leader Volodymyr Shcherbytsky suddenly acknowledged the existence of the Ukrainian famine in a speech during a relatively early stage of Glasnost, especially in Soviet Ukraine. It was not the first official acknowledgement of the famine from a Soviet source, but it was the most important since it signified a dramatic change of policy within the Soviet party. Thereafter the emphasis of the debate shifted from the existence of the famine to its causes. In the USSR these were years when Gorbachev had turned on the Soviet legacy, and victims of the period were being rehabilitated daily in the press. In 1990 an international conference on the famine was held in Kyiv, attended by various leading scholars from the West, including Mace, and the USSR, such as Ukraine's Stanislav Kulchytsky, the leading historian of collectivization in Ukraine. The general conclusion was that the Ukrainian famine was an act of genocide perpetrated against Ukrainians as a civic *nation* rather than a result of Stalin's economic policies.

This new theory represented an important change of direction. If the famine was an act of genocide, then it represented one of the greatest crimes of the 20th century, at least in its scale. Mace and Kulchytsky noted the simultaneous elimination of the Ukrainian cultural elite in this same period, and the attack on the Ukrainian language and other manifestations of what was called "national deviation." Had Stalin turned on Ukrainians because they were Ukrainians or because they were predominantly peasants who farmed the best soil in the USSR? Harvard scholar Terry Martin has maintained that the conflict may have arisen from conflicting territorial demands between Russia and Ukraine, with both republics making appeals to the Soviet center in support of their own claims. The famine debate was one element in Ukraine's move to sovereignty in 1990, though certainly not the only one. It raises the question of Stalin's goals in permitting such a situation to continue. An American scholar, Mark B. Tauger, has maintained (Tauger, 1991) that the 1932 harvest was not as good as initially thought and has suggested that there was no policy of deliberate starvation of peasants. Rather economic and climatic conditions had made the situation much worse than hitherto. Four years later, Tauger, together with R. W. Davies and S. G. Wheatcroft (Davies, Tauger, and Wheatcroft, 1995), concluded that the Soviet grain stocks on the eve of the famine were much smaller than previously thought. Though their conclusions do not exempt Stalin from major responsibility for the Great Famine, they maintain that, since the state was a monopoly supplier of grain to the towns and the army, had such grain been used to feed the peasants, mass starvation would have resulted in the towns. Stalin certainly was well informed about the critical state of affairs in Ukraine and other regions affected by drought. Therefore, one can at least say that he made a decision not to alleviate the suffering caused in 1932–1933.

One of the difficulties about studying the Ukrainian famine and its causes is its obscurity. The Moscow-based correspondents of the Western media either did not know of its existence, or else chose not to report it (and this statement applies to Walter Duranty, correspondent of *The New York Times*), or else their statements were received with incredulity by their editors at home (as was the case of the freelance journalist Malcolm Muggeridge, who visited famine regions without permission in 1932). An entire generation of Western scholars writing in the 1960s and 1970s gave barely a passing mention to the famine, including in some of the most acclaimed works of their time. They can hardly be blamed for their lack of knowledge. Various visitors to the USSR in the 1930s were given guided tours to Potemkin (imaginary) villages, to model collective farms that had been prepared carefully for the occasion and where food was plentiful and living conditions far above normal. These reports fed a domestic public wanting to believe that Stalin was creating a Soviet utopia that was not affected by crippling events like the Great Depression in the West. It was almost inconceivable that Stalin was willing to kill millions of his fellow countrymen and, moreover, the producers of the food that was to supply the growing urban population.

The existence of the famine was known to select circles in the West from a variety of sources. Walter Duranty told the British Embassy privately of the scale of the suffering, while declining to publicize it in his articles for the newspaper. One reason for his negligence (or callousness) may have been a desire not to offend the Soviet censor or his elevated position as the leading and most respected foreign correspondent in Moscow. The Italians and the Americans were also aware of the tragedy through their embassies. The United States was in the sensitive position of commencing diplomatic relations with the Soviet Union. It therefore chose to give the Stalin regime the benefit of the doubt when the latter claimed that there was no famine in the country. The famine represented the end product of a war against the peasantry that had begun with War Communism in 1918–1921, and had been resurrected and imposed in more violent form by Stalin in the early 1930s. It was the culmination point of the Soviet regime's war against the peasantry, which itself constituted an extreme reversal of the revolutionary populism of the 19th century. The peasant population represented the essence of the former Russian Empire, its great mass force. The events of collectivization and its extreme results such as famine indicated the great rupture that had been formed between the Soviet leadership and the rural population.

The debate on the famine is now a cause of the growing rift between the governments of Russia and Ukraine. However, more information is becoming available. The 1937 census has now been revealed and examined by Western scholars, and indicates that population losses in Ukraine were indeed higher than suggested by the later census. In Ukraine and the North Caucasus it is now clear that, based on orders from Extraordinary Commissions led by Molotov, Kaganovich, and Pavel Postyshev, entire villages were cordoned off and systematically starved. The famine ended in 1934 when the USSR provided relief to the affected areas. Thus there was no sustained campaign to eliminate peasants of Ukrainian origin, though the Soviet leadership could always have come to its senses and recognized the futility of an attempt to destroy a national group. According to the memoirs of Nikita Khrushchev – which, it must be said, are not always reliable – Stalin would have deported the entire Ukrainian nation after the Second World War but for the fact that it was too numerous. However, by 1944–1945, the USSR was facing considerable opposition from guerrilla movements in the western borderlands; and the statement, if Stalin really uttered it, would surely have been affected by the events of the war. In 1932–1933, Stalin may have been concerned about an anti-Moscow cultural and national movement in Ukraine but he, along with Kaganovich, was one of its instigators. The famine likely occurred because of excessive grain requisitions and brutal laws that prevented the producers of the grain from feeding themselves. The farmers and their families were sacrificed for Stalin's plans, the needs of the urban workforce, and the appetite of a large army, but there was also a clear ethnic component.

Completion of collectivization

The question of machinery was always a priority for Lenin, and so it proved for Stalin, too. The new collective farmers had to use tractors, harvesters and other equipment for the new farms to operate successfully. However, the authorities were never willing to allow the peasants to own such machinery – it had to be leased out through organizations known as the Machine-Tractor Stations (MTS), which were usually created in all rayons (districts) of an oblast. The MTS were a watchdog on the new farms. During peak activity, the Soviet leadership formed MTS political sections, made up of reliable personnel, usually from outside the villages, who were called upon to perform special tasks, such as ensuring the collection of the harvest or conducting purges of the kolkhozes and the village party organizations. The MTS political sections were short-lived and appeared at three peak periods: in 1933; during the war; and in 1948–1949 when the leaders decided to enforce mass collectivization in the newly incorporated western borderlands. Collectivization in the USSR as a whole was completed during the years of the 2nd Five-Year Plan, by which time there were almost a quarter of a million collective farms in the country, embracing 93 percent of peasant households.

By 1935, when the Statute of the Agricultural Artel was issued, it indicated that, on paper, the collective farm was an autonomous organization in which decisions were made by a general meeting, and the farm itself run by a board of directors that included a chairman, an inspector, and a chief agronomist. The collective farm was distinct from a larger entity – the state farm, or sovkhoz – which was essentially a Soviet factory in the countryside and represented for Stalin the optimal form of rural farming. However, the kolkhoz also had few rights. Peasants were tied to it, paid for their membership into the indivisible fund and thereafter maintained a miserable subsistence livelihood without any real incentive to improve their situation. One of the most poignant aspects of the accounts written by German troops who came through the Soviet countryside after the summer of 1941 are the descriptions of the dilapidated farms they found and the primitive nature of the villages that appeared to them little changed from medieval times.

The start of industrialization

The 1920s had seen some progress toward industrial development, though in essence this period focused on traditional industrial centers of the former Russian Empire, such as the Moscow region and Ukraine. Ukraine in particular had seen both reconstruction and the development of new factories in metallurgy, machine-building, iron ore, and the coal industry. The other regions of the country saw little major development, though in Azerbaijan the oil industry of Baku had become a key area. In the Belarusian SSR, the third Slavic republic, agriculture still predominated, and only forestry and forestry-related industries made much progress. Clearly, by late 1928, the regime had decided to embark on a radical change of policy. At that time, an all-Union conference was held to discuss a new state plan, which included scientists and workers in the economy. By December, Soviet newspapers published figures for the coming five-year plan. In March 1929, the State Planning Commission – Gosplan – approved two variants of the plan, an initial stage and an optimal one, in which figures were about 20 percent higher. Rykov, who was already falling out of favor, preferred the initial version, but the consensus was to opt for the more ambitious targets.

In this same month, a meeting of the Collegium of People's Commissars decided to select the optimal variant, and approved a final draft on April 23, covering the period from 1928–1929 to 1932–1933. The plan was linked to the original plan to electrify the country – the GOELRO (State Commission for Electrification of Russia) – but it went much further. In May the 5th All-Union Congress of Soviets gave its assent. It anticipated a capital investment of 64.5 billion roubles, just over one-third of which was designated for major construction in industry. This figure represented an increase of more than three times the previous five years. The five-year plan, according to official propaganda, intended to transform the country into an industrial powerhouse, along with collectivized agriculture, and the elimination of illiteracy. The policy of industrialization was a return to idealized socialism. As an incentive to the workers, the authorities introduced "socialist competition" in the factories, by which individual factories or teams of workers were to compete with each other for high production. Before long the key contests took place within one workplace. At critical times, emphasis was on shock work or shock workers, particularly at the end of a month or the end of an annual plan period. Socialist competition officially got under way in March 1929 when an appeal of Leningrad workers for national socialist competition was published.

The 1st Five-Year Plan was undertaken on a grandiose scale. High targets were set in virtually every sector, and the plan began with a wave of fanfare and publicity that permeated all sectors of urban life. The 16th Party Congress, which took place in June 1930, was referred to as the Congress for the advance of socialism on all fronts. However, many of the plans had been initiated at the previous congress. One of the major ideas was the creation of a new metallurgical center at Magnitogorsk, known as the Ural–Kuznetsk Combine. The construction at Magnitogorsk symbolized the party's intent to broaden the economic basis of the country, and to begin industrial development beyond the Ural Mountains in areas that were rich in resources, but where local conditions often provided a formidable impediment to construction. Bolshevik propaganda stressed that no problems were too great for Soviet workers to resolve. On the other hand, it is hard to overcome the perception that the plan was worked out in piecemeal fashion, with huge problems encountered from the outset. The plan timetable was the first casualty. The five-year period was reduced, on Stalin's orders, to four years and three months.

Magnitogorsk was representative of the scale of new construction. In year two of the plan, one of the new developments was a railroad that would link Western Siberia and Turkestan. On June 17, 1930, at Stalingrad a huge tractor factory was completed with great ceremony, but unfortunately it proved incapable of producing any tractors owing to the lack of engine parts. Other tractor factories were built at Kharkiv in Ukraine, and Chelyabinsk east of the Ural Mountains. The Rostov factory produced its first tractor on June 15, 1930. When progress was reviewed at a meeting of economic workers in 1931, Stalin laid down "six conditions," which demanded proper organization of the workforce in the factories and, above all, the abolition of the notion of egalitarian wages. What Stalin wanted most was the creation of a technical intelligentsia from the Soviet workers and peasantry, and an end to the former reliance on bourgeois or foreign specialists. It hardly needs to be said that some of these efforts were crude and shortsighted. However, in many areas of Soviet industry, the results were quite impressive.

In his report of January 7, 1933, Stalin announced that the 1st Five-Year Plan had been completed in four years and three months. However, overall the plan indices were not fulfilled, despite the most intense efforts of the party. True, industrial output exceeded the prewar level by 1930, and was some three times higher by 1932. The country had seen the construction of over 1,500 new factories, some of which were the largest in Soviet industry. A hydroelectric power station was constructed on the Dnipro river, two giant combines were built in Kuznetsk and Magnitogorsk, and machine-building had developed rapidly. By 1932, this industrial branch accounted for about one-quarter of Soviet output as compared to less than 7 percent prior to the First World War. In some areas, none the less, the results were disappointing. The USSR had failed to meet targets in the important area of ferrous metallurgy and continued to import metal from abroad. In the coal industry, the output of 65 million tons was 10 million below the target. The oil industry fared better at first, but then suffered a lapse in the later years of the plan. National income rose by 59 percent, as compared to a projected 130 percent. The Soviet planners did not manage to achieve a significant rise in labor productivity, nor were they able to lower significantly the high cost price of production. Output in agriculture declined by 14 percent over the plan years, against a projected rise of 5 percent each year.

In the early 1930s the Soviet regime was still heavily reliant on the skills of foreign engineers, many of whom came voluntarily, thankful to escape the misery of the Great Depression. By 1931 there were about 5,000 foreign specialists in the USSR, about 40 percent of whom were Americans. The aim of the Soviet leadership was to develop a skilled homegrown workforce, but the process was difficult and lengthy. The period of the 1st Five-Year Plan saw a mass migration from the countryside to the towns, creating a new proletariat, but one that was largely unskilled. Most of these new workers were employed in heavy industry, which was the focal point of the plan. By 1933 the USSR had a workforce of about 23 million, more than double the figure of 1925–1926, at the peak of the NEP. About a quarter of the workers were employed in large factories, and initially there was a significant migration to the emerging factories in Soviet Asia. Women also began to enter the labor force in greater numbers than ever before, and comprised about 1 million industrial workers in the period 1929–1933. After 1929 the factories never shut down. An employee worked five days and then took a day off, in a rotational system. Each worker had his own workbook, with his performance noted in it. The graded wage system favored by Stalin was introduced in 1934.

The towns became grim and horribly overcrowded. By 1931 the USSR had eliminated unemployment and had begun to experience labor shortages. Accommodation was sparse, and generally several families would share an apartment and bathroom facilities, often growing up together. Family life became communal, often appearing like the transfer to the towns of a system familiar in the countryside, with the proviso that, in the villages, space was not at a premium. The collectivism of Soviet life was made more acute by the rapid industrialization. At first, it did not seem to matter. Though Soviet propaganda has created myths about the euphoria of the time, there is little reason to doubt the various accounts of the high spirits with which many workers approached the new era. They were building socialism, and moreover at a time when capitalism appeared to be on the verge of collapse. Though most people lived in harsh conditions, food was generally scarce, and the rules of the workplace became increasingly restrictive, many workers believed firmly that they were creating a better livelihood for their children, and that the Soviet Union would become the new utopia for workers. These beliefs were bolstered by official propaganda, and by films and plays, which played an important role in convincing a workforce with a peasant mentality that they were building a new future.

The centralized planning system continued with the 2nd Five-Year Plan of 1933–1937. Just as it was beginning, the 17th Party Congress – termed the Congress of Victors – was held. It followed a major purge of the Soviet Communist Party apparatus in 1933. That process was a bitter one for those involved. Many party members had no prior warning that they were to be singled out for attention, and little idea on what areas the accusations might focus. Generally the purges examined family background – whether the accused came from a bourgeois family, for example, or whether he himself had at one time been a kulak, or whether he had married in a church, or whether any family members possessed icons. The accused eventually were prevailed upon to confess their sins, just as Trotsky, Zinoviev, and Kamenev had done. The confessions were a familiar part of the later trials, and may have owed something to the Stalinist style, noted as early as Lenin's funeral, to endow public life with a quasi-religious element. By the time of the party congress, therefore, the party had been through three great trials: collectivization, with its elimination of the kulak stratum and the famine; the 1st Five-Year Plan in industry; and a fundamental purge of the party that removed some 800,000 members and replaced them with "clean" proletarians.

The period of the second plan saw a new emphasis on output, on exceeding work norms in the factories, and on raising individual labor productivity. The authorities were more ingenious than in the frantic period of the first plan. In early 1935, in the aviation industry, a movement called the *otlichniki* (literally: "the excellent workers") was born, of workers who met or exceeded state targets, with products of the highest quality. It was the forerunner of a movement that was to become much more famous. On August 31, 1935, a Donbas coal miner named Aleksey Stakhanov mined 102 tons of coal in a single seven-hour shift at the Tsentralnaya Irmino coal mine, thus exceeding the average work norm by fourteen times. His achievement sparked a series of record-breaking performances in the coal industry. By early September, Stakhanov had returned to the coalface to hew an unlikely 175 tons in a shift, before the totals became more surreal when another Donbas miner, Nikita Izotov, mined 240 tons of coal in one shift. The feats were immediately publicized in the local and all-Union press, and Stakhanov became a national hero. By November, the First All-Union Conference of Stakhanovites was held, and record-breaking became the norm for Soviet economic life.

Several points are worth noting about the beginning of the Stakhanov movement. The conditions in which Stakhanov set his record were artificial. He was relieved of all tasks other than to hew coal, while his comrades took up other aspects of his job. Raising the norms was considered progressive, but it occurred at the expense of the coal mine, as the miners simply worked available seams, neglecting safety problems. Further, record-breaking was not particularly popular among all members of the workforce, whose daily quota was now deemed inadequate. By January 1933, Soviet industry operated according to a system of labor days, namely the amount of time it should normally take to complete a given task. The Stakhanovites made a mockery of such norms and increased the requirements of labor days to levels that were simply unrealistic. The stress on shock work could not help but lower general quality control at the workplace. Factory managers began to cut corners to meet plans, break records, or compete with neighboring factories. They were rewarded for good results, but poor performances concomitantly raised suspicion. Why was the factory falling behind? Could it be that the manager was really a saboteur, perhaps in league with foreigners, and trying to undermine Soviet industry?

The Stakhanovite movement faded away, along with its creator, who reportedly became an alcoholic and died in obscurity in his late seventies, his feat forgotten. (In 1985, Gorbachev commemorated the 50th anniversary of the movement in a somewhat misguided effort to engender enthusiasm at the workplace once again and raise labor productivity.) Conditions in factories by the end of the decade, with war on the horizon, were much more severe than at the start of the 1st Five-Year Plan. Absenteeism became a criminal offence; and the workers, who earlier in the decade changed jobs on average three or four times per year, were not allowed to leave the factory without permission from the authorities. The working day became longer. Though the eight-hour workday officially remained in place, the working week was

Plate 4.1 Portrait of Stalin hanging on a building, 1936.
Image: Bettmann/CORBIS

extended to seven days without any rise in salaries. During the 2nd Five-Year Plan, the rate of industrial growth was substantially less than expected. In March 1939 the 18th Party Congress approved the 3rd Five-Year Plan (1938–1942), which envisaged the completion of "socialist construction" and a gradual transition to Communism. The plan proposed to accelerate industrialization in the eastern regions especially. However, the threat of war led to the prioritization of military goods, the production of which grew by almost 40 percent annually. By 1940 the military was using up about one-third of the state budget, and in the following year the plan was halted by the outbreak of war. (Plate 4.1)

The purges

Trials, including public ones, were a familiar occurrence from the earliest years of the Soviet state, and included an early instance with Socialist Revolutionaries in Moscow in 1922. However, the beginnings of the purges that reached a culmination point in 1937 can be traced in origin to the late 1920s, when several trials, both open and closed, took place. They included the Trial of the Industrial Party in late November to early December 1930, allegedly headed by Professor L. K. Ramzin. The party supposedly united groups of "wreckers" or "saboteurs" intent on disrupting Soviet industry. The leaders received death sentences, which were subsequently commuted to ten years' imprisonment. Most of the accused received pardons, and Ramzin was later the recipient of a Stalin Prize in 1943 for his inventions during wartime. A 1931 trial of Mensheviks focused on the noted theorist D. B. Ryazanov, who lost his place in the Communist Party for his past associations with the rival group. Lastly, in April 1933, there took place the trial of experts of the Metropolitan Vickers Company, six of whom were citizens of the United Kingdom. Once again the intent was to demonstrate acts of sabotage in Soviet industry – the firm had reportedly supplied faulty turbines. The British government intervened to ensure the release of the engineers, and the trial did not cause any long-term stoppages to Anglo-Soviet trade.

The 17th Party Congress appeared to signal the triumph of Stalin. His former enemies – several of whom were making a final appearance on the public stage, such as Zinoviev, Kamenev, Rykov, Tomsky, and Preobrazhensky – were now making speeches in praise of Stalin's outstanding personal characteristics. Stalin was reaching the level of a benevolent despot (at least according to the public image). The ten members of the Politburo comprised Stalin's closest associates, both old and new – Kaganovich, A. A. Zhdanov, Molotov, Voroshilov, Ordzhonikidze, Kirov, A. A. Andreev, S. V. Kosior, Kuibyshev, and Kalinin. The members of the important Secretariat were Stalin, Kaganovich, Zhdanov, and Kirov. Of these figures, Kirov was the most popular. Some analysts of this Congress have claimed that several delegates, tired of the excesses of Stalin, turned to Kirov with an appeal to lead the party. They note also that Kirov took their appeal directly to Stalin. It is also held that, at the time of the new elections to the Central Committee of the party, about 300 delegates voted against Stalin, but the Soviet leader ordered that all but three of these ballot papers be destroyed. Correspondingly, according to these same reports, Kirov received more votes than Stalin.

There is no hard evidence to these theories, but they are persuasive enough to contain at least partial truths. It would be surprising, given the scale of the suffering caused – particularly in the famine of 1932–1933, which had already become a state secret, as unmentionable as Lenin's Testament with its demand for Stalin's removal – if there were not some dissatisfaction with the route being taken. Yet this theory benefits from hindsight and the subsequent unprecedented measures taken by the Soviet leadership against Old Bolsheviks in particular. Already the country was pervaded by a general atmosphere of suspicion. How far this sentiment pervaded individual households, especially in the urban centers, is a moot point. There were no sociological surveys conducted to ascertain whether the citizens of Soviet towns lived in fear by early 1934. Further, the trumpeting by the regime of the foreign threats was continuous, the improved relations with the United States notwithstanding. For Stalin, the external enemy was a necessary facet of his power. He appeared in propaganda cartoons so frequently that the hidden enemy – be he a kulak, a supporter of Trotsky, or a spy working (most likely) for the British or Japanese governments – became a reality in the public mind. On the one hand was Stalin, defending the regime against the capitalist menace; and on the other were internal enemies, intent on subverting the socialist state and replacing it with a capitalist system.

Several signals of a storm brewing appeared after the 17th Party Congress. On July 10, Genrik Yagoda, a ruthless figure completely devoted to Stalin, was appointed as First People's Commissar of Internal Affairs. A new exchange of party cards was announced on August 20 to restore discipline in the party structure. Then, on December 1, 1934, there occurred the mysterious assassination of Kirov, who was shot in the party headquarters at the Smolny Institute in Leningrad by a demoted party functionary, Leonid Nikolayev, who had twice entered the building, evidently without raising any suspicions. Several scholars have published books on the assassination, and the consensus until recently appeared to be that, though the event proved convenient for Stalin, there is no conclusive evidence of his direct involvement. Nikolayev's diaries, revealed to the public only on December 1, 2009, suggest that the assassin acted alone, and out of revenge. Stalin, however, took extreme measures. He took a train to Leningrad the following day, along with several associates, and admonished the local NKVD for its lack of vigilance, even slapping the local commander across the face as a sign of his anger. Within hours of Kirov's death, Stalin personally introduced a new decree, "The Law of 1st December," which changed fundamentally the criminal code of the USSR. The decree, which was never formally approved by the Soviet government, demanded that within ten days new anti-terrorist measures had to be introduced. Prosecutors could question suspects in court without witnesses or defense lawyers, without appeals, and then order their execution immediately after a conviction. At the same time the NKVD quickly uncovered a Leningrad Center, and executed fourteen of its alleged members shortly after Kirov's death.

Further harsh measures were introduced in 1935. A new law declared that all family members of "enemies of the Motherland" were automatically guilty and all children over the age of 12 were liable to prosecution. Mass arrests of alleged Trotskyites and Zinovievites followed. In early January 1935, the regime implicated Zinoviev and Kamenev in the death of Kirov through a Trial of the Moscow Center, a contrived trial that encompassed nineteen people, including the two unfortunate former associates of Stalin. The victims were accused of forming an underground counter-revolutionary organization that intended to carry out terrorist acts, and which had also taken part in the assassination of Kirov. Zinoviev was sentenced to ten years in prison and Kamenev to five. The other defendants were also jailed for various lengths of time. In the spring of the same year, all works by Trotsky, Zinoviev, and Kamenev were taken out of Soviet libraries, and a new party purge began, ostensibly to ensure that no supporters of the former United Opposition remained within the ranks of the party. A society for Old Bolsheviks was abolished in May. By June, one could receive the death penalty for attempting to cross the Soviet border into Poland or the Baltic States. A bizarre Kremlin affair was uncovered in this same summer, in which government workers were accused of preparing to assassinate Stalin. Plainly conditions were in place for a major attack on alleged enemies of the regime.

A series of show trials followed, and these are often identified as the main "purges" of the 1930s. They remain one of the most discussed issues of the Soviet period inasmuch as, despite new archival evidence including Stalin's own letters to Molotov during this time, the motivation for such events is unclear. Some historians have argued that Stalin was paranoid; others have seen the show trials as an attempt to cover completely the traces of Stalin in his revolutionary phase, which might reveal his past as a bank robber or his secondary role in the Revolution. We have noted earlier that Stalin sought to create the image of a state surrounded by enemies. The revolutionary state required an outside force in order to justify harsh measures, or economic failures, or even for that matter opposition to Stalin's policies. The public spectacle of former Old Bolsheviks and reliable party figures confessing their sins in public, along with the fantastic crimes they had reportedly committed, has often been described as a form of public theater, with Vyshinsky the Prosecutor-General in the role of director, and Stalin behind the scenes monitoring – and sometimes watching – the trials. One can assert that the worst purges, the victims of which were arrested, sometimes executed, and sometimes removed to the Gulag, occurred behind the scenes. The sight of the black Maria outside an apartment building in the middle of the night was a signal that a new class enemy had been uncovered. Many of these victims simply vanished, and died virtually forgotten in the distant camp system of the Gulag. For the public, however, the confirmation that there were hardened enemies in their midst had to be constantly reaffirmed.

BOX 4.1

Reaction of Soviet citizens to the Terror

Did Soviet residents live in a perpetual state of terror during the 1930s? Historians have been divided on the issue. Given the lack of availability of Soviet archives for much of Soviet history, Western scholars had to resort to inspired guesswork to calculate the scale of the purges and their impact on the population. Robert Conquest's book *The Great Terror* remained for many years the standard text in the English language. In 1985, J. Arch Getty's *The Origins of the Great Purge* questioned some of Conquest's figures and argued that the purges were far from being the initiative of a single dictator, as Conquest had suggested. According to Getty, the chaotic conditions in the USSR in the 1930s did not allow for the planning of a systematic purge, while Stalin's subordinates had considerable leeway in their local domains. In a new edition of his book published in 1990, Conquest retorted that his statistics had in fact been underestimates, as newly opened Soviet archives now revealed. A group of social historians has also provided new insights into various aspects of Russian history, from the Revolution to the Great Purge, and encompassing the works of scholars such as Sheila Fitzpatrick (Fitzpatrick, 1996, 1999) and Lynne Viola (Viola, 1998). Much of their work has focused on grassroots life in a calculated attempt to steer clear of the "top-down" analyses of more traditional scholars. Robert Thurston has argued persuasively but controversially (Thurston, 1986, 1998) that Soviet citizens for the most part led relatively normal lives in the mid-1930s, and that the purges did not cause widespread fear among the population.

> The various reactions to arrest . . . suggest that general fear did not exist in the USSR at any time in the late 1930s. Usually, only those who were actually arrested came to understand that the innocent were being widely persecuted. People who remained at liberty often felt that some event in the backgrounds of the detained individuals justified their arrests. The sense that anyone could be next, the underpinning of theoretical systems of terror, rarely appears. If by the "Great Terror" we mean that many innocent people suffered at the hands of the state, that is an acceptable statement; to say that all, or probably even the majority, were terrorized is as unacceptable for the USSR in the 1930s as it is for Germany at the same time.
>
> (Thurston, 1986, p. 230)

However, in certain circles, as Thurston acknowledges, the purges were devastating – Old Bolsheviks, the army, the NKVD, and the elites of the national republics, perhaps the only group that could not be replaced adequately for at least a generation. The purges were proportionally more widespread in the non-Russian republics, but many of the consequences (mass executions of victims at burial sites well away from the main urban centers) remained secret until the late 1980s when a number of mass graves of NKVD victims were uncovered. One can also determine the regime's focus on certain sectors of the population at different times: Old Bolsheviks in 1936–1938; the military in 1937; the NKVD in 1938; and border populations in 1939–1941. Conquest notes that peasants made up a very high ratio of terror victims, just as they had in the earlier part of the decade. All this suggests perhaps a clearer purpose to the Terror than was ever apparent at the time. Interrogations invariably inculpated a vast number of people who had little or no knowledge of the crimes they were alleged to have committed.

Between August 19 and 24, 1936, the first show trial began in Moscow's House of Trade Unions, of an "Anti-Soviet United Association of the Trotskyite–Zinovievite Center". On trial were sixteen people, headed by Zinoviev and Kamenev (dragged from their prison cells yet again after being subjected to the harshest of regimens). Most of the others were second-rank Bolsheviks, clearly placed there in order to incriminate figures of the top rank. They included G. E. Yevdokimov, I. P. Bakayev, V. A. Ter-Baganyan, and others. All confessed to playing a role in the death of Kirov, to being in league with the exiled Trotsky, and to plotting against Stalin. Among the names that were liberally spilled around the courtroom as associates of the accused were Radek, Pyatakov, Sokolnikov, L. P. Serebryakov, and the three leaders of the Right Opposition: Bukharin, Rykov, and Tomsky. The last committed suicide two days after the trial ended, having few illusions of what was about to follow. The accused were all executed, thus ending the tragic careers of Zinoviev and Kamenev, whose families had been hounded but who were convinced until the very end that their former comrade, Stalin, would spare them. Following the trial, on September 30 (some sources state September 26), the police chief Yagoda was suddenly dismissed and replaced by an even harsher leader, N. I. Yezhov, the man who gave his name to this period of the purges known as the *Yezhovshchina* ("the time of Yezhov").

Yezhov was a party careerist with little formal education. Born in St Petersburg in 1895, he had been a factory worker in the famous Putilov works, and had served in the tsarist army on both the Western and the Northern Fronts. Having joined the Bolsheviks in 1917, he enlisted in the Red Army the following year. In the 1920s he attended party courses on Marxism-Leninism, which constituted his basic education. Subsequently he served the party in a number of positions in various parts of the country, from Semipalatinsk to Kazakhstan, where he played a leading role in the horrendous collectivization campaign that left up to one-third of the Kazakh peasants dead. His ruthlessness was noted, and in 1933 he was made chairman of a commission to supervise a major party purge. By 1934, Yezhov was a member of the party Central Committee, a member of the party's Organizational Bureau, and the Commission of Party Control (by February 1935 he had been appointed chairman of the latter). Yezhov was a committed follower of Stalin, utterly without scruples and apparently without a conscience. His rise to power had been rapid, given his relative obscurity. He took particular pleasure in the campaign against Zinoviev and Kamenev, and once in charge of the NKVD he began to fill the organization with sadists and criminal types. Yezhov often compiled the lists of people who were to be shot. His name will always be associated with the darkest days of the official purges, gaining him the title of the Iron Commissar.

Two other events coincided with this first show trial. These were a series of explosions at Russian coal mines in Kemerovo – the possibility that they were carried out by the authorities has to be considered – and a major purge of the NKVD apparatus, which was now claimed to be riddled with Trotskyists and other counter-revolutionaries. Mass arrests followed in the coal-mining and transport industries before the new trial, the "Trial of the Trotskyist Parallel Center," which took place between January 23 and 30, 1937. At this trial, seventeen people were accused of forming a counter-revolutionary center to carry out acts of sabotage. The accusations were plainly directed at the industrial leaders of the country, including Stalin's long-time associate Ordzhonikidze, but the major names among the seventeen accused were Pyatakov, Sokolnikov, and Radek. The existence of the center provided an explanation for the acts of sabotage but more conveniently for the unsatisfactory performance of the 2nd Five-Year Plan. Thirteen of the accused were given the death penalty, and all seventeen had confessed their responsibility. The NKVD derived confessions through typical tactics of interrogation, including deprivation of sleep, threats, blackmail, and torture. Pyatakov was executed on February 1. Sokolnikov and Radek received ten-year prison sentences and died in labor camps two years later.

In February–March 1937, the Plenum of the All-Union Communist Party approved a period of Terror against enemies of the regime, and over the next two years the repressions were conducted on a mass scale. Once again, the passage of time has not clarified the number of victims. Western historians are divided over the extent of the repressions within the Communist Party. J. Arch Getty calculates that there were about 180,000 victims within the party, while others place the figure at more than 1 million. In the party's Central Committee, note Russian historians V. I. Menkovsky and O. I. Yanovsky, ninety-eight out of 139 members were arrested; and the same fate befell 1,108 of the 1,966 delegates to the 17th Party Congress. The numbers imprisoned were vast – at least 3.5 million and possibly as many as 10 million; many became slave laborers on some of the huge Stalin projects in the White Sea and other regions. In the non-Russian republics, the extent of the purge was even greater than in Russia itself, and affected in particular the elite of society, from the Communist Party to the Academy of Sciences, high-level management, the universities, the writers' unions, and other cultural spheres. It has been estimated that one in every three families lost a member during this period. Stalin's associates each played their own role in the process. Beria was responsible for the purges in Georgia, Kaganovich was sent to the West Russian city of Smolensk, Malenkov took responsibility for Belarus and Armenia, and the troublesome Ukraine saw the appearance at various times of Molotov, Yezhov, and Khrushchev, who eventually became the party chief there in 1938.

In May 1937 the purge extended to the Red Army, with the arrest of several commanders, including M. N. Tukhachevsky, I. Ye. Yakir, and I. P. Uborevich. These trials were held in camera by military tribunal, and on June 11 the country's military leaders received death sentences for espionage and treachery. In the ensuing purge that reached every level of the Red Army, three of the five marshals (the highest army rank) and about 40,000 officers were removed. There is evidence that the Germans deliberately planted the rumor that Soviet military leaders collaborated with them. Then, on March 12–13, 1938 there took place the last great show trial, the Trial of the Anti-Soviet

Right Trotskyist Bloc, involving the remaining Old Bolsheviks who were accused of Kirov's murder, plots against Stalin, and industrial sabotage, thus encompassing all three of the previous major accusations. The twenty-one people included Bukharin, Rykov, Kh. G. Rakovsky, N. N. Krestinsky, and Yagoda (there is a certain satisfying justice to the appearance of the former secret police chief), and seventeen received the death sentence. Bukharin, who like his former comrades had earlier confessed his sins, was accused also of trying to assassinate Lenin and Stalin in 1918 in a bid to take power himself. He defiantly asserted his innocence at this trial, much to the disgruntlement of Vyshinsky. He remained in many respects the most likeable Bolshevik, leaving behind his young wife to cherish his memory.

The focal point of the purges was Trotsky, who had settled in Mexico after periods of asylum in Turkey, France, and Norway. In the last country, under pressure from the Soviet Union, he was eventually confined to house arrest. However, with the support of Mexican president Lazaro Cardenas, he moved there in 1937 and lived for a time at the home of the painter Diego Rivera. In 1938 he initiated the creation of the Fourth International, intended as a rival organization to the Comintern, which was dominated by Stalin's Soviet Union. Trotsky was a prolific writer, and among his works in exile was a savage indictment of Stalinism entitled *The Revolution Betrayed* (1936). In 1939, Trotsky took up residence in the Mexico City suburb of Coyoacan, by which time he was in poor health and believed his death to be imminent. He wrote his final Testament on February 27, 1940. However, his death was to be a violent one, conducted by a Spanish-born NKVD agent called Ramon Mercader, who had fought in the Spanish Civil War. He befriended Trotsky and, on a visit to his home on August 20, attacked him with an ice pick, injuring him severely. Trotsky was taken to hospital where he died the following day. Mercader received a twenty-year prison sentence, and having served his time moved to Cuba. In 1960 he moved to the Soviet Union (then led by Nikita Khrushchev) where he received the title Hero of the Soviet Union for the murder of Trotsky. Trotsky's writings remained banned in the USSR until the late 1980s and he was never officially rehabilitated, though the Gorbachev administration treated him sympathetically. However, it is rare to encounter contemporary Russian works that do not offer severe criticisms of his career.

As a result of the Terror, Soviet society was decapitated, deprived of its leaders. It also became increasingly dangerous to show initiative. People were reluctant to take on positions of responsibility in political or economic life. Many specialists and skilled workers had been removed. The party, the leading organization in society, was devastated. Its history could now be rewritten according to the gospel of Stalin, since no Old Bolsheviks from the revolutionary period remained alive. On December 8, 1938, Yezhov was removed from office, arrested, and replaced by Beria. The main figure in the Great Terror was also to become a victim, like his predecessor Yagoda. On February 4, 1940, Yezhov, who had been condemned for plotting against

Stalin and indulging in homosexual practices, was executed. As he had done with early collectivization, Stalin declared that some local party organizations had made mistakes during the Purge, despite its generally good results. Some 327,000 people were freed from the Gulag after the 18th Party Congress in 1939, including some prominent military leaders who would play crucial roles in the coming conflict with Germany. In this way Stalin managed to maintain an image of an honest and wise leader. Clearly, his personal authority increased because of the Terror. He had moreover successfully propagated the image of a Soviet state surrounded by enemies who had penetrated deep inside the Soviet hierarchy. The public was not too far from the period of civil war and foreign intervention. In 1938, Soviet troops were fighting with the Japanese on the Mongolian border.

In the 1930s there had also been significant achievements. It is always difficult to distinguish between the application of mass terror and the impression of a society in the course of construction of a new economy and new social life. In May 1935, for example, under the guidance of Kaganovich, there opened the Moscow metropolitan railroad, an extraordinary accomplishment with 6.8 miles of track and thirteen stations. It was officially called the Kaganovich Metro until 1955. A new Soviet Constitution was issued in draft form in June 1936 and was approved in its final version six months later. The Constitution declared the rights and freedoms of the population. Intended mainly for foreign consumption, it propagated the view of a democratic society at the first stage of Communism. The gap between the rights of people on paper and in reality could hardly have been wider, and the Constitution appeared at the height of the repressions. Similarly, for all the economic changes in the country, the system overall was inefficient and exploitative. Labor productivity remained much lower than in capitalist countries, and arguably the collective farm system hardly worked at all.

Despite the purges, the size of the Communist Party continued to increase, affording the possibility of dramatic career rises for those members fortunate enough to avoid the purges. Between 1930 and the beginning of 1941, the party almost doubled in size, reaching 3.8 million by the latter date. It could also count on the support of over 5 million members of the Komsomol, the party's youth movement, and 27 million members of the trade union movement, which was also under tight party supervision. The party pervaded every area of Soviet life to some extent by the late 1930s. It had control over life and death, over employment, over education, over thought and culture. The ideological aspect of the Bolshevik Revolution had been shelved after 1917, but it was arguably completed under Stalin. However, despite official rhetoric, the Soviet achievement to date had been less to establish a Marxist regime than to establish a personal dictatorship, in the name of the proletariat, and one that was attaining unprecedented heights for its toll of civilian lives. The vast majority of those purged were innocent of any crime, and many would be rehabilitated under Khrushchev and Gorbachev. (Plate 4.2)

Plate 4.2 Nikolay Bukharin, President of the Communist International, in 1929. He would be the last of the major victims of Stalin's purges.
Image: Bettmann/CORBIS

Socialist Realism begins

In April 1932 the authorities dissolved all existing writers' associations, replacing them with a single organization, the Union of Writers of the USSR, which held its first congress in August 1934. The chairman of the new union was Maksim Gorky (the pseudonym of Aleksey Maksimovich Peshkov), a 68-year-old native of Nizhny Novgorod who had earlier been one of the Bolsheviks' fiercest critics but became a close associate of Stalin. The move heralded the beginning of an official cultural policy, that of Socialist Realism. Henceforth, Socialist Realism became mandatory for Soviet writers and artists. According to the official statutes, Socialist Realism was "the fundamental method of Soviet creative literature and literary criticism." It demanded from the artist a "truthful, historically concrete depiction of reality in its revolutionary development." The idea was that all forms of culture should reflect Soviet life. Critical realism, the term used to describe the work of the past, had outlived its usefulness. According to Gorky, who presented the report to the First Congress of Soviet Writers, "this form of realism has never served and cannot serve to educate a socialist personality. It never affirmed anything and at worst, it returned to affirm the very things that it had criticized." Gorky was one of the pioneers of Socialist Realism and one of its accepted practitioners. Others were Vladimir Mayakovsky, Mikhail Sholokhov, and Aleksandr Fadeyev. In other fields, the movement's representatives were film directors such as Sergey Eisenstein and Vsevolod Pudovkin, and composers such as Dmitry Shostakovich and Sergey Prokofiyev. There followed writers such as Nikolay Ostrovsky and Aleksandr Tvardovsky. The ideological state had thus entered a new era – an ideological culture that was to depict the progress of the state in a non-critical manner.

BOX 4.2

....

Vladimir Mayakovsky (1893–1930)

Born on July 19, 1893 in Baghdati, Georgia, Vladimir Mayakovsky was one of the leading Russian poets of the Revolution era. At an early age he became a Marxist devotee and joined the Russian Social Democratic Workers' Party. He began writing poetry while imprisoned in the Butyrka prison in 1909. After his release, he joined the Russian Futurists, a group that advocated the freeing of the arts from academic traditions. His first significant Futurist publication, written in 1912, was called *A Slap in the Face of Public Taste*. In 1915 he completed his first major poem, *A Cloud in Trousers*, which included themes of love and revolution. He also produced pro-Bolshevik propaganda for the Russian Telegraph Agency (ROSTA) after being inspired by the October Revolution. In 1924 he became renowned throughout Russia for composing an elegy on the death of Lenin. Initially he was one of the few cultural figures allowed to travel freely, but this privilege was soon taken away as his work began to be accused of being non-proletarian and anti-Soviet. Mayakovsky gradually became more alienated and disillusioned. His last two satirical plays, *The Bedbug* (1928) and *The Bathhouse* (1930), criticized the increasingly bureaucratic nature of the Stalinist regime. On April 14, 1930, he committed suicide.

There were some distinct features of Socialist Realism. It was divided into two basic concepts – *narodnost'* and *partiynost'*. The former maintained that literature must represent the common worker, and be written in simple, comprehensible language without stylistic experiments or the avant-garde devices that had been used by writers in the 1920s. There was also a strong element of chauvinism in the way Soviet characters were to be depicted according to this method. Writers were to fashion them as upright and honest, self-confident, whereas foreigners were to be devious, miserable, and self-seeking. In practice, they were often outright villains. The second concept, *partiynost'*, demanded that writers should not vary from the official party line, while maintaining an air of optimism. Writers in short had to work on behalf of the Soviet regime. Creativity and experiment in literature and art were ended. Stalinist society, officially, had reached a stage of universal harmony with no internal conflict. If the novels were to portray evil, then one could be certain that it was represented in the figure of the foreign capitalist, usually American or British. The regime was specific about the need to end "bourgeois formalism" in literature, whereby authors could take liberties with writing techniques. Added to the characteristics of Socialist Realism was the quest for hero figures depicting the revolutionary period. Literature, in short, had become a form of state propaganda. This became evident in some of the earliest works of Socialist Realism, devoted to socialist construction and the five-year plans, such as Mikhail Zoshchenko's *Istoriya odnoy zhizni* (*History of One Life*, 1935) about the building of the White Sea–Baltic Canal and Ilya Ehrenburg's *Den' vtoroy* (*The Second Day*, also 1935). Others wrote novels stressing the need for a strong military defense, such as Petr Pavlenko's *Na vostoke* (*In the East*, 1937).

Architecture and art also reflected the great movements of the 1930s, and represented the way the USSR liked to present itself to the outside world. The yearning for grandiose buildings was a feature of the Stalinist system (it was also the case in Nazi Germany), as though the dictator liked to provide an image of greatness through size. At the same time, the buildings reverted to classical and neo-classical forms, from schools, palaces of culture, railway stations and stadiums. The Moscow Metro was perhaps the supreme example of this form of Socialist Realist architecture. It coincided with a general plan for the reconstruction of the city of Moscow, which was approved by the party's Central Committee in 1935. Sculpture became very important in Soviet architecture. Along with statues of Lenin and Stalin, one could also find the work of Vera Mukhina, the proletarian man and the collective farm woman standing defiantly together with hammer and sickle. The sculpture was the highlight of the Soviet Pavilion at the 1937 international exhibition in Paris, and made Mukhina the most celebrated sculptor in the Soviet Union. Such monuments would become even more typical when war memorials were created after the Second World War. In general their main features were hugeness and the representation of the Soviet worker and peasant as hero figures. Stalin himself was the key figure both in architecture and in art. In the latter, his pronouncements delineated the future path of Soviet art in the 1930s.

BOX 4.3
....
Vera Mukhina (1889–1953)

The greatest sculptor of the Soviet Union, Vera Mukhina was born in Riga to a merchant family on July 1, 1889. In 1912, she traveled to Paris and attended the art school Académie de la Grande Chaumière. Her style was imbued with captivating propaganda, and she eventually became one of the leading and most influential Soviet artists. Her most notable

Box 4.3 continued

and celebrated sculpture was the 24-meter (79-foot), 75-ton monument called *Worker and Kolkhoz Woman* (1937), made of sixty-five separate stainless-steel pieces. It was a glorification of the Communist ideology and the triumphs of workers. Her works prior to 1937 included the lesser-known *The Wind* (1926–1927) and *A Woman's Torso* (1927). Portraits were also an enduring interest for Mukhina, and consisted mainly of her husband and war heroes such as B. A. Yusupov and I. L. Khizhnyak (1942). A monument of Maksim Gorky originally intended for Moscow was stationed instead in the city of Gorky (now Nizhny Novgorod). Mukhina died in Moscow on October 6, 1953.

Soviet art was also to be harnessed as an ideological weapon. Several Soviet leaders became involved in ascertaining the intellectual roots of Socialist Realist art, including both Stalin and Voroshilov. Between 1937 and 1940, Soviet publications included books about the pronouncements on art of Marx, Engels, Lenin, and Gorky. The chief arbiter of Soviet art, however, was Stalin himself. Perhaps more than other cultural genres, art was to be used to produce paintings that the Soviet people could easily understand. Practically every painting was commissioned on themes developed by committees and approved by the party leadership. Artists such as Vasily Yefanov (1900–1978) and Aleksandr Moravov (1878–1951) focused on subjects such as Stalin greeting a delegate to a Kremlin conference and recruits being called up for service in the Red Army. The cult of Stalin was a major focus for artists and for Soviet propaganda. Stalin had usurped Lenin in the role of a father figure of the Soviet people, curiously detached from the other party members, in spite of the upheavals of the 1930s. If Soviet residents, particularly peasants or inmates of the Gulag, felt a sense of betrayal, quite often it was directed against the Communist Party rather than against Stalin (similarly, protests in Germany during the difficult times of the 1930s centered on the Nazi Party rather than on Hitler personally). The Stalin cult had not reached a peak, but it had grown considerably since its inception on Stalin's 50th birthday in December 1929. Soviet artists and sculptors played an important role in cultivating this image.

BOX 4.4

Aleksandr Moravov (1878–1951)

Aleksandr Moravov was a leading representative of Socialist Realism. He was born on December 20, 1878. He studied at the Moscow College of Arts, Sculpture and Architecture from 1897 to 1902. Initially he was part of the *Peredvizhniki* (the Russian school of Realist painters) movement, whose members were made up of realist artists who often critically depicted many facets of social life. With the increasing demand for art to be more accessible and appreciated by the masses and in opposition to the

▶

Box 4.4 continued

avant-garde style, the Association of Artists of Revolutionary Russia (AKhRR) was formed in 1927. Membership of AKhRR included those who were already established artists prior to the October Revolution in 1917, Moravov among them. He produced paintings such as *Portrait of Leo Tolstoy* (1909), *The Ancient Hall* (1913), *Haymakers* (1915), and *Meeting of the Village Poor Committee* (1920). As representatives of Communist ideals in the arts, they laid the foundations for the Socialist Realism style that succeeded it. Moravov was known for his modern pictorial culture – his paintings contained coarse texture and intense colors. They were also noted for traditional themes and motifs pertaining to peasant life, in accordance with the artistic demands at the time, such as *Counting Up the Labor Days* (1939). He received the title of honored artist of the Russian Soviet Federative Socialist Republic (RSFSR) in 1946.

Foreign policy in the 1930s

In January 1933, Hitler came to power in Germany, which had been the USSR's closest partner in the early postwar years. For the Soviet Union, though the immediate danger may not have been apparent – the Weimar regime, after all, had seen several chancellors come and go between 1930 and 1932 – it became plain that the earlier foreign policy would no longer guarantee safety. Britain and China were perceived as hostile powers. Germany and Italy were natural allies. Poland had long been hostile. In the Far East, Imperial Japan had invaded Manchuria and established a puppet state in 1931. The Japanese virtually controlled the government. And now Germany, the other outsider in international politics, was under the Nazi leader Adolf Hitler. By 1934 the situation in Germany had become clearer. The SA brownshirts had been purged by the summer in what was known as the Night of the Long Knives. Henceforth, the elite black-shirted SS made up the personal bodyguard of Hitler, who formed a working alliance with the German army, the Wehrmacht. In Rome, in 1933, Britain, Germany, France, and Italy signed a pact that once again seemed to isolate the USSR.

In late 1933 two important powers recognized the Soviet Union. On November 16, diplomatic relations were restored with the United States following the visit of Maksim Litvinov to Washington; and, on December 12, China and the USSR renewed relations in a move to forestall further Japanese aggression in China. Conversely, military cooperation with Germany, which had developed since the Treaty of Rapallo, came to an abrupt end. The USSR's foreign-policy experts, Molotov and Litvinov, both declared that Nazi Germany posed an acute threat to the security of the Soviet Union. At the 17th Party Congress, Soviet leaders discussed the coming of a new war and advocated the adoption of a policy of collective security. Their main hopes lay with France, as long as Foreign Minister Louis Barthou remained in office.

Barthou had in mind an "Eastern Pact" as a form of collective security in Eastern Europe, the basis of which would be a Franco-Soviet treaty. At the same time, France also invited the USSR to join the League of Nations. However, the situation became less clear when Barthou died on October 9, 1934 under suspicious circumstances. Pierre Laval, his successor as foreign minister, was less disposed to an Eastern Pact and preferred to improve relations with Germany. In addition, both the United States and Britain had opposed this idea.

None the less, France was the main sponsor of the USSR's entry into the League of Nations, a move that ended its international isolation and made Stalin a major player in European politics. Thirty states signed the invitation to the Soviet Union, and three nations opposed it (Portugal, Holland, and Switzerland); and in the period 1934–1939 the USSR took part in the League and began to support a program of collective security, i.e. for forming a defensive alliance against the aggressor states, which, as far as the Soviet Union was concerned, were Germany and Japan. On May 2, 1935, France and the USSR signed a defensive treaty, which noted that the two countries should consult with each other and render mutual aid in the event of one being attacked by a third power. Two weeks later, a treaty of mutual aid was signed in Prague between the USSR and Czechoslovakia. According to this, if a third power attacked Czechoslovakia, the Soviet Union would come to its aid, with the proviso that France would make the first move. As there was no border at that time between the USSR and Czechoslovakia (and Poland was firmly opposed to allowing the Red Army passage through its territory), Stalin's obligations were minimal.

In 1934 the Soviet Union also established diplomatic relations with a number of countries in Central Europe, such as Czechoslovakia, Hungary, Bulgaria and Romania. In the spring of 1935, after the sale of the Chinese Eastern Railway to the puppet government of Manchuria, differences were buried with Japan, and a formal treaty was signed on March 23. For the Soviet Union, it appeared that, for every step it made toward consolidating a defensive security system, it was undermined by some act of aggression in Europe. The role of Britain and France, the formal leaders on the European continent, also appeared very ambiguous to the suspicious Stalin. He was positive that the real goal of these powers was to use a policy of appeasement toward Germany and Italy in order to foment a war between Germany and the USSR. The Western democracies seemed prepared to tolerate acts of aggression by the authoritarian states as long as the actions did not lead to a major war.

Thus, early in October 1935, the Italian army advanced into Ethiopia, and the League of Nations agreed only to the imposition of sanctions, which were never very effective. In March 1936, German troops marched into the demilitarized zone of the Rhineland, with instructions to retreat if the French army intervened. In this same period, Tukhachevsky provided a report about the need to modernize the Red Army in light of the new German threat. Given the weakness of the League of Nations, the USSR was prepared to advance collective security by broadening its support for political movements across Europe in the form of "united" or "popular fronts." The mechanism for this policy was the international Communist movement, and specifically the 7th Congress of the Comintern, which was held from July 25 to August 25, 1935 in Moscow. Sixty-five Communist parties were represented at the congress, which had decided the previous year to re-examine the operations of the Comintern's leading organs. Present at the Congress from the Soviet side were Stalin, Andrey Zhdanov, and Dmitry Manuilsky, a former First Party Secretary of Soviet Ukraine and Secretary of the Comintern's executive committee in the period 1928–1943.

The main speaker, however, was the Bulgarian Communist leader, Georgi Dimitrov (1882–1949), who declared that the main aim of Fascism was the destruction of the Soviet Union. In the face of this dire threat, Communists alone lacked sufficient forces, and therefore it was necessary to form a working alliance with the Social Democratic parties. Stalin (and for that matter his predecessor Lenin) would have regarded this dramatic suggestion as anathema in an earlier period. Now it was a time for healing the differences within the working class to take into account those with more moderate views. Simultaneously, the Social Democrats had to be persuaded to part company with their bourgeois allies and act with the Communists. The latter would also work to cooperate with the international trade union movement. Though the change of policy was radical, the Comintern agreed to be bound to an official policy of "democratic centralism." There was no question, however, of the USSR relinquishing control over the movement. Ironically, at the moment when it appeared that the Soviet leadership might start to cooperate with socialists across Europe, Stalin was about to embark on a purge of Old Bolsheviks in Moscow and other centers. To some extent, therefore, the new policy was a façade, but it was a movement that appeared quite convincing at first.

Popular Fronts

The initial manifestation of united fronts was in Spain, where a fragile Popular Front government was elected, and was soon in a bitter struggle with rebels led by the Spanish army, and in particular by the Morocco-based army leader General Francisco Franco. In July, full-scale civil war broke out in Spain. France and Britain proposed a non-intervention agreement, which all countries backed, but almost at once Mussolini violated the agreement and began providing military aid to Franco. Hitler soon joined in, using Spain as a training ground for the Luftwaffe. The two dictators had much in common with Franco. There was no immediate reaction from Stalin, who appears to have been making an assessment of the ability of the Spanish Republic to defend itself. On October 23, 1936, Ivan M. Maysky, the Soviet ambassador to Britain, protested at German–Italian aid to the Spanish rebels, and declared that the USSR no longer considered itself tied to the policy of non-interference. Soviet military advisors were dispatched to Spain, along with weapons such as tanks and guns.

Stalin's aid to Spain was limited in several respects. The USSR intervened officially through the Comintern rather than as an individual state. Though the NKVD sent substantial forces to Spain, their main role appears to have been to carry out ruthless purges of anarchists and Trotskyists, thus contravening the principles of a united front. Fighting was conducted through International Brigades (which did not include Soviet volunteers), and often these brigades were hopelessly inept at military strategy. The population regarded the republican side as anti-clerical and anti-property, and thus the two powerful forces of the church and the landowner were behind the rebels. There is some question as to Stalin's motives and long-term goals. A socialist Spain was not a priority and may not even have been desirable. What was important and useful was to ensure that the war dragged on as long as possible, thereby occupying Hitler and Mussolini and allowing the Soviet Union a breathing space during a period of domestic upheaval. And yet intervention in Spain – in contrast to the hapless policies of the French and the British – was a significant propaganda boost to the Stalin regime. Only the USSR had made a stand against the Fascist aggressors. Those who fought in Spain had different views of the Soviet role, and especially of the NKVD's ruthlessness, but to the outside world the policy of a united front appeared to have been upheld.

In the same period, the fall of 1936, the build-up of forces against the USSR appeared ominous. A formal Axis, or military–political union, between Italy and Germany was concluded on October 25, 1936 in Berlin, dividing up the spheres of interest of the two states. In November, Germany and Japan concluded an Anti-Comintern Pact, which included a secret protocol that was clearly directed against the Soviet Union. Italy was to join the pact later. In the period that followed, the USSR had little impact on Germany's revisions of the Treaty of Versailles. In March 1937, for example, the Soviet leaders protested at the German–Austrian *Anschluss*. During the Sudentenland crisis of September 1938, the Soviet Union was not permitted to take part in the agreement signed at Munich between Germany, Italy, France, and Britain. On October 2, the USSR again protested and laid the blame on France for failing to fulfill its commitments to Czechoslovakia. Soviet sources maintain that the USSR used Klement Gottwald as an intermediary and informed President Eduard Benes that the Soviets would come to the aid of the Czechs provided that the Prague government approach Moscow first with a request for aid. It seems very unlikely that Stalin would have committed himself to such a move. The victory of Franco in the Spanish Civil War by the spring of 1939 further undermined the USSR's position, though Franco's demands on the German Reich proved too much for Hitler, and thus Spain did not join the Axis.

Stalin's chief worry in this tumultuous period was that the USSR would be involved in a two-front war against Germany and Japan. By the summer of 1937, the Soviet leadership had begun to put pressure on the Chinese Communists to join forces with the Kuomintang in a common struggle against the further encroachments of Japan. On August 21, 1937, the USSR and China signed a Non-Aggression Treaty for five years, and followed this up with military technology and credits. Soviet military specialists were sent to China to provide advice to the government, which had to be moved several times as the Japanese approached. Meanwhile the Chinese Communists mounted guerrilla warfare against the Japanese in north China. In 1938 skirmishes between Soviet and Japanese troops broke out near Vladivostok, on the Soviet border with Manchuria and Korea. The fighting lasted for two weeks. Between May 11 and August 31, 1939, armed conflict broke out around Khalkin-Gol, in which Soviet and Mongolian forces successfully repelled Japanese attacks. Among the Soviet commanders who distinguished themselves was Georgy Zhukov, one of the few military leaders of note to have survived the purges of 1937.

Toward the Nazi–Soviet Pact

After the Munich Treaty, Europe enjoyed a brief and illusory interlude of peace that lasted for almost six months. In mid-March 1939, however, German troops incited demands of autonomy from the Slovaks, and intervened in the republic once again, occupying the remaining territories. The far-eastern region of Transcarpathia at first established a weak independent state, but Hitler allowed Hungary to occupy the territory in March 1939. Hitler also added a further revision to the Versailles Treaty by forcing the Lithuanians to cede Memel, the German enclave on the west coast. Meanwhile Britain and France decided to offer a guarantee to Poland, promising aid to preserve its independence. Similar guarantees were also extended to Romania, Greece, and Turkey. The Polish question was clearly at the top of Hitler's agenda: the need for a corridor to East Prussia, and the desire to regain as a German city the important port of Danzig, with its predominantly German population. Britain and France thus decided to hold talks with the Soviet Union in March, though the discussions dragged on inconclusively into August. Stalin's goal was for a defensive alliance whereby the states would come to each other's aid in the event of aggression against one of the three or against any of the East European states bordering the USSR, and located between the Baltic and Black Seas.

Because there was no border between the Soviet Union and Germany, it was imperative that Stalin should come to some agreement with Poland, so that the Red Army would be permitted to cross into Polish territory in the event of further acts of aggression by Hitler. The Polish government understandably was reluctant to allow this, particularly having been the subject of hostile and even violent propaganda from the Soviet regime for a number of years. To Stalin, the British and the French were typically duplicitous and likely had no real intention of coming to an agreement with the Soviet Union. His main fear was that the Western democracies would be quite content to see a war of attrition break out between the two dictatorships. Consequently he began to seek an alternative policy, one that would stave off war for a few years and permit the Soviet Union time to build up and modernize its military forces. The only alternative was to come to some kind of agreement with his ideological enemy, Hitler. The first step toward this new policy was the removal of the Jewish Foreign Minister Litvinov and his replacement by Molotov. Litvinov had favored an agreement with the British, whereas Molotov wasted little time in making contact with the Germans.

On August 19, 1939, the Soviet Union and Nazi Germany signed a trade agreement, a clear sign that a policy switch was in the offing. Evidently on his own initiative, Joachim von Ribbentrop, the German Foreign Minister and outspoken Anglophobe, flew to Moscow on August 23 and signed a Non-Aggression Treaty with Molotov, as Stalin hovered in the background. This treaty was shocking enough – at least to many international Communists – but it was followed by a secret protocol that divided Eastern Europe into spheres of interest between the two powers. In particular, Poland was to be divided more or less in half, along the boundary of the Vistula, San, and Narew rivers. Germany was to be recognized as the principal power in Lithuania, and the USSR in Estonia and Latvia. The USSR's special interest in regaining the territory of Bessarabia from Romania was also recognized. The Protocol was one of the most cynical pieces of land-grabbing of the century. It suggested that Stalin was happy to play the game of Great Power politics favored by Hitler. The notion that he was simply buying time does not stand up to close analysis. True, he was acquiring a defensive buffer zone, and retaking territories that had been part of the Russian Empire; but some lands, such as Northern Bukovyna, had no history of Russian rule. After the August 23 meeting, the two sides toasted each other, and Stalin offered a toast to Hitler. For the immediate future, the propaganda campaigns of each side against the other would also cease.

For world Communists, the Nazi–Soviet Pact was a puzzling and even bewildering affair. Overnight the enemies had become friends. It was no longer possible to perceive the world in black and white. Some Communists became disillusioned; others made the best of it, arguing that it was a temporary solution to the problem of German expansionism. On September 1, Germany invaded Poland and quickly overwhelmed the Polish army. Stalin waited for sixteen days before ordering the Red Army to cross the border. Officially there was no invasion. Soviet propaganda stressed that the Polish government had fallen, and therefore it was incumbent upon the USSR to take measures to protect the "blood brother" Ukrainian and Belarusian population. Oddly nothing was said about the need to protect the large Jewish population, perhaps in deference to the Germans. The statements also raised the question: From what did the population need protecting? As the Red Army crossed the border, there were no fellow Communists to greet the "liberators." The Comintern had dissolved the Communist parties of Western Ukraine and Western Belarus, along with their mother organization, the Communist Party of Poland, in July 1938 on the grounds that Trotskyites had penetrated them. Their leaders had been summoned to Moscow and executed. On September 22, after some initial confusion, the dividing line between the Wehrmacht and the Red Army was demarcated, and the two armies held a joint parade of triumph in the city of Brest (subsequently an event that was something of an embarrassment to the Soviet side). General Heinz Guderian was present, along with the Soviet commander, Semyon Krivoshein.

The Soviet takeover of these territories is quite instructive regarding the thinking of the Soviet authorities in the fall of 1939. For one thing, they were tentative. Britain and France had guaranteed the integrity of the Polish state, and thus it was considered important to stress to the world that this state no longer existed. In reality part of the Polish army was still fighting. Second, the Soviet leaders went through a show of democratic procedure, convoking assemblies in Lviv in Western Ukraine and Bialystok in Western Belarus to decide the future of these territories. Meanwhile Polish officials were quickly rounded up and sent eastward to Soviet labor camps. Poles in general were disenfranchised prior to the elections, which were held on October 22, 1939. Red Army soldiers were permitted to vote and even to stand as candidates in the elections. Because there were not enough local Communists to run as candidates, a group sympathetic to the USSR was set up, and ran as the only official body tolerated in the elections. Ukrainians in Western Ukraine were at least nationally conscious and had maintained cultural institutions throughout a difficult period of Polish rule. Belarusians had no conception of forming their own state or joining their territory to the Belarusian SSR.

The Soviet authorities took no chances with the organization of the elections. First, provisional administrations were formed in Western Ukraine and Western Belarus. In the latter region, every single step of the process was ordered by P. K. Ponomarenko, the leader of the Communist Party of Belarus, a man who had carried out Stalinist purges with brutality in this republic. On October 4, 1939, the party was to convoke an assembly of representatives of the various provisional administrations and inform them of the decisions of the all-Union party. Belarusian party leaders were given various tasks, including organizing elections to the People's Assembly of Western Belarus. They also were ordered to work out all the decisions of this assembly beforehand, such as the approval of the expropriation of landed estates, joining the BSSR, nationalizing banks, and other measures. All the leaders of the regions were selected before the assembly met, and a delegation of fifty people from Soviet Belarus was to visit the assembly in the town of Bialystok – doubtless to convince its handpicked members of the benefits of joining the USSR. Thus nothing was left to chance, and anything that happened spontaneously could only be attributed to an unforeseen accident. In reality, there were unlikely to be any problems because of the thoroughness of the takeover of the new territories.

Before the elections took place, on September 23, 1939, the USSR and its new ally revised the Non-Aggression Pact with a "Treaty of Friendship and Borders." The Soviet Union was now given hegemony over all three Baltic States, while Germany received territory around the city of Warsaw, signifying that it possessed a slightly larger area of Poland than did the USSR. Soon Molotov made an agreement with Lithuania, whereby the city of Wilno (Vilnius), in which several nations and ethnic groups had deep cultural roots – including Jews, Poles, Belarusians, and Lithuanians – along with the surrounding area, was transferred to Lithuania. The elections in the former Eastern Poland followed the Soviet ritual of very high turn-out and almost unanimous support for the "people's candidate," followed by the calling of the People's Assemblies, which in turn petitioned the USSR Supreme Soviet for these territories to be added to the Soviet Union, as part of the Ukrainian and Belarusian Soviet republics. At an Extraordinary Session of the USSR Supreme Soviet from October 31 to November 2, 1939, the process of annexation was completed. The Soviet Union had expanded westward, gained more than 10 million people, and at remarkably little cost. However, the incorporation of Western Ukraine paradoxically completed the inclusion of most ethnic Ukrainian territories in one republic and increased considerably nationalist sentiment.

In late September and early October 1939, the Soviet Union forced all three Baltic States to sign agreements on mutual aid, which allowed the establishment of Soviet military bases on their territory. The arrangement was clearly a prelude to outright annexation of the three republics, which had been independent during the interwar period. A similar request was made of Finland, along with the demand for border territories, but the Finns refused. On November 26, war broke out with Finland. In his memoirs, Khrushchev maintained that the Soviet Union had no legal claim to Finnish territory (Finland had been part of the Russian Empire for over a century), but it had a moral right to protect itself. The attack on Finland led the League of Nations to expel the Soviet Union from membership on December 14, and Stalin's state became an international pariah. World opinion was on the side of the Finns in this David-and-Goliath struggle. Moreover, the Red Army, under the command of the hapless Kliment Voroshilov, was neither equipped nor prepared for a winter campaign, and the first phase of the war, from November 1939 to February 10, 1940, was disastrous for the Soviet forces. The Red Army was beaten back repeatedly at the Mannerheim Line and at the Karelian Isthmus, and suffered disproportionately high losses. On January 7, Semen Timoshenko replaced the ineffective Voroshilov, and a new offensive was planned with massive artillery strength and tanks. The Red Air Force gained control of the skies.

Not only had the war illuminated some of the failings of the Red Army, but also the possibility of a new international coalition against the USSR seemed likely to the Soviet leadership. It was thus essential to bring the Finnish war to an end as rapidly as possible. The new attack on the Mannerheim Line (the main defensive line in Southern Finland) occurred on a bitterly cold day, February 11, 1940, and the overwhelming force of the Red Army quickly broached the Finnish defenses. By March the city of Vyborg had fallen into Soviet hands; and, on March 4, General C. G. E. Mannerheim, the commander-in-chief of the Finnish armed forces, told his government that further resistance was pointless. By March 7, the two sides had entered an armistice, with Sweden acting as the mediator, and a peace agreement was signed on March 12, 1940. As a result, the Soviet border was pushed northward ninety-three miles into formerly Finnish territory, and the Hanko naval base was transferred to the Soviet Union for a thirty-year period. The Karelian Isthmus, including the town of Vyborg and portions of the Rybachi and Sredny peninsulas, also became part of the USSR. Stalin gained a vital defensive zone to prepare for a coming war, but at a great price. Red Army losses were around 127,000 dead and wounded, including 6,000 officers and commanders, and about six times the number of Finnish losses. Finland barely retained its independence but had fought valiantly. Moreover, it now sought the first opportunity to gain revenge on the USSR for its unprovoked attack.

The three Baltic States provided an easier target. Between June 14 and 16, the USSR sent diplomatic notes to Latvia, Estonia, and Lithuania, accusing them of violating the agreement on mutual cooperation, and of advocating anti-Soviet positions. Almost immediately afterward, the Red Army occupied the small countries, and by June 21 all three had Soviet governments installed. By July 21, Estonia, Latvia, and Lithuania became Soviet Socialist Republics, thus bringing to a premature end the brief period of independence. The United States refused to recognize these actions. Also on Stalin's list for annexation by the USSR were Bessarabia and the northern region of Bukovyna, both of which became part of Romania in 1918. The Soviet Union simply sent a curt note to the Romanian government on June 28, 1940, requesting the return of Bessarabia (thus equating directly the territory of the former Russian Empire with that of the Soviet Union, which was revealing about Stalin's thinking), and linking it with Bukovyna. The only claim to the latter – and a very flimsy one at that – was that its population was linked to Ukraine through language and national composition. In fact the population of Bukovyna was multinational, consisting of Jews, Romanians, Ukrainians, and other groups. The Romanian government was in no position to resist Soviet demands, and vacated these territories; the Red Army crossed the border and occupied the main towns of Chernivtsi in the north, Kishinev, the main city in Bessarabia, and Akkerman and Izmail in the south.

On August 2, 1940, without any resort to Soviet-style elections as in the annexed Polish territories, the USSR proclaimed the formation of the Moldavian SSR, which was made up of the former Moldavian Autonomous Republic and the Moldavian parts of Bessarabia. Northern Bukovyna and the southern Akkerman–Izmail region were appended to Soviet Ukraine. Molotov was delighted with this accomplishment – in a speech to the Supreme Soviet, he pointed out that the agreement with Germany had brought great benefits to the USSR. Within one year, the Soviet population had risen by 23 million people, at very little cost, other than the war against Finland (Karelia became the Karelo-Finnish Republic). The aggressive intentions of the USSR were a source of concern to Hitler. Stalin had been slow to take advantage of the Nazi–Soviet Pact, but within a year had gained more than the Germans. The indigenous population of most of these regions was removed, and Soviet officials were dispatched from neighboring regions. In Western Ukraine, for example, the local party organizations were staffed with leaders from Eastern Ukraine. In Western Belarus, measures were quickly taken against the Poles, and the NKVD conducted a series of purges against various sectors of the population.

Generally, Soviet policy upon taking over new regions was to gain favor with the titular group of the new republic by pushing its members into leadership positions, opening schools and other institutions in the native language, and retaining a fairly tolerant attitude toward local political parties and churches before the spring of 1940. In this way, a case could be made that the local population had been "liberated" from foreign rule, particularly Polish rule over territories in which Poles had remained a minority. It would take some time before these lands could be Sovietized, and the Soviet authorities were concerned that the population had been under "bourgeois influence" during the interwar period. Therefore, many of the early steps concentrated on eradicating such influences through a new educational system and other measures. For example, on December 1–2, 1939, the Communist Party of Belarus issued a decree on the organization of popular education in the western regions of the republic. All schools were affiliated to the state, separate and private schools were eliminated, and the teaching of religion and religious education was banned. However, party workers were advised to implement these measures without insulting believers. The language of all the schools in the region became Belarusian; but, again, this was to be introduced slowly, so that a sufficient number of teachers proficient in the language could be properly trained. The focus of this decree was also on eliminating adult illiteracy.

Propaganda aside, the key element in the westward expansion of the USSR was security. The USSR in effect now shared a border with Nazi Germany; and, given the volatile nature of the Hitler regime, it became essential to bolster the country's defensive system. In 1938 the USSR had spent about 18.7 percent of its total budget on military needs, but by 1940 the proportion was an astounding 32.4 percent. The size of the Red Army and the Red Fleet was increased substantially. On September 1, 1939, the USSR introduced universal military service, and in certain sectors the term was raised from two to three years, with the age limit for entry into the Red Army lowered from 21 to 19, and 18 for those who ended their education at the middle-school level. Consequently, the size of the Red Army was increased from 1.9 to 5.4 million people (though the training of new recruits was incomplete when war broke out). Stalin himself gave a speech to graduates of a military academy on May 5, 1941. Seventy-seven new academies had opened between July 1939 and December 1940, and by the summer there were more than 200 in operation. By this time the country's economy was on a war footing. New tanks were soon coming off the production line – the T-34 and the KV – as well as the Il-2 fighter plane, the PE-2 bomber, and others. Artillery also made significant advances, including the BM-8 and BM-13 (Katyusha) designs. About 40 percent of the population wore some sort of uniform by 1940–1941.

The 1930s had thus seen some significant changes in Soviet foreign policy: an attempt at rapprochement with the Western democracies, which was abandoned in midstream with accusations of bad faith; an attempt at intervention in Spain, which also failed, though there was no real loyalty to the Spanish Republic; a pact with the devil, Hitler, that required a radical change of policy and official propaganda, and which could never be regarded as more than a temporary expedient; and a significant territorial expansion that resulted in a war with Finland, and fairly brutal occupation regimes in most of the annexed territories. During this decade Stalin had matured into a skilled negotiator, using Molotov, his ruthless but intellectually limited associate, as his main negotiator. There is no indication that Stalin was prepared to break his ties with Germany in the summer of 1941; but, on the other hand, strained and tense relations had replaced the friendly banter of August and September 1939. In November 1940, Molotov had visited Berlin to press for Soviet desires in the Balkans, and according to the German side he had lectured them "like a school master." German assertions that the British were all but defeated were belied by an RAF air raid that forced Molotov into an air-raid shelter. By December, Hitler had already developed plans for Operation Barbarossa, but his intentions were complicated by fighting in Yugoslavia, after the expulsion of a pro-German regime in April 1941. As for the USSR, a neutrality pact with Japan was signed on April 13 that appeared to offset the dangerous implications of the Anti-Comintern Pact, though Stalin never trusted the Japanese.

The atmosphere in the USSR in the summer of 1941 was tense, but to that point Soviet foreign policy had been remarkably successful as well as ruthless. Poland had ceased to exist, and already some 26,000 Polish officers had been murdered at three holding camps on Soviet territory (a fact not revealed until 1943 and not acknowledged by the Russian side until the late 1980s), one of which was in the Katyn Forest near Smolensk. On June 14, TASS, the Soviet news agency, issued a declaration denying the "unfounded rumors" about the coming war with Germany. Soviet trains containing raw materials for the German war industry were still regularly crossing the border. Stalin had implemented a traditional Russian foreign policy of securing a buffer zone for the country, and at the same time extending the territorial boundary while appealing to national sentiment in neighboring republics.

Questions for discussion

1. Why was collectivization of agriculture sometimes described as the Revolution from Above?

2. Why was Stalin willing to allow mass famine to develop in Ukraine and the North Caucasus?

3. What were the main achievements of the 1st Five-Year Plan?

4. Why did Stalin carry out the Terror that culminated in 1937, and who were its main victims?

5. What steps did the Soviet Union take to improve its security in the period from 1933 to the summer of 1939?

Recent works

Apor, Balázs. *The Leader Cult in Communist Dictatorships: Stalin and the Eastern Bloc.* Basingstoke: Palgrave Macmillan, 2004.

Applebaum, Anne. *Gulag: A History.* New York: Anchor Books, 2004.

Brackman, Roman. *The Secret File of Joseph Stalin: A Hidden Life.* London: Frank Cass, 2001.

Brent, Jonathan. *Inside the Stalin Archives: Discovering the New Russia.* New York: Atlas, 2008.

Brent, Jonathan. *Stalin's Last Crime: The Plot against the Jewish Doctors, 1948–1953.* New York: Perennial, 2004.

Butler, Rupert. *Stalin's Instruments of Terror: CHEKA, OGPU, NKVD, KGB from 1917 to 1991.* Staplehurst: Spellmount, 2006.

Conquest, Robert. *The Great Terror: A Reassessment.* Oxford: Oxford University Press, 2008.

Cunningham, Kevin. *Joseph Stalin and the Soviet Union.* Greensboro, NC: M. Reynolds, 2006.

Davies, R. W., and Stephen G. Wheatcroft. *The Years of Hunger: Soviet Agriculture, 1931–1933.* Basingstoke: Palgrave Macmillan, 2004.

Davies, Sarah. *Stalin: A New History.* Cambridge: Cambridge University Press, 2005.

Dobrenko, Evgeny. *The Landscape of Stalinism: Art and Ideology of Soviet Space.* Seattle, Wash.: University of Washington Press, 2003.

Edmunds, Neil. *Soviet Music and Society under Lenin and Stalin: The Baton and Sickle.* London: RoutledgeCurzon, 2004.

Fay, Laurel E. *Shostakovich and His World.* Princeton, NJ: Princeton University Press, 2004.

Frolova-Walker, Marina. *Russian Music and Nationalism: From Glinka to Stalin.* New Haven, Conn.: Yale University Press, 2007.

Furst, Juliane. *Late Stalinist Russia: Society between Reconstruction and Reinvention.* Abingdon: Routledge, 2006.

Gitelman, Zvi. *Revolution, Repression, and Revival: The Soviet Jewish Experience.* Lanham, Md: Rowman & Littlefield, 2007.

Gorlizki, Yoram. *Cold Peace: Stalin and the Soviet Ruling Circle, 1945–1953.* Oxford: Oxford University Press, 2004.

Gottfried, Ted. *The Stalinist Empire.* Brookfield, Conn.: Twenty-First Century Books, 2002.

Harris, Jonathan. *The Split in Stalin's Secretariat, 1939–1948.* Lanham, Md: Lexington Books, 2008.

Hoffmann, David L. *Stalinism: The Essential Readings.* Malden, Mass.: Blackwell, 2003.

Hostettler, John. *Law and Terror in Stalin's Russia.* Chichester: Barry Rose, 2003.

Hryn, Halyna, ed. *Hunger by Design: The Great Ukrainian Famine and Its Soviet Context.* Cambridge, Mass.: Ukrainian Research Institute of Harvard University, 2009.

Ilic, Melanie. *Women in the Stalin Era.* Basingstoke: Palgrave Macmillan, 2001.

Kenez, Peter. *Cinema and Soviet Society from the Revolution to the Death of Stalin.* London: I. B. Tauris, 2001.

Khlevniuk, Oleg V. *The History of the Gulag: From Collectivization to the Great Terror.* New Haven, Conn.: Yale University Press, 2004.

Khlevniuk, Oleg V., and Nora Seligman Favorov. *Master of the House: Stalin and His Inner Circle.* New Haven, Conn.: Yale University Press, 2009.

Koganovsky, Lilya. *How the Soviet Man Was Unmade: Cultural Fantasy and Male Subjectivity under Stalin.* Pittsburgh, Pa: University of Pittsburgh Press, 2008.

Konstantin, Anatole. *A Red Boyhood: Growing Up under Stalin.* Columbia, Mo.: University of Missouri Press, 2008.

Kuromiya, Hiroaki. *Stalin.* Harlow: Pearson/Longman, 2005.

LaPorte, Norman, Morgan, Kevin, and Matthew Worley. *Bolshevism, Stalinism and the Comintern: Perspectives on Stalinization, 1917–53.* Basingstoke: Palgrave Macmillan, 2008.

Lewin, Moshe. *The Soviet Century.* London: Verso, 2005.

Litvin, Alter. *Stalinism: Russian and Western Views at the Turn of the Millennium.* London: Routledge, 2005.

Lustiger, Arno. *Stalin and the Jews: The Red Book. The Tragedy of the Jewish Anti-Fascist Committee and the Soviet Jews.* New York: Enigma, 2003.

McCauley, Martin. *Stalin and Stalinism.* Harlow: Pearson Longman, 2008.

McDermortt, Kevin. *Stalin: Revolutionary in an Era of War.* Basingstoke: Palgrave Macmillan, 2006.

McLoughlin, Barry. *Stalin's Terror: High Politics and Mass Repression in the Soviet Union.* Basingstoke: Palgrave Macmillan, 2004.

Mawdsley, Evan. *The Stalin Years: The Soviet Union 1929–1953.* Manchester: Manchester University Press, 2003.

Medvedev, Roy A. *The Unknown Stalin: His Life, Death and Legacy.* New York: Overlook Press, 2004.

Medvedev, Zhores A., and Roy A. Medvedev. *The Unknown Stalin.* London: I. B. Tauris, 2003.

Montefiore, Simon Sebag. *Stalin: The Court of the Red Tsar*. New York: Knopf, 2004.

Montefiore, Simon Sebag. *Young Stalin*. New York: Alfred A. Knopf, 2007.

Overy, R. J. *The Dictators: Hitler's Germany and Stalin's Russia*. London: Allen Lane, 2004.

Pauley, Bruce F. *Hitler, Stalin, and Mussolini: Totalitarianism in the Twentieth Century*. Wheeling, Ill.: Harlan Davidson, 2003.

Platt, M. F., and David Brandenberger. *Epic Revisionism: Russian History and Literature as Stalinist Propaganda*. Madison, Wis.: University of Wisconsin Press, 2006.

Polian, P. M. *Against Their Will: The History and Geography of Forced Migrations in the USSR*. Budapest: Central European University Press, 2004.

Pollock, Ethan. *Stalin and the Soviet Science Wars*. Princeton, NJ: Princeton University Press, 2006.

Rayfield, Donald. *Stalin and His Hangmen: The Tyrant and Those Who Killed for Him*. New York: Random House Trade Paperbacks, 2005.

Rees, E. A. *The Nature of Stalin's Dictatorship: The Politburo, 1924–1953*. Basingstoke: Palgrave Macmillan, 2004.

Riasanovsky, Nicholas V. *Russian Identities: A Historical Survey*. Oxford: Oxford University Press, 2005.

Roberts, Geoffrey. *Stalin's Wars: From World War to Cold War, 1939–1953*. New Haven, Conn.: Yale University Press, 2006.

Rossman, Jeffrey J. *Worker Resistance under Stalin: Class and Revolution on the Shop Floor*. Cambridge, Mass.: Harvard University Press, 2005.

Saccarelli, Emanuele. *Gramsci and Trotsky in the Shadow of Stalinism: The Political Theory and Practice of Opposition*. New York: Routledge, 2008.

Shearer, David R. *Policing Stalin's Socialism: Repression and Social Order in the Soviet Union, 1924–1953*. New Haven, Conn.: Yale University Press, 2009.

Shukman, Harold. *Redefining Stalinism*. London: Frank Cass, 2003.

Siegelbaum, Lewis H. *Stalinism as a Way of Life: A Narrative in Documents*. New Haven, Conn.: Yale University Press, 2004.

Stalin, Joseph. *The Stalin–Kaganovich Correspondence, 1931–36*. Compiled and edited by R. W. Davies. New Haven, Conn.: Yale University Press, 2003.

Suny, Ronald G., and Terry Martin. *A State of Nations: Empire and Nation-Making in the Age of Lenin and Stalin*. Oxford: Oxford University Press, 2001.

Suvorov, Viktor. *The Chief Culprit: Stalin's Grand Design to Start World War II*. Annapolis, Md: Naval Institute Press, 2008.

Tauger, Mark B. *Natural Disaster and Human Actions in the Soviet Union, 1931–1933.* Pittsburgh, Pa: Center for Russian and East European Studies, University Center for International Studies, University of Pittsburgh, 2001.

Usdin, Steven T. *Engineering Communism: How Two Americans Spied for Stalin and Founded the Soviet Silicon Valley.* New Haven, Conn.: Yale University Press, 2005.

van Ree, Erik. *The Political Thought of Joseph Stalin: A Study in Twentieth-Century Revolutionary Patriotism.* London: RoutledgeCurzon, 2002.

Viola, Lynne. *Contending with Stalinism: Soviet Power and Popular Resistance in the 1930s.* Ithaca, NY: Cornell University Press, 2002.

Viola, Lynne. *The Unknown Gulag: The Lost World of Stalin's Special Settlements.* Oxford: Oxford University Press, 2007.

Volkov, Solomon. *Shostakovich and Stalin: The Extraordinary Relationship between the Great Composer and the Brutal Dictator.* London: Little Brown, 2004.

5

....

The Great Patriotic War and aftermath, 1941–1953

Early stages

The early stages of the war remain an enigmatic period. The USSR contained five border districts in the summer of 1941: the Baltic, Western, Leningrad, Kyiv, and Odesa. On the night of June 21, the ruling Politburo decided to form another front, and decided that if the country were to be attacked, then the war would be taken into enemy territory, following an active defense in the early hours. The same evening, several key Politburo members gathered in the Kremlin to discuss the emerging crisis, along with Soviet military leaders. A directive was then sent to the border to place military facilities in a state of readiness, including the concealment of planes, but at the same time to take such a step without provoking the German army. The accounts of this meeting suggest a disagreement within the Soviet leadership. Timoshenko and Zhukov were suggesting that the entire border be placed on high alert. Stalin was in opposition, feeling that there was no need to antagonize the Germans in light of his agreement with Hitler. The Soviet border troops were even warned not to respond to certain provocations. Whatever the content of the dispute within the Kremlin, it is certain that the directive to go on the alert did not reach the border regions.

In *Khrushchev Remembers: The Glasnost Tapes*, Nikita Khrushchev recalls angrily that:

> To argue that we did not expect a German attack is just plain stupid, particularly coming from the military people who were close to the general staff. No one with an ounce of political sense should buy the idea that we were caught flat-footed by a treacherous surprise assault. Even to suggest such a thing is irresponsible. Yet such phrases have often been used in newspaper articles, which means that they serve a certain political purpose. They're used to cover up for those who were responsible for the preparations of the army and the country, and who failed in their responsibility. People are trying to justify either themselves or Stalin – his genius, his foresight, and his vigilance. If he really was vigilant, where was the treachery?
>
> (Khrushchev, 1990, p. 49)

Stalin had ample warning about the coming onslaught from various sources. His master spy in Japan, Richard Sorge, had even provided a date of June 21, 1941 for such an attack. Churchill had also warned Stalin; but the Soviet leader, who had also become the Chairman of the Council of Ministers on May 6, 1941 (replacing

Molotov), did not trust the British prime minister. The Red Army was much improved since the purge of 1937. Gathered in the border region were 2.9 million troops, equipped with more than 9,000 tanks, some 8,400 planes, and more than 46,000 guns and mortars. Yet this huge army had its weaknesses. There were problems with communication between the field and headquarters, a lack of automatic weapons, and the local commanders were less skilled and showed less initiative than their German counterparts. Because of the purges, commanders were generally cautious and lacked military experience. If a blow was to come from Germany, it was also unclear in which direction it would come. Stalin based a lot of troops in Ukraine, but he does not seem to have allowed for a three-frontal attack. The Germans had fewer men and weapons than the Red Army, though not in the border regions.

The Germans and their allies attacked the USSR at 4.15 a.m. Moscow time on June 22, 1941, on a front that stretched from the Baltic to the Black Sea. The Soviet leadership at once lost contact with the front as connections and communication lines were cut. The losses of planes in particular were huge, with about 1,200 being destroyed on the first day of the war, about two-thirds of them on the ground. In the Kremlin, Stalin met other Soviet leaders – Molotov, Beria, Timoshenko, L. Z. Mekhlis, and Zhukov. Again they appear to have convinced themselves that nothing serious had occurred, merely some provocations. Early that same morning, Count Schulenberg, the German ambassador to the USSR, had handed Molotov a memorandum which declared that Germany could not accept such a dangerous situation on its eastern border. In Soviet eyes, the attack was deemed "treacherous." This adjective was used constantly, partly because to Stalin and Molotov the signing of the Nazi–Soviet Pact had been seen as a guarantee that no such attack would take place. It was also to convince the public that the Soviet leadership could not possibly have been prepared for a sudden invasion. Thus at 12 noon, Moscow time, almost eight hours after the German attack had begun, Molotov went on Soviet radio and announced that Germany had treacherously attacked the Soviet Union, and that a war in defense of the Motherland had begun. The enemy, he asserted, would be destroyed – "Victory will be ours."

Preparation to counter invaders was piecemeal and confused. It proved to be virtually impossible to form non-Russian brigades in the Caucasus, or among Kazakhs and Tatars, partly because these troops did not comprehend Russian, and partly because of their unwillingness to take part in this conflict. Creation of the Latvian, Lithuanian, and Estonian divisions also proved hard to organize in the first days of the war, with German troops entering these territories and being welcomed as liberators. At the fortress of Brest, the defenders prepared to fight to the last man under the command of Major P. A. Gavrilov and NKVD Colonel E. M. Fomin, one of the few examples of Soviet heroism at this stage of the war. Even the Germans could only admire the fortitude with which the defenders fought, though one reason for the lengthy resistance was that the invaders had little time to clean up resistance and the fortress had a network of underground tunnels. On June 23, the Stavka, the

Chief Command of the Armed Forces of the USSR, was created, led at first by Timoshenko, the People's Commissar of Defense, with Zhukov in command of General Headquarters. Molotov, Voroshilov, Budenny, and Stalin were also included. The Stavka had a body of advisors, including the two marshals of the USSR to survive the purges, G. I. Kulik and B. M. Shaposhnikov, along with some prominent political leaders, such as Kaganovich, Beria, and Malenkov.

But to highlight this body is to insert order where none really existed. One advisor, General K. A. Meretskov, who had been made a Hero of the Soviet Union the previous year for his role in penetrating the Mannerheim Line in Finland, was accused of espionage on June 24, and imprisoned in the Lubyanka. The two marshals were dispatched to the front, and several other military leaders were punished for gross incompetence. These problems were not resolved until the war was three weeks old. Since the Germans had broken the communications system, the leaders in Moscow found it impossible to get news from the Front, and thus reported wildly optimistic stories about repelling enemy attacks. The Soviet press during this period also refused to admit the defeats, though the people could ascertain the speed of the German advance from the location of the reports. Two days after the war began, the Soviet leadership created punitive battalions, ostensibly to guard factories against saboteurs or parachutists dropped behind the lines, but equally to take action against those Red Army soldiers who retreated or showed cowardice. About 328,000 people were recruited for this work, and were directly subordinated to the NKVD.

The Germans moved rapidly during the first days of the war, using Panzer strikes supported by the Luftwaffe. They frequently applied pincer movements to surround unsuspecting Soviet divisions, taking large number of prisoners. The Soviet leadership had refused to allow these divisions to retreat, so German successes were greater than they might have been. In just eighteen days, the Germans and their allies advanced between 280 and 370 miles to the east. Progress was particularly fast for Army Group North, which moved toward Leningrad, and Army Group Center, which used the major route from Poland into Belarus toward Minsk. Soviet casualties were already over 100,000, and 40 percent of Soviet tanks were destroyed in this same period. By mid-July the Germans occupied all three Baltic States, and the Belarusian, Moldavian republics, as well as a large part of western and central Ukraine. It was evidently the fall of Minsk on June 30 that led to Stalin's personal breakdown, though he had been notably reticent since the start of the war. This defeat occurred as a result of a large part of the Soviet Army of the Western Front being surrounded, and was up until then the biggest disaster of the war. The fall of Minsk also left open the main route through to Smolensk, Vyazma, and Moscow. Stalin declared that he refused to lead the country further, and left for his dacha in the country.

Malenkov, Voroshilov, Beria, and Molotov gathered at the Kremlin. Mikoyan and Voznesensky were sent to Stalin's dacha to tell him of a plan to set up a new organ of government to oversee the war. The visit does not appear to have made much impression on Stalin. It seems likely that he expected to be dismissed at any moment for the disgrace he had brought upon the country. There was evidently some suggestion that Molotov should continue to run the country for the time being, but the majority of the leading group (not necessarily all the Politburo, which does not seem to have met in full very often) resolved that another effort should be made to convince Stalin to return to the Kremlin. This time, the group informed Stalin that they would all take responsibility for the failure to be vigilant and prepare adequately for the German invasion. Molotov reportedly was the one who convinced Stalin that the war was not yet lost. Stalin agreed to return and to invest power in the new State Defense Committee (GKO), which would direct the war effort. The committee would have five permanent members and two plenipotentiary members, Mikoyan and Voznesensky. Though the GKO technically dates from June 30, it likely emerged in practice a few days later, once Stalin had returned to the Kremlin.

Though Stalin was now clearly in charge, he did not make particularly wise or intelligent decisions at the outset. On July 3, he spoke on Soviet radio, urging the country to resist the invader. He addressed the public as "brothers and sisters," and advocated a scorched-earth policy toward the invader. Anything that could not be transported to the east was to be destroyed, particularly grain and gasoline. He also advocated the establishment of partisan units in territories under German occupation. The Germans had to be eliminated without mercy. At first the lack of mercy was mainly evident against Soviet commanders and the public. As early as June 29, a government and party decree was issued for a ruthless struggle with "panic-mongers" and those spreading false rumors. By July 4, spreading rumors had become a criminal offense. In Belarus, volunteer units that had sprung up to fight the invaders were disbanded because the NKVD had no control over them. By July 10, Stalin had taken over command of the Stavka, and war operations were now firmly under his control. Cronies who had remained with him through the purges – Molotov and Beria, and military leaders from the civil war period and later, such as Budenny, Timoshenko, and Voroshilov – offered him advice and served in various functions. The GKO, which ran day-to-day business, included more political figures, such as Kaganovich and Malenkov; while Voznesensky seems to have had several roles, and eventually was responsible for military supplies.

In reality, the administrative leadership during the war consisted of Stalin and several chosen subordinates, who might differ from one meeting to another. The government, the GKO, and the Stavka were really one, and as the war developed Stalin accumulated much more power. Publicly, however, it became essential for a collective leadership to be perceived, at least as long as military reverses continued. In the early stage of the war, blame for the setbacks was placed on cowardly generals and officers, who retreated rather than stand and fight, or who allowed themselves to be surrounded by the advancing Germans. In addition, the looseness of the system was not necessarily a bad thing, since it allowed for rapid decision-making. Yet the distances of the country, the vast space between the GKO and the armies in the field, and the fact that all key decisions came from Moscow were a disadvantage. Often, by the time an order was given, it had already been made obsolete by the speed of the German advance. The GKO worked better in terms of administration over materials, transport, and the evacuation of factories. Almost 10,000 decrees were issued in the four years of the German–Soviet war, or an average of more than seven per day.

The evacuation of factories started two days after the war began, organized by a Council for Evacuation under N. M. Shvernik, assisted by A. N. Kosygin and M. G. Pervukhin. The Council had to decide where the factories should be located, the number of railway wagons required to transport them, and the number of buildings needed. The factories located in the western borderlands, in general, could not be saved; but approximately 1,500 large factories and a similar number of smaller ones were moved to the towns of eastern European Russia or else east of the Ural Mountains. New industrial centers dedicated to the war effort sprang up in Central Asia, the Volga region, and Western Siberia, while some 2 million workers had to be transported east to devote themselves to producing military goods. By all accounts the system worked extraordinarily well, though there was a gap between the evacuation and the start-up of production at the relocated factories. Some accounts suggest that the time lag was as little as 1.5–2 months, but it seems likely that it was often longer. Also a lot of valuable equipment had to be left behind in the occupied regions. During the period of preparation for production, the country was at its weakest.

The Germans began to attack major centers. After the fall of Minsk, the Soviet army retreated to Smolensk using the forces of four fronts against Von Bock's German Army Group Center. In the north, Leningrad came under attack by July 10; and, in the south, the long struggle that culminated in the capture of Kyiv had also begun. The Germans took an enormous number of prisoners. In some cases – particularly in the borderlands – the people were reluctant to take up arms against the invader. In others, the leadership was less than competent; and in others defeatism was evident – a general belief that the German army was invincible. Though there was always a distinction between the behavior of the German army and of the organizations that generally followed it into the USSR, such as the SS and the Gestapo, part of the problem was that no provision had been made for such a large number of prisoners. According to a Russian estimate, the figure after three weeks of fighting was in the region of 3 million men. This sullen mass was rounded up and incarcerated, and barely kept alive in terms of food. Perhaps the Germans could not have fed such a large group adequately – it was equivalent in size to the entire German invasion force – but their total lack of attention to and disdain for the prisoners of war was in contrast to the treatment of prisoners on the Western Front. Thousands died from hunger or from internment-camp diseases such as dysentery and cholera.

The question has been raised whether more benign treatment would have helped the German campaign. But, for one thing, Hitler had no intention of using the services of captured troops from the Eastern Front. To him they were less than human. The Germans also rounded up Communists, Jews, and other groups as they captured towns. In Lviv, two Ukrainian units arrived with the German army, and under their influence a Ukrainian state was proclaimed on the city's radio station on June 30 by members of the Organization of Ukrainian Nationalists (Bandera faction, or OUN-B). But it was short-lived and soon dismantled by the Germans. Stepan Bandera, the OUN-B leader, was held in Germany under house arrest for most of the war. Thus it became evident to the non-Russian people that the Germans were not their protectors, but had come to enslave them. However, in the first weeks of the war, even mistreatment by the Germans failed to unite the Soviet population. By mid-July a system of military commissars had been established in the Soviet army. The commissars' goal was to inspire troops to fight (and to shoot deserters), and back up all major military decisions. It need hardly be added that such a system was disastrous at a time when there was already a delay in orders reaching the fronts. The commissars dated back to the period of military purges, and inspired fear in military commanders. The system also created a dual authority in the army until it was abolished in the fall of 1942. Meanwhile, the police and state security organs were merged into the NKVD on July 20, 1941 and under the control of Lavrenty Beria. In the first month of the war, political and security organs had taken on a leading role.

The power of the NKVD was formidable. It had control over a vast empire of prisons, camps, major economic enterprises, and intelligence-gathering. The Special Assembly of the NKVD carried out more than 26,000 executions in 1941 alone, and this had risen to over 77,000 in 1942. On August 16, 1941, Stalin signed Order 270 for the arrest and trial of commanders who had retreated without being ordered to do so. By March 1942, thirty Soviet generals had been executed. Stalin appears to have been genuinely afraid that the German attack might lead to a counter-revolution in the country. As the Germans crossed the Soviet border, NKVD troops were instructed to execute prisoners before they retreated. This harsh action not only led to thousands of unnecessary deaths (mainly of Poles, Ukrainians, Belarusians, and members of the Baltic nationalities); it also served to alienate the border population from the Soviet regime. Before the war ended, the Germans could still find support in these regions and were able to form SS divisions to fight against the Red Army.

On the other hand, because of the heavy losses and the large number of Soviet troops taken prisoner, Stalin and Beria could not conduct repressions on the same scale as in the 1930s. Instead they had to release prisoners to bolster the war effort. In the first four months of the war, 175,000 former prisoners were mobilized. One of those released was the Polish-born general K. K. Rokossovsky, who proved to be one of the most renowned of Soviet military commanders. General Ivan Konev would have been imprisoned at the start of the war but for the intervention of Zhukov. General Meretskov, a Hero of the Soviet Union, was also freed at this time, though numerous other generals were shot without a trial. Specialists, technicians, and people needed for the wartime economy were set free without hesitation during this period, even while the NKVD carried out its grisly role against deserters and those not fully committed to the all-embracing struggle. A. N. Tupolev, the famous airplane-builder of later years, also received an amnesty to work in the armaments industry. These people, however, were never really trusted. Rather more faith was placed in party leaders at the regional, oblast, and rayon levels, who were entrusted to fight on under occupation and form underground cells. In some cases party leaders were parachuted back into their regions to incite the local population. Such actions did not really begin to pay dividends until later in the war.

The assault on Leningrad and Kyiv

Army Group North advanced steadily toward Leningrad, a city that Hitler wished to see utterly destroyed. Assisted by the Finns, the Germans captured Pskov on July 1, and moved toward Novgorod and Luga, about ninety miles from Leningrad. Erich von Manstein, a ruthless and efficient general, led the ground attack. On July 28, the Estonian capital of Tallinn fell under German control, and the Baltic Fleet had to be transferred to the Kronstadt base. A tremendous battle took place for control of the Karelian region, initiated by the Finnish troops on July 28 and encompassing the estuaries of Ladoga and Onega. It took the Germans until August 19 to occupy Novgorod; eleven days later, they had reached Kolpino, in the suburbs of Leningrad, though they were temporarily forced back. After a further attack from the south, the Germans placed Leningrad under blockade, determined to cut off the population from supplies and to starve it into surrender. By September 9, the Germans were again in the suburbs and were able to cut tramlines between the town of Uritsk and the city center. Zhukov was sent to the Leningrad Front to bolster the defenses.

The population of Leningrad at this time was about 3 million. According to some reports, most of the children were removed from the city before the blockade began. Other accounts suggest that as many as 400,000 remained behind. By the end of September, the German advance had been halted, and the Wehrmacht resorted to bombing rather than a frontal assault that would likely have proved costly. Factories continued to work, though food rations grew increasingly low. For a brief period, the Germans managed to sever the railroad between Leningrad and Moscow. Leningrad came to a virtual standstill, but it did not surrender. It remained under blockade for almost 900 days and with a loss of about 1 million people. In contrast, Kyiv, the USSR's third city, fell on September 19, and the results were particularly disastrous because of Stalin's refusal to let the Red Army retreat. General M. P. Kirponos, the commander of the Southwestern Front, was killed, and troop losses were exceptionally high. The German pincer movement encircled the Red Army soldiers, and another 300,000 prisoners were taken. The NKVD laid mines along the Kreshchatyk, the main street in the city center, timed to explode when the German army entered. Kyiv remained Hitler's biggest prize on the Eastern Front. Odesa, Ukraine's chief port, was also occupied, after a much longer struggle that lasted from August to October 16, 1941.

Operation Typhoon: the attack on Moscow

The German military leadership, the OKH, had embarked on Operation Barbarossa with the goal of capturing Moscow, the Soviet capital, the heart of the Soviet communications system, and an important industrial area. Hitler, however, diverted troops to the different fronts after the initial invasion, in the belief that they could always rejoin Army Group Center for the final victory. By the time that the Germans were ready to begin a final assault on Moscow – known as Operation Typhoon – they were in control of a very important part of the European USSR. Around 40 percent of the total population was by now under occupation, in an area that before the war had produced about one-third of gross industrial production, and almost 40 percent of the country's grain. The industrial regions under foreign occupation had provided over 60 percent of the country's coal supply, 58 percent of steel, and almost 70 percent of cast iron. Control over such an area convinced Hitler that the fall of Moscow would end the war. The huge number of Soviet prisoners in German hands could only have bolstered his viewpoint. It appeared that the Red Army no longer wanted to fight. On October 2, 1941, Hitler ordered the start of Operation Typhoon, confident that total German victory was now at hand.

At first, all went according to plan. Army Group Center concentrated its forces in one rapid strike group and encircled Soviet armies at Bryansk and Vyazma. Konev and Budenny were responsible for this fiasco, and only the personal intervention of Zhukov prevented Stalin from venting his fury on the former. The losses at these two towns seemingly left Moscow open to the invaders. Four armies had been entrapped at Vyazma, and two at Bryansk, with 663,000 troops taken prisoner. The Germans, however, began to suffer several setbacks in the next stage of the battle. Heavy rain turned the roads to mud, making them virtually impassable for the largely horse-drawn German army. By late October the rain had ceased, but the temperature dropped and the ground became rock hard. The Germans had not been given adequate winter clothing, and thousands of troops began to suffer from frostbite. Tanks would not start in the morning unless they had been kept heated throughout the night. The climate had come to the aid of the Red Army. German diaries of the period testify that many soldiers were becoming disillusioned. They could not deal with the vastness of Soviet territory, the routine of constant advances through almost identical countryside but seemingly never getting anywhere.

Zhukov was ordered to save Moscow, and soon the city's entire population was conscripted to prepare the defenses. Women and children dug ditches, and a people's militia was formed that would plug any holes in the defensive lines. The NKVD and students from military academies were also added to the mobilized forces. Zhukov, meanwhile, began to bring reserve troops to the capital from the Far East. Most of these were stationed behind the city in preparation for a counter-attack. Yet the Germans kept moving forward. Within Moscow itself, their arrival was expected almost daily. The Soviet government evacuated several departments, offices, and personnel, and there was a rumor that Stalin also had left the capital. Party members tore up their cards. German voices could be heard on Soviet radio; this came as a huge shock to the population, accustomed to the monotonous voices of Soviet propaganda extolling the great Stalin and Soviet achievements. The war had gone so badly up to this point that many citizens were ready for a German occupation. On October 8, the authorities drew up a list of the factories in Moscow that were to be destroyed as the Germans entered. A virtual uprising broke out in the town of Ivanovo a week later, when it became known that the Soviet government had abandoned Moscow.

Again, there is some question regarding Stalin's activities at this crucial time. Moscow was under siege between October 16 and 19. It was reported that Beria had already made provision for peace with the Germans and that Stalin was suffering from depression. City life had come to a standstill, and most of the population was chronically short of food. As in 1921, many residents were gathering their belongings and fleeing to the southeast. Women and children did so by order, but many others left without permission. In retrospect, this moment may have been the defining point in the entire German–Soviet war. How close the Germans came to victory may never be known. On paper, it would seem unlikely that they could have occupied much of the USSR for the long term, but by pressing on with Operation Typhoon they had come perilously close to obtaining a Soviet surrender. Stalin's nerve, however, did not fail him this time. If he had indeed left the city with other government members, then he had certainly returned by November 6, when he made a speech at the Mayakovsky metro station; the following day, the traditional Revolution Day parade was held in Moscow, with Stalin on the podium. Gunfire could be heard in the distance. To the troops and the public, Stalin's presence meant a great deal, and was reassurance that the Soviet government had not conceded defeat.

Stalin's speech also broke new ground for a Communist leader. Having commented on the great "liberation struggle" of the Red Army, he evoked the memory of the renowned Russian military warriors of the past – Nevsky,[1] Donskoy,[2] Pozharsky,[3] Suvorov,[4] and Kutuzov.[5] The dramatic link to the Russian past symbolized the changing propaganda of the Soviet leadership during the war. Henceforth, the Soviet soldier fought not for the Communist Party but for the Motherland – an emancipating concept that appeared to herald a new future once the invader had been removed. The Russian Orthodox churches were reopened, and people were encouraged to worship. The Soviet–German war thereafter became the Great Patriotic War. Stalin, under circumstances he had helped to create, was less a Communist leader than a tsar – a transition aided by the obsequiousness and hyperbole of Soviet propaganda. Soviet soldiers fought – For the Motherland! For Stalin! This change was gradual but its starting point was November 6–7, 1941. A combined devotion to both the Motherland and the Soviet leader suggested a number of changes in official propaganda. First, it indicated that the USSR by itself lacked appeal for the masses during a period of great instability. Second, it indicated that the Stalin leadership was identifying itself with an imperial past, suggesting a direct link between the tsarist period and the Soviet counterpart. Third, it would lead eventually to a new attempt to legitimize the Soviet regime through the "Great Patriotic War" rather than the "Great October Revolution." The change of direction represented the first clear compromise between the Soviet regime and Russian nationalist sentiment, though the latter had also been evident during the civil war.

Just a week later, the Germans began their second attempt to capture Moscow, and moved slowly through the forests on the outskirts of the city, narrowing the distance from twenty-five to 15.5 miles. Lead units got within six miles of the city, and could see the spires of the Kremlin. Each step of the way cost the Germans heavily, but Hitler was convinced that the Soviets had no reserves. On December 5, Zhukov's counter-attack came as a complete surprise to the Germans. It was only made once Richard Sorge, the Soviet master spy in Japan, had convinced Stalin that the Japanese would not join in with their German allies and force the USSR into a two-front war. Sorge was aware that the Japanese were planning an attack on the Americans. By January the Germans had been pushed back all along the front of Army Group Center, from sixty miles to 155 miles westward. Though the retreat was chaotic at first, Hitler demanded that the Germans retreat only to their supply dumps, after which the line had to be held. Several generals might have preferred to hold a defensive line even further to the west, but Hitler's orders were carried out. As village after village fell into the hands of the Red Army, the GKO felt that it might be possible to capitalize on the success and drive the Germans out of the USSR. This feeling illustrates Stalin's inexperience as a military commander. The Germans, it was declared, would be driven back from Lake Ladoga to the Black Sea, and the war could be over by 1942. These appeals came just one month after the USSR had faced defeat, but it was not realistic. Zhukov, Shaposhnikov, and Voznesensky warned Stalin of the foolhardiness of such a plan, but the Soviet leader ignored their advice.

The result was the failure of the Soviet drive, which took place in three directions – to the west, to the northwest and to the southwest. The Soviet troops outpaced their supplies, and the Germans were able to counter-attack effectively, using their traditional pincer movements once again to take large numbers of prisoners. The Germans recaptured the city of Kharkiv, capital of Ukraine until 1934, before the spring thaw, with the flooding of the huge Soviet river systems, put an end to the fighting. The Germans had recovered from the shock counter-attack, but their military leaders by now realized the magnitude of the task ahead. Far from being short of troops, the number of new recruits into the Red Army appeared to be unlimited. Hitler's constant interference in decision-making had once made sense, but on the Eastern Front such interventions detracted from intelligent solutions and local initiatives. Consequently, most of the leading generals resigned, were dismissed, or fell ill in late 1941 and early 1942, including Walther von Brauchitsch, the Commander-in-Chief of the German army, Von Runstedt, Von Leeb, Von Bock, and Guderian. Hitler

Plate 5.1 Families identify the dead in Kerch, Crimea, January 1942.
Image: The Dmitri Baltermants Collection/CORBIS

assumed overall command. Thus, for the moment, the brilliant generals who had captured much of Western Europe and Poland were absent. The Germans still possessed capable leaders, but henceforth the Soviet military leaders were probably on an equal footing, and as the war progressed Soviet wartime leadership became superior to its German counterpart. (Plate 5.1)

The Partisan movement

Officially the Partisan movement dates from the very first days of the war. On June 29 and July 18, 1941, the Soviet government and the Communist Party gave instructions for the formation of a Partisan movement at the rear of the German-Fascist army. In Belarus and Ukraine, similar directives were given on July 1 and 5 respectively. However, during the first ten months of the war, there was little serious Partisan activity in the areas occupied by the Germans. The numbers of Partisans were very small, though the movement developed gradually in response to various acts of cruelty by the new rulers. Moreover, when the Partisan movement did develop it did so in a variety of ways and under very different circumstances. The Germans in general focused their attention on major towns and communication routes, like roads and railways. They lacked the numbers to control the immense areas of the Soviet Union. But the

Partisans required certain conditions in order to survive – forests, a water supply, and access to food from sympathetic villages. The best areas for this sort of activity were most of Belarus, the northwest part of Ukraine, and western and central Russia.

The Partisan movement was formalized on May 30, 1942 when a Central Headquarters of the Partisans was created, led by Ponomarenko, the infamous Belarusian First Party Secretary. At the end of August, the Partisan leaders met in Moscow to elaborate strategy. On September 5, 1942, the Supreme Chief Command of the movement gave an order outlining the Partisans' roles, which included attacks on German communication routes, assassination of German leaders, and the political indoctrination of the population. The beginning of the Partisan movement resembles the early stages of the war itself, with the party and the NKVD taking an active role, curtailing local initiatives, and ensuring that as far as possible the movement be centralized. In reality, such control proved impractical. The impact of the Partisans at first was relatively minor, and the Germans deployed Axis non-German troops for the most part to counter them. However, once the German army ended its offensive operations and began to retreat, just like Napoleon's Grande Armée – weakened similarly by Partisan raids – it also began to suffer. As the Partisan movement grew in size – it reached a peak of around 250,000 in the summer of 1943 – its effectiveness grew, and its leaders, such as the coarse but effective Ukrainian-born Partisan leader Sydir Kovpak, gained reputations for heroism. In modern-day Belarus, the Partisans are still regarded as heroes and have acquired almost mythical status. They included the Jewish Partisan movement led by the Bielski brothers (Tec, 2009). Perhaps the Partisans' most famous action was to sever some 470 miles of railway lines in the Kursk region during the fall of 1943. By this time, however, Stalin had resolved that the Partisans were acting too independently, and dissolved the Central Headquarters of the movement. Henceforth each Partisan section had to operate separately from its fellows.

Stalingrad

Following the failure of the Soviet drive of early 1942, it was clear that the Germans would resume their advance the following summer. They had consolidated their positions alongside supply dumps on the major river systems. Stalin believed that Moscow would be the logical target, since the enemy had come so close to capturing the capital the previous winter. Hitler, however, was now a free agent as far as planning was concerned. To him it made more sense to capture the oil regions of the Caucasus, particularly the Maikop oilfields, which the German drive needed in order to continue. At the same time, the city of Stalingrad was something of a magnet for the German leader. From the military perspective, the city had to be neutralized so that the German forces driving into the Caucasus were not attacked from the rear. In the summer of 1942 the Luftwaffe retained almost complete control of the air, making such an attack seem feasible. Stalingrad, originally called Tsaritsyn but named after Stalin to commemorate his real and alleged civil war feats, was a large industrial city on the west bank of the Volga, previously known for producing tractors, but by now for its output of heavy tanks. To Soviet military leaders, it was essential to hold the city at all costs, not least because of the symbolism of its name.

Hitler divided Army Group South into army groups A and B. The former was to move into the Caucasus, and the latter toward Stalingrad. In this region of southwest Russia, the Soviet forces suffered some disadvantages – most of the divisions that moved there were reservists lacking military experience, and they were short of transport and artillery. The Germans had twice as many planes, and four times as many tanks as the Russians at the outset of the campaign, though the ground forces were roughly equal. By August, the 6th Army under General Friedrich von Paulus had reached the outskirts of the city, and the 4th Panzer Army was redirected to join it. The Russian 62nd Army, led by General A. I. Lopatin, was in the city. On August 23, the Luftwaffe subjected Stalingrad to one of the heaviest bombardments to date. Though Zhukov was sent there five days later, the situation was critical, with German tanks massing to drive to the Volga. Gradually Von Paulus' infantry advanced until on September 12 they had reached a line that in places was only 1.25 miles from the city center. The next day another great German attack began, which penetrated to the railway station. By late September, the Germans had reached the Volga both in the northern and southern districts of the city. Soviet forces were defending a narrow central front that looked increasingly fragile.

The great battle, however, had become one of attrition. Stalin replenished the leadership on the spot with commanders who were prepared to fight to the death. On July 28, 1942 he issued Order 227, sometimes known as "Not a step backward!", by which NKVD units called *zagradotryady* (blocking units) were set up on every front with orders to shoot cowards. Over 130,000 soldiers were sent to penal battalions, and a much smaller number – around 1,000 – were executed. From September 1942, the 62nd Army was under the command of General Vasiliy Chuikov. Andrey Yeremenko commanded the army of the Stalingrad Front from August to December 1942, and Konstantin K. Rokossovsky led the army of the Don Front, which made several intrusions into the German lines during the Stalingrad campaign. The city became the subject of much publicity in both Soviet and German propaganda. Yet, whatever the costs involved in terms of casualties, the situation favored the Soviets once the German war machine lost its maneuverability and was forced to fight a war of attrition, trying to take factories and buildings one by one. One of the Soviet propaganda slogans was that "Every house is a fortress," and would not be taken until every defender was killed. From this battle there are numerous tales of individual heroism that have become Soviet legends. Even Western sources have publicized the epic struggle. The Hollywood movie *Enemy at the Gates*, for example, depicts the story of the sniper Zaitsev. The Stavka held an important meeting in September 1942, attended by Zhukov, the Deputy Chairman of the Supreme Chief Command, Vasilevsky, as head of the General Headquarters, and Stalin; and it was resolved to relieve Stalingrad by mounting a counter-attack with the hope not only of defeating the 6th Army but also of trapping German forces in the Caucasus. As these plans were being made, the German grip on the city gradually increased, and by mid-November about 90 percent of it was under the invader's control.

The counter-attack was meticulously planned. Though the Germans had fought well, their flanks outside the city were held by weaker forces – Romanian and Italian troops less committed to the cause and beginning to suffer under winter conditions. The movement of troops and material to the region of the city – on the east bank of the Volga – negated the German advantage in artillery and tanks. By the time the counter-attack was mounted, the Soviets had clear superiority in equipment and tanks, and – for the first time – slightly more planes. The campaign was to be conducted by three armies: the Southwestern Front, commanded by Lieutenant General Nikolay F. Vatutin, the Don Front (Rokossovsky), and the Stalingrad Front (Yeremenko). On November 19, as Hitler was anticipating the imminent surrender of Stalingrad, these armies began a formidable counter-attack under the name of Operation Uranus. Within four days the two main armies (Vatutin and Yeremenko) had broken through the lines of the Axis forces and joined up some twenty-five miles to the west of Stalingrad, cutting off the 6th Army and part of the 4th Panzer Army inside the city.

For the Germans, the situation was critical but far from lost. The circle was weak in several areas and could easily have been breached by a determined break-out. Hitler, however, refused permission for this and continued to demand that the entire city be captured. Von Manstein received orders to relieve the 6th Army; while Goering promised, without much clear thinking, that the Luftwaffe could relieve the besieged army from the air. On most days the Luftwaffe drops were far from adequate, supplying less than a third of subsistence needs. The situation for the Germans grew perilous, and at one point Von Paulus – who was in regular correspondence with Von Manstein – lost his nerve. The latter's army made good progress from the south, reaching within twenty-two miles of Stalingrad, but Von Paulus did not make any effort to break out and join forces. Hitler in the meantime was content to have the 6th Army occupy large numbers of Soviet forces in the protracted and epic battle that had focused the attention of the Soviet military leadership. By early January, the German forces in Stalingrad had been divided into two pockets. Later in the month the Soviets captured the main German airport, after which the Germans could not ship out their wounded. Though Von Paulus was promoted to Field Marshal, he surrendered to the Soviet forces on February 2, 1943.

Historians continue to assess the scale and results of this great battle. The German 6th Army, with about 90,000 troops, Von Paulus among them; one of the few German officers ever to emerge from captivity, he spent his remaining few years in East Germany. One Soviet estimate suggests that German losses overall were in the region of 700,000 troops. Soviet losses, however, were extraordinarily high, for they combined both military and civilian deaths. There was simply no distinction in the conditions in which the battle was fought. About 1.5 million Russians may have died in this massive conflict, raising the question whether the Stalingrad victory was as decisive as it is often described. It was, none the less, the first major defeat of the German army, or the second if one considers the Battle of Moscow a Soviet victory. It meant the end of German expansion in Russia; this could not have gone on indefinitely, with German armies fighting so far from home. The distances were too great, and the Soviet reserves often decisive. Stalin and Zhukov were prepared to sacrifice men for territory and for a great psychological victory. Of the many aspects of Stalingrad that Western audiences find hard to fathom, that of sacrifice is paramount. As the war continued, the Russian wave attacks would constantly push the Germans back, albeit at great cost.

The Soviet military leaders planned four counter-offensives in the winter of 1941–1942, of which only two were carried out. Whereas Operation Uranus brought about a turn of the tide at Stalingrad, further to the north Zhukov and Konev undertook Operation Mars, which was intended to remove the German 9th Army under General Walther Model in the Rzhev region, not far from Moscow; and ultimately to eliminate Army Group Center. Both operations were planned in September, but Operation Mars received little publicity subsequently because it was a failure and resulted in very heavy Soviet losses. It began on November 25 against the Rzhev Salient, where at first some 200,000 Soviet troops attacked a German defense of about 40,000. The attack and all subsequent ones failed to dislodge the Germans. An attempt to capture the city of Bely in this area also failed. As Colonel David Glantz has noted, Operation Mars "was a shambles." The Soviet side reportedly suffered losses of almost 500,000, as well as 1,700 tanks – equivalent to the entire number of tanks used for the operation in the south. Glantz points out that Zhukov barely mentions Operation Mars in his memoirs; and Stalin, similarly, was silent because nothing was supposed to detract from the glorious victory at Stalingrad (Glantz, 2009a). Thus Operation Mars, along with a number of subsequent failures on the Eastern Front, received almost no publicity. Moreover, the record of Zhukov likewise remained untarnished even though it seems clear that his rash assaults in unfavorable conditions were responsible for the enormous Soviet losses.

By the second half of 1942, the Soviet economy was beginning to outperform its German counterpart, particularly in key areas such as the production of guns, tanks, and military equipment. The workers labored for long hours, often in dire conditions, and with rations at subsistence level. The lack of food was a consequence of the disruption to agriculture. Not only were the Germans occupying the most important grain areas, but also the work on farms was generally in the hands of women

Plate 5.2 War on the Eastern Front, July 1942.
Image: Bettmann/CORBIS

and children, because of a critical labor shortage. However, the Soviet people were by now united against the common enemy. It was plain that the invader had come to enslave rather than to liberate. The Stalin regime guided this new wave of patriotism, through public announcements, propaganda, and other measures. People were encouraged to join the Communist Party, which had been an exclusive sect before the war. Membership almost doubled despite huge losses in membership as a result of the war, and German reprisals against any Communists they could identify when entering villages and towns. By early 1943, the siege of Leningrad was partially broken by armies of the Volkhovsky and Leningrad Fronts. In February the Red Army captured the cities of Voronezh and Kursk. The Germans were on the run. (Plate 5.2)

Wartime culture: the peak of Socialist Realism

The war years gave rise to new forms of cultural propaganda, particularly after the Battle of Stalingrad when the media were once again allowed to focus on Stalin, this time in his new role as war leader. Even in the early months of the war, however, the importance of cultural figures was paramount. Prominent writers, musicians, artists, film directors, and poets, such as Sergey Eisenstein, Anna Akhmatova, and Boris Pasternak, were evacuated from Moscow to ensure their safety. Both

Eisenstein and Sergey Prokofiev were commissioned by Stalin to work on a film about Ivan the Terrible, a follow-up to director Eisenstein's prewar film *Aleksandr Nevsky*. As noted by Solomon Volkov (Volkov, 2008), however, Eisenstein's films, though critically acclaimed, never had mass appeal, and Soviet audiences preferred to watch the film *Chapayev*, made in 1934 by Georgy and Sergey Vasilyev. The film was about the Russian Civil War and starred actor Boris Babochkin. It was perhaps the most popular of all Soviet films, and Stalin was one of the chief admirers. Ilya Ehrenburg had returned to Moscow from Paris in 1941 and took on the role of international propaganda chief for Stalin. His best-known writings during the war were publicized in *Pravda*, *Izvestiya*, and *Krasnaya zvezda*, and included inflammatory prose that was also distributed among frontline troops, perhaps the best-known being his leaflet "Kill," which included the statement "If you have not killed at least one German a day, you have wasted that day." During the war Ehrenburg was a member of the Jewish Anti-Fascist Committee. In less incendiary tone was the poem of Konstantin Simonov about a wartime woman waiting for her lover to return from the front. Reportedly, thousands of Russian soldiers kept copies of the poem with them at all times. Aleksandr Tvardovsky published a poem "Vassily Terkin" about a regular soldier who remains upbeat despite the horrors of war, thus providing an antidote to official reports that referred mainly to the roles of Stalin and high-ranking officers.

BOX 5.1

Ilya Ehrenburg (1891–1967)

Born on January 27, 1891 into a Jewish family in Kyiv, Ilya Ehrenburg was a prominent poet and writer, winning the Order of Lenin twice in 1944 and 1961. After the February Revolution, he became involved with the Bolsheviks' revolutionary activities; this led to his arrest in 1908 by the Okhrana, followed by five months' detention. He emigrated to avoid further arrests and chose Paris, knowing that Lenin was residing there at the time. During his stay in France, he began to write poetry. In 1917, following the October Revolution, Ehrenburg returned to Russia. There, he opposed the policies exercised by the Bolsheviks, which he expressed in his poem *Prayers for Russia* (1917). During the 1920s he published several popular novels that criticized both the capitalist and the communist systems. Ehrenburg began working as a foreign editor outside the Soviet Union for *Izvestiya* in 1932. He was a war journalist in the Spanish Civil War from 1936 to 1939 and, during the Second World War, wrote very popular propaganda poems directed against the German occupants. In 1952 he received the Stalin Prize. His novel *The Thaw*, published in 1954, tested the limits of censorship during the period of de-Stalinization under Khrushchev. In 1960, he began to write *People, Years, Life* (1961–1966), a depiction of the purges of writers. Ehrenburg died on August 31, 1967.

Socialist Realist art enjoyed its zenith during the war as artists were conscripted to produce paintings of various war scenes. Arkady Platov from the Simbirsk region, who excelled in painting village scenes, produced "The Germans Are Coming" in 1941 showing idyllic scenes from Soviet village life on the eve of the war. In the following year his painting "A German Plane Passes Overhead" depicted the aftermath of a German air raid, showing a young child and cattle dead, and a dog howling toward the sky. In similar vein was V. Serov's "The Enemy Was Here," which shows a dead girl stretched out on the grass and two partisan-like male figures examining the scene. In each case it is clear that the intent of the paintings is to equate the Germans with death and destruction. Aleksandr Deneika's "Defense of Sevastopol," completed in 1942, depicts dark-clad Germans fighting Soviet soldiers wearing white, heroically defending their port. At the front of the canvas lies a dead German. Konstantin Yuon, a Moscow-born painter who was partly of Swiss origin and a teacher at the Surikov Art Institute in Moscow, portrayed the famous commemoration of the revolution in Red Square on November 7, 1941 in his painting "Parade on Red Square," though the picture was not completed until after the war. Ya. Nikolayev's impressionistic painting "Leningrad 1941" (1942) shows huddled figures lining up for bread during the early stages of the German siege of the city. Sergey Gerasimov's early watercolors are considered masterpieces, but like other artists of the Soviet era he was obliged to switch to the Socialist Realist style and one of his most famous wartime offerings is "Mother of a Partisan" (1943), which features a barefoot peasant woman standing defiantly in front of a brutish German soldier who is trying to arrest her Partisan son. Fyodor Bogorodsky won the Stalin Prize in 1945 for his "Glory to the Fallen Heroes."

However, the artist who might be considered typical of the era is the now much maligned Aleksandr Gerasimov (no relation to Sergey cited above), who rose from humble peasant origins in Tambov region to become the godfather of Socialist Realist art and a close acquaintance of Stalin. A. Gerasimov's patron was Kliment Voroshilov, who was an early subject for his canvases, though Gerasimov also painted Lenin and eventually (1933) a portrait of Stalin at the 16th Party Congress (Bown and Taylor, 1993). Unlike some other artists of the period, A. Gerasimov appeared genuinely to endorse Socialist Realism, and expressed his disgust at Western art and its avant-garde themes. During the war, having returned from his evacuation in Tblisi, Georgia, the artist completed his "Hymn to October" concerning Stalin's speech at the Bolshoy Theatre with the Germans at the gates of Moscow in November 1941. By mid-July he was endowed with the title "People's Artist of the USSR." Both "Hymn to October" (1942) and "The Four Oldest Artists" (1944) received the Stalin Prize, an award that Gerasimov received four times in his career. His preference in his spare time was for painting nudes, but he is better-known as a portrait painter of Soviet leaders. After the war he became president of the USSR Academy of Arts at the time when critical attacks on any kind of experimentation in art were the norm. A. Gerasimov always stressed the serf background of his ancestors and was a heavy consumer of vodka.

BOX 5.2

Aleksandr Gerasimov (1881–1963)

Aleksandr Gerasimov was one of the leading advocates of Socialist Realism and produced many well-known realist paintings such as "Lenin on the Tribune" (1929–1930). He was born on August 12, 1881 in Kozlov (now Michurinsk) in Tambov region. From 1903 to 1915, he attended the Moscow School of Painting, Sculpture and Architecture. He served in the Russian army during the First World War and the Red Army during the Russian Civil War, and upon his return home authored plays that glorified the Revolution and the Soviet government. His works often depicted prominent revolutionary leaders as great heroic figures. He was a founding member of the Association of Artists of Revolutionary Russia (AKhRR) in 1927, and remained with them until 1932. He then chaired the Moscow section of the Union of Soviet Artists (MOSSKh) from 1937 to 1939. In 1941 he won the Stalin Prize, the first of four he would receive during his career, for his painting "Stalin and Voroshilov in the Kremlin" (1938). Between 1939 and 1954 he chaired the Union of Soviet Artists and went on to become the president of the USSR Academy of Art – founded in 1947 – until 1957. Like other well-known Socialist Realist artists, he was a strong opponent of formalism, especially later in his life, and criticized it particularly during the period of Andrey Zhdanov's ascendancy immediately after the Second World War. He died on July 23, 1963.

Though such paintings may have been inspirational, they are considered practically worthless today. However, Gorky deployed Socialist Realism in particular as a means to incite the Soviet population to embrace Communism, and subsequently Russian patriotism during the war years and on through the Cold War. In addition to Gorky, the other upholder of art for political purposes was Stalin, who became its chief subject. In later years, particularly under the leadership of Brezhnev, memory of the war years and Soviet heroism and losses was commemorated through monuments; but, while the war was in progress, art, poetry, prose, and music played a critical role. In the last sphere were patriotic symphonies composed by Shostakovich (Seventh Symphony, or "Leningrad"), Khatchaturian (Symphony No. 2, officially written for the 25th anniversary of the October Revolution) and Prokofiev (Sixth and Seventh Sonatas) among others. In 1942, Stalin asked Sergey Mikhalkov, a writer of children's literature, to come up with lyrics for a new national anthem ("Hymn of the Soviet Union"), the music for which was composed by Aleksandr Aleksandrov; and it was adopted officially at the start of 1944, replacing the former anthem of the Internationale. Aleksandrov teamed up with Vasily Lebedev-Kumach to write perhaps the most famous Soviet song of the war years called "Svyashchennaya voina" ("Sacred War"), completed shortly after the German invasion. Many of the wartime hymns and songs remained popular until the end of the Soviet period and beyond. Mikhalkov, for example, was asked to write new lyrics in 1977 and again in 2001 when the original tune was also restored as the national anthem of Russia.

BOX 5.3

Sergey Prokofiev (1891–1953)

Sergey Prokofiev, born on April 27, 1891, is one of the most celebrated Russian composers of the 20th century. As a young composer, he left the Soviet Union after the October Revolution, despite pleas to stay, and toured Europe and the United States. His first major success came in Chicago in 1920 with the opera *The Love for Three Oranges*. Abroad, response to Prokofiev's works was mixed, but when he embarked on a tour of Russia in 1927 he was welcomed as a national hero. By 1936 he had decided to reside permanently in Moscow. Prokofiev soon took an interest in film music and the theatrical stage, producing numerous successful scores such as *Hamlet* (1937), *Aleksandr Nevsky* (1939), and *Ivan the Terrible* (1942–1945). During the war years, he wrote the opera *War and Peace* (1943–1953), completed the war-inspired Sixth Sonata (1940) and Seventh Sonata (1942), the latter winning the Stalin Prize, and his best-known score, the Fifth Symphony (1944), which also earned the same award. Soon afterward, his health began to worsen; and the passing of the Zhdanov Decree in 1948, which targeted him as a formalistic composer, exacerbated the decline of his health. Still, he continued to compose various scores, including his Seventh Symphony (1951–1952), which earned the Lenin Prize in 1957, a posthumous award. He died on the same day as Stalin – March 5, 1953, with his death symbolically overshadowed by the passing of the Soviet leader.

The Battle of Kursk Salient

By the spring of 1943, the Soviet military had gained supremacy not only on the ground but also in the air. Germany could no longer fight along the entire Eastern Front, but had to resort to an elastic defense, enticing the Red Army forward and then mounting incisive counter-attacks, in the hope of encircling units that had advanced too far too quickly. In retrospect this policy was relatively successful. Against formidable odds, the Germans kept fighting in the USSR, though they were gradually pushed westward. Not until the summer would the Soviets achieve the overwhelming offensive demanded by Stalin. By the summer of 1943, Hitler planned one last major drive, involving the southern army groups, and with the intention of exploiting a Soviet "bulge" west of Kursk. German production had improved under Armaments Minister Albert Speer. Moreover, the Germans had improved the design of their tanks, such as the Tiger, the Panther, and the Ferdinand. They were now better-armored than their Soviet counterparts, though less mobile. The attack on Kursk Salient was to deploy tanks, and fifty crack German divisions, about 43 percent of all forces on the Eastern Front. Success would perhaps once again bring the USSR to its knees, by eliminating up to seven Soviet armies. The German plan was very simple – they would attack the salient from the north and the south – but failure would be very costly, since the Germans had little in reserve. The campaign would be known as Operation Zitadelle. It had the approval of Hitler and his chief of staff, General Kurt

Zeitzler, but many of the more experienced tank commanders had grave reservations about the wisdom of attempting a new advance in this fatalistic fashion.

Once again, the timing of the operation proved to be critical for the Germans. Had the operation taken place in May, as Hitler wished, then possibly the Germans might have broken through Soviet lines before they had time to prepare defences adequately, but the required tanks were not available until the beginning of July. As for the USSR, its major tanks, the T-34 and the KV-1, had performed superbly in earlier conflicts. By 1943 the key tank was the T-34c, which could outpace any German tank. In addition, Soviet intelligence had uncovered the German plans, and now the Soviet forces had time to organize. Following a familiar pattern, Zhukov was appointed Commander of the Kursk Front, and ordered his men to build bunkers and tank traps, lay mines, and dig trenches. The scale of the defensive operation was remarkable – around 3,100 miles of trenches along a line that extended about ninety miles from north to south. Two army fronts were created – the Central Front under Rokossovsky, and the Voronezh Front under Vatutin. The Steppe Front, under Konev, was kept in reserve. As Douglas Lee Welsh points out in *The Russian War Machine* (Mayer, 1977), the Soviet goal was to separate the German infantry from German armor, without which it would be highly exposed. The Red Air Force was basically in control of the skies above the salient, and the battle clearly favored the defender.

Before the attack, the Germans launched an artillery barrage – a clear sign to the Soviets that the attack was expected – and then a large group of tanks and infantry went into battle on July 5, under the command of Model and Manstein. At first, German success was stunning as the enormous Tigers burst through the Soviet lines, eliminating the T-34s and KVs before they could get close enough to be effective. As the Soviet infantry retreated, the lack of machine-gun fire indicated that the new German tank had not been equipped with protection against infantry. Possibly Hitler never anticipated that his new tanks could be in a situation in which they faced only infantry. Once the fleeing Red Army soldiers realized that they were not vulnerable, they turned on the tanks, using grenades or firing through the hatches at the drivers. The effect was as notable as the early reverses. The culmination point of the battle was at the village of Prokhorovka, where at one point there were 1,200 tanks on the battlefield. Amid the mayhem and slaughter, each side lost about 400 tanks without obtaining a decisive breakthrough. It became evident that the German assault had failed; and, on July 12, Hitler called off Operation Zitadelle, a war of attrition that had not achieved the desired result.

Zhukov ordered a counter-attack that saw the Red Army achieve success after a hesitant start. The Soviet push involved armies from several fronts – the Steppe, the Voronezh, the Western, the Central, and the Bryansk. By August 5, Orel and Belgorod had fallen into Soviet hands. On August 23, the major prize of Kharkiv, the largest city in the southwestern USSR, was recaptured. German losses in this campaign were huge – more than 1,500 tanks had been destroyed, along with 3,700 planes. Human casualties were around 500,000 troops, the last remaining hope of the German army. Though the battle at Kursk Salient was not such an emphatic victory as Stalingrad, it was arguably more decisive. Henceforth, the Germans would be unable to mount a significant offensive in the east. In September, a battle began for control of the Dnipro river, Germany's main line of defense. In the southeast, the city of Donetsk changed hands on September 8. November saw a major offensive during which the Red Army crossed the Dnepr. The Ukrainian capital of Kyiv was reoccupied on November 6.

In general, after 1942, the Soviet drive was relentless despite several reverses. Stalin and Zhukov were anxious to retake the lands the USSR had occupied by the summer of 1940. Speed was considered essential. Whereas, in the early part of the war, Stalin's constant demand of his allies was for a second front, in the latter part of the war, with one notable exception, the goal was to advance as quickly as possible, whatever the weather and whatever the defensive fortifications of the Germans. By 1944 the Red Army had reverted to the tactics that Zhukov had tried so disastrously in early 1943. Rather than focus energy on one particular point on the front, the goal was to attack on several fronts simultaneously, simply to overwhelm the Germans by numbers. The defenders might eliminate the first few waves but would eventually be overrun. Fortified by a large shot of vodka before they went into battle, the first waves were sacrificed for the ultimate goal. The early part of 1944 saw one German defeat after another. By the beginning of March, the blockade of Leningrad, already weakened, was finally lifted. In the Korsun region the armies of the First and Second Ukrainian Fronts under Vatutin and Konev encircled a large group of Germans. Konev managed a remarkable feat in March by advancing during the harsh flood conditions of the spring thaw. As a result, the Army of the Second Ukrainian Front had reached the Romanian border by March. In the south, the Crimean peninsula was also retaken. The Red Army was now preparing for the final stage of the reconquest of the USSR.

Stalin and his allies

The relationship between the three wartime leaders, Stalin, Churchill, and Roosevelt, has prompted much debate. The three personalities were very different, and one could assert that none operated according to traditional methods of diplomacy. Churchill was probably the most outspoken anti-Soviet statesman of the early 20th century, and one of the key supporters of Allied intervention in Russia after the Bolshevik Revolution. He was a man for the grand occasion, and his carefully rehearsed speeches had rallied the British in the critical period after the collapse of France in June 1940. Roosevelt was less open, and always anxious to allay Stalin's natural fears that the two English-speaking nations would join together against the Communist ally or even join forces with the Germans. By June 1941, Churchill had achieved a complete volte-face after the German invasion of the USSR – a moment of great joy to him, as it signified that the war would no longer be confined to the British Empire, on the one hand, and the Axis Powers, on the other. He immediately offered British help for the Soviet Union, even though the British had been unable to provide aid to Poland, the country whose integrity they had guaranteed in March 1939.

Roosevelt was more circumspect, content at first to offer both the British and the Soviets aid through Lend-Lease rather than entering the war. He was always aware through Churchill's letters and his own devices. In July 1941, Britain and the USA anticipated joint operations in a war against Germany, and formally recognized this agreement by the signing of the Atlantic Charter on September 24, 1941, by which the three states declared a common goal to struggle against Fascism. On September 29, 1941, representatives of the three countries met in Moscow – Molotov on behalf of the Soviet Union; Averell Harriman, the advisor to President Roosevelt, for the United States; and Lord Beaverbrook for Britain. The Moscow conference agreed on further supplies to Britain and the Soviet Union from the United States up to the summer of 1942, and led to the formal inclusion of the USSR in the Lend-Lease Program on November 7, 1941.

By 1942 the three allies were on a firmer footing. On May 26, 1942, Britain and the USSR signed an agreement for a united and common war effort against Germany and its allies in Europe, with an addition about cooperation and mutual aid once the war had been brought to a successful conclusion. The next month, a similar treaty was signed between the United States and the Soviet Union. Another meeting in Moscow followed between Stalin and Churchill, and then a major conference was held there from October 19 to 30, 1943. Present were Molotov, British Foreign Minister Anthony Eden, and US Secretary of State Cordell Hull. The conference discussed ways to bring the war to a rapid close, particularly in view of the surrender of the Italians, and their new role as a participant on the Allied side. The Allies signed an agreement on future world security, and set a definite time for the opening of a second front in the west for May–June 1944. Stalin and Churchill had by this time signed an agreement on bringing the Nazis to justice for crimes against humanity, thus establishing the foundations for the Nuremberg trials. The Moscow meeting paved the way for the first formal conference of the three Allied wartime leaders, which took place in Tehran, from November 28 to December 1, 1943.

The Tehran meeting anticipated a postwar settlement following joint operations to eliminate the German forces in Europe and ratified the Moscow decision to open a second front in the West. However, no decision could be finalized on the future borders of Poland, as Stalin consistently demanded that the borders established after September 1939 be recognized. The question was put off until the next major summit, and in the meantime the Red Army crossed the old Soviet border into these territories. To Stalin, control over Eastern Europe was essential. Some countries made his task easier. On the initiative of Eduard Benes, the USSR signed an agreement with Czechoslovakia on December 12, 1943 concerning postwar friendship and cooperation. Benes may have been naïve, but he was unlikely to forget the betrayal of his country by the Western democracies at the Munich summit. The following May, the two countries reached an agreement on military relations after the arrival of the Red Army. Of all the East European countries, Czechoslovakia on paper had least to fear from the Red Army. The liberation of the Motherland, however, was to be followed by new conquests. Since the victory at Stalingrad, Soviet propaganda had begun to extol Stalin's military wisdom, and his role as the protector of his people. By this time, Stalin was rarely seen out of military uniform. Indeed, in paintings of the period, he is always depicted in uniform, often fictitiously at the front, taking an active part in the war. In fact, Stalin rarely left the Kremlin. A significant gap had emerged between the perception of the dictator and the reality. The war had not changed Stalin, other than to render him wise enough to allow his talented generals to take charge of the intricate features of military planning. In retrospect, there is no reason to maintain that the true nature of the Stalinist system changed during the war; rather the malevolence and the desire for retribution were focused on the avowed rather than the imaginary enemies of the Soviet state.

It was at the three leaders' second conference that tensions emerged. The Yalta conference took place in the Livadia Palace in the Crimea from February 4 to 11, 1945. Stalin had other advantages over his Anglo-American counterparts besides the fact that the conference took place on Soviet soil. Roosevelt was gravely ill by this time. The USSR, through bugging devices, could monitor the discussions of the Allied teams before the meetings. Third, the areas under dispute were controlled by the Red Army, which by now had won a series of massive victories. Stalin had become the leading arbiter over the destiny of Europe; the Western leaders could only pick up the pieces and try to limit the territory that would fall under the sway of the USSR. Before Yalta, the focus on the European front had fallen on Poland. In the summer of 1944, the GKO launched Operation Bagration, the attack on Belarus using four army groups that copied earlier German tactics by encircling and then eliminating German armies. Minsk was recaptured on July 3, along with other Belarusian towns such as Vitebsk and Mogilev. The captured Germans were then forced to march through the streets of Moscow before a jeering crowd, in a parade presided over by Stalin, who liked nothing better than a public spectacle that degraded his enemies.

Later in 1944, events on the Eastern Front went according to plan from the Soviet perspective. Between July and October, the armies of the 3rd Belarusian Front entered the Baltic States, while in July and August the troops of the 1st Ukrainian Front moved into Western Ukraine, capturing the city of Lviv, and advancing into Poland as far as the Vistula. There, Rokossovsky halted, waiting for supplies and allowing his men to recover from the rapid advance. Moscow Radio, however, enticed the Polish Home Army in Warsaw to choose this moment for an uprising against their German rulers. The implication was that the Soviet troops would come to their aid. The uprising was duly launched, and though it achieved some initial success the Poles could not beat five German divisions without outside aid. Both the British and the

US governments appealed to Stalin to allow his troops to support the Poles, or at the very least to permit Allied planes based in northern Italy to fly over Warsaw and drop supplies, while picking up the wounded and refueling on Soviet-occupied territory. Stalin refused, maintaining that a group that was anti-Soviet had initiated the uprising. The consequences for the Polish Home Army were fatal. The Germans repressed the uprising brutally and then razed Warsaw, so that the only options for the Home Army were to fight to the last man, flee, or to take refuge in the sewers of the city. More than six decades on, it seems that the Soviet version of events, that the armies of the 1st Ukrainian Front were not in a condition to attack Warsaw, was accurate. All the same, Stalin could easily have allowed his Western allies to supply aid, which at the very least would have prolonged the conflict. For Stalin, it was preferable that the Home Army be defeated emphatically.

By July, Stalin also had in mind the formation of the future Polish government. A Polish Committee for National Liberation was formed under Polish auspices; by August it was based in the city of Lublin, which was made the temporary capital of Poland as long as Warsaw remained under German occupation. In early 1945 the Soviet government recognized the Lublin Committee as the future government of Poland. By the end of 1944, all of Poland was under Soviet occupation. These matters posed serious dilemmas for Roosevelt and Churchill. The former had been re-elected as president for a third term, partly through the backing of Americans of Polish ancestry who supported the Democratic Party. Churchill led a country that had guaranteed the integrity of the Polish state that emerged after the First World War. London was the home of the Polish Government-in-Exile that had been recognized by the Soviet Union until the Germans uncovered the mass graves at Katyn. Thus, in the run-up to the Yalta summit, it was evident that the Polish question would be high on the agenda. The treaty's goal was to lay the foundations of postwar society. Plainly the Germans and their remaining allies were about to lose the war. East European countries had already pulled out of the Axis. By September 1944, as the Soviet army advanced southwest into Romania and the other countries of the Balkans, Romania and Bulgaria quickly came to terms. Admiral Horthy in Hungary was willing to do the same, but the SS deposed him and mounted a last-ditch stand in Budapest. In the north, Finland pulled out of the war on September 1944 and signed a peace treaty with the Soviet Union and Britain. On October 20, the Yugoslav People's Army of Tito, a loyal devotee of Stalin at that time, liberated Belgrade. These victories all bolstered Stalin and Molotov's position at Yalta.

On some matters, there was basic agreement at the Yalta meeting – Germany was to be completely disarmed and ordered to pay reparations for the damage caused by its armies during the war. A United Nations was to be established after the war. Stalin maintained that, once it was created, all the republics of the Soviet Union should be permitted seats. The summit compromised by agreeing that, in addition to the Soviet Union, the Ukrainian and Belarusian republics should be allotted places in the new body as compensation for the suffering endured during the war. Once the war in Europe had ended, Stalin agreed that within three months the USSR would attack Japan, thus violating the non-aggression pact signed with that country in 1941. As a result, the USSR hoped to regain territory lost by the Russian Empire to Japan during the Russo-Japanese war of 1905. Once again Stalin was demonstrating his Great Russian attitude in foreign policy affairs. On matters pertaining to central Europe, however, the first signs of the coming Cold War were already evident. With great reluctance, the Western allies recognized the Curzon Line as the Soviet–Polish border, signifying that the territories of Eastern Poland annexed by the USSR in September 1939 would not be returned to Poland. Instead, Poland would be given large chunks of German territory in the west, including German Silesia, West Prussia, and Pomerania. East Prussia would be divided between Poland (south) and the USSR (north), with the latter gaining the valuable port of Koenigsberg, which would be promptly renamed Kaliningrad (as was the newly created province) after the longstanding Soviet Prime Minister. Poland in fact had been moved about 100 miles to the west – the city of Katowice, which had been located on Poland's southwestern border, was now firmly in the center of the country. Lastly, the Allies agreed that after the war the governments formed in Eastern Europe would be both democratic and friendly toward the USSR. This clause of the treaty was bound to elicit future arguments as to what constituted a "democratic state." Perhaps, of all the Yalta provisions, this one was cited most regularly as demonstrating the bad faith of Stalin, who never intended to allow Western-style democracies to be established on the USSR's western border.

Was Yalta another version of the Munich Treaty, with the Soviet Union now cast in the role of the aggressor? Stalin certainly got the better of his two wartime allies, but they were at a serious disadvantage. Roosevelt and Churchill had to negotiate for territories that were already occupied by the armies of the various Soviet Fronts. Perhaps the Western Powers could have gained certain advantages had they decided to invade Europe in 1943 rather than in 1944, i.e. to abandon the campaign to attack Italy through what Churchill termed "the soft underbelly of Europe." This would have involved very heavy casualties, but it might have forced the issue in Europe, and permitted the Western armies to penetrate much further eastward than turned out to be the case. However, such supposition has its reverse side – a deep Western advance would likely have tied up more German armies on the Western Front, thereby permitting a rapid Soviet advance from the east. Montgomery and Eisenhower did not agree over tactics to be pursued in the West, but operated according to the premise that the Soviet Union was an ally, and not a future enemy. Stalin, on the other hand, appears to have had more foresight, likely because he never trusted his temporary partners in the first place. As in other facets of policy, his goal was to gain every advantage possible, using subterfuge if not outright lies. The Yalta Treaty represents the culmination point of Stalinist foreign policy, a veritable triumph that paved the way for Soviet domination of Eastern Europe, and first and foremost Poland, for more than four decades after the end of the war.

Victory in the West and in the East

The year 1945 was in some ways the most dramatic of the war, both in the scale of the battles and in their consequences. In January–February 1945, the two northern fronts of the Soviet forces – the First Belarusian Front under Zhukov and the First Ukrainian Front under Konev – advanced from the Vistula to the Oder rivers. The attack began partly at the request of the Western allies, who were being placed under severe pressure in the Ardennes region. The Red Army by contrast marched over 300 miles in just over three weeks, and during this period occupied all interwar Polish territory. East Prussia, which had been cut off from the rest of Germany on January 24, held out until April 1945 when the last German remnants in Koenigsberg were defeated. At the Oder, Soviet forces halted, while the Germans prepared themselves for a last stand in front of their capital. Stalin incited Soviet soldiers to take revenge during this campaign. In the former German and Austrian territories of Central Europe, the Red Army began a systematic campaign of looting, torture, and rape, as though to release all the pent-up energy of the savage fighting. One explanation for these excesses may have been that Soviet soldiers had uncovered the Nazi death camps, freeing living skeletons and uncovering mass graves. However, the pattern of the atrocities was rather familiar, and the majority of the victims were equally innocent.

The German 9th Army had fourteen poorly equipped divisions to defend its capital, calling up the Hitler Youth and other raw recruits. They faced 110 Soviet infantry divisions with a formidable arsenal of artillery and guns. The campaign was one of the most difficult of the entire war, despite the overwhelming advantages possessed by the Soviet commanders. It took sixteen days for the Soviet armies to capture the ruins of Berlin, with casualties of around 360,000 men, some of whom were lost at the Battle of Seelow Heights (April 16–19), with Zhukov again leading the attack. Hitler, the coveted prize, committed suicide on April 30, five days after Konev's forces met the Americans, at Torgau on the Elbe, cutting Germany in two. The Americans had stopped at the Elbe, allowing the Soviet forces to capture territories within reach of their armies – a decision that was to cost the Allies greatly in the coming years. On May 6, the armies of the First Ukrainian Front began an operation to capture Prague that ended on May 11, the last day of fighting in Europe. Germany capitulated on May 8, and Stalin gave a victory speech in Red Square the next day, the date that was to be commemorated throughout the Soviet period and beyond as Victory Day. The official victory parade took place in Red Square on 24 June. Zhukov received the victorious troops, who included 1,000 personnel from every front during the war, and Rokossovsky was in command of the soldiers on parade. The leaders of the party and the government, headed by Stalin, stood on Lenin's Mausoleum. A 1,400-strong orchestra played, and Zhukov told the gathering that they had achieved a victory the like of which had never been known.

The postscript to the war from the Soviet perspective was the operation against Japan, which occurred against the background of the testing and deployment of the atomic bomb by the Americans. The Japanese had anticipated that the USSR might perform the role of mediator in the war against the United States, but the Soviet government had denounced the neutrality agreement on April 5, 1945. On the night of August 8–9, the Red Army crossed the border into Manchuria. Three fronts were established: the Baikal under Marshal R. Ya. Malinovsky; the First Far Eastern Front under Marshal Meretskov, whose career following his removal at the beginning of the war had come full circle; and the Second Far Eastern Front under General M. A. Purkayev. Overall command was in the hands of Marshal Vasilevsky. Though Soviet and Russian sources have stressed the quality of the troops facing the Soviet armies, it appears that the Japanese had little stomach for another conflict against the Russians. The Red Army moved rapidly and advanced about fifty miles per day before the Japanese Kwantung army surrendered on August 18. In the Far East, the Red Army had fought for nine days, but by early September the rewards were considerable: Stalin's troops controlled the northeast part of China, North Korea, all of Sakhalin Island, and the Japanese Kurile Islands. General K. N. Derevyanko was present at the ceremony for the official capitulation of Japan on September 2, 1945. Ultimately, however, the USSR was not permitted to play a role in the future administration of Japan, though it did retain the Kurile Islands, thereby reversing and adding to the 1905 Treaty of Portsmouth with Japan.

The results of the Great Patriotic War

The war replaced the October Revolution as the most important event in Soviet history. It was used to legitimize Soviet rule, and as the foundation for an expanding new empire that would extend into Eastern and Central Europe, the Far East, and the Near East. The German Fascist threat would be portrayed as the greatest danger ever posed to humankind. It had been overcome, according to the official Soviet version of events, only by the unity and resolution of Soviet forces under the leadership of Stalin (whose role would be downplayed by 1956 and especially after 1961). The war was also identified with a great victory of Russians above all other peoples of the USSR. In part, this attitude reflected Stalin's belief that many non-Russians had acted disloyally and often treacherously at the beginning of the war. There were of course Russian traitors (the former Soviet general Andrey Vlasov is the best-known) as well as those of other Soviet nationalities. But after 1945 the conjunction of Russians with Soviets became commonplace. The Russians emerged as the leading force in Soviet society. Their prime role was recognized. Russian achievements were magnified and exaggerated, whereas other nationalities were told to show gratitude to the Russians for liberating them from the Fascist occupants.

The scale of the war simply defied belief for future generations. Nothing had been seen like it before. The size of the German invasion force was the largest ever encountered, and the ferocity of the battles also appeared to be without precedent.

Yet, whatever the suffering, Soviet propaganda raised the war to a new platform. It could not simply be portrayed along the lines of defeat, occupation, and then victory. Instead, following Molotov's earlier example, it was depicted first of all as a "treacherous" invasion (even though widely anticipated at some point), following which the entire Soviet people fought to remove the hated invader, and did so, freeing Europe in the aftermath. The role of the Western Allies was largely ignored. Victims of the Jewish Holocaust on Soviet territory were never singled out, but rather included anonymously among the Soviet dead. Sixty-five years on, this version of the war still remains in place in many Russian cities (and even non-Russian cities, such as Minsk). As such, perspective on the war, even the questioning of events, battles, alignment of forces, has remained almost impossible. By 2009 it was designated a criminal offense to do so.

In the Soviet period, every textbook on Soviet history dwelled at length on the results of the Great Patriotic War, emphasizing the tremendous losses and the damage caused by the invader. That such losses occurred is not in doubt. However, to the impact of the occupier can be added some equally destructive actions by the Soviet forces themselves. Two Soviet republics, Ukraine and Belarus, bore huge losses. Proportionally the latter lost more civilians during the war than any other nation worldwide – one in every four people. As for Russia itself, it had borne great battles at Moscow, Leningrad, Stalingrad, and Kursk. The war affected many parts of Russia but in different ways. Asian Russia provided troops and industrial goods for the war effort, as did the eastern part of European Russia. The fighting, however, penetrated only part of Russia. Some areas suffered Nazi occupation for three years, others for a matter of weeks. For years, Soviet works did not focus on human losses, possibly because of the sheer scale of Soviet casualties. The Soviet regime celebrated a great victory and did not wish to belittle the achievement by revealing the ratio of its losses vis-à-vis the Germans. Instead the regime declared that about 25 million people had been deprived of the most elementary of housing, and focused on the destruction of towns, villages, bridges, and railways.

According to Russian statistics, by May 9, 1945, more than 6.9 million Axis troops had perished in the war, of which about 2.8 million (or about 40 percent) had died on the Eastern Front. Soviet deaths in the army are calculated at 8.6 million. However, population deaths in the USSR – military and civilian – were around 27 million (as compared to 6 million in Germany). Thus the ratio was about 4.5:1 Soviet over German deaths. Of the 27 million Soviet dead, more than three-quarters were men, all born between 1901 and 1931. These figures overlook certain factors. Some Soviet citizens (an estimated 500,000) chose not to return to the Soviet Union. Stalin deported seven entire nations from their homelands in 1944–1945 for alleged cooperation with the enemy – the Crimean Tatars, the Kalmyks, the Chechens, the Ingushetians, the Karachai, the Balkars, and the Meshketian Turks – while the Volga Germans had suffered the same fate earlier in the war. Likewise the purges and executions of alleged traitors, panic-mongers, and officers who refused to stand and fight to the last man – mainly at the beginning of the war – added to the immense death-toll. Whatever the cause of the deaths, the impact on the demographic makeup of the population was extraordinary – women of reproductive age outnumbered their male counterparts by about 4:1 in the European part of the country, with the imbalance being particularly high in the villages. In 1946 in the Soviet Union as a whole, there were 96.2 million women and 74.4 million men.

The first task for the Soviet authorities at the end of the war was demobilization of the army. At the beginning of the German–Soviet war, the Red Army's active troops numbered 2.9 million. By the end of the war the figure was 11 million. Demobilization began in 1945 but took three years to complete, leaving an active army of 2.5 million troops. The youngest members of the army were the last to return to civilian life. Many of these were restless recruits who had no great desire to search for jobs because the army had been their first and only experience in life. Victory in the war undoubtedly generated a great optimism in society. This sentiment even pervaded the growing Gulag camp system, where inmates were confident of a general amnesty. Instead the camp population grew with the arrival of new prisoners, who included not only alleged traitors and collaborators but also troops who had seen service outside the borders of the Soviet Union, and soon DPs (Displaced Persons), some of whom had been forcefully repatriated from camps in Central Europe. Many of them were arrested upon their return. Others were happy to come home, but still some of them were interrogated and detained. In many respects, the late 1940s were one of the most difficult periods in Soviet history – the country needed a long respite from the effects of the war, but it continued to be run like a military camp.

Two further major conferences took place in 1945 as the war approached its end. From April 25 to June 25, 1945, a Conference on the United Nations took place in San Francisco, attended by forty-two nations. The Soviet delegation for the first two weeks was led by Molotov, as the Commissar of Foreign Relations, and then subsequently by the dour Belarusian Andrey Gromyko, then at the beginning of his long diplomatic career. Gromyko had been appointed Soviet ambassador to the United States and emissary to Cuba in 1943, and he had been present at the meeting in Washington in 1944 that gave formal agreement to found the UN. The conference set up the formal network of the organization, which would work to establish international peace and security, amicable relations between the world's nations, and international cooperation in resolving problems. Three weeks after the San Francisco conference ended, the Allied powers met for the last time, at Potsdam, in the ruins of suburban Berlin. Stalin represented the USSR, Truman the United States, and Churchill Britain. The last had to return to Britain for an election during the conference and was defeated in a landslide by the Labour Party under Clement Attlee. The Potsdam Conference was far from friendly. It concurred on the need to remove all Nazi influences from Germany, on reparations, and on the establishment of the western border of Poland. It confirmed also the transfer to the Soviet Union of East Prussian territories, including the city of Koenigsberg.

Economic recovery

The devastation of the war years remained for some time, but industry recovered more rapidly than agriculture. The State Defense Committee was abolished on September 4, 1945, and the industrial ministries reverted to civilian heavy industrial organizations. Machine-building replaced the production of tanks. The establishment of industries in the areas to the east of the Urals provided a basis for the further industrial development. However, the productive capacity of the country had declined by about two-thirds. Between March 12 and 19, 1946, the USSR Supreme Soviet approved the 4th Five-Year Plan for the years 1946–1950 – the 3rd Five-Year Plan having been disrupted by the war. At the same meeting the government of the USSR, the Council of People's Commissars, was given the more formal and less revolutionary title of the Council of Ministers. Stalin remained the Premier (Kalinin remained formal head of state as the Chairman of the Supreme Soviet until his resignation for health reasons in April – he died in June – but already his fall from favor was evident when Stalin had his wife arrested after the end of the war). The Presidium of the Council of Ministers was filled with Stalin's closest colleagues: Molotov ran Foreign Affairs; Beria was given the chairmanship of a special committee for atomic energy; Voznesensky became the Chairman of the State Planning Committee (Gosplan); A. A. Andreev was in charge of agriculture; and Mikoyan became the Minister for Foreign Trade.

The energies of the country were channeled into industrial recovery along with investment. This decision was as much for security as for economic reasons. The Soviet Union declined to participate in the Marshall Plan – which was aimed at European recovery – because it regarded it as an American provocation, so it was essential to concentrate on alleviating the main problems arising from the war. By 1948 the authorities said that industry had reached its prewar level of output, and by the end of the plan period the targets had been exceeded – an achievement as extraordinary as those of the initial five-year plan of 1929–1933. After September 1946 a wage differential was created according to the nature and amount of skill required for a job. The recovery of the towns, however, could hardly conceal the lamentable situation in the countryside, where an acute labor shortage marked the early postwar years. The number of working people on the collective farms had declined by 32.5 percent from the level of 1940. Then, for example, there had been almost 17 million males working in agriculture. At the beginning of 1946, only 6.5 million remained. The concept of a wage or payment on collective farms remained only on paper. In practice, the collective farmers in the early postwar years worked for nothing other than the food on their tables.

The government made no attempt to relieve the situation in the villages. Private plots were overtaxed, and state purchase prices for grain remained low. The tasks of the 4th Five-Year Plan, though modest, proved impossible to fulfill because of the reduction of sown area by more than 50 percent. As before the war, the recovery of industry – and the development of heavy industry in particular – was to be financed through taxation of the villages. Ration cards were supposed to be abolished in 1946, but the authorities found it unwise to carry out such a policy in the difficult conditions that emerged. In 1946 an acute drought occurred in many areas of the USSR – it was particularly acute in Eastern Ukraine where a new famine broke out – and the Soviet leaders postponed the end of the ration card system until 1947. A decree of February 1947, issued by the party's Central Committee, focused on "measures to raise agriculture in the postwar period." It demanded that the prewar level of agricultural output be attained within three years, but in the circumstances of the postwar village such a task proved impossible. Only in December 1947 was the ration card system eliminated, but the measure did not signify that Soviet residents now had enough food. In Moscow and Leningrad, sufficient food reserves were built up, but elsewhere the elimination of ration cards caused an immediate food crisis as people struggled in vain to find such basic requirements as bread, butter, and sugar.

In December 1947 the Soviet economic authorities introduced a monetary reform, made necessary by the inflation during the war period. Old money was changed for the new currency at a rate of ten old roubles to one new rouble. The ostensible goal was to undermine speculators, but it affected more deeply the elderly and villagers, who traditionally did not keep their surplus money in savings banks but with them. Many lost their lifetime savings overnight, though reform did stabilize the financial system. It is fair to say that all the countries involved in the Second World War faced similar problems in the early postwar years, but many others benefited from US credits. The Soviet Union decided to finance its own economic recovery, and the result was an extended period of hardship, particularly in the countryside. Soviet leaders paid little attention to the acute difficulties in agriculture, though they did begin to devise new programs for the extensive development of the countryside, and to demonstrate that the Soviet state, and Stalin in particular, would not baulk at controlling nature.

Two examples may suffice to illustrate this new attitude – one involved the scientist Trofim D. Lysenko, a man born in the Poltava region of Ukraine in 1898, a holder of the title Hero of Socialist Labor (1945), and a three-time recipient of the Stalin Prize (1941, 1943, and 1949). Lysenko was a charlatan, who essentially told the Soviet leaders what they wished to hear, namely that an organism could change its genetic characteristics through its interaction with the environment – a form of dialectics of nature. These characteristics could then be passed down to the next generation on a selective basis so that only those most desired would be developed in the offspring. The theory seems closer to Nazi science than to reality, but it suited the Stalin regime since it implied that the Soviet Union could revive agriculture by transforming one species of seed into another. From 1940 to 1965, Lysenko headed the Institute of Genetics of the Soviet Academy of Sciences with the direct support of Stalin. All opponents of his surreal theories were removed; many of them were imprisoned, including the distinguished geneticist Nikolay Vavilov (1887–1943), who was arrested and sent to the Gulag in Kolyma, where he died.

Stalin was always interested in grandiose schemes to alter the course of nature. In November 1948, a new Stalin Plan was announced, whereby a massive new hydroelectric station would be built in Western Siberia, with dams linking it to the Pacific Ocean, and an artificial sea would be built. Stalin had already initiated the White Sea Canal, which was built by slave labor from Gulag camps. In May 1952 the authorities also heralded a similar scheme, the Volga–Don Canal, also constructed by prison workers. The postwar years were a time of confidence and Soviet prestige. As early as June 1945, the victory over the Germans was attributed first and foremost to the Russian people. In the late Stalinist period, Russian achievements were propagated throughout the country, embracing both high-level scientific achievements and past history. Thus virtually every major invention was "discovered" to have been created by a Russian. Stalin was the infallible leader, a Russian by choice rather than by birth, but he identified with and promoted these new ideas. Tsarist history, previously considered a period of colonial rule over subject peoples, was transformed into a mission to civilize and educate backward regions, a progressive task over the centuries.

Armed resistance

The war did not end conflict for Soviet forces. In several borderland regions, fighting continued after the demise of the Germans, carried out by bands of insurgents who fought fanatically against the return of Soviet rule. One area was Western Ukraine, where a Ukrainian Insurgent Army (UPA) was founded in 1942, and reached a peak of around 40,000 members. Since the region had only been incorporated into the USSR for some twenty months in 1939–1941, it had not been subjected to Sovietization. On September 27, 1944, the party issued a decree "On deficiencies in party work in the western regions of Ukraine." The decree was premature as the war was still in progress, but it showed concern with the weak influence of the Communist Party in this important border region. Though the Germans had departed, the authorities targeted a new phenomenon – the "Ukrainian–German nationalist." The term signified alleged collaboration between the insurgents and the German occupiers, an incitement to the people to expose and eliminate the enemies within. For some time, however, the Red Army had other priorities, and it was left to the internal police, the MVD, to fight pitched battles against the insurgents, who could use the terrain to melt into the forests, certain of being supplied by sympathetic villagers.

The UPA fought battles with a variety of enemies at one time or another. During the war, it had several skirmishes with Polish forces (neither side showed the other the least mercy) and with Soviet Partisans who came through the region. It had some encounters with the Germans as they retreated. However, the main enemy was always the USSR, and the hope was that the Western allies would reject their former ally, Stalin, and enter a new conflict with the Soviet Union. The receipt of aid parachuted into the region by the Americans served only to bolster this hope. The insurgents frequented a border region that encompassed not only Soviet territory but also parts of Poland and Czechoslovakia. In June 1945, the USSR forced Czechoslovakia to cede Transcarpathian Ukraine, which became the westernmost region of the Ukrainian SSR. It had been under Hungarian rule before the end of the First World War, and then became part of Czechoslovakia in the interwar period. It had much in common with Ukraine, but also possessed its incumbent nationalist movement. However, its inclusion in Ukraine simplified the struggle against the UPA because it created a Soviet–Czechoslovak border. In 1947 the police forces of the USSR, Poland, and Czechoslovakia combined to hunt down the insurgents, forcing the movement underground. Under its leader Roman Shukhevych, the UPA continued the fight into the early 1950s, relying on terrorist raids and assassinations in the tradition of the prewar Organization of Ukrainian Nationalists under Stepan Bandera. In 1950, Shukhevych was killed in a skirmish near L'viv. Gulag observers such as Solzhenitsyn have noted the large proportion of Ukrainian nationalists in the camps, a good portion of them emanating from the UPA movement.

In 1948 the Soviet authorities initiated mass collectivization in the western borderlands, as well as in Eastern Europe. Though the movement failed in Poland and Hungary, it was introduced with typical ruthlessness in Soviet territories, using the experience of the 1930s without altering the methods. In the Baltic States it was introduced in 1949–1950, and here, too, the Soviet forces faced a local guerrilla movement before collectivization could begin. Delegations of local farmers were sent to model collective farms around the USSR, while Communist Party members were directed for permanent work in these regions. The kulak emerged once again as a target figure, but this time he was identified with bourgeois nationalists who were resisting Soviet rule. Collectivization certainly cut off the food supply for the insurgents, who responded with equal brutality by victimizing anyone in the village who had joined the new farms voluntarily. Machine-Tractor Stations were established in each district, and in 1949 the MTS political sections were re-established to enforce the movement. Before collectivization was completed, the Soviet authorities carried out a series of deportations of the native population to Siberia, particularly in 1948–1949. Russians, Central Asians, and other nationality groups replaced them. In Western Ukraine, Eastern Ukrainians again formed the basis of the party leadership, but in all regions outsiders were transferred to the area. Similarly, the authorities used an agreed population exchange with Poland to ensure that potentially troublesome Ukrainians were moved to areas of industrial labor shortages rather than to farms.

As a result of these measures, collectivization of the western borderlands was completed by the early 1950s. By 1951 more than 90 percent of households had been collectivized in Latvia, Estonia, right-bank Moldavia, and Western Ukraine, with Lithuania and Western Belarus fully collectivized by the middle of the decade. Stalin was dealing with populations that had demonstrated a noted lack of loyalty during the war. As such, these small regions took on an importance out of proportion to their size. They became the focal point of new plots, involving not only the Germans – who were, after all, defeated – but also sinister machinations by "Anglo-American imperialists," and subsequently by a new enemy, Zionism. In 1950 the US authorities founded under the auspices of the CIA the radio stations Radio Free Europe and Radio Liberty, to serve as surrogate broadcasters of news to the subject populations of the USSR. The western borderlands, more than any region except Poland, represented for the Soviets the most sensitive region – they had long been under bourgeois influence, they formed the gateway to the West, and they contained bitter anti-Soviet elements that were to resurface for the remainder of the Soviet period.

The period of High Stalinism

Postwar Stalinism may be divided into two periods. In the first, the government made an attempt to impose cultural uniformity under the leadership of Andrey Zhdanov, the Leningrad party boss. After Zhdanov's death in 1948, Stalin again began to pre-pare new purges at the highest level, while Soviet propaganda took on an anti-Semitic hue, against external Zionism and the alleged plots involving Soviet Jews. However, the two periods were linked and can be regarded as the zenith of High Stalinism. In the aftermath of the war, and in contrast to the relatively moderate trends toler-ated during the war, the postwar years saw a return to the repressive atmosphere of the 1930s. The campaign began with a party decree of August 14, 1946, which con-demned two Leningrad journals, *Zvezda* and *Leningrad*, for publishing articles by Anna Akhmatova and Mikhail Zoshchenko. Zhdanov led the attack, pointing out that Akhmatova was a reactionary and an individualist, while Zoshchenko wrote vulgar prose that tried to ridicule Soviet life and the Soviet people. At Zhdanov's behest, the Union of Writers withdrew their membership. The decree heralded a new era, in which writers had to adopt a policy that was fundamentally anti-Western. Stalin and Zhdanov maintained that several Soviet writers had demonstrated servility toward the West, or glorified Western achievements. Such unwarranted adulation was to be replaced by reverence for the Motherland, and praise for all aspects of Russian cultural and material achievement. No amount of hyperbole could be considered excess-ive. Those who opposed such a way of thinking were not loyal Soviet citizens. Rather they were rootless cosmopolitans. The Soviet press and radio added more illustrious names to the ranks of offenders, including Boris Pasternak and Yury German.

The new stipulations had profound effects on Soviet literature, art, and music. Soviet writing took on a rigid, formal style which was hardly distinct from official propa-ganda. Experiments in form and style were frowned upon. In all books and poems, the authors were required to lavish praise on the Soviet system, to praise its achievements, applaud Stalin and the benevolent role of the Russian people, and heap scorn on non-Soviet society. The most feared criticism among writers of this period was to be accused of being pro-Western. Cultural works were to be optimistic about the future and to emphasize the harmony of Soviet life. The new style was also reflected in postwar architecture and art. Classicism was the chief form, with the prime project being the prospective Palace of the Soviets, on the site of the Church of Our Savior, a giant edifice with a statue of Lenin at the highest point, soaring into the sky. It was never completed. On August 5, 1947, any autonomy enjoyed by Soviet artists ended after the establishment of an Academy of Arts of the USSR, which was subordinate to the Committee for Artistic Affairs. The party henceforth could command Soviet art. The key focus of postwar artists was Stalin. Typical was the work "Generalissimo of the Soviet Union I. V. Stalin" by Fyodor Reshetnikov. Similar renditions appeared under the authorship of Viktor Puzyrkov and Aleksandr Gerasimov. They depicted Stalin as aloof, separate from the people, a godlike figure. Often individual artistry gave way to artistic teams or brigades, a practice that had begun in the late 1930s. This sort of system precluded individual achievement in art and promoted uniformity. Art in this way became a form of organized propaganda. Brigades were also responsible for a series of new sculptures of Stalin and Lenin. Massive monuments to the victory in war were perhaps to be expected. They culminated in the statues to Mother Russia at Stalingrad and Kyiv. Yevgeny Vuchetich contributed a similar massive monument to the Treptov Memorial Park in Berlin.

BOX 5.4

Fyodor Reshetnikov (1906–1988)

Born to iconic painters on July 28, 1906 in Sursko-Lovskoe village in Ekaterinoslav region (now Dnipropetrovsk Oblast), Ukraine, Fyodor Pavlovich Reshetnikov was a renowned Soviet painter and regarded as one of the greatest artists of Socialist Realism. His famed works include "Generalissimo of the Soviet Union I. V. Stalin" (1948) and "The Great Oath" (1949). He was orphaned at an early age and raised by his brother. In the early 1930s while attending Vkhutein, an elite art college in Moscow, he gained notoriety for his realist representations and was employed as an artistic reporter. By the late 1940s, Reshetnikov had established himself as a distinguished Socialist Realist artist. He received many awards for his contributions to Soviet culture, including the prestigious Stalin Prize in 1949 and 1951. He became an appointed member of the Academy of Arts in 1953 and remained in the institution for over thirty years, becoming its Vice-President in 1974. Throughout his life he was a strong opponent of formalism and expressed his disapproval of "bourgeois" artistic movements in the book he authored entitled *Secrets of Abstractionism* (1963). He died in Moscow on December 13, 1988.

Many renowned cultural figures ran into trouble with Zhdanov's new uniformity. Eisenstein's *Ivan IV, Part 2*, portrayed the 16th-century ruler as a demonic tyrant, which proved offensive to a regime that had seen its leader compare himself consciously to the former tsar. Several composers stood accused of "formalism" and "anti-populism" in music. Their works were ideologically subjective and departed from contemporary themes. Foremost among them were Sergey Prokofiev, A. I. Khachaturian, Dmitry Shostakovich, and N. Myaskovsky. Much of their work was too experimental for official tastes. Like art and literature, the themes had to be clear and simple, and with the goal of elevating the Soviet regime and its leader. Not surprisingly, therefore, the period of cultural uniformity produced little of lasting cultural value. Authors continued to write, artists to paint, and musicians to compose, but the results were impersonal and the themes predictable. Stalin and Russia were now beyond criticism. The October Revolution was perceived exclusively as a Russian revolution, and the Russian Empire with its imperial past was perceived officially as a period of cultural enlightenment for backward peoples.

BOX 5.5

Dmitry D. Shostakovich (1906–1975)

Born on September 25, 1906 in St Petersburg, Dmitry D. Shostakovich was a composer best-known for his fifteen symphonies and fifteen string quartets. He was also awarded the Order of Lenin in 1946, 1956, and 1966. Shostakovich's first musical success came in 1926 when he wrote his First Symphony, which was heavily influenced by the works of Prokofiev and Stravinsky. He had marginal success in his career until 1934 when his opera *Lady Macbeth of the Mtsensk District* gained immediate success and popularity. None the less, in 1936 he suffered the first of two denunciations by the Communist Party for *Lady Macbeth*, which the authorities accused of being formalist; it was banned for almost thirty years. Despite this denigration, he received the support of Maksim Gorky, who interceded with Stalin on his behalf, earning him a reprieve in late 1937 with the completion of his Fifth Symphony, described by author Solomon Volkov as a "symphony novel" and interpreted as a reflection of the years of the Great Terror. Worldwide success came in 1941 when he completed his Seventh Symphony, dubbed "Leningrad," which symbolized the resistance to Nazi totalitarianism in both the West and in Russia. In 1948, Zhdanov issued a decree denouncing Shostakovich and other composers for formalism, but nevertheless the latter survived the assault. He was appointed a deputy to the Supreme Soviet in 1951 and joined the Communist Party in 1960. Five years later he signed a letter as part of a campaign to prevent the rehabilitation of Stalin. Thereafter, his health began to deteriorate. He wrote his last piece, the Fifteenth Symphony, in 1971 and died of lung cancer on August 9, 1975.

BOX 5.6
....

Aram Khachaturian (1903–1978)

Born on June 6, 1903 in Tiflis (Tblisi), Georgia, to a poor Armenian family, Aram Khachaturian was a composer best-known for his ballets *Gayane* (1942) and *Spartacus* (1956), as well as for his Piano Concerto (1936). His early works were influenced by contemporary Western music, and his later works often contained elements of Armenian, Georgian, and Russian folk music. He was trained at the Gnesin State Musical and Pedagogical Institute in Moscow and at the Moscow Conservatory. In 1943 he wrote his Second Symphony for the 25th anniversary of the Russian Revolution and composed the Armenian national anthem. He was a loyal supporter of Communism and joined the CPSU in 1943. Despite this commitment, he still fell victim to *Zhdanovshchina* that prevailed in the early postwar years. In 1948, he was denounced for his allegedly formalist style, along with Dmitry Shostakovich and Sergey Prokofiev, by the Communist Party. Khachaturian was forced to apologize publicly in order to restore his reputation. Following Stalin's death in 1953, he openly condemned the accusations of the Communist Party, but withdrew his statement a few years later. In 1959 he was awarded the Lenin Prize. The rest of his life was spent performing all over the world. He died in Moscow on May 1, 1978 at the age of 74.

As the cult of Stalin reached a new peak in the postwar years, the leader himself grew increasingly remote, often relying on subordinates to carry out his key policies. New enemies were soon targeted. In November 1948, the Jewish Anti-Fascist Committee, a wartime organization, was abolished and its members arrested. One of the goals of the committee was to form a new homeland for Soviet Jews. Early in 1949 a new official campaign was launched against "cosmopolitanism," which was defined as a movement that rejected patriotism and advocated a theory of world citizenship. In 1949 the MGB (Ministry of State Security) announced the exposure of a new conspiracy, called the "Leningrad Affair," in which several leading party activists reportedly wished to detach Russia from the Soviet Union and establish Leningrad as the state capital. One of its alleged ringleaders was N. A. Voznesensky, who was removed from the Politburo on October 27, 1949 and arrested, along with A. A. Kuznetsov, M. I. Rodionov, and Ya. F. Kapustin. All the leaders were executed on October 1, 1950. Voznesensky remained the most prominent victim of the postwar purges, which were building in a familiar crescendo. In May 1951, a new trial was held featuring the Jewish Anti-Fascist Committee. Its leaders received the death sentence for their role as "despicable hirelings of imperialism and Zionism," while others received long terms in labor camps.

From October 5 to 14, 1952, the 19th Party Congress took place in Moscow. It was the first party congress for thirteen years and the last one in Stalin's lifetime. As it was the first such meeting since the end of the war, the Congress recognized fallen heroes and those party leaders, such as Zhdanov and Kalinin, who had died since the war's end. Various dignitaries from the satellite states of Eastern Europe attended the Congress, such as East German leaders Walther Ulbricht and Erich Honecker, and Czechoslovakia's Communist leader Klement Gottwald. Stalin's health had begun to deteriorate by this time, and Malenkov presented the main speech. The Congress heralded an ambitious new five-year plan (the 5th) and noted the rapid expansion of hydroelectric power and oil and gas. The long gap between the congresses was indicative of the new power structure of the USSR. Though party membership had almost tripled since the 18th Congress, real authority was now invested in the few men at the top, who had ruled through the GKO and now struggled for supremacy within the Presidium. Stalin as ever was suspicious of his subordinates. In mid-January 1953, *Pravda* announced the uncovering of a new plot against the Soviet leadership, focused on a group of Kremlin doctors, at least half of whom were Jewish. The doctors were accused of murdering Zhdanov in 1948 and planning the death of other prominent leaders – significantly Beria was not among the group to be eliminated, evidence that he was among those to be victimized in the new purge.

The Doctors' Plot seemingly anticipated a new series of purges but it did not come to fruition. On February 28 the Soviet leadership held a meeting at Stalin's dacha at Kuntsevo. On March 2, Stalin fell ill, and four leaders – Beria, Malenkov, Bulganin, and Khrushchev – left for his dacha. Before he died on March 5, he opened his eyes several times. Stalin's death occurred in suspicious circumstances, but to date historians can only speculate on the course of events. Radzinsky (1996), who provides the most detailed and colorful version, outlines several possible scenarios that may have followed Stalin's initial stroke. He implicates Beria as possibly bearing the main responsibility for ensuring that Stalin did not recover, and preventing medical aid from reaching the incapacitated leader. Beria's troops surrounded Red Square on March 9, 1953 for Stalin's funeral, and as a result the masses in attendance had no means to leave the square. Hundreds died in the crush to pay tribute to the great leader, whose body was placed alongside that of Lenin in the Mausoleum. Throughout the Soviet Union, and even in the Gulag, there was genuine grief at Stalin's death. The public considered itself leaderless. Stalin, for all his crimes, his brutality, and his utter ruthlessness, had guided the people through momentous times. By sheer repetition the propaganda about his personal attributes was believed by many. Even his enemies would have granted that his loss would leave an enormous void. Stalin had set the path for future leaders, but none would ever match his power and authority. Though in official propaganda he was described as the successor and devoted follower of Lenin, the leader of the October Revolution had never sought or even anticipated the sycophantic devotion that Stalin seemed to crave. Stalin had been the sole ruler of the Soviet Union for twenty-five years, and he had been at least joint ruler for twenty-nine. Under Stalin an agrarian nation had begun a transformation to an industrial state that emerged after the Second World War as a global power.

Notes

1 Aleksandr, Duke of Novgorod (1220–1263) defeated a Swedish army on the Neva River in 1240, and was known thereafter as "Nevsky."
2 Dmitry, ruler of Muscovy (1350–1389), defeated Tatars on the Don River in 1380, thus acquiring the appellation "Donskoy."
3 Prince Dmitry Mikhailovich Pozharsky (1578–1642) led the army that liberated Moscow from the Poles in 1612, signaling the end to the so-called "Time of Troubles" and the accession of the first Roman tsar, Mikhail, in 1613.
4 Aleksandr Vasilevich Suvorov (1729–1800) was a Russian general who never lost a battle, and is best-known for a series of victories over the Turks, as well as against the Poles, and French revolutionary armies in Italy.
5 Prince Mikhail Illarionovich Golenishchev-Kutuzov (1745–1813) was a protégé of Suvorov, and attained his highest fame for the defeat of Napoleon's Grande Armée during its Russian campaign of 1812.

Questions for discussion

1. Why was Stalin so unprepared for the German invasion on June 22, 1941?
2. Why did the German army fail to take Moscow in the winter of 1941?
3. How was the Soviet regime able to rally the Russian population during the war years?
4. Who gained the most from the Treaty of Yalta?
5. Has propaganda superseded historical accuracy in our knowledge of the Soviet victory in 1945? Which events in particular might have been distorted?

Recent works

Berthon, Simon. *Warlords: An Extraordinary Re-Creation of World War II through the Eyes and Minds of Hitler, Churchill, Roosevelt, and Stalin.* Cambridge, Mass.: Da Capo Press, 2006.

Broekmeyer, M. J. *Stalin, the Russians, and Their War: 1941–1945.* Madison, Wis.: University of Wisconsin Press, 2004.

Edwards, Robert. *The Winter War: Russia's Invasion of Finland, 1939–1940.* New York: Pegasus Books, 2009.

Filtzer, Donald A. *Soviet Workers and Late Stalinism: Labour and the Restoration of the Stalinist System after World War II.* Cambridge: Cambridge University Press, 2002.

Glantz, David M. *After Stalingrad: The Red Army's Winter Offensive, 1942–1943.* Solihull: Helion, 2009[a].

Glantz, David M. *To the Gates of Stalingrad: Soviet–German Combat Operations, April–August 1942.* Lawrence, Kan.: University Press of Kansas, 2009[b].

Gottfried, Ted. *The Great Fatherland War.* Brookfield, Conn.: Twenty-First Century Books, 2003.

Hasegawa, Tsuyoshi. *Racing the Enemy: Stalin, Truman, and the Surrender of Japan.* Cambridge, Mass.: Harvard University Press, 2005.

Hill, Alexander. *The Great Patriotic War of the Soviet Union: A Documentary Reader.* Abington: Routledge, 2009.

Jones, Jeffrey W. *Everyday Life and the "Reconstruction" of Soviet Russia during and after the Great Patriotic War.* Bloomington, Ind.: Slavica, 2008.

Kirschenbaum, Lisa A. *The Legacy of the Siege of Leningrad, 1941–1995: Myth, Memories, and Monuments.* Cambridge: Cambridge University Press, 2006.

Lukacs, John. *June 1941: Hitler and Stalin.* New Haven, Conn.: Yale University Press, 2006.

Manley, Rebecca. *To the Tashkent Station: Evacuation and Survival in the Soviet Union at War.* Ithaca, NY: Cornell University Press, 2009.

Merridale, Catherine. *Ivan's War: The Red Army 1939–45.* London: Faber & Faber, 2005.

Nagorski, Andrew. *The Greatest Battle: Stalin, Hitler, and the Desperate Struggle for Moscow That Changed the Course of World War II.* New York: Simon & Schuster, 2007.

Pleshakov, Konstantin. *Stalin's Folly: The Tragic First Ten Days of World War II on the Eastern Front.* Boston, Mass.: Houghton Mifflin, 2005.

Rees, Laurence. *World War II behind Closed Doors: Stalin, the Nazis and the West.* New York: Pantheon Books, 2008.

Tec, Nechama. *Defiance.* Oxford: Oxford University Press, 2009.

Volkov, Solomon. *The Magical Chorus: a History of Russian Culture from Tolstoy to Solzhenitsyn.* New York: Vintage Books, 2009.

Weeks, Albert L. *Stalin's Other War: Soviet Grand Strategy, 1939–1941.* Lanham, Md: Rowman & Littlefield, 2002.

6

....

Khrushchev's reforms, 1953–1964; and postwar foreign policy

The succession question

Stalin, in contrast to Lenin, had not been preoccupied with the question of a successor. Had he done so, the person selected would have immediately been the subject of suspicion and intrigue, and likely would not have survived for long. Because of this lack of decision, the leadership of the country was in dispute for several years. The idea of collective leadership emerged, but this concept was far from satisfactory given the rivalry between the various personalities. The three most prominent party leaders were Beria, Malenkov, and Molotov. The last was the best-known figure but by this time the weakest of the three. In Stalin's later years, Molotov had fallen out of favor. During the war, through Stalin's machinations, government organizations superseded those of the party in terms of authority and decision-making. Thus, when Nikita Khrushchev became the party secretary, it did not signify that he was the leading candidate to succeed Stalin. Khrushchev was a lower-rank leader at this time. Malenkov was the Chairman of the Council of Ministers, and his four deputies were Beria, Molotov, Bulganin, and Kaganovich. In terms of rank, Khrushchev was number six, with little chance in theory of succeeding Stalin as leader.

The first opportunity to take power, however, fell to Beria, Stalin's trusted lieutenant for many years, an odious but contradictory character. During the short period of his ascendancy he introduced some important changes of direction in several key sectors. In the republics, the policy of Russification stopped abruptly. The Doctors' Plot was exposed quickly as a fabrication. Beria also wished to defuse international tension, particularly over Yugoslavia, which had been removed from the Cominform on Stalin's instructions in 1948. He proposed in addition to re-examine the enforced socialist construction in East Germany and to reduce the number of Soviet "advisors" in the satellite countries of Eastern Europe. Why did Beria adopt such moderate policies? One possible reason is that he believed that a period of toleration was necessary after the harsh Stalin dictatorship. Better perhaps than any other leader, Beria was aware of the alienation caused by centrist policies that belittled the rights of the national republics. In addition, the change of policy would allow the uprooting of the Stalin team and the installation of a new government that could include his most loyal supporters. However, Beria moved too quickly and too transparently. In particular, he wished to reduce the power of the Communist Party, thus posing a direct threat to his fellow leaders.

Malenkov and Khrushchev also had their differences, but together with Zhukov they were powerful and united enough to prevent Beria from taking over. On March 14, 1953, the country elected a new Secretariat under the leadership of Khrushchev, though he remained lower in the Soviet hierarchy than Malenkov. The following month, a decree of the CC CPSU (as the all-Union party was now called) focused on the activities of the Georgian Ministry of State Security, exposing a Mingrelian nationalist organization led by Beria. On June 26, 1953, Beria was formally arrested during a meeting of the Presidium. Zhukov and K. S. Moskalenko carried out the arrest, and the majority of the Presidium supported the action (Mikoyan was opposed). Some time during the next six months, Beria was executed as an enemy of the people, who allegedly had been spying for the British for several years. At a Central Committee Plenum of July 2–7, 1953, Beria was removed from the Central Committee and deprived of his party membership. On July 10, he lost his other major posts, those of the First Deputy Chairman of the Council of Ministers (directly subordinate to Malenkov) and of Minister of Internal Affairs. Evidently several members of the Presidium wavered as to the sentence that Beria and his associates would be given, but Molotov demanded the death penalty, in the belief that otherwise Beria's political recovery was possible. It should be borne in mind that Beria kept files on all the party leaders and was a feared figure. Following Beria's death, the Ministry of Internal Affairs was abolished. The KGB replaced it in 1955, and was transferred from government to direct party control. The move greatly strengthened the authority of the party and, by the same token, Khrushchev personally.

However, Malenkov initially enjoyed a brief spell as the leading figure, even though he did not occupy the leading position in the party. With the removal of Beria, Molotov was the highest-ranking leader as the First Deputy Chairman of the Council of Ministers and the Foreign Minister. The next-ranking figure in the spring of 1953 was Kliment Voroshilov, the Chairman of the Supreme Soviet. Thus, in the first eight postwar years, the key decision-making role was taken by leaders of the Soviet government. Both Beria and Malenkov took positive steps toward removing the harshest aspects of Stalinism, though neither can really be cited as an anti-Stalin figure. Malenkov created a commission to investigate the repressions of the Stalin period; and on March 27, 1953, just over three weeks after Stalin's death, a government decree "Concerning Amnesty" – an initiative of Beria – resulted in the liberation of over 20 percent of all political prisoners serving short-term sentences in Gulag camps. A similar number was released before Khrushchev acquired full powers, as noted by the Russian historian Vadim Kozhikov. Thus Khrushchev's role was to continue the initiatives started by his peers, Beria and Malenkov. At the same time he began by various means to try to undermine the political leadership of the latter in order to bring about his own takeover of power.

In August 1953, Malenkov made an important speech about the need to reprioritize the Soviet economy to produce more and better consumer goods and basic foods.

He relieved the collective farms of their debts and raised the prices for agricultural products. He also proposed the expansion of private plots of collective- and state-farm workers. At the same time, Malenkov's position was never consolidated. He bore responsibility for the agricultural shortcomings of the country, had been foolish enough to declare that the country "had resolved" the grain problem, and his position had also been undermined by the Leningrad Affair, during which he had been one of the most outspoken supporters of a new purge. Malenkov initiated the move to elect Khrushchev as the First Secretary of the CC CPSU in early September 1953, evidently underestimating his comrade's own desire to take over the leadership of the country. Almost immediately upon taking up his new position, Khrushchev made a speech in which he ridiculed Malenkov's comment that the agricultural problems had been solved, and also maintained that the government had failed to give adequate guidance to the oblast and local committees of the Union republics, and to backward collective farms. The latter had been subjected to an amalgamation campaign in 1950 – a program supported by Khrushchev – and for several years this reform caused enormous problems in the village.

In early 1954, as a move to commemorate the 300th anniversary of the Treaty of Pereyaslav, the Crimean peninsula – with the exception of the city of Sevastopol, which remained under Russian jurisdiction – was officially transferred from the Russian Republic to Ukraine. The official decree, issued on 1 February 19, noted as the reasons the economic and cultural links between Crimea and Ukraine. Though Voroshilov signed the decree as Chairman of the Presidium of the Supreme Soviet and N. Pegov as its Secretary, it was reportedly an initiative of Khrushchev, using his position as party leader. With the deportation of the Tatars during the war, the population of the peninsula was predominantly Russian, and it was also a key naval center, as the port of Sevastopol for many years had been the base of the Black Sea Fleet. Some Russian historians today maintain that the transfer occurred illegally because the original decision was made at a party plenum that lacked a quorum. The transfer at the time was more symbolic than anything else, as Ukraine was not an independent republic, but it would come to have much more meaning after the collapse of the Soviet Union.

Slowly but relentlessly, Khrushchev undermined Malenkov's position. In April 1954 the proposed victims in the Leningrad Affair were rehabilitated. At a CC Plenum between January 25 and 31, 1955, Khrushchev attacked Malenkov for the move away from heavy industry toward light and consumer industries, the former being the traditional priority of the centralized socialist state. As a result, Malenkov lost his position as Chairman of the USSR Council of Ministers at the same plenum and was replaced by N. I. Bulganin on February 8, 1955. Malenkov supposedly lacked the attributes for such a prominent position. Along with his removal, Zhukov, cast into the wilderness by the jealous Stalin after his triumphs in the German–Soviet war, returned to favor as USSR Minister of Defense. Thus, almost two years after the death of Stalin, the nature of the new administration had been clarified. Khrushchev emerged on center stage as the new leader, supported particularly by Bulganin and Zhukov, with other figures like Mikoyan in the background. Before long he would readjust the power structure to ensure that the party once again played the dominant role in Soviet life. In 1955, however, the longevity of the new leader in his elevated position was a moot point. Who was Khrushchev and to what did he owe his rise to power?

Nikita S. Khrushchev is a larger-than-life figure. He has been the subject of several recent biographies, including one written by his son Sergey, who resides in the United States. More significant, however, have been his autobiographical works based on his diaries and tape recordings after his enforced retirement in late 1964. Most recently, three volumes of Khrushchev's memoirs have been published under the editorship of his son. Overall they promote the view that Khrushchev was a reformer who returned the country to the path of Lenin and whose leadership constituted a major turning point in Soviet history. Mikhail Gorbachev perpetuated that viewpoint when he took over the leadership of the party in 1985. However, it is a simplistic and inaccurate perspective. Khrushchev may have nurtured the image of a reformer, and he was certainly less cruel and malevolent than Stalin. He was, none the less, never suited to the role of a humanitarian and might be better-described as a petty authoritarian who made decisions on the spur of the moment and rarely consulted with his colleagues in the Presidium. Moreover, as a leader he was dangerously unpredictable, and caused unprecedented tension abroad and chaos at home.

Khrushchev was born in the village of Kalinovka, Kursk guberniya, on April 17, 1894 into a coal-mining family. In his early years he took up physical labor, both as a metalworker and a coal miner in the Donbas region of Ukraine (the area to which his family had migrated in 1908), the republic with which he is most closely associated. Khrushchev joined the Bolshevik Party in 1918, using the patronage of Lazar Kaganovich, a party worker raised in Ukraine, who had joined up in 1911. After taking part in the civil war, he was further involved in economic work in the Donbas and in Kyiv. In 1929 he studied at the Industrial Academy in Moscow, and took up positions in the party apparatus of Moscow Oblast. By January 1934 he had risen to be the First Secretary of the Moscow city and oblast party committees, and in this same year he was elected to the party's Central Committee. A loyal Stalinist at this time, Khrushchev took an active part in the early purges in Moscow, frequently complaining that the number of people being arrested was too low, before being appointed First Party Secretary of the Ukrainian SSR in January 1938. He also became a Candidate Member of the Politburo, being promoted to full status the following year. In Ukraine he continued purges – they had virtually ended in Moscow – particularly after the Soviet westward expansion that incorporated into the republic the former eastern territories of Poland.

Khrushchev had an active war record, serving on the Southwest Front, in Stalingrad, Voronezh and the First Ukrainian Fronts as a political commissar and member of the Military Council. After the war, he returned to Ukraine as the leader of the Ukrainian government, in addition to his role as party chief. In March 1947 he briefly lost his leadership over the Ukrainian party organization, evidently for his inability to eliminate the insurgents of UPA – the task was given to Kaganovich – but he returned to this same post in December of that year with his powers intact. After December 1949, Stalin brought him back to Moscow as the First Secretary of the Moscow committee of the party. Khrushchev can be described as an ideological Communist, a robust, stocky man with a bald pate, crude and ruthless, but at the same time a far more human figure than Stalin. Like his former allies Beria and Malenkov, Khrushchev recognized the need for a more tolerant period in Soviet life. On several occasions Stalin had taken his advice on agricultural affairs, and Khrushchev considered himself an expert and even a pioneer in this troubled sphere. Khrushchev was a restless man of great energy, and in several respects a more dangerous adversary for the Western powers than the more predictable Stalin.

His style of leadership was markedly different from that of his predecessor. He was constantly on the move, touring the country and making speeches. He also made appearances at party congresses in Poland and Czechoslovakia. His friends were promoted to eminent positions. They included the first woman to be prominent in the political leadership (and eventually in the Presidium), Yekaterina Furtseva, who was put in charge of the Moscow party organization; Ivan Serov, who took over the KGB; and Frol Kozlov, who was placed in control of the Leningrad party apparatus. Premier Bulganin was also loyal to his new master. Khrushchev did not hesitate to expand his areas of influence, particularly in foreign policy. From the first, he frustrated the grim Molotov by delving into foreign affairs. In December 1954, Khrushchev and Bulganin went to China on a trip that was a publicity triumph, but one from which Molotov was, inexplicably, excluded. More and more frequently, party decrees would be passed on Khrushchev's signature alone, which led to many members of the Presidium being unaware of some events of major importance. Khrushchev's impulsive character would also lead to several dangerous moments for the country.

Younger than the Stalin generation by some fifteen years, Khrushchev seems to have revelled in his newfound power. Perhaps more than any Soviet leader, Khrushchev was an ideological Communist. He tried to combine the Stalinist concept of the Motherland, and more specifically Great Russia, with party authority and party infallibility, creating in citizens an image of the triumphs of the Soviet state specifically. In doing so, he deliberately competed with the main adversary, the United States, at every opportunity. Whereas Stalin worked quietly and deviously to undermine the capitalist giant, Khrushchev expressed the world conflict openly, being both disparaging and dismissive about the rival power. He was frequently intoxicated in public, a liberty that Stalin would never have taken, thus appearing almost comical. There are probably more Soviet anecdotes about Khrushchev than about any of the other leaders. He is remembered for anti-American phrases such as "We will bury you!" and for his boasts and bluster when it was plain that the USSR was not in the superior position that it claimed to be. Because of this attitude, Khrushchev's brief time in power assumed much more importance than was warranted by the figure who seemed to have leapfrogged into power. It was a time of extremes, of experiments, of early successes but of very fundamental failures. Khrushchev was the first Soviet leader to take over a global power, and he very much wanted to rule in his own stead, without the personality cults, but with most other facets of the leadership, including personal decision-making, intact.

The Virgin Lands Program

Under Khrushchev, a reform movement was initiated in agriculture almost immediately. At the September 1953 Plenum of the Central Committee, various authorities in the USSR discussed the question of increasing grain production. By January 1954 the CC CPSU had issued a memorandum entitled "Ways to resolve the grain problem," which was circulated among local party organizations. The goal was to cultivate the so-called Virgin Lands, remote regions of the country that could be devoted to grain production, and which would add around 13 million hectares to the sown area by 1955. Khrushchev devised the plan and he was very much associated with its success and its failure. The locations for the program were Kazakhstan, the Volga region, Siberia, the Urals, and the North Caucasus. By 1954 the party was asking for volunteers – primarily through the Komsomol – to travel to the Virgin Lands to take part in the new program. Many of Khrushchev's colleagues had reservations about the plan, which contained typical elements of any Khrushchev program, such as great enthusiasm, the desire for an immediate return on investment, a radical transformation of Soviet agricultural practices, and a general lack of foresight about the likely results. Essentially it took the form of a youth movement to the countryside. In theory, priority was to be given to volunteers with agricultural or technical skills. They traveled on special trains, while equipment and building materials were quickly transported to the east of the country.

Most of the volunteers traveled on Komsomol permits. By May 1954 those arriving in the Virgin Lands of Kazakhstan comprised some 130,000 new settlers, and by the following year the figure had risen to more than 360,000. One in seven were members of the party or the Komsomol of the Virgin Land regions, but the European settlers evidently were in control of the newly established state farms. Khrushchev's goal was to get some 1,220 poods of grain from the new lands, using 120,000 tractors, 10,000 combines, plus plows and seeding machines. The new arrivals came from almost all the Union republics of the USSR. Once at their destination, new state farms were founded. Several key party officials were on hand to guide the volunteers, including P. K. Ponomarenko, the former Belarusian party chief, and 48-year-old Leonid I. Brezhnev, a trusted associate of Khrushchev, who was appointed the First Party Secretary of Kazakhstan in August 1955. Reliable party workers from the major cities of Russia, Ukraine, and Belarus arrived to run local party committees; in the first two years of the Virgin Lands Program, some 26,000

Communist Party members moved to these areas, helping to set up party organizations. Conditions were very difficult. The new settlers found no infrastructure when they arrived. They slept in tents and worked long hours, suffering intensely dry summers and heavy snowfalls in winter.

At first, the scheme was quite successful. By 1955 another 13 million hectares of new lands had been plowed, making a total of almost 36 million hectares by 1956. More than 50 percent of these lands were in Kazakhstan. In 1954, which was a difficult year for agriculture in the European part of the USSR, the Virgin Lands accounted for 43.5 percent of gross agricultural output. The country was agog with publicity about the success of the program, which was identified closely with the First Party Secretary. Almost 94,000 Virgin Landers received awards and medals, and 262 received the revered title of Hero of Socialist Labor. The program continued, but it never reached such heights again. Khrushchev had simply been very lucky. There were record harvests in the early years, but the climatic conditions ensured that these would be a passing phenomenon. The Virgin Lands lay in a zone that was fundamentally unsuited to agriculture. Moreover, with the investment required for such a program, funds had to be diverted from other agricultural regions, which suffered greatly as a result. The food question was not resolved, and before long it was to get worse. Khrushchev's ambitious plan was of his own making, but it was the first of several rash ideas. By 1957 he had made the bold prognosis that within a four-year period the USSR would catch up with and overtake the United States in the production of dairy products – and especially meat – per head of population.

The dairy production program soon overrode all other concerns in agriculture. Individual oblast and district leaders began to organize the mass slaughter of livestock to meet the extravagant figures demanded by the party leader. There are some famous examples of how these targets were reached, such as the story of A. N. Larionov, the party leader in Ryazan oblast, who declared that he would produce five times his assigned quota of meat. He more than fulfilled his target by slaughtering all the livestock in the region, and was rewarded with fame and his photograph in *Pravda*, largely at the behest of Khrushchev, who thereby received free publicity for his program and could demand similar performances from other regions. However, in the following year the Ryazan oblast could not possibly match the same target, and eventually Larionov, having received the Order of Lenin in the previous year, committed suicide. Meat production in the early 1960s was considerably lower than in the 1950s, largely as a result of Khrushchev's program. The proposed dramatic rise in livestock raised the question of corn production for animal feed. In 1959, Khrushchev visited US president Dwight Eisenhower at Camp David, and during the trip toured farms in Iowa; here he appears to have become convinced of the merits of growing corn. He seemed to believe that the American example could simply be imported without regard for Soviet conditions. Soviet farmers planted some 37 million hectares with corn, much of it in areas that were too cool and too damp. Many agricultural regions suffered as a result.

Khrushchev dabbled with the structure of agricultural organization. In 1958, again on the instructions of the Soviet leader, the Machine-Tractor Stations were abolished, and transformed into Repair Tractor Stations. The goal was to allow the farms to build up their technical base and remain the sole proprietors of the land. The farms could then purchase whatever technology they required. Like other reforms, this one was conducted in great haste. As the MTS wound down their operations, the collective farms bought out their goods and began to run up large debts. In the late 1950s an attempt was made to make the collective farms larger and then to transform them into state farms, which were considered closer to the ideal for the construction of Communism in the Soviet Union. By the early 1960s, Soviet agriculture had reached crisis point. Prices for meat and butter rose, and the grain harvests were no longer adequate to feed the people, particularly in the cities. The Soviet Union became for the first time an importer of grain, a situation that was to remain throughout the rest of the Soviet period. By June 1962 there were accounts of mass protests about the food supply in the country, and in the city of Novocherkassk a workers' uprising ended in brutal suppression by the authorities and the execution of some 7,000 protestors. Khrushchev's experiments in agriculture had not only failed to alleviate the problems; they had made things worse.

The 20th Party Congress

On November 22, 1955, the Military Collegium of the USSR Supreme Court re-examined the affair of the Jewish Anti-Fascist Committee and concluded that there were no grounds upon which to convict its members. The following month, an earlier initiative was continued, namely the formation of a Commission for Rehabilitation, which was given the task of examining evidence from the 1930s purges of the party and candidate members who had been elected at the 17th Party Congress, along with other Soviet citizens purged in the same period. These measures formed the prelude to the convocation of the 20th Party Congress, which opened in the Great Kremlin Hall in Moscow on February 14, 1956. More than 1,350 delegates represented 7 million party members. The latter included both old and new – almost 22 percent of those present had joined the CPSU during the war years, and 34 percent in the period between 1931 and 1940. The Congress, which as usual included foreign visitors, proceeded normally, discussing the 6th Five-Year Plan. But members were called back at midnight for a closed-door session, which featured a lengthy speech by Khrushchev entitled "About the cult of personality and its consequences." Several other delegates also spoke on the same topic, but it was Khrushchev who gave the main speech in a move to dissociate his government from that of Stalin.

Essentially, Khrushchev stated that Stalin had deviated from the correct policies of the party during the period of the purges. The speech did not question the actual measures, such as collectivization and removing the kulaks, but rather the extortionate methods used. The goal, therefore, was to return to the path laid out by Lenin (whose teachings and measures by implication were infallible). Since Khrushchev himself had been a key actor in the drama of the mid- and late 1930s, he had to tread carefully. One may ask why he chose to take such a step at all. The answer likely lies in the control that the Stalinists still exerted over the party, particularly Stalin's old followers and devoted admirers, such as Kaganovich and Molotov. The latter two, however, were not singled out in the speech. Rather the focus lay on the two NKVD chiefs of the 1930s, Yagoda and Yezhov. Hundreds of innocent victims of the purges were rehabilitated, but hundreds more remained, at least on paper, guilty as charged. Moreover, there was no suggestion that the purges had been as devastating in the national republics. A copy of the speech found its way abroad where it was published later in 1956. It did not appear in print in the Soviet Union for another thirty-two years. It implied that a personality cult was a dangerous thing, and that it had led to distortions of Lenin's teaching. Stalin deserved some praise for his leadership of the country, but he had to take the blame for the fact that the purges got out of control, and also for his lack of preparedness at the outset of the German–Soviet war.

Khrushchev's speech inaugurated a new, somewhat more tolerant era in Soviet politics. However, the immediate impact was shock and protest that he should have attacked Stalin in such a way. Mass demonstrations broke out in Georgia, demanding the restoration of the good name of Stalin and under slogans such as "Down with Khrushchev!" and "Away with Bulganin!" On March 9, Khrushchev ordered Soviet tanks to intervene and suppress the protests. Gradually the official movement away from Stalin filtered into the official press and official propaganda. On March 28, an article appeared in *Pravda* entitled "Why the cult of personality was alien to the spirit of Marxism-Leninism." The CC CPSU issued a decree only on June 30, 1956 with the same title as the secret speech, but much more tentative and moderate in tone. For the first time, Soviets were to hear of events that they had hardly dared discuss hitherto. The shock they received can only be imagined. Yet the document was mild. Circumstances had dictated that there would be certain restrictions on freedom, particularly the presence of anti-Soviet imperialists seeking an end to the Soviet government. Stalin had performed some important tasks, especially in the struggle against the deviations of Trotsky and his followers. During the war, however, Stalin had taken all the credit for the victories, which was a distortion of the facts. Obsessed with his own image, he had developed a personality cult.

According to the decree, there was a parallel development in the country during this period. On the one hand was the damaging personality cult of Stalin, which caused serious harm to socialism and to the building of Communism in the country. Yet, on the other hand, the party and the working class continued to follow the teachings of Lenin. The CPSU leadership was collective and continued the process of socialist construction. Thus it was possible, after Stalin's death, to recover from the harm and to return to a correct approach. The speech and then the decree caused immediate problems for the Soviet leader. In several countries of Eastern Europe, a political crisis developed. On the other hand, the liberalization was a benefit to many Soviet citizens. In late April the victims of Stalin's wartime deportations were allowed to return home; several were partially rehabilitated and their national republics once again given autonomy (Chechens, Ingushetians, and Kalmyks). Khrushchev's rivals in the Presidium could no longer afford to delay before making a move to unseat him. Molotov lost his position as Minister of Foreign Affairs on June 2, and was replaced by Dmitry T. Shepilov. The opposition faction therefore decided to remove Khrushchev, selecting as the opportune moment his state visit to Finland with Bulganin, his closest ally, in June 1957.

The conspirators were a mixture of old Stalinists, Malenkov, Molotov, and Kaganovich (Voroshilov was another who gave support to the plot), and younger economic leaders doubtless perplexed by Khrushchev's frenetic and unpredictable reforms. When Khrushchev returned from Finland, the Presidium immediately held a vote, and he was voted out of office by eight votes to four. Khrushchev refused to accept his dismissal, arguing that the motion was invalid because it required a vote of the full Central Committee plenum. Though outnumbered at the Presidium level, Khrushchev had some powerful allies. Through Zhukov he had the support of the army, and through Serov he had behind him the powerful organization of the KGB. The four plotters found themselves unable to resist the call for a full Plenum to discuss Khrushchev's position, and this took place between June 22 and 29, 1957. A tense affair, the Plenum developed into a virtual trial of Malenkov, Molotov, and Kaganovich; they were depicted as a Gang of Three, who had opposed openly the decisions of the 20th Party Congress. Molotov, it was noted, had tried to prevent conciliatory moves toward Yugoslavia and he had opposed the State Treaty with Austria that led to the removal of Soviet troops from that state in 1955. The three plotters, however, were permitted to offer their criticisms of Khrushchev, and they attacked his style of leadership and rash promises such as overtaking the United States in the production of meat and milk. It is likely, however, that few of those present could look forward without trepidation to the potential elevation of three figures so closely associated with Stalin. Zhukov was evidently ready to divulge information about the gang's role in the purges and was particularly incensed at the removal and execution of many of his former colleagues in the purge of the military.

Thus, at the end of the Plenum, Molotov, Malenkov, and Kaganovich were removed from the Presidium and the Central Committee of the party. Their ally Shepilov lost his position as a Secretary of the CC CPSU and candidate membership in the party. Henceforth they were to be referred to as the Anti-Party Group. Khrushchev, however, did not take the traditional route of a public trial, followed by pleas of guilt and executions. His three opponents, all well known to the public, were given demeaning roles instead. Malenkov was put in charge of a power plant in Central Asia, Molotov the diplomat was given an ambassadorship in Mongolia, and Kaganovich, Khrushchev's former mentor and patron, was sent to Sverdlovsk in the

Urals and given responsibility for a cement works. Thus ended ingloriously the active careers of three faithful followers of Stalin. Molotov was no longer in good health, and eventually Khrushchev agreed that he could take up an easier position as the leader of the Soviet delegation to the Commission on Atomic Energy in Vienna. In 1984, when Molotov turned 90, the Brezhnev regime readmitted him into the party. Kaganovich lived a long life reclusively in Moscow, relying on his state pension. The relatively mild sentences show that Khrushchev's regime promised a departure from the past, but the demotions owed as much to political in-fighting as to a change in political direction.

Khrushchev's power was consolidated by the advancement of his allies into prominent positions. Furtseva and Brezhnev were admitted to the Presidium, and Aleksey Kosygin became a Candidate Member. The treatment of Zhukov, however, was quite different. Zhukov had been indispensable to Khrushchev on two occasions – the removal of Beria and in fending off the Anti-Party Group. However, Khrushchev believed that the wartime hero had become too powerful. Moreover, Khrushchev had decided to cut military spending by 1955–1956, one facet of which was a substantial reduction in the size of conventional military forces. The fear of a military coup was never far from Khrushchev's mind. Thus, in October 1957, he removed Zhukov from his state and party positions while the latter was on a state visit to Yugoslavia, replacing him with Marshal Rodion Malinovsky. According to the official communiqué, Zhukov was dismissed for "crude violations of the Leninist principles of leadership over the armed forces," meaning that the army had escaped for too long the grasp of party control. Under Malinovsky the army was to become part of the ruling structure, but more compliant. The next month Mao visited Moscow, another occasion when the two world Communist leaders stood side by side, evidently united.

Over the next decade, party membership expanded at a rate exceeding even that of the war years. Almost 5 million new members were added, making over 11.5 million in total or 8.5 percent of the adult population, as opposed to only 5 percent in 1955. Khrushchev's own title was simply Secretary until September 1953, after which it was changed to First Secretary, and in February 1956 he also occupied the position of head of the Bureau of the Central Committee of the CPSU in the Russian Republic. Conversely, it was not until late March 1958 that he decided to take the position also as Chairman of the Council of Ministers of the USSR, dismissing Bulganin for his alleged support of the Anti-Party Group. Thereafter, Khrushchev's power was to rest on the party structure, which reverted to the prewar years. Not until the mid-1980s with Perestroika did the party lose its ascendancy again and, in contrast to the later Stalin years, congresses were once again convened on a regular basis, though they served less as forums for discussions than for announcements of the latest grand initiative of the Soviet leader.

Khrushchev soon began to delve into the Soviet bureaucracy, introducing changes in the way industry was organized. Specifically he switched from the branch to the

territorial principle, creating Economic Councils (*Sovnarkhozy*) to replace the role of
the ministries. One of the problems of the Soviet structure was that, with the centralized structure, ministers made decisions about factories located hundreds of miles
away and without any detailed knowledge of the area in question. So Khrushchev
eliminated twenty-six industrial ministries and created 104 *Sovnarkhozy* at a Central
Committee plenum of February 13–14, 1957. The Councils were answerable to the
governments of the Union republics. Khrushchev maintained that under the old
system the ministers tended to operate within their departmental boundaries, often
creating structures that operated parallel to each other. Now the Economic Councils
controlled Soviet heavy industry and energy resources in particular. Once again,
however, the existing structure did not lend itself well to change. The concept was
original, but the result was the development of more regionalized bureaucracy,
with a haphazard control over the factories and plan targets. One of the goals of the
reform was to allow for the production of consumer goods, an area neglected by
the centralized planned economy with its focus on military and heavy industry.
Khrushchev's moves made him unpopular in Moscow circles, where ministers saw
their power being undermined. Moscow was very much the hub of the country,
with a superior lifestyle and standard of living. Already party officials were enjoying
several perks of office. However, the establishment of numerous economic councils
at the regional level only caused confusion and resentment.

On July 31, 1957, again on the initiative of Khrushchev, a decree was issued to deal
with the acute housing problem in urban areas. In Khrushchev's period, there had
been a significant migration of population from villages to towns, exacerbating the
already complex housing situation of the Stalin years. Khrushchev scoffed at what
he saw as "architectural excesses." The workers needed a roof over their heads, and
the buildings could be simple and inexpensive. Thus he commandeered the construction of the "*Khrushchevky*" or "*Khrushchoby*" – the Khrushchev "slums" as they were
referred to by the public (the second term rhymes with the Russian word for slums,
trushchoby) – five-story high-rises built according to one design and still all too
visible today in the suburbs of the major cities. The aim was to ensure that each family should enjoy the basic requirements of working life: a home of its own, television,
refrigerator, a moderate-sized pension and some time to enjoy it. Thus Khrushchev
raised the minimum pension for workers, and allowed men to retire at 60, women
at 55. However, at 63, he had no intention of retiring!

In 1959 the government also reformed the banking system, eliminating a number
of banks and dividing their functions between the two remaining banks, the State
Bank of the USSR and the State Construction Bank. Khrushchev also tampered with
the school system, introducing a change whereby the ten-year system of education
was reduced to eight, and the two additional years were to be spent in industry or
in agriculture. Schools became associated with local factories or enterprises. It also
became impossible for students to enter university without having gone through this
practical experience, along with the support of a party or trade union official. For

the factories themselves, however, the new system meant that they had to deal with an influx of untrained young students. The trade taught was predetermined by what sort of factory existed in the neighborhood. Therefore students were not necessarily able to work in an area most suited to them, or follow the sort of career that they or their parents may have envisaged. Khrushchev was always adamant that the sons and daughters of workers and peasants should have ready access to universities. He resented the notion that students from members of the party and government hierarchy should receive preferential treatment. In the early 1960s he went one stage further and introduced the principle that government and party officials should serve limited terms and then step down.

Underlying these piecemeal measures – none of which was to survive him for long, and several of which were reversed even during Khrushchev's administration – was the notion that a workers' state was under construction. Unlike other Soviet leaders, Khrushchev anticipated that the construction of socialism would bear fruit before long. A Soviet utopia would be created. By 1959, when the authorities convoked an Extraordinary 21st Congress of the CC CPSU, some of Khrushchev's visionary claims received official status. The victory of socialism had been completed, it was announced. Therefore the path for the future was to create Communism. The basis for a Communist society was to be a newly introduced Seven-Year Plan for the development of the USSR that would see the Soviet Union (in theory) lead the world not only in overall output of production but also in consumer goods. The largest increases were to take place in industry, which was expected to enjoy a growth rate of more than 8 percent per year. The rise in agriculture, albeit much lower, was to see the continued focus on the development of animal husbandry, increasing the yields per hectare of various crops, but especially of grain. Though these targets proved to be unrealistic, Khrushchev persisted with the concept of pursuing a Communist utopia. The next occasion was the 22nd Party Congress, which took place from October 17 to 31, 1961 and at which a new party program was introduced. The first such program was based on the original Communist Manifesto of Marx and Engels in 1848, and announced at the 2nd Congress of the Russian Social Democratic Workers' Party in 1903. The second program had been announced in 1919 at the 8th Congress of the Bolshevik Party of Soviet Russia, with the aim of building a socialist society.

In his opening speech to the Congress, Khrushchev defined the world as falling into two clearly defined camps – the socialist camp and the capitalist camp. The former represented socialist progress, and the latter reaction, oppression, and war. The two systems had switched positions, Khrushchev declared, in that socialism had now forged ahead in a decisive sphere of activity – that of material production. Henceforth there would be two clearly defined periods for the USSR. From 1961 to 1970, the country was to establish the material base for Communism, overtake the United States (portrayed in the opening speech as a declining power), and ensure that a high standard of living was attained for the Soviet people. The second stage was to last from 1971 to 1980 and would achieve the technical basis required for full Communism. The goal would require a colossal economic surge – an overall rise in output of around 250 percent over the nineteen-year period, a fourfold increase in the production of meat, and the doubling of grain output. Labor productivity, Khrushchev anticipated, would increase by up to 350 percent over the same time-span.

How was this utopia to be realized? Khrushchev's solution was to announce several grandiose power and electrification programs, particularly using the great rivers of Siberia. Irrigation schemes would divert northern rivers so that they could reach the arid farmlands of the south. Oil and gas would be rapidly developed. As in the past, Khrushchev felt that the distinction between the town and the village would gradually disappear. Farms would be larger, and eventually the kolkhoz community would merge with the town, and concomitantly living standards for the farmers would catch up with those of their urban counterparts. Along with the rise in labor productivity that would be attained over the coming two decades, the working week would gradually be cut down to thirty-five hours with two days off in the first period, and even shorter working hours in the final decade. The decentralization policies introduced with the *Sovnarkhoz* were to be reversed, and the economy would be run by a Supreme Economic Council, under the chairmanship of Dmitry F. Ustinov, who had been appointed Minister of Armed Forces in 1946 and subsequently, after a merger of this ministry with aviation, the Minister of Defense in March 1953. The Supreme Economic Council supervised the National Economic Council, the National Building Association, and the State Planning Committee. Khrushchev now wished to strengthen party control over the economy and to end his experiment with the regions.

The 22nd Party Congress is also remembered for Khrushchev's definitive split with Stalin. Many of the measures initiated at the 20th Party Congress were now completed. Stalin's victims were said to be in the millions, and Khrushchev acknowledged that the Soviet leader had signed the death warrants for thousands. Stalin could therefore no longer fittingly remain in the Mausoleum beside Lenin; his body was removed and buried in the Kremlin wall, in a rather prominent place, since his bust is clearly visible from the entrance to Lenin's Tomb. Portraits of Stalin were taken down, and towns and villages bearing his name had to be renamed. Most poignant was the decision to rename Stalingrad – site of the most famous of all Soviet military victories – Volgograd. In Georgia, however, Stalin's name remained sacrosanct. Why did Khrushchev return to his anti-Stalin campaign? The most logical explanation is that he needed a diversion from his agricultural and international failures; with regard to the latter, the final break with Stalin was also a direct affront to China. Khrushchev's relations with Mao had deteriorated badly, but China had adhered to Stalinism and the memory of the USSR's wartime leader. This time, the reaction to Khrushchev's policies was more muted.

The attack on the Russian Orthodox Church

After the death of Stalin, it appeared likely that, like other sectors of society, the Russian Orthodox Church might also expect further growth, particularly after the cooperation between the Soviet government and the church during the war years. The immediate postwar years saw the rebuilding of churches damaged by wartime conflict. However, Khrushchev's return to "Leninism" signified that more attention would be paid to official ideology. Stalin could thus be accused of being somewhat lax toward religion. In turn, this policy gradually translated into a wholesale attack on the church and its priests, resulting in closures and often destruction of churches and monasteries. The prelude appears to have been a party decree of July 7, 1954, which noted that young people were being drawn into the church as a result of the activity of priests, church newspapers, and pressure on individuals. The decree urged the Education Ministry and the Komsomol to take a more active role in indoctrinating Soviet youth against church activities and religion. But, like many Soviet decrees, it took some time to take effect; and a serious attack on the church did not begin until Khrushchev consolidated his power, and especially in 1958–1964. The move evidently had the support of Mikhail Suslov, who was responsible for ideological policy, as well as of Khrushchev himself in his quest to build a society that brought the country closer to pure Communism. Responsibility for the attack on the church was given to the Agitation and Propaganda (AgitProp) section of the Central Committee, which used for its purpose the Council for Russian Orthodox Church Affairs headed by KGB agent G. G. Karpov.

A May 1958 report by AgitProp focused on defects in "scientific–atheistic propaganda," noting that the decree of July 7, 1954 had not been properly carried out. This was followed in October by a secret resolution of the Central Committee, which instructed Karpov's Council to ascertain whether the church had violated state laws. On October 16, the Soviet government raised taxes on monasteries and increased in particular impositions on factories responsible for producing church candles. Limits were placed on the publication of religious literature, and on the organization of religious conferences that might attract young people. Under pressure from the government, the church authorities were obliged to start closing down monasteries and hermitages. Young people under 30 were no longer permitted to enter monasteries, and the latter could no longer receive external subsidies without the approval of the Council for Russian Orthodox Church Affairs. That Council under Karpov, however, was under intense pressure from the government to fall in line with the new anti-church campaign. The number of dioceses was to be reduced, and the closure of monasteries proceeded apace from 1959 in particular. In 1960 the target was the closure of fifteen monasteries; and, as author Tatiana Chumachenko points out (Chumachenko, 2002), eleven of these had already stopped their activities by August 1, 1960.

Churches underwent a catastrophic decline in numbers. One argument used by the government was that in the western borderlands the churches had been in the zones occupied by the Germans. These could now be "legitimately" closed down. In Belarus, for example, the number of Orthodox churches fell from 1,250 at the end of the war to around 400 by 1964. However, the campaign did not end with the closure of these churches. Priests were restricted to churches within the areas of their residence permits. Thus many churches were unable to hold services for extended periods. After a six-month period had elapsed, the local government would demand that the church be closed, after which no attempts to reopen it would be tolerated. In 1959 alone, 309 churches disappeared from the registry. People under 18 were not permitted to serve in a church, while those attending seminaries might suddenly be whisked away for military service. Intense propaganda was mounted by the state, which was not always confined to media ridiculing the morals and behavior of priests. Young hooligans would often be adopted to attack church property and to harass priests. By 1958, too, the authorities began to cut down the number of priests, encouraging them to take up other professions or moving them to other jobs immediately. Organizations linked to the church were prohibited from undertaking any sort of charitable activity. Author Dmitry Pospielovsky points out that, when a church was to be dissolved, the move would be preceded by a village meeting that involved the consumption of all the communion wine by local officials and police, and then a wholesale physical attack on the church and beatings of the elderly parishioners – thereby ensuring that, of the 25,000 Russian Orthodox churches functioning in 1958, fewer than 8,000 opened their doors in 1965 (Pospielovsky, 1984). Thus the church was subjected to the sort of pressure reminiscent of the late 1920s and the 1930s. Under Khrushchev, "Scientific Atheism" was not only encouraged; it was elevated as a state priority. The famed Monastery of the Caves in Kyiv, founded in 1015, was closed as a result of this campaign.

Cultural thaw

Stalin's death brought an end to the heyday of Socialist Realism in Soviet culture. Ilya Ehrenburg's 1954 novel *The Thaw* heralded the arrival of a more tolerant era. It took time, however, for conditions to be truly normal. Those who appeared to go too far, such as Aleksandr Tvardovsky, editor of the reformist journal *Novy mir* (*New World*), suffered temporary dismissal. After the 20th Party Congress, however, writers began to be more ambitious. In 1956, two symposia held under the title of "Literaturnaya Moskva" ("Literary Moscow") offered criticisms of conditions inside the Soviet Union. Hundreds of writers were released from the Gulag and from prisons in the general amnesty that followed Stalin's death. Slowly new discussions began in the press about the lamentable state of Soviet literature. In December 1953, Vladimir Pomerantsev had published an article in *Novyi mir* which declared that Soviet literature was insincere and dishonest, simply listing slogans rather than focusing on the real problems of Soviet society. Several other writers joined in the criticisms, including Ehrenburg and Zoshchenko. The Union of Writers expelled several of them. However, after 1956, a new and distinctive period in Soviet culture emerged that had several characteristics. First, many of the "icons" of the Stalin years fell from grace, particularly those who could not bring themselves to desist from veneration of Stalin. These included Konstantin Simonov and Aleksandr Gerasimov, both of whom had become famous during the years of the German–Soviet war. Two new theaters originated in the years of Khrushchev's ascendancy: the Sovremennik (Contemporary) in 1956 under the leadership of Oleg Efremov, and the Taganka in 1963 led by the actor Yuri Lyubimov. The latter's founding date meant that it belonged more to the Brezhnev period than to the period of Thaw.

Although a more tolerant era had emerged, artists and writers found it difficult to discern the limits on their activities. Frequently, these depended on the personal whims and moods of the new leader. The classic example is that of Boris Pasternak's famous novel *Doctor Zhivago*, which originated in the difficult times of Zhdanov's pre-eminence and control over official ideology, and was based on the author's relationship with his lover, Olga Ivinskaya, who had been arrested and sent to a labor camp in this same period. Once the novel was completed, Pasternak recognized that its setting in the period of the 1917 revolutions and Russian Civil War might cause consternation among Soviet censors, and he sent it to several foreign publishers. Eventually it was published in Milan, in late November 1957, and a year later it won the Nobel Prize for Literature. Pasternak immediately came under furious attack from Khrushchev and the head of the Soviet Komsomol, Vladimir Semichastny. When was translated into English, the novel received acclaim in the West. However, Pasternak was not permitted to go to Stockholm for the award ceremony, and under intense pressure from the Soviet authorities he declined to accept the award. According to Vladislav Zubok, Khrushchev used Ivinskaya as a means to put pressure on the author by releasing her from camps and exile after seven years, but with the implicit threat that she might be returned (Zubok, 2009).

BOX 6.1
....

Boris Pasternak (1890–1960)

A poet and the author of the Nobel Prize-winning novel *Doctor Zhivago*, Boris Pasternak was born in Moscow on January 29, 1890 to a prominent Jewish family with an artistic background (his father was a professor and a painter, and his mother was a concert pianist). He began with a musical interest but gave it up to study philosophy at the Marburg University of Germany in 1910. Returning to Moscow in 1914, he published his first collection of poetry, but it went unnoticed. He first gained recognition with his poem *My Sister Life*, published in 1922. By the late 1920s, Pasternak found difficulty molding his style to the doctrine of Socialist Realism. He attempted to conform to the cultural demands by producing long poems such as *Lieutenant Schmidt* (1927), *The Year 1905* (1927) and

Box 6.1 continued

The Second Birth (1932). Although he was spared during the purges, he fell out of favor with the Soviet government, and began translating various poems and Shakespearian plays as a source of income. He started to write his most famous work, *Doctor Zhivago*, in 1945. It was first published in Italy in 1957, and in 1988 in the Soviet Union. When it was awarded the Nobel Prize in 1958, he opted not to receive the award under pressure from the Soviet government, which frowned upon this work. When Pasternak died of lung cancer on May 30, 1960, his funeral became an occasion for mass mourning and was attended by hundreds despite the lack of official recognition for a world-famous author.

The entire period was far from uniform. Toleration was followed by repression, and then moderation returned again. After further de-Stalinization that occurred during the 22nd Party Congress (1961), however, Aleksandr Solzhenitsyn's radical depiction of the Gulag system, *One Day in the Life of Ivan Denisovich*, appeared uncensored in November 1962 in serial form in *Novyi mir*. Khrushchev himself was the ultimate arbiter of Soviet literature and art. In the case of the Solzhenitsyn book, he evidently read it while on vacation in the Crimea – in contrast to *Doctor Zhivago*, which he had condemned without reading. Khrushchev's backing of Solzhenitsyn's short documentary novel arose from its anti-Stalin sentiment, which was in line with official policy. Its publication was also a major coup for the journal's editor Tvardovsky. However, almost simultaneously, in the world of art, young artists received an antithetical response. The occasion was an exhibition of art at the Manezh Central Exhibition Hall in Moscow displaying works of young artists of the New Reality Artistic Academy founded by the Russian visual artist Ely Belyutin in 1948, which was commemorating the 30th anniversary of the Moscow Union of Artists and opened on November 26, 1962. To the surprise of the exhibitors, Khrushchev arrived with his entourage and tore into the artists, describing their modernistic works as "dog shit." At a Politburo meeting three days later, the Soviet leader attacked formalism in art and declared he was ready to start arresting transgressors.

Following this outburst, which left cultural leaders confused, Khrushchev ordered a crackdown against formalism in the media and at artistic establishments. He identified himself with simple workers and peasants against a new cultural intelligentsia obviously imbued with Western styles and philosophies. In March 1963, at a gathering of cultural leaders at the House of Unions, Khrushchev continued the assault, singling out Andrey Voznesensky, an avant-garde poet who had been criticized by one of the speakers for commenting on the generation gap in the country. Although Voznesensky tried to defend himself, he stood little chance against the venom and invective of the Soviet leader, who accused him of being a servant of foreign agents and announced that the Thaw was over. The scene was quite remarkable as other party leaders joined in the symbolic condemnation of Voznesensky and other young artists. Zubok notes that Aleksandr Shelepin, former head of the KGB, berated Voznesensky as a "damned beatnik" for coming to the Kremlin without wearing a shirt and tie (Zubok, 2009). The purge that followed influenced all walks of cultural life, particularly of the followers of Belyutin, but it also affected writers, musicians, and film-makers. The vast majority was obliged to reject their own works and acknowledge the correctness of Khrushchev's new line. Several scholars have noted that this savage new attack on culture began directly after the fiasco of the Cuban missile crisis, thus suggesting that after a humiliating defeat in foreign policy the Soviet leader needed to assert his will at home. While there is some truth in this line of argument, the crackdown also reflected Khrushchev's real views and prejudices. On the one hand, he was out of touch with the younger generation; but, on the other hand, he was a cultural philistine with little understanding of art and music. The events indicate also that at heart Khrushchev remained something of a Stalinist as well as an autocrat.

Foreign policy during the early Cold War, 1945–1963

Germany and Eastern Europe, 1945–1948

The victory over Nazi Germany was achieved despite the wartime alliance as much as because of it. The goals of the Allied Powers, and particularly of the three leaders, were rarely the same. There were three parallel concepts of the way the West should conduct the war. It would be an error to perceive the Western allies in unity against the new Soviet power once the war ended, though it certainly seems true that relations improved after the death of Roosevelt in April 1945. Stalin had been content at Yalta to make a few minor concessions while holding on to his gains in Eastern Europe, and ensuring that Roosevelt – a man inexperienced in foreign policy and with little interest in the fate of small countries in Central and Eastern Europe – was never very close to Churchill. The British leader staked his career on the defeat of Nazi Germany, a goal that for a long time superseded any others on the world stage. Once it became clear that the Germans would eventually be overcome, however, Churchill seemingly switched to his former role as an anti-Soviet politician who was determined to preserve both the British Empire and an independent, "free" Poland. It says much for the frustration of the British prime minister that he entered into a bizarre negotiation with Stalin in September 1944, in which the two leaders, at Churchill's behest, divided Europe by means of a percentage-of-interest system.

In acting in this fashion before Yalta, Churchill presented Stalin with a mandate for the latter's future claims. Yalta was a most unsatisfactory treaty for the Western allies, made worse by the rapid advance of the Red Army. Stalin was in a powerful position but made the concession that there would be democratic elections in the countries of Eastern Europe once the war was over. Only Czechoslovakia could genuinely be termed pro-Soviet. However, Stalin intended to use the Red Army's presence to merge various political parties and harness them to the local Communist parties.

The first step was the formation of the Lublin Committee as a future Polish government. This immediately undermined the Polish Government-in-Exile, which Stalin regarded as hostile. The Allies agreed, however, that the Lublin Committee could serve as the basis for a future government, with the addition of some Cabinet members from the Government-in-Exile.

Stalin also showed some restraint. Though Germany was to be divided between the three powers and France, the Soviet Union never made any claims to the zones in Western hands, other than the delivery of industrial goods – part of the reparations demanded from Germany for instigating the war. Stalin also had not intervened in the civil war in Greece, allowing the British to help the government suppress the insurgents. (Tito, however, a more ideological leader, did come to the aid of the Communists.) In this respect he was consistent. The Soviet Union would allow the Western allies to administer zones under their occupation as they saw fit. In return, they should not interfere in the Soviet "zones." This sort of vision fitted well within the traditional European spheres of influence that had been prevalent in conflicts over the previous centuries. It did not coincide with the outlook of the new power within Europe, the United States. However, as far as the USSR was concerned, the American presence was temporary. The United States already had extensive commitments in the Pacific, and it was anticipated that the country would eventually send home its troops and retreat into its former isolationism. This viewpoint made it essential that the Soviet Union did not retreat from its holdings in the meantime, and took a firm line when dealing with Western requests and demands. Possibly the inconsistency and unpredictability of Western policy was a larger problem for Stalin's regime than its support for a democratic Poland, or the non-recognition of new governments in Romania and Bulgaria while under Soviet occupation.

The United States had two presidents who were not well versed in foreign policy. Paradoxically, it was a president who was – theoretically at least – the best-qualified in this area, John F. Kennedy, who was partly responsible for the débâcles at the Bay of Pigs and later in Vietnam. If Roosevelt was able to accumulate knowledge from the experience of the world's worst-ever conflict, Truman was clearly reliant on his advisors at the outset. He seems to have vacillated between a desire for compromise and outright irritation at Soviet behavior. In May 1945, before the Potsdam Summit, by which time Churchill was already furious at what he regarded as Soviet duplicity, Truman sent his aide Harry Hopkins to Moscow, in the hope that the wartime diplomat could once again reach a satisfactory agreement with Stalin. Before the month ended, however, US Lend-Lease aid to the Soviet Union was suddenly halted. By this time, the United States was making good progress on the Manhattan Project. Truman seems to have decided, therefore, that the policy of conciliation would not work, and that the Soviet Union should be made aware of the formidable economic and military power of the United States. The presence of the bomb also relieved Truman of the need to rely on the Red Army to assist in the defeat of Japan, as stipulated by the Yalta Treaty.

By the time the three powers met at Potsdam, the impasse between the two leading powers was already evident. Germany had been defeated and was being rapidly demilitarized. Germany and Austria were joint zones of occupation. Both old capitals, Berlin and Vienna, lay within the Soviet sphere, and already the Soviet occupation regime had demonstrated a distinct lack of sympathy with the local population, in spite of the fact that Stalin always made a distinction between the ruthless Nazi leadership and the benign German workers. Stalin and Molotov made more demands at Potsdam, requesting that the USSR take over the mandate of the Italian colonies in Libya – a request that the Allies turned down point blank – that the Ruhr industrial region be made an international zone, and that significant annexations be made in the south at the expense of Turkey. The Western allies were not anxious to see Germany permanently crippled and additional burdens placed on the taxpayers of their countries through reparations. Though Truman informed Stalin about the testing of the atomic bomb just before the conference began, the comment made minimal impact. Stalin was already aware of the weapon, but could not believe that it would be used against the Soviet Union. Secretary of State James Byrnes represented the United States at the Council of Foreign Ministers in London in September–October 1945, and once again tried to reach an accommodation with the Soviet side, including the statement that the USSR might have a role in the future administration of Japan.

Yet the United States was already moving to a new policy of containment. The strategy owed much to George Kennan, the US ambassador to the Soviet Union, a Soviet specialist who believed that Soviet foreign policy was based primarily on ideology and long-term insecurity that made it impossible for the Communist state to reach any serious agreements with a rival power. Already, Moscow was exerting control over the Communist parties of neighboring states, and the result would be the collapse of weak regimes around the world. Kennan's views, expressed in his *Long Telegram* (February 22, 1946), gained the support of the disillusioned Byrnes. The diplomat and the politician seemed to have good grounds for their skepticism. Powerful Communist parties in France and Italy seemed destined to take power or to have a decisive influence over the governments. Civil war continued in Greece. Communist parties were gradually taking control in Eastern Europe. Soviet troops refused to leave their zone of Iran, as scheduled, on March 2, 1946. Containment – the taking of a firm line and adhering to it no matter how great the pressure – seemed the only logical response. At the same time, the United States had no wish to prolong the colonial empires of the European powers that had been weakened by the war. Britain and France, the main democratic Western powers of Europe during the interwar period, had both suffered humiliating defeats during the war (France at home and Britain in Southeast Asia), and the United States was at best half-hearted in supporting their attempts to regain their overseas possessions. Both, in fact, were close to bankruptcy.

Kennan's views, however, implied that the Americans had for the moment to tolerate imperialist empires in the face of the greater threat – Soviet Communism, or, as Stalin usually envisaged and called it, the expansion and influence of Russia. Thus the Americans and the British acted firmly on Iran, with the result that the Red Army withdrew in May 1946. Truman then came to the aid of the British, when the Attlee government declared in February 1947 that, because of economic constraints, it could no longer continue to support the Greek government. Churchill had requested the renewal of the wartime partnership during his speech at Fulton, Missouri, on March 5, 1946 when, in the presence of President Truman, he declared that an Iron Curtain had fallen over Europe "from Stettin in the Baltic to Trieste in the Adriatic." Churchill was no longer in office and thus free to be outspoken. There could be no clearer indication of his anger at his former wartime ally, Stalin. The delay in the move from deep suspicion to outright hostility between the two superpowers, however, was most likely because of US reluctance to prop up the British Empire and its desire to open up world markets to American trade. Though Soviet propaganda railed against a single entity, which it termed "Anglo-American imperialism," Stalin was well aware of the tensions between the English-speaking powers. The Americans had been negotiating a huge loan to the British in late 1945, but the tough terms engendered a furious outcry in Britain. The United States was also growing more reluctant to share its nuclear secrets with its wartime allies.

Stalin's position was considerably weaker than it appeared. The USSR entered a period in which it was forced to concentrate on domestic recovery rather than on further extending its power. It possessed by far the largest army in Europe once the United States began to send troops home and divert others to the Far East, but the military also required replenishing. It had suffered huge losses and now had to deal with postwar administrations, control over neighboring states, as well as insurgencies within the USSR itself. The best hope for Stalin was that the United States would leave the scene. In contrast, on March 12, the Truman Doctrine was introduced, whereby the Americans resolved to come to the aid of countries facing Communist insurgencies, and offered immediate financial assistance to Greece and Turkey. The commitment was huge and theoretically universal. To the Stalin regime, it also seemed illogical and unfair. The United States was attempting to take the position of world policeman to promote US economic interests and imperialism. In June 1947 these beliefs were bolstered by the introduction of the Marshall Plan to assist European recovery. Initially, assistance was offered to all the countries of Europe, including the USSR. The plan came too late to assist the full recovery of the Western Europeans, but it immediately placed Stalin and Molotov in a quandary – how to respond to an offer that would represent foreign intrusion into the economic affairs of the Soviet Union and its allies. Initially, Molotov received instructions to consider approving the plan.

At a meeting of the European powers in Paris concerning the US aid program, Molotov met with the most enthusiastic supporters, Britain and France. He requested that Germany be excluded from the Marshall Plan. The Western powers had no wish to get into a prolonged debate that would delay American credits, and thus a serious rift developed with the Soviet Foreign Minister. On July 1, Molotov received a telegram from Stalin and the following day he spoke out strongly against the Marshall Plan, which was depicted as an intrusion into national sovereignty and a means of enforcing US control over recipient countries. Moreover, the Soviet Union then put pressure on Eastern European countries, such as Czechoslovakia, which at first were also in favor of the idea. In official Soviet jargon, the plan would establish control over German industry by the US "monopoly capitalists." Where the truth lay was debatable. Most likely, Stalin and Molotov feared that the plan would push Soviet citizens into more contact with the West, thereby subjecting them to the corruptions of bourgeois influence. The Soviet Union had begun to isolate its citizens in the tense postwar atmosphere. At the same time it could not afford to allow its satellite states to be drawn into the Western sphere, either. Thus the Soviet Union had to come up with an alternative to the Marshall Plan, something that would bring together the Eastern Europeans under a single economic umbrella.

The answer was the Communist Information Bureau, commonly known as the Cominform, initiated in September 1947 at a meeting in Warsaw attended by the Communist parties of the Eastern European countries and also those of France and Italy. The main speaker at the conference was Andrey Zhdanov, the rising star of the Politburo, and the party leader of Leningrad. Zhdanov, the enforcer of cultural uniformity within the USSR, noted that Italian and French workers were already on strike against US plans to enslave Europe. However, the speaker noted, those parties had missed a golden opportunity to take power when the Second World War ended. It was necessary in addition for the assembled to unite against the same threat, and to maintain constant communication in order to prevent the outbreak of a new war. In theory, the Cominform would now coordinate the activities of the various Communist parties. In practice, there was to follow a period when the leaderships of the satellite states had to pay homage to the benevolence and wisdom of the Soviet leadership in Moscow. The smaller countries were obliged to exhibit their gratitude to the Soviet "elder brother." Henceforth, non-Communist parties in these countries would no longer be tolerated. Either they were dissolved or else – assuming that they were sufficiently left-leaning – they would be merged with the Communists. The USSR also began to sign treaties of "friendship, cooperation, and mutual aid" with its Western neighbors, beginning with Romania, Hungary, and Bulgaria in November 1948.

Both Finland and Czechoslovakia at first remained outside this new Union. In February 1948, the Finnish problem was resolved by a Soviet–Finnish military alliance. Stalin had no wish to begin a new military conflict with his northern neighbor. Czechoslovakia was a different matter entirely. On paper it was the country most likely to seek accommodation with the USSR, but Prime Minister Klement Gottwald had been among the first to welcome the Marshall Plan, before he was summoned to Moscow and instructed to reject its terms. In 1946 in the only democratic elections in postwar Eastern Europe, the Communist Party had won 38 percent of the vote and had begun to play a prominent role in the government. The vote was influenced by the fear of Germany, and also by a general suspicion of the Western democracies.

Gradually, however, Stalin prepared for the demise of independent Czechoslovakia using control over the police forces and intimidation by Soviet troops that had begun to mass over the border in Austria. Liberal leaders began to resign from the government. By the summer of 1948, the Socialist Party had been merged with its Communist counterpart and a new constitution drawn up, based on the Soviet model. President Benes resigned rather than accept such subservience, but Czechoslovakia was now firmly part of the Cominform group.

Of the East European countries, Yugoslavia, which had got rid of the German occupiers by means of its own forces rather than by the presence of the Red Army, was the most independent. For some time Tito was the most loyal of all Stalin's supporters, and equally ruthless. By 1946, Yugoslavia had introduced a Soviet-style constitution, and began its first five-year plan a year later. Though Tito favored local trading blocs with neighboring states in the Balkans, there is no evidence that he was trying to form a breakaway group. Thus in 1948, when Stalin suddenly turned on his disciple, it could only have come as a profound shock. What were Tito's faults? In Soviet official missives he was referred to as a renegade and a spy, a hireling of the imperialist powers, and a Hitlerite–Trotskyite agent. Plainly he had not followed orders to Stalin's liking, particularly in the reluctance to develop heavy industry at the expense of consumer goods. He had also not ruled out trade with the West and was anxious to develop close economic links with neighbors in order to improve living standards for Yugoslav citizens. To Stalin, it may have appeared that these contacts took precedence over subservience to Soviet diktat. Gradually links were severed. In the spring of 1948, Stalin recalled Soviet advisors from Yugoslavia, along with military specialists. An attempt to spark civil war in Yugoslavia by declaring the country's leader a traitor failed manifestly. The population was not ignorant of the sort of fate that might await it were it to follow Stalin's lead. The brief entry of the Red Army into the country in 1945 was remembered as an interlude of mayhem. Instead it was the hardened Stalinists who were arrested for disloyalty as the two leaders exchanged a series of angry messages. On September 28, the USSR ended diplomatic relations with Yugoslavia, which was expelled from the Cominform. Titoists were hunted and purged in neighboring states, and Stalin waited for the inevitable fall of his new adversary. The United States stepped in and offered aid and a new trading partner. Ideology was superseded by the opportunity to create a chink in the Soviet armor. Not until 1955 would relations be restored between Yugoslavia and the USSR, and Khrushchev rather than Tito would make the conciliatory steps. (Plate 6.1)

The Berlin Crisis

In the European climate of 1948, it appeared that a new war could break out at any time. The crucial area was clearly Germany, divided among the Allies and ruled by the Allied Control Council that allowed the military leaders of either side to visit the other's zones. The main conflict arose between the Americans and the British, on the one hand, and the Soviet Union, on the other. Berlin was the battleground, an

Plate 6.1 Soviet soldiers watching the Czechoslovakian Independence Day parade, 4 November 1949.

Image: Bettmann/CORBIS

island of capitalism in the Soviet zone and located only thirty miles from the Polish border. Stalin's views on postwar Germany often changed. At certain times he appeared to favor a reunification of Germany on condition that reparations would continue and the country would develop as a modest agricultural region with a major role for the Communist Party. He was also aware that the key industrial regions lay under Western control. Economically the Soviet zone did not constitute a viable future state. The greatest fear for the Soviet Union was the remilitarization of Germany. The second fear was a US attack on the USSR in the period 1946–1948. When such an attack did not take place, Stalin grew more confident. He was also aware of the progress of the atomic bomb project behind the Ural Mountains, supervised by Beria, but using the resources of some brilliant scientists, such as Igor Kurchatov and Andrey Sakharov. The bomb would eventually be detonated on August 29, 1949, initiating a new phase in the Cold War – the arms race.

The US and British authorities merged their occupation zones in January 1947 into what became known as Bizonia. They wanted to introduce a common currency and to allow the zone to benefit from the resources of the Marshall Plan. To the Stalin leadership, these measures were signs that the easy terms for Soviet purchases in Germany were about to end and, more seriously, that the Western powers had reneged on the agreement that Germany should remain demilitarized. At a meeting in Paris in April 1946, the USSR had put forward this view on the grounds that such a policy had been agreed upon at Yalta and Potsdam, but the United States was no longer willing to recognize that the decisions taken during the war years should be adhered to in the new postwar circumstances. In December 1947, when the Council of Foreign Ministers met in London, the Soviet delegation reiterated its demands, but the Western nations refused to accept them; they held several private meetings, excluding the Soviet delegation, with a wish to maintain the division of Germany, and to unite the (then) two Western zones into a new federation of Western Germany. The following summer, the foreign ministers of the main socialist countries met in Warsaw, and not only agreed that the dismantling of all weapons from Germany should be completed, but also resurrected the idea of four-power control over the Ruhr industrial zone. Matters finally came to a head when the Western powers announced plans to carry out monetary reform (France joined Bizonia in the summer of 1948), extending the new currency into West Berlin. The prospect of two Germanys suddenly became a real one.

On May 20, 1948, the Soviet delegates abruptly left the Allied Control Council. Ten days later they began to restrict communication routes between Berlin and the western zones of Germany. The Berlin blockade was an attempt by Stalin to alter the gradual but relentless process of transforming occupied Western Germany into a new federal state that would have access to Western aid and technology. The emergence of such a state would redefine the limits of Soviet control. Whether Stalin intended to occupy all of Berlin remains a moot point. It seems more likely that he was using Berlin as an instrument to prevent the division of Germany and the formation of a potentially dangerous new state in the West. Also, the USSR in the early postwar period could not hope to match the United States in terms of economic power. Gradually Western links with Berlin became more and more restricted. Trains were no longer allowed to leave Berlin for the western zones. Only air links remained. Stalin found it hard to believe that the Western powers would care whether the 2.5 million citizens of Berlin – their avowed enemy only three years earlier – fell under Soviet rule. Geography alone suggested that they would have to comply with the Soviet move. There was no real need for a contingency plan in the unlikely event that the Allies would resort to force, because the USSR could always end the new controls at any time. The official reason for the closure of the rail and road routes was that there were "technical difficulties" in the Soviet zone, which would continue "for a long time."

The decision of the United States and Britain on June 24 to use an airlift to supply West Berlin throughout the winter of 1948–1949 changed the nature of the Cold War. It also led irrevocably to the formation of two German states. The western zones were combined into the Federal Republic of Germany with the capital in Bonn; in response the German Socialist Unity Party (SED), on the instructions of the Soviet Politburo, formed the German Democratic Republic (GDR) on October 7, 1949, presided over by the well-known German Communist Wilhelm Pieck, though real power lay in the hands of the chairman of the Socialist Unity Party, Walther Ulbricht. The Soviet military administration turned over the government to the new entity, which would enjoy a brief inglorious forty years of existence highlighted mainly by drug-induced sporting triumphs; and, as a Soviet creation, it would constantly bear the hallmarks of its painful birth. Stalin's decision to blockade Berlin, which was to be ended by May 1949, also catalyzed the formation of a Western defensive alliance, the North Atlantic Treaty Organization (NATO), which was an expansion of a smaller European defensive pact and initially comprised twelve nations, including the United States and Canada. The Federal Republic of Germany would be included in NATO by October 1954 after a treaty signed in Paris. The USSR formally ended its state of war with Germany in January 1955, but responded officially to West Germany's acceptance into the Western alliance by forming its own military union, the Warsaw Pact, on May 11–14, 1955. By this time the Cold War was at its height, and the world had been divided into two notably hostile camps, split in Soviet propaganda into capitalist and socialist.

Though the creation of the Warsaw Pact occurred after the death of Stalin, it lies within the scope of postwar Stalinist foreign policy. In one respect, Stalin's worst suspicions had been confirmed – as he had suspected would happen during the war, the Western powers had finally linked their cause with that of Germany in a campaign against the Communist East. However, it is also clear that in their later years Stalin and the heavy-handed Molotov lacked subtlety in their approach to foreign relations. There was a cruelty and a ruthlessness in their attitude to satellite states that, for the most part, would not have objected to a friendly Soviet Union on their border provided that they could have formed governments of their own making. The blockade of Berlin was a gamble but it also represented a fundamental misreading of American intentions. The relative tolerance of the wartime Soviet Union had undergone a metamorphosis into the most brutal of dictatorships, transcending in its nature – though not in numbers of victims – the prewar regime. The Allied Control Council provided the USSR with a permanent presence in Western meetings, but the leadership chose to leave it. And mistakes made over Berlin were to be repeated only a year later, when the Soviets walked out of the UN Security Council, thereby allowing the UN to become involved in the Korean Crisis – a war that Stalin clearly knew about, and of which he may even have been the chief architect.

Stalin and Molotov, however, were now actors on a world stage and felt that they could adopt a more aggressive attitude. The wartime victories and the new atomic weapon permitted a confidence that was not exhibited in the early war years. When Stalin died in March 1953, Yugoslavia had seemingly been lost to the cause. Moreover, Stalin did not even trust the victorious Chinese Communists and their leader Mao Zedong, though the Chinese treated the veteran Soviet leader with great deference. On February 14, 1950, the USSR and China signed a Treaty of Friendship, Cooperation, and Mutual Aid, following Mao's bizarre and drawn-out visit to the USSR; during this he was left alone for long periods and rarely given the sort of treatment that merited a fellow Communist leader, who was arguably, after Tito, only the third such leader to have gained his eminence through genuine popular support. In later years Stalin grew more distant from Molotov, but foreign policy remained constant, marked by general suspicion and malevolence. Stalin's strategy and Soviet foreign policy were one and the same thing. By late 1948, Zhdanov, the apparent successor to Stalin, had died. Soviet policy was essentially that of a single man. Perhaps because of such a precedent, Khrushchev also continued the same general policies – belligerence, bullying, cajoling, refusal to tolerate dissent, and using every opportunity to promote Soviet interests vis-à-vis the United States. In January 1949, at an economic summit, the USSR initiated the Council for Mutual Economic Assistance (CMEA), an organization that lasted until 1991 and through which the USSR channeled aid and traded with fellow socialist countries.

Soviet involvement in the Korean War, 1950–1953

The Korean War saw the expansion of the Cold War into Asia. It was an important event in several respects. It was the only time during the Cold War that all three major powers (the USA, the USSR, and China) were actively engaged in a conflict, and to some extent it defined the limits of both Communist expansion and Western will to resist. The war, moreover, resulted in an armistice but never formally ended. Even after the fall of the Berlin Wall in Europe, Korea remained the dividing line between East and West, with UN and North Korean border guards facing each other at the DMZ village of Panmunjom. The Korean War, however, has often been taken out of the context of the Cold War and portrayed as a civil conflict between two hard-line governments – that of Kim Il Sung in the north and that of Syngman Rhee in the south. Through the opening of Soviet archives, and the work of historian Kathryn Weathersby and others, that assessment has been revised. That the Soviet Union was closely involved in the Korean War is no longer in doubt; but the main questions revolve around the outbreak of the war in 1950, and the USSR's continued commitment to it. Negotiations between three countries occurred separately – between North Korea, the USSR, and China. Of the three major figures (the third being Mao), Stalin was by far the most senior, the most experienced, and the one who had acquired most international prestige. Stalin by the late 1940s was a skilled manipulator of foreign policy.

The official Soviet version of the outbreak of the war was that it had begun because of aggression by South Korea, including provocative moves at the 38th parallel. At the end of the Second World War, the USSR and the USA had divided Korea at the 38th parallel following the surrender of Japan, which had occupied the peninsula during the war. In 1949, North Korea was militarily weak, and evidence suggests that the Stalin regime feared that the South could mount an invasion. However, Kim Il Sung had ambitions to unite Korea under his own leadership, and form a Marxist state. How the United States would respond to an invasion was not known. The international climate, from the Soviet perspective, appeared favorable. US troops had withdrawn from Korea, and the closest available forces were based in Japan. They were far from battle-ready. Alluding to the US assigned defensive perimeter in Southeast Asia, Secretary of State Dean Acheson had notably excluded Korea, while some US senators maintained that eventually Korea would be taken over by the Communists. Furthermore, Japanese rule, which had been predictably harsh, had widened social tensions among the population, enhancing the popularity of the Communists under Kim Il Sung. To the North Koreans, the time for an invasion was ripe, and their task was to persuade their patron, Stalin, that he had nothing to lose from supporting such a venture. An invasion could not take place without Soviet support. The Chinese Communists were close to victory but had yet to consolidate their regime. The North Koreans lacked planes (especially) and modern weapons with which to stage a successful occupation of the South. In April 1949, the USSR and North Korea signed an agreement on military–technical assistance, whereby Moscow would dispatch to its allies planes, tanks, machine-guns, ships, and other goods.

For Stalin, the essential matter seems to have been to avoid a major confrontation that could result in a Third World War. Some historians, particularly at the height of the Cold War, saw the invasion as part of Stalin's plans for world domination. Weathersby in particular has argued persuasively that this was not the case (Weathersby, 1999). In 1949, Stalin consistently rejected North Korean pleas to support an invasion on the grounds that preparations were insufficient, the South Koreans would not necessarily support such an invasion and, moreover, such a decisive action would compel the Americans to intervene on behalf of the South Koreans. At some point, however, Stalin changed his mind. North Korean military preparedness had improved by late 1949 and early 1950. The Soviet international situation looked much stronger, too. Mao's victory in China signified that the Soviet Union now had a partner that had attained Communism independently, without the support of the Soviet army. Also in 1949, the Soviet Union had detonated its own atomic bomb. At the same time, having suffered the reverses of the Berlin blockade, and with the formation of NATO, there was an understandable desire to achieve a short but complete military triumph that would raise the country's prestige. All these factors made the case for supporting North Korean aggression much stronger. Stalin also demanded that, in return for Soviet support, the North Koreans start to supply lead to the USSR. Kim Il Sung meanwhile had been requesting a visit to Moscow to plead his case. He was allowed his wish in April 1950, shortly after a visit by Mao. Though Stalin and Mao discussed the developing crisis in Korea, Stalin evidently never divulged the invasion plans to the Chinese leader.

Stalin wanted the war to be brief and successful, presenting the Americans with a *fait accompli*. Soviet military advisors drew up the battle plans, which then had to be translated into Korean. Stalin instructed Kim Il Sung to inform the Chinese about the preparations for the invasion; the North Korean leader did so, indicating that the Soviets were fully behind the plans. Though Stalin had decided to back the invasion, however, the commitment was largely kept secret. The war began with subterfuge reminiscent of the German attack on Poland in September 1939. North

Koreans wore South Korean uniforms and mounted an assault on their own border guards. Thus the fiction could be propagated that the South Koreans had begun an invasion of the North. The Communist regime would therefore defend itself and take the fight into South Korean territory. This interpretation of the start of the war stood the test of time, and would remain convincing to some for several decades. It could be corroborated by a protracted correspondence between Moscow and Pyongyang throughout 1949 concerning the dangers of an attack from South Korea over the 38th parallel. South Korea was also militantly nationalistic and regarded by the Communists as essentially a puppet regime put together by the United States, without much grassroots support from the Korean population.

There seems no question that the Soviet leader retained some reservations about the operation, and these became more pronounced with the failure of the North Koreans to achieve a swift and convincing victory. Though US response (through the United Nations, the USSR having temporarily given up its veto power by walking out of the assembly in protest at the failure to provide a seat for Communist China) was far from rapid, once intervention began, US forces immediately gained control of the air. In early July, Kim asked Stalin how his forces should proceed, and Stalin agreed to send more Soviet military advisors. In September, after General Douglas MacArthur had engineered the landing at Inchon, effectively trapping the North Koreans between UN forces there and at Pusan, the situation for the Communists began to look desperate. The USSR suddenly became very scathing about the North Korean military performance. Stalin was obliged to agree to send Soviet pilots to the border region, with strict instructions that they should not venture far from the Yalu river. The North Koreans would have preferred to see the arrival of the Soviet army to participate directly in the fighting. Stalin, unwilling to raise the stakes to such a degree, was prepared to evacuate North Korean forces from the peninsula, and be ready for a liberation movement at some time in the future. The Soviet-backed operation had clearly been a failure.

In October 1950, communication between the USSR and China regarding the situation in Korea began to increase sharply. Like Stalin, Mao did not really wish to become embroiled in what promised to be a prolonged struggle. There would come a point, on the other hand, when Chinese territorial security might come under threat. President Truman, swayed by the optimism of MacArthur, was prepared to take the war into North Korea in an attempt to unify the peninsula. This program went well beyond the original UN agreement to remove the North Koreans from land south of the 38th parallel. Even so, the Chinese response depended heavily on Stalin's commitment to future aid. Only with a firm Soviet promise would China agree to form "volunteer" detachments to join with the North Koreans (in North Korean uniforms) in fighting UN forces. Stalin's commitment was genuine but always limited. Air support was spasmodic at best. The Soviet leader's main concern was that no Soviet pilots should fall into UN hands. They were dressed in Chinese uniforms – ironically, therefore, captured Chinese were less likely than Soviet troops to be found in their own uniforms – and were not permitted to carry identification documents. On the other hand, Stalin took considerable interest in downed planes from the US side, using captured technology to support the Soviet military program. The USSR began to exploit the Korean War for its own purposes once it became clear that no military victory was in sight. The Chinese could hold off the UN forces indefinitely, while the Soviets supplied thousands of military advisors and occasional air support around the Yalu river region. With the stalemate situation, President Truman also wished to limit the scope of the war, refusing MacArthur's request to take the war into China.

Why, then, did the Korean War drag on for so long? The answer is that Stalin had become the main impediment to the peace process. There were without doubt other major issues, such as the controversial question of returning prisoners of war, some of whom (on the Communist side) were less than willing to be returned to their homeland, and also the treatment of such prisoners, adjudged by some to have been unnecessarily harsh on both sides. However, without the opposition of Stalin, the war would likely have ended much sooner than it did, as is witnessed by the relatively quick armistice that followed Stalin's death in March 1953. For the Soviet Union, Korea may have been a proxy war, but it was conducted cleverly. The American enemy, through the UN forces, was largely preoccupied for three years. Paradoxically, the Soviet Union was then weakened badly by the loss of its leader with no clear replacement. Between 1949 and 1953 the Soviet Union's world position had grown stronger. Another Communist power, using Soviet technology, had prevented the collapse of Kim's regime, despite an unexpected intervention by the forces of the UN (the United States and some fifty supporting countries). That power, China, was now stronger, but still regarded the Soviet Union as the senior partner. The relative success in Korea partly made up for the failure to remove Tito from the Cominform. On the other hand, Soviet prestige was ultimately lowered somewhat by the second-hand form of commitment to North Korea. It was China that had emerged as a Communist regime more prepared to support its neighbors.

Foreign policy under Khrushchev

Under Khrushchev, Soviet foreign policy was at first directed toward trying to restore the unity of the Communist world that had existed at the end of the Second World War. Khrushchev and Bulganin visited China between September 29 and October 12, 1954, and signed a new Sino-Soviet Treaty that handed the Liaotung Peninsula to the Chinese. Soviet troops left Port Arthur, the base that had been defended with such tenacity against the Japanese in 1904–1905. In May 1955 the Soviet leaders visited Yugoslavia to try to restore relations with Tito's regime. The Soviet side clearly played a conciliatory role as Tito was more or less able to dictate the terms by which Yugoslavia would restore relations with the Soviet Union. Khrushchev's immediate concern, however, was the proposed entry of the Federal Republic of Germany into the NATO alliance, as a result of the Paris Peace Treaty on Germany signed by the Western allies in December 1954. The response was the formation of the military alliance known as the Warsaw Pact, which included the USSR, Poland, Hungary, Czechoslovakia, Romania, Bulgaria, and Albania, in May 1955. All those involved had already signed bilateral treaties with the USSR. Now they were obliged to sign a joint Treaty of Friendship, Cooperation, and Mutual Assistance. The pact might be seen as the belated Soviet response to NATO, or to the emergence of a militarized West Germany, but it can also be perceived, perhaps more accurately, as a guarantee both of Soviet hegemony in Eastern Europe and the preservation of the Eastern European alliance. The pact did more to prevent Eastern European countries from breaking away from Soviet control than it did to oppose NATO aggression.

The pact was also useful for the Khrushchev regime in that it initiated discussion on various issues. The individual armies of the satellite countries had been effectively under Soviet control since the later years of the war. Now the key institution for the next decade was the Political Consultative Committee (PCC). The Joint Staff of the Warsaw Pact consisted of the deputy ministers of defense of the signatory nations, which in turn established a Joint Staff, with each nation represented. The pact was scheduled to last for twenty years, but would be renewed for a further ten years automatically unless any of the member nations renounced it. In theory, the pact would be quietly dropped if the Western nations could be persuaded to disband NATO and sign a collective security agreement for Europe. The Soviet side made this request repeatedly, apparently with little real hope of success. Rather it was an effective propaganda ploy to place NATO in the role of the aggressor. Khrushchev pursued the policy with the visit of West German Chancellor Konrad Adenauer to the USSR in September 1955, after which diplomatic relations began between the two states. One week later, Khrushchev recognized the existence of the GDR, a state created by the USSR, by signing a formal Treaty of Friendship and Cooperation with the East Germans. The withdrawal of Soviet troops from Austria in 1955 was another important act, and one that symbolized the professed peaceful desires of the Soviet Union in Europe. However, the Western states never responded in the way that Khrushchev wished.

The crisis of 1956

In his early years in office, Khrushchev was put under tremendous pressure both by Western moves and by incidents of disobedience and protest within the Soviet bloc. Soviet tanks had been used to pacify East Germany after protests in 1953. The formation of NATO, while a response to actions taken by Stalin rather than by Khrushchev, heralded a new era of arms build-up in Europe. Though the Soviet Union had detonated a hydrogen bomb in August 1953, the country remained well behind the United States at this stage of the Cold War. Khrushchev's response to Soviet "backwardness" was to bluster and boast about Soviet capability, which only prompted the United States to act more belligerently. The internal instability and Khrushchev's own struggle for power ensured that the Eastern Europeans would take some action to free their states from the Soviet stranglehold. The catalyst was Khrushchev's denunciation of Stalin, which appeared to undermine the position of hardline Communist leaders in countries such as Poland and Hungary. The key question was how far the Soviet regime would be prepared to allow Eastern Europeans to promote new leaderships, often with people who had been rehabilitated in the more tolerant post-Stalin environment. Following the Congress, Khrushchev dissolved the Cominform – evidently his prime motive was to improve relations with Yugoslavia – and replaced the stone-faced Foreign Minister Molotov with Shepilov. By October, however, riots had broken out in Poland; and, on October 18, Zhukov placed Soviet armed forces on high alert. An invasion of Poland seemed only a matter of time.

October 1956 was dramatic. On October 19, the date scheduled for the 8th Plenum of the Polish United Workers' Party (PUWP), a Soviet plane carrying almost the entire Politburo landed in Warsaw. The initial intention may have been to prevent Wladyslaw Gomulka from taking over as the leader of the PUWP. The Polish party had become fractured and mired in bitter disputes over who was to run it. Gomulka, who had been removed from the leadership in the late 1940s, played the nationalist card, arguing that the Soviet military had been in control of its Polish counterpart to the extent that Soviet–Polish relations had been adversely affected. Among Gomulka's demands were the removal of Soviet military forces and the replacement of Konstantin Rokossovsky, the Polish-born marshal and Soviet war hero, as Minister of Defense. Rokossovsky, a supporter of Stalin though at one time a victim of the purges, was a symbol of Soviet military dominance over Poland. Under Gomulka, the PUWP managed to heal the splits in the party, and its members united under his leadership. Rokossovsky and other hardliners were excluded from the newly elected Politburo by a vote on October 17 (though the results would only be ratified by the forthcoming Plenum). The situation was then conveyed to Moscow by the Soviet ambassador to Poland, Ponomarenko. Thus when the Soviet delegation stepped off the plane – it included Khrushchev, Zhukov, Konev, Mikoyan, Molotov, Kaganovich, and Antonov – the situation looked ominous for the Poles. Ponomarenko seemed to expect that a major purge of the newly elected Polish leadership would take place.

After a few heated exchanges, however, Gomulka and the Polish military leaders were able to convince the Soviet leaders that they would be best-advised to accept the more moderate Polish regime. Worker protest could be held in check, whereas a Soviet invasion would meet sustained resistance. Gomulka's Poland would remain loyal to the Warsaw Pact and follow Soviet foreign policy guidelines. To that extent, Poland would be permitted to follow its own path to socialism, though there would be no opposition to Communist rule. The compromise ended the impasse in Poland and the threat of the most important buffer state leaving the Soviet-led alliance. It was a close call. Khrushchev in any case had a larger problem. The riots in Poland had had repercussions in other states, most significantly in Hungary. Imre Nagy, the new Communist Party leader, was prepared to go much further than Gomulka by making Hungary independent and withdrawing from the Warsaw Pact. Communist control was to be ended. In the meantime student protestors had demanded the removal of statues to Stalin and an end to the control of the Communist Party over political life. A domino-like collapse of the Soviet buffer zone seemed imminent. On October 24, Soviet troops stationed in Hungary entered Budapest and, on the following day, shot dead more than a hundred people in the city's central square. Thousands more were injured. By October 30, a massive Soviet invasion, involving more than 200,000 troops, was under way. More than 25,000 Hungarians were killed after vicious conflicts. By November 4, the insurrection was over and the Soviet Operation Vertex – to restore the "national-democratic" government of Hungary – had succeeded. Nagy was arrested and executed. His replacement was Janosz Kadar, a firmer leader who was ready to comply with Soviet demands.

Why was the Soviet Union prepared to act with such force in Hungary, but not in Poland? Poland had always been a more sensitive issue, a country that had been formed as virtually a new state in the postwar period, but without the democratic structure favored by the Western Powers. Gomulka had used diplomacy to assuage the angry Soviet leadership. He was fortunate that the leaders came to him, and that he could convince them of his own popularity and of the need to end the fractures within the PUWP leadership. Nagy had gone much further. Moreover, he had done so during a major international crisis, the attack on Egypt by Britain, France, and Israel following General Nasser's nationalization of the Suez Canal. This event involved all the major wartime powers, but for once the Soviet Union and the United States were in agreement that the attack had to end. Khrushchev threatened to resort to nuclear weapons unless the British and the French ended their invasion. Though Suez ended quietly, with a humiliating withdrawal for Britain and France, its timing was fortunate for the Soviet Union. The Hungarian rebellion was quashed without any form of Western intervention. Though such a Western response was probably impossible, Hungarians had been encouraged in their resistance to Soviet hegemony by broadcasts from Radio Free Europe. When protests came from the UN after the brutal intervention, the Soviet Union proposed a non-aggression pact between NATO and the Warsaw Pact.

Germany, spy planes, and the Cuban Missile Crisis

By the time of the Khrushchev administration, an arms race had begun between the Cold War powers. Both sides had detonated hydrogen bombs by 1953, but the United States had amassed a far greater number of nuclear weapons than the USSR, outnumbering them by at least ten to one. American B-52 bombers posed a serious threat to the Soviet Union. Though Khrushchev feared US military technology, he was confident that his country could catch up. In the interim the Soviet authorities staged a cunning display of bombers over Moscow on Aviation Day in June 1955, when aircraft made repeated sorties to give the impression of greater numbers. The United States had devised a sophisticated spy plane, the U2, which was able to cover long distances at high altitude. The plane proved useful for spying on Soviet military facilities, so – whatever Khrushchev's subterfuge – Eisenhower's administration soon knew that the United States was ahead in the arms race. On the other hand, he was unlikely to make any kind of public statement about it. He had no wish to reveal his sources, and Washington was only too well aware that the Soviet Union was capable of matching the US military build-up in relatively short time. It was Khrushchev rather than Eisenhower who was naturally aggressive. Whether Khrushchev fully understood the nuclear threat is debatable, but he combined his official quest for "peaceful coexistence" with public comments about a victorious nuclear conflict.

There were fears that the Soviets posed a genuine threat to the security of the United States. There were questions also about the validity of the Allied approach to European security, which had been based on a nuclear deterrent to a conventional attack by Warsaw Pact forces. Was the West morally able to carry out such a response? Moreover, would it even be effective, given the comments of the Soviet leader, now solidly in power after the defeat of his enemies, concerning the possibility of victory in a nuclear war? Khrushchev had raised the stakes considerably, not being content, as Stalin had been, to bolster Soviet security in neighboring countries. In that sense, Khrushchev was more of a messianic leader, a confirmed Communist who believed that an aggressive stance could be successful. On August 26, 1957, the USSR tested successfully its first inter-continental ballistic missile (ICBM), once again ahead of its American rival. Only in the following year did the United States begin to respond in kind. The focal point of the Cold War, none the less, was not space but Berlin, the island of capitalism within the GDR. The city was Khrushchev's obsession. Almost his entire Cold War policy can be explained by the desire to end the existence of West Berlin.

Two years earlier, the former wartime allies had met in Geneva, at a conference attended both by Eisenhower and by Khrushchev. Up until then, all initiatives for reducing international tension – whether serious or for propaganda – had been made by the Soviet side. In Switzerland, Eisenhower suggested that each side be permitted to fly planes over the other's territory to inspect military forces. Khrushchev regarded the proposal as a provocation. He had no wish to expose the military strength of the Soviet Union to his main adversary. In general, however, the Geneva summit did ease international tension. In this same year, the Soviet Union had withdrawn from Austria and recognized the Federal Republic of Germany. The positive atmosphere of Geneva did not last long – above all, because of the brutality of the invasion of Hungary, and the surprising support for such action by Yugoslavia and by Poland's new leader, Gomulka. Khrushchev appeared to have united the Soviet bloc once again and he was clearly prepared to use force to preserve the Soviet position. By November 1958, he turned again to the German question, announcing his intention to turn the matter over to the GDR, which would then have the authority to stop Western access to West Berlin. Khrushchev then boldly set a six-month ultimatum for the problem to be resolved; during that time all foreign troops should leave Berlin, which would be declared a "free city" by the United Nations. The demand was in clear contravention of the four powers' administration over Berlin agreed at the Yalta summit. The Americans could hardly be expected to accept such a demand. Instead, Eisenhower gave consent for the US to attend a foreign ministers' conference in Geneva just two weeks before the expiration of the ultimatum, in May 1959. There, Khrushchev extended the deadline.

As the talks continued in Geneva, a US cultural exhibition opened in Moscow in July, attended by Vice-President Richard M. Nixon. Nixon's visit was enlivened by some heated exchanges with Khrushchev, with both men using the occasion to make political capital. Though neither gave any quarter, the Kitchen Debate, as it became known, was a prelude to an invitation to Khrushchev to visit the United States in September. His arrival caused a mixed reaction among Americans. To some observers, he represented a hostile nation and had shown himself unprepared to make compromises. For Khrushchev, the visit was of great symbolic significance. No Soviet leader had visited the United States, and he wished to be recognized on an equal footing with the other major nuclear power. The two leaders discussed the Berlin question, with Eisenhower promising that he would seek a fair solution, provided the ultimatum was lifted. A new summit would also be held, made up of the former wartime allies. It was, at best, a temporary reprieve to the tension, but Khrushchev was swayed by the mood of the moment, and agreed to the suggestions. Overall, his trip boosted his prestige at home but did not alter his thinking on the German question or indeed his general perception of the United States as a hostile power, though one to be emulated and surpassed economically and militarily.

The summit of the four powers was to take place in May 1960. It would be followed by a visit by Eisenhower to the Soviet Union. Both events were critical to the Khrushchev leadership, a huge propaganda ploy that would raise the international prestige of the Soviet Union. To Khrushchev, the public perception of two equal powers and two leaders of similar standing was of equal importance to the matter of nuclear weapons, and second only to the German issue. The Americans, however, continued the U2 missions over Soviet territory that had begun in 1956. CIA director Allen Dulles believed they gave the Americans an advantage since they could take photographs of the Soviet landmass without detection. The missions contained a high degree of risk, but as long as they remained undetected they would proceed. U2 flights could take off from a variety of bases to the west, northwest, and south of the Soviet Union, with a total range of around 5,000 miles. Only the President could authorize them. The flights caused problems for both leaders. Eisenhower had detailed information about the state of the Soviet arms build-up, and it revealed that the Americans maintained a significant lead. However, he could not divulge the source of his information, and therefore the US public was not privy to such knowledge. Instead a myth persisted of a "bomber gap," that the US administration had permitted the country to fall behind the USSR. Conversely, Khrushchev was soon told about the missions, but was also reluctant to divulge such news, since it would demonstrate Soviet inferiority. The goal instead was to shoot down one of the planes.

Eisenhower made the rash decision – one of several in the early 1960s – to allow two more U2 missions before the Paris summit, in order to ensure that he was fully acquainted with the Soviet military situation. The aircraft involved in the second of these flights, on May 1, was reported as missing. Soviet sources reported a crash in Russia, but the US authorities did not anticipate that the pilot, Gary Francis Powers, might have survived. Khrushchev's position was difficult. He did not wish to cancel the summit, but on the other hand was under pressure to condemn the spying mission. His anger was probably genuine. The US decision to send two spy planes at such a time could only indicate that the enemy was attempting to glean information that it could exploit in Paris. He decided on a public spectacle, showing both pilot and plane on Soviet television, and demanding an apology from Eisenhower. Several factors came into play. Eisenhower had to consider his Western allies, one of whom – Charles de Gaulle, recently elected as the new president of France – was anxious to develop a nuclear deterrent independently of NATO and adopt policies that would reduce the French commitment to the alliance. Britain, under Harold Macmillan, was more amenable, but still smarting from the disastrous intervention in the Suez crisis when the United States had notably refused to support the British action. Eisenhower decided not to apologize, though he did take responsibility for the missions – a rare acknowledgement by a world leader that his country had been involved in spying.

Khrushchev then decided on more gestures, arriving in Paris early for the summit, and taking the floor immediately as soon as the conference started in order to reprimand Eisenhower. Khrushchev denounced the United States, and demanded that the summit be postponed for six to eight months. He also told the Americans that the invitation for them to visit Moscow no longer stood, and repeated his demand for an apology from the US president. Khrushchev's behavior shocked the conservative politicians who had gathered in Paris. The French in particular were appalled at the crudity of the Soviet leader. Macmillan got an opportunity to voice his displeasure when both he and Khrushchev were at the UN General Assembly in September, the occasion of its 15th anniversary. While the British prime minister spoke, Khrushchev listened, visibly agitated, frequently intervening with caustic remarks. Finally Khrushchev took off his shoe and pounded the table with it in protest. He and Gromyko, the Foreign Minister, then added to the spectacle by banging on the table with their fists. Later, Khrushchev deliberately sought out the new Cuban leader, Fidel Castro, and the two men embarked on a propaganda tour of Harlem. Khrushchev's boorish manners bordered on the ludicrous – not until Boris Yeltsin in the 1990s would a Russian leader make such a public spectacle of himself again. Yet the events reflected the precariousness of Khrushchev's position. He had to express his anger openly, and from then on he would seek the first opportunity to get revenge – some gesture that would serve as a counter-ploy to the US spying missions. An opportunity appeared to have presented itself with the surprising and very narrow defeat of Richard Nixon in the US presidential elections by the 43-year-old

Democrat, John F. Kennedy, who took up his office in January 1961. Khrushchev decided to exploit the situation to resolve the Berlin question in the USSR's favor.

Khrushchev's behavior owed much to his position at home – his reform failures, particularly in agriculture, necessitated some sort of spectacular foreign policy success – and in his relations with China, whose leaders perceived him as unraveling Stalin's legacy and failing to stand up to the United States. The confrontation on Berlin that began with Khrushchev's ultimatum had essentially seen the Soviet side back down. In June 1961 the two leaders met in Vienna. The meeting had been requested by Kennedy and desired by Khrushchev. There could hardly be a greater contrast between the two superpower leaders – the young patrician Kennedy, rich and well educated, reliant on academic training to resolve some of the pressing international questions of the day, and the boisterous, emotional Khrushchev, with his peasant habits and often outrageous public antics. In Vienna, Khrushchev at first suggested that Berlin's long-term future should be left to the people of Germany to decide. Kennedy replied by noting that the American presence in the city had been agreed to by the Allied powers. The Soviet leader then accused the President of seeking a military conflict over the issue, and once more raised the notion of turning Berlin over to the East Germans. Kennedy, who was suffering from acute back problems during the summit, would not be moved by the threats, but the impression was of Khrushchev making threats, and the American responding mildly and – in so far as it was possible – in conciliatory fashion. The Vienna summit represented at least a token victory for the Soviet side.

On the other hand, Khrushchev had hardly acted subtly. His objectives were clear, and Kennedy was determined to be firmer on the question of Berlin. Soon after the summit, Kennedy began an expansion of the US military at the same time as Khrushchev decided to reduce conventional Soviet armed forces. The US president appeared to be determined to defend West Berlin should it prove necessary. For the Soviet side, the major factor was becoming less the division of the city in the middle of Communist territory than the wave of migrants leaving East Berlin for the West. Many crossed the border regularly since their places of employment were in West Berlin. The border was thus open, and many of these workers could choose not to return. Usually, it was the young and skilled East Berliners who decided to remain in the West. The gap in living standards was only too obvious. The Kennedy administration was aware of the sensitivity of the problem for the Soviet Union. One solution, the closure of the border, was always an option, and for the Americans a more preferable one than the enforced annexation of West Berlin, since this would have brought a response from the Western allies. But did the Americans encourage the border closure? As with the question of the Korean peninsula in 1949–1950, US intentions were rather hard to decipher. Certainly some leading statesmen favored such a move as a temporary solution to the German question. The East German leader, Walther Ulbricht, on the other hand, was becoming frantic. Ulbricht demanded that all routes between the two Germanys be closed off to stem the flood of East German refugees. The viability of his quasi-state was coming into question. Its population, at around 17 million, was already small. It was under pressure from Ulbricht that Khrushchev agreed to the border being closed at the end of July.

By August 12, barbed wire was in place, and the Soviet authorities began to build a more permanent barrier – a heavily fortified wall. West Berlin would not be sealed off; rather the East Germans would be sealed in. The most memorable edifice of the Cold War, in many ways its most enduring symbol, was created, like the Warsaw Pact, to hold the fragile Eastern European alliance together. The building of the wall did, however, sever Berlin families, and it was hardly a positive outcome to the German problem. The Kennedy administration did not respond to this move on the part of the Soviets and East Germans. In theory, if the Americans were to act, then they had to do so quickly, before the wall became consolidated. Would such an action have resulted in a new war? It is possible. In retrospect, however, the construction of the Berlin Wall was an act of desperation, the aim of which was to prop up a collapsing state, East Germany. For the Kennedy administration, it provided a temporary respite – as long as the President could convince West Berliners that they would not be cast aside (something he was to achieve with his speech the following year) and the lack of response was not interpreted as a sign of weakness. For Khrushchev, the Berlin Wall did not constitute good publicity, but he had very much forced the issue of Berlin on the West.

The culmination of this policy was the Cuban Missile Crisis, which may be seen as another rash gamble to gain ground on the Berlin question. Having been made aware of the ability of the U2 flights to photograph missile bases, one can only wonder how Khrushchev expected to get away with installing missile bases on Cuba. Yet, by agreement with Castro who feared a second US attempt to invade Cuba following the abortive Bay of Pigs operation in 1961, Khrushchev began the installation of missiles in secret in the summer of 1962. The missiles were SS-4s and SS-5s, with a range of about 1,250 and 2,500 miles respectively. From Cuba these missiles could reach most parts of the United States, and posed a particular threat to the cities of the eastern seaboard. Why did Khrushchev make such a move? Neither recent work by historians nor the memoirs and tapes of Khrushchev himself have provided a satisfactory answer. In theory, the aim was to protect a new Communist state, tiny Cuba, from an invasion by the United States. It also provided a response to the US Jupiter-C missiles in Turkey that could easily reach Soviet territory. The use of Cuba as a bargaining point strengthened Khrushchev's hand in Berlin. Added to this is the general impression that Khrushchev enjoyed the subterfuge and the idea that he could pose a genuine threat to the United States, one that was not possible with missile systems based on Soviet territory. The United States had deployed U2 planes secretly for years. He could now exact some revenge. This is largely supposition, but it seems to tie in with the personality of the ebullient Khrushchev. Ultimately, organizations far less sophisticated than the CIA could have uncovered the secret. Trucks carrying the lengthy cylinders caused havoc on Cuban streets whenever they turned corners, destroying mailboxes and impeding traffic. On October 14, 1962, a U2 flight confirmed the existence of missile launchers.

The world crisis raised questions about the way that the two leaders communicated with each other. The American side would wait for Radio Moscow announcements, while messages from Khrushchev arrived slowly, and appeared to contradict one another. The two powers also relied on proxies, such as the Attorney General, Robert Kennedy, the President's brother, and the Soviet Ambassador to the United States, Anatoly Dobrynin. The US president adopted a patient approach to such a blatant attempt to gain ground in the Cold War. It seems certain that Khrushchev wished to use the crisis to improve his position at home, where his standing had fallen considerably as a result of the crisis in agriculture and a variety of failed reforms. The impasse over Cuba was also based on the Soviet guarantee to Cuba that it would not stand by if the United States invaded the island. On October 22, when Kennedy went on television to announce the existence of Soviet missiles on Cuba, an international crisis began. NATO voiced its full support for the United States, as did the Organization of American States.

After the US decided to impose a naval blockade – the least risky of several options open to the Executive Committee of the National Security Council (EXCOM) – the two superpowers entered a new phase of direct confrontation. Khrushchev said that, if the blockade were enforced, the Soviet Union would use its submarines to break it. On October 24, however, Soviet ships turned back. It seems plausible that their captains had been given orders ahead of time to avoid being boarded by US naval personnel. On October 26, the US Embassy in Moscow received a new letter from Khrushchev that was more conciliatory in tone than earlier ones. It offered to withdraw the weapons provided the United States provided a guarantee that Cuba would not be invaded. A subsequent letter, received on October 27, added to this request the demand that the United States remove its missiles from Turkey. It seemed as though Khrushchev was being inconsistent, and on any given day he might be bolder or more fearful than on the previous one. The United States was not averse to the demands of the second Khrushchev letter, but Kennedy would not be seen publicly to be in agreement with the demand about Turkey. Discussions by now took place on several different levels – through the Soviet Embassy, through the UN, and through news reporters. Even now, the restraint of the Kennedy administration seems admirable. It continued despite the downing of a U2 flight over Cuba while negotiations were in progress.

The Soviet loss of prestige during the Cuban crisis was enormous, but the gains made, curiously, were much greater than they first appeared. For Khrushchev, a leader who relied on public image, they were not enough to save his leadership, mainly because the agreement specified that they could not be announced publicly. In return for the Soviet removal of atomic weapons from the island, the United States agreed to remove its Jupiter missiles from Turkey (they were fairly obsolete), and not to invade Cuba in the future. The Communist foothold in Central America thus remained. In addition, the two sides established a hotline for quick contact to prevent the risk of an accidental nuclear war. Thus the Soviet side had made significant progress in the strategic conflict, even though it had lost the diplomatic war. Above all, the bullying tactics of Khrushchev, first witnessed at the Vienna Summit with Kennedy, appeared to have failed. The Soviet regime would never again offer such a direct challenge to the United States. It was convinced that, without the removal of the missiles, an air strike would be imminent, likely followed by an invasion of Cuba. Of all the parties affected by the crisis, Cuba was probably the one that would have resorted to aggression, had it been in a position to do so. Paradoxically, however, it was now safe, thanks to the incautious action of Khrushchev. Castro would survive long after Kennedy was assassinated and Khrushchev forced into retirement.

The growing arms race

Under Stalin, the USSR had made an ambitious start to the arms race that culminated with the detonation of the hydrogen bomb in 1953, matching the US achievement of the previous year. Thermo-nuclear bombs initiated a new stage in the arms race, but in the 1950s the United States had a commanding lead. Its pronounced policy for some years had been one of proposed massive retaliation to any conventional Soviet attack on Western Europe. This policy threatened a Third World War should the two superpowers ever be involved in a direct confrontation. Stalin had carefully avoided any discussion of such a situation, and though he occasionally took risks – as in Korea – he would never endanger the survival of the Soviet Union in a dispute over territory that lay outside his immediate strategic priorities. Khrushchev, ironically in a weaker position than Stalin vis-à-vis the United States, was much more outspoken. His main desire lay in enhancing Soviet prestige and being regarded as an equal partner with the United States in international standing. Such a goal was feasible only as long as the gap in nuclear weapons and long-range bombers was never revealed publicly (as with the Soviet silence over the U2 flights prior to the shooting down of Gary Powers). Under Kennedy and his Secretary of State, Robert McNamara, the policy of massive retaliation was replaced with flexible response. The United States would not be committed to waging all-out war in the face of Soviet aggression, but could offer a response in stages, building up to full escalation. The flexible response correspondingly made the American counter to a Soviet attack unpredictable. In 1962, the policy called counter-force posited that the US side would attack military installations rather than cities. These policies rendered the possibility of a more active move and even of a first strike by the United States on the Soviet Union.

Domestic policy under Khrushchev was in a constant state of flux, but to the Soviet public there was some indication that the country was moving toward a brighter future. Khrushchev's mistake was that he decided to bring about that future through party decrees and by providing a date for the unfathomable – the attainment of pure Communism by the Soviet Union. Propaganda was a key facet of Soviet life. Its most publicized event in the West was the Soviet exhibition held in the USA in June 1959.

But, within the country, the greatest success in these years lay in the development of weapons, and particularly in space. By 1957 the country had launched an ICBM, an SS-6 missile, several thousand miles into Siberia. This showed that missiles had become more important than weapons delivered by bombers, against which the United States had begun to take elaborate precautions. By implication, the threat to the West now rose significantly. The Soviets had also taken the first steps toward an effective submarine-launched ballistic missile, though until the early 1960s these could be launched only when the submarine was on the surface, and the range was not much more than 600 miles. The first such submarine missile was called the SS-N-4 Sark.

On July 27, 1954, the country witnessed the operation of the world's first atomic power station for civilian purposes. Almost three years later, on October 4, 1957, the 184lb capsule *Sputnik*, hurled into an orbit around the Earth by an SS-6 rocket, broke new ground and thrust the USSR ahead of the Americans in the space race. On this same day the USSR also announced the launching of the world's first atomic icebreaker. In November a much heavier satellite (over 1,100lb) with a dog on board was sent into orbit. For the United States, the launches were a sign that they were falling behind in the race in technology and missiles. For Khrushchev, these were events to publicize. The prestige of the country was further boosted by cosmonaut Yuri Gagarin, the first man to orbit the earth, on April 12, 1961. Gagarin, a 27-year-old pilot from the Smolensk region, was a national hero. There was genuine celebration in the streets at the news of his extraordinary feat, which reflected well on the Soviet regime, and likewise grief when he died in a plane crash at the age of only 34. Of all Soviet achievements, the conquest of space received the most publicity and impelled the United States to invest heavily in its own program. The race to put a man on the Moon had begun. The Soviet space lead proved to be brief, but it provided some soul-searching in the United States, particularly since, until 1961, the US public was still ignorant of the true facts about nuclear weapons.

Another plot

The combination of domestic blunders and adventures in foreign policy were enough to convince Khrushchev's fellow leaders that he could not be allowed to continue as Soviet leader. Given the failure of the previous plot in 1957, however, the plotters had to maneuver much more carefully. Khrushchev had alienated many of the forces that had supported him in the past – the ministers, the army (incensed at the cuts to conventional forces, and the apparent loss of face during the Cuban Missile Crisis), and also the KGB when he had tried to limit its authority. Serov, Khrushchev's ally, had been transferred to the GRU in the early 1960s and his successors as chairmen of the KGB, Aleksandr Shelepin and Vladimir Semichastny, were at the heart of the plan to remove the Soviet leader. Frol Kozlov, another close ally of Khrushchev, suffered a stroke in May 1963, and never regained his health.

Brezhnev, meanwhile, had enjoyed mixed fortunes. In April 1962 he was elected Chairman of the Presidium of the USSR Supreme Soviet, a largely ritualistic position that had been occupied for many years by Kalinin. For two years it appeared that Brezhnev's ambitions would come to nothing. However, in July 1964, he replaced Kozlov as the Second Party Secretary of the CC CPSU while Mikoyan took over the ceremonial presidency. Another major figure was Mikhail Suslov, the so-called "gray cardinal," a former chief editor of *Pravda*, who was to play major roles in the administrations of Stalin, Khrushchev, and Brezhnev. By 1964, Suslov was also clearly a key supporter of the plan to get rid of Khrushchev.

Publicly, Khrushchev's removal was a simple affair. On October 14, 1964, when he was on vacation in the Crimea, the Presidium voted to remove him. Khrushchev's moves came under close scrutiny by the KGB – his telephones were bugged, and the plotters had ensured that the vote could not be reversed in the Central Committee. According to the official account, Khrushchev was in poor health and had retired on a state pension. The Central Committee Plenum that followed his removal cited his failures, particularly his erratic reforms and the establishment of a new personality cult. Khrushchev went into retirement under fairly generous conditions, and officially became a non-person, disappearing almost totally from the Soviet press. When he died in Moscow on September 11, 1971, his death merited only a brief paragraph on the back page of *Pravda*. However, his retirement was spent in writing his memoirs, some of which were also recorded on tape. In these he attempted to justify his various policies and to add to them an order that was hardly evident at the time. Khrushchev's removal ended active party leadership for two decades. Henceforth, the Presidium (soon to be renamed the Politburo) would ensure that no one person became so powerful that he could introduce and pass decrees without the consent of the other members.

With the removal of Khrushchev, three leading figures emerged in political life, none of whom had played a leading role in the KGB-engineered coup. Brezhnev became the First Party Secretary; Aleksey Kosygin became the head of the government; and Nikolay Podgorny became Chairman of the Presidium of the Supreme Soviet by November 1965, with the retirement of Mikoyan. In March and April 1966, when the 23rd Congress of the CC CPSU took place, Brezhnev became General Secretary. Other changes were in place by 1967, solidifying the new leadership. A. A. Grechko became the Minister of Defense with the death of Marshal Malinovsky; and, in May, Yuri Andropov became the Chairman of the KGB, replacing Semichastny, one of the key figures in the plot to remove Khrushchev. Khrushchev's reforms in the party sphere, particularly the attempts to decentralize administration and limit party leaders' terms in office, were quickly reversed by the new administration. Brezhnev essentially was a mediocrity. He had few new ideas or desires to make major changes. Rightly he recognized that the country needed a period of stability; and, though he was as ambitious as he was conceited, it would be some years before Brezhnev began to assert himself as the "first among equals" within the party leadership. (Plate 6.2)

Plate 6.2 Nikita Khrushchev taking a walk.
Image: The Dmitri Baltermants Collection/CORBIS

Questions for discussion

1. How was Khrushchev able to defeat his rivals in the years after Stalin's death?
2. How did Khrushchev's ideological policies affect the Russian Orthodox Church?
3. What was "The Thaw", and what were the limitations on freedom of artistic expression in 1954–1964?
4. Account for the different Soviet responses to movements for change in Poland and Hungary in 1956?
5. What were Khrushchev's major reforms in agriculture, and why are they considered failures?

Recent works

Brzezinski, Matthew. *Red Moon Rising: Sputnik and the Hidden Rivalries That Ignited the Space Age.* New York: Times Books, 2007.

Chumachenko, T. A. *Church and State in Soviet Russia: Russian Orthodoxy from World War II to the Khrushchev Years.* Armonk, NY: M. E. Sharpe, 2002.

Daniloff, Nicholas. *Of Spies and Spokesmen: My Life as a Cold War Correspondent.* Columbia, Mo.: University of Missouri Press, 2008.

Dobbs, Michael. *One Minute to Midnight: Kennedy, Khrushchev, and Castro on the Brink of Nuclear War.* New York: Alfred A. Knopf, 2008.

Dobson, Miriam. *Khrushchev's Cold Summer: Gulag Returnees, Crime, and the Fate of the Reform after Stalin.* Ithaca, NY: Cornell University Press, 2009.

Frankel, Max. *High Noon in the Cold War: Kennedy, Khrushchev, and the Cuban Missile Crisis.* New York: Ballantine Books, 2004.

Fursenko, A. A. *Khrushchev's Cold War: The Inside Story of an American Adversary.* New York: Norton, 2006.

Garthoff, Raymond L. *A Journey through the Cold War: A Memoir of Containment and Coexistence.* Washington, DC: Brookings Institution Press, 2001.

Gottfried, Ted. *The Cold War.* Brookfield, Conn.: Twenty-First Century Books, 2003.

Grogin, R. C. *Natural Enemies: The United States and the Soviet Union in the Cold War, 1917–1991.* Lanham, Md: Lexington Books, 2001.

Hanson, Philip. *The Rise and Fall of the Soviet Economy: An Economic History of the USSR from 1945.* London: Longman, 2003.

Hardesty, Von. *Epic Rivalry: The Inside Story of the Soviet and American Space Race.* Washington, DC: National Geographic, 2007.

Herrmann, Richard K. *Ending the Cold War: Interpretations, Causation, and Study of International Relations.* Basingstoke: Palgrave Macmillan, 2004.

Ilic, Melanie. *Soviet State and Society under Nikita Khrushchev.* London: Routledge, 2009.

Ilic, Melanie. *Women in the Khrushchev Era.* Basingstoke: Palgrave Macmillan, 2004.

Jones, Polly. *The Dilemmas of De-Stalinization: Negotiating Cultural and Social Change in the Khrushchev Era.* Abingdon: Routledge, 2006.

Khrushchev, Nikita. *Memoirs of Nikita Khrushchev*, Vol. 1, *Commissar (1918–1945)*; Vol. 2, *Reformer (1945–1964)*; Vol. 3, *Statesman (1953–1964)*. Edited by Sergei Khrushchev. University Park, Pa: Pennsylvania State University, 2004–2007.

Kozlov, V. A. *Mass Uprising in the USSR: Protest and Rebellion in the Post-Stalin Years.* Armonk, NY: M. E. Sharpe, 2002.

Lan'kov, A. N. *From Stalin to Kim Il Sung: The Formation of North Korea, 1945–1960.* New Brunswick, NJ: Rutgers University Press, 2002.

Leffler, Melvyn. *For the Soul of Mankind: The United States, the Soviet Union, and the Cold War.* New York: Hill & Wang, 2007.

McWilliams, Wayne C. *The World since 1945: A History of International Relations.* Boulder, Colo.: Lynne Rienner, 2005.

Mastny, Vojtech. *War Plans and Alliances in the Cold War: Threat Perceptions in the East and West.* London: Routledge, 2006.

Motyl, Alexander J. *Russia's Engagement with the West: Transformation Integration in the Twenty-First Century.* Armonk, NY: M. E. Sharpe, 2005.

Newman, Kitty. *Macmillan, Khrushchev and the Berlin Crisis, 1958–1960.* Abingdon: Routledge, 2007.

Siddiqi, Asif A. *Sputnik and the Soviet Space Challenge.* Gainesville. Fla: University Press of Florida, 2003.

Szalontai, Balazs. *Kim Il Sung in the Khrushchev Era: Soviet–DPRK Relations and the Roots of North Korean Despotism, 1953–1964.* Washington, DC/Stanford, Calif.: Woodrow Wilson Center Press/Stanford University Press, 2005.

Taubman, William. *Khrushchev: The Man and His Era.* New York: Norton, 2003.

Thornton, Richard C. *Odd Man Out: Truman, Stalin, Mao, and the Origins of the Korean War.* Washington, DC: Brassey's, 2001.

Wettig, Gerhard. *Stalin and the Cold War in Europe: The Emergence and Development of East–West Conflict, 1939–1953.* Landham, Md: Rowman & Littlefield, 2008.

Zubok, V. M. *A Failed Empire: The Soviet Union in the Cold War from Stalin to Gorbachev.* Chapel Hill, NC: University of North Carolina Press, 2007.

Zubok, Vladislav. *Zhivago's Children: The Last Russian Intelligentsia.* Cambridge, Mass.: The Belknap Press of Harvard University Press, 2009.

7

....

The Brezhnev regime and its successors, 1964–1984

Introduction

Though often stereotyped as a period of stagnation and decay, the years of the Brezhnev administration represented perhaps the most successful period of the USSR in terms of the consolidation of military and economic power. The dual leadership of Brezhnev and Kosygin embarked on an ambitious agricultural reform that sought to provide incentives for collective farmers and to reduce significantly the various impediments to production on collective farms. The regime increased the number of livestock that could be raised on private plots, and abolished the antiquated labor-day system, replacing it with a guaranteed monthly wage. Bonuses were to be paid for exceeding work targets, and collective farmers received the same benefits as urban workers – the right to a passport, a pension, and social insurance. The government also raised investment in the agricultural sector, and almost immediately saw a sharp rise in agricultural output. Unfortunately, the improvement was somewhat cosmetic and could not offset the damage inflicted on valuable agricultural land by the kolkhoz experiments of the past. In the mid-1970s there was a further effort to improve the situation by building roads in the villages and developing non-black-earth regions of the country.

In the 1960s and 1970s migration from the villages to the towns continued. The agricultural population declined to 25 percent of the total by the end of the 1960s (at the beginning of the collectivization campaign, in 1928, the figure was 80 percent). The regime's main focus was on a rapid build-up of industry based on impressive development and a focus on beating five-year and annual plans. In September 1965, a Central Committee Plenum announced major reform of Soviet industry, dissolving Khrushchev's economic councils and restoring the branch system of administration. The Soviet Union introduced a five-day working week, but in every other respect began a massive program of expansion in areas such as heavy industry, construction, oil and gas development, and the arms industry. Priority lay with what was called the "military–industrial complex." By 1970 the USSR had overtaken the United States in several fields of output – iron ore, coal, tractors, and oil. The period 1966–1970 was notable for the dramatic rise in national income, labor productivity, and living standards. The urban population enjoyed certain basic commodities, such as televisions and refrigerators, and the privileged even bought automobiles. Oil and gas development in Siberia proved to be the catalyst of the economic boom. Oil exports were an important source of hard currency, though output began to slow down in the late 1970s.

Despite the improvement in living standards, there were some serious defects in Soviet society and economic development. Emphasis was often on the grandiose, and on immediate rather than on long-term gains from investment: for instance, expansive and harmful irrigation projects; the stress on quantity rather than on quality; and boasts about Soviet achievements. Housing remained a constant problem, since the number of people living in urban regions always exceeded the available space. Because of the economic focus on heavy industry and military technology, consumer goods were generally neglected and certain items were always in short supply. When such an item did appear at a store, a long line-up would result. Queues became a familiar feature of Soviet existence. Public transport was overcrowded and chaotic. Healthcare was relatively poor for a developing industrial nation, let alone for a military superpower. The divide between the privileged elite and the mass of the population grew wider. Party officials, senior managers, the military elite, and the KGB enjoyed lifestyles that included private cars with chauffeurs – Brezhnev's Volga with its darkened windows used the exclusive middle lane in Moscow – access to special stores and goods, as well as large and well-equipped dachas.

Furthermore, the surge in output could not be maintained. By the early 1970s, the industrial growth rate, the principal measure of progress for the Brezhnev regime, had begun to decline. The five-year-plan model may have worked for industry beginning more or less from scratch, but in a situation that the government called "Developed Socialism" it proved increasingly inadequate. Bottlenecks and shortages seemed to be unavoidable. Prices were set by the state; wages were relatively high but did not match productivity. Moreover, though citizens had a ready supply of cash, there was little of worth to be purchased. By the late 1970s industrial growth had slowed almost to a halt, introducing what was later depicted as an "era of stagnation," though this phrase was probably inaccurate, and a reflection of the nature of the ruling group rather than of the Soviet economy. In the era of developed socialism, the regime also advocated the concept of the merger of nations, meaning that the different national groups that formed the Soviet Union would eventually form a coherent whole. The Slavic republics were encouraged to promote Russian as the language of business, and newspapers and journals increasingly were published in the Russian language. At the same time, in republics such as Ukraine and Belarus there was a significant groundswell of protest. In 1972, Petro Shelest, the Ukrainian party chief, was removed for his alleged promotion of Ukrainian interests. In 1980, Petr Masherov, Belarus's popular party leader, a man noted for his asceticism and marked lack of corruption in contrast to the Moscow-based leaders, was killed in a car crash under suspicious circumstances.

Leonid Ilich Brezhnev

Presiding over the country was the benign but uninspiring party apparatchik, Leonid Ilich Brezhnev, who was 58 years of age when pushed into power by the coup that overthrew Nikita Khrushchev, ostensibly as a puppet leader. However, Brezhnev was gradually able to consolidate his personal authority and to emerge as one of the strongest Soviet leaders. By 1970 he was in firm control of the country and gradually tried to stamp his influence on Soviet life. Brezhnev was a native of Kamenskoe, later renamed Dniprodzerzhinsk, one of the large industrial cities to be developed on the Dnipro river. He trained at the Kursk Technical Institute for Land Improvement and the Dniprodzerzhinsk Metallurgical Institute. Having joined the Communist Party in 1931, he played a part in the harsh collectivization campaign in the Urals region where he was responsible for rounding up kulak farmers. Before his rise through the party hierarchy, he was employed as an engineer at a metallurgical works. Brezhnev was a party careerist who benefited from the extensive purges of the 1930s and rose much more rapidly than might have been expected given his modest talents. By 1939 he had progressed through the party structures of Dniprodzerzhinsk and Dnipropetrovsk to become the Party Secretary of the latter. His war record was undistinguished, though it was later elaborated to give the impression that he had been a war hero – there are numerous stories of Brezhnev defending his position against hordes of Germans, firing round after round of his machine-gun after all his comrades had been killed.

After the war, Brezhnev was sent to the western border, where he headed the political administration of the Transcarpathian military district, but he returned to Ukraine in 1946 as leader first of Zaporizhzhya oblast and then once again of Dnipropetrovsk. In July 1950 he was appointed the First Party Secretary of Moldavia, and by 1952 he was a Candidate Member of the Presidium and a member of the Central Committee of the party. Under Khrushchev, he was moved to the party leadership of Kazakhstan, and by 1957 was a full member of the Presidium. Arguably Brezhnev was regarded as an ideal leader by the 1964 plotters precisely because he was such an unthreatening figure. Increasingly bulky and overweight, he was noted for his big bushy eyebrows. He was no public speaker, though his later shambling public performances were a result of his failing health. Brezhnev does not seem to have been particularly malevolent. He made a half-hearted attempt to restore the name of Stalin, but backed down when it appeared that there would be significant opposition. Above all, he was vain, and despite his limited talents he wished to elevate himself to the sort of heights that Stalin had enjoyed. Cynics referred to his leadership as a "personality cult without a personality." There was no more familiar sight in the Soviet press or on television than the view of Brezhnev receiving another medal on his already well-decorated chest. As such he became a figure of fun, just as Khrushchev before him for his drunkenness and boorish public behavior.

The titles and medals became almost ridiculous. Brezhnev was named a Hero of the Soviet Union no fewer than four times – 1966, 1976, 1978, and 1981. In 1973 local and regional party organizations discussed a memo on the need to strengthen the authority of "Comrade Brezhev, L. I." Consequently, in 1976, he was given the same title with which Stalin had adorned himself, that of Marshal of the Soviet Union. In 1977 he added to his titles the term President, when he took over the chairmanship of the Presidium of the Supreme Soviet, formerly a ceremonial position. It was said that through this he could conduct negotiations on equal terms with his American counterpart, Jimmy Carter. On February 20, 1978, he was awarded the Order of Victory. Brezhnev even took to writing, and the result of his turgid tomes – compulsory reading for all party members – was the award of the Lenin Prize for Literature, perhaps the most outrageous of all his awards. He also received the International Lenin Prize for advancing the cause of world peace. In 1976 he suffered a stroke, and his health began to deteriorate, but the party leadership tried to keep this from the public, who could only have been bemused to see their leader in action. Plenums and Congresses were occasions to lavish praise on the leader. At the June 1980 Plenum, for example, Eduard Shevardnadze, the Georgian party leader, described Brezhnev as a Leninist who was both bold and wise. The press described him as a "wise Leninist," and the "father of the peoples of the USSR." In 1981, when Brezhnev spoke to the delegates of the 26th Party Congress, his speech was interrupted seventy-eight times for applause. The party leadership seemed remote, cut off from the population, and living in a sort of fantasy world where real problems were hidden by propaganda and the trumpeting of Soviet achievements. (Plate 7.1)

The economy

The introduction of an ambitious reform program associated with Prime Minister Aleksey Kosygin coincided with the demise of Khrushchev's Economic Councils (*Sovnarkhozy*). In September 1965, at a party plenum, the centralized ministries were re-established, signifying that the "branch" principle again replaced the "territorial" one. The bureaucratic structure of the latter had proved even more complicated than that of the ministries, and thus twenty-nine Union and Union Republican ministries emerged. However, the intention now was to provide enterprises with more economic stimulation and thus receive more returns for capital investment. First, the planning system was to be improved by making it more efficient and allowing more decision-making at the factory level. Factory managers were to have more authority over the distribution of profits, and over prices – hitherto fixed arbitrarily by the state – which were to be based primarily on actual costs. In turn, the number of plan indices set by the central authorities in Moscow was to be reduced significantly. Factories could decide in theory their own production output targets, create direct contacts

Plate 7.1 Kuznetsk coal basin, 1990. The Kuznetsk basin in Russia is one of the largest coal-mining areas in the world, covering approximately 27,000 square miles.
Image: Bernard Bisson/Sygma/CORBIS

with suppliers and consumers, set wages according to level of skill and work rate, and then decide what to do with profits. Workers were to receive benefits in the form of social welfare, recreational facilities, and better housing. It was felt, too, that the reform, introduced on the eve of the 8th Five-Year Plan (1966–1970), would introduce some market elements into the Soviet economy.

Gradually the new program was introduced to the majority of enterprises in the Soviet Union. It resulted in some positive consequences, particularly in overall plan results by 1970. However, the first problems occurred in the area of price formation, which was established by the central planners rather than the enterprises, and did not correspond with market conditions or reflect the scarcity of some products. The Soviet economy remained divided according to areas of state priority. In other words, the "military–industrial complex," i.e. factories devoted to armaments and related industries, took priority, received the most investment, and achieved the best results. Profits accrued also in the energy sphere, particularly in the oil and gas industries. But some important heavy industries, such as coal, ferrous metallurgy, and meat processing, failed to improve and were even operating at a loss. Also, perhaps the chief criticism that can be aimed at the Kosygin Reform was that the Soviet central planners themselves were averse to any fundamental changes that would decrease their authority. Ultimately, the ministries and the Communist Party still had over-all responsibility for industry in a centrally planned economy, but now they had less control. The reform thus created confusion and, according to William Tompson, "jeopardised the central balancing of inputs against outputs" (Tompson, 2003).

Soon, the country became even more reliant on the success of the energy complex. The omens were good. With the outbreak of war in the Middle East between Egypt and Israel in 1973, the oil-producing countries of the Organization of Petroleum Exporting Countries (OPEC), as well as Egypt and Syria, introduced an oil embargo, targeting those countries that had supported Israel. The market price of oil rose accord-ingly from $3 to $12 per barrel, and continued to rise for the next decade. These events coincided with a world recession and stock market crisis, but for the Soviet Union they created new opportunities, resulting in the investment of huge sums for oil and gas exploration, particularly in Western Siberia. Over the 1970s, profits from the sale of oil increased dramatically, raising the country's fund of hard currency (*valyuta*). In turn, that currency could be used to purchase advanced technological equipment and consumer goods, as well as grain. But searching for and producing oil in remote regions was also expensive, particularly once the easily available resources had been exploited, and costs rose from about $4 billion annually at the beginning of the 1970s to about $9 billion by the end of the decade. Also, much depended on the fluctuations of the world market, and it was therefore far from ideal that the Soviet Union became so narrowly focused in its quest for economic success.

The energy question also illustrates another phenomenon of the 1970s, namely the change of key industrial spheres from the European part of the country to Siberia and the Far East. To enable such development, the authorities approved in 1974 the building of the Baikal–Amur Railway (BAM), which was described by the government as "the construction project of the century." The program was not new, as earlier sections had been built in the 1930s and 1940s. During this second phase, it was built using volunteers – mainly from the Komsomol – as opposed to the prison labor from the Gulag deployed in the initial phases, but it was not completed, even in theory, until the early 1990s. The railway covered a distance of 2,500 miles about 400 miles north of the Trans-Siberian Railway and through even more forbidding territory covered by permafrost for eight months of the year. Its western point was Taishet, a town in Irkutsk Oblast about 185 miles east of Krasnoyarsk, and it ended at the former naval base of Sovetskaya Gavan (harbor) in Khabarovsk region, at the northern part of the Sea of Japan. It was considered potentially more reliable as a conduit than the Trans-Siberian line, as the latter runs very close to the Chinese bor-der and during the 1970s relations between the USSR and China were increasingly hostile. The project was plagued by cost overruns, poor infrastructure, and lack of facilities for the workforce in such remote regions.

In addition to the energy industries of Western Siberia, Soviet planners opted to reduce past focus on development of the giant coalfield of the Donbas (stretching from Eastern Ukraine into the Rostov Oblast of Russia), a mainstay of the Russian economy since the 19th century, and invest heavily in new opencast coalfields in Siberia at Pavlodarsk-Ekibastuz and Kansk-Achinsk. Coal production, like other key industrial sectors, was centered on huge organizations called territorial-production complexes. These organizations lumped together different industries in order to share materials, labor, and energy, and most of them were located in Siberia and the Far East, particularly in remote northern regions. To be successful, however, they required close cooperation at the ministerial level by the respective leaders in Moscow. Shortly, overall output of coal in Siberia surpassed that of the Donbas, and productivity in the eastern mines was about nine times higher than in the European coalfields, but problems emerged over transportation, as well as over adverse working environments in the new mines. In Siberia and the Far East as a whole, living conditions prompted a "flight of labor" by the early 1980s. The lasting legacy of the Brezhnev years in industry was seen with the collapse of the Soviet Union a decade later, when many of the newly formed towns as well as older industrial centers were largely abandoned.

Despite the emphasis on the development of Siberia, as well as high investment in the arms industry that continued throughout the 1970s, the Brezhnev years are perhaps most notable for increased investment in and attention to agriculture, particularly from the outset of the 9th Five-Year Plan (1971–1975). However, the results were dismal, particularly on collective and state farms. One key factor was losses of the harvest after its collection as a result of transportation problems, poor storage facilities, the remoteness of some of the farms, and, doubtless, petty theft. Perhaps one-fifth of the total harvest was lost annually this way. At the same time, the amount of foodstuffs produced on the small private plots of collective and state farmers – less than 3 percent of the overall sown area – accounted for extraordinary proportions of output: about one-third of meat, vegetables, and milk, and around 60 percent of potatoes. However, these totals were not enough to offset the low production and generally poor quality of such goods produced in the state sector. Soviet citizens were adept at growing vegetables on their dachas, pickling most of the products for the winter months. The government introduced so-called "agro-industrial associations," reminiscent of Khrushchev's ideas for the integration of the village and the town, with the goal of connecting the collective and state farms with relevant industries. However, these proved of short duration and were abandoned by the mid-1980s. Well before then, the government recognized that the agricultural sector was in a crisis, particularly in the output of grain and other foodstuffs. Despite investing far more per head of agricultural worker than the advanced industrial countries of the West, the Soviet Union could not attain self-sufficiency in food production, and imports of grain continued to rise.

The Soviet grain harvest declined quite dramatically between 1978 (a peak of over 237 million metric tons) and 1981 (about 158 million metric tons). By this time the country was importing annually about 46 million metric tons, three times more than in 1978, and an amount that was the equivalent of almost one-third of the total harvest. This dire situation prompted the last major reform of the Brezhnev period known as the Food Program (in the Central Committee, the secretary responsible for agriculture was Mikhail Gorbachev), introduced in May 1982. The program once again raised investment in agriculture, proposed more support for private plots, and demanded that the Ministry of Agriculture take on more responsibility in the planning and control of agriculture. Various commissions were created to direct agricultural activities, including processing and distribution of products. Investment was redirected to certain target sectors, including the long-neglected rural amenities (especially roads and housing). The state agreed to raise purchase prices for agricultural products, while lowering those paid out by farmers for fuel and fertilizer. In short, the Food Program offered familiar solutions to persistent problems. Moreover the 1982 harvest, though somewhat better, was less than anticipated (Goldman, 1992). As with reforms in other sectors, they ran into opposition from the more conservative sections of the party leadership, which was opposed to radical changes. The Soviet village received some incentives such as the writing off of existing debts, but it was a declining entity. By the early 1980s, the rural population embarked on a mass exodus for the towns, a process that would continue throughout the decade and seriously upset the demographic balance of the country. Many villages simply disappeared.

The decline of Soviet agriculture led to several related problems, the most serious of which were a drop in health standards brought about in part by difficulties in the supply of food, and a deteriorating ecological situation caused by some of the more ambitious schemes. The latter included the diversion of major river systems to irrigate arid regions such as Central Asia, as a result of which the Aral Sea declined by about two-thirds in size, and other natural wonders such as Lake Baikal and Lake Ladoga were also damaged. Many Soviet towns were affected by extensive industrial development leaving formerly quiet residential areas in the middle of industrial zones. Though the situation was to get far worse, the late Brezhnev period saw a marked slowdown in the increase of population, particularly in the Slavic republics and the Baltic States, where the average annual rise was between 0.1 and 0.6 percent. Exacerbating these conditions was the failure of the Soviet Union to keep pace with the West (and the United States in particular) in scientific–technical innovations and developments. The Soviet economy was characterized by high costs, poor and outdated equipment that often could not be replaced by more modern designs, a high proportion of manual labor, and low productivity. The failure of the consumer sector to provide adequate supplies to a population with growing purchasing power was particularly apparent. Past methods, such as grandiose projects, were no longer feasible partly because the country had exhausted easily accessible resources and refused to alter the existing planning system. Yet the growing dilemma was masked by official reports of successes and favorable comparisons with the situation in the West. (Plate 7.2)

Plate 7.2 Dachas and gardens near Petropavlovsk, Kamchatka, Russia, ca. 1977–1998.
Image: Wolfgang Kaehler/CORBIS

The Constitution of 1977

In October 1977, the Brezhnev regime issued a new Soviet Constitution, the first since the Stalin Constitution of 1936. It was based on the concept of Developed Socialism, which was a signal that Khrushchev's vision of Communism would not be attained by 1980, as forecasted in the 1961 Party Program. Instead there would be a slower movement to the ideal society through Developed Socialism, a society in which no crises or contradictions existed. The idea first emerged in 1967, when Brezhnev presented a report on "Fifty Years of the Great Achievements of Socialism." Now, sixty years after the October Revolution, the country had developed the material and technical basis for Communism; it had reached a new stage of societal development. Centralized management would be combined, in theory, with the independence of units, and management would be free of bureaucracy and red tape. As for the new Constitution, it was the first to state openly the leading role of the Communist Party in Soviet society (article 6), and one that stood for the interests of the working class. The new Constitution reaffirmed the goals of the Soviet state as the leader of an anticipated world transition from Capitalism to a classless Communist society. It also confirmed the right of citizens to free education and healthcare, pensions, and housing.

As in 1936, the Constitution hardly reflected reality. In the late 1970s, the Soviet structure became both bureaucratic and corrupt. Such a development was made more likely by the stability of the Brezhnev administration. By the end of his tenure as General Secretary, the USSR possessed 160 all-Union ministries, a vast and centralized empire. The Communist Party had reached the peak of its power. No state organizations were free of its control, from the Komsomol to the trade unions, to the Supreme Soviet. The government avoided hostility by raising social services and through a barrage of slogans and propaganda. The latter was also associated with the growing Soviet world role as a military power with tentacles in every continent, and a navy that operated in every ocean. The regime focused in particular on the development of arms, and reached approximate parity with the United States. It was also, increasingly, chauvinistic. In the late 1970s, the regime mounted a new initiative to promote the teaching and use of the Russian language in non-Russian republics. In this way, it was hoped, a "merger" of the Soviet nations would occur. In reality, the campaign was a lost cause in the Caucasus and the Central Asian republics, where the population was increasing much more rapidly than in the Slavic republics. The move, made partly because of the prospect that Russians would soon be a minority of the Soviet population (the Muslim populations had a much higher birthrate), was to ensure the hegemony of Russians over the Soviet empire. The task was not impossible given the centralization of control in Moscow. But it was applied clumsily and in ways calculated to arouse opposition.

Language and political questions in the national republics

It seems that the language question was one that concerned Brezhnev personally, though by the time the new policy reached its fruition the leader himself was incapacitated and relatively ineffectual. When, in the spring of 1978, the authorities in Moscow attempted to eliminate the status of Georgian, Azeri, and Armenian as state languages in the respective republics of the Caucasus, mass protests ensued, particularly in Tblisi, and the government was forced to back down. Nevertheless, the promotion of the Russian language continued. It manifested itself in official publications – books, journals, and newspapers in Russian were promoted and had much higher circulations than native-language publications in the various republics. Russians for some time had migrated into non-Russian republics, so much so that in Latvia, Estonia, and Kazakhstan the native peoples barely maintained a majority of the population. Russians, and to a lesser extent Ukrainians and Belarusians, comprised between 35 and 45 percent of the population. The Russian language began to be implemented at all levels of the educational system, from kindergarten through to university. Moreover, students found that their choice of career would be more limited without a knowledge of and fluency in Russian. In one respect, the policy made some sense. For a vast contiguous territory, a common language for communication was essential. On the other hand, in so far as Soviet policy was based on the teaching of Lenin, nationality policy had to recognize the rights of the individual republics. In theory, these republics had the right to break away from the Union. Though such a right remained only on paper, the issue was a very sensitive one. Officially Russian was promoted as the "intra-national" language, and the language of business.

On the other hand, in the non-Slavic republics, the languages of the indigenous or titular populations continued to flourish. In turn, members of the titular nationality did benefit from state policies. In his provocative study (Brubaker, 1996), Rogers Brubaker maintains that even the Stalin regime was never intended to destroy the nations of the Soviet Union, though he is careful to note that nations represent groups of persons rather than territorial areas. Ronald Suny perceives national formation as a constant process during the Soviet period, initiated by the state through the system of national republics (Suny, 1993). The more traditional view would hold that the Soviet Union was intent on promoting Russian interests to the detriment of those of the national republics. By the mid-Brezhnev period, one can say that two parallel trends were in evidence: on the one hand, key positions were preserved for trusted representatives of the Russian (and, to a lesser extent, Ukrainian and Belarusian) nationalities; and, on the other hand, within the designated territories of the national republics, a certain amount of national enhancement did occur. The compromise between a proclaimed Communist regime in Moscow and national self-assertion in the periphery was at its most pronounced in the states of Central Asia. It manifested itself in a very high level of corruption, which occasionally was "uncovered" by the official media, with the consequent resignation of officials. There was never, however, any systematic attempt to eradicate the high levels of corruption in republics such as Uzbekistan.

Of all the national groups of the USSR, the Russians were by this time the least confined to their national territory. About 25 million ethnic Russians lived outside the RSFSR, for example, and made up significant proportions of the population in republics such as Ukraine, Belarus, Kazakhstan, Latvia, and Estonia, though a reversal of this process began by the early 1980s as conditions in urban centers, especially in Central Asia, began to decline. Russians also migrated extensively into Siberia (as they had done for several centuries). In the Brezhnev era, the large-scale development of oil and gas in Western Siberia encroached on the lands of the native populations (such as the Khanty-Mansi autonomous region), while the development of Eastern Siberian resources (especially gold and diamonds) again saw a large influx of Russian and other Slavs into areas such as Yakutia and the Far East. Russians often occupied the key managerial positions in these new territories. Autonomous regions were in a much weaker position than the national republics. The Soviet system may have paid lip service to the fifteen republics, but it did permit development along national lines while curtailing political freedoms. The concepts touted by the regime – the merger of nations and the emergence of the New Soviet Man – were mere propaganda. Increasingly, the national boundaries established by the Soviet state became exactly that – potential borders of a future state, even when many other elements of state formation were lacking. Brubaker notes that non-titular groups within titular republics may have suffered, particularly with regard to the retention or development of their national languages. As a result, when the USSR eventually collapsed, there were many internal conflicts, often between different ethnic groups, or between smaller ethnic groups and the titular nation. The somewhat arbitrary division of republics also made a transition to a national state more complex in the 1990s. However, Brezhnev and his associates never looked beyond the hypothetical world of an ideal state in which the national question had been resolved.

In the Slavic republics, the danger was somewhat different from that of regions such as Central Asia and the Caucasus but none the less of equal importance. We have noted the removal of Petro Shelest as the party leader of Ukraine in 1972. As in the other critical moments of the Soviet period – the aftermath of the October Revolution and the Great Patriotic War – Ukraine played an important and yet contradictory role in the Soviet equation. As fellow Slavs, Ukrainians took on key leadership roles. The region of Dnipropetrovsk in particular was an important industrial base and one in which Brezhnev himself had been raised. Frequently officials from this region were promoted rapidly, over the heads of their superiors, and sometimes as far as the Politburo itself. One example is Nikolay Tikhonov, who replaced Kosygin as the Chairman of the Council of Ministers of the USSR in 1980, at the age of 75. On the other hand, the important factor in such promotions was not national residence but party power. The majority of inductees from Dnipropetrovsk and other parts of industrial Eastern Ukraine were non-Ukrainians (like Brezhnev). Ukrainians were needed, as Slavs, to prevent other nationality groups from gaining ascendancy. In the 1960s and 1970s, furthermore, members of the indigenous groups had successfully used the Soviet system and emerged as local leaders. It was a natural phenomenon, but its implication was the loss of control by Russians (and, to a lesser degree, by Slavs) over the positions of authority within the empire. In the late Brezhnev period, the regime set about resolving this dilemma with an astounding lack of sensitivity. Nationalities policy and the fear of non-Russian self-assertion would eventually become a self-fulfilling prophecy.

By the late 1960s and early 1970s, the indigenous populations in most of the non-Russian republics could be found in positions of authority. In the Baltic republics, particularly Lithuania, Russians had been virtually excluded from the power struc-ture. In Central Asia, the progress had been slower, but already the native populations comprised more than half of the ruling party elite. Was this phenomenon a sign of the success of the Soviet regime or of its failure? The ageing masters of the Kremlin decided the latter. In Belarus, Russians dominated the party leadership; but, in Minsk, Petr Masherov had distanced himself from the corruption and intrigue of the Kremlin. He had remained a more steadfast Communist and moreover one significantly more popular than Brezhnev himself. Masherov's role was important in keeping alive a Belarusian entity. Belarusians in this period generally had a good standard of living and were free from the political intrigues and high-level official farce in Moscow. At the same time, the Russian language had assumed a position of control over state and urban life. The vast majority of books, journals, and newspapers were published in Russian. Because of the similarity of the Belarusian and Russian languages, and the "invisibility" of the large Russian minority, an acute level of Russian linguistic assimilation took place in the republic, making it much more difficult for subsequent national self-assertion. In Moldavia, the leadership was under firm Russian and Slavic control. One may exaggerate the dilemma that arose before the Politburo by the mid-1970s – the ruling elite itself was Russian (including ten out of twelve members of the Politburo elected in this decade). As the Politburo grew in size, Russian membership was maintained. The authorities also tried to stress the natural friendship and links between the three Slavic nations, their common roots in the Kyivan state of the 10th century, and a common history in which the key aspect was Russian friendship and guidance of the "younger brothers." Often state propaganda would revert to the war years, to a theme of common actions against a foreign occupant, heroism, and love for the Motherland. In turn, the growing Soviet power in the world was also a common topic. The period had hardly been a successful one for the rival power, the United States, which had suffered badly – particularly in terms of internal protests – during the war in Vietnam. The Brezhnev regime therefore sought to present an image of a state that was united and based on the friendship of its peoples. National distinctions thus were blurred as far as possible. Yet they were never eradicated and would re-emerge during the Gorbachev period as a new and pressing dilemma for the Soviet leadership.

Foreign policy under Brezhnev

Introduction

Under Brezhnev, the foreign policy pursued several aims. In Eastern Europe, it faced threats of Communist Party reform and, toward the end of Brezhnev's leadership, the creation of an independent trade union in Poland. In the developing world, the Soviet Union took advantage of decolonization to spread its influence in India and Afghanistan; in several African countries it established a foothold either directly or by proxy. Relations with China were hostile, and resulted in several military clashes on both sides of the border. At this time China became the main enemy of the Soviet Union. Finally, in the Cold War conflict with the United States, the Soviet leadership was able to reach a position of approximate parity, to promote détente and an official peace campaign. The culmination point was the signing of a SALT-2 Treaty with the United States in Vienna, though the latter did not ratify this, preferring first to ensure that the missile situation in Europe was made more even. By the mid-1970s, the signing of the Helsinki agreement brought a practical end to the Second World War, recognizing the current boundaries, the two German states, and the agreement of the Soviet Union to respect human rights. The period 1964–1982 can be regarded as one of Soviet consolidation and military growth. It saw two Soviet invasions of neighbors – one within Europe and one in the Near East. These were to be justified by the so-called Brezhnev Doctrine, but they revealed that the Communist giant was in essence an imperial regime that would use force to expand its power or to ensure that its satellite states did not try to break the links with Moscow.

The invasion of Czechoslovakia

By the end of the 1950s, the Warsaw Pact had carefully integrated the armies of the East European states under Soviet control. The period of consultation with military leaderships of the smaller states was replaced by a Soviet command system. The Warsaw Pact from this point embarked on a series of military exercises. Superiority – in numbers at least – over conventional NATO forces in Europe was a source of concern to the West. Of the European socialist states, only Yugoslavia and Albania remained outside the Soviet orbit. Romania nominally took an independent line partly because its Constitution did not allow it to become involved in Warsaw Pact aggression without domestic consent, and it can be regarded as a fringe state of the Warsaw Pact. The key ally up to 1968 was Czechoslovakia, the most openly pro-Russian country of Eastern Europe. However, it was a nation in name rather than in reality. Under President Antonin Novotny, economic performance was sluggish, and the Slovaks felt that they had been relegated to a secondary position by the country's leadership. This situation changed on January 5, 1968, when Alexander Dubcek, a Slovak, replaced Novotny as party leader. Under Dubcek the Communist Party began to reform the economy, while public activists, especially students and journalists, started to campaign for an end to media censorship imposed by a law of 1966. Novotny resigned in March, and by the end of the month Ludvik Svoboda, a member of the Czechoslovak Legion in the Russian Civil War, was elected as president. Barely a week later the Communist Party released a new "Action Program," which proclaimed the development in Czechoslovakia of "socialism with a human face." It advocated a multi-party system, in which the Communists would face opposition in elections, and it initiated an experiment in the development of "democratic Communism." However, Svoboda and Dubcek did not question Czechoslovakia's commitment to the Warsaw Pact. Unlike the Hungarians, they were not acting disloyally. Rather they were attempting the sort of ideological change that many felt should have come from Moscow, had the mother country been demonstrating adequate ideological guidance.

Some groups wanted to go further than the party leaders. May Day 1968 in Prague turned into a massive rally of support for the new political direction. In June, reformers issued a manifesto called Two Thousand Days, which supported not only democratization but also the re-establishment of the Social Democratic Party, banned since 1948, and the creation of citizens' committees. Dubcek felt that the Manifesto went too far, and turned it down. In the meantime, his government ended the censorship of the press. The activities in Czechoslovakia did not go unnoticed in Moscow. In May the Czechoslovak leaders were in the Soviet Union, being admonished for the changes to Communist Party control. Soviet military leaders visited Czechoslovakia in May, to lay the groundwork for a series of new military exercises. Ostensibly the aim of these exercises was to intimidate the reformers and to reassure the more hardline Communist officials in Prague that the USSR was behind them. At this stage, there did not seem to be any real danger of intervention. Moscow did not expect the sort of crisis that had been faced in 1956. In July, after a meeting in Warsaw, representatives of the five major Communist Parties of the Warsaw Pact (the USSR, Poland, the GDR, Hungary, and Bulgaria) sent a warning to the new Czechoslovak government (by now it was under the leadership of Oldrich Cernik) that Prague was undermining the position of the other socialist countries in the alliance. Dubcek rejected this argument, maintaining that the party was building its position among the public, and would create a genuinely popular force.

In Moscow, Brezhnev and Kosygin were under some pressure. It came, paradoxically, less from Eastern European governments than from Soviet republics. First among them was Ukraine, under party leader Petro Shelest, who maintained that the liberal direction being followed in Czechoslovakia would spill over into Ukraine. Shelest, who was to be removed as too "nationalistic" only four years later, was the most hawkish republican party boss, and favored Soviet intervention. To the north, the Belarusian SSR under Masherov also strongly supported an invasion. Within the Warsaw Pact alliance, the GDR under Ulbricht and Poland under Gomulka also feared the impact of the Czechoslovak movement on their regimes. With these pleas in mind, the Soviet leadership began talks with their Czechoslovak counterparts in late July at Cierna-nad-Tisou. Over three days, the Soviet delegation dismissed Dubcek's arguments that the party could only benefit from the reforms being implemented. Four states – the USSR, Poland, the GDR, and Hungary – had already begun military exercises very close to Czechoslovakia's eastern border in Transcarpathian Ukraine. The culmination was a high-level Warsaw Pact meeting in Bratislava, the Slovakian capital, on August 3 (without the participation of Romania). Several Czechoslovak delegates handed a letter to Brezhnev demanding an intervention to prevent the spread of sedition and threat to Communist control. At this meeting, the USSR first expressed the Brezhnev Doctrine, that it was permissible to intervene in a Warsaw Pact country if a bourgeois, i.e. pluralistic, system ever emerged. The doctrine would be fully developed by Brezhnev in November.

The invasion was thus, at least in part, a response to pleas from anti-reform Communists in Czechoslovakia, contrived and ritualistic though they may have been. Timing became an issue because the Czechoslovak Communist Party's Congress was due to take place on September 9. It was evident that the liberal wing, including Dubcek, would be targeted for expulsion. On the other hand, the chances of a liberal success and further change were self-evident, given the popularity of the reforms. Two hardline leaders, Drahomir Kolder and Alois Indra, were asked to evaluate a report of the situation drawn up by Jan Kaspar of the Information Department of the Central Committee of the Czechoslovak Communist Party. Kolder and Indra were to play more than bit parts in the drama that unfolded. Loyal in the Stalinist tradition, they expressed their worst fears to Stepan Chervonenko, the Soviet ambassador in Prague. Though one version of events has the Presidium of the Czechoslovak party requesting "fraternal aid" from the Warsaw Pact, Kolder and Indra's assessment of the Kaspar Report was probably directly responsible for the actions. The troops had crossed the border before the request for help, with the sort of timing that was a feature of Soviet invasions. Evidently Andrey Grechko, Soviet Defense Minister, was committed to the invasion, regardless of the Western response. On the night of August 20, 500,000 Warsaw Pact troops (including more than 80 percent from the Soviet Union in twenty-three divisions, in addition to two East German, two Polish, and one Hungarian division) invaded Czechoslovakia. Prague recognized the futility of resistance – in truth it had made few preparations – and its troops remained in their barracks. The invading army arrested several leading Communist reformers, including Dubcek and Cernik.

Despite the decision not to resist the invasion, there was widespread support for the Dubcek Communists during this period. The population daubed walls with graffiti and remonstrated with invading troops. Portraits of Svoboda and Dubcek were put up in the streets. Moscow was sensitive to such protests and did not immediately replace Dubcek. By August 21, the Soviet media were stressing the progressive nature of the invasion, that it was necessary for the protection of the working class and socialism. The Czech Communists' request to Brezhnev to resolve the political crisis was given as the reason for Warsaw Pact intervention. The same day there was an encounter between angry citizens and Soviet troops in Prague's Wenceslas Square. Tanks fired on several historic buildings. Dubcek and others were taken to Moscow and harangued by Soviet leaders into denying parts of the reform program and accepting the presence of Warsaw Pact troops. On August 25, the Czechoslovak leaders signed the Moscow Protocol, which in essence accepted the new conditions. The backlash came quickly, even though Dubcek kept his position for several months. Censorship of the media was re-established, and many local activists lost their high-level jobs and were given menial tasks. On October 28, in an effort to placate the Slovaks, the country was designated as a federal republic. Only in April 1969 was Dubcek, the symbol of the reform movement rather than the instigator, replaced by Gustav Husak, a leader who was more faithful and willing to adhere to Soviet instructions. Dubcek became a forestry inspector in his native Slovakia. Opposition leaders made an effort to revamp the Communist Party in its original reform and to hold the banned Congress privately. For some time the sentiments of reform continued. The Warsaw Pact invasion was not a bloody affair like the 1956 invasion of Hungary because resistance was passive rather than active. Rather it was a limited campaign, imposed with overwhelming force, with little chance of encountering disaster. It embodied the new policy of the Brezhnev Doctrine.

The doctrine itself was expressed fully by Brezhnev in a speech to the Polish United Workers' Party at its Congress in Warsaw in November 1968. It has been translated and printed many times as it came to encapsulate Soviet foreign policy in this period. Brezhnev noted that it was the duty of the USSR, together with the other socialist countries, to consolidate the socialist community. The attack was not one against self-determination, but one to prevent threats to socialism within both Czechoslovakia and neighboring socialist states:

> Each Communist Party is responsible not only to its own people, but also to all the socialist countries, to the entire socialist movement. Anyone who forgets this and emphasizes only the independence of the Communist Party takes a one-sided position. He deviates from his international obligations. Marxist dialectics . . . demand that each separate situation be scrutinized seriously, linked to other events and other processes. As Lenin instructed . . . one or another socialist state . . . cannot act independently of the common interests of that community.

The events in Czechoslovakia thus had to be taken in conjunction with those in the socialist world generally. A "counter-revolution" in one socialist state necessarily affected the others. Ultimately, Brezhnev noted, the most important duty of a Communist Party was to support the struggle against the opposing system of Capitalism. He cited Lenin's dictum that one must decide which side to join; those who were not on the side of the Communist social system were, *ipso facto*, enemies of that system. One can read this as saying that such a change could only come if all Communist parties were in agreement. It also signified that a country that had a Communist government could not reject that government, even if popular forces within the country supported such a move. If the process in Czechoslovakia had gone unchecked, then NATO troops would have been able to cross the border from West Germany. Thus the Soviet Union and its allies had been forced to act in the way they did. Five of the twenty-three Soviet divisions remained behind to "guard" the country against the incursions of "imperialism" from the West. (Plate 7.3)

The beginning of détente

Though the intervention in Czechoslovakia was the most extreme action taken by the USSR in foreign policy in the 1960s, there were other important initiatives. The Brezhnev leadership was not dissatisfied with the current situation in Europe, as long as the forces of the West did not grow stronger. Accordingly, it advocated a policy of détente, the essential part of which was the Soviet recognition of the existence and borders of the Federal Republic of Germany, and the latter state's acceptance of the loss of its eastern territories as a result of the Second World War. The legitimacy of such recognition was never properly explained. West Germany, after all, was a state created from Western occupation regimes until German citizens voted for their own government. In 1970, West Germany and the Soviet Union signed the Treaty of Moscow,

Plate 7.3 Leonid Brezhnev and Helmut Schmidt in Bonn, West Germany, in May 1978. Brezhnev paid a state visit to Germany.

Image: pa/dpa/CORBIS

which promoted trade agreements and through which the German side agreed to sign the nuclear non-proliferation treaty. The two states also recognized the postwar borders as inviolable. For the West Germans, the price was worth paying, though Chancellor Willy Brandt always stressed that, while acknowledging the existence of two Germanys, he had not reneged on the concept of reunification. East Germans who came to the West continued to be granted automatic citizenship.

The culmination of this policy was the signing of the Helsinki Accords in 1975, which constituted the final document that resulted from the end of the Second World War. The Accords, in turn, owed as much to the *Ostpolitik* policy of Brandt as they did to Brezhnev's foreign policy. Détente, however, was useful in many ways for the

USSR. It signified an easing of tensions with the West, and of direct confrontation in various parts of the world, which had been a feature of the Khrushchev leadership. The rapprochement allowed the Soviet leaders to develop initiatives in new directions, to attempt to win the global conflict between Communism and Capitalism by a war of attrition. Détente could hardly satisfy the East Germans. Walther Ulbricht, the GDR leader, opposed it strongly; but, in 1971, Erich Honecker replaced him. Ulbricht was probably wise to be so reticent because the policy of détente allowed closer contacts between Western and Eastern Europe. Eastern Europeans recognized the benefits of Capitalism and began to lose their partly Soviet-induced fear of NATO. However, any weakening of the Communist alliance was probably compensated by the introduction of a much broader Soviet foreign policy that sought to spread Soviet influence into the Third World.

Expansion into Africa

The collapse of the European empires in Africa in particular opened new opportunities for the Soviet Union. The development began under Khrushchev, but intensified by the mid-1960s, as Britain, France, and Belgium in particular gave up control of vast territories. One example of how the USSR became involved in Africa is that of the former British colony of Somalia. For the Soviets, friendly links opened up the possibility of acquiring major naval bases in the Gulf of Aden. Further south, a Marxist government in South Yemen, which gained its independence from Britain in 1967, had already given the Soviets the chance to use Aden. Relations between the USSR and Somalia began with a peace treaty of July 1974, but became complicated when Somalia's main enemy, Ethiopia, proclaimed itself a Marxist-Leninist state in 1977. Somalia was anxious to secure the Ogaden region from Ethiopia, which was populated mainly by Somalis. In November 1977, Somalia abruptly ended its links with the USSR and expelled Soviet military advisors. With appeals to the United States to help, the Somalis invaded the Ogaden. The Brezhnev regime was quick to respond to an attack on a "fraternal" country, but began the practice of using the troops of "friendly" countries, while directing affairs through their own advisors. Using the services of more than 18,000 Cuban troops, the Ethiopians recaptured the Ogaden, and the Soviet navy was given access to a new port at Massawa. The events are not important for Soviet history but they indicate the Machiavellian nature of Brezhnev's foreign policy. The ideology of the African state mattered less than the end results for the USSR. By using Cubans, Soviet action appeared less calculated. The fiction was maintained that the struggle was one to support a socialist regime against an imperialist one. In truth, once the United States became more involved on the African continent, its rationale was no more clear-cut.

An extended conflict was to develop in the territories held by Portugal, which were maintained until a change of government in Lisbon in 1974. The two main Portuguese colonies were Angola and Mozambique. In Angola a civil war developed, with the two superpowers backing opposite sides. This was one struggle in which the United States, in the aftermath of defeat in Vietnam, and with Jimmy Carter as the new president-elect, appeared to lose its nerve. The USSR backed the forces of the Popular Movement for the Liberation of Angola (MPLA) against the National Union for the Independence of Angola (UNITA). Once again the Cubans proved to be the decisive factor, as Castro's crack troops turned the tide of the war, allowing the establishment of a Marxist government in Luanda, which then promptly signed a friendship treaty with its mentor, the Soviet Union. Such influence over a country with huge reserves – especially of oil – appeared to give the USSR decisive advantages in the quest for influence in Africa, but Soviet gains were not as clear as they appeared. For one thing, the USSR had to bear most of the costs of maintaining the Cuban troops even after the apparent victory. For another, Soviet control rested on the survival of the then leader, Agostinho Neto (he died in 1979). There were limitations to the amount of economic aid the USSR could give a former African colony of Portugal, and for weapons sales Soviet interest rates were high and terms of payment relatively brief. By contrast US-based corporations had a more advantageous position in the long term, and the US political administration could hardly fail to detect the new Soviet threat on the African continent. Initially, the decolonization received wholesale support from the United States. The iniquities of the former systems were self-evident to Washington. The question soon arose, however, of how to permit decolonization without weakening the newly independent states, economically and politically.

For a brief time in the later 1970s, the West seemed to suffer one setback after another in the giant continent. Using the Cubans as their principal military force, the Soviets were able to help several governments that declared their political orientation to be Marxist. Several African leaders were trained in Moscow institutions. The main power in the north was Libya, which became very anti-Western after 1969, when the monarchy was overthrown and Colonel Muhammar al-Qaddafi came into power. Qaddafi's early years were characterized by the nationalization of foreign companies and the closure of British and US bases. Marxist regimes appeared in the Congo and in Benin. After the collapse of the former Portuguese empire, the last remnants from the colonial period were in the south – Rhodesia, a British colony that had declared unilateral independence to maintain white rule, and Namibia. In South Africa, an apartheid government remained in power, opposed by the Organization for African Unity (OAU), an idealistic body that believed in the common interests of the continent, free from the incursions and influence of the superpowers or former European colonists. In the early years of the Carter administration, the United States had adopted a firm stand on the moral righteousness of decolonization while remaining wary of international involvement that could result in another Vietnam. For a brief period, therefore, the USSR could act with impunity. The main beneficiary was the expanding Soviet navy, which now patrolled all seas of the world, but especially the Indian Ocean and the Red Sea, a menacing threat to Western interests. Only in 1978, when Cuban-trained guerrillas began an insurgency in Zaïre, did the United States react, and then only after the French had decided to support the Zaïre government.

Ultimately the United States may have decided to raise the stakes in Africa for economic reasons. Gradually, too, the limitations of Soviet "aid" became evident to various African governments from Ethiopia to Algeria. The ideological aspect of Soviet influence might be a suitable topic for a doctoral thesis at a Western university, but it would prove to be a short one. By the late 1970s, the Soviet Union had ceased to have a serious ideological mission. The contest in Africa had become purely and simply one for power, both military and economic, over a new continent. The governments formed were corrupt, undemocratic, and brutal, but they were hardly long-term players in a contest for minds. The United States had lost a lot of ground, but it could always raise the stakes, particularly in the area of missile development. Guided by his National Security Advisor, Zbigniew Brzezinski, Carter eventually responded to the Soviet threat, in Africa and in the arms race. The African embroilment was unlikely to result in a major breakthrough for either side once the United States adopted a policy of supporting regimes or movements that opposed the Soviet client states.

The SALT talks

The arms situation was regarded as critical by both sides. During the early period of détente, the two powers had signed an interim agreement on May 26, 1972 to limit strategic offensive arms, known more commonly as the SALT-1 Treaty. As a temporary agreement, SALT-1 came into effect in October 1972 and was to last for a five-year period. Both sides agreed not to build any more fixed ICBM launchers after July 1, and not to convert old launchers into more modern variants for post-1964 ICBMs. Similarly, modern ballistic-missile submarines were not to be constructed after the date of the treaty, i.e. only those already under construction could be completed. Each superpower was restricted to two defensive missile sites to protect its capital city. The treaty was signed after protracted debates over a number of issues, the most important of which were ABM systems, the guidance systems, multiple independent targeted re-entry vehicles (MIRVs), and multiple re-entry warheads. It followed the 1970 Non-Proliferation Treaty, which had been signed by the USSR, the United States and Britain (though not France or China).

SALT-1 marked a breakthrough in the arms race, but it left both sides examining their position and seeking means of gaining an advantage. At the time of the signing, the USSR had the lead in ICBMs, but was adrift as far as bombers and missiles were concerned. By the mid-1970s, the Soviets appeared to be redressing their disadvantage in these areas. They had tested a MIRV before the beginning of the Carter administration, and it was known that a new long-range bomber was under construction. The Americans introduced several new weapons systems, which were transitory but appeared very threatening to the Soviet side. Trident missiles were the linchpin because no area in the Soviet Union was safe from them. The Cruise missile was also introduced in this period – a small self-piloted missile that could evade radar in reaching its target. New supersonic aircraft were also brought into operation (B-1 bombers). In brief, the United States increased the technological competition, partly to ensure that the Soviet side signed the new treaty, the SALT-2. Though the SALT-2 Treaty was indeed signed in Vienna by Carter and Brezhnev on June 18, 1979, the US Senate refused to ratify it. The reason was that the Soviets had begun to install a new missile, the SS-20, which had a range of 3,100 miles. It operated from a MIRV and could reach selected targets in Europe in less than thirty minutes. The new missile appeared to the United States to alter the balance of power in Europe. NATO had installed Pershing I missiles in Western Europe in 1969. It now began to replace these with Cruise missiles and a new generation of Pershings. The ratification of SALT-2 was delayed indefinitely (President Carter shelved the treaty after the Soviet invasion of Afghanistan in December 1979), and the Brezhnev administration looked for a new response to the more belligerent stance of NATO. The period of détente appeared to be over.

Soviet policy in the Middle East

In the Khrushchev period, the Soviet Union had begun to cultivate allies in the Arab world. The Suez Crisis of 1956 was the pivotal event, with Israel attacking Nasser's Egypt, and the British and the French landing forces in one of their last major actions as colonial powers. The tough response of the Soviet Union, added to the disapproval of the United States, forced the two Western European powers into an ignominious withdrawal. Bulganin had acted in bellicose fashion, threatening nuclear attacks on London and Paris, and the complete destruction of Israel if it did not withdraw its troops from occupied lands. The Soviet Union was clearly backing the Arab states against Israel, which received military aid from the United States. Nasser proved a useful ally. In June 1967, however, Israel launched a pre-emptive strike, occupying the Sinai, and defeating Egypt, Syria, and Jordan in turn. The weakness of the Arab states around Israel was apparent. The USSR decided to fill this void by becoming the main arms supplier, to Egypt in particular. The relationship was never an easy one. However, between 1968 and 1970, when a war of attrition took place, the Soviet Union virtually controlled Egypt's air defense, while supplying more than 20,000 military advisors. Though Nasser died in 1970, his successor, Anwar Sadat, seemed willing at first to continue wholesale dependence on Soviet aid. On May 27, 1971, the USSR and Egypt signed a treaty of friendship and cooperation that was scheduled to last for fifteen years. Sadat, however, was dissatisfied with the quality and variety of weapons Egypt had received. After two visits to Moscow to try to solicit more sophisticated weapons proved fruitless, he first removed the pro-Soviet politicians in the Cabinet, and then expelled Soviet advisors on May 26, 1972. Sadat had begun to lose faith in his ally. He believed, among other things, that the SALT-1 Treaty demonstrated that the USSR and the USA had their own plans for the Middle East.

The Soviet–Egyptian relationship, however, did not end there. The USSR simply had no other reliable allies, even though they had developed some ties with Syria and Iraq. Brezhnev had committed too much military hardware to Egypt to abandon the former ally. Sadat, on the other hand, had ambitious plans for the recovery of the Sinai. Since the Israelis had proved so devastating in the air, he proposed to use surface-to-air missiles to negate any new threat. The cautious Brezhnev was anxious that no new war should break out, but Sadat would not be restrained, and launched an attack on Yom Kippur, October 6, 1973. Taken by surprise, the Israelis at first suffered heavy casualties, but proved tactically superior. Eventually, the USSR was more concerned that Egypt should survive the war, and together with the United States (which had supplied Israel with arms when it appeared to be in difficulty) negotiated an armistice. Israel and Egypt ultimately signed a peace treaty at Camp David, mediated by Jimmy Carter in September 1978, at which Israel relinquished the occupied territories. Muslim fanatics assassinated Sadat in 1981. This Soviet venture into Middle Eastern conflict was not very successful, mainly for two reasons. First, Israeli troops were better-organized and more efficient than the Arabs. Second, the quality of their equipment, which was American, proved superior to Egypt's, which was Russian-made.

Soviet Middle Eastern policy consisted otherwise of arms sales to client states and the attempt – largely successful – to displace the British and the French from areas they had formerly controlled. In this way, the Soviet navy could gain important naval bases, particularly in Yemen. Was there a goal to eliminate Israel? The Soviet authorities never took such a plan seriously, despite the occasional anti-Semitism and propaganda denouncing international Zionism. The anti-Israel policy was, rather, a response to US unequivocal backing of the Jewish state. The constant Arab defeats in the wars since 1948 hardly raised Soviet prestige. On the other hand, another close ally, India, had been much more successful in a border war with China (1959 and 1962) and a war against Pakistan (1970–1971). The Middle East remained critical for the supply of oil to the Western world. The Soviet Union had mixed fortunes when dealing with Muslim leaders. The replacement of the pro-Western Shah of Iran by a Muslim leader, Ayatollah Khomeini (1979), was equally disastrous for the Soviet Union, whose policy toward Muslims both within and outside the country was basically intolerant.

Hostilities with China

China had taken exception to Khrushchev's denunciation of Stalin at the 20th Party Congress in 1956. Subsequently relations between the two Communist states deteriorated. Frequently the two leaders indulged in slanging matches. China had several grievances. The Soviet Union, despite promises, had refused to share its nuclear technology with China (the agreement was to give a nuclear weapon to the Chinese as a model for developing its own nuclear program). In 1959 an agreement signed five years earlier for the USSR to provide technical aid to China was terminated by the Chinese. Soviet advisors and technicians were expelled from China. Khrushchev had then overtly supported India in a territorial war over the border regions that erupted in 1959 and again in 1962. By then, Communist client states supported China or the USSR, but never both. Under Brezhnev the situation did not improve. By

1964 the Chinese had detonated an atomic bomb (they developed a hydrogen bomb only three years later), and henceforth China became manifestly less reliant on the former Soviet mentor. However, in 1965, the Chinese entered into the period of internal turmoil known as the Cultural Revolution. In February 1967 the Soviet embassy in Beijing evacuated most of its personnel amid riots by young Chinese Red Guards. The following year, serious border clashes broke out on the Ussuri and Amur rivers. From being a rival Communist power, China had emerged as one of the main enemies of the Soviet Union. The development slowly began to change the balance of power in the Cold War. In vain, Brezhnev began to seek Asian allies to form a partnership to contain China. Aside from Vietnam, a country the Chinese invaded briefly in 1979, the quest was unsuccessful.

In 1972, on the initiative of US President Richard Nixon and his Secretary of State, Henry Kissinger, the United States and China established diplomatic relations. This breakthrough represented a major setback for the Soviet Union, which suddenly faced the prospect so feared by Stalin – being surrounded by hostile states. After the death of Mao in 1976, there was some hope in Moscow that more cordial relations with China might be restored. However, the two states could find no common ideological ground. China continued to maintain that the Soviet Union was an imperialist state – an accusation it backed up with reference to the 1968 invasion of Czechoslovakia and, before long, to the Soviet campaign in Afghanistan. Instead, China developed closer links with the West. In 1971, China received a seat on the UN Security Council. Meanwhile relations with the USSR foundered on several issues: the support of opposing client states in Southeast Asia – particularly Chinese support for Cambodia and Soviet support for Vietnam; the Soviet military presence in Mongolia; and the war in Afghanistan. On the last, the Chinese refused to establish normal relations with the Soviet Union unless it pulled out its entire occupation force. On Brezhnev's death in November 1982, the two countries had begun talking once again, but it was only under Gorbachev's leadership that tensions began to ease. Brezhnev appears to have been a Sinophobe, and unwilling to take conciliatory measures to improve relations. The hostile relationship with China was a hindrance to Soviet policy during the Cold War. Not only did it provide an advantage for the West, but it also lowered the international standing of the Soviet Union as a leader of world Communism. Both sides acted with a lamentable lack of subtlety.

The decision to invade Afghanistan

By 1980, the period of Soviet global ascendancy – which existed more on paper than in reality, given that the United States always maintained technical superiority – had been undermined by a number of factors. Eastern Europe, which had been relatively stable since 1968, once again became a focal point with the creation of an independent trade union, Solidarnosc, in a Gdansk shipyard in 1980. The trade union expanded rapidly as a result of public disillusionment with the Polish leadership and its failure to alleviate economic problems. Within a year it had a membership of 10 million,

25 percent of the Polish population, making it a political force that posed a serious threat to the Communist leadership. The Soviet authorities responded by staging a series of military exercises in Belarus, with the obvious threat of invasion. Under General Wojciech Jaruzelski, the Polish leadership and security forces banned the trade union and declared martial law in 1981. Though unpopular, the Jaruzelski regime had forestalled a Soviet invasion. The move was also welcomed in Moscow. By 1981, the Soviet military was already preoccupied in Afghanistan, and faced a resilient new administration in Washington under President Ronald Reagan. It could not afford another major issue in its European hinterland. Further, the issues the country faced in foreign policy were becoming overwhelming. What sort of response could be offered to the new NATO deployment of Cruise missiles and Pershing IIs in Europe? On which Eastern European ally could it depend, now that Poland had come so close to falling apart?

The invasion of Afghanistan has been seen as a pivotal event in the eventual collapse of the Soviet system. It has been compared with the impact of the Vietnam War on the United States. The decision to invade was a catastrophic error. The lessons of history alone should have made the Soviet leadership aware of the perils of trying to control the mountainous country. Since the 1950s the Soviet Union had been providing economic assistance to Afghanistan, which was outside the US strategic orbit. Of more concern among Western countries were the pro-Soviet inclinations of India, to the extent that the Soviet Union sent advisors to India during its 1959 border war with China. The United States, meanwhile, supported the military government of Pakistan. Partly at Soviet behest, Communist followers in Afghanistan formed the People's Democratic Party of Afghanistan (PDPA) in January 1965. It modeled itself closely on the CPSU, under the leadership of Nur Mohammed Taraki and his associate Babrak Karmal. The presence of a small Communist Party within a large Muslim population was hardly a cause for concern to the Afghan government. Within two years, the PDPA had split into several factions, the most significant of which were the Khalq (the people) and the Parcham (the banner). The Khalq, as the name suggests, had a larger base among rural communities, though it could hardly be considered a large party. In 1973, Mohammed Daoud overthrew the ruling monarchy and ruled the country as president, following an earlier period in office. Thereafter the country descended into a period of political intrigue. For the Soviet Union – which had now become Afghanistan's main economic partner, and had constructed several buildings and roads, in addition to helping to develop new industries – the political situation was important.

In April 1978 a coup removed Daoud and brought the PDPA to power under the Khalq leader, Taraki. In December the USSR and Afghanistan signed a treaty of friendship and cooperation. Taraki's outspoken atheism, his wish to "liberate" Muslim women, and his initiation of land reform may have been solid socialist policies, but they made him immediately unpopular. The Moscow government relied for its information on Aleksandr Puzanov, the Soviet ambassador in Kabul. The Soviets evidently believed that Taraki's prime minister, Hafizullah Amin, was the main troublemaker. When Taraki visited Moscow in September, evidently the advice given to him was to remove Amin and appoint the Parcham leader Babrak Karmal as his prime minister. Amin, however, had other ideas, and in another coup, on September 14, 1979, Taraki was killed and Amin took over. On paper, Amin was more pro-Soviet than his predecessor. Moscow, however, never trusted him. There was a fear among Brezhnev's administration, and within the KGB, that Amin was making overtures to the United States. Perhaps unwisely, Amin also began to reduce the number of Soviet advisors in the country. Ideologically, Amin was also suspect. Though a socialist, he was not convinced that Afghanistan needed to adhere closely to the Soviet experience or model of socialism. It could forge its own route. He was highly unpopular outside the capital, but the PDPA even at its height could command support from no more than a tiny fraction of the Afghan population. Could the Soviet regime have controlled Amin? The point is academic. There is not much evidence that he was willing to seek aid from the United States, or indeed do much more than permit himself some freedom of maneuver in political decision-making. For the USSR, however, there was a better alternative as president, namely the Parcham leader, Babrak Karmal. A decision was made to terminate the leadership of Amin through a Soviet-engineered coup.

Clearly several factors influenced the Soviet decision. High among them was the apparent passivity of the United States. The kidnapping of US diplomats in Iran, which had become a Muslim republic under Ayatollah Khomeini, was a key event. The presidency of Jimmy Carter was heavily preoccupied with this. The USSR appeared to be free to act with impunity in Afghanistan. The Soviet military, like the KGB, was willing to intervene, under the leadership of Marshal Sergey Sokolov. Karmal was already on Soviet soil, in Dushanbe, Tajikistan. He was a compliant and reliable leader who would not pursue an independent policy. The military commitment would, it was felt, not need to be heavy. There was already a vast contingent of military advisors in Afghanistan, and the Soviets had built most of the major roads there. They were familiar with the territory. Thus, in December 1979, using a limited contingent of troops, and with military planes carrying Special Forces to Kabul airport, the Soviet invasion began. Amin was executed and Karmal installed. The action caused shockwaves around the world. Most UN states condemned the invasion, including many countries of the developing world that had often voted with the USSR in the past. The United States withheld grain supplies, and threatened to boycott the summer Olympic Games, which were to be held in Moscow (the boycott was in fact carried out). The USSR was by now experienced in efficient and rapid invasions that caused minimal casualties. How long Soviet troops intended to stay was a debatable point. There is no indication that the Soviet authorities envisaged more than a limited campaign. Quite why the Brezhnev leadership felt that Karmal would be a leader acceptable to the majority of Afghans, however, is another matter. The Khalq faction at least had some support in the countryside. The Marxist, urban-based Parchamis had almost none. From the beginning, the Karmal regime was isolated in the towns surrounded by a hostile and, shortly, rebellious countryside. Moreover, the longer the rebellion persisted, the higher were the chances that the United States would begin to step up aid to the opposition.

Babrak Karmal was a figurehead in the Quisling tradition. His seven years as Afghan leader saw him under virtual house arrest by his Soviet guardians. He was provided with Russian mistresses, in the best traditions of the KGB, and barely able to make a decision without permission from his Moscow bosses. Russians guarded him around the clock. The uprising against his rule began almost at once and continued until Gorbachev agreed to his replacement with a Muslim, Mohammad Najibullah. The new red flag that had been introduced by the PDPA, the atheism of the new leaders, and their total subservience to a foreign power would have alienated a population far more placid than the Afghans. The Mujahideen, factionalized in the past, could unite against a common enemy. Before long they would be supplied with US military technology. The Mujahideen avoided direct confrontation with Soviet artillery, and retreated to the mountains. An exodus of Afghan refugees, mainly into Pakistan, had begun earlier in the 1970s and now it continued. The Soviet forces began to use chemical weapons to deprive the guerrillas of food. Increasingly airborne missions were used, as helicopters sought to ferret out guerrillas. It was a protracted, almost futile affair. The number of Soviet troops soon rose from 30,000 to more than 100,000. Moreover, it was rotational. Central Asian troops were deployed at first, but they sometimes fraternized with the Afghans (particularly ethnic Tajiks). Soon, European troops from the Soviet Union began to be used more frequently – Russians, Ukrainians, and soldiers from the Baltic States. The death rate – about 15,000 over the decade of the war – was relatively low, but the casualty rate was alarmingly high. More Soviet troops fell victim to disease (hepatitis) than to the weapons of the Mujahideen – an indicator not merely of adverse local conditions but of the general inattention to health and hygiene among Soviet soldiers. Others, disillusioned, succumbed to drugs. Others fought bravely, to no avail. Increasingly the war became unpopular in the USSR.

The decision to undertake an invasion and occupation of Afghanistan was made during the last days of the Brezhnev leadership. Nominally Brezhnev himself was responsible, though it is unclear whether he fully understood the implications. It revealed how far the USSR had over-reached itself in foreign policy. The attempt to operate on a global scale was very much a feature of the later Brezhnev years, and certainly supported by the Foreign Minister Gromyko, and by the KGB. Altogether, some 650,000 Soviet soldiers served in Afghanistan. The results for that country were devastating, with some 1.5 million casualties and up to 5 million refugees leaving the country. The years of Soviet aid to Afghanistan were negated by the invasion; the Soviet soldier was detested. The USSR also lost much in international prestige. Many former sympathizers wondered how the Brezhnev Doctrine could apply to Afghanistan, despite Babrak Karmal's desire that the country should become the sixteenth Union republic of the USSR. What possible security threat could Afghanistan, a small mountainous country, pose to the USSR? And would not the Muslims in Central Asia be alienated by Soviet brutality? Since the regime never addressed these questions, the war dragged on into the Gorbachev era with little hope of a positive result. The Soviet army could avoid defeat but could not win. The Afghan War drained the country economically and changed the balance of power in the Cold War. It also ended the myth that the Soviet Union did not have imperial ambitions. It had stepped outside its frontiers, confirmed by the Helsinki Agreement of 1975. It was folly of the highest magnitude committed by a leadership that had lost its way.

In general, Soviet foreign policy was heavy-handed. It over-reached in several areas even though the Brezhnev leadership was considerably more conservative than Khrushchev had been. One senses that, with time, Brezhnev became more confident. He possessed formidable military technology, which was used efficiently when a rapid response was required. In Czechoslovakia, while the forces deployed were simply overwhelming, they had been successful. Similarly the initial takeover of the Afghan government was carried out skilfully by the Special Forces. By the late 1970s, however, the USSR had begun to take calculated risks, based on the belief that the United States, badly weakened by Vietnam, had lost the will to respond. It was a dangerous assumption. Just as Khrushchev had regarded Kennedy as too in-experienced to constitute serious opposition, so Carter, with his strictly moralistic foreign policy, seemed indecisive. The failure to resolve the Iranian crisis only confirmed Soviet views – the country was now in a position to achieve global dominance. But the Brezhnev leadership had lost its bearings. There is no other way to explain the series of irrational decisions made in the late 1970s. One factor may have been Brezhnev's illness and physical deterioration; and yet, as his speech in Tashkent in March 1982 indicated, he was still capable of coherence and clarity of thought. The USSR may have achieved approximate nuclear parity, but it was losing the techno-logical war. By the 1980s, there would be no possibility to catch up in weapons technology. Yet it was precisely the emboldened approach displayed in Afghanistan that provoked the Americans into research programs such as the Strategic Defense Initiative (SDI). Can one pinpoint when Soviet power weakened? Perhaps, for a brief period in the late 1960s, there was a perception that the USSR had taken the lead in the Cold War. Yet it was a fleeting moment and undermined by the obvious limitations of the Brezhnev–Kosygin leadership. After 1979, Soviet foreign policy was clearly leading nowhere. It had no mission and no long-term goals.

Culture under Brezhnev

The first notable event signaling the attitude of the post-Khrushchev administration to the cultural world was the trial of two Leningrad-based writers – A. Sinyavsky and Yu. Daniel, who had published under pseudonyms works in the West critical of the USSR. The best-known Soviet author of the 1970s, Aleksandr Solzhenitsyn, documented the plight of political prisoners in a massive and embittered three-volume study entitled *The Gulag Archipelago* in December 1973, which was banned from publication in his own country, and for which Solzhenitsyn was deported the following year. The work followed up his earlier *One Day in the Life of Ivan Denisovich* by reassessing the origins of the Terror and the Gulag system, concluding that ultimate responsibility lay with the first Soviet leader, V. I. Lenin. Focus on Lenin ensured that the book would not be published inside the Soviet Union and that the author would be punished. Yuri Andropov, leader of the KGB from 1967, discerned connections between Western intelligence services, Russian émigrés, and Russian nationalists. Solzhenitsn belonged to the last category. He had also attracted enormous international attention with his 1962 novel, partly for the quality and style of his writing, which was free from the usual Soviet platitudes and ritualistic acknowledgements of the attainments of Communist leaders. Following his deportation, Solzhenitsyn traveled to several countries before finally taking up residence in Vermont in the United States.

BOX 7.1

··

Andrey Sinyavsky (1925–1997)

A renowned and controversial writer of the Soviet Union, Andrey Sinyavsky was born on October 8, 1925 in Moscow. He often wrote under the pseudonym Abram Tertz. His first novel, *The Circus*, was published in 1955. During the period of Khrushchev's Thaw, he gained prominence for being one of the leading liberal voices in the Soviet Union. Sinyavsky established himself as a writer in the West by publishing satirical novels in France which described the realities of Soviet life. In 1965 his publications were accused of being anti-Soviet, and he was arrested, along with fellow writer Yuli Daniel. They were tried in the infamous Sinyavsky–Daniel show trial where only senior party members and KGB officials were allowed to attend. They received sentences of seven years in the Gulag, which caused an outcry both within the Soviet Union and world-wide. By 1971, Sinyavsky had been released, and in 1973 he moved to Paris where he became Professor of Russian Literature at the Sorbonne. In France he publisheded numerous works, including *A Voice from the Chorus* (1973) and *Walks with Pushkin* (1976), written in prison, and the autobiographical *Good Night* (1984). He died of cancer in Paris on February 25, 1997.

Another focus of the authorities in the late 1960s and the 1970s was the Taganka Theater under Yuri Lyubimov, the plays of which were regularly prohibited by the Ministry of Culture. Lyubimov sometimes managed to avoid censorship by appealing directly to Brezhnev and also by disguising the message of some of the productions. Clearly, the theater was the most popular in Moscow, and some of its actors became cult figures in their own right. With the manufacture of tape recorders in the Soviet Union in the 1960s, bohemian cultural figures created the phenomenon known as *magnitizdat*, the dissemination of underground music and literature through taped copies. In this way, an unofficial culture emerged that superseded by far officially sanctioned music and literature but was known for the most part only to the urban population of the USSR, and particularly to residents of the major cities, Moscow and Leningrad. Three key figures who were completely dissimilar in background and output merit attention, and listed in chronological order they are: Aleksandr Galich, Bulat Okudzhava, and Vladimir Vysotsky. Of the three, only Galich was forced to leave the country, and he spent the last three years of his life in Norway and Germany, having adopted a strongly anti-Soviet position.

BOX 7.2

Aleksandr Galich (1918–1977)

One of the great bards of the Soviet Union, Aleksandr Galich was a prominent Russian poet, playwright, and singer. He was born on October 19, 1918 into a well-educated Jewish family in Ukraine. In 1955 he became a member of the Soviet Writers' Union and began writing plays, and started to perform his songs on the guitar. Though his songs were not overtly political, because they centered on the lives of the Gulag prisoners and the Second World War his music did not gain official approval. However, this did not hinder his popularity among the Soviet public. Galich's work was distributed by illegal recopying of live audio-tape recordings. He became increasingly critical of the Soviet regime when his works were banned or censored and, as a result, he was expelled from the Soviet Writers' Union in 1971 and from the Union of Cinematographers in 1972. He was forced to flee his country in 1974 and moved to Norway. By 1975 he had moved to Munich in Germany where he joined the anti-Communist organization the National Alliance of Russian Solidarists (NTS). His recordings outside the USSR gained enormous popularity for being openly critical of the Soviet regime. In 1977 he gave his last concert in Venice and died twelve days later on December 15. He was posthumously awarded the USSR State Prize in 1987.

BOX 7.3

Bulat Okudzhava (1924–1997)

Known best as a skilled bard, Bulat Okudzhava was born on May 9, 1924 in Moscow's Arbat district to a Georgian father and Armenian mother, both prominent Communist Party members originally from Tbilisi, Georgia. He was an immensely popular musician despite minimal official backing in his early musical career and a lack of official training. Though his lyrics were rarely overtly political, they frequently spoke of the detriments of war and the bitter-sweetness of Soviet city life. During the Great Purge in 1937, his father was executed and his mother was sent to the Gulag. At the age of 17, he volunteered as an infantryman for the Red Army and participated in the war. In 1956, he joined the Communist Party and headed the poetry division of the newspaper *Literaturnaya gazeta*. During this

▶

Box 7.3 continued

time, Okudzhava began to compose and to perform his own songs on stage. Unauthorized recordings were created and copied, and were soon distributed throughout the USSR. By the mid-1960s, he was an esteemed artist genuinely admired by the public for his sincere lyrics and unique vocals. Official releases of his music finally came in the late 1970s and were followed by immediate success. Okudzhava was awarded the State Prize (formerly known as the Stalin Prize) in 1991 and the prestigious Russian Booker Prize in 1994. He died in Paris on June 12, 1997.

The three figures symbolize what became known as Soviet Bards: musicians who would offer simple but effective songs that conveyed honestly both the immediate environment and past events. They defended persecuted cultural figures like Pasternak, evoked memories of the war years, or offered songs about love. In the case of Okudzhava he continued a gypsy tradition, whereas Galich frequently focused his songs on the Gulag camps or the fate of Soviet Jews, or just as easily moved to topics like alcoholics and prostitutes. Of the three, the youngest and most popular was Vysotsky, a chain-smoking drug addict whose effectiveness emanated in part from his powerful, sharp and witty lyrics, his captivating voice and his impressive energy and charisma. He died during the period of the 1980 Olympic Games in Moscow, but that did not deter his followers from paying tribute to a figure who had acquired cult status – ironically, he had attained the sort of adulation that Soviet leader Brezhnev craved but never received. The popularity of Vysotsky also illustrates the growing gap between official propaganda and Soviet realities. Audiences would warm not only to nostalgic songs but also to those with which they could identify and that reflected the idiosyncrasies of Soviet life.

BOX 7.4

Vladimir Vysotsky (1938–1980)

An iconic actor, lyricist and singer, Vladimir Vysotsky was born in Moscow on January 25, 1938 to a Russian mother and Jewish father. In 1955 he attended the Institute of Civil Engineering but left a year later to pursue a career in acting. He became a professional actor in 1960 and starred in plays such as *Hamlet* and *Don Juan*, and would go on to be featured in twenty-six motion pictures. Although he was a leading actor at the Taganka Theater in Moscow, Vysotsky's fame came from his career as a poet, a songwriter, and a singer. Soviet officials permitted only a few of his songs to be released, as they were largely critical of the Soviet government and society. His followers accessed his works via his appearances in clubs, and universities, and especially through home-made tapes that were illegally mass-produced. His popularity peaked during the mid-1970s. A vinyl

Box 7.4 continued

record containing his songs was officially released in the latter part of the decade. During his later life, Vysotsky became increasingly dependent on various narcotics including amphetamines and opiates, and he was a known alcoholic. He died of a heart attack at the age of 42 in Moscow on July 25, 1980, having produced over 600 songs, which had all been officially released by the 1980s.

The dissident movement

During the 1960s and 1970s, an internal movement developed that was critical of the Brezhnev regime and its infringements of the Soviet Constitution. There were several catalysts for such a movement, which wanted reform of the existing structure rather than replacement. The Sinyavsky-and-Daniel trial sparked protests across the Soviet Union and initiated the formation of public opinion, vented through underground works or *samizdat*. There were different types of dissidence, ranging from a national form – Jewish, Ukrainian, and other groups – to literary and scientific. The literature focused on the plight of the persecuted and on political prisoners, particularly the large population of the Gulag camps scattered across the remote areas of the country. Some journals became widely known both inside and outside the country, and Western views also permeated the closed Soviet society through the same process. The Soviet response was to persecute dissidents and often sentence them to long spells in prison or to hard labor. On August 25, 1968, dissidents took their protests to Red Square before the KGB rounded them up. Various events catalyzed dissidence, but the Soviet invasion of Czechoslovakia in 1968, in response to the democratization of the Czechoslovak Communist Party, was among the most important, along with attempts by members of the Soviet Jewish community to seek the right to emigrate to Israel.

Andrey Sakharov, the noted scientist and academician, spoke out that year on behalf of political prisoners. Sakharov had worked on the atomic bomb project and had become disillusioned with the arms race and its likely results. As such he was a public embarrassment to the Brezhnev regime. Sakharov felt that the two predominant systems, capitalism and socialism, were not incompatible but could be merged through the adoption of the best features of each system – there could therefore be convergence of the two systems rather than competition or conflict between them. Soviet society, in his view, needed to be more open and pluralistic. In December 1975, Sakharov was awarded the Nobel Peace Prize, a move that was criticized by the Kremlin. By 1980, the famed physicist had been exiled to Gorky, along with his wife, the noted writer Yelena Bonner. Sakharov had spoken out strongly against the Soviet decision to invade Afghanistan in December 1979. In 1976, Yurii Orlov created a group to ensure that the regime would fulfill an agreement signed with the Western powers in Helsinki in 1975 that would ensure the recognition of human rights within the Soviet Union. A particularly strong Helsinki Group emerged in Ukraine.

The Soviet regime responded harshly and clumsily to the spate of dissidence. Though the number of dissidents was relatively small – several thousand – they served to undermine the Soviet regime in a number of different ways. In particular they highlighted the contrast between official propaganda about the freedom of Soviet citizens and the regime's desire for international peace and the grim reality of domestic life in which citizens were not free to assemble or to express their views, and the KGB was omnipresent. Many dissidents were interned in psychiatric hospitals and injected with drugs; others were arrested and imprisoned, or, as in Solzhenitsyn's case, deported. In addition to those seeking political reform, there were also religious dissenters – Baptists, Ukrainian Catholics, and Lithuanian Catholics. Through meetings and underground literature, they kept alive persecuted churches. Another form of dissidence was underground music. A virtual alternative culture appeared in which the models presented by the Soviet regime were rejected.

The last years of the Brezhnev regime

Brezhnev's last years were dominated by corruption and disillusionment. The leadership grew increasingly out of touch with the population and lacked the economic stability that had bolstered the regime in the 1970s. By 1981 the average age of Politburo members was 70. It would have been even higher but for the presence of Gorbachev, appointed a candidate member of the Politburo in 1979, and rising to full membership in 1980 at the age of 49. Old cronies of Brezhnev, such as his faithful clerk Konstantin Chernenko, were promoted to high office. Little attention was paid to their abilities; what was needed to attain promotion was loyalty and adherence to the general creed of preserving power and the perks of the Soviet nomenklatura. The war in Afghanistan dragged on with no end in sight. Soviet strategy became more harsh; chemical warfare was applied, and some 3 million Afghans (out of a population of 15 million) became refugees, most of them in Pakistan. Agriculture had become a huge burden on the economy despite the ambitious start in 1965 with the Kosygin reforms. Villages were becoming depopulated, and the Soviet Union imported increasing amounts of grain. Ideologically there was none of the fervor of the Khrushchev period (rhetorical as it was), and the policy of Developed Socialism tried to recognize past achievements without delineating a way forward. Technologically, the country was falling behind the West.

The Politburo seemed oblivious to the many problems facing the country, choosing instead to publish long lists of figures illustrating the economic successes of the Soviet system. Within the Politburo, there were at least two (and probably more) factions developing: those who wished to maintain the status quo, such as Moscow party leader

Viktor Grishin and the notorious Leningrad party leader Grigory Romanov; and those who sought change, albeit without substantial reform of the structure of society, such as former KGB chief Yury Andropov and his protégé Gorbachev. Yet neither Andropov nor Gorbachev could be called radical. Rather, both were sickened by the rampant corruption, the nepotism, and the reluctance – if not outright refusal – on the part of the leadership to indulge in any form of self-criticism. There were deaths in the leadership from 1980 onward, and the Moscow public was treated to a long succession of state funerals. Suffering from a heavy cold, Brezhnev attended the November 7 parade, standing above Lenin's Mausoleum in Red Square. Three days later he was dead. Mourning was brief. An agreement had been reached between the rival factions that ensured that Andropov would be the immediate successor, with the hapless Chernenko waiting in the wings. Brezhnev had left behind a military super-power, but with a vast and archaic party bureaucracy, and a government in which all-powerful centralized ministries made decisions for a huge territory.

The interlude: Andropov and Chernenko

It is plausible that Yury Andropov might have become one of the most important leaders of the USSR. Several factors were in his favor. He had headed the KGB, perhaps the one institution not riddled with corruption; he had been ambassador to Hungary during the Soviet invasion, and thus had first-hand experience of how to deal with troublesome satellite states; though a cruel and ruthless, ideological Communist, he recognized the need for reform, greater discipline, and a new work ethic in Soviet industry. He began at once to weed out some of the more superfluous and backward-looking ministers in the Soviet government, and the struggle against corruption became the new slogan. Many appeals to the population from late 1982 and 1983 have a Stalinist ring to them: "To live better we must work harder" was one. Idlers and spongers were rounded up in raids in the towns, and it became more difficult for workers to justify periods of absence from work. At the same time, the KGB propaganda machine went to work on creating a better image for this hardline, almost faceless character. The Western media were fed with information. Andropov was a cosmopolitan figure, a man who was prepared to direct the country toward the West, who loved jazz and could converse in English and other foreign languages; in short, a cultured man with whom the West could deal. There was little or no truth in these assertions. In Andropov, none the less, the Soviet Union had a potentially strong leader. However, his health was very poor, and before long he became incap-able of carrying out the duties of office.

According to Gorbachev's memoirs, the political leadership of the country was divided into two factions in late 1982–1983, with one group opposing the onset of major reforms led by Konstantin Chernenko and including Viktor Grishin, the Moscow party boss, Volodymyr Shcherbytsky, party leader of Ukraine, and the Chairman of the

Council of Ministers, 77-year-old Nikolay Tikhonov. Supporting a reformist platform, on the other hand, were Gorbachev, G. A. Aliyev, party leader in Azerbaijan, Grigory Romanov, the party leader of Leningrad, and Eduard Shevardnadze, who held the equivalent post in Georgia. In some republics, up to one-third of the leading officials were replaced, and at the center the count was about one-fifth. During the brief but frenzied attack on corruption, introduced to restore "socialist discipline" in the workplace, the most prominent victim was the son-in-law of Brezhnev, Yury Churbanov, who was accused of taking more than $1 million in bribes from party leaders in Uzbekistan. These officials had fabricated official figures for cotton production in order to make fantastic profits. Churbanov's wife, Brezhnev's daughter Galina, was subsequently alleged to have links to a Moscow diamond-smuggling ring. The arrests would later be held up as examples of the corruption and stagnation of the Soviet Union under Brezhnev. Essentially, however, they only marked the beginning of what was to have been a rigorous cleansing of society.

There is considerable speculation about what Andropov intended to do had his health remained good. Some historians believe that he planned to resurrect the memory of Stalin, to rename Volgograd Stalingrad, the name it had held for thirty-five years until Khrushchev's de-Stalinization campaign of 1961, and to improve relations with countries that had retained a Stalinist political bent, such as China and Albania. When confrontation did occur with the West, Andropov generally adopted a harsh tone. On September 1, 1983, a Soviet military jet shot down a Boeing-747 passenger plane operated by Korean Airlines, which had wandered off course. Two hundred and sixty-nine passengers and crew were killed. The Soviet authorities at first denied the event, and then claimed that the airliner had been on a spying mission. The impasse put an end to the strategic arms limitation talks that were currently under way, and raised Cold War tensions once again. Andropov, however, was unable to play an active role in political life during his final six months in office. Although the Soviet media tried to maintain an image of a leader still capable of carrying out his duties, the façade fooled few people. On February 9, 1984, Andropov died, to be replaced by Chernenko, Brezhnev's protégé, a man with neither the qualifications nor the intellectual capacity to take on the position of General Secretary of the CC CPSU. Chernenko symbolized the decline of the Soviet regime – an uneducated clerk, a faithful servant of Brezhnev for many years, and now promoted, ludicrously, to the highest office. Chernenko was born in Siberia in February 1911. Now he was suffering from a variety of ailments. His emphysema made his speech at Andropov's funeral incomprehensible. It was obvious that this Soviet leader would not last long.

The year 1984 might be called a watershed in Soviet history. More than two decades after Khrushchev's prediction that a Communist stage would emerge by 1980, the Soviet Union was beset with economic and social problems. Perhaps there were few signs of impending disaster, but decline was evident in several walks of life. Economic growth had slowed to a trickle compared with the boom years of the early 1970s. The oil and gas industries that had helped fuel this growth were contracting, thereby reducing the supply of hard currency in the USSR. Ambitious land reclamation and irrigation schemes continued, but they had harmed the environment, as rivers dried up and disappeared, and huge industrial factories polluted the land. Agriculture remained in decline, and the Soviet village – the kolkhoz structure aside – resembled something from the feudal period. The United States had recovered from the débâcle of Vietnam and embarked (at least in theory) on a new program to build the Strategic Defense Initiative, which involved the creation of a shield to protect US territory from nuclear missiles. Such a policy had profound implications for the Soviet economy and Soviet military policy, yet for the first time since the end of the Second World War the Soviet Union was unable to respond. It had fallen behind in technological development, and the army was bogged down in the quagmire of the Afghan War. In Eastern Europe, the situation was unstable. Martial law in Poland had averted an immediate crisis with the growth of the Solidarnosc trade union, but the heavy-handed tactics of Polish police had alienated many supporters of the ruling Communists.

Above all, the party had lost its way, its raison d'être. In essence the Brezhnev structure remained in place, including the 1977 Constitution that had acknowledged the dominant role that the party played in Soviet society. The party was bloated, privileged, corrupt, and no longer motivated by ideology; it had hardly been affected by the brief reforms of the Andropov period. It went through the motions of celebrating the Soviet calendar – Lenin's birthday, the anniversary of various exploits during the Great Patriotic War, Army Day, and the Great October Revolution. Slogans still adorned major factories and streets exhorting workers on to greater efforts and sacrifice. Success, however, was in the past. And how could a Soviet public compare Lenin, Stalin, or even Brezhnev with the feeble Chernenko, whose portrait was to be found on the front page of *Pravda* and *Izvestiya*? The temporary collusion between patriotism and the CPSU appeared to be losing its meaning and relevance. The ruling Politburo mirrored the rest of the nomenklatura in its corruption. It was virtually cut off from the realities of Soviet life. Old men, making decisions around a polished table, sought mainly to retain their elitist position. The state structure, it appeared, would last indefinitely whatever its problems, and most of the latter were hidden from the general public behind Soviet statistics and reports of economic successes. The people seemed cowed and passive, and would accept hardships as they had done throughout the Soviet period. On the other hand, so much had been promised for so little return. Dissidence had not disappeared.

Despite his mediocrity, the career of Chernenko has been graced with an English-language biography. Zemtsov (1989) describes him as "an enterprising and resolute individual," but notes that he had little opportunity to make an impact on Soviet life. In theory the country was run by a collective leadership, but in reality it had already divided into at least two factions, one of which – led by Gorbachev, Gromyko, Ustinov, and Vorotnikov – appeared to be waiting simply for the interim leader to serve out his term. Because of his poor health, Chernenko had to leave most of the business of running the country to Gorbachev, and the future leader seems to have been at times less than respectful to the older man. Chernenko, Zemtsov maintains, had "good intentions," but was in no position to do anything positive. He appears to have sought popularity, the sort of acclaim (albeit superficial) given to Brezhnev, and wished to gain closer ties with the West, following the return to Cold War ideology under Andropov and his adversary, US president Reagan (who coincidentally was the same age as Chernenko). By early 1985, Chernenko was merely going through the motions, supported by the Leningrad and Moscow party bosses, Romanov and Grishin, who had the most to lose with his demise. He died on March 10, 1985, quietly and expectedly, and with virtually no mourning in Moscow. A period of great turbulence was about to begin.

Questions for discussion

1. What were key facets of the Kosygin reforms?
2. What was the "merger of nations" policy?
3. Was the Soviet Union a superpower by the late 1970s? What were its main strengths and weaknesses?
4. How did Soviet citizens create their own cultural environment in the 1970s?
5. How do you account for Brezhnev's longevity in office?

Recent works

Bacon, Edwin, and Mark Sandle. *Brezhnev Reconsidered.* Basingstoke: Palgrave Macmillan, 2002.

Combs, Dick. *Inside the Soviet Alternate Universe: The Cold War's End and the Soviet Union's Fall Reappraised.* University Park, Pa: Pennsylvania State University Press, 2008.

Gorelik, G. E. *The World of Andrei Sakharov: A Russian Physicist's Path to Freedom.* Oxford: Oxford University Press, 2005.

Kozlov, Vladimir A. *Mass Uprisings in the USSR under Khrushchev and Brezhnev: Urban Unrest under Khrushchev and Brezhnev, 1953–82.* Armonk, NY: M. E. Sharpe, 2002.

MacFadyen, David. *Red Stars: Personality and the Soviet Popular Song, 1955–1991.* Montreal: McGill-Queen's University Press, 2001.

Mlechin, Leonid M. *Brezhnev.* Moscow: Molodaya gvardiya, 2008.

Nuti, Leopoldo. *The Crisis of Détente in Europe: From Helsinki to Gorbachev, 1975–1985.* London: Routledge, 2008.

Ouimet, Matthew J. *The Rise and Fall of the Brezhnev Doctrine in Soviet Foreign Policy.* Chapel Hill, NC: University of North Carolina Press, 2003.

Parker, John. *Persian Dreams: Moscow and Tehran since the Fall of the Shah.* Washington, DC: Potomac Books, 2009.

Tompson, William. *The Soviet Union under Brezhnev.* London: Longman, 2003.

Ward, Christopher J. *Brezhnev's Folly: The Building of BAM and Late Soviet Socialism.* Pittsburgh, Pa: University of Pittsburgh Press, 2009.

Wishnick, Elizabeth. *Mending Fences: The Evolution of Moscow's China Policy, from Brezhnev to Yeltsin.* Seattle, Wash.: University of Washington Press, 2001.

8

....

Gorbachev, Glasnost and Perestroika, 1985–1991

Introduction

The advent of the Gorbachev regime in March 1985 did not immediately herald a period of substantial change. During the brief Chernenko leadership, Gorbachev had taken over the role of Second Secretary with responsibility for agriculture. In fact, he was chairing Politburo meetings and filling in for the regularly absent Chernenko. Gorbachev was a protégé of Andropov, who like many other prominent figures had visited the Stavropol region during the period when Gorbachev was party leader there. Mikhail Sergeevich Gorbachev had trained as a lawyer at Moscow State University, the leading higher-educational institution in Russia. Brezhnev appointed him to the Politburo in 1980 – one of the few signs that the latter was prepared to rejuvenate the ageing leadership. As a native of the Caucasus, Gorbachev would have been expected to have a better understanding than his predecessors of national problems within the Soviet Union. Within a short distance from Stavropol, one could find Chechens, Ingushetians, and Dagestanis, not to mention the national groups in the south, such as Georgians, Armenians, and Azerbaijanis. Though Gorbachev had no special qualifications for becoming the key figure in the party hierarchy, his promotion was certainly a welcome alternative to the pathetic array of leaders that had passed away in rapid succession. He was relatively young, robust, active, and intelligent. His wife Raisa was an expert in and tutor of Marxism–Leninism, and the first Soviet First Lady to appear regularly in public alongside her husband.

Did Gorbachev have a plan for the future, a vision of what the country should be like? In his book, *Perestroika: New Thinking for Our Country and the World*, the new Soviet leader provided a highly critical analysis of the failures of the country since the late 1970s:

> The country began to lose momentum. Economic failures became more frequent. Difficulties began to accumulate and deteriorate [sic!], and unresolved problems to multiply. Elements of what we call stagnation and other phenomena alien to socialism began to appear in the life of society. A kind of "braking mechanism" affecting social and economic development formed. And all this happened at a time when scientific and technological revolution opened up new prospects for economic and social progress.
>
> (Gorbachev, 1987, p. 5)

Economic stagnation, in turn, had led to what Gorbachev termed "a gradual erosion of the ideological and moral values of our people." In short, the country had lost its way. The party was no longer the great guiding force of society, but was more and more detached from the public. Society had lost the solidarity forged during the great moments of Soviet history, such as the Revolution, the five-year plans, and the Great Patriotic War. It had descended into a degenerate lifestyle of drug addiction and alcoholism. The ageing Soviet leadership had proved immune to change and had become engrossed in the handing out of titles and awards, which themselves concealed the real failings in administration of Soviet society.

Such an analysis, while surprising from any Soviet leader since Khrushchev, reflected realities, but was not necessarily pessimistic. Gorbachev had not lost faith in the Soviet system, but felt that former qualities and spirit needed to be revived and reinstated. Essentially, he sought a return to the correct path of Leninism, eliminating the corruption and the resistance to change. In the economy, it would be necessary to improve discipline in the workplace, to boost the technological base of industry, and to rework the system of planning and management. At the same time, in late August 1985, Gorbachev was one of the initiators of the celebration of the fiftieth anniversary of the feats of Stakhanov, an event that perhaps symbolized many of the irrational Soviet approaches to economic production. In 1985, the observer perceives several examples of this phenomenon – a critique of the current situation without really thinking beyond the confines of former methods and approaches. Even Brezhnev and Kosygin had begun with a reform program, and by distancing themselves from some of the more irrational experiments of Khrushchev. Gorbachev likewise had begun in the same fashion. Why would his leadership prove to be any different? The party hierarchy could be excused for imagining that, once they had waited out the initial flurry of reforms, life might continue as before, their privileges intact.

And yet the public image was already very different from that of the recent past. Gorbachev seemed to delight in meeting the public, albeit sometimes with his own large entourage in front, in order to avoid difficult questions. He spoke Russian awkwardly, often making grammatical mistakes, but in most respects he was a much better educated and more sophisticated leader than his predecessors (with the possible exception of Andropov). Western analysts contrasted him with the elderly US president Ronald Reagan, and pondered whether the US leader would be able to match Gorbachev in debate. The first example of the contrast with earlier leaderships lay in his personal behavior. Gorbachev adopted a moral approach, choosing first to focus on alcoholism – perhaps the most obvious social predicament, but hardly one that was new or likely to change. In May 1985 the CPSU Central Committee issued a resolution against drunkenness and alcoholism, raising the penalties for crimes related to alcohol, and reducing the number of outlets selling it. At diplomatic functions, much to the horror of many delegates, alcohol was prohibited. Russians began to call the new General Secretary "Comrade Orange Juice." Sugar disappeared from the stores as the distilling of illegal *samogon* increased. Though not a major attempt at reform, little was calculated to irritate Russians more than an attempt to curb consumption of vodka in particular. Moreover, vodka was a prime source of national income. The experiment, flawed as it was, did indicate that Gorbachev was serious in his efforts to raise the morality of Soviet society.

At first he was still surrounded by members of the Chernenko Politburo, many of whom had been in office since the Brezhnev period (and often lingering there for decades). Not all the Politburo members regarded Gorbachev favorably. Changes were essential and expected. Several of the early appointees to the Politburo consisted of men whose careers had blossomed under Andropov. They were solid but reform-minded Communists – Nikolay Ryzhkov, Viktor Nikonov, and Yegor Ligachev. Ligachev had been a party member for forty years and a full member of the Central Committee since 1976. At first, his main role in the Politburo was responsibility for party ideology. By 1987 his influence within the ruling body began to decline, as Gorbachev relied more on the maverick figure of Aleksandr Yakovlev, a former ambassador to Canada, and the architect of the Glasnost (frankness) that was to be a hallmark of the period. Andrey Gromyko, the long-serving Soviet Foreign Minister and the man who had nominated Gorbachev for the leadership of the Party, was given the ceremonial position of Chairman of the Presidium of the Supreme Soviet (or nominal president) of the USSR. Potential opponents of Gorbachev and some of the more corrupt elements of the leadership were removed gradually. They included Grigory Romanov, the leader of the Leningrad party organization, who lost his position in July, and Viktor Grishin, the Moscow party boss, who retired in December 1985. Grishin's replacement was the Urals protégé Boris Yeltsin, who was elevated to a Candidate Member of the Politburo by February 1986. By the time of the 27th Party Congress (February 25–March 6, 1986), most of the former Politburo team of the Brezhnev years had been removed, along with 45 percent of government ministers and 40 percent of the Central Committee.

The Congress was the first opportunity for Gorbachev to outline his intentions. The Soviet leader emphasized the need for Glasnost and self-criticism in Soviet life, so that defects and shortcomings could be exposed rather than concealed. He also stressed the need for radical reform, though the extent of that reform was to be limited. Alongside increased discipline, more emphasis on engineering and improvement in productivity, Gorbachev recommended a partial decentralization of the economy in light industry and agriculture, and supported the notion that cooperatives should be permitted to develop along with some selected private enterprise. The cooperative movement had been boosted before the Congress by a Politburo decree, which anticipated its enhanced role in the production of consumer goods, in the development of restaurants, and in other services. In January it had been revealed that GNP growth had slowed to around 2 percent. The heavy emphasis on the military budget had been made evident. Military spending took up about 25 percent of the Soviet outlay. For Gorbachev, it was essential to approach problems honestly. However, many of his colleagues on the Central Committee did not anticipate serious changes. As Gorbachev noted a year later, many of those present considered that Perestroika was essentially a campaign rather than a long-term platform, and regional party leaders proved reluctant to advance the careers of those supporting Perestroika and change in society. That is perhaps why Gorbachev constantly reiterated the essential point: Soviet citizens and party members in particular had to change their way of thinking. It was a formidable task.

How far had Glasnost progressed by the 27th Party Congress? There had been some signs that problems in Soviet society were to receive greater publicity; moreover those who had criticized the USSR in the past received a more sympathetic hearing from the new Soviet leadership. In mid-January 1986, for example, the daily government newspaper *Izvestiya* carried a report of a serious accident on the Trans-Siberian Railway, which blocked the line for almost three days. There was no indication, however, of the number of casualties. Just a month later, the Soviet press reported the loss of a cruiser, and even printed an interview with its captain. However, these events were relatively minor mishaps. Gorbachev invited the well-known Soviet dissident scientist Andrei Sakharov to return to Moscow from his exile in the closed city of Gorky (Nizhny Novgorod), with his wife, Yelena Bonner, and allowed the latter to visit family in the United States. Gorbachev did not respond, on the other hand, to a letter from Sakharov pleading for the release of all political prisoners. Another notable event during Gorbachev's first year as party leader was a televised "Citizens' Summit" between Leningrad and the US city of Seattle, during which Americans could ask basic questions of representatives of Soviet society, from military veterans to workers and students. On the whole, the responses to questions were rather strained and often defensive, particularly on the continuing Soviet war in Afghanistan. There was a partial opening of Soviet society by the spring of 1986, but there was little indication of the upheaval that was to follow. One of the chief catalysts of change was an accident at a nuclear plant in northern Ukraine. (Plate 8.1)

The Chernobyl disaster

The Soviet civilian nuclear program had begun to develop in the 1970s, and accelerated toward the end of the decade when it became plain that the Soviet energy industry could not rely indefinitely on supplies of oil and gas. There were several facets of the nuclear industry that related to the political structure of the USSR and its Eastern European partners. Many, though far from all, nuclear plants were located in the European USSR, particularly close to the western border. Most of the Soviet population lived in this area, and a joint grid was set up with Eastern European countries that lacked energy resources, such as Bulgaria, Czechoslovakia, Hungary, and East Germany. Countries were invited to invest in building new Soviet reactors and would then receive appropriate compensation in the supply of nuclear-generated electricity. The USSR regarded the nuclear program as a source of prestige. Its RBMK, or graphite-moderated reactor, evolved from the nuclear weapons program and was not exported. This type of reactor was considered efficient because it could

Plate 8.1 Mikhail Gorbachev, October 1985.
Image: Reuters/CORBIS

be refueled on-line, keeping shutdown times to a minimum, but it contained a fundamental construction flaw: it became unstable if operated at low power. The second type of reactor, the VVER (water–water–energetic reactor) was produced both in the USSR and in Czechoslovakia, and exported widely to Eastern Europe, Finland, Vietnam, and Cuba, among other countries. By the spring of 1986, this reactor was being more widely developed, but the RBMKs still operated and were under construction at stations near Leningrad, Smolensk, and Kursk in Russia; Ignalina in Lithuania; and Chernobyl in Ukraine.

The Chernobyl plant had been the subject of numerous complaints from local residents at the time of its construction in the late 1970s. By the spring of 1986 it had four reactors in operation, built in twin units. Another complex close by the main unit contained the partially built fifth and sixth reactors. The station was built 7.5 miles north of the old medieval town of Chernobyl (Chornobyl in Ukrainian), and two miles south of Pripyat, a town for the plant workers and their families, which had a population of 45,000 by the time of the accident. On April 25, at the start of a long holiday weekend, two electrical engineers were asked to repeat an experiment to ascertain how long safety equipment would remain in operation during a shutdown. Neither the plant director nor the chief engineer was on site at the time. Since the plant had shut down in the past when the experiment was attempted, all of its safety devices were dismantled. One of the operators made an error, and a power surge occurred at 1.32 a.m. that blasted the roof of the fourth reactor building, causing a graphite fire that threatened to spread to unit three. The Pripyat fire brigade came to the scene before more fire engines were sent from Kyiv. Working in appalling conditions, about forty firemen and first-aid workers lost their lives in the early hours of April 26. However, though some residents of Pripyat and nearby farms had seen the glow in the sky (and in some cases even felt a shudder during the power surge), no general alarm had been sounded. That Saturday in Pripyat was like any other – two weddings were held, residents went fishing, and children played in the parks or attended Saturday schools.

Only some forty hours after the event was a general warning issued and an evacuation undertaken of a zone with a radius of 6.2 miles around the reactor. Residents of Pripyat were told to gather belongings for a brief evacuation, and buses were sent from Kyiv to take them to new destinations. Many local party officials, fearing the consequences of the disaster, simply fled from the scene. There was a notably muted reaction from the Ukrainian party authorities, led by the 68-year-old Brezhnev appointee Volodymyr Shcherbytsky. The official response from Moscow was also decidedly bland. It acknowledged an accident that had caused two deaths and announced the appointment of a government commission to investigate it. That announcement appeared to have been prompted by inquiries from Sweden, where nuclear plant workers at the Forsberg station had discovered high levels of radiation on their shoes before starting work. The newspaper *Izvestiya* was denied permission to publish a detailed account (in so far as information was known) on the following day. In short, the Soviet leadership was responding in a manner that had become familiar: to limit the amount of information reaching the public in an effort to eliminate the effects of the accident before news could reach a wider audience. In this instance, however, the accident was to prove global in its dimensions, and a Soviet-style cover-up continued.

The next stage of the aftermath was a frantic campaign to contain the release of radiation into the atmosphere and below ground into the water table. Coal miners were brought in for the latter operation, tunneling under the reactor and constructing a concrete shelf. By May 2, two Politburo members, Ligachev and Ryzhkov, arrived on the scene. The zone of evacuation was duly extended to 18.6 miles (30 kilometers). Helicopters dropped lead, boron, and sand into the gaping hole of the reactor in an attempt to limit radiation releases (in reality this only pushed the reactor downward). With the use of robots, a cover was constructed hastily over the reactor, while coal miners constructed a concrete shelf to prevent the destroyed reactor from reacting with the ground water. After ten days, the releases of radiation had basically ceased. Some of the efforts were truly heroic, such as the removal of graphite from the reactor roof. At first, the government commission used the services of volunteers, most of whom worked on a thirty-day rota. Later, military reservists were called up, often working well beyond their assigned hours, and often unaware of the amount of radiation their bodies had absorbed. Soviet Geiger counters, in so far as they were available at all, only registered totals up to 25 rems. Mistakes were inevitable. Offers of Western help were generally refused. The Soviet media began to focus not on the effects of the accident, but on the emotional and sometimes exaggerated Western reaction to it. *Izvestiya* published a dubious account of accidents that had occurred over a number of years at nuclear power stations in the West, while noting that Chernobyl was the first and only such accident to have occurred in the Soviet Union, and itself an outright distortion. Gorbachev had remained silent during this first and crucial test of his leadership. Arguably he was waiting until he could acquire accurate and detailed information, but the lack of leadership was noticeable.

On May 14, Gorbachev appeared on Soviet television. The broadcast dealt briefly with the accident before the party leader launched into an attack on the "heaps of lies" that had appeared about Chernobyl in the Western media. He also equated the impact of the nuclear accident with fallout from a nuclear attack, thus justifying his policy of removing all nuclear weapons from the face of the Earth by the year 2000. The accident was also proof of the danger to Europe as a whole, which related to another of Gorbachev's early themes – that of a "common European home." This sort of response to an international incident was consistent with Soviet policy. It suggested that little of substance had changed within the leadership. Chernobyl had been exploited for official propaganda. However, it proved impossible for the Soviet regime to sustain such a position. For one thing, the Soviet Union was a founder member of the International Atomic Energy Agency, and the IAEA was now anxious to hold an inquiry into the causes of the worst civilian nuclear disaster in history. Second, the attempts to contain the effects of Chernobyl had taken on the appearance of a mass patriotic campaign. Many observers, at the behest of the authorities, openly compared the campaign with resistance to the Germans in the Great Patriotic War. The analogy was simplistic but appealing. In the spring and early summer of 1986 it was impossible to estimate the number of casualties that might result from Chernobyl. Estimates of future cancers worldwide varied from a few hundred to 500,000. The radiation cloud that had moved north and northwest after the explosion had subsequently moved south with the change in wind direction, and caused some panic in the city of Kyiv, eighty-five miles south of the plant, with a population of 2.5 million.

In August a Soviet scientific delegation led by Valery Legasov traveled to Vienna to present an account of events to the IAEA. The report was praised for its relative frankness, though it put most of the emphasis on human error rather than on the technical flaws of the RBMK reactor, of which Legasov was well aware. Nevertheless the appearance of a Soviet delegation indicated that the country was now willing to share details with Western scientists. Eventually certain "technical" improvements were made to the RBMK reactor: the plant director and chief engineer were obliged to be present during the conducting of experiments; the reactor's shutdown time was reduced from around twenty seconds to four; and the amount of enriched uranium in the reactor core was increased. In the summer of 1987, officials considered most responsible for the disaster went on trial in the town of Chernobyl. Other than the first and last days, the trial was held in camera, and the plant director Viktor Bryukhanov was given ten years' hard labor. His chief engineer got five years, and lighter sentences were imposed on other officials. The Soviet actions suggested that suitable scapegoats had been found, but the trial elicited remarkably little reaction. It was unconvincing.

There were other aspects of Chernobyl that diminished the standing of the Soviet government in the eyes of the population in the affected regions. Information on health was soon classified, and on a number of occasions illnesses associated with increased radiation were attributed to other causes – one of the favorites was "vegeto-vascular dystonia." Meanwhile local officials, including the Ukrainian Minister of Health, tried to convince the population that the environment had been made completely safe. It was claimed that the covering over the fourth reactor – the so-called sarcophagus – would last "for eternity" despite the fact that it could never be more than temporary. By the fall of 1986, reactors one and two were back in service (the third was to follow in December 1987). A new phenomenon emerged, which Soviet officials termed "radio-phobia," the fear of radiation. Panic-stricken villagers and even residents of Kyiv and the Belarusian city of Gomel began to attribute every ailment, from serious afflictions to the common cold, to the effects of radiation. Already there was skepticism toward official pronouncements. In Kyiv, rumors abounded that red wine and vodka was an appropriate cure for radiation. Meanwhile, journalists trying to uncover information received condescending responses from the Soviet scientific community. Before long a discernible rift developed between the centralized ministries and scientific institutions and regional groups in the republics of Ukraine and Belarus, which maintained that the real truth about Chernobyl had yet to be revealed. This gap between the center and the republics began to widen.

In retrospect, it is easy to see why the government's attempt to compare the struggle against radiation to the epic battle against the German occupants of 1941–1944 resulted in failure. The Germans had represented an identifiable and barbarous enemy, forcing Soviet citizens to make sacrifices in order to survive. Radiation was an invisible enemy. Mass deaths had not resulted, but the accident had led the public to fear for their future. In Soviet mythology, the future was always critical – belief in the success of the Soviet system for the coming generation had been an important motivator in difficult times. In addition, the concept of an external enemy had been maintained throughout Soviet history, whether this happened to be the British (the earlier period), the Germans (during the war), Anglo-American imperialists (the immediate aftermath of the war), or the Americans alone (the latter part of the Cold War years). After Chernobyl, the myth that the Soviet regime was in control of events could no longer be maintained. Its helplessness was apparent. It resorted to lies and secrecy, to accusations against the West for seemingly exploiting a tragedy, but it could not offer the population in the affected areas much hope that the dangers would be overcome. Doomsayers were much in evidence in the post-accident months and years. They received much more attention than they deserved. The central powers were held responsible for Chernobyl, which was added to some of the tragic events of the 20th century, both in Ukraine, which had endured much suffering, and in the Soviet Union as a whole.

The Gorbachev leadership had begun to change, too. Under the influence of Yakovlev, a genuine public opinion began to develop. Though encouraged to question and criticize policies of the Stalin leadership in particular (the official stance taken by the Gorbachev administration), the Soviet media soon turned their attention to the prevailing issues of the day. The environment had become a prime concern. For decades, Soviet industrial and agricultural planners had paid little heed to the ecological impact of their decisions. After Chernobyl, the public began to focus on risky and ill-thought-out projects, particularly in the realm of land improvement, heavy industry, chemical plants and the like. Nuclear power was the initial focus. Within the Soviet Union, massive demonstrations began to take place against virtually every nuclear power station, and particularly those still at the construction stage. One such station was being built in a seismic zone near Kerch on the Crimean peninsula. Russians demanded that construction work stop at the Rostov nuclear power station, located only 7.5 miles from the city of Volgodonsk. Lithuanians campaigned for the closure of the Ignalina station, a giant RBMK plant with 1,500-megawatt reactors. Chernobyl seemed to have woken up the public to environmental concerns. There was also a strong political element to these protests: namely, decisions about the location and operation of nuclear power stations in the republics and Russian regions were in the hands of Moscow-based bureaucrats who might never have visited the areas in question. Predictably these protests were often one-sided – ignoring, for example, the high casualty rates in the country's other energy industries. Yet they began a process of alienating the political center from the non-Russian periphery in particular. Non-Russian republics had begun to demand a greater say in the establishment and operation of industries and over the exploitation of natural resources. In this way, the Chernobyl accident began to change the political climate of the USSR.

The Chernobyl disaster focused attention on the Gorbachev regime, and became the subject of lengthy debates among scholars and scientists world-wide. In the spring of 1989, the Soviet press was permitted to publish new maps illustrating the extent of radiation fallout. The area proved to be far more extensive than the official 18.6-mile (30-kilometer) zone, encompassing about one-fifth of Belarus, one-eighth of Ukraine, and a large area of Russia, including Bryansk and Smolensk oblasts. Because of the official decision to base the contaminated zones on cesium content of the soil, those living in affected areas numbered around 3.5 million. Once again, the public considered itself to have been deceived. Those who discovered that they had been living in a contaminated zone for three years had the option of being evacuated (provided that radiation levels were sufficiently high). The health effects at that time were limited mainly to the firemen, first-aid workers, and clean-up crews (called "liquidators" in Soviet parlance). Only later did thyroid gland cancer start to develop, especially in children. A United Nations study of 2002 suggested that the evacuations after Chernobyl caused more problems than they cured. It seems likely that the post-1989 evacuations may have been the most problematic of all. Suddenly Chernobyl re-emerged as an issue. Reports from the city of Kyiv suggested that radiation hotspots had been discovered there. In another region of Ukraine west of Chernobyl, official records uncovered by diligent journalists suggested that radiation levels immediately after the accident had been three times higher than those in the 18.6-mile zone.

In general, Chernobyl was a public relations disaster for the Soviet regime. Moscow acted indecisively – often, it seems, taking the wrong decisions. On the other hand, it is difficult to say whether a Western, democratic country would have acted better. Many problems were unique. Plainly nuclear power had been geared for rapid results, and it had been operated without due regard for safety. The concealment of health statistics – and their complete disappearance in Belarus – was the act of a nervous totalitarian system. Gorbachev had used the accident for propaganda purposes, but Politburo records of the time suggest that he was trying gainfully to discover the root causes of the disaster, though without much success. The familiar Russian phrase "Who is to blame?" echoed across the land. There were reports of widespread (and often unconfirmed) deaths, though the overall total was in the hundreds rather than in the thousands – the Bhopal disaster in India had killed more people, for example. The standing of the scientific community fell dramatically, as did that of the IAEA, which only belatedly (in 1994) declared that Chernobyl was a dangerous nuclear plant that should be shut down. Within the USSR, Chernobyl had sparked the progress of public opinion and of Glasnost. Released from the shackles of a Stalinist system, the Soviet media began to question the policies and uncover the problems both of the present and of the past. The self-examination would be lengthy, revealing, and at times an exercise in self-destruction. It began in Moscow.

The development of Glasnost

The word Glasnost has been applied to various sectors of life to describe the opening of Soviet society in the Gorbachev era. The first notable evidence of change was the wider and more accurate reporting of events that illustrated some of the problems within Soviet society. In October 1986, for example, infant mortality statistics were published in the Soviet press, revealing a rate more than three times higher than that in Western countries. The comments accompanying the figures stressed that the rate had decreased since the late 1970s. There were also more frequent reports of protests at factories against new, austere measures of quality control. In July 1987, *Pravda* reported a new rise in alcohol consumption (the rate had fallen between 1985 and 1986 as a result of the anti-alcohol campaign), noting that deaths had occurred in the recent past from the consumption of alcohol substitutes, such as *samogon*, antifreeze, cheap perfume, and methanol. The Soviet press had been given a free hand to report social problems in the country, though this freedom was tied to official policy. Matters were made easier by changes in the editorship of several prominent journals and newspapers, and essentially the openness in reporting came from the top rather than from grassroots pressure. Generally, the more "progressive" reports could be found in the central rather than in the republican press, with the notable exception of the Baltic States.

Official de-Stalinization soon found its way into the press. Though somewhat startling in its scale, it merely furthered what had occurred in the period of Khrushchev. The Gorbachev administration, highly critical of the Brezhnev regime, refrained from attacking Khrushchev. Rather, that period was considered a viable attempt to move away from the excesses of Stalinism. In January 1987 the Soviet media began to discuss the revolutionary roles of much maligned (and rarely mentioned) figures such as Zinoviev, Bukharin, and later even Trotsky. It was to be some time before the last received any sort of flattering mention. Bukharin was the first to be rehabilitated. On February 5, 1988 the USSR Supreme Court dismissed the charges that had been laid against Bukharin and Rykov, the so-called Right Opposition, and supporters of the New Economic Policy. Though a radical step, the reprieve was in line with Gorbachev's public praise for the NEP and the claim that it was the preferred policy of Lenin. Gradually, other major figures from the 1930s – old Bolsheviks – were rehabilitated, with details published in *Pravda* and *Izvestiya*. Officially, Stalin's policies and crimes were seen as deviations from Lenin's vision, from the correct party policy; and there was always the underlying assumption that, although the country had lost its way in the 1930s, the Communist Party remained the leading force and path to the future. De-Stalinization was a means of stabilizing the contemporary regime, not of tearing it apart. Once begun, however, the process could not stop.

Since open opposition had been declared to Stalin and Stalinism, it also became common for new crimes of that era to be uncovered. In several areas, mass graves of victims were found (or rediscovered), often posing uncomfortable problems for local authorities. In May 1988, for example, the Belarusian archeologist and historian, and the future founder of the Belarusian Popular Front, Zyanon Paznyak revealed the presence of mass graves in the Kurapaty Forest in the suburbs of Minsk. Thousands gathered at the site, prompting the republican leaders to agree to an official inquiry into the massacre. The inquiry, which occurred despite the protests of war veterans and hardened Communists, was conducted hastily and proved inconclusive. The investigation team included members of the KGB, former partisans, and Communist officials, as well as Paznyak. Many of them had no desire to lay blame on the Stalin regime or on the NKVD. Though more than fifty witnesses were found who could testify to seeing the black Marias make their way to the execution site, the investigators concluded that it was most likely that the killings had been carried out by the Germans. The outcome revealed the extent of opposition to de-Stalinization in some areas. But other mass graves were found, including one at Bykivnya, near Kyiv. Some writers began to seek more information about the Famine and the extensive purges that had also occurred in Ukraine. They noted, for example, that one of the perpetrators, Lazar Kaganovich, was still living in Moscow. The Poles began to seek information about the executions of Polish officers at Katyn and other sites in 1940.

As a result of the inquiries into the mass repressions of the 1930s, an all-Union group called Memorial was founded on January 28, 1989, in memory of all the victims of the Soviet state. However, at first the focus was on the victims of Stalin. Some form of backlash was likely following the general denigration of the Soviet record. It came in a letter from Nina Andreeva, a lecturer at Leningrad Technological Institute. Likely with the full support of staunch Communist leaders such as Ligachev, she published the letter in the newspaper *Sovetskaya rossiya* on March 13, 1988. It appeared to many observers to be a turning point, a sign that Glasnost had ended, particularly given the lack of response from the Gorbachev leadership over a three-week period. The letter denounced some of the developments of the time:

> I have been reading and rereading sensational articles. For example, what can you gain (apart from disorientation) from revelations about "the counter-revolution in the USSR in the late 1920s and early 1930s" or about Stalin's "guilt" for the rise to power of Fascism and Hitler in Germany?

In the view of the author, the attacks on Stalin and Stalinism were being used to reject the entire epoch of "unprecedented feats," such as collectivization, industrialization, and "cultural revolution" – the events that raised the country from a backward agrarian nation to a great world power. In particular, plays and movies had, in her view, advocated a form of nihilism. Though Andreeva was no Stalinist – one of her relatives had been a victim of the purges and had then been rehabilitated under Khrushchev – the force of Stalin's personality was undeniable. Indeed, none other than his Cold War nemesis Winston Churchill had evoked it. Andreeva therefore stated plainly:

> I think that no matter how controversial and complex a figure in history Stalin may be, his genuine role in the building and defense of socialism will sooner or later be given an objective . . . assessment.

Not only Stalinism had come under assault in the period of Glasnost, Andreeva continued, but also Russian national pride. Whereas the latter was depicted as "Great Russian chauvinism," the movement of "militant cosmopolitanism" and refusedniks was regarded as a manifestation of democracy. In short, those rejecting the system are elevated over those who defended it at great sacrifice throughout the Soviet period. Aside from the underlying anti-Semitic implications of this statement, the author was declaring that true Russian values were being lost. "Principles were not given to us as a gift," she remarked, "we have fought for them at crucial turning points in the history of the motherland."

Though Gorbachev eventually responded to the points made in the letter through *Pravda*, the debate over the statements continued for some time. How was it possible to criticize all aspects of the Soviet period, to ridicule Lenin – something alluded to by Andreeva in the plays of Mikhail Shatrov – and to deny past achievements? It was only possible by a complete denunciation of the entire past, a form of whitewash of all Soviet achievements. The writers of the Glasnost period were therefore lacking in responsibility and objectivity. In several parts of the letter, the author referred to "liberals" and those who followed the dictates of the West in the name of "democracy." Paradoxically, the Andreeva letter was distinctive because it went against the prevailing tendency. It was a sign of how far matters had gone. The most outspoken writers and playwrights began to wonder whether some form of repression was about to occur, whether Gorbachev might be thrown out of power. However, despite opposition, Glasnost was to continue. As Andreeva noted, the revelations about the past were one-sided, but the reasons were logical enough. The goal was not to rationalize historical events but to expose crimes, many of which had been long hidden. No one could have expected that the results would be dispassionate or detached. Yet, because a significant portion of Soviet society – and particularly the older generation – could not free themselves from long-held views about the war or about Soviet achievements, society gradually became polarized.

One institution that had suffered from the beginning of the Soviet regime was the Russian Orthodox Church. The Gorbachev administration proved to be much more tolerant of the official church, restoring dissident priests to their parishes – Father Gleb Yakunin was one – and permitting foreign church dignitaries to visit the USSR. On August 18, 1987 the Ecumenical Patriarch Dimitrios of Constantinople arrived; he visited several holy sites and held a formal meeting with the Russian Orthodox Patriarch Pimen. No such meeting had taken place for four centuries. Two days later, Mother Teresa visited the victims of Chernobyl. The following April, Pimen was invited to the Kremlin to meet Gorbachev. The Soviet authorities had decided to commemorate the Millennium of Christianity in Kyivan Rus' of 988, when Prince Vladimir (Volodymyr) had chosen Christianity for his subjects, above all other religions. The decision was a momentous one for the Soviet state for a number of reasons. First, it indicated that Gorbachev was prepared to distance himself from the official – and much abhorred – embracing of militant atheism and recognize the traditional

Orthodox religion. A Communist state was celebrating a thousand years of Christianity, despite the limitations imposed on the church since the time of Peter the Great, and the harsh persecution of priests that began during the 1920s. Though there had been a rapprochement of sorts during the Great Patriotic War, the early postwar years had seen little change in official policy. Yet the Russian Orthodox Church had survived intact, despite church closures and the fact that church congregations tended to be predominantly elderly.

Gorbachev, inadvertently or deliberately, was also recognizing the Soviet interpretation of a common root for the Eastern Slavic peoples of the 10th century, i.e. that Russians, Ukrainians, and Belarusians emanated from the Kyivan Rus' state that was destroyed in the invasions of the Golden Horde in the 13th century. The Ukrainian historian Mykhailo Hrushevsky, who perceived a direct link between the Kyivan state and modern Ukraine, rejected such an interpretation. Hrushevsky, however, believed that Russian roots were different. Likewise, nationalist historians in Belarus did not see a common thread between the three groups, and argued, among other interpretations, that the "White Rus" had Scandinavian origins. The Moscow celebrations, which began on June 5, 1988 with wide international publicity, were therefore not well received by all churchgoers across the Soviet Union. On the other hand, Gorbachev was prepared to recognize some churches banned by Stalin. In December 1989, for example, the Ukrainian Catholic (Uniate) Church, dissolved in 1946, was permitted to register congregations like other groups. Just one month later, the study of Marxism–Leninism was dropped as a compulsory subject at Soviet universities. Was Gorbachev resorting to the more traditional forms of Russian nationalism? If so, one can say only that the support for such a policy was developed in a negative fashion, through the slow undermining of the linchpins of Soviet society – the Party, Leninism, the rehabilitation of victims, and the release of dissidents such as the remarkably popular scientist Sakharov, whose funeral was attended by more than 100,000 people following his death on December 14, 1989.

The restoration of the Russian Orthodox Church in particular was tantamount to an admission that Bolshevik ideology had failed. The destruction of the church in the 1920s had been replaced by a new ideology, that of Leninism, or Marxism–Leninism. The mummified first Soviet leader had become close to a deity, his name invoked everywhere – in books, in newspapers, at party congresses, and in everyday speech. All major towns of the Soviet Union had a statue of Lenin, whether he had visited them or not. Occasionally, the regime had been obliged to veer from its official policy, particularly at times of crisis. During the war, when churches had been opened, there was a temporary respite as the authorities realized that the names of Lenin and Stalin alone may not have been enough to inspire the Soviet people to fight. Gorbachev may have responded to the injustices of persecution of the church rather than to the failure of Soviet ideology. However, this resurrected a new popular force, one that had not faded with time or been sullied by ageing and corrupt leaders, who seemed to have forgotten what the regime stood for. It also enhanced

Russian patriotism, and undermined the long-held alliance between exclusively Russian and Soviet interests. How could the regime have two ideologies after all? Was there still a Soviet ideology? Other questions would soon arise.

Through Glasnost, the Soviet Union had begun to develop a civic society. Yet what would be the limitations of Glasnost? How far could critics go? Would the regime continue to provide guidance? Western observers had already noted that some journals and newspapers were going much further than others. The largely foreign-language *Moskovskie novosti* (*Moscow News*), for example, under Yegor Yakovlev, and *Ogonek* (*The Flame*), under the editorship of Vitaly Korotych, were leading the way. Other outlets, especially those in the republics, were hopelessly behind, their editorial boards often divided between hard-line Communists and rebels anxious to use their relative freedom to investigate new subjects. During this period, two other facets of Soviet life began to attract attention – one was the high rate of crime in the country and the second was the elitist life of party officials. The former was hardly new, but it rarely made headlines. By the spring of 1991, the authorities acknowledged that crime levels were higher than at any time since the Great Patriotic War. The public resented the party nomenklatura, with its special stores, dachas, and personal chauffeurs, particularly as economic conditions worsened and the causes were debated in the media. The Gorbachev regime was also very unfortunate in terms of suffering disasters. The superstitious in Soviet society – and there were many – attributed the ill fortune to the leader himself. Following Chernobyl, a number of railway accidents occurred, and more than 300 people drowned when two ships collided in the Black Sea. Then, on December 7, 1988, while Gorbachev was visiting the United States, a major earthquake occurred in Armenia, killing over 40,000 people and making even more homeless.

No doubt the image of the regime suffered from such adversity. The contrast between the Gorbachev regime and that of his mentor Andropov was evident from a bizarre incident that occurred in May 1987, when a 19-year old West German citizen, Matthias Rust, flew over Soviet territory, somehow evaded the Soviet air defense system, and landed his single-engine plane in Vasilevsky Spusk, close to Red Square, much to the bemusement of Muscovites and tourists. With international attention focused on the incident, retribution was relatively light. At his trial on September 2, Rust received a four-year jail sentence for "hooliganism," but was released after less than a year. Defense Minister Sergey Sokolov, a Hero of the Soviet Union, was fired over the incident. The affair reflected badly on the Soviet military, which had already been harmed by the long and largely unsuccessful war in Afghanistan. The prestige of the regime, a fundamental part of rule, had begun to decline. Attention was focused on the lack of security in a country that had always been so security-conscious, with formidable restrictions to entry.

Glasnost had a huge impact on art and culture, and sparked a revival in many spheres. Relative liberty became apparent. Several writers banned in the past were now openly discussed – Akhmatova, Bulgakov, and Mandelstam being the most prominent. In

1983 the Ukrainian poet Irina Ratushinskaya had been given a seven-year prison sentence for advocating human rights, but she was released on October 10, 1986. On the other hand, bastions of the system, those writers who had adhered to the official line and received promotion, became subject to criticism. Books once banned began to appear after 1987, including Pasternak's *Doctor Zhivago*, written in the 1950s but now published for the first time in the Soviet Union. Art exhibitions became a familiar sight in Moscow and Leningrad, including modern art, which had not been seen by Soviet citizens since Khrushchev's days (Khrushchev detested modern art). The works of banned authors, artists, and musicians became much sought after, while figures recognized by the state were largely scorned.

In the film industry, new experimental films were now permissible. The era of *chernukha* (based on the Russian word for "black") began, with depictions of the harsh realities of Soviet life as well as graphic images and sexual scenes that included nudity. Epitomizing this genre was the film *Malenkaya Vera* (*Little Vera*), directed by 27-year-old Vasily Pichul, which portrayed a blue-collar family living in a small town, with an alcoholic father who has a violent confrontation with Vera's boyfriend Sergey. The film includes a scene with a gang fight in a park (fairly typical of the time), and injects belatedly a reference to the fact that the parents had a second child (Vera) only in order to acquire a larger apartment. The era in general offered negative, nihilistic films that showed the violence, horror, and hopelessness of life. It included films such as Isaak Fridberg's *Kukolka* (*Little Doll*) (1989), Yurii Kara's *Vory v zakone* (*Thieves in Law*, meaning organized crime leaders) (1988), and Roman Balayan's *Ledi Makhbet mtsensogo uezda* (*Lady Macbeth of Mtsensk District*) (1989), based on the story by Nikolay Leskov (and the subject of Shostakovich's 1934 opera), as well as documentaries such as Stanislav Govorukhin's *Tak zhit' nel'zya* (*This Is No Way to Live*) (1990). However, Soviet audiences also liked more conventional melodramas, and detective stories enjoyed new popularity in this period. The Soviet film studio Goskino collapsed in 1991, and funding for future films became very difficult to acquire. But with the development of Glasnost the film industry's portrayal of late Soviet life was a very negative one that highlighted and exaggerated many of the worst ills of society.

Politics under Gorbachev

Gorbachev's frustration at opposition among the party hierarchy to his reforms was always apparent. Though he had made significant personnel changes, the general resistance to fundamental reform was always evident. Gorbachev's policies, however, were not consistent. Like previous Soviet leaders, he was prone to long, rambling speeches that would last for up to four hours, without deviating substantially from official (and largely meaningless) rhetoric. How was he to reform the Soviet system? What would it mean to the leading role of the Communist Party? Few observers had any clear ideas. How could a leader who had risen through the Soviet system, abided by its tenets, relied on patrons, and socialized with prominent leaders suddenly reject the past and embark on a completely new path? The simple fact is that he could not. Such a program was inconceivable to Gorbachev at first. There is no evidence of any long-term plan to curb the authority of the Party. What Gorbachev did see, however, was the impossibility of continuing in the Brezhnev style, ignoring basic problems, closing one's eyes to corruption, to the lack of direction and declining power of the Soviet Union. At first, he sought broader powers of decision-making, and to widen the base from which party leaders were selected. He also began to promote the more open-minded and reformist party leaders, such as Yeltsin. As he did so, he immediately began to face opposition from those perturbed by the elevation of people dedicated to changing the system. This predicament continued throughout the nearly seven years of Gorbachev's leadership, and it was one that he never resolved satisfactorily. His team was never united; and, while one might say the same of previous Soviet administrations, an official press in the past had always publicized the unity at the top.

In January 1987, at a Plenum of the CC CPSU, Gorbachev called for multi-candidate elections to leading party posts and to local government organizations. He also advocated that non-party citizens take on more prominent positions. The Soviet leader emphasized that in the factories the workforce, not the local party administration, should be responsible for appointing managers. At an election the following month in the Kemerovo oblast, Western Siberia, two candidates ran for the post of party First Secretary. By the summer, there were multi-candidate elections for local soviets across the country. The change had been implemented successfully. Meanwhile, in Moscow, there was widespread discontent among the city bureaucracy at a much-publicized anti-corruption campaign undertaken by party boss Yeltsin. Bowing to pressure, Gorbachev removed Yeltsin in November 1987, telling his friend that his party career was probably over. Yeltsin received a compensatory (but relatively minor) post as a deputy minister in the construction industry. His replacement was Lev Zaikov, an older and more traditional Communist. Yeltsin, the official announcement declared, had made "mistaken assessments" about party work and the necessary speed of Perestroika. The rift between Gorbachev and Yeltsin was to grow with time; ironically, the more democratic political system initiated by Gorbachev was to permit a revival of Yeltsin's political fortune just over a year later.

The year 1988 saw momentous changes. Soviet intellectual society had become a debating ground. By May, several informal groups had joined together to form the Democratic Union, based mainly on membership from Moscow, Leningrad, Siberia, and Ukraine. The Democratic Union, though not registered as such, was the closest the country had come to an alternative political party. The 19th Party Conference was held in Moscow a month later. On paper, it was of no special significance since party conferences did not offer binding decrees, but rather were normally discussion meetings. However, Gorbachev used this occasion to push for significant reforms of the ruling structure for the first time, significantly undermining the authority of the

CPSU. He proposed the formation of a new body, the Congress of People's Deputies, which would be made up of 750 deputies from public organizations (trade unions, cultural societies, the Komsomol), along with 1,500 elected by area. It would be the duty of the new Congress to elect the members of the Supreme Soviet from its own body. The Congress would also elect a president of the country. Furthermore, Gorbachev demanded that the positions of Party Secretary and Chairman of the Soviet be merged throughout the country, thus reducing the bureaucratic structure and making the position considerably stronger. Elections were set for the following March. The Conference was the scene of some extraordinary debates, including attacks on the Soviet leader. Discussion was far from free – indeed, it often took extraordinary efforts by delegates to get a hearing – but it was the first serious attempt by Gorbachev to change the way in which the country was ruled.

What were his goals? In retrospect – and perhaps to add order to events that did not appear so clear-cut at the time – Gorbachev had embarked on a policy to restrict the authority of the Communist Party, which he perceived as the main obstacle to his reforms, while providing some semblance of real authority to the Soviet system. The balance of power between the soviets and the Party had varied over the Soviet period. During the war, Stalin took on the title of Premier, thus symbolizing that he represented the Soviet government first and foremost. However, in other periods, the Party had always been the key institution, and under Brezhnev the Supreme Soviet became merely symbolic. Brezhnev, as a former Chairman of the Presidium of the Supreme Soviet during one of his darker periods, would have realized only too well how meaningless that position was. Gorbachev wished to give real power to the Congress and to the Supreme Soviet, but to what extent did he wish to restrict the power of the Party? Was the move a device to push through a reform program, after which he would continue to allow the Party to play the main role in society? After all, was not Gorbachev the archetypal Leninist? In October 1988, Yakovlev's position as the man responsible for Soviet ideology was made more secure when Ligachev, his main adversary, was demoted to agriculture. Another reformer, Vadim Medvedev, was promoted to the Politburo. With the retirement of Gromyko, and the lack of candidates willing to stand against him, Gorbachev took over the position of Chairman of the Presidium of the Supreme Soviet at the beginning of October 1988. The position was allegedly a key one as a prelude to the election of a "Soviet president" the following summer.

By January 1989, nominations began for deputies to the new Congress, with many seats being contested by a large number of candidates, including a significant portion of non-party people for the first time in a Soviet election. In the 1,500 regional constituencies, about 75 percent of elections had more than one candidate, while some had as many as seven. In Moscow, Boris Yeltsin emerged as a highly popular candidate. Many former dissidents also ran. In Ukraine, one of the successful candidates was Yury Shcherbak, the Chairman of the Green World environmental association. In the Baltic States, candidates from the Popular Fronts contested the elections.

For the first time, the media played a key role in helping competition. The results were unpredictable, even though the Communists remained the USSR's only official party. In fact, reform-minded Communists were Gorbachev's best hope – those who had supported his initiatives without distancing themselves from the Soviet regime. Voter interest and turnout was high at around 85 percent. Elections were won if and when a candidate received more than 50 percent of the vote; hence many results were decided only with a second round. The outcome embarrassed the Party and its candidates. In the three Baltic States, it was virtually shut out by the Popular Fronts of Estonia and Latvia, and the Sajudis in Lithuania. Many so-called "safe" seats were lost. Yeltsin was elected with almost 90 percent of the vote in his Moscow constituency. However, around 85 percent of delegates elected to the Congress were party members.

Before the Congress met, a plenary meeting of the CC CPSU accepted the resignation of several members, including Gromyko and the former Chief of Staff, Nikolay Ogarkov. The discussions of the Congress were broadcast on television and radio, and had a profound effect on a population that had been kept out of political debates. Before long, tensions were evident between the more radical elements and those who worried about how much the existing system would be changed. Yeltsin, together with Sakharov, was clearly one of the leading demagogues with a flair for the dramatic. Yeltsin failed narrowly to get elected to the Supreme Soviet on May 27, 1989, until another deputy gave up his seat. Yeltsin was also one of the creators of an inter-regional group of deputies that pushed for further reforms. By early 1990, the changes in the balance of power became more significant. Public organizations lost their guaranteed seats in local soviets. On February 7, 1990, at Gorbachev's behest, the CPSU recommended a constitutional amendment to abolish its monopoly on power (it was approved by a parliamentary vote of March 1990 and agreed with the notion of creating a presidential system of government). Soon the Supreme Soviet sanctioned the establishment of an executive president, who would be the head of state and the commander-in-chief of the armed forces, but otherwise would have less power in practice than the General Secretary of the CC CPSU had wielded. The country was becoming more democratic. Though no one was prepared to oppose Gorbachev as the nominated president, the signs of dissatisfaction with his leadership were becoming evident. He received 1,329 votes with 495 votes against him – a notably high figure given that by this time the delegates from the Baltic States had decided to boycott the whole procedure. Gorbachev had changed the system of the country by reducing the authority of the Party, the vehicle by which he had come to power. This situation raised questions about the legitimacy of Gorbachev's leadership and why, as a democratic leader, he did not risk an electoral vote in the country as a whole. It appeared that he was clinging to power and losing support.

None the less, he went ahead with the appointment of the Presidential Council, which was a mixture of known reformers and more hard-line figures – often in the West the latter were called "conservatives," a misleading appellation because of its political connotations in Western democracies. They were conservatives in wishing to maintain the status quo, but had little in common with the European variety. The radicals included Eduard Shevardnadze the Foreign Minister, Yakovlev, and the progressive economist Stanislav Shatalin; the traditionalists were made up of the representatives of major public organizations such as the KGB (Vladimir Kryuchkov), the Chairman of the USSR Supreme Soviet (Anatoly Lukyanov, an ex-officio member), the Ministry of Internal Affairs (Vadim Bakatin), the Ministry of Defense (Dmitry Yazov) and the State Planning Committee (Yury Maslyukov). Altogether it was not unlike the Politburo in its orientation and outlook. Almost at once the new ruling body was faced with a major task – to preserve unity in the face of increased pressure to decentralize the country. The decentralization movement was led by Russia, by far the largest of the Soviet republics, though arguably it had originated with the Baltic States. Conceivably, the USSR could lose the Baltic States and still preserve its entity; to lose Russia, however, would bring the system crashing down. The subject deserves a brief explanation.

Since the end of the war, when Stalin raised his toast to the "Russian people," Russians had occupied the prime place in Soviet society. That Russians would always be predominant in the Soviet Union might seem to be stating the obvious, given the large proportion of the country occupied by the Russian Federation. Yet the Union existed, and non-Russians did play a significant role in Soviet life. Some Russians argued that the Soviet Union, far from being a Russian empire, discriminated against Russians, who lacked their own party organization and Central Committee. Many Westerners, and quite often the Western media, failed to make the distinction between the Soviet Union and Russia, using both terms as synonymous. By 1989, however, Russians made up slightly more than 50 percent of the Soviet population. Even the Slavic population seemed likely to fall below that mark by the time of the first post-1989 census. About 25 million ethnic Russians lived outside the Russian Federation. In some areas, such as Belarus or Eastern Ukraine, their presence was hardly noticed amid a generally Russian-speaking population. But in republics such as Kazakhstan, Latvia, or Estonia the indigenous population often resented the presence and predominance of Russians in political and economic life. The Russian Federation's standard of living was notably lower than that in the Baltic States, though somewhat higher than that in the republics of Central Asia. The issue of the position of Russians in the Soviet Union is a difficult one; and a full gamut of views is held on the question of whether they were a privileged group or one exploited for the benefit of the Soviet system – the argument that Russian resources supplied most of the Soviet republics, in addition to the countries of Eastern Europe.

The misfortunes of ethnic Russians had been a theme of Russian nationalists since the early 1970s, when espoused by the dissident writer Aleksandr Solzhenitsyn. The author had also developed his ideas further in a pamphlet that advocated the formation of a Slavic community, embracing Russia, Ukraine, Belarus, and parts of Kazakhstan. In the third volume of *The Gulag Archipelago*, Solzhenitsyn includes a curious plea to Ukrainians, practically pleading with them to reject separatist nationalism and combine their interests with their fraternal brethren, the Russians. Solzhenitsyn's views for a time represented mainstream Russian nationalist thinking. He regarded the Russian Revolution as a takeover of the state by foreign elements, noting that the Cheka, like the Bolshevik Party, contained a large group of non-Russians, particularly Latvians. Solzhenitsyn also maintained that Lenin himself was only one quarter Russian (cited in Dunlop, 1983, p. 143). Thus the only major element of the Russian nation prevalent in the Soviet Union, according to this school of thought, was the Russian language. Nationalists perceived its retention and widespread dissemination more as a matter of convenience than as a desire to spread the Russian cause in the non-Russian areas. Plainly, however, Soviet politics was contradictory, and in the early postwar years the Soviet regime exhibited traits of Russian chauvinism that were reminiscent of the late tsarist period or the years of War Communism.

By the following decade, demagogues such as Vladimir Zhirinovsky, who was to challenge Yeltsin for the Russian presidency in 1991, were taking up the nationalist cause. Zhirinovsky's form of Russian nationalism has been described as a form of "national Bolshevism." How does one explain the apparent contradiction between a state giving priority to Russians, and yet at the same time denying Russians the sort of recognition offered to other republics, such as a separate branch of the Communist Party and even their own newspaper prior to the 1970s? Nationalist Russians sought a Russia outside the imperial domain. Their writings returned to the village, to peasant institutions of the 19th century. As Hosking has noted (Hosking, 2001, p. 567), "What they had diagnosed . . . was the continued dominance of Russian imperial over Russian ethnic and civic priorities." Great Russia (*Rossiya*) had superseded Russian national interests, and in the process the Russian national identity had been undermined. In the Gorbachev period, this sentiment became more pronounced with the manifestations of national identity in the non-Russian republics. It signified that in Russian political life any prospective politician had to consider an appeal on the nationalist card. To ignore it would be fatal. If Gorbachev recognized this factor, he never tried to exploit it, and it was to cost him dearly.

In 1990, Boris Yeltsin managed to take over the leading position in the Russian Federation and to press successfully for privileges vis-à-vis the Soviet Union and what was termed, disparagingly, the Moscow center. In a very close contest in late May 1990, Yeltsin was elected Chairman of the Supreme Soviet of the Russian Federation, defeating Aleksandr Vlasov, Chairman of the RSFSR Council of Ministers. Almost immediately, the Russian government proclaimed its sovereignty over resources on its territory, and the non-Russian republics followed suit. In Belarus, the proclamation of sovereignty on July 27, 1990 is still considered by the nationally conscious elements in society to be the most important day of the year. The declarations of sovereignty weakened the USSR, but did not deal it a fatal blow. They can be considered the end point of the long series of protests that had begun after the Chernobyl accident. Putting into practice the proclaimed sovereignty was to take some time; and sovereignty was not the same thing as independence. Yeltsin, however, did not stop there. On June 16, Russia formally abolished the one-party system. Three days later, a Communist Party of the Russian Federation was created and held a conference (this had last occurred in 1925). The convocation of this conference was timed to take place immediately before the 28th Congress of the CC CPSU, perhaps the least publicized and certainly the most ineffective and meaningless party congress in the Soviet period. Yeltsin had not begun the process whereby the CPSU began to disintegrate, but his actions served as a catalyst.

Already party membership had begun to decline as prominent and rank-and-file members began to leave in droves. In the first half of 1990, the number of party members who resigned, no longer paid their dues, or were expelled was close to 800,000 (almost 10 percent of total membership). The situation alarmed party stalwarts, and even Gorbachev felt obliged to re-examine his priorities. When Shevardnadze resigned as Foreign Minister in December, he warned of an impending coup d'état. In fact, Gorbachev began an attempt to regain some of the authority he had lost to the republics. On September 24, the Supreme Soviet granted him the power to rule by presidential decree for eighteen months in order to see through his program for economic reform. Yeltsin meanwhile had begun an ostentatious "presidential-style" tour of the Russian Federation. In late December, when the Congress granted Gorbachev enhanced powers, the President nominated Gennady Yanayev as his Vice-President – a strange choice. Only at the second attempt, and after prolonged

Plate 8.2 Police officers in Red Square, ca. 1990.

Image: David Katzenstein/CORBIS

persuasion from Gorbachev, could Congress be persuaded to accept it. Yanayev was a dull apparatchik with no interest in reforming the Soviet system. Other appointments made by Gorbachev in the same period did not augur well for the future of a reform program and democracy – Boris Pugo as the chief of police, and Kryuchkov as the head of the KGB – while the loss of Shevardnadze and especially of Aleksandr Yakovlev suggested that the President had made a significant about-face. By early 1991, Gorbachev had begun to demand restrictions on freedom of the press. Mass demonstrations in Moscow were banned. The experiment in political change appeared to be over. Gorbachev's challenge, clearly, was the growing power of the republics, and of Russia in particular. (Plate 8.2)

The perils of Perestroika

By most calculations, the introduction of Glasnost into Soviet society has to be considered a success, even though the open criticisms of the Gorbachev administration served to lower its credibility and Gorbachev appeared to resent personal attacks on his leadership. Perestroika proved much more difficult. Soviet reports on the economy had never been frank, particularly the reporting of harvests and other economic statistics. The state continued to fix prices for goods and to subsidize struggling firms. There is no doubt that the economy was a key priority for the Soviet leader, but what was the goal of Gorbachev's proposed economic reforms? Was it even possible to reform the archaic system? If so, how far could Gorbachev go? That there should be some decentralization, concessions to local decision-making, redistribution of profits and the like seems self-evident. Constant reiteration of words like "efficiency," "discipline," and "acceleration" are to be found in Gorbachev's early speeches.

The obstacles to be overcome, on the other hand, were "bureaucracy" and "formalism." How far could he hope to progress in areas such as agriculture when the Communist Party elite refused even to consider a dismantling of the collective farm system? Gorbachev, by any standard, was exceedingly unlucky. He could not be held responsible for the fall in world oil prices that had brought an end to the brief boom period of the 1970s. Nor could he do much about the weather, which brought about a series of poor harvests. His government had suffered two unexpected and costly disasters in Chernobyl and the Armenian earthquake. Yet it is hard to avoid the conclusion that he said much but essentially "dabbled" with the economy and the vast ministerial bureaucracies centered in Moscow. Only by 1988 was it evident that he wished to undermine the authority of the Communist Party through more radical changes to the economy and the political structure of the country. By that time most Soviet families had already suffered a substantial decline in their living standard.

In the early years of Perestroika, results were mixed. GNP growth was reduced from that of the Brezhnev period, but it nevertheless continued to increase. However, the rise in national income did not keep pace. At the 19th Party Conference, Gorbachev repeatedly demanded that enterprises have more control over decision-making and introduce better technology, and that the country should concentrate on the production of more consumer goods and better housing. But this was a familiar refrain to the public. In addition, he also suggested that price reform should be introduced that provided a more accurate picture of supply and demand. Subsidies should be aimed at consumers so that living standards did not fall too dramatically. The result of the Conference was a new package of measures that inaugurated the further development of cooperatives. The USSR encouraged joint ventures, particularly in information technology and banking.

Moscow began to take on a different look by the summer of 1988. Several foreign companies had opened stores – Pizza Hut being the best-known. Cooperative restaurants were increasingly common. Yet the reforms were piecemeal – they did not deal with the fundamental problem that general standards of living had begun to decline, not only for the average worker, but also even for the party elite. As usual, agriculture stood out as a seemingly unsolvable dilemma. The administration was reluctant to tamper with the collective farm system, but the 1987 harvest was only 195 million tons, the lowest since Gorbachev came to power. The shortfall had to be made up by a substantial purchase of grain from the United States. Though considered an expert in agriculture, Gorbachev could come up with no workable solution. He approved in principle the concept of leasing land, but believed that to dismantle, or attempt to dismantle, the collective farm system would lead to social upheaval in the countryside. By 1989 the economic situation had become critical. In July coal miners in the Kuznetsk Basin of Siberia declared a strike, demanding better working conditions and higher wages. The strike spread to the Donbas, the oldest coalfield in the USSR. Eventually almost 500,000 miners were on strike. The movement was well organized, with miners demonstrating peacefully in the streets of Moscow, Kyiv, and other cities. In the past, the Soviet regime had dealt harshly with such protests. Gorbachev, however, felt obliged to try to meet most of the demands, promising to satisfy them. In Ukraine, the strike became more political with the formation of an unofficial miners' union, which superseded the meaningless local trade union committee. In future the coalminers would be prepared. Mining conditions had become deplorable, and the accident rate in the last decade of the USSR was alarmingly high. On the other hand, the mines of the Donbas had become prohibitively deep, the coal contained high ash content, and methane gas explosions were common. Whether the mines were economically viable was a question the Soviet leadership was not prepared to address.

Alongside industrial slowdown and strikes, the greater awareness of the fragility of the environment after Chernobyl led to the postponement or abandonment of several of the more ambitious economic plans. The infamous "Sibaral" project, whereby waters from the Ob–Irtysh river system were to be diverted to irrigate the arid lands of Central Asia, was cancelled indefinitely in August 1987. Of the many irrigation and land-improvement schemes in the USSR, "Sibaral" was the most outrageous. Greens and environmentalists organized rallies against other projects, particularly in the non-Russian republics. In Armenia, various rallies took place against environmental pollution, leading to the closure of a power station near Yerevan. Following the disastrous earthquake of December 1988, the Armenian nuclear power plant, located close to the seismic zone, was closed in the spring of 1989. By November of that year, the USSR Supreme Soviet issued a resolution to halt and reverse ecological degradation in the country. New projects required an environmental study to assess the likely consequences for the environment. The authorities decided to reappraise the nuclear power program, and to reduce the use of chemicals in agriculture. It became impossible for Soviet planners to make decisions in Moscow without having studies made of the area in which an industry was to be located. By 1990, Ukraine declared a moratorium for five years on the further commissioning of new nuclear power stations or the expansion of stations already in service. In the same year almost 75,000 more people were evacuated from the contaminated regions of Belarus and Ukraine.

Such concern can be regarded as a forward step given the lamentable Soviet record on the environment since the 1st Five-Year Plan. Yet the impact on industrial growth and development was significant. Mega-projects became unfeasible. Meanwhile economic decline could no longer be concealed. The failure of Perestroika countered the success of Glasnost and precisely during the period of political disunity.

Plate 8.3 Daily life in Russia, 1989. Soviet army officers pass a bread line in a Moscow street. This photograph was made possible only by the easing of restrictions during the era of Perestroika.

Image: Ed Kashi/CORBIS

Inflation had begun to rise alarmingly, while the authorities revealed that, in 1989 and 1990, GNP and labor productivity had begun to decline. There were several voices advocating a radical overhaul of the Soviet economy, but the Soviet leadership preferred to tinker rather than introduce some form of "shock treatment." In December 1989, Ryzhkov introduced a plan for self-management in the economy without the loss of state control. The Congress accepted the plan without demur. Within the Russian republic, the economist Stanislav Shatalin introduced a plan to switch to a market economy within 500 days, a program supported by Yeltsin. In October 1990, Gorbachev introduced a more moderate version of the same plan. Conditions in the USSR, however, were no longer conducive to such superficial measures. National income fell by 5.5 percent in 1990, and the labor force became restless and progressively assertive. Perestroika may possibly have worked had a radical program been introduced at the beginning. It could not work in an atmosphere of industrial disputes, environmental protests, and political instability, at a time when the Union itself was being called into question. By the end of 1990, few Soviet people had any faith that the Gorbachev administration could reverse the consistent trend of a fall in living standards, inflation, and general decline. (Plate 8.3)

Foreign policy

Western observers regarded Gorbachev's promotion to the Soviet leadership in March 1985 with a mixture of interest and trepidation. After a succession of decrepit leaders who did not necessarily lack initiative but did not remain healthy long enough to make any impression on foreign policy, Gorbachev appeared to be energetic and likely to remain in office for a prolonged period. The war in Afghanistan showed no signs of slowing in the spring of 1985; rather the government stepped up efforts to achieve a decisive victory over the Mujahideen. In May, on the initiative of the USSR, the Warsaw Pact countries renewed the treaty for a further thirty years. On the 40th anniversary of the end of the Great Patriotic War in Europe, Gorbachev even gave Stalin some praise in a speech to the Soviet military. So what was new, some observers wondered, about the Gorbachev leadership? In the West, the leaders of the main adversaries of the Soviet Union – the United States and Great Britain – appeared hawkish. President Ronald Reagan had begun a second term, and Soviet citizens recalled his dismissal of the Soviet Union as an "evil empire." He had formed a partnership with British Prime Minister Margaret Thatcher, whose popularity had been restored by a military victory over Argentina three years earlier in the mini-war over the Falkland Islands. By postwar standards the West appeared to be fairly united, although European countries had expressed concern about the US intention to build an anti-nuclear shield over their country – the so-called Strategic Defense Initiative, or Star Wars – because this program, ambitious though it may have been, implied the removal of US troops from protecting Western Europe and a return of the US to isolationism. In brief, in 1985 there seemed to be little reason to hope that the Cold War would end in the immediate future.

Gorbachev's initial focus was on the need to reduce or eliminate nuclear weapons. He spoke frequently of his desire for "a common European home"; indeed that was the title of a speech he presented to a Czechoslovakian audience in April 1987. The nuclear problem could lead to the extinction of the human race, Gorbachev stressed:

> We live in a time in which we are faced with difficult and, perhaps, even baffling questions concerning the destiny of the world, the future of the human race. Today world nations are linked together, like mountain climbers attached to one rope. They can either climb together to the summit or all fall into the abyss. To prevent this from happening political leaders must rise above narrow-minded considerations and realize how dramatic is the contemporary situation. This underlines the essential need for a new way of political thinking in the nuclear age. Only this way of thinking will lead to all nations taking urgent measures to prevent a nuclear disaster, a disaster that would wipe out the human race.
>
> (*Pravda*, April 11, 1987)

Even before Chernobyl, it is clear that Gorbachev would begin his foreign policy with an emphasis on the nuclear question. On August 6, 1985, the 40th anniversary of the dropping of the atomic bomb on the city of Hiroshima, the Soviet leader declared a five-month moratorium on further nuclear tests. This announcement followed a decision to place a short moratorium on the plan to place medium-range nuclear missiles on European soil. Such moves could be considered ploys to provoke a response from the United States. In his second term of office, President Reagan had moderated his tone and expressed interest in a summit with Gorbachev. Though inconsequential – the two leaders met in Geneva on November 18–21, 1985 without accomplishing anything of note – it was only the first of numerous meetings that would see the two men become very familiar with each other's style and adopt a friendly approach. Both clearly liked a television camera. In early 1986 the two provided prerecorded television speeches, Gorbachev to the American audience and Reagan to Soviet listeners. Gorbachev's constant travels and speeches to European audiences were described in the US media as a "charm offensive." Not everyone was convinced that such an approach carried anything of substance; some considered it potentially sinister, a means to dupe the West into a false sense of security.

Reagan and Gorbachev met once more in the Icelandic capital of Reykjavic in October 1986; but, again, the results were inconclusive because the Soviet side was insistent that the SDI program should be stopped before any real progress could be made. Reagan's advisors ensured that no such concession would be forthcoming. Several prominent Americans attended an International Peace Forum in Moscow in February 1987, including Norman Mailer, Shirley Maclaine, Yoko Ono, and Paul Newman. In

December of this same year, Gorbachev traveled to Washington and the two leaders signed the INF Treaty to eliminate all medium-range nuclear missiles – a significant breakthrough in superpower relations, and one that heralded a new détente. Of the various foreign policy issues between the two sides, Soviet involvement in Afghanistan remained. In the early period of the Gorbachev administration, Soviet operations had intensified, but the Soviet situation was increasingly controversial and undermined by domestic criticism. Prominent statesmen, such as Andrey Sakharov, were outspoken in their condemnation of the war, which had become a Soviet quagmire similar to that of the Americans in Vietnam, though significantly smaller in scale. After the signing of the INF Treaty, Gorbachev agreed to pull Soviet troops out of Afghanistan, signing agreements in Geneva on April 14, 1988 with Afghanistan, Pakistan, and the United States. Soviet official losses amounted to around 50,000 troops; some 2 million Afghans had been left homeless, and thousands were dead. For Gorbachev, it had become a meaningless war with no clear outcome or gains to be made. By February 15, 1989, the last Soviet soldier had left Afghanistan.

By the summer of 1988, with the internal situation in the country becoming ever more precarious, Gorbachev's foreign policy took on new dimensions. The year that followed was a period of momentous decisions, triumphant appearances, and general hero-worship for the Soviet leader among the peoples of the United States, and Western and Eastern Europe. In many respects, the success was highly personal. Like Khrushchev, Gorbachev relished international media attention. Unlike Khrushchev, he responded to the occasions appropriately dressed and well behaved, usually accompanied by his wife Raisa. In late May 1988, Reagan came to Moscow, a largely symbolic visit but one during which the friendship with Gorbachev was consolidated. In December, Gorbachev arrived in New York to speak at the UN. There he made a grand gesture – he announced that the USSR would reduce Soviet military forces by 500,000 within two years. In April he was a guest of Margaret Thatcher, the British Prime Minister, who was a long-time admirer of Gorbachev. The next month he was in China, the first time a Soviet leader had visited a Chinese leader in three decades. Gorbachev wasted no time in announcing more dramatic news – he would withdraw 200,000 Soviet troops from the Chinese border to normalize relations with the rival Communist power. Was the Soviet Union still committed to spreading revolution, and to maintaining its firm hold over the satellite governments of Eastern Europe? The events of the summer of 1989 indicated a startling reversal of long-held policies. The change was signaled by Foreign Minister Shevardnadze, who visited East Berlin on June 9, and announced that it was the imperative of each country to choose its own route for reform (or lack of reform) – a plain hint that the USSR would no longer take on the responsibility of safeguarding the ramshackle regimes of Eastern Europe.

The Eastern Europeans soon exploited the sudden removal of Soviet control. In Poland, Solidarity had already achieved a decisive electoral victory. In a speech to the Council of Europe on July 6, Gorbachev said that the Soviet Union would not consider it correct to interfere in the internal affairs of another nation. To many observers this comment was tantamount to a repudiation of the Brezhnev Doctrine that had guided Soviet foreign policy since 1968. Gorbachev visited East Berlin on the occasion of the 40th anniversary of the DDR. The crowds cheered him, but not East German leader Erich Honecker. While row upon row of East German soldiers paraded past, Gorbachev warned Honecker that he had to begin reform. On November 9, with the fall of the Berlin Wall, the Cold War was effectively over in Europe. Gorbachev was to win the Nobel Peace Prize in 1990 for his role in ending the Cold War, but how far had he really controlled matters? Was there a deliberate policy to release Eastern Europe from a system imposed forty years earlier at the end of the Great Patriotic War? Was there a link between the 1985 statements expressing a fear of nuclear war and what happened four years later? Only the most blinkered of analysts could suggest that there was a premeditated plan for the events that occurred, and only Gorbachev's firmest supporters would acknowledge that he was more than a symbolic figure (compare, for example, Brown, 1996 and Dunlop, 1993). The most difficult matter of all to analyze is how policy A led to a result B, unforeseen and unanticipated, and not necessarily welcomed – at least not to a man who always referred to his political outlook as Leninist.

The most obvious explanation is that at some point Gorbachev lost control over foreign policy; the forces unleashed by his moderation took on a form of their own. As a course of decentralization began in the Soviet Union, the Eastern European countries responded accordingly. Another possibility, and one that is not negated by the previous one, is that Gorbachev considered foreign policy as secondary to the implementation of change at home. Most important was a period of international stability that would allow the leadership to place emphasis on reform of the domestic economy. In that case, however, why would the Soviet leader have announced so many new initiatives, such as unilateral reductions of the Soviet military? Would not the consequences of such a policy have been evident? And were such announcements a result of prolonged debate in the USSR or rather formulated by Gorbachev on the spot, without prior discussion with his peers? Gorbachev's own memoirs do not provide any clear answers to these questions. As with any former leader writing his recollections, the memoirs suggest a more sustained and rational policy than was clear to observers at the time. The consequence by the end of 1989 was a Soviet leader idolized in the West but increasingly alienated from his countrymen. The loss of "empire" does not necessarily bring about the fall of the leader in power, particularly if that leader appears to have no other options available, no force with which to alter circumstances, and so forth. But in Gorbachev's case there is no evidence that he intended to sever Eastern Europe from Soviet control. The comments of Gorbachev and his associates renouncing the Brezhnev Doctrine occurred only after the Eastern Europeans had already begun to reject Communist rulers. The alliances of the Cominform and the Warsaw Pact had never been comfortable. Within the four decades there had been numerous revolts, several interventions by Soviet tanks, and only the fiction of a shared defensive alliance in which all countries would have a voice. Yet the Soviet position of a superpower was dependent upon the retention of control over territories overrun by the Red Army at the end of the war.

In 1989, at least, the Soviet Union had gained the most favorable world opinion since the war years. At the end of the year Gorbachev said that the Cold War was coming to a close, and symbolically met with the Polish Pope John Paul II, re-establishing Soviet ties with the Vatican. Gorbachev now had to deal with a new US president, George Bush (who came into office in January 1989), in order to resolve a new dilemma – the question of German unification. There had been long debate about this in the Soviet Union. In principle, the idea had its attractions in the early Cold War period, when Stalin had envisioned a weak German state, deprived of its industrial resources, that might be ripe for a Communist takeover. The circumstances of late 1989 and early 1990 implied that unification would involve the powerful West German state swallowing up the 17 million East Germans. The USSR could do little about this development. Gorbachev did, however, express his opposition in February 1990 to any notion that the united Germany could join NATO. In April the United States rejected the concept that the new Germany could simultaneously be a member of NATO and of the Warsaw Pact. By July the Soviet leadership had agreed to the inevitable – a unified Germany had joined NATO. There could hardly have been a clearer demonstration of the USSR's loss of international prestige. The West German entry into NATO in 1955 had been seen as an act of provocation by the West, and led directly to Khrushchev's formation of the Warsaw Pact. Much of the tension of the Cold War could be related to the same question and to the anomaly of West Berlin, a Western oasis in the Communist heartland. By October 1990, however, a unified Germany in NATO had become a reality. The prevailing opinion in both East and West was not merely that the lengthy conflict had ended, but that the Soviet Union had "lost" the Cold War.

The loss of standing of the USSR was even more evident in the first major international crisis of the Bush presidency, when Iraq invaded Kuwait. Following initial discussions by telephone, Gorbachev and Bush met in Helsinki to discuss the UN response to the invasion. Gorbachev was strongly opposed to a military attack on Iraq, offering himself in the role of mediator. His efforts were largely ignored, and his position relegated to that of a benign observer, his intervention rejected. Operation Desert Storm was the first such action in many decades in which the Soviet Union's role was negligible. In November 1990 the members of the Warsaw Pact agreed on the number of conventional forces to remain once Soviet troops left their countries. By March 1991 the military alliance ended after forty-six years. In six years the Soviet Union had lost its status as a superpower, acknowledged its defeat by pulling troops out of Afghanistan, given up or lost the effective buffer zone it had gained from the victory over the Germans, and now acceded to a situation in which NATO was the only military alliance remaining in Europe. On the other hand, the tension of the Cold War had also been removed, and Gorbachev was the figure most responsible for what many hoped would be a new era of peace. What about the Soviet Union? Could the country survive the dramatic drop in international clout – no matter how cosmetic its position as a superpower – and what sort of country would remain? In July 1991, Bush came to Moscow, and the USA and the USSR signed the START Treaty, heralding a "new age" of warm relations between the former adversaries. For the Soviet state, the new age was to be brief, largely because, of all the problems that the country faced by the middle of 1991, the nationalities question loomed largest. Together with the failure of Perestroika, the disaffection of Yeltsin's Russia, and the withdrawal of the USSR from the Cold War, it was to signal the death knell of Lenin's state.

The national question

The Soviet Union had begun its existence as a "great compromise" engineered by Lenin – a state that could be national in form and socialist in content. As the state reached its optimal size in the 1930s and 1940s (expanding again after the Second World War), the privileges granted in the 1920s to the national republics had evaporated. Their right to secession, guaranteed by the Stalin (1936) and then the Brezhnev (1977) Constitutions, existed only on paper. The three seats held by the Soviet Union at the United Nations (USSR, Ukraine, and Belarus) were likewise no more than a façade since there was no prospect that the delegates of each republic would ever disagree with each other on any issue. It has been argued that the Soviet Union was indeed a federal state, in which the benefits for the largest group, the Russians, were less clear-cut than might be imagined; that Russian resources were used to benefit poorer republics; and that the relationship was less colonial than that of a central beneficiary scattering largess to poorer neighbors. As noted above, Stalin had demonstrated his deep distrust of non-Russians in 1941–1945 with the deportation of several nations for alleged collaboration with the German and Romanian occupiers. Other nations had suffered disproportionately during the period of purges. The two Slavic republics, Ukraine and Belarus, had been deprived of virtually their entire intellectual elite; their histories were depicted as identical to that of the Russians. The latter were regarded officially as some sort of Big Brother to the smaller nationalities, not only in the Soviet period but also even in the tsarist past, when Russian settlers brought a "new civilization" to backward regions.

The great compromise had had a better beginning. Lenin's goals may have been predatory or expedient, but there is ample evidence that he recognized the complexity of forming a federal state in which numerous national groups existed. The fifteen republics that emerged after the occupation of the Baltic States were an imprecise but logical response. The Stalin regime had begun an ill-fated experiment to settle Soviet Jews in Birobidzhan, in the harsh climate of eastern Siberia. Large regions of Russia became autonomous, including Yakutia (now the Republic of Sakha), a resource-rich region of just over a million residents, but occupying territory that comprised one-fifth of the Russian Federation. Tatarstan, another wealthy region west of the Urals, also had the same status. The centralized state developed under Stalin did not, however, allow much freedom of maneuver for the non-Russian republics and autonomous regions. Some republics had been linked to Russia for a long period. Georgia, for example, had become part of the Russian Empire in 1800 and was connected by the Orthodox religion (though it contained a number of ethnic groups). Also in the Caucasus, Armenia's presence in the Soviet Union formed a kind of protective custody from the Turkish-speaking and Muslim neighbors. Coercion held this conglomeration of republics together, however. Though one cannot speak of independence movements for most of the Soviet period (the Baltic States excepted), most of the Union republics were sensitive about their rights, national cultures and language. Ironically, the formation of national republics had helped to foster such awareness in areas such as Belarus and Moldova. Ukraine existed within boundaries that formed part of Stalin's compromise with Hitler in August 1939. These borders united most Ukrainians in one state, bringing more nationally conscious elements together with more "sovietized" counterparts.

In Soviet propaganda, no animosity existed between national groups. The nationality question had been "resolved" in official parlance. By 1985, however, several issues had festered, lying dormant until the political atmosphere allowed them to emerge. One was the deportation of the Crimean Tatars in 1944–1945. Khrushchev had permitted several groups to return to their homelands after 1956. The Tatars had not been included. The Chechens and Ingushetians had been allowed to return but not to resettle in the mountainous regions, their traditional homes. A second issue was more basic – the nature of the annexation into the Soviet Union of the three Baltic States in 1939–1940. In contrast to Ukraine, where the Ribbentrop–Molotov Pact united disparate territories, the Baltic States lost their briefly won independence as a result of Soviet military intervention. A third issue dated back to the 1920s – the presence of an Armenian-populated region, Nagorno-Karabakh, administered by the Azerbaijani SSR. Taken alone, these three issues may not have seemed to present any insuperable problems; but, combined with the more tolerant attitude to public expression, national issues also soon came to the fore. Gorbachev and his administration were well aware of the delicate nature of the national question. As a native of the Caucasus, Gorbachev grew up among many different nationalities. However, he never attempted to impose any conception of the national question on Soviet citizens. There were few indications that he differed markedly from his predecessors on such matters.

The first manifestation of national protest in the Gorbachev period occurred as a result of changes in the ruling Politburo. Among the more obvious hangovers from the Brezhnev period were two figures that seemed to epitomize the alleged stagnation of that time – Ukrainian party leader Volodymyr Shcherbytsky and his counterpart in Kazakhstan, Dunmukhamed Kunayev. Gorbachev decided to leave the faithful servant Shcherbytsky in place. Since his appointment in 1972, Ukraine had been relatively quiet. Kunaev's regime, on the other hand, was notoriously corrupt. His replacement was anticipated, but the attempt to elevate Gennady Kolbin, an ethnic Russian, led to demonstrations and riots, mainly by students, in the Kazakh capital of Alma-Ata. Several deaths were reported. The incident remained an isolated one until 1987, when several demonstrations took place in the Baltic States on August 23, the 48th anniversary of the Molotov–Ribbentrop Pact. Later the same year, the Nagorno-Karabakh question began to escalate with protests in the Armenian capital of Yerevan demanding the return of the autonomous region to Armenia. By the following spring, the protests had mounted and had provoked, in turn, counter-protests from Azerbaijan. In the city of Sumgait, the capital of the region, there were violent ethnic clashes leaving thirty-two dead with scores more injured. Soon, both sides began to prepare for a major showdown. In November 1989, Moscow urged Azerbaijan to give more autonomy to Nagorno-Karabakh; and, when the Azeris refused, it eventually imposed direct rule from Moscow, though these measures did not end the violence.

Gorbachev also inherited the Crimean Tatar issue, and his government made a commendable attempt to resolve it. The Tatars began to protest in the streets of Moscow in the summer of 1987, and these protests continued for several months. In general, the reaction was positive. In May 1988, the first 300 Tatar families were allowed to return to the Crimea, posing a potential demographic predicament for the peninsula that was the holiday resort for many Soviet citizens, with a majority Russian population and the key naval base of Sevastopol, home of the Black Sea Fleet. In general, the returning Tatars formed a poor microcosm in Crimean society, though before long they made up more than 15 percent of the population on the peninsula. Ethnic clashes in various parts of the Soviet Union had become common by 1988–1989, often resulting from age-old issues. Uzbeks and Meshketian Turks (like the Tatars, original deportees of Stalin) were involved in violent skirmishes, for example, in the Fergana region of Uzbekistan in the summer of 1989; Georgians and Abkhazians were also in conflict in this same period in Sukhumi, capital of the Abkhazia Autonomous Republic.

Though one can point to the above specific issues as key points of the national question, there is no doubt that the de-Stalinization campaign conducted under the auspices of Glasnost lifted national issues on to a higher plane. *Pravda* and *Izvestiya* began to list victims of the purges, now rehabilitated, on a daily basis. The discovery of mass graves became more common, especially in non-Russian republics. In several republics, local activists began to focus on the way that Moscow had incorporated their homeland into the Soviet Union. We noted earlier the brutal invasions of Georgia and Azerbaijan. These events, however, were superseded by the more recent and highly contested annexation of the three Baltic States in 1940. That the latter had occurred under the auspices of the Nazi–Soviet Pact only helped catalyze movements to denounce that pact as illegal. The secret protocols to the pact had not been published hitherto in the Soviet Union, but the Estonians issued the full text in their local press in 1988, prompting the formation of a Supreme Soviet Commission to investigate the matter. Officially, the USSR denied the existence of the secret protocols and, after their publication, rejected the notion that they were linked to the so-called voluntary movement to join the Baltic States to the Soviet Union (Lapidus, Zaslavsky, and Goldman, 1992) and maintained that the Nazi invasion of the Soviet Union had rendered the pact null and void. The issue was critical, because a rejection of the pact would nullify – at least in the minds of the nationally conscious Baltic citizens – the reasons for Estonia, Latvia, and Lithuania joining the USSR.

These regional actions were directed against the central government in Moscow. As early as June 1988, activities in the Baltic States had developed to the point of forming an opposition party. Lithuania, a Catholic enclave, with a firm majority indigenous population, led the way. In June 1988 the Lithuanian Perestroika movement "Sajudis" was formed, a popular front comprised of both Communists and non-Communists. Popular Fronts were set up in Estonia and Latvia by October of the same year. The local Communist Party in Latvia was far from unpopular in so far as it had begun to steer a course independent of Moscow and the central line. Estonia, a tiny republic, with a language that was close to Finnish, had always enjoyed a certain freedom of expression. Estonians, however, were fearful of further immigration from Slavic groups (particularly Russians and Ukrainians) that might leave the native population in a minority. Consequently the government was prepared to test Moscow's resolve. In mid-November 1988 the Estonian Supreme Soviet declared that Estonia was a "sovereign" nation with the right to veto Soviet laws, and to use its natural resources as it saw fit. The announcement, premature though it may have been, pointed the way for the immediate future. The Baltic States soon reverted to their pre-Second World War national anthems and flags. More important, the local Communist Parties began to identify exclusively with local interests.

Popular Fronts became the established form of political opposition in the Soviet national republics. On October 30, 1988, the Popular Movement of Ukraine for "Perebudova", the Rukh, was born on the initiative of three reform-minded Communists: Ivan Drach, Volodymyr Yavorivsky, and Dmytro Pavlychko. The next month, the Uzbek "Birlik" Popular Front was created in the cotton-growing Central Asian Republic. The Moldavians followed suit in May 1989. In Belarus, the Communist government was stronger, and the Popular Front "Adradzhene" was compelled to hold its founding congress in Vilnius. An immediate media campaign was begun against the new movement, which was equated falsely with collaboration with the Nazi occupation regime in Belarus. The Popular Fronts coordinated local movements for self-assertion and, in the case of the Baltic States, a direct movement toward independence. In May 1989, Lithuania emulated Estonia and declared itself a sovereign state. The Soviet leadership in Moscow strongly condemned such moves, frequently sending Politburo members to the Baltic States to put pressure on the governments to withdraw their declarations. In late July, Latvia also declared its sovereignty. Though the three Baltic States were as notable for their contrasts as for their similarities, they formed a partnership in the movement to re-establish their independence. They were therefore the catalyst of the national self-expression, the touchstone by which Moscow could measure the degree to which it had lost control over its regions.

From the perspective of more than a decade, what strikes one about these events is the rapidity with which they developed, and the passivity and general inertia in the reaction from Moscow. In one sense, Gorbachev, by encouraging public opinion through Glasnost, had fostered such sentiments. Late-20th-century nationalism was an unexpected phenomenon to a confirmed Marxist, a retrogressive movement that appeared to hark back to an earlier century. On the other hand, new states were rediscovering their past, their history and their culture. This statement applied not only to the larger titular nations of the USSR but also to groups of non-Russians living in the Russian Federation, from the Chechens and the Tatars down to the Small Peoples of the North (which included groups that had long been on the verge of extinction). The Baltic States, however, appeared to be in the strongest position to begin the push toward independence. Lithuania led the way, especially after the Sajudis had gained a majority in the Lithuanian Supreme Soviet in February 1990. One month later, on March 11, Lithuania declared its independence. Moscow's response was, for once, prompt. A long column of tanks and armored trucks entered Vilnius, and a blockade of the republic began that prevented vital resources, such as coal and oil, from entering the territory. The outside world, particularly the United States, which had never recognized the Soviet annexation of the Baltic States, remained silent, torn between its principles and its desire to ensure that Gorbachev remained in office. On June 30, the Lithuanian government decided to postpone its decision to declare independence, and the blockade was removed.

Though, in general, Soviet forces did not intervene during the mass movements in the various republics, they did make several clumsy and ill-directed efforts to control the situation, or to mediate between groups during ethnic clashes. Invariably these cost the Gorbachev government dearly in terms of support. In April 1989, Soviet troops turned on a nationalist demonstration in Tblisi with toxic gas and then waded in with sharpened spades, killing several protestors. Georgian alienation from Moscow dates from this event, though the violent confrontations in the small republic involved Georgians and Ossetians, and Georgians and Meshketians, rather than ethnic Russians. Soviet troops also entered Baku with similar force in January 1990 in an attempt to restore order. The death toll this time was much higher. In Dushanbe, the capital of Tajikistan, the local population rioted in protest at the large number of refugees that had entered the country from Armenia after the December 1988 earthquake. Kyrgyz and Uzbeks fought in Kyrgyzstan in the summer of 1990. The Soviet Union had degenerated into a hotbed of ethnic conflict. It was no longer possible for the Moscow center to control the situation by force. Furthermore, while some republics were relatively homogenous (Ukraine and Belarus, for example, contained a large majority of Slavs) and free of ethnic conflict, others possessed the ad hoc Soviet borders that were a recipe for trouble.

The movement toward sovereignty in the summer of 1990 at times reached the heights of farce. Decentralization might have been logical in republics with significant populations, a common history and language, but it made less sense in tiny regions where the asserting group might number no more than a few thousand. Abkhazia and Tatarstan had declared their sovereignty by this time. In November 1990, the Chechen–Ingush autonomous region declared itself detached from both the Russian Federation and the Soviet Union, a prelude to the bloody conflict that was to break out between Russia and Chechnya in 1994. Bloodshed did occur in Lithuania early in 1991. In December 1990 the three parliaments of the Baltic States held a joint session, requesting that Soviet troops withdraw. They appealed to the Western powers for diplomatic recognition, and asked Moscow for acknowledgement of a gradual move to independence. How far Gorbachev was involved in the response that followed is a moot point. Soviet troops and armored vehicles attacked the radio and television centers in Vilnius in a sudden display of brute force that left thirteen people dead and dozens injured. Public opinion within the USSR turned strongly against Moscow's reaction, although the world seemed prepared to accept Gorbachev's statement that the actions had occurred without his assent.

1991 – the year of collapse

It was time, however, for the Soviet leader to deal with the splintering Union. It was already too late to try to keep the Baltic States within the USSR. The Communist parties, like the Popular Fronts, supported independence. On February 9, 1991, Lithuania put the question of independence to a popular vote, with more than 90 percent supporting the notion, and a turnout of more than 84 percent. The Estonians and Latvians followed suit on March 3, with 79 percent and 74 percent respectively in favor of independence – likely a reflection of the reticence of the Slavic populations on this issue. Gorbachev tried to save what was left. On February 6, he had appeared on Soviet television to announce a referendum on a new Union Treaty that would endorse a new Union of Soviet Sovereign Republics. The new treaty anticipated extensive concessions to the republics, which would be recognized as sovereign, determine their forms of government, and be allowed to negotiate directly with foreign countries (though not on foreign policy). The Moscow central government requested the right to legislate foreign and defense policies, and to remain in charge of taxation – a key issue as it would later transpire in its relations with the Russian Federation. Russia requested its own president, and in several republics additional points were added to the referendum, mainly concerning support for republican sovereignty. The draft treaty represented less a federal than a regional solution, with a very real possibility that the central government, now deprived of its party ruling base, would

exert little more than symbolic power. Nevertheless, it was Gorbachev's last opportunity to preserve the state that had been created by Lenin and consolidated and
expanded by Stalin.

The referendum was held on March 17. The result was a ringing endorsement
for the revised Union, with particularly strong support in Central Asia. Overall
support for the Union was around 76 percent. Though six republics did not take
part officially in the referendum (the three Baltic States, Moldova, Armenia, and
Georgia), some residents still voted, again with a significant majority supporting the
new structure. For the government the result was positive, but almost immediately
the signs of disintegration became apparent. Russia added the question of electing
its own president to the referendum, an issue that immediately cast doubt on the
viability of the new Union. The leading contender was again Yeltsin, who announced
that he would hold a rally of support in Moscow. The statement posed an immediate challenge to Gorbachev. Such a rally would undermine the results of the referendum and raise the question of whether he or Yeltsin controlled the capital. On the
advice of his police chief, Boris Pugo, he banned the rally and placed restrictions on
the media. The police did not, however, attempt to prevent the rally, which was held
in spite of Gorbachev's orders. Facing ignominious defeat, Gorbachev reacted at first
by trying to conciliate Yeltsin and forming a new alliance with him. But it was a pact
with the devil, since Yeltsin had no inclination to support the central power. The main
hope for Gorbachev now was that he could use the referendum to forge a new
Union, but it became apparent that several republics had little interest in remaining
in the USSR.

Georgia held a referendum on independence early in April, with more than
90 percent supporting the move. Zviad Gamsakhurdia, Chairman of the Georgian
Supreme Soviet, then declared Georgia to be independent of the USSR, with a
period of two to three years for full independence to take effect. With six republics
determined to take no further part in all-Union activities, Gorbachev was obliged
to meet leaders of the remaining nine – Russia, Ukraine, Belarus, Azerbaijan,
Uzbekistan, Kyrgyzstan, Tajikistan, Turkmenistan, and Kazakhstan. On April 23, they
signed a pact agreeing to a new Union Treaty, a draft of which would be ready in late
June. Two demagogic republican leaders then received convincing victories in local
presidential elections. Gamsakhurdia won the Georgian election of May 26 – a
result that was of limited significance because of Georgia's unwillingness to support
Gorbachev's initiatives. Then, on June 12, Yeltsin won the presidency in the Russian
Federation, defeating former premier Ryzhkov and Zhirinovsky, the populist and Russian
nationalist. Yeltsin's victory was ominous for Gorbachev, as his former friend and
now fiercest rival would immediately embark on a power struggle with the Moscow
center once he was sworn in as president on July 10.

Yeltsin took several steps that appeared to threaten the remaining fabric of the
Soviet state. He banned the Communist Party from the workplace (August 4),
demanded that enterprises on Russian territory pay taxes directly into the coffers of

the Russian Federation, and began to lay the foundations for Russia to develop its own military and security policies. Within the USSR a futile attempt was made by the Supreme Soviet to reduce the powers of President Gorbachev. However, several reformers, including Yakovlev, Shevardnadze, Shatalin, Gavriil Popov, and Anatoly Sobchak formed a Movement for Democratic Reform. The key issue, however, was the confirmation of the new Union that was to take place on August 20, and would reduce permanently the authority of the central powers in Moscow. This forthcoming event, and Yeltsin's push to amass his own personal power in Russia were decisive in the move by hard-line Communists to reverse the process of decentralization in an attempted putsch on August 19–21. The putsch, sometimes seen as the decisive event of 1991, was reminiscent more of Kornilov's pathetic effort to take over Petrograd in August 1917. Gorbachev, in this respect, resembles Kerensky in his general ineffectiveness and inability to stop a new popular force, in this instance led by Boris Yeltsin. On August 18, the plotters, all members of Gorbachev's administration, and led by KGB chief Vladimir Kryuchkov, police chief Boris Pugo, and Vice-President Gennady Yanayev, placed Gorbachev under house arrest in the Crimea, where he was vacationing with his wife Raisa. Gorbachev was ordered to declare a state of emergency in the country and to hand over power to a State Committee to deal with the crisis. However, whatever the plotters might have promised him, Gorbachev did not agree.

The attempted putsch had little chance of success. Though tanks moved through Moscow in the early hours of August 19, the plotters had left far too many loopholes to make good on their threats. Though placed under surveillance, Yeltsin somehow managed to leave his dacha and make his way to the Russian White House, where he stage-managed the resistance, at one point climbing on to a tank to express his defiance. He was able to send messages through a Moscow-based Internet service and with the help of Radio Liberty. The plotters were too feeble or too drunk to attempt to use force against protests on the streets. There was no public backing for a move to turn back the clock and restore central authority in Moscow. At a press conference on August 19, the State Committee declared that Gorbachev was ill and therefore Yanayev had taken over and declared a state of emergency. Protestors began to discuss the situation openly with the troops, and quickly set up barricades. This was Yeltsin's finest moment in more ways than one. While publicly he could pose as the defender of public liberty, Glasnost, and democracy, behind the scenes he could exploit the backlash to consolidate his authority. He called openly for the release and restoration of the Soviet President while ensuring that, if and when Gorbachev did return to Moscow, he would be virtually powerless. The putsch thus accelerated events, but other than that it constituted no more than high-level drama, publicized on CNN, featuring several apparatchiks who were making decisions on the spot as events unfolded. At his press conference, Yanayev's hands were shaking so badly that few observers paid much heed to him. By August 20, some 200,000 people had gathered at the White House to oppose the putsch. By the next morning the leaders of the rebellion were either in flight, or – in the case of Pugo and his wife – had committed suicide. Some went to the Crimea to consult Gorbachev and were returned to Moscow on the presidential plane. For the Soviet president and his wife, it had been a terrifying ordeal. For the rest of the country the key event was Yeltsin's usurpation of power.

By the time Gorbachev returned to Moscow, Yeltsin had gained control over the armed forces of the Soviet Union. He paraded Gorbachev before the Congress, denouncing the Soviet leader's apparent attempt to speak in favor of the Communist Party – an astonishing comment to have made under the circumstances. Yeltsin pointed out that the plotters were all Gorbachev appointees. The Communist Party was placed under a temporary ban and its assets frozen. On August 24, Gorbachev resigned as General Secretary of the CC CPSU (though he remained Soviet president), and a mob tore down the statue of Feliks Dzerzhinsky outside the Lubyanka in central Moscow. In the wake of the failed putsch (and in two cases even during it), the Soviet republics began to declare independence, with Estonia, Latvia, Ukraine, and Belarus leading the way. The Baltic States were merely confirming earlier decisions, and by early September both the United States and the USSR had recognized their independence. Eventually the Central Asian republics, which had remained more docile and passive, also decided to proclaim their independence. The development was less straightforward than it appeared. In Moldova, for example, a breakaway Trans-Dnestr SSR was formed in September, with the backing of the Soviet military, and it seemed unlikely that the Moldavians would be able to sustain an independent state. Some republics declared independence not to fulfill any age-old dream but simply because there appeared to be no alternatives – Belarus, for example, lacked a strong independence movement even in the parliament where there were only thirty-two divided opposition deputies. Ukraine had proposed a referendum for December 1 to confirm independence, and the question was whether the move would be secession from the Soviet Union or from a revitalized Russia.

The Russian Federation did not declare independence in the summer of 1991. Rather it continued to take part in a power struggle with the Soviet Union throughout the rest of the year. By November, Yeltsin had declared himself the Russian prime minister, and asserted that the Russian Council of Ministers was the de facto authority on the territory of Russia. What remained for Gorbachev and the Congress of People's Deputies? Essentially, his power was limited to the walls of the Kremlin. On December 1, the electorate of Ukraine voted overwhelmingly for independence, with a majority vote even in the disputed territory of the Crimea, which had retained its autonomous status earlier in the year. Leonid Kravchuk, the former Communist Party ideological chief in Ukraine and Chairman of the Parliament, was elected President on the same day. The final act was to take place in Belarus, when Yeltsin and Kravchuk flew to Minsk to meet with Belarusian parliamentary chairman Stanislau Shushkevich. Kazakhstan's President Nursultan Nazarbayev had also been invited but declined to attend. Yeltsin attended only on condition that Gorbachev was not invited. Consequently, the meeting acquired the air of subterfuge. The three leaders adjourned to a hunting lodge on the Belavezha estate in the western part of the republic where they proclaimed the dissolution of the Soviet Union and its replacement by a loose federation called the Commonwealth of Independent States. Though two of the leaders had received public backing in elections (Yeltsin and Kravchuk), none really had the authority to arrogate such powers to the meeting. Gorbachev predictably regarded the move as a betrayal of the agreement to a new Union Treaty. Whether a USSR remained was a matter for conjecture, but Gorbachev was undoubtedly justified in his statement that these three figures could not legitimately decide its fate over drinks in this rural setting. None the less, the Belavezha meeting brought the Soviet period to an end. Other republics were invited to join the new federation, the existence of which made the Soviet Union superfluous. On December 25, the Soviet flag was taken down, and by the end of the year the USSR ceased to exist as a fact of law.

The Soviet legacy in retrospect

How should one define the Soviet legacy? We have argued that since the conflict of 1941–1945 the Soviet image was quietly linked with that of the ethnic Russian population. Links with the tsarist past were discovered and maintained by Soviet historians. In the 1980s, however, all the graven images of the Soviet Union collapsed, and the country ceased to be a world power. Russia ultimately proved stronger than the USSR – a factor that was exploited by Yeltsin, who had the cunning to undermine and remove Gorbachev and install a system of ruling clans, operating through control of resources. One could argue that Yeltsin was hardly the most powerful figure and that frequently he responded to the demands of new oligarchs. Dimitri K. Simes points out (Simes, 1999) that it is impossible in any of Yeltsin's writings, or those of his associates, or that author's own meetings with the former Russian leader, to discern any political philosophy. In Simes's view, Yeltsin had no vision or conception of what sort of Russia he wished to create. He was, none the less, the pivotal figure for some time, and his re-election in 1996 determined the direction that Russia would take for the next several years. To many Communists, Yeltsin is an even greater traitor than Gorbachev. The latter made mistakes and struggled to find a clear policy, but Yeltsin deliberately cast aside the former system and linked himself with the West, at least in so far as economic policy was concerned. Such analysis is simplistic in that the system had begun to crumble long before Yeltsin applied the final coup de grâce. Was there anything in the former system worth preserving? Was it, as Ronald Reagan once said, "an evil empire"?

It may be too early to write dispassionately about the Soviet Union. To many, it ended in failure. This failure may have been a result of the way in which the Bolsheviks seized power – a small group taking control of a vast nation that owed them little allegiance. There were certain notable landmarks in its 74-year history: the social upheaval of 1929–1933, the purges, and the victory during the war being the most obvious. There were also some significant achievements. In the Soviet period, rural Russia became a modern industrial society; for a short time it led the world in the space race, and rivaled the United States in the accumulation of weaponry. It eliminated illiteracy and developed in the natural sciences particularly an educational system of world renown. Soviet athletes competed with the world's best and excelled in many areas. Behind these attainments was the façade of a democratic state united behind the ideas of Lenin and – for a significant period – Stalin. The goal of spreading revolution and attaining an inevitable victory in a lengthy conflict with capitalism remained in place until the Gorbachev period. It seems in retrospect to have been a forlorn hope, but at certain times, such as 1949 when China became Communist and the Soviet Union detonated an atomic bomb, the capitalist world did fear this conflict. The Cold War derived partly from fear of Russia, fear of the Soviet Union. Once Stalin had decided that the state would become stronger, rather than wither away, as Lenin had forecast, then centralization of power solidified. The state also adopted Russian imperialist goals from the past. Soviet and Russian goals for a period became indistinguishable. The promotion of Russia and Russians throughout the empire caused resentment in the non-Russian republics. It was never an official policy but it existed none the less from 1945 onward.

Ultimately the Soviet period will be seen as a demonstration of the failure of the Communist experiment in the 20th century; of the failure of the ideas of Marx and Engels, combined with the doctrine of Lenin. Many critics claim that the form of Communism adopted in Russia became truly Russian in form, and that it was hardly representative of what a socialist state might turn out to be. Still others believe that a socialist state would always suffer from certain flaws, and that the Soviet Union was a typical example of the problems that arise from the attempt to establish an egalitarian system. The form that the Soviet Union took was a result of a combination of historical circumstances and political and military conflict. It also developed into the Stalin dictatorship, one that bore some resemblance to the tsarist past, tying peasants to the land and establishing a ruling elite. However, it was much more intrusive and thorough. The 1920s and particularly the 1930s were the formative years. Historians continue to debate this era even more than the years of the war. It has been argued that civic life in this period was less cataclysmic than it appears from the death toll. On the other hand, can there have been a period that caused so much suffering to a people in peacetime? Even Nazi Germany's gruesome record was accumulated mainly after the outbreak of the Second World War. For residents of the Soviet Union, there was little to match in horror the two periods 1914–1921 and 1929–1945. Though the events of those periods took place mainly in the European part of the country, the Asian areas were hardly immune. The Gulag camp system spread widely here; and much of the war effort stemmed from new factories in Siberia.

The Western observer is struck by the relative passivity of Russians during a time of conflict. Life continued amid the storm. Workers moved to the factories and, at least for a time, believed that they were building a new society, a Soviet utopia. Citizens made extraordinary sacrifices on behalf of their country. During the war, Hitler, for example, could never understand how the Soviet Union could continue to fight after losing more than 600,000 troops at Vyazma, west of Moscow; or after the loss of 90 percent of Stalingrad (the French and the Dutch had not been willing to endure much smaller losses). Why were residents prepared to fight for a regime that had wrought such havoc on them, taken away their food supply, and purged members of one in three families? Without resorting to platitudes (and bearing in mind the pat response that there was little choice given the ruthlessness of the occupation), one can say that there is something exclusively Russian about this attitude, a superior resilience despite apparent reluctance to rebel against tyranny imposed by one's own state. The call of the Motherland was the rallying cry during the period of German occupation. Stalin above all was quick to recognize also the need for an external enemy, whether fictional or real, and many of the events of the Cold War could be justified in this way. Propaganda played a key role in the survival and expansion of the Soviet Union. It became more sophisticated and convincing with time. Perhaps it was precisely when the USSR did attain military parity with the West that it was at its weakest; as the external threat receded, attention focused on internal anomalies and injustices.

Finally, the USSR was held together by force and coercion. The Party, the army, and the KGB were the key tools. As long as they remained in place, there could be no internal opposition in Russia, and only minimal dissension within the non-Russian republics. By the Brezhnev period, both the military and the KGB had representatives in the ruling Politburo. After the demise of Beria, the KGB did not pose a threat to the authority of the Party, but remained subordinate and working toward the same goals. The internal repression decreased after 1953 but it did not disappear entirely. Occasionally the regime would resort to violence and to force against perceived enemies. The KGB remained active throughout the Soviet period (with a variety of acronyms and tasks). At times it was a formidable source of power; at others it made some astonishing blunders. The KGB ultimately could not foment world revolution, but it could defend the state against its enemies. Often it exceeded its assigned limits, contravening the Constitution. But, like any secret service, it did not determine future relations with the West, it was not responsible for any major political changes, and its flaws have to be measured together with its assets. The Communist Party, Lenin's creation, was the decisive factor in the stability and continuation of the Soviet experiment. It was an elite force that resembled a collection of gangsters in Stalin's time, but became the arbiter of the future of families and careers. In contemporary Russia, and in the post-Soviet states, former party members remain in control just as in the past. In contrast, former dissident leaders have faded into political oblivion. Without the Party, as it declined and was ultimately destroyed by Yeltsin and Gorbachev, the system created by the Bolsheviks was doomed to failure.

Questions for discussion

1. How would you define Perestroika, and what did it entail?
2. Why did the national question emerge as a crucial issue under Gorbachev?
3. Did the Soviet Union develop a civil society in 1985–1990?
4. How important was the Cold War in bringing about the collapse of the Soviet Union?
5. Discuss the successes and failures of Gorbachev's attempts to limit the power of the Communist Party.

Recent works

Adlam, Carol. *Women in Russian Literature after Glasnost: Female Alternatives.* London: Legenda, 2005.

Bain, Mervyn. *Soviet–Cuban Relations, 1985 to 1991: Changing Perceptions in Moscow and Havana.* Lanham, Md: Lexington Books, 2007.

Breslauer, George W. *Gorbachev and Yeltsin as Leaders.* Cambridge: Cambridge University Press, 2002.

Brown, Archie. *Gorbachev, Yeltsin, and Putin: Political Leadership in Russia's Transition.* Washington, DC: Carnegie Endowment for International Peace, 2001.

Brown, Archie. *Seven Years That Changed the World: Perestroika in Perspective.* Oxford: Oxford University Press, 2007.

Daniels, Robert V. *The Rise and Fall of Communism in Russia.* New Haven, Conn.: Yale University Press, 2007.

Earley, Pete. *Comrade J: The Untold Secrets of Russia's Master Spy in America after the End of the Cold War.* New York: G. P. Putnam's Sons, 2007.

Goldman, Marshall I. *The Piratization of Russia: Russian Reform Goes Awry.* London: Routledge, 2003.

Gorbachev, Mikhail S. *Conversations with Gorbachev: On Perestroika, the Prague Spring, and the Crossroads of Socialism.* New York: Columbia University Press, 2002.

Grachev, A. S. *Gorbachev's Gamble: Soviet Foreign Policy and the End of the Cold War.* Cambridge: Polity, 2008.

Graebner, Norman A. *Reagan, Bush, Gorbachev: Revisiting the End of the Cold War.* Westport, Conn.: Praeger Security International, 2008.

Hale, Henry E. *Why Not Parties in Russia? Democracy, Federalism, and the State.* Cambridge: Cambridge University Press, 2006.

Harkins, Susan S. *The Fall of the Soviet Union, 1991.* Hockessin, Del.: Mitchell Lane, 2008.

Harris, Jonathan. *Subverting the System: Gorbachev's Reform of the Party's Apparat, 1986–1991.* Lanham, Md: Rowman & Littlefield, 2004.

Head, Tom. *Mikhail Gorbachev.* San Diego, Calif.: Greenhaven Press, 2003.

Herspring, Dale R. *The Kremlin and the High Command: Presidential Impact on the Russia Military from Gorbachev to Putin.* Lawrence, Kan.: University Press of Kansas, 2006.

Jordan, Pamela A. *Defending Rights in Russia: Lawyers, the State, and Legal Reform in the Post-Soviet Era.* Vancouver: UBC Press, 2005.

Langley, Andrew. *The Collapse of the Soviet Union: The End of an Empire.* Minneapolis, Minn.: Compass Point Books, 2007.

Marples, David R. *The Collapse of the Soviet Union, 1985–1991*. Harlow: Longman, 2004.

Matlock, Jack F. *Reagan and Gorbachev: How the Cold War Ended.* New York: Random House, 2004.

Njølstad, Olav. *The Last Decade of the Cold War: From Conflict Escalation to Conflict Transformation.* London: Frank Cass, 2004.

O'Connor, Kevin. *Intellectuals and Apparatchiks: Russian Nationalism and the Gorbachev Revolution.* Lanham, Md: Lexington Books, 2006.

Sandle, Mark. *Gorbachev: Man of the Twentieth Century.* London: Hodder Arnold, 2005.

Sherlock, Thomas. *Historical Narratives in the Soviet Union and Post Soviet Russia: Destroying the Settled Past, Creating an Uncertain Future*. Basingstoke: Palgrave Macmillan, 2007.

Shevchenko, Iulia. *Central Government of Russia: From Gorbachev to Putin.* Aldershot: Ashgate, 2004.

Shulgan, Christopher. *The Soviet Ambassador: The Making of the Radical behind Perestroika.* Toronto: McClelland & Stewart, 2008.

Skinner, Kiron K. *Turning Points in Ending the Cold War.* Stanford, Calif.: Hoover Institution Press, Stanford University, 2008.

Stoner-Weiss, Kathryn. *Resisting the State: Reform and Retrenchment in Post-Soviet Russia.* Cambridge: Cambridge University Press, 2006.

Zemtsov, Ilya. *Gorbachev: The Man and the System.* Edison, NJ: Transaction Publishers, 2008.

9

From Yeltsin to Putin: Russia's decline and recovery, 1992–2008

The failure of the Soviet experiment was followed by a decade of uncertainty and lack of leadership in Russia. Initially, from the Western perspective, hopes were high that Russia would embark on a program to transform the economy while maintaining and developing the democratic aspects of the state that had begun in the Gorbachev period. Prime Minister Yegor Gaidar had control over the economy and began by freeing prices on January 2, 1992. The decision was an unpopular one and caused great hardship among the population. Yet hopes remained high. Western countries announced a $24 billion aid package to Russia in April. Considerable progress was also made on arms reduction; and, by January 1993, Russian President Boris Yeltsin and US President George Bush met in Moscow to sign the Treaty on the Further Reduction and Limitation of Strategic Arms (START II). Relations between the two superpowers were notably good. However, the Yeltsin administration faced significant internal problems, particularly the division of authority between the government (essentially the presidency) and the legislature (the Congress of Deputies). The latter opposed market reforms and resented Yeltsin's cavalier approach to such measures, believing that they were being forced on Russians by outside forces.

What was the Russian Federation? The vast territory, stretching over six time zones, contained eighty-three "federal subjects," made up of forty-six oblasts (provinces), twenty-one autonomous republics, nine territories (krais), four autonomous districts (okrugs), one autonomous oblast, and two federal cities (Moscow and Leningrad). In March 1992 a Federation Treaty was signed based on the work of a commission to assess the future relationship between the central government and the regions. Inevitably perhaps, it was an unsatisfactory affair that left much undecided. Moscow made separate agreements with several republics, most notably Sakha, Bashkortostan, and Karelia. Some republics had vast resources and had options for even more autonomy. Some of the issues would be resolved with the approval of the so-called Yeltsin Constitution in December 1993, accepted only after a bitter conflict with the Russian Parliament. The first problems facing the President were a result of the lack of clarity in relations between the center and the regions. There appeared to be a serious danger that the provinces – on paper, less powerful than the regions – might also be disaffected if Moscow did not permit significant autonomy, decision-making, and control over resources. The situation was a natural consequence of Perestroika, which had led to the withdrawal of power from the center and to the empowerment of regional leaders, many of whom were firmly established in office.

Russia also emerged as the natural heir to the Soviet Union. This development was not as obvious as it may have seemed. To the international community, Russia represented the post-Soviet world. Soviet embassies, for example, quietly became Russian. Moscow began to assume the role of watchdog over the territories of the former USSR. The Russian Federation, even in 1991, had begun to express concern about activities in what was termed the Near Abroad. Many Russians were now cut off from Russia, whereas previously they had been living in distant regions of one empire. When conflict broke out, such as the civil war in Tajikistan, it seemed natural that Russian troops would be called in to maintain order. A form of mini-imperialism was apparent, whereby Russia was the main arbiter of disputes in the former Soviet Union. In larger states, such as Kazakhstan and Ukraine, Russia's role became more complex. Kazakhs, like leaders of the Baltic States, were anxious to begin to erode Russian influence, but it was difficult as long as the West recognized Russian interests in the former Soviet regions. As in the past, Ukraine was the critical region, particularly since its borders were those established by Stalin during the Great Patriotic War, and it retained the Crimean peninsula, transferred to Soviet Ukraine from Russia in 1954 to mark the 300th anniversary of the Treaty of Pereyaslav, when Russia and Ukraine joined forces against the Poles. Crimea had a majority Russian population and, along with Russians living in Estonia and Latvia, represented Yeltsin's chief concern in 1991–1992. In addition to these border questions, Ukraine also possessed nuclear weapons. Whereas the other states in this position, Belarus and Kazakhstan, quickly agreed to transfer these weapons to the Russian Federation for dismantling, Ukraine debated the issue, fearful of Russian pretensions to Ukrainian territory.

Yeltsin had the unqualified backing of the West at this point, specifically of the United States and its Western European allies, which placed pressure on Ukraine to give up its weapons. Under Kravchuk, Ukraine eventually complied. When it did so, however, it gained equal favor with the West, thereby weakening Yeltsin's position. Until 1994, Russia would retain the status of most favored post-Soviet nation in terms of loans, credit, aid, and international recognition. However, after the start of the war in Chechnya in December 1994, this situation would change as Ukraine replaced Russia as the key ally of the United States in the former Soviet landmass. By that time, Russia arguably was no longer a democracy. The internal struggle had turned into a civil conflict, albeit one that took place only in the streets of Moscow. By March 1993, by which time Viktor Chernomyrdin had replaced Gaidar as Prime Minister, the government had made an attempt to break down the obstinate Parliament, which was – in his view – blocking the path to reform. The Congress Speaker was a Chechen, Ruslan Khasbulatov, and on March 23 he called for the impeachment of Boris Yeltsin. An initial conflict was averted by a referendum in Russia on April 25, which expressed support (though hardly unqualified) for the President and his reforms. Just over 60 percent of the electorate took part in the referendum; 58.7 percent expressed confidence in Yeltsin's presidency, and 53 percent supported his social and economic policies. These were far from convincing results, and it was no more than a temporary truce as both sides prepared for a final showdown. On September 21, 1993, the President dissolved the Congress of People's Deputies and the Supreme Soviet, and demanded the election of a new Federal Assembly. In the meantime Yeltsin began to rule by presidential decree.

Much of 1993 was taken up by an acute struggle over a new Constitution for the Russian Federation. After the referendum, Yeltsin tried vainly to push forward an alternative plan for the Constitution that would have strengthened presidential vis-à-vis parliamentary authority. Parliament, in turn, firmly blocked these new initiatives. In the summer, the President and Parliament agreed to the formation of a Constitutional Commission. During this period, Russia came as close as at any time to civil war. Both sides refused to give way, and each backed its views with marches and demonstrations by its supporters. Though Yeltsin might be considered to have been struggling against revanchist forces, it is clear that he violated his constitutional authority when he dissolved the legislature. Yeltsin had also proposed a new referendum on December 12 on the new Constitution and elections to a two-tier parliament – the State Duma and the Council of the Federation. Such maneuvers also incensed V. D. Zorkin, Chairman of the Constitutional Court, and it seemed conceivable that Yeltsin might be impeached. In the meantime, two days after its dissolution, and on the initiative of Khasbulatov, an extraordinary Congress of Deputies "relieved" Yeltsin of his duties, and appointed in his stead Aleksandr Rutskoy, a veteran of the Soviet war in Afghanistan.

A violent confrontation followed, as Rutskoy at once began to establish a military headquarters in the Russian White House and to collect weapons of various kinds. Zorkin pleaded for a compromise that would have seen the annulment of all decrees issued by both sides from September 21, but the time for compromise had passed. Parliament briefly gained the upper hand when forces loyal to it attacked the Ostankino television station and occupied the Mayor's office. Ultimately, however, the Russian military and the Defense Minister, Pavel S. Grachev, remained loyal to the President. After several skirmishes on the streets of Moscow on October 2–3, tanks turned on the White House, the scene only three years earlier of Yeltsin's defiant stand against the attempted putsch. At least 150 people died inside the parliament building, and scores more were injured. Russia was to become a presidential republic. Was this a victory for the forces of democracy? Hardly. Ironically, the hard-line parliamentarians should have benefited from the support of the guardians of Russian democracy. The international community remained virtually silent during the violent clashes, shocked at the sudden deterioration in Russia but relieved that Yeltsin had succeeded. In truth, the West did not have another champion. The question arises why Yeltsin, the populist Russian president, should have resorted to Soviet-style measures to maintain the authority of the presidency. The answer, however, is disarmingly simple. Yeltsin was a political leader of limited vision, nurtured by the Communist Party and used to getting his way by ruthless use of force. His truculence had already been displayed several times during the Gorbachev era. It was seen more nakedly once he gained power. No one should have expected a Western style or even an Eastern European style of new democrat. The champion of the new Russia was in reality preoccupied with maintaining and promoting his own authority.

After his victory, the Russian Federation structure was revamped and the Congress of People's Deputies and Supreme Soviet were eliminated and replaced by a federal structure in the Yeltsin Constitution of December 12, 1993. The country was now run by a Federal Assembly that consisted of two houses: the lower house, or State Duma, consisting of 450 deputies; and the upper house, the Federation Council, made up of 176 deputies. The name Federation Council had also been used since 1990 to encompass the Chairman of the Supreme Soviet of the Russian Federation and the chairs of local councils of the different regions and districts. According to the 1993 Constitution, the Federation Council includes two representatives from each "subject" of the Russian Federation. Based on an amendment of December 1995, these representatives are the head of the legislative sector and the head of the executive branch. Although membership of the Federation Council changed with new elections in the republics and the regions, the Council is a permanent body. The Council has authority to approve or reject laws adopted by the Duma and in theory can sanction the removal of the President with a two-thirds majority. Members of the Duma were elected for four-year terms (amended to five years in 2008). Until the 2007 elections, one half of its members were elected according to a system of proportional representation and the other half through a plurality of votes in single-member constituencies, with members being required to be at least 21 years of age. After 2007, all members were elected by proportional representation according to party lists, and with a minimum 7 percent required for the party to acquire seats in the assembly.

Under Yeltsin in the 1990s, Russia continued to founder. A new business elite emerged with close ties to the government, intent on rapid enrichment through the control of minerals and natural resources, and close ties to the former ruling nomenklatura. Such a development was not unusual, since the Russian consumer industry had long subsisted on the black market. The official economy began to deteriorate. The Russian rouble, which some economists anticipated could take over as the new currency in the nations of the Near Abroad, plummeted on October 11, 1994. By February 1995, 500,000 Russian coal miners announced a new strike for higher salaries. The Gaidar years were over, economic reform already denounced as unworkable. For millions of residents of the Russian Federation, shock therapy was a disaster – a Western cure for the troubles of Russia that was destined to fail. Yeltsin's popularity fell faster than that of Gorbachev in 1990–1991. Yeltsin increasingly relied on a close network of associates, led by the office of the Prime Minister and the Security Council. In late November 1994, the Security Council took the lead in the decision to send Russian troops into the breakaway republic of Chechnya, which had declared independence in 1991 (Dunlop, 1998; Lieven, 1999). The invasion began on December 12, and by the end of the year Russian troops had advanced to the Chechen capital of Grozny.

The decision to go to war was a fateful one. The Russians were not adequately prepared for protracted guerrilla warfare, though they were clearly superior to the Chechens in direct ground campaigns. Why was the decision taken? Did the Chechens constitute a threat to the security of the Federation? Or was the war intended as a diversion from the disastrous domestic situation? It reflected above all the weakening grasp of the President over state policy.

Parallels with Brezhnev were only too evident. Like the former Soviet General Secretary, Yeltsin also suffered from poor health in his sixties. In July 1995 he suffered his first heart attack, with a second in late October. Corruption became widespread, with Yeltsin's family and oligarch friends the main beneficiaries. The President became very much a peripheral figure, sick for lengthy periods and returning to the Kremlin only at brief intervals. He depended upon his subordinates for the conduct of day-to-day business in the Kremlin. However, there was no stability in office; replacements of key officials, particularly of the Prime Minister and the Foreign Minister, were frequent. The war in Chechnya went badly. In January 1995, Russian troops had captured the presidential palace in Grozny, after which Chechen leader Dzhokar Dudayev abandoned the capital city. Dudayev was killed by a laser-guided missile in April 1996, by which time the Chechens had resorted to guerrilla warfare and terrorism, tactics that were much more successful against the conventional Russian army. The death of Dudayev coincided with a new presidential election campaign. Yeltsin's opponents, particularly the Russian Communist Party under Zyuganov, seemed destined to win a famous victory. Yeltsin took the blame for the poor economic state of the country, the catastrophic drop in living standards of many Russian citizens, the high levels of crime and gangsterism. Along with the failure to defeat the small forces of the Chechens, Yeltsin's recovery appeared almost impossible.

However, in a grand finale to his political career, Yeltsin succeeded in winning a new term in office. Prior to the election, he once again played the Russian nationalist card that had served him well in the past. In March 1996 he signed an agreement for closer relations with Belarus, Kazakhstan, and Kyrgyzstan. A few days later, Yeltsin and Belarusian president Alyaksandr Lukashenka put their signatures to the formation of a new alliance between Russia and Belarus, expected by both parties to be the prelude to a formal union between the two neighboring states. Yeltsin also turned his attention to Ukraine, reviving issues that had led to harsh words between the two countries in 1991 – the question of the status of the Russian language in Ukraine, and the division of the Black Sea Fleet. Within a year, Yeltsin and Leonid Kuchma, the new Ukrainian president, were to sign a new Treaty of Friendship and Cooperation, which shelved the language issue and divided up the fleet, with Ukraine leasing to Russia two bays at Sevastopol. Yeltsin also had powerful friends, including figures such as Boris Berezovsky and Vladimir Gusinsky, who between them controlled the major television stations. Zyuganov, an earnest but dull politician, offered little that was new. Even his Communism was watered down by rhetorical platitudes on

Russian nationalism. On July 3, Yeltsin defeated Zyuganov in a run-off election, and began his second term as President of the Russian Federation.

From a period of crisis in 1992–1996, Yeltsin's final years as president degener-ated into unseemly farce. This began in late 1996 with a humiliating peace accord with the Chechens, known as the Hasavyurt Treaty, following the end of combat operations in July. Yeltsin was not around to witness this débâcle (the treaty was signed on Russia's behalf by General Aleksandr Lebed) as he was undergoing quintuple bypass surgery. Many observers wondered whether he would survive the operation. Though he did so, he remained for the rest of his term a virtual invalid, hardly coherent when he spoke, and absent from Moscow for long periods of convalescence. The year 1997 was notable for the signing of several treaties, inspired mainly by the astute Foreign Minister, Yevgeny Primakov. They included the treaty with Ukraine, confirmation of a new Union Treaty with Belarus in early April, and a Founding Act on Mutual Relations, Cooperation, and Security between NATO and the Russian Federation. This treaty, signed with US President Bill Clinton, permitted Russia a voice in a new permanent joint council that was responsible for NATO's decision-making. The agreement alleviated Russian isolation, though it did little to prevent the con-cept of expansion of NATO, which was taking place despite the protests of Russia, and involving at first the Czech Republic, Hungary, and Poland. In June 1998 the Russians also mediated an end to the civil war in Tajikistan.

In 1998, Russia experienced a dramatic financial collapse. It coincided with increased tension between the President and the Duma (which had replaced the former Congress of Deputies and the Supreme Soviet). It took place amid a flurry of high-level political changes as the President desperately sought scapegoats for the economic problems. On March 23, Yeltsin dismissed Chernomyrdin, reorgan-ized the Cabinet, and announced the appointment of Sergey Kiriyenko as the new Prime Minister. After protracted debates, the Duma accepted the new appointment on April 24. Kiriyenko was young, a businessman, and a reformer. He was also virtually unknown. By mid-August, the Russian stock market had plunged. Western financiers, such as George Soros, called for the devaluation of the rouble. On August 14, Yeltsin insisted that he would never take such a step. Three days later, Kiriyenko announced the devaluation, with the Russian market desperately short of liquid assets. One week later, Yeltsin appeared on the Moscow scene to remove the entire Cabinet, announcing that he would reappoint Chernomyrdin as acting Prime Minister. The Duma refused to sanction the appointment, twice turning it down. A brave and healthy president might have dismissed the Duma at this point (a move considered by Yeltsin when it had appeared that he might lose the 1996 election). Instead he put forward Primakov as the new Prime Minister, which by now could be regarded as no more than a temporary post. Primakov was to last eight months before being replaced by Sergey Stepashin. In May 1999 a vote to impeach the President failed in the Duma. In August, Stepashin was also removed and replaced by Vladimir Putin, a former aide to Anatoly Sobchak, the late mayor of St Petersburg. By this time, the situation in Chechnya was again causing alarm following a sortie into Daghestan by Chechen rebels led by Shamil Basayev in August and September 1999. In September there were bomb blasts in two Moscow apartment blocks, killing more than 130 people. Other explosions occurred in Volgodonsk and at the Russian army base in Buynaksk. Putin advised a new invasion of the rebel province, which began on October 1.

The eight years of Yeltsin's presidency were an adverse time for most Russians, though his successor, Vladimir V. Putin, exaggerated the extent of the crisis to promote his own regime. Speaking in New York in March 2002, former president Gorbachev, another partial observer, described them thus – "Chaos in the economy, chaos in the social sphere, chaos in the federation, chaos in the army, chaos everywhere." The country seemed to have lost its way after its sudden emergence from the ashes of the Soviet Union in January 1992. To take power, Yeltsin had used the newly created office of Russian President and the disaffection of Russians for the Soviet system. Yet the post-Soviet state was troubled from the outset by the tumultuous events of the Gorbachev years. It required a period of recovery, but instead it entered an economic battle zone, as ruthless "businessmen" fought over the spoils of a collapsed state. These spoils had to be negotiated with the former nomenklatura (or, more accurately, the second-string nomenklatura following the removal of the top level). The leading figures – who became oligarchs – amassed fortunes. The Yeltsin family was similarly enriched, which may have been one reason why the sick president clung on to power. Another may have been his fear of retribution. The constant changes of prime minister may have reflected Yeltsin's desire to choose a successor who would not turn against him. With the appointment of Putin, that question had been resolved. Curiously, Yeltsin's standing both in Russia and internationally had not fallen completely. There were still acolytes who had not lost their faith in him. One was Boris Nemtsov, the young governor of Nizhny Novgorod who had become the First Deputy Prime Minister in the latter part of Yeltsin's presidency, and continued to speak admiringly of Yeltsin's achievements. The notable feature about the Yeltsin presidency was the relatively short-lived demise of dismissed officials. Regularly they were returned to some high office. The leadership resembled a clan system, in which it was virtually impossible to fall far from grace unless the sin committed was too great to be forgiven.

The country's social system was also fluid enough to allow mercurial social mobility and the accumulation of unheard-of wealth. This largess manifested itself in a number of ways: the appearance of foreign cars, clogging the streets of Moscow and St Petersburg; the flight of new capital to foreign bank accounts; conflict between rival groups – though the scale of the fight for control of resources began to taper off by the late 1990s; in addition to the appearance of Russian businessmen in foreign centers such as New York and Toronto, Western Europe, and Cyprus. During this rapid transformation of Russian society, nothing disappeared more rapidly than the Soviet legacy. Only the older generation paid tribute to past events, such as the victory in the war over Germany, the November 7 Revolution Day, or Lenin's birthday. For those under 40, change came easily, and a younger generation that could barely remember more than a few years in the Pioneers quickly adapted to a new life that was unstable but offered rewards mainly outside the official economy. The new oligarchs, for their part, were happy with the Yeltsin regime as long as it allowed them to pursue their own interests with impunity. They feared Zyuganov and the Communists because of their support for state control over enterprises and resources.

During this interim period – for it appeared to be a time of virtual anarchy until Russia restored its customary authoritarian rule under Putin – there was a distinct lack of ideological and spiritual guidance for Russian citizens. For more than sixty-five years, the cult of Lenin had been in place, and for many of those years Lenin represented Russia more than the Bolshevik Party. As an object of worship, Lenin, in turn, had replaced the Orthodox Church for much of the Soviet period. Though Bolshevik rule had descended into a ritualistic conformity, it continued to provide some hope for Russians. The concept of a better future existed for a long time; it became an integral part of Communist Party doctrine. Though that concept died out in the later 1980s, Yeltsin's new Russia seemed to epitomize many long-held ambitions in late 1991. Russia could now develop as a nation state and take its place in the world. It was not associated with the recent disasters. It was Gorbachev who had "lost" Eastern Europe, dissolved the Warsaw Pact, and conceded defeat in the Cold War. And Russia was now free of the burden of supplying weak Eastern European states with badly needed resources. Appearances, however, were illusory. Russia was called upon to join the US Partnership for Peace program, while at the same time it proved ineffective in trying to halt the eastward advance of NATO. Russia was no longer a global player; its power could only be used in a regional dimension. In the short term, Russia faced a serious task merely to hold together its disparate parts. In short, it faced an identity crisis.

A similar difficulty arose with regard to the Near Abroad – Russia's relations with the republics of the former Soviet Union. The countries that emerged from the Soviet Union developed very differently. Few sought integration with Russia in the early 1990s. The three Baltic States quickly severed ties and began to negotiate for entry into the European Union. The states of the Caucasus became embroiled in a variety of local conflicts. Central Asian states, which had been the most reluctant to leave the Soviet fold, barely changed at all. Often the pre-independence leadership remained intact, and enhanced its authority. Even Ukraine, which many Russians regarded as an integral part of Russia's history, proved unwilling to move close to Russia under its first two presidents. The one country that did wish to restore past relations – Belarus – represented a potential economic millstone should the two economies become entwined. Ultimately Russia did begin to pursue greater integration, but it moved cautiously. The CIS never represented more than a loose confederation, the prime goal of which was to bring about the collapse of the Soviet Union and Gorbachev. In Belarus, Lukashenka, re-elected as president following a virtually unrecognized election in September 2001, was now isolated internationally. In Ukraine, President Kuchma was badly tainted by a political scandal, in which he appeared on tape to demand the removal of a journalist; the tapes were subsequently smuggled out of the country. The journalist Georgy Gongadze, editor of the newspaper *Ukrainska pravda*, was later found decapitated in a forest outside Kyiv.

On December 31, 1999, Yeltsin suddenly tendered his resignation and appointed Putin as Acting President pending new elections the following March. Russia appeared to be directionless and in deep depression. Its forces were still involved in a war in Chechnya that had aroused widespread condemnation for its brutality. Most citizens had suffered a significant fall in living standards over the decade. The Russian population itself was declining at an alarming rate. Though some residents had chosen emigration, the main factor was that the death rate was now much higher than the birth rate. This in turn was a sign of a drastic decline in health standards. The average lifespan for men was around 59, some twenty years less than for those in the West or in Japan. Estimates suggested that by the year 2025 there could be as few as 130 million Russian residents (compared with the 145 million in 1991). Putin was concerned enough by the population fall to declare it a matter of national security. He called for strong measures to improve health, and to reduce alcoholism and drug addiction, especially among young people. Yet under Putin, a former employee of the KGB in East Germany for seventeen years, Russia began to recover from its economic, social, and spiritual decline.

Vladimir V. Putin

Yeltsin's choice as successor was his fifth prime minister and perhaps the most obscure of them all. Vladimir V. Putin is a native of St Petersburg (then Leningrad) where he was born on October 7, 1952 into a family of blue-collar workers. At school he excelled in sports as much as in academic subjects, and after graduating he completed a law degree at Leningrad State University in 1975. In 1983 he married Lyudmila Shkrebneva, a flight attendant from Kaliningrad, with whom he had two daughters, born in 1985 and 1986. Putin had learned German at school, a language eventually acquired by the whole family and which was to prove useful to his future career in the KGB. Evidently Putin had made up his mind to join the KGB at the age of 16, and he spent the first decade with the agency's Foreign Intelligence Department in Leningrad. One of his first tasks was to monitor foreigners arriving in the city. In September 1984 he was transferred to the Red Banner Institute near Moscow, where he went through an intense program of physical training that prepared him for his first foreign posting, to the city of Dresden, in the German Democratic Republic. His five years working with the notorious Stasi coincided with the period of Perestroika in the USSR, and ended with the fall of the Berlin Wall in November 1989.

Obliged to leave the defunct state of East Germany early in 1990, Putin and his family returned to Leningrad, where he remained on the KGB reserve list and took a position as Deputy Rector for International Affairs at Leningrad State University. A former professor, Anatoly Sobchak, had become mayor of the city and invited Putin to be a personal assistant, thus becoming his first patron in the political world. After resigning permanently from the KGB on August 20, 1991 (the day the putsch in Moscow began to fall apart), Putin rose to become the Deputy Mayor of St Petersburg (as Leningrad was now called) by the spring of 1994. He had a reputation as an incorruptible figure who could solve problems and whose loyalty to his boss never wavered. However, Sobchak failed to win re-election as mayor in 1996, and Putin returned to his studies to complete a Candidate degree at the St Petersburg Mining Institute. At the same time he was also invited to join the Presidential Administration in Moscow by Pavel Borodin, director of the Kremlin's property department. His duties included a position as First Deputy Chairman dealing with Russia's regions in 1998, and then as Chairman of the FSB, the Russian Security Services. By the spring of 1999 he was also a secretary to Yeltsin's powerful Security Council. Thus he was an influential figure with an impressive background when he was elevated to the position of Prime Minister by Yeltsin.

Putin's public persona was unsmiling and serious. Small in stature but athletic, he rarely betrayed his emotions in public, in contrast to his predecessor as president, Yeltsin. He conveyed his views best by public press conferences that were televised, and usually with preset questions. Nevertheless, he gave an impression of spontaneity in his answers, which demonstrated that he was articulate and had a wide knowledge both of Russian affairs and of world affairs generally. At times, particularly when referring to troubles in Chechnya, corrupt officials, or his political enemies, he resorted to crude language. Yet he was charming enough to win over many better-known international statespersons. Politically he came to power as an unknown. He was not a member of any Duma faction and did not appear to hold any strong political positions other than that Russia should seek to regain its position as a major world power. He often appeared before the camera in military uniform, and engaged in adventurous pursuits such as flying planes or skiing down mountainsides. Thus Russians had as leader a man of action with a long background as a KGB agent and who could be contrasted with the corrupt businessmen who hitherto had dominated political and economic life in Russia. Some writers have pointed to a virtual "cult of Putin," as exemplified by posters and dolls, and opinion polls which indicated that Putin was Russia's leading sex symbol among women, particularly those of middle years. In short, the average Russian could identify with him, particularly when he expressed his regrets at the fall of the Soviet Union, and emphasized the important historical place in national memory of the victory over the Germans in the Second World War. In this sense he created a link between the Soviet past and the Russian state, a connection that had been abruptly severed by Yeltsin.

Putin commanded respect by his skilful diplomacy, quiet demeanor, and flexibility at key moments, particularly after the terrorist attacks on the United States on September 11, 2001. Unlike Yeltsin, he did not claim to be leading Russia along a path to Western-style democracy, and his leadership was notable for its closer control over the regions (including Chechnya) and the curbing of the power of regional leaders, a reduction of the freedom of the media, and growing state ownership of flagship companies. Notable also in the first four years of Putin's leadership was the significant change in foreign policy, from one that went through the motions of a would-be global power to one that was more concerned with regional security and integration with Russia's closest neighbors, Ukraine, Kazakhstan, and Belarus. Putin had to deal with some acutely difficult situations, particularly the requested passage through and sojourn of US troops in one of the most sensitive areas of the former USSR, Central Asia, after the 9/11 terrorist attacks on New York and Washington. He also witnessed the expansion of NATO to include not only countries of Eastern Europe such as Poland and the Czech Republic, but also republics that were part of the old Soviet Union, such as the Baltic States, along with Washington's support of future membership for Ukraine and Georgia.

Political events, 2000–2008

Putin was elected president formally on March 26, 2000, when he attained almost 53 percent of votes on the first ballot in the new presidential election. The achievement, while impressive, appeared less decisive than may have been the case had the contest gone to a second round. His closest rival was Zyuganov, the leader of the Communist Party of the Russian Federation (Russian acronym: KPRF), who received almost 22 million votes or 29.21 percent of the ballot. The other candidates – there were eleven altogether – all received less than 6 percent of the vote, the highest being Grigory Yavlinsky (5.8 percent), Aman Tuleyev (2.95 percent), and Vladimir Zhirinovsky, the flamboyant leader of the Liberal-Democratic Party of Russia (2.7 percent). Though the election proceeded smoothly, critics of the government maintained that Putin had received an unfair advantage by being appointed Acting President several months before the election, and being designated as Yeltsin's chosen successor. Nevertheless, Putin's rise in popularity was undeniable, and from being a little-known bureaucrat and former KGB employee, one almost unknown in the country and with a footing only in his native St Petersburg, he had achieved the pinnacle of power. In the spring of 2000, his weakest area of control was the capital, Moscow.

The new president moved quickly to increase central authority vis-à-vis Russian regions. Through Decree 849, issued on May 13, 2000, Putin transformed Russia into seven federal districts, each of which would be placed under a presidential representative who would ensure that the region or province adhered to federal laws. In practice, this decree undermined the authority of regional governors, many of whom were replaced. The seven regions were as follows: Central, Southern, Northwestern, Far Eastern, Siberian, Urals, and Volga. By July, Putin had also gained the right to remove regional leaders. Local leaders were soon also stripped of their parliamentary immunity from prosecution, and after August 5 they were no longer automatically elected to the Federation Council. The process of recentralization was under way. After his inauguration as president on May 7, 2000, Putin appointed Mikhail Kasyanov as his Prime Minister. Kasyanov was a former leader of Gosplan, and Minister of Finance in Yeltsin's administration in 1999. He was regarded as a member of the Yeltsin "family," and his relationship with the new president became increasingly difficult once Putin distanced himself from his predecessor. However, in 2000, Putin had also agreed that the former president and his relatives must be free from prosecution, and there was no immediate indication that dramatic changes of policy would occur.

The early period of power brought an immediate crisis when an explosion in a nuclear submarine, *Kursk*, located in the Barents Sea, caused the death of a crew of 118. Though the precise cause of the explosion was not known at the time of the accident on August 12, 2000, a government commission subsequently determined that there had been two explosions, the second at the front of the submarine, and that a leakage of torpedo fuel had been the root cause of the disaster. Putin was on holiday in the Crimea when the accident occurred and was lamentably slow to react. Not only did he not go immediately to the accident site, but also almost instinctively he turned down offers of help from Norwegian and British ships in the area, while the media speculated that the accident had been caused by a collision with another boat. The adverse public reaction to such attitudes was immediate, and the new president learned the lesson well. The only comparable crisis in his first term occurred on October 23, 2002, when armed Chechens entered the Dubrovka Theater in Moscow and took 850 members of the audience hostage for three days, demanding that all Russian forces pull put of Chechnya within a week. Putin's response was to send in security forces, which used nerve gas to subdue the terrorists. As a result, 124 of the hostages as well as thirty-nine captors died from inhaling the gas, while another five hostages died from gunfire. The government's response may have been extreme, but it was difficult to say whether the costs would have been higher had Putin not stood firm and adopted such an approach. Putin's leadership during the second crisis brought him support throughout Russia.

The attack on the oligarchs

Once in office, Putin quickly took steps to curb the authority of powerful oligarchs such as Gusinsky and Berezovsky. The crux of the issue between the government and influential businessmen who had ensured that Yeltsin remained in power at the 1996 election was an informal agreement of 2000 that these people would not become involved in politics. Some, such as Roman Abramovich, the governor of Chukhotka, adhered closely to the arrangement. Abramovich, a 37-year-old joint owner of the Russian oil company Sibneft, in partnership with Berezovsky, broke with his partner in 2000. He held 50 percent of the shares in "RusAl," which controlled the supplies of Russian aluminum, and also purchased the shares that Berezovsky owned in the Russian television company ORT, as well as about one quarter of the shares in Aeroflot, Russia's national airline. Abramovich bought homes in the UK, and became the owner of Chelsea Football Club. Like other oligarchs, the way in which Abramovich achieved his sudden fortune gave rise to speculation about insider trading, and harsh comments on the way that the Russian government allowed businessmen to purchase holdings in key natural resources of Russia at bargain prices.

Putin was not innately opposed to such wealth accumulation as long as it did not represent a threat to his political authority. However, he targeted Gusinsky's Media-Most empire as early as May 2000. The company owned the television station NTV, a popular channel noted for its independent views and critiques of the Russian leadership, as well as the Media-Most Bank, and a number of newspapers, most prominent of which was *Segodnya* (*Today*). Gusinsky was detained briefly after a raid on the Media-Most offices and moved abroad in the summer of 2001, citing fear of further arrests. A similar fate befell Boris Berezovsky, whose companies – they included the car manufacturer Avtovaz, the television station ORT (49 percent stake), as well as the former Soviet airline Aeroflot – were targeted for tax evasion as a result of the sell-offs of the mid-1990s. After Putin's election as president, Berezovsky had formed an opposition faction in the Duma called Liberal Russia. In November 2000, however, he fled to Britain, and subsequently fought off several extradition requests from Russia. Once his companies had been abandoned they were quickly taken over by the state. Berezovsky remains Russia's best-known exile, and remains on the wanted list of the Russian government, which has also tried to pin the blame on him for high-profile assassinations in Moscow and elsewhere.

The fortunes of another oil baron, Mikhail Khodorkovsky, took a similar turn. At the end of October 2003, the Russian authorities arrested Khodorkovsky, the 40-year-old chief executive officer of the Yukos oil company, on charges of fraud and avoidance of taxes, on the eve of an apparent merger between Yukos and Sibneft. Yukos had produced almost one-fifth of Russia's oil in 2002, and its growth in production in that year was an impressive 19.3 percent. Yukos produced about 2 percent of the world's supply of oil in this same year. Most of these reserves were located in a sensitive zone of Western Siberia, crossing into the Khanty-Mansi autonomous region. About 50 percent of the output of the companies owned by Yukos was exported to the West in 2002. Khodorkovsky had become Russia's richest man. At first, his reputation was somewhat tarnished by lurid tales of money-laundering and trafficking in women, but his advisers worked hard to cleanse such an image. He was also reported to apply the most modern technology to his companies. Unlike Abramovich, however, he did not steer clear of politics, offering large subsidies to a variety of political parties before Duma elections, including to the Union of Right Forces (which had supported Boris Yeltsin during his term as president) and Yabloko, a liberal pro-market party, as well as the KPRF, which traditionally had performed well in elections in post-Soviet Russia. Khodorkovsky's benevolence led analysts to believe that he planned to run for president himself in 2008 – a time when, according to the Russian Constitution, Putin must step down, as he would be at the end of his second term.

The arrest of Khodorkovsky (he received a nine-year prison sentence at his trial in May 2005) resulted in the resignation of Putin's chief of staff, Aleksandr Voloshin, apparently in protest at the growing power of the security forces under Putin. It also alienated Kasyanov, who felt that the arrest undermined the international image of Russia. The events were symbolic of the changing power base in Russia, from one dominated by oligarchs to one controlled predominantly by security leaders, most of whom had a base in St Petersburg. Putin also began to find political allies in the Duma, making no secret of his support for a new political group formed from Unified Russia and the Motherland faction under Moscow mayor Yury Luzhkov. The faction, called Unified Russia, was placed under the leadership of the Interior Minister, Boris Gryzlov, to contest the December 7, 2003 parliamentary elections. In those elections, Unified Russia attained a victory, eclipsing the Communists with 38 percent of the electoral vote to 12.8 percent. In terms of seats, the results gave Unified Russia a total of 221 in the 450-seat legislature, but several smaller parties and independent delegates were also supporters of the president. In brief, therefore, and for the first time since independence, the 2003 election provided Putin with control over the parliament. That he had achieved success without dispensing with democratic procedure (and notwithstanding government control over the media and propaganda conducted during the elections) only solidified his now impressive power base. The election also saw the virtual demise of the parties containing leaders responsible for the dramatic transformation to a market economy early in 1992, such as the Union of Right Forces (4 percent of votes, three seats) and Yabloko (4.4 percent, four seats).

Presidential elections of 2004

On March 14, 2004, Putin was re-elected for a second term as president, winning 71.2 percent of the vote on the first ballot. Of more than 66.3 million votes cast, the incumbent president received almost 49 million. His closest rival of the previous election, Communist leader Gennady Zyuganov, opted not to run; and the candidate who represented the KPRF was a member of the Agrarian Party, Nikolay Kharitonov, who received a disappointing 13.7 percent of votes cast (9.4 million); while the other four candidates all received less than 5 percent of the popular vote. They included Sergey Glazev, aged 43, who was elected to the Duma as part of the Motherland bloc and was originally born in Zaporizhzhya, Ukraine; Irina Khakamada, aged 48, the daughter of a Japanese Communist immigrant who was linked the Union of Right Forces, although she ran as an independent; Oleg Malyshkin, who took over the role of Vladimir Zhirinovsky, and represented the Liberal-Democratic Party; and Sergey Mironov, a former regional campaign manager for Putin, who inexplicably ran against him with a policy of combating corruption. The circumstances under which the election took place led to criticisms of the abandonment of democracy in Russia and violations of electoral laws. It seems plain, however, that Putin's popularity was genuine and that, even had conditions for the candidates been equal, he would have won a convincing victory.

How was Putin able to achieve such an impressive standing so quickly? The prelude to the 2004 election was notable because of Putin's gradual severance of the links with his predecessor and mentor, Yeltsin. In February 2004 he had dismissed Kasyanov, the last remaining political statesperson from the Yeltsin years. His replacement, 53-year-old Mikhail Fradkov, from a Jewish family in Samara, had been Minister of Foreign Economic Relations and Trade in 1997 and then Minister of Trade in 1999, but he was not regarded as a major political player and he had been dismissed from that post when Putin came to power and moved into a position as a tax inspector. His re-emergence and elevation to such a prominent post was a surprise to many observers because he was an outsider, not known to have affiliations with the former oligarchs so powerful under Yeltsin or with the security forces that were now becoming prominent under Putin. Most likely, however, given his later appointment (2007) as head of the Russian Foreign Intelligence Services, he may have had connections with the KGB or the FSB. Fradkov's long period in office was unusual for a prime minister, testifying to his popularity and his abilities, as well as to his distance from any particular factions within the government.

Putin had by this time curbed the authority of the regional governors, undermined the powerful oligarchs, and led Russia to a significant economic recovery and growth, largely through the unexpected rise in the prices for world oil and gas. He was aided, in part, by Russia's response to an international period of crisis between 2001 and 2004, which included the terrorist assault on the United States and the coalition-led attack on Iraq and the removal of the regime led by Saddam Hussein. Russia had economic links to Iraq through the conglomerate "Lukoil," which it vowed to preserve, although arguably more critical were the contacts and trade connections with Iran, which was using Russian technology and advisors in the construction of a controversial nuclear power station at Bushwehr. Putin was the first world leader to come to the support of the United States after September 11. Russia also joined the international coalition against terrorism despite opposing the US-engineered invasion of Iraq. Putin could hardly have opted for a different policy. A survey of October 2002 indicated that only 2 percent of Russians supported military intervention in Iraq; 45 percent favored a peaceful solution; and 33 percent maintained that, in the event of a war, Russia should not become involved. Putin did, however, consult with several other interested parties before taking his stance, including France and Israel. The final argument put forward by the Russian government was that only the UN Security Council had the authority to approve an invasion of Iraq, and the Council had not provided that approval.

Russia and its neighbors

Relations with neighboring states improved markedly in the first term of Putin's presidency, although Putin's relations with Belarusian president Alyaksandr Lukashenka ran into some difficulties over the terms of the Russia–Belarus Union. Responding to the Belarusian claims that the Union could only be carried out on equal terms, Putin declared in the summer of 2002 that as Belarus's economy was only 3 percent the size of Russia's no such equality should exist, and one option was for Russia to incorporate its neighbor as a new western region, much as it had done during the period of the Russian Empire. A monetary union – the extension of the Russian rouble into Belarus scheduled for January 2005 – was also quietly shelved. Nevertheless, Russia offered Belarus a major loan in the summer of 2004, part of which was to be used for the purchase of Russian gas, and Russian troops continued to use Belarus as a training ground and as a base for its Early Warning System (Hantsavichy) and communications with its atomic submarines (Vileyka). Earlier, Putin had openly supported Lukashenka's re-election in a campaign that was severely criticized by the EU and the OSCE for its contravention of democratic procedures. While Lukashenka appeared a troublesome figure with some popular support among the Communist sector in Russian society, he seemed to represent for Putin the safest alternative as Belarusian leader, as the leading members of the opposition parties would likely have tried to orient Belarus toward future membership of the EU, and partnerships with Poland and the Baltic States. However, as personalities, Putin and Lukashenka were incompatible, the restrained Russian leader contrasting with the brash and outspoken former state farmer in Minsk.

Relations with Ukraine were occasionally strained, too. In October 2003, Russia asserted a dubious claim to Tuzla Island, off the Kerch peninsula of Crimea – an issue that had been set aside amid the signing of a new treaty on a common economic space between Russia, Ukraine, Belarus, and Kazakhstan. Putin appointed Vladimir Chernomyrdin as the plenipotentiary ambassador to Ukraine in May 2001, a signal of how important he considered relations with Russia's close neighbor. In 2002 he announced the celebration of "Days of Ukraine" in Russia – in the following year Ukraine reciprocated with a display of "Days of Russia" in Ukraine. Of the numerous summits between Putin and Ukrainian president Leonid Kuchma, perhaps the most revealing of Russian attitudes was the one in Kyiv in January 2004. At that time Putin outlined a policy of new unity and friendship with Ukraine to coincide with the 350th anniversary of the Treaty of Pereyaslav, which the Russian side – like its Soviet predecessor – perceived as a period of common unity between the two republics against a common enemy, Poland. The commemoration and its interpretation of history according to the Soviet version elicited widespread criticism among historians both in Ukraine and abroad. Putin, however, did not stop there. During a visit to the Pecherska Lavra (Monastery of the Caves) he declared that it was on the Dnipro River that Prince Vladimir had begun to baptize "Russia." Kuchma joined in by expressing his wish that the Orthodox churches in Ukraine and Russia could be united. Presumably Putin's intentions were friendly, but his reluctance to accept the existence of an independent Ukraine was notable. His attitude toward Ukraine reflected a general tendency of Russia that had persisted since 1991 of looking at the former Soviet republics as part of a Near Abroad, in which Russia is relatively free to impose its wishes.

Relations with Ukraine entered a tense period in late 2004 during the presidential election campaign. Along with Ukrainian President Kuchma, Putin implicitly supported the candidacy of the leader of the Donetsk government, Viktor Yanukovych, in his campaign against the leader of Our Ukraine, Viktor Yushchenko. A conference of Ukrainians in Moscow led to Yanukovych's picture being displayed around the Russian capital, and Putin visited Kyiv twice during the campaign, appearing in public alongside Kuchma and Yanukovych. In October 2004, after a rigged second round of voting that inflated the votes cast for Yanukovych, thousands of Ukrainian residents gathered in the central square of Kyiv, protesting at the outcome. Putin, however, immediately endorsed Yanukovych's "victory." Ultimately, the second round had to be held again, Yushchenko won, and a period of tense relations with Ukraine began. A key issue was the Russian Black Sea Fleet's lease of two bays in the port of Sevastopol, which had an expiry date of 2017. Yushchenko declared that the lease would not be renewed and that the Russians should prepare themselves a new base on Russian territory. The Ukrainian president began to revisit some of the controversial events of the Stalin period in Ukraine, promoting the view that the 1932–1933 famine in Ukraine was a genocide perpetrated by the government in Moscow, and advocating that anti-Soviet insurgents of the Ukrainian Insurgent Army (UPA) receive recognition as veterans of the German–Soviet war. Ukraine also pushed for membership of the EU and NATO, while the Moscow government considered that its counterpart in Kyiv was deliberately pursuing anti-Russian policies.

Although Putin has been depicted as a "neo-Soviet" political leader for his style and policies, he has always recognized the innate weaknesses and failures of the Soviet system. Richard Sakwa says:

> Putin's post-Sovietism recognises not only that the Soviet Union was a failed utopian experiment (this is accepted even within the framework of his neo-Sovietism), but also accepts that this failure was rooted not only in the inadequacies of communist ideology but also in Russia's typically exaggerated views of its abilities, capacities and importance.
>
> (Sakwa, 2004, p. 36)

During his first term, Putin was able to moderate Russia's world role. In a global world, in which the one dominant power was the United States, he appeared to accept his country's transition from a superpower to a regional player, and his attitude toward the Americans often took a high moral tone – sympathy after 9/11, cautions regarding the invasion of Iraq, criticism over the US disavowal of the 1972 arms treaty, and the like. He also presided over the transition to a market economy that was far from smooth but at least circumvented the massive social upheavals of the Yeltsin years. In short, he seemed prepared to relinquish the concept of Russia as a rival to the United States. This was not to say that he relished Russia's new role or that he anticipated the future path of Russia as a minor world power, largely confined to Eurasia and as an observer of critical events in the Near East or elsewhere. Putin's Russia, while fearful of NATO's expansion, and apprehensive as to its future direction, expressed concern only over the possible transfer of nuclear weapons to adjacent or nearby territories, such as Poland and the Baltic States. At the time of the 2004 presidential election, domestic concerns were uppermost, internal enemies had been vanquished, and an economy that had appeared to be in virtual collapse only six years earlier had begun to grow at a significant pace. All these factors, as well as the election results, established Putin more firmly in power than either Gorbachev or Yeltsin had been.

During Putin's second term, 2004–2008, foreign policy became a larger issue. A fundamental gap was evident between US and Russian perceptions of the world. US policy was geared toward unilateral assistance to democratization; interference in countries in which the regimes were based on force, repressions, and authoritarianism; and direct or indirect support for so-called color revolutions in the countries of the former Soviet Union. In response, Russia tried to undermine the new governments installed by such revolutions, while ensuring that the opposition domestically was completely stifled. In this period as well, Russia frequently expressed concern at a proposed Membership Action Plan that would expedite the entry of Ukraine and Georgia into NATO. In turn, Russia adhered to its traditional spheres of interest, the rule of law, recognition of the key role of the UN in resolving international crises, and above all the preservation of national integrity and an alternative perception of the world outside the sphere of the USA. At times this was interpreted as the right to become involved in crucial elections in neighboring states. Putin's blatant interference in the flawed Ukrainian elections of 2004 was much resented by sections of the Ukrainian electorate. Russia also intervened in Georgia's war with its autonomous regions, supporting the right to independence of South Ossetia and Abkhazia, pushing the OSCE for support for the illegal regime in Trans-Dnestr region, which had broken away from Moldova, overt opposition to the Estonian government for moving a wartime statue to the memory of Soviet soldiers, and others.

The period also saw Russia remain oriented toward Europe rather than toward countries to the south or the east. Such a policy was perhaps self-evident given the upheaval in the southern regions of Asia – protracted conflicts in Iraq and

Afghanistan, repressive regimes in Central Asia, instability in Pakistan – and uncertainty in the east. Russia and China have some common interests but have never cemented a firm friendship; relations with Japan are still limited by Russia's refusal to discuss the future of the Kurile Islands, which it has occupied since the end of the Second World War. Russia gradually became more assertive, as exemplified by its suspension of the CFE Treaty on July 14, 2007, claiming that it had become "meaningless," which was partly in response to a proposed US policy of installing interceptor missiles in Poland and radar bases in the Czech Republic to counter the possibility of a "rogue state" attacking USA – a clear reference to Iran, where Russia was providing technology and fuel for the nuclear power station. Such maneuvers appeared to the Russian leaders to constitute a direct threat to their geostrategic position, and thus a strong response was warranted (President Barack Obama subsequently abandoned the missiles program). Whereas the early years of the 21st century saw Russia recover somewhat its international standing, by 2008 the country was beginning to assert itself as the major player in the region, and demanding once again recognition as a world power.

Chechnya: terrorism and the resumption of war

In September 1999 the Russian government sanctioned air raids over Chechnya as a prelude to a resumption of the 1994–1996 war. On October 1, as Prime Minister, Putin declared that the government of Chechnya under President Aslan Mashkadov was illegitimate. Russian troops stormed into the republic; and after several weeks of brutal fighting, with atrocities on both sides, they occupied the capital, Grozny, on February 2, 2000. By May of this same year, the Russian Federation assumed direct control over Chechnya, and the main rebel forces retreated into the mountains. A new Constitution was issued for Chechnya in April 2003, which allowed considerable autonomy to the republic, but ensured that it would become once again part of the Russian Federation. A powerful clan leader, Akhmad Kadyrov, switched sides and declared his allegiance to Russia, thus enabling him to become the first official president of the Chechen Republic on October 5, 2003. However, on May 9, 2004, he was assassinated at a football stadium while attending a ceremony for Russia's Victory Day, commemorating the 59th anniversary of the end of the war in Europe. His replacement as president was Alu Alkhanov, a police officer who had fought on the Russian side during the first Chechen war, though the real authority was Akhmad's son Ramzan, who would succeed Alkhanov as president shortly after he turned 30, the minimum age required, in February 2007.

The defeated Chechen rebels increasingly resorted to terrorist actions, many of which made headlines around the world. On May 5, 2003, a bomb exploded on a train in Stavropol, killing forty-six people and injuring 170. On February 6, 2004, a suicide bomber detonated a bomb at the Avtozavodskaya metro station in Moscow along the route to Paveletskaya station on the Zamoskvaretskaya line. Forty people were killed and more than 120 hurt. On August 24, a more ambitious attack occurred under the leadership of Shamil Basayev that resembled the 9/11 attacks in the United States. Explosions occurred on two passenger aircraft departing from Moscow's Domodedovo airport. The first occurred in Tula region on a Tu-134 plane flying from Moscow to Volgograd, killing thirty-four passengers and nine crew. The second plane to be targeted was a Siberian Airlines Tu-154 flying from Moscow to Sochi, and resulting in the death of thirty-eight passengers and nine crew. It seemed as though the rebels could attack at will anywhere in Russia and in this way reassert the cause of an independent Chechen state. As with the theater bombings of October 2002, the terrorists were quite willing to sacrifice themselves and could thus strike at will.

As Putin's second term began, a radical Muslim faction called al-Riyad al-Salihin consisting of thirty men and two women, all heavily armed and wearing belts, took control of a secondary school in the settlement of Beslan in Northern Ossetia on September 1, 2004. Subsequently, Chechen warlord Basayev again claimed responsibility for the attack. Teachers, pupils, and a number of family members of the latter were taken hostage, and the terrorists demanded that, in order for them to be released, all Russian troops must be withdrawn from Chechnya. The assault on children horrified most Russians. The response of the President was to dispatch Special Forces troops, who, together with local militia, stormed the school two days later in a ferocious but costly raid that resulted in the death of 344 civilians (mostly children), eleven Russian soldiers, and most of the hostages, though Basayev escaped. The Russian media blamed al-Qaida for the attack. It raised fears about Islamic terrorist attacks elsewhere in the Russian Federation and prompted the detention of about 10,000 Muslim migrants in Moscow, not all of whom were Chechens. Two years later, on July 11, 2006, Russian Special Forces succeeded in assassinating Basayev by detonating explosives close to his car in a rural area of Ingushetia.

Gradually the Russian forces, with the help of President Ramzan Kadyrov, pacified Chechnya. Putin introduced a policy called Chechenization, whereby local Chechen forces took over from the Russians in stabilizing the republic. The embattled city of Grozny was partially restored, but Ramzan Kadyrov introduced a brutal regime known to detain and torture opponents at will. Several high-profile deaths occurred of those who reported for or worked with human rights organizations in Chechnya and other parts of Russia. Author and journalist Anna Politkovskaya, a fierce critic of Putin and Kadyrov, was gunned down in the elevator of her Moscow apartment on October 7, 2006, Putin's 54th birthday. She had worked for the newspaper *Novaya gazeta* and had spent much time in the previous decade reporting on Russian atrocities in Chechnya as well as on the authoritarian nature of the Russian government. Natalya Estemirova was a close friend and translator for Politkovskaya, and a worker for the Russian human rights organization Memorial. On July 15, 2009 she was abducted in broad daylight from a street in Grozny, pushed into a car, and later found some 90 miles away in a wooded area of Ingushetia. Like Politkovskaya she had been a strong critic of Ramzan Kadyrov and his police squads. In general the death toll of investigative journalists working in Chechnya, Daghestan, and Ingushetiya was very high, and Russia was declared to be the third most dangerous place for journalists to work, after Iraq and Algeria, by the Committee for the Protection of Journalists based in New York.

BOX 9.1

....

Anna Politkovskaya (1958–2006)

An award-winning journalist born on August 30, 1958 in New York City to Ukrainian parents, Anna Politkovskaya openly criticized the Putin regime for its corruption and disregard for human rights. She attended Moscow State University, studying journalism. In 1999 she became a columnist for the independent newspaper *Novaya gazeta* and immediately began reporting on the war in Chechnya, where she chronicled the crimes committed by the Russian military during the First Chechen War of 1994–1996 and the Second Chechen War after 2000. She was awarded the Amnesty International Global Award in 2001 and the Olof Palme Award for her courageous efforts in reporting under potentially life-threatening conditions in 2004. Politkovskaya also authored several books including *A Dirty War: A Russian Reporter in Chechnya* (2001) and *Putin's Russia* (2004). Her books denounced the Putin government, particularly the Federal Security Service (FSB), which she accused of violating human rights with the intention of establishing a dictatorship. Throughout her journalistic career, she received numerous death threats, and in 2001 Russian troops detained her and subjected her to interrogation and beatings in a Chechen village. She was shot in the elevator of her apartment building on October 7, 2006, coincidentally Vladimir Putin's 54th birthday. Though there have been numerous suspects, no one has been charged with the murder.

Partnerships

Russia worked officially through several organizations to promote economic stability and economic security, some of which originated from the early years of independence. They included the following:

(a) *The Eurasian Economic Community*

Russia opted to combine a pro-European orientation with a Eurasian one, through the Eurasian Economic Community – which eventually comprised six states (Russia, Belarus, Kazakhstan, Kyrgyzstan, Tajikistan, and Uzbekistan) – the goals of which were declared to be a full customs union and common market, joint rules for the security of borders, and general agreement on rules for trade in goods and services. Ratified in 2001, the Community originally had five members until Uzbekistan joined in 2005, while Armenia, Ukraine, and Moldova had observer status.

(b) *The Collective Security Treaty Organization (CSTO)*

The CSTO came into being in 2002 based on the original 1992 Collective Security Treaty of six former Soviet republics – Russia, Armenia, Kazakhstan, Kyrgyzstan, Tajikistan, and Uzbekistan – with Azerbaijan, Georgia, and Belarus added in 1993. It became the CSTO in 2002, and recently pressure has been placed on Turkmenistan to join in. The CSTO is willing to work with the OSCE, but its members are closer to Moscow. In 2009, after some initial reluctance from Belarus, the partners agreed to form a Special Forces military group that could respond to emergency situations in the region.

(c) *The Shanghai Cooperation Organization (SCO)*

The SCO was originally called the Shanghai Five – Kazakhstan, China, Kyrgyzstan, Russia, and Tajikistan – with Uzbekistan added in 2001. In 2004 it created a Regional Anti-Terrorist Structure, and the following year saw a Peace Mission Exercise involving Russian and Chinese troops. In 2007 the SCO and CSTO signed an agreement in Dushanbe to develop cooperation. In the SCO, Iran, India, Pakistan, and Mongolia have observer status, while a request for such status by the USA in 2005 was rejected.

Russia is the dominant force in these new institutions, which are not especially powerful, but are none the less efforts to formulate a common policy in its immediate neighborhood – as well as a sign that the CIS is largely defunct. This Eurasian policy, which includes eventual membership in the WTO (something that seems highly unlikely in the short term given that Georgia is likely to veto it), is an indicator of the restored power of Russia in the east and south that has taken place simultaneously with its more focused orientation toward Europe.

The 2007 parliamentary elections

Putin's Russia established a party of power in a largely controlled parliament. Opposition movements were limited in activities, and subjected to arrests and harassment. Since 1993, when Yeltsin sent tanks to blow up the Russian parliament, Russia has been a presidential republic with the role of parliament greatly reduced. The December 2007 elections accentuated this trend. Prior to the election, the rules were amended so that only parties that attained a minimum of 7 percent would receive seats in the Duma. This was in addition to the new system of proportional representation whereby each party would present a list of candidates for general acceptance. The pro-Kremlin Unified Russia party, victorious in the 2003 election, was backed by Putin, and received 64.1 percent of votes cast (resulting in 350 seats in the 450-seat Duma). However, that figure belies the magnitude of the victory. The Liberal-Democratic Party, which came third with 8.2 percent, was noted for its ultra-nationalist position and was a strong supporter of the Putin government, as was the A Just Russia, which gained 7.8 percent. The only opposition party to win seats was the Communist Party, with 11.6 percent. None of the democratic parties, such as Yabloko or Union of Right Forces, attained anywhere near the 7 percent marker.

The Vice-President of the Parliamentary Assembly of the OSCE, Kimmo Kiljunen, remarked that the election had been fair and democratic, but then divulged the fact that, in Chechnya, 99 percent had voted for Unified Russia, which was not something he considered possible. Putin, approaching the end of his second term as president, allowed his name to be put forward as the future prime minister, leading to specu-lation that the new president, following the elections of March 2008, might be a mere puppet controlled by the popular Putin, with a resulting strengthening of the office of prime minister. On December 10, Putin declared that he fully supported the candidacy as president of First Deputy Prime Minister Dmitry Medvedev, a fellow native of St Petersburg and one of his most loyal acolytes. The choice raised criticism outside Russia, and there were assertions that the election would constitute a farce. Several prospective candidates, such as former Prime Minister Mikhail Kasyanov, were barred from running because of alleged improprieties on their nomination lists or – in the case of former dissident Vladimir Bukovsky – the fact that he had not been resident in Russia for ten years prior to the election as required by the Constitution. Former world chess champion Garri Kasparov, a prominent opposition figure, was also declared ineligible to run. Medvedev won the election easily in the first round with more than 70 percent of the vote, which was higher than Putin ever achieved. His campaign was assisted by the virtual monopolization of positive media and of course the backing of Putin. (Plate 9.1)

BOX 9.2

Dmitry Medvedev (1965–)

Born in Leningrad on September 14, 1965 to parents who were both university professors, Dmitry Anatolyevich Medvedev was trained as a lawyer at Leningrad State University and, as with Putin earlier, one of his professors was Anatoly Sobchak. After completing his Candidate of Juridical Sciences degree, he taught for almost a decade in St Petersburg State University. At the same time he worked as an advisor to the chairman of Leningrad City Council. At the age of 23 he was baptized into the Russian Orthodox Church. By 1999 he was the deputy leader of the Administration of the Russian President. He has also served in all the leading positions of the Gazprom Company, of which he was chairman of the Council of Directors in 2001–2008, with one short break. From October 2003 he was the head of the administration of the Russian president, and First Deputy Prime Minister after 2005. In 2008 he succeeded Putin and became the third presi-dent of Russia. Diminutive, mild-mannered and described as "studious," he has had a long business career alongside his political one, He is married to Svetlana (née Linnik), with whom he was at university; their son, Ilya, was born in 1996. He is known to be a devotee of British classic rock music, including such bands as Deep Purple and Black Sabbath.

Plate 9.1 Dmitry Medvedev and Vladimir Putin, December 2007.
Image: Alexander Zemlianichenko/epa/CORBIS

Notably, Medvedev has no affiliation with the Security Services. One could consider him rather a pro-market and pro-European businessman with little previous interest in day-to-day politics. He was inaugurated as president in early May 2008, and one day afterward he appointed Putin prime minister, thus initiating a period of dual rule. There was much speculation that Medvedev's term as president would be short and thus allow Putin to return as president after a few months. However, the partnership appeared to work quite smoothly over the first year, despite the world recession and some harder economic times in Russia. Medvedev allowed himself to be interviewed by one of the most objective newspapers in Russia, *Novaya gazeta*, thus giving the impression that he might bring about a more tolerant atmosphere. At the same time, when war broke out in Georgia in August 2008, Medvedev did not hesitate to adopt the harshest of language, in line with statements made by his prime minister, and he immediately authorized the intervention of Russian troops inside not only the breakaway regions but also Georgia's heartland. Above all, the coming to power of Russia's third president indicated that the policies introduced by Putin – or what some have termed "Putinism" – would be continued.

Gazprom and economic revival

In the 21st century, Russia has been able to recover economically from the turbulent Yeltsin years, most notably by building up the gas and oil sector and by ensuring that the former came under state control. The curbing of the power of the oligarchs and the reassertion of central power over the regions, which had become profitable power bases for local satraps, also assisted the economic revival. Gas exports required the conveyance of supplies through pipelines to consumers in Central and Western Europe, mostly through Ukraine and Belarus, though several new pipelines were proposed or under construction by 2008. Russia has the world's largest reserves of natural gas (1.680 trillion cubic feet), and is the world's main gas exporter (6.6 trillion cubic feet, or just under one-third of its average annual production). The chief recipients of Russian gas are countries of Central and Western Europe, led, in terms of quantity received, by Ukraine, Germany, Belarus, Turkey, Italy, and France. In some countries, imports of gas from Russia compose very high percentages of domestic gas consumption, making up 100 percent in Slovakia, Finland, Macedonia, and Georgia, and 96 percent in Bulgaria. Thus gas became the mainstay of the Russian economy in the 21st century. In June 2000, Putin's close ally Dmitry Medvedev became chairman of the board of directors of Gazprom, then still largely in private hands, but now a target for a government takeover in a new era. Gradually the government began to buy up shares in the company, taking advantage of the demise of existing shareholders. In 2004 the government share of the company rose from 38.4 to 50.0 percent. In September 2005, Gazprom's power was enhanced significantly when it acquired a 72.6 percent stake in the company Sibneft.

One of the critical questions that arose for the government-owned company was what price to charge for the gas. For some time, Russia's neighbors that were formerly Soviet republics had been receiving gas at well below official market prices. Pressure was placed on Ukraine and Belarus; and, by 2008, Ukraine was paying $179.50 per thousand cubic metres (tcm) and Belarus $119, as compared to $230 in Georgia, and $280 in each of the three Baltic States. On 1 January 2006, Gazprom promptly stopped supplies to Ukraine as a result of lack of payment, causing a gas crisis throughout Europe, which relied on the supply of gas through the Ukrainian pipeline. A similar crisis prevailed early in 2008, much to the consternation of the European Union, which raised questions about the reliability of supplies from Gazprom, and particularly via the route through Ukraine. Observers blamed the impasse on political disagreements between the two states. Belarus also had problems meeting payments for Russian gas, relying on loans from the International Monetary Fund and – somewhat ironically – Russia. Russia and Belarus also reached an agreement whereby gas prices would rise gradually to world levels by 2011, by which time Russia would acquire a 50 percent stake in the main transit company, Beltransgaz.

Despite disputes over gas prices and difficulties with the transit of gas, the energy sphere brought about significant increases in Russian GDP in the early years of the 21st century: 4.2 percent in 2003, 6.7 percent in 2005, and 8.1 percent in 2008. However, the world recession in late 2008 brought a sudden end to the economic resurgence, and in 2009 growth was expected to drop sharply by at least 5 percent in real terms (allowing for inflation), as a result of a sudden drop in the prices of commodities, as well as a reduction in demand from consumers. Unemployment constituted 9.5 percent of the workforce, and the budget for 2009 had to be revised because of a serious shortfall in anticipated revenues. The Russian rouble also dropped sharply against the dollar on the international exchange. However, prognoses were that Russia would start to recover from the crisis by late 2010.

Historical memory and the modern state

With the disappearance of the Soviet Union and the rise of the new Russia, a definite link can be discerned between the time of the Russian Empire and the present. The Soviet period no longer constitutes such a clean break as it did earlier, although the revolutions of 1917 may still be seen as a turning point and a time of dramatic changes. For Russians there are still some constants that provide connections with the nineteenth century and even earlier. One is a deep affection for the land and for nature, which has been emphasized more of late because of the impact of environmental pollution and degradation, the disappearance of villages, and the shrinking of lakes. The feeling for the land is illustrated by the fact that despite industrialization since the 1930s and the vast migration of Russians from villages to towns throughout the century, but particularly since the 1960s, all Russians seem to sense the connection with the countryside. It manifests itself through such pursuits as mushroom- and berry-gathering, picnics, fishing, and perhaps above all the survival of the dacha as a summertime retreat as well as a means of supplying a variety of vegetables and plants.

A second constant is the Russian Orthodox Church, which had little real authority by 1917 and then came under assault from Lenin's Russia. With a respite during the war years, the Soviet government continued to attack the church for most of the Soviet period before Gorbachev changed course. The number of churches dropped from over 55,000 on the eve of the February Revolution to just over 7,000 by the mid-1980s, and the number of monasteries accordingly from 550 to eighteen. From 1917, with the separation of church and state, the Russian Orthodox Church not only lost state support; the authorities actively promoted militant atheism, destroyed churches, arrested priests and nuns, or forced them into secular positions. The church itself after the 1950s was deeply penetrated by the KGB. Nevertheless, despite also some significant differences with the Vatican, disputes over ownership of parishes outside the territory of the Russian Federation, and a virtual invasion of Russia by fundamentalist Christian groups, not to mention the growth of other denominations, the Russian Orthodox Church has survived and remains a symbol of the Russian nation.

A third constant is veneration for the past, particularly in the form of patriotism and memory. Today, the key event in terms of national commemoration, monuments, and official narratives is the Great Patriotic War, defined as 1941–1945. This book devotes a relatively large space to the war years because they represented a critical moment for the Soviet state, one that forged new links with the tsarist past quite deliberately and illustrated that, for the average citizen, devotion to Russia appeared more important than love for the USSR. In turn, the Soviet state founded in 1917 gained a raison d'être in the sacrifices of its citizens, Russians and non-Russians, in the great conflict against the Germans and under German occupation. After the war Stalin designated some "hero cities" – Stalingrad, Leningrad, Odesa, and Sevastopol. On June 22, 1961, to mark the twentieth anniversary of the outbreak of war, a statute was issued formally, and the number of cities was expanded by the addition of Kyiv and Moscow, while Brest, the former western border outpost, was declared a Hero Fortress under Brezhnev in 1973–1976, and three more cities were declared Hero Cities, namely Kerch, Novorossiisk, and Minsk. In 1985, Murmansk and Smolensk were added to the number before Gorbachev halted the process in 1988. At that time it appeared that the commemoration of the war might be toned down. During the time of Boris Yeltsin's presidency, although the war was commemorated each year, the ceremonies were subdued.

Yet in 2005 the Russian government not only revived the practice but also introduced a new concept, "Cities of Military Glory," in order to add to number of heroic cities. In April 2007 the new title was awarded to Belgorod, Kursk, and Orel. Six months later, five more cities and small towns also received the same honor from President Putin – Vladikavkaz, Elnya, Elets, Malgobek, and Rzhev. A monument was erected in each one with the coat of arms of the city and the text of the presidential decree. The fact that most of the new cities were unfamiliar to non-Russians illustrates that the commemoration of the war has taken on a new life. Today any town or settlement that can provide records of brave resistance to the Germans can apply to receive the title. In May 2009, President Medvedev announced the formation of a special commission to investigate alleged attempts to rewrite the history of the war in versions that are damaging to Russian prestige. Simultaneously, the Unified Russia faction that controls the Russian Duma sanctioned the draft of a new law that will give prison sentences of three to five years for anyone convicted of "rehabilitating Nazism." The commission and the new law reflect historical revisionism about the war years in the former Soviet republics rather than in Russia. Medvedev referred to Estonians and Latvians who fought alongside the Germans, as well as to Ukraine's efforts under President Viktor Yushchenko to treat the 1932–1933 famine as an act of genocide that was targeted against Ukrainians as an ethnic group.[1]

These recent events indicate that the Great Patriotic War has been co-opted by the Russian state as its most important historical memory. The number of living participants in that conflict is dwindling, but the anniversaries will continue – May 2010 marked the 65th anniversary of the victory, and 22 June 2011 the 70th anniversary of the German invasion of Soviet territory. With archival access increasingly difficult in Russia, it seems unlikely that there will be much hope of penetrating the fog of propaganda about the war period that has now been revived in the 21st century. The role of the Western allies is all but forgotten. In 2008 the Russian authorities dissociated themselves from overt attacks on the leadership of Stalin. In fact, in several statements, Putin suggested that the achievements of Stalin should be noted. At the same time, there does not seem to be the same fervor over the October Revolution, perhaps because most Russians still cannot perceive that event as one that united them against a common enemy as the war and the occupation did. The war also brought about a plethora of new poems, articles, paintings, sculptures, and – as noted – ultimately monuments. Though Russia has been at war with its own republic of Chechnya, and experienced a lengthy and costly war in Afghanistan in 1979–1988, there are few commemorations of the latter and none of the Chechen engagement. Thus the selection of the Russian/Soviet defeat of Fascism is a deliberate choice, as is the decision to prosecute people who may disagree with the official interpretation.

However, the fourth constant, which may continue without sanction of the authorities, is Russian culture. The 20th century provides a long narrative of courage of cultural figures in the face of official repression, of musicians, playwrights, writers, and artists who circumvented the official Socialist Realist style or others who conformed but nevertheless still maintained an independent existence. The Russian love of poetry is well known, and even the Stalin leadership commemorated the centennial of the death of Aleksandr Pushkin in 1937. There is a long tradition in Russia of songwriters and bards, symbolized perhaps by the great popularity of Vladimir Vysotsky in the 1970s, as well as by a culture that has been influenced strongly by Jews and gypsies, as well as by Russians. The new Russia has been subjected like other countries to a global culture. The Internet brings to Russians a largely Westernized perspective. Since the late 1980s, the streets of Russian cities and towns have been replete with the giant commercial enterprises of the West – fast-food outlets, restaurants, car manufacturers, and the like. With the end of the USSR, there was a time in Moscow and St Petersburg when it seemed that the population embraced this new perspective. Yet one could also sense an underlying wave of resentment against the global culture, and under Putin there has been a reassertion of Russia's separate path and mission. The films of Nikita Mikhalkov and the stories of Tatyana Tolstaya, for example, both in their own way continue the traditions of post-Soviet Russian culture largely unaffected by its associations with the West. Mikhalkov, who has starred in many of his own movies, might be described as a Slavophile who wishes to defend Orthodoxy in Russia, Serbia, and elsewhere.

> ### BOX 9.3
>
> ....
>
> ### Tatyana Tolstaya (1951–)
>
> One of the leading writers of the post-Soviet era, Tatyana Tolstaya was born on May 3, 1951 into a well-educated family of eminent authors. She is the granddaughter of Aleksey N. Tolstoy (1883–1945, a science fiction writer who was a propagandist for the Soviet Union) and the great-grandniece of Leo Tolstoy. Her work centers primarily on the dissonance between her characters' dreams and the inescapable reality. She studied Classics at Leningrad State University, and after graduation worked at the Nauka publishing house in Moscow. Her literary career began when her short story "Na zolotom kryltse sideli" ("On a Golden Porch") appeared in *Avrora* magazine in 1983. In 1987 she published her first collection of stories under the same title, which established her as a serious author. During the late 1980s and the 1990s, she spent most of her time in the United States teaching at various institutions, including Princeton University and Skidmore College. Back in Russia she has co-hosted a popular television show, *The School for Scandal*, where she interviewed various cultural and political Russian figures. Her first novel, *The Slynx* (translated 2003), completed in 2000, took fourteen years to complete. Tolstaya's translated works also include *Sleepwalker in a Fog* (1992) and her collection of essays *Pushkin's Children: Writings on Russia and Russians* (2003).

The question that arises is whether it is possible today for any highly industrialized state to develop in isolation culturally and economically. Alarmist reports appear in Western outlets about the emergence of extreme nationalism, including Nazi-like youth movements such as Nashi, which until recently received official support from the government, or of racist attacks on foreigners in Russian towns. The Western media almost universally have criticized the current Russian government as authoritarian, secretive, and perhaps above all threatening. In 2008, when Georgia attempted to reassert control over its breakaway republics of South Ossetia and Abkhazia, Russia intervened immediately and occupied several Georgian ports and towns, including Stalin's birthplace Gori. Some materials were ferried to the Russian army from Sevastopol, much to the embarrassment of the Ukrainians, whose president, Yushchenko, had declared his support for Georgia. Talk abounded of a new Cold War, and international condemnation followed from most Western countries. Yet, from Russia's perspective, Russia was reasserting its influence in an area once part of the Russian Empire and the Soviet state. The Russian government was incensed when the state of Kosovo was formed by a unilateral declaration of independence on February 18, 2008, and it tried repeatedly to reassert its power and resist what it saw as constant Western encroachments in its backyard. These include the establishment of anti-radar bases in Poland and support for Ukrainian and Georgian membership of NATO, both of which have been perceived as overt and deliberate threats to Russia.

Nationalism, anti-Western sentiment, and isolationism are historical phenomena that have recurred periodically throughout Russian history. Nineteenth-century Populists had tried to focus on the natural goodness of the Russian peasant and limit harmful influences from the West. The image inculcated in official Russia's interpretation of the war years is one of a brave people, neglected and forgotten by the rest of the world and left to face a Fascist onslaught alone. That image has been reinvented under Putin and Medvedev, and applied to new world ambitions with a lack of subtlety that presents an unfortunate image today of ruthlessness, and – the noun used most often – authoritarianism. Writer Boris Kagarlitsky, on the other hand, has termed Russia's system a "neo-liberal autocracy." Russia, many analysts maintain, is naturally authoritarian and should not be expected to take a democratic path. Democracy was tried and failed in 1917 and in the period 1987–1999 – in the latter instance, mainly because Russia was not the United States and could not adapt to a Western-style system. Thus in the post-Soviet environment the country lurched from one path to another, but eventually the patrimonial state re-established itself, this time with a former KGB man at the helm and security forces in the ascendancy and a parliament (Duma) with no more power than its tsarist ancestor of 1906–1914. In turn, from his position as Prime Minister, the powerful figure of Vladimir Putin is still in practice the most influential political leader in the country. But, for most Russians, as verified by opinion polls over the past few years, the situation today is preferable both to the uncertainty and changes of Perestroika and the economic chaos of the Yeltsin years. The loss of democracy is of far less importance than improved standards of living, guaranteed wages, and pensions. A century of experiments has only strengthened this need for stability and security.

Note

1 In late October 2009, however, Medvedev declared publicly that the mass killings under Stalin during the repressions of the 1930s could not be justified (Agence France Presse, October 30, 2009).

Questions for discussion

1. What were the causes of the dispute between President Yeltsin and the Russian parliament in 1993?
2. Account for the collapse of the Russian economy in 1998 and its recovery under Putin.
3. How did Putin deal with the oligarchs?
4. How would you define "Russian-ness" today?
5. Do Russians have less freedom today than in the Gorbachev period?

Recent works

Yeltsin period

Andrews, Josephine T. *When Majorities Fail: The Russian Parliament, 1990–1993*. Cambridge: Cambridge University Press, 2002.

Barnes, Andrew S. *Owning Russia: The Struggle over Factories, Farms, and Power*. Ithaca, NY: Cornell University Press, 2006.

Brudny, Yitzhak. *Restructuring Post-Communist Russia*. Cambridge: Cambridge University Press, 2004.

Chandler, Andrea. *Shocking Mother Russia: Democratization, Social Rights, and Pension Reform in Russia*. Toronto: University of Toronto Press, 2004.

Clark, Terry D. *Changing Attitudes toward Economic Reform during the Yeltsin Era*. Westport, Conn.: Praeger, 2003.

Colton, Timothy. *Yeltsin: A Life*. New York: Basic Books, 2008.

Desai, Padma. *Conversations on Russia: Reform from Yeltsin to Putin*. Oxford: Oxford University Press, 2006.

Eklof, Ben. *Educational Reform in Post-Soviet Russia: Legacies and Prospects*. London/New York: Frank Cass, 2005.

Ellison, Herbert J. *Boris Yeltsin and Russia's Democratic Transformation*. Seattle, Wash.: University of Washington Press, 2006.

Goldfarb, Alexander. *Death of a Dissident: The Poisoning of Alexander Litvinenko and the Return of the KGB*. New York: Free Press, 2007.

Felkay, Andrew. *Yeltsin's Russia and the West*. Westport, Conn.: Praeger, 2002.

Herrera, Yoshiko M. *Imagined Economies: The Sources of Russian Regionalism*. Cambridge: Cambridge University Press, 2005.

Kagarlitsky, Boris. *Russia under Yeltsin and Putin: Neo-Liberal Autocracy*. London/Sterling, Va: Pluto Press, 2002.

Kempton, Daniel R. *Unity or Separation: Center–Periphery Relations in the Former Soviet Union*. Westport, Conn.: Praeger, 2002.

Klein, Lawrence R., and Marshall Pomer. *The New Russia: Transition Gone Awry*. Stanford, Calif.: Stanford University Press, 2001.

Kort, Michael. *The Soviet Colossus: History and Aftermath*. Armonk, NY: M. E. Sharpe, 2001.

Kuchins, Andrew C. *Russia after the Fall*. Washington, DC: Carnegie Endowment for International Peace/Brookings Institution Press, 2002.

McGee, Robert W. *Accounting and Financial System Reform in a Transition Economy: A Case Study of Russia*. New York: Springer, 2005.

Martinez-Vazquez, Jorge. *Tax Reform in Russia*. Northampton, Mass.: Edward Elgar, 2008.

Morrison, Claudio. *A Russian Factory Enters the Market Economy*. London: Routledge, 2008.

O'Brien, David J. *Measuring Social and Economic Change in Rural Russia: Surveys from 1991 to 2003*. Lanham, Md: Lexington Books, 2006.

Pallot, Judith. *Russia's Unknown Agriculture: Household Production in Post-Communist Russia*. Oxford: Oxford University Press, 2007.

Russell, John. *Chechnya – Russia's "War on Terror"*. London: Routledge, 2007.

Shevtsova, Lilia. *Russia Lost in Transition: The Yeltsin and Putin Legacies*. Washington, DC: Carnegie Endowment for International Peace, 2007.

Shleifer, Andrei. *A Normal Country: Russia after Communism*. Cambridge, Mass.: Harvard University Press, 2005.

Skinner, Kiron K. *The Strategy of Campaigning: Lessons from Ronald Reagan and Boris Yeltsin*. Ann Arbor, Mich.: University of Michigan Press, 2007.

Spulber, Nicolas. *Russia's Economic Transitions: From Late Tsarism to the New Millennium*. New York: Cambridge University Press, 2003.

Szászdi, Lajos F. *Russian Civil–Military Relations and the Origins of the Second Chechen War*. Lanham, Md: University Press of America, 2008.

Wegren, Stephen K. *The Moral Economy Reconsidered: Russia's Search for Agrarian Capitalism*. Basingstoke: Palgrave Macmillan, 2005.

Weigle, M. *On the Road to the Civic Forum: State and Civil Society from Yeltsin to Putin*. London: Routledge, 2007.

Putin period

Aslund, Anders, and Andrew Kuchins. *The Russia Balance Sheet*. Washington, DC: Peterson Institute for International Economics and Center for Strategic and International Studies, 2009.

Baker, Peter. *Kremlin Rising: Vladimir Putin's Russia and the End of Revolution*. Washington, DC: Potomac Books, 2007.

Balmaceda, Margarita M. *Energy Dependency, Politics and Corruption in the Former Soviet Union: Russia's Power, Oligarchs' Profit and Ukraine's Missing Energy Policy, 1995–2006*. London: Routledge, 2007.

Black, J. L. *Vladimir Putin and the New World Order: Looking East, Looking West?* Lanham, Md: Rowman & Littlefield, 2004.

Brown, Archie. *Contemporary Russian Politics: A Reader*. Oxford: Oxford University Press, 2001.

Colton, Timothy J. *Popular Choice and Managed Democracy: The Russian Elections of 1999 to 2000.* Washington, DC: Brookings Institution Press, 2003.

Fish, M. Steven. *Democracy Derailed in Russia: The Failure of Open Politics.* Cambridge: Cambridge University Press, 2005.

Goldman, Marshall I. *Petrostate: Putin, Power, and the New Russia.* Oxford: Oxford University Press, 2008.

Hedenskog, Jakob. *Russia as a Great Power: Dimensions of Security under Putin.* London: Routledge, 2005.

Herspring, Dale R. *Putin's Russia: Past Imperfect, Future Uncertain.* Lanham, Md: Rowman & Littlefield, 2007.

Horvath, Robert. *The Legacy of Soviet Dissent: Dissidents, Democratization and Radical Nationalism in Russia.* London: RoutledgeCurzon, 2005.

Jack, Andrew. *Inside Putin's Russia.* Oxford: Oxford University Press, 2004.

Jonson, Lena. *Vladimir Putin and Central Asia: The Shaping of Russian Foreign Policy.* London: I. B. Tauris, 2004.

Kotz, David M. *Russia's Path from Gorbachev to Putin: The Demise of the Soviet System and the New Russia.* London: Routledge, 2007.

Letiche, John M. *Russia Moves into the Global Economy.* London: Routledge, 2007.

LeVine, Steve. *Putin's Labyrinth: Spies, Murder, and the Dark Heart of the New Russia.* New York: Random House, 2008.

Levitt, Marcus C., and Tatyana Novikov. *Times of Trouble: Violence in Russian Literature and Culture.* Madison, Wis.: University of Wisconsin Press, 2007.

Lo, Bobo. *Vladimir Putin and the Evolution of Russian Foreign Policy.* Oxford: Blackwell, 2003.

Longworth, Philip. *Russia: The Once and Future Empire from Pre-History to Putin.* New York: St. Martin's Press, 2006.

Lucas, Edward. *The New Cold War: How the Kremlin Menaces Both Russia and the West.* London: Bloomsbury, 2008.

Lucas, Edward. *The New Cold War: Putin's Russia and the Threat to the West.* Basingstoke: Palgrave Macmillan, 2009.

Lynch, Allen. *How Russia Is Not Ruled: Reflections on Russian Political Development.* Cambridge: Cambridge University Press, 2005.

Mackinlay, John. *Regional Peacekeepers: The Paradox of Russian Peacekeeping.* Tokyo: United Nations University Press, 2003.

Mackinnon, Mark. *The New Cold War: Revolutions, Rigged Elections and Pipeline Politics in the Former Soviet Union.* Toronto: Random House, 2007.

Noel, Michel. *Development of Capital Markets and Institutional Investors in Russia: Recent Achievements and Policy Challenges Ahead.* Washington, DC: World Bank, 2006.

Nygren, Bertil. *The Rebuilding of Greater Russia: Putin's Foreign Policy towards the CIS Countries.* London: Routledge, 2008.

Orttung, Robert W. *The Dynamics of Russian Politics: Putin's Reform of Federal–Regional Relations.* Lanham, Md: Rowman & Littlefield, 2004–2005.

Peterson, D. J. *Russia and the Information Revolution.* Santa Monica, Calif.: RAND Corporation, 2005.

Politkovskaya, Anna. *A Russian Diary.* London: Harvill Secker, 2007.

Pravda, Alex. *Leading Russia: Putin in Perspective. Essays in Honour of Archie Brown.* Oxford: Oxford University Press, 2005.

Rose, Richard. *Elections without Order: Russia's Challenge to Vladimir Putin.* Cambridge: Cambridge University Press, 2002.

Rosefielde, Steven. *Russia in the 21st Century: The Prodigal Superpower.* Cambridge: Cambridge University Press, 2005.

Ross, Cameron. *Russian Politics under Putin.* Manchester: Manchester University Press, 2004.

Sakwa, Richard. *Putin: Russia's Choice.* London: Routledge, 2008.

Shevtsova, Lilia. *Putin's Russia.* Washington, DC: Carnegie Endowment for International Peace, 2005.

Streissguth, Thomas. *Vladimir Putin.* Minneapolis, Minn.: Lerner, 2005.

Stuermer, Michael. *Putin and the Rise of Russia.* London: Weidenfeld & Nicholson, 2008.

Tiknomirov, Vladimir. *Russia after Yeltsin.* Aldershot: Ashgate, 2001.

Vinhas de Souza, Lúcio. *A Different Country: Russia's Economic Resurgence.* Brussels: Center for European Policy, 2008.

White, Stephen. *Media, Culture and Society in Putin's Russia.* Basingstoke: Palgrave Macmillan, 2008.

Bibliography of older works

1 From tsarism to revolution, 1894–1917

Ascher, Abraham. *The Revolution of 1905: Authority Restored.* Stanford, Calif.: Stanford University Press, 1992.

Baron, Samuel H. *Plekhanov: The Father of Russian Marxism.* Stanford, Calif.: Stanford University Press, 1966.

Bradley, Joseph. *Muzhik and Muscovite: Urbanization in Late Imperial Russia.* Berkeley, Calif.: University of California Press, 1985.

Charques, Richard. *The Twilight of Imperial Russia.* Fairlawn, NJ: Essential Books, 1959.

Engel, Barbara Alpern. *Between the Fields and the City: Women, Work, and Family in Russia, 1861–1914.* Cambridge: Cambridge University Press, 1993.

Harcave, Sidney. *The Russian Revolution of 1905.* London: Macmillan, 1964.

Herlihy, Patricia. *The Alcoholic Empire: Vodka and Politics in Late Imperial Russia.* Oxford: Oxford University Press, 2002.

Judge, Edward H., and James Y. Simms Jr. *Modernization and Revolution: Dilemmas of Progress in Late Imperial Russia.* New York: Columbia University Press, 1992.

Laqueur, Walter. *Black Hundred: The Rise of the Extreme Right in Russia.* New York: HarperCollins, 1993.

Lieven, Anatol. *Chechnia: Tombstone of Russian Power.* New Haven, Conn.: Yale University Press, 1999.

Lincoln, W. Bruce. *The Great Reforms: Autocracy, Bureaucracy, and the Politics of Change in Imperial Russia.* DeKalb, Ill.: Northern Illinois University Press, 1990.

McDonald, David M. *United Government and Foreign Policy in Russia, 1900–1914.* Cambridge, Mass.: Harvard University Press, 1992.

Massie, Robert K. *The Romanovs: The Final Chapter.* New York: Random House, 1995.

Mehlinger, Howard D., and John M. Thompson, eds. *Count Witte and the Tsarist Government in the 1905 Revolution.* Bloomington, Ind.: Indiana University Press, 1972.

Menning, Bruce. *Bayonets before Bullets: The Imperial Russian Army, 1861–1914.* Bloomington, Ind.: Indiana University Press, 1992.

Pares, Bernard. *The Fall of the Russian Monarchy.* London: Phoenix Press, 2001.

Pipes, Richard. *Russia under the Old Regime.* New York: Penguin, 1974.

Pipes, Richard. *The Russian Revolution.* New York: Knopf, 1990.

Pomper, Philip. *The Russian Revolutionary Intelligentsia.* New York: Crowell, 1970.

Radzinsky, Edvard. *The Last Tsar: The Life and Death of Nicholas II.* Translated by Marian Schwartz. New York: Doubleday, 1992.

Raeff, Marc. *Understanding Imperial Russia.* New York: Columbia University Press, 1984.

Robinson, G. T. *Rural Russia under the Old Regime.* New York: Longman, Green, 1932.

Steinberg, Mark D. *The Fall of the Romanovs: Political Dreams and Personal Struggles in a Time of Revolution.* New Haven, Conn.: Yale University Press, 1995.

Troyat, Henry. *Daily Life in Russia under the Last Tsar.* Translated by Malcolm Barnes. Stanford, Calif.: Stanford University Press, 1961.

Verner, Andrew N. *The Crisis of Russian Autocracy: Nikolay II and the 1905 Revolution.* Princeton, NJ: Princeton University Press, 1990.

Waldron, Peter. *Between Two Revolutions: Stolypin and the Politics of Renewal in Russia.* London: UCL, 1998.

Weissman, Neil B. *Reform in Tsarist Russia: The State Bureaucracy and Local Government, 1900–1914.* New Brunswick, NJ: Rutgers University Press, 1981.

2 The October Revolution, 1917–1921

Acton, Edward. *Rethinking the Russian Revolution.* New York: Edward Arnold, 1990.

Avrich, Paul. *Kronstadt, 1921.* Princeton, NJ: Princeton University Press, 1991.

Carr, E. H. *The Russian Revolution: From Lenin to Stalin, 1917–1929.* New York: The Free Press, 1979.

Crownover, Roger. *The United States Intervention in North Russia 1918, 1919: The Polar Bear Odyssey.* Lewiston, NY: Edwin Mellen Press, 2001.

Figes, Orlando. *A People's Tragedy: The Russian Revolution, 1891–1924.* New York: Viking, 1997.

Fitzpatrick, Sheila. *The Cultural Front: Power and Culture in Revolutionary Russia.* Ithaca, NY: Cornell University Press, 1992.

Fitzpatrick, Sheila. *The Russian Revolution.* Oxford: Oxford University Press, 1984.

Footman, David. *Civil War in Russia.* Westport, Conn.: Greenwood Press, 1961.

Kenez, Peter. *The Birth of the Propaganda State: Soviet Methods of Mass Mobilization, 1917–1929.* New York: Cambridge University Press, 1985.

Koenker, Diane, William G. Rosenberg, and Ronald G. Suny, *Party, State, and Society in the Russian Civil War.* Bloomington, Ind.: Indiana University Press, 1989.

Lincoln, W. Bruce. *Red Victory: A History of the Russian Civil War.* New York: Simon & Schuster, 1999.

McDonnell, Lawrence. *October Revolution.* Staplehurst, Kent: Spellmount, 1994.

Pipes, Richard. *The Russian Revolution.* New York: Knopf, 1990.

Pipes, Richard, ed. *The Unknown Lenin: From the Secret Archive.* New Haven, Conn.: Yale University Press, 1996.

Rabinowitch, Alexander. *The Bolsheviks Come to Power: The Revolution of 1917 in Petrograd.* New York: Norton, 1976.

Read, Christopher. *From Tsar to Soviets: The Russian People and Their Revolution, 1917–1921.* New York: Oxford University Press, 1996.

Service, Robert. *The Bolshevik Party in Revolution, 1917–1923: A Study in Organizational Change.* London: Macmillan, 1979.

Service, Robert. *Lenin – a Biography.* Cambridge, Mass.: Harvard University Press, 2000.

Smele, Jonathan D. *Civil War in Siberia: The Anti-Bolshevik Government of Admiral Kolchak.* Cambridge: Cambridge University Press, 1997.

Suny, Ronald G., and Arthur Adams, eds. *The Russian Revolution and Bolshevik Victory.* 3rd edn. Problems in European Civilization. Lexington, Mass.: D. C. Heath, 1990.

Volkogonov, Dmitri. *Lenin: A New Biography.* Translated by Harold Shukman. New York: The Free Press, 1994.

3 NEP and the rise of Stalin, 1921–1928

Ball, Alan M. *Russia's Last Capitalists: The Nepmen, 1921–1929.* Berkeley, Calif.: University of California Press, 1987.

Bergman, Theodor, Gert Schaefer, and Mark Selden, eds. *Bukharin in Retrospect.* Armonk, NY: M. E. Sharpe, 1994.

Brooks, Jeffrey. *When Russia Learned to Read.* Princeton, NJ: Princeton University Press, 1985.

Chase, William. *Workers, Society, and the Soviet State: Labor and Life in Moscow, 1918–1929.* Urbana, Ill.: University of Illinois Press, 1987.

Cohen, Stephen F. *Bukharin and the Bolshevik Revolution: A Political Biography, 1888–1938.* New York: Vintage Books, 1973.

Deutscher, Isaac. *The Prophet Unarmed: Trotsky, 1921–1929.* Oxford: Oxford University Press, 1980.

Fitzpatrick, Sheila, ed. *Cultural Revolution in Russia, 1928–1931.* Bloomington, Ind.: Indiana University Press, 1978.

Fitzpatrick, Sheila, Alexander Rabinowitch, and Richard Stites. *Russia in the Era of NEP: Explorations in Soviet Society and Culture.* Bloomington, Ind.: Indiana University Press, 1991.

Gluckstein, Donny. *The Tragedy of Bukharin.* London: Pluto Press, 1994.

Jansen, Marc. *A Show Trial under Lenin: The Show Trial of the Socialist Revolutionaries, Moscow 1922.* The Hague: M. Nijhoff, 1982.

Male, Donald J. J. *Russian Peasant Organization before Collectivization: A Study of Commune and Gathering, 1925–1930.* Cambridge: Cambridge University Press, 1971.

Martin, Terry. *The Affirmative Action Empire: Nations and Nationalism in the Soviet Union, 1923–1939.* Ithaca, NY: Cornell University Press, 2001.

Merridale, Catherine. *Moscow Politics and the Rise of Stalin: The Communist Party in the Capital, 1925–1932.* Basingstoke: Macmillan Press, 1990.

Nove, Alec. "Some Thoughts on the End of NEP." In Linda Harriet Edmondson, ed. *Economy and Society in Russia and the Soviet Union, 1860–1930: Essays for Olga Crisp.* New York: St. Martin's Press, 1992.

Pethybridge, Roger. *One Step Backwards, Two Steps Forward: Soviet Society and Politics in the New Economic Policy.* New York: Oxford University Press, 1990.

Pipes, Richard. *The Formation of the Soviet Union: Communism and Nationalism, 1917–1923.* Cambridge, Mass.: Harvard University Press, 1964.

Pipes, Richard, ed. *The Unknown Lenin: From the Secret Archive.* New Haven, Conn.: Yale University Press, 1996.

Radzinsky, Edvard. *The Last Tsar: The Life and Death of Nicholas II.* Translated by Marian Schwartz. New York: Doubleday, 1992.

Rees, E. A. *State Control in Soviet Russia: The Rise and Fall of the Workers' and Peasants' Inspectorate, 1920–1934*. London: Macmillan, 1987.

Siegelbaum, Lewis H. *Soviet State and Society between Revolutions, 1918–1929.* Cambridge: Cambridge University Press, 1992.

Stone, David R. *Hammer and Rifle: The Militarization of the Soviet Union, 1926–1933*. Lawrence, Kan.: University Press of Kansas, 2000.

Tucker, Robert C. *Stalin as Revolutionary, 1879–1929*. New York: Norton, 1974.

Tucker, Robert C. *Stalin in Power: The Revolution from Above, 1929–1941*. New York: Norton, 1990.

Volkogonov, Dmitri. *Stalin: Triumph and Tragedy*. New York: Grove Weidenfeld, 1991.

4 Collectivization, industrialization, and the Great Purge, 1929–1940

Antonov-Ovseyenko, Anton. *The Time of Stalin: Portrait of a Tyranny.* New York: Harper Colophon Books, 1980.

Brackman, Roman. *The Secret File of Joseph Stalin: A Hidden Life*. London: Frank Cass, 2001.

Bullock, Alan. *Hitler and Stalin: Parallel Lives*. New York: Knopf, distributed by Random House, 1992.

Chase, William J. *Enemies within the Gates? The Comintern and the Stalinist Repression, 1934–1939*. New Haven, Conn.: Yale University Press, 2001.

Conquest, Robert. *The Harvest of Sorrow*. New York: Oxford University Press, 1986.

Conquest, Robert. *The Great Terror*. New York: Oxford University Press, 1990.

Daniels, Robert V., ed. *The Stalin Revolution: Foundations of the Totalitarian Era*. 3rd edn. Lexington, Mass.: D. C. Heath, 1990.

Davies, R. W., M. B. Tauger, and S. G. Wheatcroft. "Stalin, Grain Stocks and the Famine of 1932–1933." *Slavic Review*, 54 (Fall 1995): 642–657.

Deutscher, Isaac. *Stalin: A Political Biography.* 2nd edn. New York: Oxford University Press, 1982.

Fainsod, Merle. *Smolensk under Soviet Rule*. New York: Vintage Russian Library, 1958.

Fitzpatrick, Sheila. *Everyday Stalinism: Ordinary Life in Extraordinary Times. Soviet Russia in the 1930s*. New York: Oxford University Press, 1999.

Fitzpatrick, Sheila. *Stalin's Peasants: Resistance and Survival in the Russian Village after Collectivization*. New York: Oxford University Press, 1996.

Gorodetsky, Gabriel. *The Precarious Truce: Anglo-Soviet Relations, 1924–27*. Cambridge: Cambridge University Press, 1977.

Hindus, Maurice. *Red Bread: Collectivization in a Russian Village*. Bloomington, Ind.: Indiana University Press, 1988.

Hochman, Jiri. *The Soviet Union and the Failure of Collective Security, 1934–1938*. Ithaca, NY: Cornell University Press, 1984.

Hochschild, Adam. *The Unquiet Ghost: Russians Remember Stalin*. New York: Penguin, 1994.

Garros, Veronique, Natalia Korenevskaya, and Thomas Lahusen. *Intimacy and Terror: Soviet Diaries of the 1930s*. Translated by Carol A. Flath. New York: The New Press, 1995.

Getty, J. Arch. *Origins of the Great Purges: The Soviet Communist Party Reconsidered, 1933–38.* Cambridge: Cambridge University Press, 1987.

Getty, J. Arch, and Roberta T. Manning. *Stalinist Terror: New Perspectives.* Cambridge: Cambridge University Press, 1993.

Getty, J. Arch, and Oleg V. Naumov. *The Road to Terror: Stalin and the Self-Destruction of the Bolsheviks, 1932–1939.* New Haven, Conn.: Yale University Press, 1999.

Goldman, Wendy Z. *Women at the Gates: Gender, Politics, and Planning in Soviet Industrialization.* Cambridge: Cambridge University Press, 2002.

Jakobson, Michael. *Origins of the Gulag: The Soviet Prison Camp System, 1917–1934.* Lexington, Ky: The University Press of Kentucky, 1993.

Jansen, Marc. *Stalin's Loyal Executioner: People's Commissar Nikolai Ezhov, 1895–1940.* Stanford, Calif.: Hoover Institution Press, 2002.

Kennan, George Frost. *Russia and the West under Lenin and Stalin.* New York: New American Library, 1960.

Kennan, George Frost. *Soviet Foreign Policy, 1917–1941.* Huntington, NY: R. E. Krieger, 1979.

Kershaw, Ian, and Moshe Lewin, eds. *Stalinism and Nazism: Dictatorships in Comparison.* Cambridge: Cambridge University Press, 1997.

Khlevnyuk, Oleg. *In Stalin's Shadow: The Career of "Sergo" Ordzhonikidze.* Armonk, NY: M. E. Sharpe, 1995.

Knight, Amy W. *The KGB: Police and Politics in the Soviet Union.* Revised edn. Boston, Mass.: Unwin Hyman, 1990.

Kotkin, Stephen. *Magnetic Mountain: Stalinism as a Civilization.* Berkeley, Calif.: University of California Press, 1995.

Kravchenko, Victor. *I Chose Freedom.* New York: Garden City, 1946.

Lambert, Nick, and Gobor T. Rittersporn. *Stalinism: Its Nature and Aftermath. Essays in Honour of Moshe Lewin.* Armonk, NY: M. E. Sharpe, 1992.

Lensen, George Alexander. *The Damned Inheritance: The Soviet Union and the Manchurian Crisis, 1924–1935.* Tallahassee, Fla: Diplomatic Press, 1974.

Leong, Sow-Theng. *Sino-Soviet Diplomatic Relations, 1917–1926.* Honolulu, HI: University Press of Hawaii, 1976.

Lewin, Moshe. *The Making of the Soviet System: Essays in the Social History of Interwar Russia.* London: Methuen, 1985.

Lewin, Moshe. *Russian Peasants and Soviet Power: A Study of Collectivization.* Evanston, Ill.: Northwestern University Press, 1968.

McCauley, Martin. *Stalin and Stalinism.* New York: Longman, 1995.

Maddux, Thomas R. *Years of Estrangement: American Relations with the Soviet Union, 1933–1941.* Gainesville, Fla: University Presses of Florida, 1980.

Nove, Alec, ed. *The Stalin Phenomenon.* New York: St. Martin's Press, 1992.

Payne, Matthew J. *Stalin's Railroad: Turksib and the Building of Socialism.* Pittsburgh, Pa: University of Pittsburgh Press, 2001.

Radosh, Ronald, and Mary R. Habeck, eds. *Spain Betrayed: The Soviet Union in the Spanish Civil War.* New Haven, Conn.: Yale University Press, 2001.

Reese, Roger R. *Stalin's Reluctant Soldiers: A Social History of the Red Army, 1925–1941.* Lawrence, Kan.: University Press of Kansas, 1996.

Rittersporn, Gabor. *Stalinist Simplifications, Soviet Complications: Social Tensions and Political Conflicts in USSR, 1933–1953.* London: Harwood Academic Publishers, 1991.

Rogovin, Vadim Zakharovich. *1937: Stalin's Year of Terror*. Oak Park, Mich.: Mehring Books, 1998.

Siegelbaum, Lewis, and Andrei Sokolov, eds. *Stalinism as a Way of Life: A Narrative in Documents* New Haven, Conn.: Yale University Press, 2000.

Spenser, Daniela. *The Impossible Triangle: Mexico, Soviet Russia, and the United States in the 1920s*. Durham, NC: Duke University Press, 1999.

Tauger, Mark B. "The 1932 Harvest and the Famine of 1933." *Slavic Review*, 50 (Spring 1991): 170–189.

Thurston, Robert W. "Life and Terror in Stalin's Russia, 1934–41," *Slavic Review*, Vol. 45 (Summer 1986): 238–44.

Thurston, Robert W. *Life and Terror in Stalin's Russia*. New Haven, Conn.: Yale University Press, 1998.

Trotsky, Leon. *Preliminary Commission of Inquiry into the Charges Made against Leon Trotsky in the Moscow Trials*. New York: Pathfinder, 2006.

Trotsky, Leon. *The Revolution Betrayed*. Mineola, NY: Dover, 2004.

Trotter, William R. *A Frozen Hell: The Russo-Finnish Winter War of 1939–1940*. Chapel Hill, NC: Algonquin Books, 1991.

Tucker, Robert C. *Stalin as Revolutionary, 1879–1929*. New York: Norton, 1974.

Tucker, Robert C. *Stalin in Power: The Revolution from Above, 1929–1941*. New York: Norton, 1990.

Uldricks, Teddy J. *Diplomacy and Ideology: The Origins of Soviet Foreign Relations, 1917–1930*. London: Sage, 1979.

Viola, Lynne. *The Best Sons of the Fatherland: Workers in the Vanguard of Soviet Collectivization*. New York: Oxford University Press, 1998.

Volkogonov, Dmitri. *Stalin: Triumph and Tragedy*. New York: Grove Weidenfeld, 1991.

Ward, Chris. *Stalin's Russia*. London: Edward Arnold, 1994.

White, Stephen. *Britain and the Bolshevik Revolution: A Study in the Politics of Diplomacy, 1920–1924*. London: Macmillan, 1980.

White, Stephen. *The Origins of Détente, the Genoa Conference and Soviet–Western Relations, 1921–1922*. Cambridge: Cambridge University Press 1985.

5 The Great Patriotic War and aftermath, 1941–1953

Bacon, Edwin. *The Gulag at War: Stalin's Forced Labor System in the Light of the Archives*. New York: New York University Press, 1994.

Barber, John, and Mark Harrison. *The Soviet Home Front, 1941–1945: A Social and Economic History of the USSR in World War II*. New York: Longman, 1991.

Barros, James. *Double Deception: Stalin, Hitler, and the Invasion of Russia*. DeKalb, Ill.: Northern Illinois University Press, 1995.

Bown, Matthew Cullerne and Brandon Taylor, ed. *Art of the Soviets: Painting, Sculpture, and Architecture in a One-Party State*. Manchester: Manchester University Press, 1993.

Brooks, Jeffrey. *Thank You, Comrade Stalin! Soviet Public Culture from Revolution to Cold War*. Princeton, NJ: Princeton University Press, 1999.

Carman, Ernest Day. *Soviet Territorial Aggrandizement, 1939–1948: An Analysis of Concepts and Methods*. Washington, DC: Public Affairs Press, 1950.

Duffy, Christopher. *Red Storm on the Reich: The Soviet March on Germany, 1945*. New York: Atheneum, 1991.

Fischer, Louis. *The Road to Yalta: Soviet Foreign Relations, 1941–1945*. London: Harper & Row, 1972.

Gallagher, Matthew P. *The Soviet History of World War II: Myths, Memories, and Realities*. Westport, Conn.: Greenwood Press, 1976.

Glantz, David M. *Stumbling Colossus: The Red Army on the Eve of World War*. Lawrence, Kan.: University Press of Kansas, 1998.

Gross, Jan. *Revolution from Abroad: The Soviet Conquest of Poland's Western Ukraine and Western Belorussia*. Princeton, NJ: Princeton University Press, 1988.

Holloway, David. *Stalin and the Bomb: The Soviet Union and Atomic Energy, 1939–1956*. New Haven, Conn.: Yale University Press, 1994.

Khrushchev, N. S. *Khrushchev Remembers: The Glasnost Tapes*. Boston, Mass.: Little, Brown, 1990.

Knight, Amy W. *Beria: Stalin's First Lieutenant*. Princeton, NJ: Princeton University Press, 1993.

Kostyrchenko, Gennadii. *Out of the Red Shadows: Anti-Semitism in Stalin's Russia*. Amherst, NY: Prometheus Books. 1995.

Linz, Susan J. *The Impact of World War II on the Soviet Union*. Totowa, NJ: Rowman & Allanheld, 1985.

Mastny, Vojtech. *Russia's Road to the Cold War: Diplomacy, Warfare, and the Politics of Communism, 1941–1945*. New York: Columbia University Press, 1979.

Mayer, S. L., ed. *The Russian War Machine*. London: Arms and Armour Press, 1977.

Paananen, Eloise. *The Winter War: The Soviet Attack on Finland, 1939–1940*. Harrisburg, Pa: Stackpole Books, 1992.

Raack, R. C. *Stalin's Drive to the West, 1938–1945: The Origins of the Cold War*. Stanford, Calif.: Stanford University Press, 1995.

Radzinsky, Eduard. *Stalin*. New York: Random House, 1996.

Roberts, Geoffrey K. *The Unholy Alliance: Stalin's Pact with Hitler*. Bloomington, Ind.: Indiana University Press, 1989.

Rubenstein, Joshua, ed. *Stalin's Secret Pogrom: The Postwar Inquisition of the Jewish Anti-Fascist Committee*. New Haven, Conn.: Yale University Press, 1999.

Soifer, Valerii. *Lysenko and the Tragedy of Soviet Science*. New Brunswick, NJ: Rutgers University Press, 1994.

Spahr, William J. *Zhukov: The Rise and Fall of a Great Captain*. Novato, Calif.: Presidio Press. 1993.

Vaksberg, Arkady. *Stalin against the Jews*. New York: Random House, 1995.

Weiner, Amir. *Making Sense of War: The Second World War and the Fate of the Bolshevik Revolution*. Princeton, NJ: Princeton University Press, 2001.

Werth, Alexander. *Russia at War, 1941–1945*. 2nd edn. New York: Dutton, 1999.

Wittlin, Tadeusz. *Commissar: The Life and Death of Lavrenty Pavlovich Beria*. New York: Macmillan, 1972.

6 Khrushchev's reforms, 1953–1964; and postwar foreign policy

Adelman, Jonathan R. *The Dynamics of Soviet Foreign Policy*. New York: Harper & Row, 1989.

Brooks, Jeffrey. *When the Cold War Did Not End: The Soviet Peace Offensive of 1953 and the American Response*. Washington, DC: Kennan Institute/Woodrow Wilson Institute, 2001.

Brown, James F. *The New Eastern Europe: The Khrushchev Era and After*. New York: Praeger, 1966.

Bruce, James B. *The Politics of Soviet Policy Formation: Khrushchev's Innovative Policies in Education and Agriculture*. Denver, Colo.: University of Denver, Graduate School of International Studies, 1976.

Burlatskii, Fedor Mikhailovich. *Khrushchev and the First Russian Spring*. London: Weidenfeld & Nicolson, 1991.

Crockatt, Richard. *The Fifty Years War: The United States and the Soviet Union in World Politics, 1941–1991*. London: Routledge, 1995.

Dallin, Alexander, ed. *The Khrushchev and Brezhnev Years*. New York: Garland, 1992.

Davies, Robert William. *Soviet Economic Development from Lenin to Khrushchev*. Cambridge: Cambridge University Press, 1998.

Dockrill, Michael L. *The Cold War, 1945–1963*. Atlantic Highlands, NJ: Humanities Press International, 1988.

Eubank, Keith. *The Missile Crisis in Cuba*. Malabar, Fla: Krieger, 2000.

Filtzer, Donald A. *The Khrushchev Era: De-Stalinization and the Limits of Reform in the USSR, 1953–1964*. Basingstoke: Macmillan, 1993.

Fletcher, William C. *Religion and Soviet Foreign Policy: 1945–1970*. London: Oxford University Press for the Royal Institute of International Affairs, 1973.

Fursenko, Aleksandr, and Timothy J. Naftali. *One Hell of a Gamble: Khrushchev, Castro, and Kennedy, 1958–1964*. New York: Norton, 1997.

Gaddis, John Lewis. *The Long Peace: Inquiries into the History of the Cold War*. Oxford: Oxford University Press, 1987.

Gaddis, John Lewis. *We Now Know: Rethinking Cold War History*. Oxford: Clarendon Press, 1997.

Ginat, Rami. *The Soviet Union and Egypt, 1945–1955*. London: Frank Cass, 1993.

Hess, Gary R., ed. *America and Russia: From Cold War Confrontation to Coexistence*. New York: Crowell, 1973.

Hyland, William. *The Fall of Khrushchev*. New York: Funk & Wagnalls, 1968.

Khrushchev, N. S. *Khrushchev Remembers: The Glasnost Tapes*. Boston, Mass.: Little, Brown, 1990.

Khrushchev, Sergei. *Khrushchev on Khrushchev: An Inside Account of the Man and His Era*. Boston, Mass.: Little, Brown, 1990.

Laver, John. *The Cold War*. London: Hodder & Stoughton. 1992.

Linden, Carl A. *Khrushchev and the Soviet Leadership, 1957–1964*. Baltimore, Md: Johns Hopkins University Press, 1966.

Lynch, Michael. *Stalin and Khrushchev: The USSR, 1924–64*. London: Hodder & Stoughton, 1990.

McCauley, Martin. *Russia, America, and the Cold War, 1949–1991.* London: Longman, 1998.

Medvedev, Roy A., and Zhores A. Medvedev. *Khrushchev: The Years in Power.* Translated by Andrew R. Durkin. New York: Norton, 1978.

Nelsen, Harvey W. *Power and Insecurity: Beijing, Moscow, and Washington, 1949–1988.* Boulder, Colo.: Lynne Rienner, 1989.

Paterson, Thomas G. *On Every Front: The Making and Unmaking of the Cold War.* New York: Norton, 1992.

Phillips, Ann L. *Soviet Policy toward East Germany Reconsidered: The Postwar Decade.* Westport, Conn.: Greenwood Press, 1986.

Porter, Bruce D. *The USSR in Third World Conflicts: Soviet Arms and Diplomacy in Local Wars, 1945–1980.* Cambridge: Cambridge University Press, 1984.

Pospielovsky, Dmitry. *The Russian Church under the Soviet Regime.* Crestwood, NY: St. Vladimir's Seminary Press, 1984.

Resis, Albert. *Stalin, the Politburo, and the Onset of the Cold War: 1945–1946.* Pittsburgh, Pa: University of Pittsburgh, Center for Russian and East European Studies, 1988.

Rubinstein, Alvin Z. *Soviet Foreign Policy since World War II: Imperial and Global.* New York: HarperCollins, 1992.

Shearman, Peter. *The Soviet Union and Cuba.* London: Routledge & Kegan Paul, 1987.

Tompson, William J. *Khrushchev: A Political Life.* New York: St. Martin's Press, 1995.

Tucker, Robert C. *The Soviet Political Mind: Stalinism and Post-Stalin Change.* New York: Norton, 1971.

Ulam, Adam B. *The Rivals: America and Russia since World War II.* New York: The Viking Press, 1971.

Walker, Martin. *The Cold War: A History.* New York: Holt, 1995.

Weathersby, Kathryn. "The Korean War Revisited." *The Wilson Quarterly* (Summer 1999).

Zubok, Vladislav Martinovich. *Inside the Kremlin's Cold War: From Stalin to Khrushchev.* Cambridge, Mass.: Harvard University Press, 1996.

7 The Brezhnev regime and its successors, 1964–1984

Anderson, Richard. *Public Politics in an Authoritarian State: Making Foreign Policy during the Brezhnev Years.* Ithaca, NY: Cornell University Press, 1993.

Arbatov, Georgi. *The System: An Insider's Life in Soviet Politics.* New York: Times Books, 1992.

Arnold, Anthony. *The Fateful Pebble: Afghanistan's Role in the Fall of the Soviet Empire.* Novato, Calif.: Presidio, 1993.

Brubaker, Rogers. *Nationalism Reframed: Nationhood and the National Question in the New Europe.* Cambridge: Cambridge University Press, 1996.

Dibb, Paul. *The Soviet Union: The Incomplete Superpower.* Basingstoke: Macmillan, 1986.

Doder, Dusko. *Shadows and Whispers: Power Politics inside the Kremlin from Brezhnev to Gorbachev.* New York: Penguin, 1988.

Dunlop, John B. *The Faces of Contemporary Russian Nationalism.* Princeton, NJ: Princeton University Press, 1983.

Edmonds, Robin. *Soviet Foreign Policy – the Brezhnev Years*. Oxford: Oxford University Press, 1983.

Gelman, Harry. *The Brezhnev Politburo and the Decline of Détente*. Ithaca, NY: Cornell University Press, 1984.

Goldman, Marshall. *What Went Wrong with Perestroika*. New York: W. W. Norton, 1992.

Hammer, Darrell. *USSR: The Politics of Oligarchy*. Boulder, Colo.: Westview Press, 1990.

Kakar, M. Hasan. *Afghanistan: The Soviet Invasion and the Afghan Response, 1979–1982*. Berkeley, Calif.: University of California Press, 1995.

Kelley, Donald R., ed. *Soviet Politics in the Brezhnev Era*. New York: Praeger, 1980.

Lampert, Nicholas. *Whistleblowing in the Soviet Union: A Study of Complaints and Abuses under State Socialism*. New York: Schocken, 1985.

Rutland, Peter. *The Politics of Economic Stagnation in the Soviet Union: The Role of Local Party Organs in Economic Management*. Cambridge: Cambridge University Press, 1993.

Schwartz, Donald V. *The Brezhnev Years, 1964–1981*. Toronto: University of Toronto Press, 1982.

Steele, Jonathan. *World Power: Soviet Foreign Policy under Brezhnev and Andropov*. London: Michael Joseph, 1983.

Stevenson, Richard W. *The Rise and Fall of Détente: Relaxations of Tension in U.S.–Soviet Relations, 1953–84*. Basingstoke: Macmillan, 1985.

Suny, Ronald Grigor. *The Revenge of the Past: Nationalism, Revolution, and the Collapse of the Soviet Union*. Stanford, Calif.: Stanford University Press, 1993.

Ticktin, H. (Hillel). *Origins of the Crisis in the USSR: Essays on the Political Economy of a Disintegrating System*. Armonk, NY: M. E. Sharpe, 1992.

Zemtsov, Ilya. *Chernenko: The Last Bolshevik*. New Brunswick, NJ/Oxford: Transaction Publishers, 1989.

8 Gorbachev, Glasnost and Perestroika, 1985–1991

Aslund, Anders. *How Russia Became a Market Economy*. Washington, DC: Brookings Institution, 1995.

Babkina, M. *New Political Parties in the Soviet Union*. Commack, NY: Nova Science, 1991.

Beissinger, Mark R. *Nationalist Mobilization and the Collapse of the Soviet State: A Tidal Approach to the Study of Nationalism*. Cambridge: Cambridge University Press, 2002.

Brown, Archie. *The Gorbachev Factor*. Oxford: Oxford University Press, 1996.

Campbell, Robert Wellington. *The Failure of Soviet Economic Planning: System, Performance, Reform*. Bloomington, Ind.: Indiana University Press, 1992.

Connor, Walter. *The Accidental Proletariat: Workers, Politics and Crisis in Gorbachev's Russia*. Princeton, NJ: Princeton University Press, 1991.

Daniels, Robert V., ed. *Soviet Communism from Reform to Collapse*. Lexington, Mass.: D. C. Heath, 1995.

Dunlop, John B. *The Faces of Contemporary Russian Nationalism*. Princeton, NJ: Princeton University Press, 1983.

Dunlop, John B. *The Rise of Russia and the Fall of the Soviet Empire.* Princeton, NJ: Princeton University Press, 1993.

Egorov, Vladimir K. *Out of a Dead End, into the Unknown: Notes on Gorbachev's Perestroika.* Chicago, Ill.: Edition Q, 1993.

Filtzer, Donald. *Soviet Workers and the Collapse of Perestroika: The Soviet Labour Process and Gorbachev's Reforms, 1985–1991.* Cambridge: Cambridge University Press, 1994.

Galeotti, Mark. *Gorbachev and His Revolution.* New York: St. Martin's Press, 1997.

Gill, Graeme, and Roger D. Markwick. *Russia's Stillborn Democracy? From Gorbachev to Yeltsin.* Oxford: Oxford University Press, 2000.

Gorbachev, Mikhail. *Perestroika: New Thinking for Our Country and the World.* New York: Harper & Row, 1987.

Hanson, Philip. *From Stagnation to Catastroika: Commentaries on the Soviet Economy, 1983–1991.* New York: Praeger, 1992.

Holmes, Leslie. *The End of Communist Power: Anti-Corruption Campaigns and the Legitimation Crisis.* Oxford: Oxford University Press, 1993.

Hosking, Geoffrey. *Russia and the Russians: A History.* Cambridge, Mass.: The Belknap Press of Harvard University Press, 2001.

Hough, Jerry F. *Democratization and Revolution in the USSR, 1985–1991.* Washington, DC: Brookings Institution, 1997.

Kiernan, Brendan. *The End of Soviet Politics: Elections, Legislatures, and the Demise of the Communist Party.* Boulder, Colo.: Westview Press, 1993.

Kotz, David M. *Revolution from Above: The Demise of the Soviet System.* New York: Routledge, 1997.

Lapidus, Gail, Victor Zaslavsky, and Philip Goldman, eds. *From Union to Commonwealth: Nationalism and Separatism in the Soviet Republics.* Cambridge: Cambridge University Press, 1992.

Lewin, Moshe. *The Gorbachev Phenomenon: A Historical Interpretation.* Berkeley, Calif.: University of California Press, 1988.

McCauley, Martin. *Gorbachev.* London: Longman, 1998.

Marples, David R. *The Social Impact of the Chernobyl Disaster.* London: Macmillan, 1988.

Morrison, John. *Boris Yeltsin: From Bolshevik to Democrat.* New York: Dutton, 1991.

Moskoff, William. *Hard Times: Impoverishment and Protest in the Perestroika Years. The Soviet Union 1985–1991.* Armonk, NY: M. E. Sharpe, 1993.

Novikov, Euvgeny. *Gorbachev and the Collapse of the Soviet Communist Party: The Historical and Theoretical Background.* New York: Peter Lang, 1994.

Pankin, Boris Dmitrievich. *The Last Hundred Days of the Soviet Union.* London: I. B. Tauris, 1996.

Remnick, David. *Lenin's Tomb: The Last Days of the Soviet Empire.* New York: Random House, 1993.

Roeder, Philip. *Red Sunset: The Failure of Soviet Politics.* Princeton, NJ: Princeton University Press, 1993.

Satter, David. *Age of Delirium: The Decline and Fall of the Soviet Union.* New Haven, Conn.: Yale University Press, 2001.

Shane, Scott. *Dismantling Utopia: How Information Ended the Soviet Union*. Chicago, Ill.: I. R. Dee, 1994.

Simes, Dimitri K. *After the Collapse: Russia Seeks Its Place as a Great Power.* New York: Simon & Schuster, 1999.

Suny, Ronald Grigor. *The Revenge of the Past: Nationalism, Revolution, and the Collapse of the Soviet Union.* Stanford, Calif.: Stanford University Press, 1993.

Taranovski, Theodore, ed. and trans. *Reform in Modern Russian History: Progress or Cycle?* Washington, DC: Woodrow Wilson Center Press, 1995.

Watson, William E. *The Collapse of Communism in the Soviet Union.* Westport, Conn.: Greenwood Press, 1998.

White, Anne. *Democratization in Russia under Gorbachev, 1985–91: The Birth of a Voluntary Sector.* Basingstoke: Macmillan, 1999.

9 From Yeltsin to Putin: Russia's decline and recovery, 1992–2008

Allensworth, Wayne. *The Russian Question: Nationalism, Modernization, and Post-Communist Russia.* Lanham, Md: Rowman & Littlefield, 1998.

Anderson. John. *Kyrgyzstan: Central Asia's Island of Democracy?* Amsterdam: Harwood Academic Publishers, 1999.

Aron, Leon Rabinovich. *Yeltsin: A Revolutionary Life.* New York: Thomas Dunne Books/St. Martin's Press, 2000.

Aslund, Anders. *How Russia Became a Market Economy.* Washington, DC: Brookings Institution, 1995.

Aslund, Anders, and Martha Brill Olcott, eds. *Russia after Communism.* Washington, DC: Carnegie Endowment for International Peace, 1999.

Blasi, Joseph R. *Kremlin Capitalism: The Privatization of the Russian Economy.* Ithaca, NY: ILR Press, 1997.

Boilard, Steve D. *Russia at the Twenty-First Century: Politics and Social Change in the Post-Soviet Era.* Fort Worth, Tex.: Harcourt Brace College Publishers, 1998.

Brubaker, Rogers. *Nationalism Reframed: Nationhood and the National Question in the New Europe.* Cambridge: Cambridge University Press, 1996.

Brucan, Silviu. *Social Change in Russia and Eastern Europe: From Party Hacks to Nouveaux Riches.* Westport, Conn.: Praeger, 1998.

Christensen, Paul Thomas. *Russia's Workers in Transition: Labor, Management, and the State under Gorbachev and Yeltsin.* Dekalb, Ill.: Northern Illinois University Press, 1999.

Dunlop, John B. *Russia Confronts Chechnya: Roots of a Separatist Conflict.* Cambridge/New York: Cambridge University Press, 1998.

Eckstein, Harry et al. *Can Democracy Take Root in Post-Soviet Russia? Explorations in State–Society Relations.* Lanham, Md: Rowman & Littlefield, 1998.

Freeland, Chrystia. *Sale of the Century: The Inside Story of the Second Russian Revolution.* London: Little Brown, 2000.

Gaddy, Clifford G. *The Price of the Past: Russia's Struggle with the Legacy of a Militarized Economy.* Washington, DC: Brookings Institution, 1996.

Gleason, Gregory. *The Central Asian States: Discovering Independence.* Boulder, Colo.: Westview Press, 1997.

Goldman, Marshall I. *Lost Opportunity: Why Economic Reforms in Russia Have Not Worked.* New York: Norton, 1994.

Handelman, Stephen. *Comrade Criminal: Russia's New Mafiya.* New Haven, Conn.: Yale University Press, 1995.

Harper, Timothy. *Moscow Madness: Crime, Corruption, and One Man's Pursuit of Profit in the New Russia.* New York: McGraw-Hill, 1999.

Hewitt, George, ed. *The Abkhazians: A Handbook.* New York: St. Martin's Press, 1998.

Huskey, Eugene. *Presidential Power in Russia.* Armonk, NY: M. E. Sharpe, 1999.

Kagarlitsky, Boris. *Restoration in Russia: Why Capitalism Failed.* New York: Verso, 1995.

Kampfer, John. *Inside Yeltsin's Russia.* London: Cassell, 1994.

Kotkin, Stephen. *Armageddon Averted: The Soviet Collapse, 1970–2000.* Oxford: Oxford University Press, 2001.

Lapidus, Gail, Victor Zaslavsky, and Philip Goldman, eds. *From Union to Commonwealth: Nationalism and Separatism in the Soviet Republics.* Cambridge: Cambridge University Press, 1992.

Lieven, Anatol. *Chechnia: Tombstone of Russian Power.* New Haven, Conn.: Yale University Press, 1999.

Mandelbaum, Michael, ed. *The New Russian Foreign Policy.* New York: Council on Foreign Relations, 1998.

Pilkington, Hilary. *Migration, Displacement, and Identity in Post-Soviet Russia.* London: Routledge, 1998.

Politkovskaya, Anna. *A Dirty War: A Russian Reporter in Chechnya.* London: The Harvill Press, 2001.

Remnick, David. *Resurrection: The Struggle for a New Russia.* New York: Random House, 1997.

Sakwa, Richard. *Putin: Russia's Choice.* London: Routledge, 2004.

Simes, Dimitri K. *After the Collapse: Russia Seeks Its Place as a Great Power.* New York: Simon & Schuster, 1999.

Steele, Jonathan. *Eternal Russia: Yeltsin, Gorbachev, and the Mirage of Democracy.* Cambridge: Harvard University Press, 1995.

Webber, Mark. *The International Politics of Russia and the Successor States.* New York: Manchester University Press, 1996.

Wyman, Matthew. *Public Opinion in Postcommunist Russia.* London: Macmillan, 1996.

Index

A Just Russia, 325
Abkhazia, Abkhazians, 292, 295, 321, 332
Abramovich, R.A., 316
Academy of Arts of the USSR, 170
Academy of Sciences of the USSR, 77, 113
Acheson, Dean, 204
Acmeist movement, 80–81
Aden, 240
Adenauer, Konrad, 207
Aeroflot, 316
Afghanistan, Afghans, 14, 85, 87, 287, 322;
    Soviet invasion and war in, 234, 243,
    245–49, 253–54, 257, 263, 274, 285,
    287, 289, 331
Africa, 240–42
Agriculture, land question, 1, 44, 92–103,
    149, 165–66, 178, 180–83, 188, 222,
    228–29, 254, 257, 262, 282–83
Ak-Mechet, 61
Akhmatova, Anna (Anna Andreevna
    Horenko), 150, 169, 274;
    biography of, 80
Akkerman, 128
Al-Qaddafi, Muhammar, 241
Al-Qaida, 323
Al-Riyad al-Salihin, 323
Albania, Albanians, 207, 235, 256
Alcoholism, 261–62, 270, 312
Aleksandr I, 5
Aleksandr II, 2
Aleksandr III, 3, 11
Aleksandr Nevsky (film), 151
Aleksandra (tsarina), 12, 17–18
Aleksandrov, A.V., 153
Alekseev, M.V., 47
Aleksey (tsarevich), 12, 18–19
Algeria, Algerians, 242, 324

Aliyev, G.A., 256
Alkhanov, A.D., 322
Allied Control Council, 199, 201–02
Alma-Ata, 292
Amin, Hafizullah, 247
Anarchism, Anarchists, 42, 44, 54, 123
Andreev, A.A., 108, 122, 165
Andreeva, Nina, 271–72
Andropov, Yu.V., 218, 250, 255–58, 260–61,
    274
Anglo-Russian Joint Advisory Committee, 88
Angola, Angolans, 240
Anti-Comintern Pact, 123, 130
Antireligioznik, 76
Antonov, A.A., 52
Antonov, A.I., 208
Antonov-Ovseenko, V.A., 32, 34, 74
Appeasement, 121
April Days, 21
Aral Sea, 229
Argentina, Argentines, 285
Arkhangelsk, 47, 50
Arkos, 88
Armenia, Armenians, 11, 58, 61–62, 113,
    231, 260, 274, 282, 284, 291–92, 296,
    324–25
Arms race, 186, 200, 207, 209–11, 213,
    216–17, 222–23, 228, 235, 242, 244,
    249, 253, 286–87, 300
Artels, *see* Collective Farms
Ashkhabad, 48
Assembly of Russian Factory Workers, 3
Association of Artists of Revolutionary
    Russia, 120, 153
Atheism, 76, 190–91, 272–73, 329
Atlantic Charter, 157
Attlee, Clement, 164, 197

Austria, Austrians, Austro-Hungarian
  Empire, 15–18, 24, 39, 47–48, 69, 83,
  87, 123, 161, 185, 196, 199, 207, 210
Averbakh, Leopold, 79
Azerbaijan, Azeris, 53, 61–62, 69, 103, 231,
  260, 291–92, 296, 325

Babel, I.E., 79, 81
Babochkin, B.A., 151
Baghdad, 14
Bagritsky, E.G., 80
Baikal-Amur Railway (BAM), 227
Bakatin, V.V., 279
Bakayev, I.P., 112
Baku, 3, 48, 50, 103, 294
Balayan, R.G., 275
Balkan Wars, 15
Balkars, 163
Baltic Fleet, 4–5, 27, 37
Baltic States, Balts, 17, 48, 51–52, 62,
  126–27, 137, 140, 158, 168, 229, 248,
  270, 277, 279, 290–92, 296, 311, 314,
  319, 321, 328; *see also* Estonia, Latvia,
  and Lithuania
Bandera, Stepan, 140, 168
Banks, banking system, 187, 283
Barents Sea, 315
Barthou, Louis, 120–21
Basayev, S.S., 310, 323
Bashkir Autonomous Republic, Bashkirs, 58
Bashkortostan, 304
Basic (Fundamental) Laws of the Russian
  Empire, 9
Bay of Pigs, 195, 214
Beaverbrook, Lord (Max Aitken), 157
Behrs, Sofya Andreevna, 12
Belarus, Belarusians, 3, 17, 40–41, 48,
  51–52, 58, 61, 77, 84, 103, 113,
  125–29, 169, 190, 273, 324–25; in
  Brezhnev period, 223, 231–34, 236,
  246; Communist Party of, 129; in
  Gorbachev period, 279–80, 296, 298;
  in Great Patriotic War, 137–38, 140,
  145–46, 158–59, 163; impact of
  Chernobyl disaster in, 267–69, 284;

and national question, 290–91,
  293–95; relations with Russia in
  independence period, 305, 308–09,
  311, 314, 319, 328
Belarusian Popular Front, 270, 293
Belavezha, 299
Belgium, Belgians, 1, 15–16, 240
Belgorod, 50, 155, 330
Belgrade, 15, 159
Beltransgaz, 328
Bely (city), 149
Bely, Andrey, 78
Belyutin, E.M., 193–94
Benes, Eduard, 123, 157–58, 199
Benin, 241
Berezina river, 51
Berezovsky, B.A., 308, 315–16
Beria, L.P., 113–14, 136–38, 140, 143, 165,
  173, 176–77, 180, 186, 200, 301
Berlin, 130, 170, 196, 211; battle of, 161;
  crisis in, 199–204, 213; treaty of, 86;
  see also East Berlin, West Berlin
Berlin Wall, 203, 213–14, 288
Beslan, 323
Bessarabia, 61–62, 84, 125, 128
Bezbozhnik, 76
Bhopal, 269
Bialystok, 126
Bielski brothers, 146
Birobidzhan, 290
Black Hundreds, 9
Black Sea, 49–50, 53, 274
Black Sea Fleet, 7, 37, 178, 308, 320
Blok, Aleksandr, 78
Bloody Sunday (1905), 6, 8
Blyukher, V.K., 88
Bock, Fedor von, 139, 144
Bogorodsky, Fyodor, 152
Bogrov, D.G., 11
Bolshevik, 76
Bolshevik Party, Bolsheviks, 2, 8–9, 11,
  20, 22–24, 38–41, 43–44, 69;
  Central Committee of, 23, 28, 35, 40;
  8th Congress of, 188; and the
  October Revolution, 31–37;

in Petrograd Soviet, 26–27;
7th All-Russian Conference of, 23
Bolshoy Drama Theater, 81
Bonaparte, Napoleon, 5, 146
Bonn, 201
Bonner, Yelena, 253, 263
Borodin, P.P., 313
Bosnia-Herzegovina, 14
Brandt, Willy, 239
Bratislava, 236
Brauchitsch, Walther von, 144
Brest, 126, 136–37, 330
Brest-Litovsk, Treaty of, 39–41, 42, 48, 67, 85
Brezhnev, L.I., 32, 153, 260–61, 270, 330;
    agricultural reforms of, 222;
    background and career of, 186, 218,
    224–25, 277; corruption under, 254;
    cult of, 225, 258; cultural
    developments under, 249–53; death
    of, 255; and Developed Socialism, 223;
    foreign policy of, 234–49; illness of,
    249, 308; and Virgin Lands Program,
    181
Brezhnev Doctrine, 235–38, 248, 288
Brezhneva, G.L., 256
Briand-Kellog Pact, 88
Britain, British, 1, 5, 13, 15, 17, 21, 43–44,
    47–49, 51, 53, 82, 85, 108, 177, 209,
    212, 315; in Cold War, 195–97,
    199–201, 240–44; foreign policy
    in interwar period, 82, 85–88, 91,
    120–26; in Second World War, 130,
    156–59; in Gorbachev period, 285
Brubaker, Rogers, 232–33
Brusilov, A.A., 17, 26
Bryansk, 142, 269
Bryukhanov, Viktor, 267
Bryusov, Valery, 78
Brzezinski, Zbigniew, 242
Bubnov, A.S., 32–33
Budapest, 159, 209
Budenny, S.M., 50–52, 137–38, 142
Bukhara, 58
Bukharin, N.I., 39, 65, 67, 76, 82, 89, 91–93,
    112, 114, 270

Bukovsky, V.K., 326
Bukovyna, 125, 128
Bulgakov, M.A., 78, 274; biography of, 79
Bulganin, N.A., 173, 176, 178–80, 184–86,
    206, 243
Bulgaria, Bulgarians, 121, 159, 195, 198, 207,
    236, 263, 328
Bush, George H.W., 289–90, 304
Bushwehr nuclear power station, 318
Buynaksk, 310
Bykivnya, 271
Byrnes, James, 196

Cambodia, Cambodians, 245
Camp David, 182, 244
Canada, Canadians, 202
Cardenas, Lazaro, 114
Carpathian Mountains, 17
Carr, E.H., 44–45
Carter, James Earl, 225, 241–44, 247, 249
Caspian Sea, 50
Castro, Fidel, 212, 214, 216, 241
Caucasus, 41, 48, 61, 95, 98, 101, 136,
    146–48, 181, 231, 311
Central Asia, Central Asians, 48, 59, 61, 139,
    168, 185, 231–33, 283, 298, 311, 314
Central Bureau of Trade Unions, 21
Cernik, Oldrich, 236–37
CFE (Conventional Forces in Europe) Treaty,
    322
Chapayev (film), 151
Chechnya, Chechens, 163, 185, 260, 291,
    294–95, 314, 326; Russia's war in, 305,
    307–10, 312, 322–24, 331; and
    terrorism, 310, 315, 322–23
Cheka (All-Russian Extraordinary
    Commission for the Struggle with
    Counter-Revolution and Sabotage),
    41–44, 280; *see also* State Political
    Directorate (GPU)
Chelsea Football Club, 316
Chelyabinsk, 48–49, 104
Chernenko, K.U., 254–58, 260, 262
Chernivtsi, 128
Chernobyl disaster, 263–69, 272, 280, 282

Chernomyrdin, V.S., 305, 309, 319

Chernov, V.M., 19, 21, 37, 53

Chervonenko, S.V., 237

Chervyakov, A.G., 60

Chiang Kai-Shek, 88

Chicherin, G.V., 40, 85–86

China, Chinese, 3–5, 14, 87–89, 91, 93, 120, 124, 162, 180, 242, 287; Communists struggle for power in, 123–24, 202, 204, 300; in Korean War, 203–06; Sino-Soviet relations: under Khrushchev, 189, 213; under Brezhnev, 227, 234, 244–46; under Andropov, 256; under Putin, 322, 325

Chinese Eastern Railway, 87–88, 121

Chkeidze, N.S., 20, 22

Chuikov, V.I., 147

Chumachenko, Tatiana, 190

Churbanov, Yury, 256

Churchill, Winston S., 88, 135–36, 156–60, 164, 194–95, 197, 271

Cierna-nad-Tisou, 236

Clinton, W.J., 309

CNN, 297

Coal, coal industry, coal miners, 104, 226–28, 265–66, 283, 307

Collective farms, kolkhozes, collectivization, 62–63, 92–98, 101, 102–03, 106, 115, 165, 168–69, 178, 183, 189, 222, 224, 228, 282–83

Collective security, 120–21

Collective Security Treaty Organization, 325

Cominform (Communist Information Bureau), 176, 198–99, 206, 208, 288

Committee for Artistic Affairs, 170

Committee for the Protection of Journalists, 324

Committee for the Protection of the Motherland and the Revolution, 34

Committees of the Poor, 42, 45, 48, 62, 96

Committee for Public Safety, 35–36

Commonwealth of Independent States (CIS), 299, 311, 325

Communist International (Comintern), 82–83, 88, 114, 122–23, 125

Communist Party of Germany (KPD), 82, 122

Communist Party of Poland, 84, 125

Communist Party of the Russian Federation (KPRF), 281, 314, 317, 326

Communist Party of the Soviet Union: Corruption of, 257, 260, 274; Membership of, 115, 150, 186, 281; Programs of, 188; Purge of, 113; role in society, 230–31, 278, 301; temporary ban of, 298

Congo, 241

Congresses and Conferences Russian Communist Party:

8th Congress (1919), 62

10th Congress (1921), 59, 63

13th Congress (1924), 71

14th Conference (1925), 72

Communist Party of the Soviet Union:

1st All-Union Congress of Soviets (1922), 60

2nd All-Union Congress of Soviets (1924), 71

5th All-Union Congress of Soviets (1929), 103

15th Party Conference (1927), 75, 92

15th Party Congress (1927), 75, 93

16th Party Congress (1930), 92, 104

17th Party Congress (1934), 105, 108–09, 113, 120, 183

18th Party Congress (1939), 108, 115

19th Party Congress (1952), 172–73

20th Party Congress (1956), 183–85, 189, 191, 208, 244

21st (Extraordinary) Party Congress (1959), 188

22nd Party Congress (1961), 188–89, 193

23rd Party Congress (1966), 218

26th Party Congress (1981), 225

27th Party Congress (1986), 262–63

19th Party Conference (1988), 276–77, 282–83

28th Party Congress (1990), 281

Congress of Deputies of Russia, 304–05

Congress of People's Deputies of the USSR, 277–78

Conquest, Robert, 99, 111
Constituent Assembly, 19, 21, 23, 27–28, 37–39, 42
Constitutions
Constitution of 1918, 38
Constitution (Basic Law) of USSR (1924), 60–61
Constitution (Stalin) (1936), 61, 115, 253, 290
Constitution of 1977, 230–31, 257, 290
Constitution of 1993 (Yeltsin), 304, 307
Constitutional Democratic Party, *see* Kadet Party
Cooperatives, 262, 283
Corruption, 232, 254–56, 276, 308, 313, 318
Council of Europe, 287
Council for Evacuation, 139
Council of the Federation, 306
Council for Mutual Economic Assistance, 203
Council of People's Commissars, 34
Council for Russian Orthodox Church Affairs, 190
Council of Workers' Control, 36
Crimea, 52–53, 157, 178, 193, 297–98, 305
Crimean Tatars, 163, 178, 291–92
Cuba, Cubans, 240–41, 264
Cuban missile crisis, 194, 214–16
Culture
    Architecture, architects, 118, 170
    Art, artists, 118–20, 152–53, 157, 169–70, 193, 275
    Literature, plays, 77–82, 118, 169–70, 191–94, 249–51, 272, 274–75, 331
    Music, 169–71, 194, 250–53, 331
Cultural Revolution, 245
Curzon, George, 54n, 86–87
Curzon Line, 52, 54n, 84, 161
Czechs, Czechoslovakia, Czech Republic, 84, 121, 123, 157–58, 168, 180, 194, 198–99, 207, 235, 263–64, 309, 314, 322; Soviet invasion of, 235–38, 245, 249, 253
Czechoslovak Corps, 47–48, 50, 235

Dagestan, Dagestanis, 58, 260, 310, 324
Dan, F.I., 19
Daniel, Yu.M., 249–50, 253
Danzig (Gdansk), 124
Daoud, Mohammed, 246
Dardanelles, 86
Davies, R.W., 100
De Gaulle, Charles, 212
Death's Head Women's Battalion, 33
Declaration of the Rights of the Peoples of Russia, 34
Declaration of the Rights of the Toiling and Exploited Peoples, 36–38
Declaration on Land, 34
Demobilization, 164
Democratic Assembly, 27
Democratic Union, 276
Deneika, A.A., 152
Denikin, A.I., 13, 47–51, 82
Denmark, Danes, 87
Deportations, 163, 168, 185, 290
Derevyanko, K.N., 162
Détente, 238–40
Developed Socialism, 223, 230, 254
Dimitrios of Constantinople, 272
Dimitrov, G.M., 122
Dissident movement, 253–54, 257, 273, 301
Dnipro River, 104, 156
Dniprodzerzhinsk, 224
Dnipropetrovsk, 224, 233
Dobrynin, A.F., 215
Doctor Zhivago, 192–93, 275
Doctors' Plot, 173, 176
Domodedovo airport, 323
Don region, Donbas, 62, 91, 98, 179, 227–28, 283
Donetsk, 156
Donskoy, Dmitry, 174n
Drach, I.F., 293
Dresden, 312
Dubcek, Alexander, 235–37
Dubrovka Theater, 315
Dudayev, D.M., 308
Dukhonin, N.N., 36
Dulles, Allen, 211

Duma (Russian Empire), 6, 8–10, 18–20
Duma (Russian Federation), 306–07, 309;
Duranty, Walter, 100–01
Dushanbe, 247, 294
Dybenko, P.Ye., 32
Dzerzhinsky, F.E., 33, 41, 43, 51, 298;
    biography of, 41–42

East Berlin, 213, 287–88
East Germany, *see* German Democratic
    Republic
East Prussia, 16, 83, 124, 161, 164
Economic Councils (*Sovnarkhozy*), 187, 189,
    222, 225
Economism, 2
Economy, Economic Reform, 11, 44, 52, 61,
    115, 149, 165–67, 188–89, 225–29,
    256–57, 260–62, 282–85, 304, 307,
    310–11, 318, 321, 329
Eden, Anthony, 157
Education, 77
Efremov, O.N., 192
Egypt, Egyptians, 209, 227, 243–44
Ehrenburg, I.G., 79, 191–92; biography of,
    151
Eisenhower, Dwight, 160, 182, 210–12
Eisenstein, S.M., 6, 117, 150–51, 171
Elbe river, 161
Elets, 330
Elnya, 330
Emancipation of the serfs, 1
Enemy at the Gates, 147–48
Energy, 187, 189, 227, 263
Engels, Friedrich, 119, 188, 300
Entente (Britain, France, and Russia), 13–15,
    21, 25–26, 36, 47–49, 84
Environmental issues, 257, 267, 283–84
Estemirova, N.Kh., 323–24
Estonia, Estonians, 40, 49, 88, 125, 128, 136,
    169, 231–32, 278–79, 293, 295, 298,
    305, 321, 330
Ethiopia, Ethiopians, 121, 240, 242
Eurasian Economic Community, 324
European Union (EU), 311, 319–20, 328
Ezerum, Battle of, 17

Fadeyev, A.A., 78, 80, 117
Falkland Islands, 285
Famine, Famines, 3, 53, 64, 98–102, 109, 166
Far Eastern Republic, 51, 53, 58
Fascism, 122
February Revolution, 18–22
Federal Republic of Germany, West
    Germany, 201–02, 206–07, 210, 234,
    238–39, 289
Federation Council, 307
Federation Treaty, 304
Fellow Travelers, 79
Fergana, 292
Films, filmmakers, 194, 275
Finland, Finns, 11, 13, 25, 51, 141, 159,
    185, 198, 264, 328; war with USSR
    (Soviet-Finnish war), 127–28, 130,
    137
First World War, 15–18, 21, 45
Fitzpatrick, Sheila, 37, 111
Five-Year Plans
    First, 92, 103–06
    Second, 102, 105, 108, 113
    Third, 108, 165
    Fourth, 165–66
    Fifth, 173
    Sixth, 183
    Eighth, 226
    Ninth, 228
Fomin, E.M., 136
Food Program, 229
Foreign Policy
    In the 1920s, 82–89
    In the 1930s, 120–30
    In the early Cold War, 194–206
    In the Khrushchev period, 206–17
    In the Brezhnev period, 234–49
    In the Gorbachev period, 285–90
    In the Putin period, 314, 321–22, 333
Forsberg, 265
Fourth International, 114
Fradkov, M.Ye., 318
France, French, 1, 15–17, 21, 39, 44, 47, 49,
    52–53, 156, 198, 209, 212, 301, 319,
    328; in Cold War, 195–97, 201, 240,

242–44; foreign policy in interwar period, 82, 85–87, 120–24, 126

Franco, Francisco, 122–23

Franz Ferdinand (Archduke), 15

Fridberg, I.I., 275

Frunze, M.V., 49, 52

FSB (Federal Security Service), 313, 324

Furtseva, Ye.A., 180, 186

Gagarin, Yu.A., 217

Gaidar, Ye.T., 304–05, 307

Galich, A.A., 251–52; biography of, 251

Galicia, 16–17, 24

Gamsakhurdia, Zviad, 296

Gapon, Georgy, 3, 6

Gas, gas industry, 173, 189, 222, 226–27, 232, 256, 263, 318, 328–29

Gazprom, 326, 328–29

Gatchina, 34

Gavrilov, P.A., 136

Gdansk, 245

Geneva, 210–11, 286

Genoa, 85

George V, 18

Georgia, Georgians, 58–59, 62, 69, 84, 113, 177, 184, 189, 231, 260, 291–92, 294, 296, 314, 321, 325, 327–28, 332

Gerasimov, A.M., 152, 170, 192; biography of, 153

Gerasimov, S.V., 152

German, Yury, 169

German army, *see* Wehrmacht

German-Soviet war, *see* Great Patriotic War

Germany, Germans, 1–2, 11, 22, 24, 67, 69, 72, 82, 118–19, 328; in First World War, 15–18, 21, 36, 38–40, 42–45, 47–48, 83–84; foreign policy in interwar period, 85–86, 113, 120–30; in the early Cold War period, 194–203; in Great Patriotic War, 137–38, 161, 191, 267, 271, 330; in Second World War, 102–03; unification of, 289; Wehrmacht of, 125, 135–37, 139–42, 144–47, 149, 154–56, 162, 168;

German Democratic Republic, GDR, East Germany, East Germans 149, 176, 201–02, 207, 210, 213–14, 234, 236–37, 239–40, 263, 288–89, 313

Getty, J. Arch, 111, 113

Glantz, David, 149

Glasnost, 100, 262–63, 268–75, 282, 284, 292, 294

Glazev, S.Yu., 317–18

GOELRO (State Commission for Electrification of Russia), 103

Goering, Herman, 148

Golden Horde, 273

Gomel, 61, 267

Gomulka, Wladyslaw, 208–10, 236

Gongadze, G.R., 312

Gorbachev, M.S., 31, 42, 63, 100, 107, 114–15, 179, 255, 258, 310, 330; and agriculture, 229; and arms race; background and career of, 254, 257, 260; and Chernobyl disaster, 266, 268; and de-Stalinization campaign, 270–72; foreign policy of, 245, 285–90; and national question, 292, 294; outlook of, 256; perestroika under, 282–85; politics under, 275–82, 301; in power, 260–301; as president of USSR, 278–79; and putsch of 1991, 297–98; and the Russian Orthodox Church, 272–73, 329; unpopularity of, 288, 311; and war in Afghanistan, 248; wins Nobel Peace Prize, 288; and Union Treaty, 296, 299

Gorbacheva, Raisa, 260, 287, 297–98

Goremykin, I.I., 9

Gori, 69, 332

Gorki, 71

Gorky, A.M., 78, 81–82, 116–17, 119, 153

Gorky (Nizhny Novgorod), 263

Gorsk Autonomous Republic, 58

Goskino, 275

Gottwald, Klement, 123, 173, 198

Govorukhin, S.S., 275

GPU (State Political Directorate), 42, 66

Grachev, P.S., 306

Great Depression, 105
Great Patriotic War, 135–65, 266, 273; battle of Kursk Salient in, 154–56; battle of Stalingrad in, 146–50; casualties in, 137, 149, 155–56, 163–64; early stages of, 135–41; evacuations during, 139, 150; historical memory and, 330–31; Operation Typhoon in, 142–45; partisan movement in, 145–46; prisoners in, 142; results of, 162–64
Grechko, A.A., 218, 237
Greece, Greeks, 125, 195–97
Grishin, V.V., 255, 258, 262
Grodno, 51
Gromyko, A.A., 164, 212, 248, 257, 262, 277
Grozny, 48, 307–08, 322–23
Gryzlov, B.V., 317
Guchkov, A.I., 7, 12–13, 21, 24
Guderian, Heinz, 125, 144
GULAG (Chief Administration of Camps), 80–81, 92, 110, 113–14, 119, 164, 167, 173, 177, 191, 193, 227, 250, 252–53, 300
Gulag Archipelago, 250, 279–80
Gumbinnen, Battle of, 16
Gumilyov, L.N., 80
Gumilyov, N.S., 80
Gusev, S.I., 49
Gusinsky, V.A., 308, 315–16
Gypsies, 331

Hanko, 128
Hantsavichy, 319
Harriman, Averell, 157
Harvest of Sorrow, 99
Hasavyurt Treaty, 309
Helsinki, 289
Helsinki Accords, 234, 239, 249, 254
Helsinki Group, 254
Herriot, Eduard, 87
Hiroshima, 286
Hitler, Adolf, 68–69, 86, 92, 119–20, 122–25, 128–29, 135, 139, 141–42, 144–48, 154–55, 161, 301
Hitler Youth, 161

Hoffmann, Max, 40
Hohenzollern monarchy, 18, 39, 48
Holland, Dutch, 121, 301
Honecker, Erich, 173, 240, 288
Hopkins, Harry, 195
Horthy, Miklos, 159
Hosking, Geoffrey, 280
Housing, 65, 187, 223, 229, 283
Hrushevsky, Mykhailo, 273
Hull, Cordell, 157
Hungary, Hungarians, 15, 47–48, 83–84, 121, 124, 159, 168, 198, 207, 236–37, 263, 309; Soviet invasion of, 208–10, 235, 255
Husak, Gustav, 237
Hussein, Saddam, 318

Ignalina, 264, 268
Illiteracy, 76, 103, 129, 300
Inchon, 205
India, Indians, 234, 244, 246, 325
Indian Ocean, 241
Indra, Alois, 236–37
Industry, Industrialization, 1, 74, 94, 103–08, 142, 165–66, 178, 186–88, 222–23, 227–29
INF (Intermediate-range nuclear forces) Treaty, 287
Ingushetia, Ingushetians, 163, 185, 260, 291, 324
Institute of Red Professors, 77
Interdistrict Group, 23
International Atomic Energy Agency (IAEA), 266, 269
International Brigades, 123
International Monetary Fund, 328
International Peace Forum, 286
Iowa, 182
Iran, Iranians, 14, 85, 87–88, 196–97, 247, 249, 318, 322, 325
Iraq, Iraqis, 244, 289, 318–19, 321, 324
Irrigation, 189, 223, 229, 257, 268, 283–84
Israel, Israelis, 209, 227, 243–44, 253, 319
Italy, Italians, 87, 101, 120–23, 148, 157, 196, 198, 328

Ivan IV (the Terrible), 151
Ivanov, N.I., 16
Ivanov, V.V., 81
Ivanovo, 143
Ivinskaya, Olga, 192
Izhevsk, 49
Izmail, 128
Izotov, N.I., 106
Izvestiya, 20, 151, 263, 265–66, 270, 292
Izvolsky, A.P., 13

Japan, Japanese, 13–14, 47, 51, 53, 87, 115,
        144, 196, 203–04, 322; relations with
        Russia in interwar period, 120–21,
        123–24, 130; war with Russia in 1905,
        3–5, 206; war with Russia in 1945,
        160–62, 195
Jaruzelski, Wojciech, 246
Jewish Anti-Fascist Committee, 151, 172, 183
Jewish Bund, 2, 8
Jews, 3, 13, 52, 84, 125, 127–28, 139, 146,
        163, 244, 252–53, 290, 331; postwar
        campaign against, 169, 172–73
John-Paul II, 289
Jordan, Jordanians, 143
July Days, 24–26

Kabul, 247
Kadar, Janosz, 209
Kadet Party, 2, 6–7, 9, 13, 20, 25–26, 34, 37,
        42
Kadyrov, A.A., 322
Kadyrov, R.A., 322–24
Kaganovich, L.M., 77, 91, 101–02, 108, 113,
        115, 137–38, 176, 179–80, 184–85,
        208, 271
Kagarlitsky, B.Yu., 333
Kakhovka, 52
Kalinin, M.I., 53, 60, 64, 66, 71, 76, 97, 108,
        165, 173, 218
Kaliningrad, 160
Kalinovka, 179
Kalmyks, 163, 185
Kamenev, L.B., 22, 25, 28, 32–33, 35, 58, 67,
        69; persecution and trial of, 108, 110,

112; and power struggle in 1920s,
        71–77, 89, 106
Kamenev, S.S., 47, 49
Kansk-Achinsk coalfield, 228
Kaplan, Fanya, 43, 85
Kapustin, Ya.F., 172
Kara, Yu.V., 275
Karachai, 163
Karakhan, L.M., 40
Karatygin, E.S., 92
Karelia, Karelo-Finnish Republic, 127–28,
        304
Karmal, Babrak, 246–48
Karpov, G.G., 190
Kaspar, Jan, 237
Kasparov, G.K., 326
Kasyanov, M.M., 315, 317–18, 326
Katowice, 160
Katyn Massacre, 130, 159, 271
Kazakhstan, Kazakhs, 61, 75, 98–99, 112,
        136, 181–82, 224, 231–32, 279,
        291–92, 296, 305, 308, 314, 319,
        324–25
Kazan, 6, 48
Kemerovo, 112, 276
Kennan, George, 196
Kennedy, John F., 195, 213–15, 249
Kennedy, Robert F., 215
Kerch, 268, 330
Kerensky, Aleksandr, 20–21, 24–28, 39;
        downfall of, 31, 33–36; forms Second
        Coalition Government, 25; forms
        Third Coalition Government, 27
KGB (Committee for State Security), 177,
        180, 185, 217–18, 223, 247–48,
        253–54, 271, 301, 312–13, 329
Khabalov, S.S., 19
Khabarovsk, 89
Khakamada, I.M., 318
Khalkin-Gol, Battle of, 124
Khanty-Mansi autonomous region, 232,
        316
Kharitonov, N.M., 317
Kharkiv, 50, 104, 144, 155
Khasbulatov, R.I., 305–06

Khatchaturian, A.I., 153, 171;
biography of, 172
Khiznyak, I.L., 119
Khodorkovsky, M.B., 316–17
Khomeini, Ayatollah, 244, 247
Khorezmsk, 58
Khrushchev, N.S., 101–02, 113–14, 127, 173,
249, 270–71, 287; background of,
179–81; cultural thaw period under,
80, 115, 151, 191–94, 250, 275;
denunciation of Stalin, 183–85, 208,
244; foreign policy of, 199, 203,
206–17, 240, 289; and Great Patriotic
War, 135, 291; ideology of, 188–89,
230, 254; overthrow of, 217–18, 224;
reforms of, 186–89, 213, 228, 261;
and Russian Orthodox Church,
190–91; and space program, 217;
and succession question after Stalin,
176–79; 189; visit to United States,
211
Khrushchev, S.N., 179
Kiljunen, Kimmo, 326
Kim Il Sung, 203–06
Kirghizia, Kyrgyszstan, Kirghiz, 61, 294,
296, 308, 324–25
Kiriyenko, S.V., 309
Kirov, S.M., 73, 91, 108–10, 112, 114
Kirponos, M.P., 141
Kishinev, 128
Kissinger, Henry, 245
Kitchen Debate, 211
Koenigsberg, 16, 160–61, 164
Kokovtsov, Vladimir, 10
Kolbin, Gennady, 292
Kolchak, A.P., 49–50, 82
Kolder, Drahomir, 236–37
Kollontay, Aleksandra, 23
Kolpino, 141
Kolyma, 166
Komsomol, 96, 115, 181, 190, 227
Komsomolskaya pravda, 76
Konev, I.S., 140, 142, 149, 155–56, 161, 208
Korea, Koreans, 3–5, 14
Korean Airlines, 256

Korean War, 202–06, 216
Kornilov, L.G., 26–28, 47–48
Kornilov Revolt, 25, 26–28
Korotych, V.O., 274
Korsun, 156
Kosior, S.V., 108
Kosovo, 332
Kosygin, A.N., 139, 186, 218, 222, 233, 236,
249; reforms of, 225–27, 254, 261
Kovpak, S.A., 146
Kozhikov, Vadim, 177
Kozlov, F.R., 180, 217–18
Krasin, L.B., 85
Krasnaya zvezda, 76, 151
Krasnov, N.N., 34–35, 48
Kravchuk, L.M., 298–99, 305
Krestinsky, N.N., 114
Krivoshein, A.V., 10
Krivoshein, S.M., 126
Kronstadt, 7, 24; rebellion at, 53–54; sailors
of, 28, 33–34, 53–54, 63
Krupskaya, N.K., 22, 70–71, 73–74
Krylenko, N.V., 32, 36
Krymov, A.M., 26–27
Kryuchkov, V.A., 279, 282, 297
Kuchma, L.D., 308, 312, 319–20
Kuibyshev, V.V., 49, 59, 108
Kulaks, 44, 62–63, 74, 93, 168; liquidation
of, 95–98, 106, 224
Kulchytsky, S.V., 100
Kulik, G.I., 137
Kunayev, D.A., 291
Kurapaty Forest, 270–71
Kurchatov, I.V., 200
Kuropatkin, A.N., 4
Kurile Islands, 162, 322
Kursk, 6, 50, 146, 150, 163, 264, 330
Kursk submarine, 315
Kutuzov, M.I., 174n
Kuwait, Kuwaitis, 289
Kuznetsk, 104, 283
Kuznetsov, A.A., 172
Kyiv, 51, 84, 100, 139, 156, 170, 265, 269,
319–20, 330
Kyivan Rus', 272–73

Kyrghyz-Kazak Autonomous Republic, 58, 61
Kzyl-Orda, 61

Labor Group (*Trudoviki*), 9
Lake Baikal, 51
Lake Ladoga, 229
Language policy, *see* Nationality Policy
Larionov, A.N., 182
Latvia, Latvians, 40, 125, 128, 136, 169,
    231–32, 278–80, 293, 295, 298, 305,
    330
Lausanne Conference, 86
Laval, Pierre, 121
Law for the Protection of Socialist Property,
    98–99
League of Nations, 89, 121, 127
Lebed, A.I., 309
Lebedev-Kumach, V.I., 153
Leeb, Wilhelm Ritter von, 144
Left Socialist Revolutionary Party (Left SRs),
    32, 34–35, 37, 40, 42; uprising of,
    43–45
Legasov, V.A., 266
Lend-Lease, 157, 195
Lenin, V.I., 7, 58, 69, 76, 102, 119, 151, 173,
    176, 179, 238, 250; and centralization
    of state, 67; April Theses of, 22–23;
    and Cheka, 41–44; cult of, 73, 77, 92,
    184, 273, 311; death of, 71; dissolves
    Constituent Assembly, 37–39; foreign
    policy of, 83, 85–87, 122; and
    formation of USSR, 59–61, 232, 290,
    300; illness of, 59, 66, 70; "Letter to
    the Congress," 71; "Letter from Afar,"
    22; and literature, 78, 81; "Marxism
    and the Uprising," 28; and murder
    of Romanov family, 43; and New
    Economic Policy, 62–64, 270;
    returns to Russia in 1917, 22–24; and
    Russian Civil War, 48, 51, 53, 82; at
    2nd Congress of RSDWP, 2–3; statues
    of, 170; and October Revolution, 28,
    31–37; Testament of, 67, 70–71, 73,
    109; and Treaty of Brest-Litovsk,
    39–40; and War Communism, 45

Lenin Library, 77
Leningrad, 71–72, 97, 109–10, 137, 139, 166,
    251, 263–64, 275, 330; blockade of,
    141, 150, 156, 163; *see also* Petrograd,
    St. Petersburg
Leningrad (journal), 169
Leningrad Affair, 178
Leskov, N.S., 275
Liaotung Peninsula, 4–5, 206
Liaoyang, Battle of, 4
Liberal Russia, 316
Liberal-Democratic Party, 318, 325
Libya, 196, 241
Ligachev, Ye.K., 262, 265, 277
Literaturnaya gazeta, 252
Lithuania, Lithuanians, 40, 41, 88, 125–28,
    136, 169, 233, 254, 264, 268, 277,
    293–95
Litvinov, M.M., 85, 120, 125
Livadia Palace, 157
Lockhart, Bruce, 44
Lodz, 1, 7
London, 159, 201
Long Telegram, 196
Lopatin, A.I., 147
Lublin, 52
Lublin Committee, 195
Lubyanka Prison, 137
Lukashenka, A.G., 308, 311–12, 319
Luftwaffe, 122, 137, 147–48
Lukoil, 318
Lukyanov, A.I., 279
Lunts, Lev., 81
Luzhkov, Yu.M., 317
Lysenko, T.D., 166–67
Lviv, 16, 126, 140, 158
Lvov, G.E., 20–21, 25
Lyubimov, Yu.P., 192, 250

MacArthur, Douglas, 205–06
MacDonald, Ramsay, 87
Mace, James E., 99–100
Macedonia, Macedonians, 328
Machine-Tractor Stations (MTS), 102, 168,
    183

Maclaine, Shirley, 286
Macmillan, Harold, 212
Magnitogorsk, 104
Maikop oilfields, 146
Mailer, Norman, 286
Makhno, Nestor, 53
Maksudov, Sergey, 98
Malenkov, G.M., 113, 137–38, 176–78, 180, 185
Malgobek, 330
Malinovsky, R.Ya., 162, 186, 218
Malyshkin, O.A., 318
Manchuria, 4–5, 88–89, 120–21, 162
Mandelstam, N.Ya., 81
Mandelstam, O.E., 80, 274; biography of, 80–81
Manezh Central Exhibition Hall, 193
Manhattan Project, 195
Mannerheim, C.G.E., 127
Mannerheim Line, 127, 137
Manstein, Erich von, 148, 155
Manuilsky, D.Z., 122
Mao Zedong, 186, 189, 202–05, 245
Marinsky Palace, 33
Markhlevsky, Yu.Yu., 51
Marshall Plan, 165, 197–98, 200
Martin, Terry, 100
Martov, Yuly, 2, 20
Marx, Karl, 119, 188, 300
Marxism, Marxism-Leninism, 2–3, 23, 76, 115, 273
Marxism and the National Question, 11
Masherov, P.M., 223, 233, 236
Maskhadov, A.A., 322
Maslyukov, Yu.D., 279
Massawa, 240
Masurian Lakes, Battle of, 16
Mayakovsky, V.V., 77–78, 81, 117; biography of, 117
Maysky, I.M., 122
McNamara, Robert, 216
Media-Most, 316
Medvedev, D.A., 326–28, 330, 333; biography of, 326
Medvedev, Vadim, 277

Mekhlis, L.Z., 136
Memorial, 271, 323
Menkovsky, V.I., 113
Menshevik Party, Mensheviks, 2, 8–9, 11, 32, 34–35, 37–38, 42, 44, 59, 66, 69; and February Revolution, 19–21; in Petrograd Soviet, 23–24; in Provisional Government, 25, 27; in Russian Civil War, 48; trial of, 108
Mercader, Ramon, 114
Meretskov, K.A., 137, 140, 162
Meshketian Turks, 163, 292, 294
Metropolitan Vickers Company, 108
Mexico, Mexicans, 87
Middle East, 243–44
Mikhail (Grand Duke), 18–19
Mikhalkov, N.S., 331
Mikhalkov, S.V., 153
Mikoyan, A.I., 137–38, 165, 177, 179, 208, 218
Military-Revolutionary Committee, 32–36
Miller, E.K., 49
Milyukov, P.N., 6–7, 20–21, 24
Minsk, 8, 51, 137, 139, 158, 163, 330
Mir (village community), 10–11, 20
Mirbach, Wilhelm, 43, 45
Mironov, S.M., 318
Model, Walther, 149, 155
Mogilev, 27, 36, 158
Moldavia (Moldova), Moldavians, 3, 61–62, 128, 137, 169, 224, 234, 291, 293, 296, 298, 321, 324
Molotov, V.M., 69, 91, 180; appointed Premier, 92; and collectivization and famine, 95, 101; and foreign policy in interwar years, 120, 125–26, 128, 130; and foreign policy in postwar period, 165, 196–98, 202–03; and Great Patriotic War, 136–38, 157, 159, 163–64; and purges, 108, 110, 113; relations with Khrushchev, 180; 184–86, 208; and Stalin's succession, 176–77
Monastery of the Caves, 191

Mongolia, Mongolians, 14, 87, 124, 185, 245, 325
Montgomery, Bernard, 160
Moravov, A.V., 119; biography of, 119–20
Moscow, 1, 6, 8, 23, 31, 45, 72, 97, 166, 179, 209, 251, 275, 292, 314, 320, 330; becomes capital, 42; Great Patriotic War in, 137, 141–42, 149, 158, 163; industrial growth in, 62, 103, 187; Metro, 118; October Revolution in, 35–36; Olympic Games in, 247, 252; putsch of 1991 in, 297–98, 313; terrorist attacks in, 310, 315, 322–23; Treaty of, 238–39; Yeltsin's anti-corruption campaign in, 276
Moscow Arts Theater, 79
Moscow Conference, 157
Moscow Protocol, 237
Moscow Soviet, 7, 27
Moscow Union of Artists, 193
Moskalenko, K.S., 177
Moskovskie novosti, 274
Mother Teresa, 272
Motherland, 317
Movement for Democratic Reform, 297
Mozambique, Mozambiquens, 240
Muggeridge, Malcolm, 101
Mujahideen, 248, 285
Mukden, Battle of, 4
Mukhina, V.I., 118; biography of 118–19
Munich, Treaty of, 123–24, 158
Murmansk, 47, 50, 330
Mussolini, Benito, 123
Myaskovsky, N.Ya., 171

Na postu, 78
Nagorno-Karabakh, 61, 291–92
Nagy, Imre, 208–09
Najibullah, Mohammad, 248
Nakhichevan, 61
Namibia, 241
Narimanov, N.N., 60
Nasser, G.A., 209, 243
National Union for the Independence of Angola (UNITA), 241

Nationality policy, national question, 231–34, 260, 279–80, 290–95, 308
NATO (North Atlantic Treaty Organization), 202, 204, 206–07, 209, 212, 215, 235, 238, 243, 246, 289, 309, 320, 332; expansion into Eastern Europe, 311, 314, 321
Nazarbayev, Nursultan, 298
Nazi-Soviet Pact, 124–28, 130, 136, 291–93
Nebogatov, N.I., 5
Nemtsov, B.E., 310
Neto, Agostinho, 241
Nevsky, Aleksandr, 174n
New Economic Policy (NEP), 62–65, 73–74, 76, 87, 92–93, 105, 270
New Reality Artistic Academy, 193
New York, 314
Newman, Paul, 286
Nicholson, A., 13
Night of the Long Knives, 120
Nikolay (Grand Duke), 16–17
Nikolay II, 4–6, 8–9, 11–12, 15, 17, 19; abdication of, 13, 18–19; murder of, 43
Nikolayev, Leonid, 109
Nikolayev, Ya.S., 152
Nikonov, V.P., 262
Nixon, Richard M., 211–12, 245
Nizhni Novgorod (Gorky), 310
NKVD, 109–14, 123, 129, 137–38, 140–42, 146–47, 271
Nogin, V.P., 35
Non-Proliferation Treaty, 242
North Korea, North Koreans, 162, 203–05
Norway, Norwegians, 87, 315
Novaya gazeta, 323, 327
Novaya zhizn, 33, 81
Novgorod, 141
Novocherkassk, 183
Novorossiisk, 49, 330
Novotny, Antonin, 235
Novy mir, 191
NTV, 316
Nuclear power, 263–66, 268–69, 284
Nuremberg Trials, 157

Obama, Barack, 322
October Manifesto, 6
October Revolution, 31–54, 171, 331
Octobrist Party, 7, 9, 20
Oder river, 161
Odesa, 6, 49–50, 75, 141, 330
Ogaden, 240
Ogonek, 80, 274
OGPU (United State Political
    Administration), 75, 92, 96
Oil, oil industry, 104, 173, 189, 222–23,
    226–27, 232, 241, 244, 256, 263, 282,
    316, 318, 328
OKH (Oberkommando des Heeres), 142
Okhrana, 2–3, 44, 69, 151
Oktyabr, 78
Okudzhava, B.S., 251; biography of, 251–52
Oligarchs, 310–11, 315–17, 328
Omsk, 48–49
One Day in the Life of Ivan Denisovich, 193,
    250
Onega, 141
Ono, Yoko, 286
Operation Bagration, 158
Operation Barbarossa, 130, 142
Operation Mars, 149
Operation Uranus, 148–49
Operation Zitadelle, 154–55
Order No. 1, 20–21, 45
Ordzhonikidze, Sergo (G.K.), 59, 84, 108,
    113
Orel, 50, 155, 330
Orenburg, 61
Organization for African Unity, 241
Organization of Petroleum Exporting
    Countries, 227
Organization of Ukrainian Nationalists
    (OUN), 140, 168
Organization of American States, 215
Orlov, Yu.F., 253
ORT, 316
OSCE (Organization for Security and
    Cooperation in Europe), 319, 321, 325
Ossetiya, Ossetians, 294
Ostpolitik, 239

Ostrovsky, N.A., 117
Ostankino, 306
Otlichniki, 106
Ottoman Empire, 14, 18

Pacific Fleet, 4
Pakistan, Pakistanis, 244, 246, 248, 287, 322,
    325
Pale of Settlement, 3, 13
Panmunjom, 203
Paris, 15, 201, 212
Paris peace treaties, 40, 84, 206–07
Partisans, 138, 145–46, 167, 271
Partnership for Peace, 311
Pasternak, B.L., 150, 169, 192, 252, 275;
    biography of, 192–93
Patriarch Tikhon, 47
Paulus, Friedrich von, 147–48
Pavlenko, P.A., 118
Pavlodarsk-Ekibastuz coalfield, 228
Pavlychko, D.V., 293
Paznyak, Zyanon, 270–71
Peaceful Coexistence, 83, 87, 210
Pecherska Lavra, 320
Pegov, N.M., 178
People's Commissariat for Enlightenment, 78
People's Commissariat of Food Supply, 45
People's Democratic Party of Afghanistan
    (PDPA), 246–48
Peredvizhniki, 119
Perekhop, 52
Perestroika, 79, 260, 262–63, 282–85, 304
Pereval, 79–80
Pereyaslav Treaty, 178, 305, 319–20
Pervukhin, M.G., 139
Peter and Paul Fortress, 33
Peter the Great, 273
Petlyura, Symon, 51
Petrograd, 18–21, 23, 26, 28, 37;
    Red Terror in, 44; *see also* Leningrad,
    St. Petersburg
Petrograd Military Garrison, 19, 27–28, 32
Petrograd (St. Petersburg) Soviet, 6–7,
    19–20, 23, 27, 31, 34, 39, 42, 45,
    49–50, 71; *Petropavlovsk* battleship, 53

Petrovsky, G.I., 35, 40, 44, 60
Pichul, V.V., 275
Pieck, Wilhelm, 201
Pilnyak, B.A., 79, 81
Pilsudski, J.K., 51, 84
Pimen (Patriarch), 272
Pioneer organization, 77
Pipes, Richard, 23, 31, 67
Pizza Hut, 283
Platonov, Andrey (Andrey Platonovich
    Klimentov), 80
Platov, Arkady, 152
Plehve, V.K., 3, 5
Plekhanov, G.V., 23
Podgorny, N.V., 218
Poland, Poles, 11, 88, 137, 180, 236–37, 305,
    319–20; and crisis of 1956, 207–09; in
    First World War, 17, 40; in interwar
    period, 120–21; and NATO, 309, 314,
    321–22, 332; results of Nazi-Soviet
    Pact in, 124–30, 140, 271; in
    revolution of 1905, 7; and Solidarity
    Union, 234, 245–46, 257, 287; and
    Treaty of Riga, 84; war with Soviet
    Russia, 51–52; wartime settlement of,
    157–58, 160, 164, 195; in World War II,
    159, 167–68
Polish Committee for National Liberation,
    159
Polish Government in Exile, 159
Polish Home Army, 158–59, 167
Polish-Soviet war, 51–52, 84
Polish United Workers' Party, 208, 238
Politkovskaya, A.S., 323; biography of, 324
Pomerania, 160
Pomerantsev, Vladimir, 191
Ponomarenko, P.K., 126, 146, 181, 208
Popov, G.Kh., 297
Popular Fronts, 121, 122–24, 277–78, 293
Popular Movement for the Liberation of
    Angola (MPLA), 241
Popular Movement of Ukraine for
    "Perebudova" (Rukh), 293
Population, 1, 93, 99, 128, 141, 163–64, 187,
    222, 229, 279, 312, 329

Populism, 2, 333
Port Arthur, 4, 206
Portsmouth, Treaty of (1905), 5, 87, 162
Portugal, Portuguese, 121, 240
Pospielovsky, Dmitry, 191
Postyshev, P.P., 101
Potemkin (battleship), 6
Potsdam, 14
Potsdam Conference, 164, 195–96, 201
Powers, Gary Francis, 212, 216
Pozharsky, D.M., 174n
Prague, 11, 161, 235, 237
Pravda, 11, 22–23, 25, 75, 92, 94, 97, 151,
    173, 182, 184, 218, 270, 272, 292
Preobrazhensky, Ye.A., 25–26, 65, 108
Primakov, Ye.M., 309
Pripyat, 265
Prokhorovka, 155
Prokofiev, S.S., 117, 151, 153, 171–72;
    biography of, 154
Proletarian Culture (Proletkult), 77–78
Proletarii, 3
Provisional Government, 20–28, 33–34
Pskov, 19, 34, 141
Pudovkin, V.I., 117
Pugo, B.K., 282, 296–98
Purges, 99, 106,108–16, 126, 129, 136,
    163–64, 178–79, 184, 194, 208, 224,
    271
Purkayev, M.A., 162
Pusan, 205
Pushkin, A.S., 331
Putilov munitions factory, 6, 19
Putin, V.V., 31, 309, 311, 330; background
    and career of, 312–14; becomes prime
    minister, 326–27, 333; domestic policy
    of, 314–17, 325–26; foreign policy of,
    314, 321–22, 333; and presidential
    elections of 2004, 317–19; on Stalin,
    331; and war in Chechnya, 310,
    322–24
Putsch of 1991, 297–98, 313
Puzanov, Aleksandr, 246
Puzyrkov, Viktor, 170
Pyatakov, G.L., 74–75, 112–13

Rabochaya gazeta, 2
Radek, K.B., 74–75, 112–13
Radio Free Europe/Radio Liberty, 169, 209, 297
Radio Moscow, 215
Radzinsky, Edvard, 68, 173
Rakovsky, Kh.G., 75, 114
Ramzin, L.K., 108
Rapallo, Treaty of, 85–86, 120
Rasputin, Grigory, 12–13, 17–18
Rathenau, Walther, 86
Ratushinskaya, I.B., 275
Reagan, Ronald, 246, 258, 261, 285–87
Red Air Force, 127, 155
Red Army, 52, 59, 84, 121, 124, 128–29, 197, 301; formation of 45–47, 93; in Great Patriotic War, 136–37, 140–42, 144, 150, 154–58, 161–62, 164, 194–95, 199; invasion of Poland (1939), 125–26; purge of, 111, 113–14; in Russian Civil War, 49–51; war with Finland, 127–28
Red Fleet, 129
Red Guards, 27–28, 34, 36
Red Sea, 241
Red Terror, 42–44, 50, 53, 82; *see also* Terror, Purges
Rennenkampf, P.K., 16
Repin, Ilya, 13
Reshetnikov, F.M., 170; biography of, 170
Revolution of 1905, 5–8
Revolutionary Military Council, 48, 52
Reykjavic summit (1986), 286
Rhee, Syngman, 203
Rhodesia, 241
Ribbentrop, Joachim von, 125
Riga, Treaty of, 52, 84
Rivera, Diego, 114
Rodionov, M.I., 172
Rodzyanko, M.V., 7, 12, 19; biography of, 13
Rokossovsky, K.K., 140, 147–48, 155, 158, 161, 208
Romania, Romanians, 6, 61, 84, 88, 121, 124–25, 128, 148, 156, 159, 195, 198, 207, 235–36

Romanov, G.V., 255–56, 258, 262
Roosevelt, Franklin D., 156–60, 194
Rostov, 50, 104, 228, 268
Rozhestvensky, Z.P., 5
Ruhr, 196, 201
Runstedt, Gerd von, 144
Russian Association of Proletarian Writers (RAPP), 78–79
Russian Civil War, 45–53
Russian Communist Party (RCP), 38
Russian Federation, 295–96, 298; extreme nationalism in, 332–33; financial collapse of, 309; historical memory and, 329–31; and Near Abroad, 305, 319–22; parliamentary elections of 2007 in, 325–26; presidential elections of 2004 in, 317–19; regions of, 314–15; relations with West, 309; structure of, 304, 307
Russian Futurists, 117
Russian Orthodox Church, 12–13, 48, 66, 143, 190–91, 272–73, 313, 320, 329–30
Russo-Japanese War (1904–1905), 3–5, 8, 87, 160
Rust, Matthias, 274
Rutskoy, A.V., 306
Ryabtsev, K.I., 35
Ryazan Oblast, 182
Ryantsev, A.V., 92
Ryazanov, D.B., 108
Rykov, A.I., 35, 76, 89, 91–92, 103, 108, 112, 114, 270
Ryzhkov, N.I., 262, 265, 285, 296
Rzhev, 149, 330

Sadat, Anwar, 243–44
Safarov, G.I., 59
St. Petersburg, 1, 5–8, 314; *see also* Petrograd, Leningrad
Sajudis, 277, 293–94
Sakhalin Island, 5, 87, 162
Sakharov, A.D., 200, 253, 263, 273, 287
Sakwa, Richard, 320
SALT Treaties, 234, 242–43, 321

Samara, 48
Samizdat, 253
Samsonov, A.V., 16
San Francisco Conference, 164
Saratov, 52
Sarykamysh, Battle of, 16
Savage Division, 26
Sazonov, S.D., 14, 18
Schlieffen, Alfred von, 15
Schlieffen Plan, 15, 17
Schools, Education, 129, 187–88, 190
Schulenberg, Friedrich Werner von, 136
Seattle, 263
Second World War, *see* Great Patriotic War
Security Council, 307, 313
Seelow Heights, Battle of, 161
Segodnya, 316
Semichastny, V.Ye., 192, 217–18
Serapionovy Bratya, 79, 81
Serbia, Serbians, 14–15
Serebryakov, L.P., 112
Serov, I.A., 180, 185, 217
Serov, V.A., 152
Sevastopol, 49–50, 53, 178, 292, 308, 320,
    330, 332
Sha Ho, Battle of, 4
Shakhty affair, 91
Shanghai, 88
Shanghai Cooperation Organization, 325
Shaposhnikov, B.M., 137, 144
Shatalin, S.S., 279, 285, 297
Shatrov, M.F., 272
Shcherbak, Yu.M., 277
Shcherbytsky, V.V., 100, 255, 265, 291–92
Shelepin, A.N., 194, 217
Shelest, P.Yu., 223, 233, 236
Shepilov, D.T., 185, 208
Shevardnadze, E.A., 225, 256, 279, 281–82,
    287, 297
Shipov, D.N., 7
Shkrebneva, L.A., 312
Sholokhov, M.A., 117
Shorin, V.I., 49
Shostakovich, D.D., 117, 153, 171–72, 275;
    biography of, 171

Shturmer, B.V., 18
Shukhevych, Roman, 168
Shumsky, Oleksandr, 77
Shushkevich, S.S., 298–99
Shvernik, N.M., 139
Sibaral project, 283–84
Siberia, 10, 48, 51, 92, 95, 98, 104, 139,
    167, 181, 189, 232, 300; economic
    development in, 223, 227–28, 316
Siberian Peasant Union, 52
Siberian Provisional Government, 48
Sibneft, 316, 328
Silesia, 160
Simbirsk, 48
Simes, Dimitri K., 299
Simferopol, 53
Simonov, K.M., 151, 192
Sinai, 243–44
Sino-Soviet Treaty (1954), 206
Sinyavsky, A.D., 249, 253; biography of, 250
Skobelev, M.I., 21
Slovakia, Slovaks, 124, 235, 237, 328
Small Peoples of the North, 294
Smidovich, P.G., 35
Smolensk, 113, 130, 137, 139, 264, 269, 330
Smolny Institute, 33–34
Sobchak, A.A., 297, 309, 313
Sochi, 323
Social Democracy of the Kingdom of Poland
    and Lithuania, 41
Social Democratic Workers' Party of
    Russia (RSDWP), 2, 3, 7–8, 69;
    First Congress of, 2; Second Congress
    of, 2, 188; Third Congress of, 3;
    6th Congress of, 25
Socialist competition, 103
Socialist Party of Germany (SPD), 82–83,
    122
Socialist Realism, 81, 116–20, 150–54, 191
Socialist Revolutionary Party (SRs), 2, 8–9,
    34, 42, 66; and Constituent Assembly,
    37–38; and February Revolution, 19,
    21; in Petrograd Soviet, 23–24; in
    Provisional Government, 25, 27; purge
    of, 108; in Russian Civil War, 48–49

Socialist Unity Party, 201

Sokolnikov, G.Ya., 40, 69, 112–13

Sokolov, S.L., 247, 274

Soldatskaya pravda, 25

Solzhenitsyn, A.I., 168, 193, 249–50, 254, 279–80

Somalia, Somalians, 240

Somme, Battle of the, 17, 85

Sorge, Richard, 135, 145

Soros, George, 309

South Africa, 241

South Korea, South Koreans, 203–05

South Ossetia, 321, 332

South Yemen, 240, 244

Sovetskaya Gavan, 227

Sovetskaya rossiya, 271

Sovremennik Theater, 192

Spanish Civil War, 122–23, 129–30

Speer, Albert, 154

Sputnik, 217

Stakhanov, A.G., 106, 261

Stakhanov movement, 106–07

Stalin, I.V., 5, 11, 22, 25, 28, 31–33, 42, 50, 63, 79–80, 176, 178–80, 190, 224, 232, 331; as alleged agent of Okhrana, 41; background and personality of, 67–70; and collectivization, 93–98; cult of, 92, 119, 157, 172, 209; death of, 173, 191; denunciations of, under Gorbachev, 270; dictatorship of, 61; and famine in Ukraine, 99–102; and five-year plans, 104; foreign policy of, 82–83, 86, 89, 121–25, 127–30, 197–207, 216, 289, 301; and formation of USSR, 59, 84, 291, 300; and Great Patriotic War, 135–38, 140–41, 143, 145–50, 156, 161–62, 164, 193, 195, 277, 290, 330; as heir to Lenin, 71, 77; Khrushchev's denunciations of, 183–86, 189, 208, 213; and *On the Problems of Leninism*, 72; in postwar period, 165–71, 196; and Purges, 91–92, 108–12, 114–15, 333n; and *Socialism in One Country*, 72, 74–75; and Socialist Realism, 118–19, 150,

152–53, 192; and struggle for power in 1920s, 65, 67, 71–76, 91–92

Stalingrad, 104, 170, 189, 330; battle of, 146–50, 156, 163, 301

START (Strategic Arms Reduction) Treaty, 290, 304

Stasi, 312

State Assembly (Moscow), 28

State Defense Committee (GKO), 138–39, 144, 158, 165, 173

State Council, 9, 13

State farm, sovkhoz, 102, 183, 228

State Planning Commission (Gosplan), 64, 103, 189

Stavka, 136–38, 148

Stavropol, 260, 322

Stepashin, S.V., 309

Stessel, Anatoly (General), 4

Stockholm, 192

Stolypin, P.A., 10–12, 44, 93

Strategic Defense Initiative (SDI), 249, 257, 285–86

Struve, P.B., 14

Sudetenland, 123

Suez Crisis, 209, 212, 243

Sukhumi, 292

Sumgait, 292

Sun Yat-Sen, 88

Suny, Ronald G., 232

Supreme Council of the Economy, 36

Supreme Economic Council, 189

Surikov Art Institute, 152

Suslov, M.A., 190, 218

Suvorov, A.V., 174n

Sverdlov, Ya.M., 25, 28, 32, 35, 37, 42–43, 66, 69–70

Sverdlovsk, 185

Svoboda, Ludvik, 235

Sweden, Swedes, 87, 127, 265

Switzerland, Swiss, 121

Syria, Syrians, 227, 243

Taganka Theater, 192, 250, 252

Taishet, 227

Tajikistan, Tajiks, 248, 294, 296, 305, 309, 324–25

Tambov, 52

Tannenberg, Battle of, 16

Taraki, Nur Mohammed, 246–47

Tashkent, 249

TASS, 130

Tatar Autonomous Republic, Tatarstan, Tatars 58, 136, 291, 294–95; *see also* Crimean Tatars

Tauger, Mark B., 100

Tauride Palace, 19

Tblisi, 69, 231, 294

Tehran Conference, 157–58

Ter-Baganyan, V.A., 112

Terror, Terrorism, 2, 111, 113–15, 250

Thatcher, Margaret, 285, 287

Thurston, Robert, 111

Tibet, Tibetans, 14

Tikhonov, N.S., 81, 233, 256

Timoshenko, S.K., 127, 135–38

Tito, Josip Broz, 159, 195, 199, 202, 206

Togo, Heihachiro (Admiral), 5

Tolstoy, A.N., 78–79

Tolstoy, L.N., biography of, 12

Tolstaya, A.L., 13

Tolstaya, T.N., 331; biography of, 332

Tompson, William, 227

Tomsky, M.P., 75, 89, 91, 108, 112

Torgau, 161

Transcarpathia, 124, 168, 236

Transcaucasian SSR, 59, 61–62

Trans-Dnestr SSR, Transdnistria, 298, 321

Trans-Siberian Railway, 4, 227, 263

Treaty of Friendship and Borders, 126

Treptov Memorial Park, 170

Trials, show trials: of the Anti-Soviet Right Trotskyist Bloc, 113–14; of the "Anti-Soviet United Association of the Trotskyite-Zinovievite Center," 112; of the Industrial Party, 108; of the Mensheviks, 108; of the Moscow Center, 110; of the "Trotskyist Parallel Center," 113

Triple Alliance (German, Austro-Hungary, and Italy), 14

Trotsky, L.D., 7–8, 24–25, 27–28, 42–44, 51, 54, 69, 71, 112, 184, 270; assassination of, 114; and formation of Red Army, 45–47; and *The Lessons of October*, 71–72, 74; "New Course," 71; and October Revolution, 31–32, 34; and power struggle in 1920s, 65–67, 70, 72–76, 106; returns to Russia in 1917, 23; and *The Revolution Betrayed*, 114; in Russian Civil War, 48–49, 82; and Treaty of Brest-Litovsk, 39–40, 84

Trotskyists, 123, 125

Trud, 25

Truman, Harry S., 164, 195–97, 205–06

Truman Doctrine, 197

Tsaritsyn, 50, 82; *see also* Stalingrad, Volgograd

Tsarskoe Selo, 34

Tsereteli, I.G., 19, 21

Tucker, Robert C., 68

Tukhachevsky, M.N., 49–52, 54, 84, 113, 121

Tula, 50, 323

Tuleyev, A.G., 314

Tupolev, A.N., 140–41

Turkestan, 61, 104

Turkey, Turks, 16–17, 40, 75, 85–86, 88, 196–97, 214–15, 328; *see also* Ottoman Empire

Turkmenistan, Turkmens, 61, 296, 325

Tuzla Island, 319

Tvardovsky, A.T., 117, 151, 191, 193

U2 missions, 209, 211–12, 214–16

Uborevich, I.P., 113

Ufa, 48–49

Ukraine, Ukrainians, 3, 10–11, 17, 39–42, 45, 48, 50–53, 58, 61, 64, 77, 84, 92, 125–28, 166, 178, 248, 254, 273, 324; in Brezhnev period, 223–24, 228, 231–33, 236, 253; Chernobyl disaster in, 263–69, 284; collectivization in, 94–95; Famine of 1933 in, 98–102, 109, 320, 330; in Gorbachev period,

277, 279, 283–84, 296, 298; Great Patriotic War in, 140, 145–46, 158–59, 163; industry in, 103; and national question, 280, 290–91, 293–95; purges in, 113, 179, 271; relations with Russia in independence period, 305, 308–09, 311–12, 314, 319–21, 328, 330, 332; resistance in western regions of, 167–69

Ukrainian Catholic (Uniate) Church, 273

Ukrainian Insurgent Army (UPA), 167–68, 180, 320

Ukrainska pravda, 312

Ulbricht, Walther, 173, 201, 213–14, 236, 240

Unemployment, 105

Unified Russia, 317, 325–26, 330

Union of the Militant Godless, 76

Union of Right Forces, 317–18, 325

Union of the Russian People, 12

Union of Soviet Artists, 153

Union of Writers of the USSR, 79, 82, 116, 169, 192

Union Treaty, 295–97, 299

United Nations, 159, 164, 205–06, 209, 212, 215, 269, 321; Security Council of, 202, 245, 319

United Opposition, 74–76

United States, Americans, 5, 39, 47, 64, 82, 85–86, 101, 105, 120, 128, 144, 157, 159, 161–62, 168, 244–46, 263; in early Cold War, 195–99, 201–07; relations with Russian Federation, 304–05; relations with USSR: under Khrushchev, 180, 182, 185, 188, 209–17; under Brezhnev, 222, 231, 234, 240–43, 247–49, 257, 300; under Gorbachev, 283, 285–87, 289, 294, 298; under Putin, 314, 318, 321–22, 325

Urals, 64, 95, 104, 139, 181, 224

Uritsk, 141

Uritsky, M.S., 32–33, 43

USSR Academy of Arts, 152

Ustinov, D.F., 189, 257

Uzbekistan, Uzbeks, 58, 61, 232, 256, 292–94, 296, 324–25

Vasilevsky, A.M., 148, 162

Vasilyev, G.N., 151

Vasilyev, S.D., 151

Vatican, 329–30

Vatsetis, I.I., 47–48

Vatutin, N.F., 148, 155–56

Vavilov, N.I., 167

Verdun, Battle of, 17, 85

Versailles, Treaty of, 83, 86, 123–24

Victoria (Queen), 12

Victory Day, 161

Vienna, 266

Vienna Summit (1961), 213, 216

Vietnam, Vietnamese, 245, 264

Vietnam War, 195, 234, 241, 246, 287

Vileyka, 319

Vilnius, 51–52, 126, 293–95

Viola, Lynne, 97, 111

Virgin Lands program, 181–83

Vistula river, 158, 161

Vitebsk, 61, 158

Vladikavkaz, 330

Vladimir (Grand Duke), 6

Vladimir (Volodymyr), 272, 320

Vladivostok, 5, 47, 51, 53, 124

Vlasov, A.A., 162

Vlasov, A.V., 280

Volga Germans, 58, 163

Volga Region, 10, 48, 64, 94–95, 98, 139, 181

Volga river, 50, 147–48

Volga-Don Canal, 167

Volgodonsk, 268, 310

Volgograd, 189, 256; *see also* Stalingrad

Volhynia, 84

Volkogonov, Dmitry, 68

Volkov, Solomon, 151

Voloshin, A.S., 317

Voluntary Army of the Don, 47–48

Voronezh, 50, 52, 150

Voroshilov, K.E., 71, 91, 108, 119, 127, 137–38, 152, 177–78, 185

Vorotnikov, Vitaly, 257

Vovovsky, V.V., 85

Voznesensky, A.A., 193–94

Voznesensky, N.I., 137–38, 144, 165, 172

Vuchetich, Ye.V., 170

Vyazma, 137, 142, 301

Vyborg, 9, 13, 127–28

Vyshinsky, A.Ya., 91, 110, 114

Vysotsky, V.S., 251, 331; biography of, 252–53

Wages, 98

War Communism, 42, 44–45, 53–54, 65, 94, 101

Warsaw, 1, 7, 51–52, 84, 126, 158–59, 198, 201, 208, 236, 238

Warsaw Pact, 202, 207, 209–10, 235–37, 285, 288–89, 311

Washington, DC, 314

Weathersby, Kathryn, 203–04

Welsh, Douglas Lee, 155

West Berlin, 201–02, 210, 213–14, 289

West Prussia, 160

What Is To Be Done?, 2, 31

Wheatcroft, S.G., 100

White Army, 27, 47–53, 65

White Sea, 92, 113

White Sea Canal, 167

White Terror, 49

Wilhelm II (Kaiser), 14–15

Wilson, Woodrow, 40

Wilno, *see* Vilnius

Winter Palace, 19, 33–34

Witte, Sergey, 1, 3, 5–6, 9, 11

Women, 105, 149–50

Workers' Opposition, 63, 72

World Literature publishing house, 81

Wrangel, Petr, 52–53

WTO (World Trade Organization), 325

Yabloko, 317, 326

Yagoda, G.G., 109, 112, 114, 184

Yakir, I. Ye., 113

Yakovlev, A.N., 262, 268, 277, 279, 282, 297

Yakovlev, Ye.V., 274

Yakunin, G.P., 272

Yakutia (Republic of Sakha), 11, 232, 290–91, 304

Yalta Conference, 157, 159–60, 194–95, 201, 211

Yalu river, 205–06

Yanovsky, O.I., 113

Yanayev, G.I., 281–82, 297

Yanukovych, V.F., 320

Yaroslavl, 48

Yavlinsky, G.A., 314

Yavorivsky, V.O., 293

Yazov, D.T., 279

Yefanov, V.P., 119

Yegorov, A.I., 51

Yekaterinoslav, 50; *see also* Dnipropetrovsk

Yeltsin, B.N., 212, 262, 277, 301, 315, 330; background and early career of, 276, 278; conflict with Russian parliament, 306–07; and economy, 285, 311; foreign policy of, 302; illness of, 308–09; and nuclear weapons, 305; and putsch of 1991, 297–98; as Russian president, 280–81, 296, 298–99, 309, 312, 314

Yeremenko, A.I., 147–48

Yerevan, 284, 292

Yesenin, Sergey, 78

Yevdokimov, G.E., 112

Yezhov, N.I., 112–14, 184

Yom Kippur War, 244

Yudenich, N.N., 49–51

Yugoslavia, Yugoslavs, 130, 159, 176, 185, 199, 202, 205, 208, 210, 235

Yukos, 316

Yuon, K.F., 152

Yurovsky, Yakov, 43

Yushchenko, V.A., 320, 330, 332

Yusupov, B.A., 119

Zaire, 242

Zaitsev, V.G., 148

Zaikov, L.N., 276

Zamyatin, Ye.I., 81

Zarudin, N.N., 80

Zeitzler, Kurt, 154–55

Zemstvo Union, 20–21

Zemtsov, Ilya, 257–58

Zetkin, Klara, 71

Zhdanov, A.A., 108, 122, 153–54, 173, 198, 203; campaign for cultural uniformity of, 169–72, 192

Zhirinovsky, V.V., 280, 296, 314

Zhukov, G.K., 124, 135–37, 140–42, 144, 147–49, 155–56, 161, 177–79, 185–86, 208

Zionism, 169

Zinoviev, G. Ye., 22, 25, 28, 32–33, 35, 67, 69; as chairman of Comintern, 82, 87–88; persecution and trial of, 108, 110, 112; and power struggle in 1920s, 71–77, 89, 106; rehabilitation of, 270

Zorkin, V.D., 306

Zoshchenko, M.M., 118, 169, 192

Zubok, Vladislav, 192–94

Zyuganov, G.A., 308–09, 311, 314, 317

Zvezda, 169